Yeshua

The Unknown Jesus

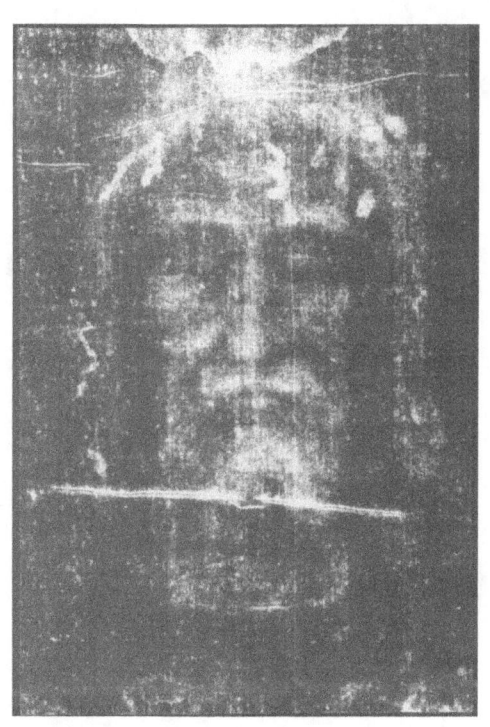

by

Lewis Keizer

© 2000-2007 by Lewis and Willa Keizer

ISBN 978-0-6151-6738-1

About the Author

Dr. Lewis Keizer is a distinguished independent Bishop, respected scholar, lecturer, and professional educator who has been writing and guiding men and women through spiritual studies for since his consecration in 1975. Through his online seminary program at www.hometemple.org he mentors and trains qualified people for non-professional sacramental and interfaith ministry. These include home churches, hospice and jail chaplaincies, and other independent volunteer ministries. One of the first Bishops to ordain and consecrate women, he has been a champion of civil rights and women's issues all his life. He is listed in *Who's Who in the World, Who's Who in Religion, Who's Who Among America's Teachers,* and many other standard reference biographies. He was inspired by his close friendship with Mother Jennie, a Spiritualist saint, under whose guidance in 1969 he developed meditation and spiritual practices not taught in seminary.

He received the Bacclaureate of Sciences with General Studies in Humanities from Portland State University in 1965. After attending the Anglican Theological College in Vancouver, B.C., for a year as a postulant for Holy Orders in the Episcopal Diocese of Oregon, he transferred to the Episcopal Theological School (now Episcopal Divinity School) in Cambridge, Massachusetts, where he undertook additional graduate courses at Harvard Divinity School and Harvard University. Graduating with the S.T.B. degree in 1968, which is now known as the M.Div. degree, he was awarded an Episcopal Church Foundation three-year grant to support his Ph.D. studies at the Graduate Theological Union in Berkeley, California. In 1969 he became an Acting Assistant Professor of Humanities at the University of California in Santa Cruz, where he taught Religious Studies and Classics. In 1973 he was awarded the Ph.D. in Biblical Studies with emphasis in New Testament by the Graduate Theological Union.

Dr. Keizer makes his UCSC college courses in Jesus Studies, Comparative Religion, Gnostic Studies, and the Western Mystery Tradition available through multimedia lecture-presentations that can be accessed through his http://wisdomseminars.org/ web site.

A multi-talented person, his expertise crosses many disciplines and includes not only academics, but music and the arts, educational, social and environmental reform, and many other areas. He co-founded the Popper-Keizer School for Mentally Gifted Children in Santa Cruz in 1979. There he served as fulltime teacher and Headmaster for twenty years, offering advanced education to high-potential low-income and minority students with grants from David and Lucile Packard and Cowell foundations. He was a candidate for California State Superintendent of Schools in 1994. Keizer also founded and conducted the Santa Cruz Chamber Orchestra for many seasons. He premiered new works of contemporary composers, showcased talented soloists, conducted award-winning sound tracks for films, and presented annual Nutcracker Ballet performances.

For most of his life he has performed world-wide as a jazz cornetist (allstarband.net). He continues to perform today, and occasionally as an all-star soloist.

An avid sailor since the 1980's, he is a U.S. Coast Guard Licensed captain and an officer of the U.S. Coast Guard Auxiliary. He sails and cruises his Cape Dory 28 *Levon* from its home port of Alameda on the San Francisco Bay.

In 1988 he founded T:.H:G:., the Temple of the Holy Grail, as a new mystery school designed to provide advanced esoteric training for 21st century men and women. In addition to the First Order Empowerments, over three decades of daily practice he developed the Christ-Melchizedek Tantra based on techniques of Tibetan Buddhist Kalachakra generation and completion stages and those of Kabbalistic *Merkevah* ascent. Information can be found at http://hometemple.org/THG.htm.

But his lifelong love has been the ongoing project of using the best insights of modern biblical scholarship to recover the historical teachings of *Mar Yeshua,* the Master Jesus. For a complete list of his academic and popular writings, go to his online resume at http://www.wisdomseminars.org/Keizer%20Resume.pdf. A more detailed list of many of his publications can be found at http://hometemple.org/Publications.htm. Several of his writings are also available for purchase at online bookstores like Amazon.com and Lulu.com, and available inexpensivelyas Kindle e-books.

Since January, 2011, Dr. Keizer has been scheduling and presenting his *Yeshua* Workshop without fee world-wide. There he sells his books and CD's at the lower workshop price to help defray expenses for travel. Information about scheduling the *Yeshua* Workshop can be found online at http://hometemple.org/Lecture-Tour.htm.

A Special Word of Thanks

It is hard for any author to proofread his own work because all too often the brain sees what he thought he wrote—not what's really there. So typos and other mistakes remain in the text. Many authors let a first draft "cool" for a few months so they can re-read and proof without that problem.

Therefore I want to thank independent Home Temple Bishop Daniel Doornbos for his careful volunteer editing and sharp-eyed corrections of my first draft. He professionally edits technical manuals in Silicon Valley, and was one of my top seminary students. As a Home Temple Priest, prior to advancement to the Episcopate, he developed an excellent volunteer jail ministry in Santa Clara County, which he still maintains. He also carried the grounding he gained in the Western Mystery Tradition from Home Temple School of Sacred Studies degree courses into his educational leadership as a high-degree Mason. He was uniquely qualified on many levels to proofread my work, and when he volunteered to do so, I immediately accepted.

PREFACE

My study of the language, context, and meaning of the teachings of Jesus began in 1966 while I was a graduate student at the Episcopal Theological Seminary (now Episcopal Divinity School) in Cambridge, Massachusetts, with additional classes at the Harvard Divinity School and Harvard University.

Recovering the Aramaic Language of *Yeshua* (Jesus)

The New Testament was written in Greek, but the language of *Yeshua* was Aramaic, a later dialect of Hebrew and a language radically different than Greek. There are no simple one-to-one correspondences between Greek and Aramaic words. The Gospels were composed by Greek-speaking gentiles (non-Jews) three generations removed from the Master and his thought-world of Jewish Messianic mysticism. Writers of the Gospels cherry-picked the sayings and parables of *Yeshua* from preserved oral and written sources that had no context in order to "spin" them to support late first-century Christian church teachings and worship. These were not the Messianic teachings and religion of *Yeshua,* but doctrines about Jesus the Christ that were developing in the new religion called Christianity.

While there are no reliable historical records about the life of *Yeshua,* both the New Testament and many non-canonical sources can be used to recover the historical religion and teaching of *Yeshua.* Because the earliest recorded sayings of the Master lack historical context, are preserved in a different language, and spun in the New Testament Gospels to support the issues and doctrines of the early Christian churches, they cannot be taken literally. But scholars can recover the authentic historical teachings using proven methods of literary-historical and textual criticism. The starting place is getting from the Greek back to the Aramaic teachings of *Yeshua.*

I first compared the New Testament Greek and language usage of the teachings of Jesus with that of the Pentateuch. By an examination of this Greek translation of Hebrew Scriptures done for Hellenistic Jews and used during the time of Jesus, I was able to determine which Greek words were used to translate Hebrew and Aramaic texts of the Old Testament. Then I examined the Diatessaron, which was the second-century translation of the Greek New Testament into Syriac—an Aramaic dialect similar to the language spoken by *Yeshua.* In the later second century, the Diatessaron was re-translated from the Greek Gospels of the New Testament back into the later Syriac alphabet by Aramaic native speakers who still understood Aramaic-Greek equivalencies used by the contemporaries of *Yeshua.* These studies yielded much of the glossary of words and concepts used by *Yeshua* that I have compiled and appended for your reference at the end of this book. It is worthy of careful study. A reader will find it helpful to refer to the glossary often while reading the novel.

I said that there are not simple one-to-one equivalencies between the Aramaic dialect of Jesus and the Greek of the New Testament. Here is one of thousands of possible examples. A key concept for *Yeshua* was *emunah*, "faithfulness, fidelity" to the covenantal love, justice and mercy of God. But the Jesus portrayed in the Greek New Testament speaks of *pistis,* "faith," meaning "belief." The faith taught by *Yeshua* was the *emunah* or faithful perseverance of a mustard seed, but the faith of the Greek New Testament was about belief in doctrines of the early gentile churches—something quite different..

The *Epistle of James*, which clearly preserves historical teachings of *Yeshua*, forcefully reminds the early gentile Christians about the faith taught by *Yeshua*: "Faith without works is dead." Faith is fidelity—not dogma. It is something that is done and proven, not something that is a matter of belief or opinion. But Martin Luther wanted the *Epistle of James* expunged from the Bible because its teaching contradicted his doctrine of Salvation by Faith—i.e., salvation through belief in correct doctrine. Modern Christian fundamentalists even stray so far as to confuse political-ideological opposition to abortion and gay rights as essential to "faith!" *Yeshua* says nothing about either issue, and the Old Testament scriptures against male homosexuality must be understood in the context of *Yeshua's* teaching, "In old times it was said…but now I say unto you." In other words, That was then, this is now.

Yeshua didn't teach people doctrine or dogma, which are ultimately nothing but human opinion—what he called the "doctrines of men." The word he used—*emunah*—was about leading a sanctified life faithful to the Way of God. When *Yeshua* used the word faith, it meant faithfulness, fidelity, perseverance—not belief. Yet most modern Christians consider their faith to consist of religious belief about Jesus

Another example: *Yeshua* never accused the Pharisees of being hypocrites as the New Testament presents it. The Greek word, which means "play-actor, pretender," is taken from a tradition of dramatic theater that did not exist in Jewish culture. Rather, *Yeshua* used an Aramaic-Hebrew idiom that could be translated as "turning up the nose at." It denotes self-aggrandizement, a sense of superiority to others, religious snobbery—not hypocrisy. That was how he criticized the fastidious ritual *mitzvoth* of Judaean Pharisees. They were not hypocrites; they were as sincere as modern-day religious fundamentalists. But like the fundamentalists, they were bigots who thought everyone except them was going to hell. *Yeshua* absolutely despised that attitude.

Again, *Yeshua* did not teach salvation. The name *Yeshua* means "liberation." He taught liberation from the bondage of evil. That implies that even though the human world is under the domination of evil forces, human souls can work with Heaven to sanctify and liberate their world. Salvation (Greek *soteria*) and redemption are proto-gnostic gentile ideas that emerged in early Christianity along with non-Jewish ascetic practices. They imply that not only the human world, but the Earth and life in flesh, are inherently evil. A Heavenly Redeemer helps human souls to abandon the human world, the Earth, and the flesh and leave it all behind—i.e., the fundamentalist Rapture. Humanity and the world are not transformed and sanctified, but merely abandoned to burn in Hell.

Yeshua taught liberation and sanctification—not salvation. Yet modern Catholic, Orthodox, and fundamentalist Christianity cling to the doctrines of a Gnostic Redeemer offering salvation from matter and flesh.

Recovering the Context of the Master's Teachings

The earliest records of *Yeshua's* words are the *logia* or short sayings and parables preserved in the hypothetical Q Source of Matthew and Luke, in the Gnosticised collection of the *Gospel of Thomas,* and scattered throughout the authentic Pauline Epistles (as opposed to the pseudepigraphical ones like I and II Timothy). They have no context. They were later woven together (redacted) and made into gospel narratives for the gentile Christian churches, who by then were in deep conflict with the more original Messianic Jews, the developing Gnostic Christians, and other religions. They applied anachronistic spin to the teachings of Jesus to support their own positions—especially their doctrine that Israel had rejected its own Messiah, and God had given a new covenant to the gentiles through Christianity, which was the New Israel.

Most important, nearly all knowledge of Jewish Messianic mysticism (prophetic, Kabbalistic, wisdom, and *Merkabah*) that informed the original *Basor-Ha-Malkuth Ha-Shamayyim* or Divine Birth Message of the Coming Sovereignty of Heaven on Earth (the Gospel taught by *Yeshua*) had been lost. Instead a completely new Greek mystery religion worshipping a Savior God (Jesus) had been spawned called Christianity.

To recover the context of Jewish Messianic mysticism, I studied the Scriptures that were sacred to *Yeshua* and his disciples before the canon of the Old Testament had been defined by later Pharisaic Rabbis. Most important were the prophecies of Trito-Isaiah, Daniel, and the wisdom and apocalyptic writings attributed to Enoch, *Yeshua Ben-Sirach* and many others that today form part of neither the main Jewish nor Christian Scriptural canon, but are known as the Apocrypha and Pseudepigrapha of the Old Testament. They were written during the three-hundred year period before the time of Jesus, after the Old Testament ended (according to the Rabbis, the Spirit of Prophecy left Israel when the Second Temple was built), and before there was a New Testament. We find some of them quoted by early Christian writers like the author of the Epistle of Jude. Today they are too Jewish for the Christians, and too Christian for the Jews, but they were the main Scripture that guided *Yeshua* and the Messianic Jews of his day.

For example, most of the content of Matthew's famous Sermon on the Mount (Luke's Sermon on the Plain) already existed in obscure revelations like the *Testaments of the Twelve Patriarchs* that were written by Pharisaic Messianic mystics a century before Jesus. Again, we find the development of the feminine aspect of Jewish Godhead in the wisdom literature as the *Ruach Ha-Qodesh,* Spirit of Holiness—the "Holy Spirit" so deeply reverenced by *Yeshua*. She was the initiator and teacher of saints and sages.

Jewish Kabbalah ("that which is given to the ear of the student from the mouth of the teacher") was hidden knowledge of the *Razim,* divine secrets or mysteries. They were transmitted orally from one master to one student—not to a group. According to the early Jewish mystics referenced in the second-century *Mishnah,* of whom *Yeshua* is one, the *Merkabah* Ascent to the Chariot-Throne of YAHWEH was never taught by men. Rather, it was a form of heavenly *manda* or *gnosis* that could be learned only in the heart of a *tzadik* or pure and righteous saint who was attuned to Heaven. The "rider of the Throne-Chariot" was taught by God, not by man. Only when two masters who had both learned to make the Ascent found by clues that they were both initiates were they then permitted by Heaven to privately discuss the *Merkabah*. Nevertheless there were many who went insane or died trying to achieve it, according to the *Mishnah*.

The first written Kabbalah was the *Sepher Yetzirah,* which according to Jewish scholars like Gershom Scholem first appeared about the time of the *Mishnah* in the late second or early third century of the Christian era. That implies the existence of many centuries of previous oral tradition. Scholem ascribes the letter-number mysticism of Jewish Kabbalah to Greek Pythagorean Kabbalah. The contact for that form of syncretism would have been in the Jewish diaspora after the Babylonian Captivity four to six centuries before the Christian era. By studying the *Sepher Yetzirah* and other early Kabbalistic traditions, we can illuminate much of the context of Messianic mysticism that informed the teachings of *Yeshua*.

Clearly there were profound oral *Razim* in prophetic and wisdom schools at the time of *Yeshua*. A careful study of clues in the wisdom and apocalyptic literature of the period allows us to recover some of its basic parameters. My study of Margalioth's *Sepher Ha-Razim*, recovered from Cairo *genizah* and representing Hellenistic Jewish magico-mystic traditions, provided more clues.

The History, Comparison, and Phenomenology of World Mystic and Initiatic Spirituality

Many denominational and church-supported Christian scholars know far too little about Judaism in general, and Hellenistic Judaism in particular. They have no real foundation for reconstructing the teachings of Jesus. Even those who have studied the contextual materials still have a major blind spot. They aren't familiar with comparative and parallel spirituality from other world religions. All they can do is elaborate on traditional Christian theological interpretations of the teachings of Jesus.

For example, a rational scholar will assume that the miracles of Jesus are all of one cloth—legends and fictions. A biblical literalist pseudo-scholar will assume they are all historical. But the truth seems to be that, while some are legends, others are not. To be able to discriminate among all these, one needs to have not only knowledge, but experience with psychic, initiatic, and yogic phenomena.

Using my knowledge of the history, comparison, and phenomenology of religions, I have been able to make careful determinations of what I present as probable history in this novel, and how I present it.

The Purpose of This Novel

I have written this life of *Yeshua* to make the insights of a modern Jesus scholar accessible to lay persons in a popular format. There is no way to recover the personal history and biography of *Yeshua.* But we can recover his historical teachings.

My hope is that a fictional biography that is true to the spirit and context of his Messianic mysticism might help Christians grow beyond mere dogmatics into the true and historical Gospel of the Master Jesus as I can best reconstruct it.

Some scholars will disagree with me on a multitude of points—that is their job. But others will applaud the overall effort. Many of the best scholars have become agnostic because they strained out the gnats and swallowed the camel. They don't grasp the mystic depths of Christianity, they don't seriously practice the *halakah* of the Master with self-examination and prayer, and their spiritual practices—other than attending public church services—are minimal or non-existent.

Scholars and critics are all too often like eunuchs. They can talk about it, but they can't do it. Therefore, I invite my severest critics to do it! Write a better historical biography of Jesus than I have done, based on real scholarship and true fidelity to the teachings of the Master—not just another tired, literalistic harmony of the gospels. If a qualified biblical scholar can improve upon my best effort, he will have my praise and gratitude.

Lewis Keizer

Aromas, California

August 28, 2007

CONTENTS

About the Author 4

A Special Word of Thanks 6

PREFACE 7

    RECOVERING THE ARAMAIC LANGUAGE OF *YESHUA* (JESUS) 7

    RECOVERING THE CONTEXT OF THE MASTER'S TEACHINGS 8

    THE HISTORY, COMPARISON, AND PHENOMENOLOGY OF WORLD MYSTIC AND INITIATIC
    SPIRITUALITY 10

    THE PURPOSE OF THIS NOVEL 10

CONTENTS 12

Chapter One: MASTER *YOSEF* 15

Chapter Two: *MIRIAM'S* GARDEN 21

Chapter Three: *YAKOB* 30

Chapter Four: *BAR-MITZVA* 36

Chapter Five: PILGRIMAGE TO THE TEMPLE 43

Chapter Six: THE BROTHERHOOD 52

Chapter Seven: SEPPHORIS 62

Chapter Eight: THE DEATH OF *YOSEF* 73

Chapter Nine: JOURNEY TO BABYLON 82

Chapter Ten: THE FELLOWSHIP OF DANIEL 94

Chapter Twelve: THE ORDEALS OF DANIEL 121

Chapter Thirteen: SHOSHANA 143

Chapter Fourteen: THE CURSE 154

Chapter Fifteen: THE WANDERER 166

Chapter Sixteen: THE WAY OF THE BUDDHA 175

Chapter Seventeen: THE *STUPA* 190

Chapter Eighteen: EGYPT AND THE *THERAPEUTAI* 200

Chapter Nineteen: THE PROPHET *YOCHANAN* 234

Chapter Twenty: NAZARETH 257

Chapter Twenty-One: THE PROPHET *YESHUA* 264

Chapter Twenty-Two: THE MARTYRDOM OF YOCHANAN 281

Chapter Twenty-Three: *MIRIAM* OF *MAGDALA* 296

Chapter Twenty-Four: FIRST JOURNEY TO JERUSALEM 304

Chapter Twenty-Five: INNER AND SECRET *HALAKAH* 324

Chapter Twenty-Six: RETURN TO THE GALILEE 337

Chapter Twenty-Seven: FINAL *PESACH* IN JERUSALEM 346

Chapter Twenty-Eight: *QIMAH* 370

A PARAPHRASE OF *YESHUA'S BASOR* OR ETERNAL GOSPEL 377

THE PRAYER OF *YESHUA* 378

AUTHOR'S COMMENTS 380

GLOSSARY OF TERMS 394

Chapter One: MASTER *YOSEF*

"This—my son—is a drunkard and a glutton."

Terror of death! He could not break free from the painful grip of the many rough hands that bowed his head to the dust. He tried to cry out, "No, Grandfather!" but they crushed his mouth into the stony earth.

"He will not hear the voice of my calling!"

The agonized old man ripped hair from his beard and sobbed under the glare of the molten sun.

"Let him suffer stoning, according to the Law of Moses."

Suddenly jolted into the center of the circle, the grandson fell to his knees to beg forgiveness. A heavy red stone was thrust into the old man's hands. For a second he wavered, then let it symbolically drop into the circle.

"Strike the head and get it done quickly," someone muttered. The eleven other bearded men began reluctantly to cast the heavy stones. Covering his head with his elbows, he recoiled in pain as the first stone broke his fingers. He heard the grunting of the men as they increased their effort to finish the awful task. Red earth, red stones, blood, crushing pain…

"Stop, stop!"

He opened his eyes. The glaring sun—no, a brilliant, white full moon streaming through the doorway. His mother was kneeling by his side.

"*Yeshe, Yeshe,* wake up," she whispered. "What is wrong? Is it that horrible dream again?"

He sat up and blinked his eyes while she held his face and kissed his forehead. Her dark, warm figure blotted out the glare of the moon.

"It's all right, Child. Nothing can harm you."

He knew that he had awakened Master *Yosef* because he could not hear his gentle snoring from the other room. How he wanted to talk to his father! But *Abba Yosef* needed his sleep. He was in charge of another building project for the rich Romans. It was over two hours journey to Sepphoris, and *Abba Yosef* was not a young man.

He drew a long breath and sighed, "I'm ready to go to sleep, *Imma*. I love you."

She tenderly kissed each of his eyes. The bright moonlight fell upon him again as she drew back. He could sense the radiance of her loving smile, although her face was only a dark silhouette. He heard her settling in with *Abba Yosef* in the other room, some muffled sleepy words, and soon the rhythmic snoring began.

He moved out of the moonlight to the West so it wouldn't come upon him again that night. He breathed slowly—seven heartbeats in through the right nostril, and seven heartbeats out through the left nostril. This was the way that Master *Yosef* had taught him to relax for sleep and balance the lunar *keseh* with solar *shemesh*. As his heartbeat slowed and his breathing became long and shallow, he heard within himself many voices, male and female, hypnotically intoning the Zadokite psalm—*Eliahu Ha-Nabi, Eliahu Ha-Nabi…*

*******   *******   *******   *******

Yosef was of the royal tribe of Judah and a master stone mason. He had apprenticed with his father *Yakob*, who had learned the trade from his father. When his eldest son

Yeshua would finally complete the trainings and initiations to become a Master Mason, he would carry the trade into its twelfth generation.

The first Master was Zerubbabel, who was born to Shealtiel in Babylon during the Captivity. He had been educated and trained by the Magian builders. He fulfilled his Apprenticeship degree as a laborer on the original foundation of the Second Temple under Sheshbazzar, then his Journeyman and Master degrees when work was resumed by the High Priest *Yeshua*.

Before the Captivity, there had been no major succession of Hebrew stone masters. Building had been a community effort to erect simple housing and defensive walls. Solomon had imported professional builders to work under Hiram-Abi of Tyre for the First Temple. King David had commissioned foreign artisans and metal-workers to make the Temple furnishings that Solomon used, and he had relied upon foreign builders to plan and supervise his great stone *hekel* or winter palace in Jerusalem. Traditionally, these builders and artisans were of the foreign lineage of Tubal-Cain, not the lineage of Seth, from whom Israel derived its Noachic origins.

Over the centuries the Egyptian, Persian, and other foreign masters had jealously guarded their secrets, teaching only one design to each Hebrew worker when new sanctuaries were built in the ancient oracle places like Beth-El and Baalbek. But with the completion of the Second Temple, Israel now had Jewish stone-masters capable of overseeing sacred architecture and building, as well as new Guilds of metal-workers and other artisans. At the dedication of the Second Temple, *Yosef*'s ancestor Zerubbabel and his Guild-brothers had been honored as founders and patriarchs of Jewish Sacred Masonry.

From this time forward, all first-born males of *Yosef*'s line had been not only trained in the mechanics of stone masonry, but educated and initiated into the sacred mysteries of the Master Builder, the *Aman*.

Yosef walked briskly like the three young Nazarene workers who accompanied him to the site in *Zippori*. The city had been burned to the ground by Herod to crush Zealot activity, then rebuilt to become his capitol city for ruling Galilee. The city was now known to the Romans as Sepphoris. Its continuous building projects by Romans and wealthy Jews supplied the Masonic Guild of Zerubbabel with more work than it could handle.

Yosef was tall, muscular, and his face was all but hidden in a white beard that had never seen a razor. The main features of his classic semitic face were gleaming eyes, high cheekbones, and a massive, angular nose that was, itself, a marvel of architecture and design. Altogether he had the appearance of a man with the face of a lion, not unlike some of the divine images used in Egyptian and Assyrian temples.

He also had the temperament of a lion—majestic, regal, and capable of evoking respect from anyone. The young workers respected him, not only for his wisdom but for his sheer physical strength and ability to use it. They referred to him as *Ha-Arizedek*, the Lion of Righteousness. His Roman patrons were never inclined to accuse him of cheating, and they paid his fees promptly on demand. He, in turn, paid his workers generously at the end of each day. He was the best *Aman* any worker could have.

They had started out on the journey before sunrise, while it was cool. After an hour's walk, fiery *Shemesh*, the morning sun, had arisen in the East over Sepphoris. They could see the grove where a little spring sometimes flowed. It was a good stopping place, being half the journey, and *Yosef* called for water, morning prayer, and rest.

They sat quietly upon stones in the sparse shade and refreshed their dry tongues from water flasks. Then *Yosef* faced South toward the Temple, kissed his prayer shawl, pulled it over his head like a cowl, and assumed the standing orant position. The young men followed suit, standing behind him.

Barukh Attah, Eee—yah—ohh—way—eee, Elohenu, Melek Ha-Olam, he intoned.

He reverently pushed his shawl back over his shoulders, then suddenly, without warning, whirled around into a martial crouch. His eyes were afire. He gripped his powerful staff in both hands, raised and leveled to the forehead of the closest intruder. His countenance was ferocious, but his voice was calm and unwavering.

"Do you want to live or die?"

The three young men dropped their hands and turned to see what was happening. Behind them were seven armed men crouching on all fours with knives drawn. They were *sicarii*, members of an outlaw zealot or band of guerrilla revolutionaries, who would kill and rob Romans or anyone who served the Romans.

"Boys, take your mallets and prepare to break these *ebenim*," he commanded. Instantly the young men grasped the hammers they used to break and chisel rough stone blocks and raised them over their heads.

Seeing the spiritual power of the Master and the discipline of his young men, the leader of the *sicarii* spoke in a sly voice without moving from the crouching position, "We are your brothers."

Yosef widened his eyes and roared, "Do you want to live or die—*brother*?"

The man knew that in his crouching position he could have his brains splattered before he could get up. His face froze.

In a lightning move, *Yosef* punched the leader's forehead with his staff. His head snapped back with his eyes bulging wide, then he slowly slumped to the ground.

Turning his leonine head slightly to face the other men, who were still crouched on all fours, he pointed his staff at the nearest one and quietly commanded, "Drop the knives."

"How do we know you won't kill us," one of the men quavered.

Bash! The next man fell unconscious into the red dust.

The man crouching on the earth next to him looked up with pleading eyes and said, "I'm dropping my knife."

He slowly dropped the knife, then suddenly scuttled backwards, rolled onto his legs, and ran down the road toward the Sea of Galilee. *Yosef* pointed to the next nearest man, who did the same, then the others dropped and ran, like a routed army.

"Shall we run after them, Master?" asked *Shimone*.

Yosef slowly shook his head, "No. But watch your backs in Sepphoris. Remember the faces of these men. They will try to avenge this humiliation."

"What about these two?" *Shimone* pointed his hammer at the men lying unconscious in the dust.

"Take their sandals. Give them a nasty walk home. Now *we* can be the thieves!"

This was not the first time Master *Yosef* and companions had faced cut-throat thieves on a wilderness journey who, after a word and a glance from *Ha-Arizedek*, had quickly decided to move on. But this was the first time they had been faced with terrorist *sicarii* who saw themselves as saviors of Israel.

Yosef was silent for the rest of the journey.

That evening *Yosef* convened a *chaburah* meal in the upper room of the inn where all the Guild members were quartered. After the intoning of prayers and psalms he raised his right hand for silence.

"Brothers, I see a great evil arising in Israel—something even more evil than Roman domination. It is the rise of the *sicarii*. They form zealot cohorts in memory of Judas Gamala under the pretext of preparing for a sacred war to liberate us from Rome. Yes, it is honorable to die in the defense of Israel. But we have a law that no one can violate with honor. "Thou shalt do no murder!" My brothers, hiding in a crowd to assassinate a Roman official by secretly stabbing him in the back and then disappearing, perhaps to let an innocent person take the blame—is this honorable and sacred warfare?"

He paused while the brethren nodded their agreement.

"Brothers, this is murder, and it violates the most fundamental laws of Israel. It is neither righteous nor honorable.

"Today we were attacked by *sicarii*. Because we trade with the Romans, we have now become traitors in their eyes, fit to be robbed and even murdered without warning. We successfully defended ourselves today because I was warned about the attack while communing in prayer. The *Ruach Ha-Qodesh* whispered into my heart and possessed the hearts of my young men so that they responded with instant obedience, without words or instruction. She taught our hands to fight, even as she inspired Father David.

"But tomorrow it may not be so. Tomorrow we might be attacked while distracted in labor or conversation. We might be attacked while separated and alone. We might be murdered in our beds while we sleep."

Slowly sweeping his gaze from right to left, he locked eyes with each person.

"Brothers, even Father David traded with the Philistines during times of peace, then faced them honorably in battle using the iron swords and spears he had bought from them. It is wisdom for us to discriminate the means we use for liberation.

"Remember the first teaching we received in the Apprentice degree: *Yah does not justify the means by the end, no matter how noble the end may be. Rather, it is the means, and only the means, by which Yah justifies human ends.* Even the liberation of Israel cannot justify cowardly murder before Yah. And with this we learned: *Build upon a foundation of rock, and lay each stone with care.* If we use rotten materials, if we cut corners, if we offer what is unacceptable to Yah, the Temple cannot stand. It will be like a man with broken legs and collapse when the first storms arrive.

"Liberation will come to Israel, brothers. But it cannot appear, and it cannot stand, if it is built upon a foundation of cowardly murder.

"Brothers, from now on when you are working in a Roman city like Sepphoris, you will never travel alone. You will always be alert for danger, and you will lock your doors and windows each night. Watch out for each other at all times on and off the job. Use your signs of recognition when an unknown worker approaches you."

Achim raised a finger and received permission to speak.

"Master *Yosef* and brothers, we know that Yah will redeem Israel by means of the Messiah ben *Yosef*—not by assassination and rebellion. But there have been many signs that Messiah will appear. What do you think? Will he be born to woman? Will he appear out of the sea, or out of the Heavens?"

Eliud raised a finger and spoke.

"Prophets have seen that the Messiah ben *Yosef* will be born of woman and will die like any other man. How will that redeem Israel? Perhaps sacred war will be the only way to break the yoke of Caesar."

Yosef raised a finger and spoke.

"The Prophet Daniel saw this: *Bar-Enash* will appear in the hidden *razim* of Yah. There will be no signs that we can interpret. There will be no announcements from Heaven. Even *Bar-Enash* must be tested, proven, and grow mature like any other son of humanity. Like a hidden spark of fire in the darkness of this world, his light will be at first invisible. My brothers, for all we know, the Messiah ben *Yosef* has already been born among us—invisible. He may be any child you see playing in the streets. Do not follow the hot-heads into premature rebellion. Have patience to see what Yah has prepared for Israel and all humanity."

With that he nodded, *Shimone* broke the loaf, and the men began to share bread and fish in silence.

Chapter Two: *MIRIAM'S* GARDEN

"If the seed is bigger, then the plant grows bigger—is that so, *Imma*?"

Miriam glanced at *Yeshe* as he hammered sun-hardened clods into usable soil. His father allowed him to use an apprentice's mallet for this work even though it would be years before *Yeshua* could be accepted for training. Normally the mallet was used with a chisel to smooth rough rocks into building stones, but for the young boy working in his mother's garden it served to strengthen his right arm. After he became a *Bar-Mitzvah* he would be tested for strength as a condition for initiation. He would have to smooth and shape twelve large stones from sunrise to noon. If his work was not acceptable, he would have a year to prepare and try again. If he again failed, he could not be initiated as a Jewish stonemason.

"What did the wise man say?" she answered.

He stopped hammering and looked up at the cloudless sky.

"He said, 'Know for Thyself.' But how can I do that, *Imma*?"

Miriam pointed to the rocky hill with terraced gardens and said, "Let's go see whether bigger seeds make bigger plants, *Yeshe*."

She took his small hand and felt the hard callouses that had formed from his week of labor. Then she felt his right forearm. It was hot and hard, but she knew from the tension in his face that his little muscles were sore when she began to gently massage them.

"It's time for a walk, dear one. I think you are making knots in your arms. Don't hurt yourself. You have many years to grow a mighty right hand."

Tenderly she took his left hand and they climbed the rocky path into the terraced garden.

"Where will we find seeds?" he asked.

"They are in the fruits and grains. Here is a new fig. Let's look at the seeds."

Yeshua pulled the skin apart and opened the fig. It was an early first-fruit, unripe and without fragrance.

"I guess we eat these seeds," he remarked. "My mouth can tell me best how big they are!" He felt them with his tongue. They were sour and astringent.

"These are small seeds, but the tree is big, *Imma*."

"That's right, *Yeshe*. Now I want to show you something really amazing." She led him to the top of the hill. It was not cultivated, but covered with natural shrubs.

"Look at that bush. It is almost the size of the fig tree, but it's only a shrub. See how thick the branches are! It is called a mustard bush. Do you think this has big seeds?"

Yeshe climbed up to the huge, spreading bush, startling several large birds who were nesting there. They raised a loud alarm and began flapping wildly in circles to protect their nests.

"Where will we find seeds, *Imma*? This bush has no fruit."

"That's right, dear one. But later it puts out flowers that form little sacks with seeds so very, very tiny that they blow away in the wind. We can harvest these little grains and grow small, green mustard shoots in our garden. They make flowers and seeds that we grind like grain to flavor our food."

"But *Imma*, how can such tiny seeds grow into these giant bushes?"

"I don't know, dear one. But the seeds are very strong and spicy to eat. They have much more flavor than many large seeds. I think they must be very strong, like your right hand will be after much practice and perseverance. Someday your *Abba* will look at your right arm and say, 'How did such a mighty arm come from my little *Yeshe*?'"

Miriam fell silent, then looked into *Yeshua*'s eyes.

"Always remember this, my Son. The mustard is a very tough and hardy bush. That is the way the Children of Abraham are. No matter what happens, there is always a remnant of our people who remain faithful to Yah, and we grow and become strong again.

"The wise man said that you must know for yourself. Most of all, you must find and know the true and innermost Torah of Yah that the Prophet tells us is inscribed not on stone tablets, but in our hearts. And when you know what is truly just and good, you must live in fidelity to that secret and hidden Torah. Then you, too, will always have the faithful *emunah* of a tiny mustard seed, and you will become like the greatest of God's people."

*******   *******   *******   *******

During the spring of each year, *Yeshua* worked with *Miriam* helping to prepare the garden. The first and most difficult job was softening the sun-baked surface and crushing it into fine soil.

"How will you do this?" his Mother asked.

Without a reply he began to pound the ground with his mallet. After a few strokes he was able to loosen a chunk of the surface, which he pulled up and pounded. Particles flew in all directions and a thick dust rose into his nostrils. It mixed with the beads of sweat on his forehead as he sneezed and rubbed his eyes. Now his face was streaked with grime.

Miriam laughed and wiped his eyes with the linen shawl she wore for protection from the sun.

"Dear one, there is a better way. Look." She spilled some water upon the crusty earth and pointed to it. "Now strike once or twice with your mallet."

It took only one strike to loosen a large piece of earth, which he pried up with his fingers. No dust, no scattered particles. When he struck it again, it easily broke into smaller pieces without dust. They were infinitely easier to pulverize into fine soil. The wetness of the new soil made it darker than the dry earth, easier to pick out small stones, and simpler to collect.

"*Yeshe*, do you know that the human heart can be like hard-baked earth? When we dry up the waters of compassion, we harden our hearts to others. Then we have excluded the *Ruah ha-Qodesh* from the temples of our hearts. She lives in the waters of compassion. When we allow the living waters to dry up, we no longer have the Presence of God dwelling within our hearts."

"But you poured water upon the dry earth, *Imma*, and it became alive again. How can we bring the living water back into our hardened hearts?"

Miriam was silent for a moment, then she dipped her fingers into the water, opened his garment, and traced the Star of David upon the little boy's chest.

"When we no longer have the Spirit of Holiness in our hearts, She commands Her angels to strike painful blows that break apart the dry earth and choke us with our own dust. Then we weep tears of self-pity that begin to soften our hearts, and again She strikes painful blows that bring more tears, until finally our hearts crumble into fine, moist soil.

Then She brings forth springs of living water that moisten our hearts with sincere compassion for others when we feel them suffering as we have suffered."

She gazed into his eyes. "Why do you think our hardened hearts must be pulverized into humble soil?"

"So they can grow into gardens?"

"Good, *Yeshe*! Our hearts can receive divine seeds that Heaven sows and bring them forth in life. But first they must be humbled through many experiences."

"Is that why people suffer, *Imma*?"

"There are many reasons why people suffer, *Yeshe*. But there is a special kind of suffering that we bring upon ourselves when we harden our hearts. This happens to every heart as we grow—no exceptions. And it will happen to you, dear one, before you become a man."

Yeshua drew back and knitted his brow. "Never! I shall never become like that, *Imma*! How can anyone let this happen?"

Miriam looked away and said, more to herself than to the little boy, "It must be so, if we are to grow…"

On the following *Shabbat*, *Yeshua* waited for the time for scrolls and psalms and then asked *Yosef*, "*Abba*, how can Yah be a woman? What is the *Ruach ha-Qodesh*?"

Yosef was surprised by the question.

"My Son, you are asking about the *Kabbalah* teachings that are not given to children, especially those who are not yet *Bar-Mitzvah*."

"But *Abba*, if I can ask the question, can I not receive an answer?"

The boy's reply pleased *Yosef*.

"We shall read tonight from the scroll of *Yeshua Ben-Sirach*," he said. He nodded to *Miriam*, and she brought the scroll. "But you will have to find your own meaning, my Son."

Yosef placed the scroll on the table before him and began to read.

"At first She will lead him by tortuous paths, filling him with craven fears. Her discipline will be a torment to him, and Her decrees a hard test, until She fully trusts him.

"But then She will come straight back to him again and bring great joy, and reveal her secrets unto him."

"But *Abba*, who is She?" There was no answer. *Yosef* rolled up the scroll and handed it to *Miriam*, who smiled warmly upon *Yeshua* and raised her eyebrows.

"The men don't teach me their *Kabbalah* either, dear one. But maybe the Garden will teach you the *Kabbalah* that I know in my heart."

Yakob nudged his older brother excitedly and whispered, "Tell me what you think the scroll means tonight when we go to bed!"

After psalms and goodnights, *Yeshua* and *Yakob* lay together in the darkness of a moonless night. *Yakob* whispered, "What do you think about the reading?"

After a silence, he answered, "Maybe if Yah is our *Abba*, we must also have an *Imma*."

"But She sounds so very strict," moaned *Yakob*. "She tests her disciples and makes trial with them until She trusts them."

Yeshua thought for a moment.

"Yes, but when they prove themselves She brings them joy and knowledge."

Yeshua remained awake long after *Yakob* had drifted off to sleep.

   *******   *******   *******   *******

For many years the young *Yeshua* worked with his mother in the garden. She often answered his questions with more questions, but always encouraged him to be aware of the spiritual lessons that the garden could teach. She often said she could feel the *Pardes* or Paradise of Adam and Eve invisibly present in their little garden.

"There will be many men who will teach you, dear one," you once told him. "But the great Teacher of all men is *Hochmah,* the Spirit of Wisdom, and you should strive to become Her disciple. She draws near unto us and instructs those with eyes to see and ears to hear through the allegories of nature."

When the moon became full, *Yeshua* often lay awake in his bed thinking about Her. Was She God? He wanted to be Her disciple, but he was not even a *Bar Mitzvah*.

On the first bright full moon of spring, which his Mother called his birth-moon, as he was about to turn seven years old, *Yeshe* made a special birthday prayer.

"Great *Abba* and God of Abraham, Isaac, and *Yakob, Baruch Attah, Melek ha-Olam,* I know that I am too young to be a disciple of your *Hochmah*. But I pray for even a glimpse of your Wisdom."

He paused, closing his eyes against the sheer brightness of the full moon, and quickly became drowsy. As he drifted into sleep, exhausted from his physical labor, he heard voices singing *Eliahu, ha-Nabi.*

He awakened suddenly at midnight. The full moon was high in the sky. A vivid dream was fresh and dancing into his mind.

He had been buried, like a dead man. It was pitch dark and he couldn't move, but he was not afraid. There was a fragrance of warm, dry soil surrounding him. He had been in this state for what seemed a very long time, but he wasn't hungry. In fact, it was as though he were indifferent to the passing of time.

But one thing was very clear. He was alone, isolated, inert.

Then he heard a gurgling of water and felt moisture all around him. Moisture became wetness. He felt his skin soaking and expanding, and somehow now he was growing hungry, even ravenous.

He was amazed to find himself surrounded by a huge store of milky food. It had been a hard, rock-like structure in which he had always been embedded, but now it had softened in the moisture that was penetrating his world. He devoured the sweet food.

But the food was soon gone, and his body had split apart and was dissolving. Now he began to feel that he was both starving and drowning. His familiar world of isolation and loneliness turned to one of panic and despair

In place of the supply of sweet, milky food, he could taste only strange and poisonous substances dissolved in the water that inexorably penetrated everything in his world of darkness. He was starving to death for want of his familiar food.

In despair he began to push a white root downward. No hope, no way out of death. Better the hasten death and sip the poisonous waters that were drowning him. With his last bit of strength, he drank and died.

But behold! Now he awakened into another world. The poisons that had killed him were now nourishing him in another kind of body. He felt a new and exhilarating energy that was connecting him with other beings outside of his world—or rather, beings that were now inside his world of darkness. He could feel them touching and penetrating him through the moisture that surrounded his new body.

The new body was growing both up and down. Beneath him was a cold, dark abyss, and above him a gentle, moist warmth. His consciousness was ascending toward that warmth, which seemed to draw him upward. Yet he knew that he was straining, working, and growing on his own in harmonious dialogue with the warmth from above.

Suddenly the dawning of a brilliant light! As he pushed his way upward through the warm soil he found himself bathed in the source of all warmth—the sun. It was the sun which had inspired and drawn him upward even from deep beneath the Earth. The sun, acting through hierarchies of soil and moisture, had called him forth into the light.

Now he was no longer supported by tightly packed soil on all sides, but in order to continue his ascent must balance and elevate himself upon his deep root. He must stiffen his resolve with an outer armor—a skin or bark that defined and protected him. No longer an undifferentiated sprout or sapling, he stood tall with a kind of divine pride generating limbs, leaves, and flowers. Birds and insects sheltered among his branches.

Finally he was full-grown, the greatest of the shrub-trees. He cast his seed into the wind knowing that he had finally become fruitful. The ancient sun smiled upon him as he cast forth the divine pattern on Earth that the *Abba-Imma* of Lights had conceived in the eternal *'Olamim* of the Heavens.

In the clear light of the full moon, *Yeshe* marveled. He knew that Divine *Hochmah,* the Wisdom of God, had spoken to him in a wordless lesson while his body slept. He knew that he had been accepted for divine instruction.

What would this mean? How would he be tested?

He remembered the suffering and doubt of the isolated seed. The food that was offered for growth was so different that it seemed poisonous. To accept it seemed to mean defeat and death. This was a test, but who did the testing? Not the Eternal One who offered the food. It was the seed himself! He was testing and torturing himself with inability—no, *unwillingness*—to accept the nourishment that would make him transform and grow.

Perhaps She, *Hochmah*, offers some kind of new, transforming nurture that is misunderstood as suffering or torture by those who seek Her. Perhaps a change in life or circumstance that seems evil can, in fact, be even better for the wise person than a continuation of his accustomed ways.

He resolved to remain faithful and accepting in all circumstances. But what was that thing his mother said? Every person, no exception, hardens his heart and brings suffering upon himself. "It must be so, if we are to grow." Would this happen to him?

Suddenly he remembered that in his dream, he was not just any seed—he was a mustard seed. Mother Wisdom was showing him that even the faithful mustard seed must suffer in isolation and die before it can live, transform, and grow to fulfillment. So even those of greatest faith must lose all hope and suffer!

He marveled and whispered aloud, "This is how the faithful test and torture their own souls. But even so, like faithful Job, they do not curse or blame God, nor do they blame themselves. They just eat the poison and die."

He would always remember the *emunah* of the mustard seed, who must suffer and die before it can live and grow.

Later in summer *Miriam* gave birth to a healthy, screaming thing named *Shalome*. Her father named her "Peaceful" with the hope that it would bring out that quality, but *Yeshe* and *Yakob* decided it had the opposite effect. Some nights she squalled for hours, and during the daytime she demanded every spare moment of her exhausted mother's attention. This was also a summer of new construction for *Yosef*, who was forced to be away in Sepphoris a great deal of the time.

Yeshua and *Yakob* were left to their own devices much more than in the past. When their work at home was finished, *Miriam* often sent them to the market place. There they sometimes made purchases for their mother or were allowed to purchase a small treat for themselves.

Other children played at the market place, both children of the vendors and older boys who wandered all over the city without supervision. These older boys were from poor families of the *amme-ha-eretz* or non-practicing Jews. They watched with envy when *Yeshua* and *Yakob* made their purchases, making jokes and whispering to each other.

Some of them belonged to a gang that was known to steal. Their families were jealous of Master *Yosef*'s modest wealth. This had instilled a sense of class alienation that discouraged the market-place boys from making friendships with *Yeshe* or *Yakob*. Some of the bolder boys were openly hostile.

Like his father, *Yeshe* was tall and feared no one. The other boys knew this instinctively and did not attempt to hinder him. But *Yakob* was a different matter. When separated from *Yeshe*, he was teased and tormented. Many times *Yeshua* had protected him from bullies, whom he called the "land boys."

One afternoon *Yakob* went ahead of *Yeshua* to the market place. He sat quietly on a rocky hill overlooking the city center waiting for his older brother to arrive. He thought he was safe, but suddenly a gang of boys appeared on the road to the market place. They spotted him alone and vulnerable on the hilltop. With hoots and jeers they approached him.

"Hey, little prince! You got some money?"

Yakob took a deep breath and stared straight ahead saying nothing.

"What—you can't talk? You got some money?" Now the biggest of the boys grabbed his garment and shook it violently.

"I don't hear any money!" he shouted.

"Let's get out of here before big brother comes," one of the other boys warned. *Yakob*'s tormentor thought for a moment and said, "Nice sandals. If I take them, you can't run home very fast."

The bully yanked both of *Yakob*'s sandals from his feet and, holding them up as a trophy, ran laughing back to the road. The whole group of boys ran following him into the city center while *Yakob* sat desolate on the hill hoping that *Yeshua* would arrive soon.

"Okay, *Yakob*. Let's go to the market place!" It was *Yeshua* on the road motioning for him to follow.

Yakob stood up.

"Where are your sandals?" his big brother asked.

Yakob stared at the ground and swallowed back his tears.

"Did the land boys take your sandals?" *Yeshua* asked, already knowing the answer.

"*Yakob*, I want you to stay here. Don't try to walk anywhere because you'll cut your feet. I'll go get your sandals."

"But *Yeshe*, there are many land boys and they are mean," *Yakob* cried. "Please don't go. They might beat you!"

"I might beat *them*!" *Yeshua* hissed, turning and striding resolutely toward the market place. "Stay here!"

Yakob was too afraid for his brother, and too curious to see what would happen, to do as he was told. Keeping a discreet distance, treading painfully over the rocky road, he followed *Yeshua* with a great feeling of foreboding.

From a great distance away, the land boys saw *Yeshua* coming. He strode with chin jutted and fists closed straight toward them.

"Here comes big brother. Maybe we better teach him a lesson," said the bully who still held the sandals in his hand. But the other boys shrank back as *Yeshua* approached, moving faster now and focusing his fierce gaze upon the bully. Suddenly the boy with the sandals knew that *Yeshua* had more power, anger, and rage than he could ever feel, and he was afraid.

Yakob ran forward to see what would happen now. He was no longer afraid.

Striding without speaking up to the bully, with both hands *Yeshua* grabbed the boy's right hand. His burning eyes transfixed the land boy, who suddenly found himself unable to move. The bully dropped the sandals. *Yeshua* quickly bent the boy's little finger backwards into an extremely painful position while he held the rest of his hand immobile in his powerful grip.

"Ow! Help! Please don't break it!" the bully whimpered in panic. He realized that *Yeshua* could snap his finger back and leave it hanging like a broken staff, and he had no power to stop him. The other boys watched awe-stricken.

Without releasing his grip, and without releasing the bully from his fierce eyes, *Yeshua* spoke.

"What I say to you, I say to all. If anyone of you harms my brother or any other child, I will come to get you at a time you least expect it."

With a powerful lurch he threw the bully to the ground and stepped on his testicles, holding up his finger to indicate that if the boy moved, he would crush them. The boy held breathlessly still. *Yeshua* continued to transfix him with his eyes.

"And I will not be nice."

"Okay," the bully whispered.

"Pick up the sandals, crawl over, and put them back on my brother's feet," *Yeshua* commanded. He released the boy, but did not step back.

"I should crawl?" the bully whispered. No answer. He slowly crawled to the sandals, then to *Yakob*. Without looking up, he brushed off the sand, replaced, and latched the sandals.

"Go away from here," *Yeshua* ordered in a soft but firm voice. The bully walked backwards, keeping his face toward *Yeshua*, then turned and ran. All the other boys also ran.

Yeshua took his brother's hand and walked silently into the market place.

"How did you know I was here, *Yeshe*?" asked *Yakob*.

"Why were you here?" he responded. They both laughed.

Next summer another little sister was born, and during the following years three baby brothers—*Shimone, Yosef,* and *Jehuda.*

Chapter Three: YAKOB

Yeshua was fascinated with the parchment scrolls that *Yosef* kept hidden in an ornamented olive-wood box. They contained the psalms and visions of Enoch that were written by the scribes of entranced Jewish *chasidim,* prophets and sybils.

On *Shabbat,* Master *Yosef* always placed one scroll on the table before him. After the blessing of the children and before the opening of the meal, he would read without explanation from the scroll, just as though it were the great Torah Scroll of the synagogue. Sometimes it told of the Ten Heavens, the *Merkabah* or Throne-Chariot of Yah, of angels and the *'Olam Ha-Ba* or Messianic Age yet to come. Other times it quoted the wisdom that the Twelve Patriarchs transmitted in sacred testaments to their children.

Yet other times it contained the words for a new psalm—one that *Yeshua* had never heard resonating from the synagogue. *Yosef* would sing the first line, and everyone would sing it back to him antiphonally. *Yeshua* always learned the complete new psalm the first time it was introduced. The next morning his mother often heard him singing and teaching it to the other children.

Yosef allowed *Yeshua* to sit at his right side and see the Hebrew and Aramaic words of the scrolls as he read them. Long before the age that he was to begin formal studies for *Bar Mitzva,* the highly precocious *Yeshua,* with occasional help from his father, had taught himself to read Hebrew script in both languages.

As Master *Yosef* prospered, his circle of professional and religious associates grew. Stone-masters and other Jewish Guildsmen often sat at the family table on *Shabbat* Eve alongside religious teachers, healers, prophets, and Rabbis. When such dignitaries were present, *Yosef,* would place the chosen scroll before *Yeshua* and point to a selection. To the amazement of guests, the boy would not only read the sections flawlessly, but intone and lead the psalm.

A first-born son, Jewish or gentile, had privileges not accorded to younger sons. Although the custom was of great benefit to him, *Yeshua* did not feel it was fair. His younger brother *Yakob* was also bright and interested in religion. Why should he be excluded simply because of age or birth?

"*Abba*, can my brother *Yakob* also sit with you and learn to read?" he asked one *Shabbat* afternoon.

"But *Yeshe*, I have only one right hand, and your mother always sits at my left hand," *Yosef* answered gently, inwardly moved by the generosity of the boy's concern for his younger brother.

"*Abba*, he can sit at my place and learn," was the reply. "I already know how to read."

Yosef closed his eyes and was silent for longer than *Yeshua* could keep from drawing a breath. Finally he said,

"*Yeshe*, you are the first-born. This was the doing of Yah, not me. You may not give your seat to your brother."

Yeshua stared at his feet.

"But my son, you may teach him to read yourself."

"What?" The boy's face lit up. "How? I have no scrolls."

"You have sand and a stick. If you can teach Yacob how to recognize and speak the Hebrew letters by Pesach, I will allow you to take out the scrolls under your mother's supervision and begin teaching them to *Yakob*."

Yeshua was elated!

"Thank you, *Abba*," and before *Yosef* could open his mouth, the boy had scampered away in search of his brother.

Miriam smiled at her husband in disbelief.

"You know, he'll do it. He'll have *Yakob* reading. Then what? Next he'll be wanting to teach his sisters to read Torah."

Yosef laughed.

"Remember, my Darling, that *Rav* Elishua taught his two daughters to read and study Torah. Perhaps *Rav Yeshua* will do the same for his sisters!"

Eagerly *Yakob* sat under a tree learning the Hebrew letters, which his older brother patiently explained.

"Look at the shape. See, it's like a house, *beth*. Here's the floor, the wall, the roof. And here's the open door. So we call it *beth*, and it makes the sound 'buh'.

"Okay, what's this? Good! Now, how do your say this sound? Very good, *Yakob*! You are learning faster than I ever did!"

On Pesach Eve as his sisters were preparing the table, *Yeshua* kissed his father's prayer shawl and said,

"*Abba*, your son *Yakob* knows all the letters. Would you like to test him?"

Yosef pretended to be very surprised. He stood up, removed the olive-wood chest from its place, and retrieved one of the scrolls.

"*Yakob*, come sit on my lap. Now, what is the name of this letter?"

"That is *nun*, *Abba*. It has a different shape when it comes at the end of a word. It makes the sound 'nuh'."

Yosef was very pleased. He continued the test until he had verified that *Yakob* knew every Hebrew letter. Then he placed the scroll onto the table, shifted *Yakob* to his left knee, and set the laughing *Yeshua* on his right knee.

"I suppose you want to start learning to read the scrolls now, *Yakob*? I promised this to your brother, who loves you very much and wanted to give you his first-born seat at the table. I wouldn't let him give up his seat, because that would not be *zadik*. Do you understand?"

"Yes, *Abba*."

"But I have something new for both of you. We now have a *Chazzan* at the synagogue."

Yeshua's eyes brightened as he asked, "A Torah Teacher?"

"Yes. And he has agreed to take both of you as students. You will meet with him two mornings each week and begin what you must learn to become a *Bar Mitzva* when you are thirteen years old. If you are good students, he will answer any questions you wish to ask.

"His name is Eleazar Ha-Zedek. He knows very much. He is a dear old friend of mine, a retired Master Mason. When he was young, he was raised and educated by the desert prophets known as the Essenes."

"Who are the Essenes, *Abba*?" asked *Yakob*.

"They are saints of Yah, my Son. They have collected all the scrolls of prophecy and wisdom that are not known in the synagogue—the same scrolls that we read from on *Shabbat*. They do not sacrifice animals on altars, but offer eucharist and praise of bread and wine, as we do every *Shabbat* Eve. They are the true Priesthood who make intercession for the sins of Israel. They keep themselves pure from the abominations of those who control the Temple and politics of Jerusalem."

Later that night when the children were asleep, *Miriam* put her hand on *Yosef*'s shoulder.

"The Essenes are ascetics who look down their noses at natural families, yet they want to take our brightest children for indoctrination. Their price for education is the souls of our children. Will Eleazar try to steal our *Yeshe* and our *Yakob* from us?"

Yosef stroked her forehead.

"Eleazar was expelled from the Essene community because he expressed these very thoughts. He has been my Guild brother, my friend, and my *chaburah* brother for many years. I know his deepest thoughts and motives. His loyalty is to the School of Hillel, and he knows not only Torah, but the Prophets and the Later Writings. Even more, he is a Messianic brother who knows how to ascend in the *Merkabah*. Do you see how *Yeshua* reaches out for deep instruction? Eleazar will know this and answer all his questions, even concerning the *Kabbalah* mysteries."

Miriam sighed and lay her head upon *Yosef*'s chest.

The Pesach full moon ruled like a Queen over the Sea of Galilee and its verdant fields. Birds were singing as though it were high noon. But all the inhabitants of Nazareth were sleeping soundly. All except one.

Yeshua was awake, but not his body.

He looked down upon his sleeping body, and then drifted over above *Yakob*. Dimly he realized that he was still sleeping, but no longer dreaming.

"Is this real? Where are *Abba* and *Imma*?" he thought.

Instantly he found himself floating above their sleeping figures. *Abba* was not snoring, but he was not awake, either. Then *Yeshua* saw something like a cord of silver moonlight extending from the crown of *Abba*'s head straight up through the roof.

"What is this?" he thought. Instantly he was floating upward, following the cord through the roof where it disappeared in the silvery brilliance of the moonlight. He looked down and became afraid. Suddenly he felt himself falling backwards and a shock like striking the ground awakened him, heart pounding. This time he was awake in his body, breathing hard and trying to sit up. But his muscles wouldn't move.

A few more breaths and he began to feel more normal. He sat up and tried to remember what happened. He listened for his father's snore, but there was only silence. He crept on all fours to the screen that separated the children's room from their parent's and peeked around the corner. *Abba* was asleep, but not snoring.

He stood up and walked to the open door. It was midnight and the moon was directly overhead, lighting up the Galilee so brightly that he could see individual trees and fields. He quickly put on his sandals, stepped outside into the courtyard, and then out the front entrance. Hesitating for a moment, he suddenly felt drawn to one of his favorite places—a grassy hill overlooking Nazareth from the West.

Picking his way between the larger boulders that protruded from the earth and gRabbing bushes for support, he ascended the stony path. Finally he was able to crawl up and over the large boulder that held the grassy earth in place, where he stood for a moment looking at the placid lake known as the Sea. Then, facing Southeast toward the Temple in Jerusalem, he raised his hands in the orant position and intoned the prayer that *Yosef* often used.

"*Barukh Attah, Ee-yah-oh-way-ee, Elohenu, Melek Ha-Olam…*"

He felt a strange excitation of energy at the crown of his head and at the root of his spine. He intoned the Divine Name of Yahoweh again, this time drawing it out slowly and letting the tone resonate in his nostrils.

"*Eeee-yaaah-oooh-way-eeee; Eeee-yaaah-oooh-way-eeee; Eeee-yaaah-oooh-way-eeee.*"

Now he felt like a glowing coal. He stopped his breath, staring fixedly at trees and bushes. They seemed to glow as well. No, they seemed to actually burn! He drew in a deep breath and intoned the Divine Name again. The experience became even more intense. All the earth, the sky, the Sea of Galilee were no longer separate, but all part of one fiery matrix that glowed a golden-reddish radiance. The moon was no longer silver, but aflame with a fiery radiance.

"Moses saw the Fire of Yah in a burning bush, but I see the Fire of Yah everywhere. All the Earth is sacred to Yah—not just one place or another. I am standing on sacred ground, but I don't need to remove my sandals, because they are sacred, too. I am sacred. I…Am…sacred. All beings are sacred."

He sat upon the flaming grass with his back against a large boulder. Closing his eyes, and put his head between his knees, as Elijah had done on Mount Carmel. In his mind, he began to intone the Pesach psalm to the Prophet Elijah,

"*Eliahu Ha-Nabi, Eliahu Ha-Nabi…*"

Soon he could hear the psalm being intoned by many men with deep voices. The psalm was singing itself without any effort from him. His mind became quiet and he listened to the hypnotic chanting. Then he fell asleep.

He dreamed of Elijah the Prophet, of Moses, and of Enoch. They showed him beautiful things he could scarcely remember later, but he knew that somehow, in some way, he had actually been with them. They were living, like him, in some kind of body.

"*Yeshe,*" a voice whispered. He felt a gentle tugging on his shoulder. "What are you doing? Everyone is out looking for you."

He opened his eyes and saw *Yakob*. It was morning and the sun had already risen.

"*Abba, Imma*! I found him! He's up here!" *Yakob* shouted.

As the boys scuttered down the steep path, *Yeshua* saw his father standing with his staff and frowning. *Imma* was not in sight. She must still be looking for him.

"*Yeshe*, I want to talk to you alone," said *Yosef*. *Yakob* exchanged a glance with *Yeshua*, then ran up the road looking for *Imma*.

"What were you doing, my Son?" Master *Yosef* was far more upset than he allowed himself to appear.

"I couldn't sleep, so I went up to my special place and, well, I guess I fell asleep up there. I'm sorry, *Abba*."

"*Yeshe*, listen to me. There are men—bad and misguided men—who want to do us harm because I work for the Romans. I don't think that they will come to Nazareth, but they could. From now on, when you want to be alone in prayer, take care that someone knows where you are."

Yeshua searched his father's eyes.

"How did you know that I was in prayer?" he slowly asked.

"I know you, my Son. And so does your brother *Yakob*."

Chapter Four: *BAR-MITZVA*

Eleazar the Righteous was short, broad, and bearded. His knees were calloused and scarred because, unlike the *Chasidim* of Nazareth who stood with hands raised for prayer, Eleazar always knelt. He was a mystic and practitioner of hidden *Kabbalah.*

He arrived early for *Shabbat* and, after a formal introduction by *Yosef*, sat cross-legged at the corner of the room with eyes closed and hands resting palms up on his knees.

Yeshe stole furtive glances at his Torah teacher, who seemed to have become almost invisible. Yet he felt Eleazar's glowing eyes fixed upon him. How could the teacher have his eyes closed and yet be gazing intently at him? *Yeshe* did not find this to be an invasive experience. It actually seemed very familiar and friendly, as though Eleazar were one of many invisible friends who watched over him day and night.

During the *seder, Yosef* invited Eleazar to offer the Blessing over the Cup. He drew a deep breath and then began quietly humming a deep tone that slowly transformed itself into the sacred word *B-a-a-r-u-u-u-ch*, which he intoned several times followed by the full Blessing.

Yeshe had heard his father intone the Blessing every week, but never had he known it this way—vibrated with such power and sanctity. It was as though he were hearing, feeling, and experiencing the Blessing for the first time. Suddenly he had ears to hear. He realized now why his *Abba* had arranged for this man to be his tutor.

Yeshe was inspired with a deep reverence and awe for both the Blessing and for Eleazar. A lump of deep feeling arose in his throat with a yearning to achieve the sanctity of Eleazar and the skill to reveal divine Reality to others through his voice.

During the *Shabbat* meal, there was none of the usual light conversation and joking. Instead, *Yosef* and Eleazar talked about the responsibilities of a *Bar Mitzva,* the long and perseverant study that was required, and the transformation from boyhood to manhood that was symbolized in the ceremony. *Yosef* would make a commitment to bring both *Yeshe* and *Yakob* regularly to the *Shabbat* morning synagogue worship to hear Torah read and to attend the class offered by Eleazar as *Chazzan* of the synagogue. But the two boys would also meet with him once during the week for private tutorial.

Toward the end of the seder, *Yosef* asked *Miriam* to bring the scroll that he had obtained for this occasion. It was not like the scrolls that *Yeshe* was used to seeing, and the letters were written in a different form of Hebrew script.

"This is Torah, my sons. The language is much more ancient than what you have seen in the scrolls we have at home. It is also sometimes more difficult to understand the meaning. You will learn to read and chant Torah."

Yosef handed the scroll to Eleazar, who now spoke for the first time to the boys.

"You will also read the Targums, which translate the Prophets into language that our people in the synagogue can understand. We sing Torah, then recite and explain Targum. In order to chant Torah, you will not need to understand it. You will memorize Torah portions that will be sung in synagogue each week of the year and others for holy days. What questions do you have?"

Yeshe was amazed that he was invited to ask questions of the *Chazzan*, but responded quickly.

"Master, will I be able to ask any questions I want?"

Now it was Eleazar's turn to be amazed. He hesitated for a moment, then answered, "Any serious question that enters you heart, I shall try to answer."

"Master, why do we only sing Torah, but recite and explain Targum?"

Eleazar smiled. "Torah contains the laws and statutes of Adonai which we already know and are taught from the days of our youth. They are holy and good, so we praise them by chanting them, just as we praise Adonai by singing the psalms.

"But the Prophets were holy men burning with divine fire, like the bush that Moses saw. They speak to us in plain language about the deep interior purity and righteousness that allows the *Ruach Ha-Qodesh* to dwell in the temple of our hearts, to inscribe the higher mysteries of Torah on our hearts. The *davrim* of the Prophets draws us upward to the Divine Throne, where the angels teach us directly from the mouth of Adonai. That is why it is important to recite and explain the writings of the Prophets."

After a brief silence, *Yosef* reached out and pulled *Yakob* onto his lap.

"Well, my little one, do you know that your brother has taught you to read the *davrim* of the Prophets? That is what we recite on every *Shabbat,* and that is what you have learned to read. Now, see how well you can recite what is written here in Torah."

Yosef unrolled the scroll and pointed to the beginning of the Torah. "Now we'll see just how well your brother has taught you."

Yakob worked laboriously through the words. "At the start of…the making…of the Elohim…I don't know these words. What are '*tohu*' and '*vohu*'?"

Yeshe bent across his father's bosom and stared at the Hebrew letters. They didn't make any sense to him, either.

Eleazar slowly drew the scroll to himself and rolled it up. "This is a mystical language. It reveals how Adonai formed all things from the substance of His Divine Light, and how He generated Humanity as one male-female being."

"What does 'generated' mean?" asked *Yakob*.

"It means that Adonai brought forth or emanated all things from within Himself as a Father and Mother bring forth children," *Yosef* replied.

"Then, is that why we call Adonai our *Abba*?" asked *Yeshe*. Without waiting for the reply, he asked, "Why does it call Adonai the *Elohim*? Is not Adonai One?"

"Adonai is One, Two, Three, and Many," replied Eleazar. "When He is Two, He is both Father and Mother. When He is Many, He is us."

There was silence. Eleazar handed the scroll to *Miriam* and began to hum a tone. Soon the tone grew into the first line of a Psalm. "*Baruch Attah.*" He paused. *Yosef* and the two boys sang the same phrase responsively in the same meter and with the same melody used by Eleazar. Continuing, the Essene *Chazzan* intoned the Holy Name: "*Ee-ah-oh-waoy-ee.*" For this he was joined by *Yosef* and the boys, for it was common in Galilean Judaism to intone the Sacred Name. Then Eleazar intoned the next phrase and paused for the response: "*Tzu-u-u-u-u-udy.*"

As the three responsively returned the phrase, *Yeshe* recognized the Psalm, which was sung at times of great oppression against Israel. "Blessed art Thou, YHWH, my Rock, Who teaches my fingers and hands to fight and wage battle."

When the Psalm had been sung, all placed their right palm over the heart with left palm over the right. This was the *nacham* or posture of submission to the guidance and protection of YHWH. This was usually done merely as a gesture, but Eleazar remained in the *nacham* for what seemed a very long time before taking a deep breath, rocking forward and backward, and intoning a threefold *A-a-mayn*. *Yosef* and the boys joined in.

Yeshe was in deep awe of Eleazar. After the Essene sage had taken his leave, *Yeshe* asked his father, "Why did we sing the Psalm for struggle and battle, Father?"

Yosef looked deeply into the eyes of both boys with what seemed to be both sadness and joy.

"My boys, you will be training to be Sons of the Covenant and to stand as men in Israel. There are dark forces that oppose you and all Israel. You will be tested many times. That is how men are made. You will learn to be warriors of the Spirit. You will learn from your wounds."

Yeshe was silent for a moment, then asked, "Father, will we be tested by Adonai or by *Hochmah*?"

Without hesitation, *Yosef* responded, "Do I, your father, test you? Does your mother test you?"

Yakob replied, also without hesitation, "No, Father. You protect us and feed us. You give us only good things."

"Well spoken, little one!" *Yosef* answered. "And neither does Adonai test you, even through the Voice of *Hochmah*."

"But Father, we have read in the scrolls that *Hochmah* tests us until She trusts us," *Yeshe* objected.

"Dear One, sometimes we have to interpret the scrolls. Sometimes we understand things differently and better than the great saints who wrote them, just as we understand things better when we are men than when we are young boys. Things that were written in old times are holy and sacred *only* if our understanding is holy. Do you understand?"

"Yes I do, Father," *Yeshe* replied thoughtfully.

"I will tell you the true *Kabbalah* of the scroll, which was written by *Yeshua* ben Sirach. When you read, you must reverse the pronoun genders, because all *talmidim* and seekers after Divine Wisdom are female with respect to Adonai. That is because we are not mere *nefeshim*, but eternal *yechidoth*. Our highest souls are female and destined to Holy Union as the Bride of Adonai. So in the future when you read this passage, you will identify Wisdom with Adonai and a *talmid* with *yechida*, his feminine high self, and say,

"At first He will lead her by tortuous paths, filling her with craven fears. His discipline will be a torment to her, and His decrees a hard test, until she fully trusts Him.

"But then He will come straight back to her again and bring great joy, and reveal His secrets unto her."

Yeshe was silent for a moment, then asked with measured speech, "And so...it is the *talmid* who must trust Adonai's Wisdom—not the other way around?"

Yakob continued his brother's question without waiting for an answer. "And *Abba*, the *talmid* is not tested or tortured by Adonai, but by His Torah?"

"Not by Torah or discipline, but by his own reaction—his own response—to the Way of Wisdom, which is not the way of human will or desire," *Yosef* replied. "It is not Adonai, but we ourselves who bring spiritual trial to our own souls—sometimes out of ignorance, and other times through the instrumentality of our own high self. The issue is not who or what tests us, but how we respond, because tests and trials *must* be experienced by those who seek Wisdom, just as children must fall many times before they can walk."

"Now...I understand what the prophet meant when he said that in future days the true Torah would be inscribed in our hearts. These are the future days, and those were the old times. This must be the *Kabbalah* that Eleazar will teach us. Is it so, *Abba*?" asked *Yeshe*.

"That is so, *Yeshe*. Now you will begin to understand why I have asked Eleazar to be your tutor," *Yosef* replied with a glance at *Miriam*, who nodded in agreement.

"Yes, and I too understand," said *Miriam*.

"But know this, my sons. *Kabbalah* cannot be taught. It can only be known and learned. Eleazar will not teach you doctrine. He will merely give you the tools you need to understand what Adonai has already inscribed in your hearts."

******* ******* ******* *******

When *Yeshe* was very young, *Yosef* had met only with his Masonic *chaburah* for *Shabbat* Torah study. But when Eleazar had moved to Nazareth to become *Chazzan* of the synagogue, *Yosef* began attending *Shabbat* Torah study at the synagogue after services. He was joined by many of his Guild apprentices. The boys had attended synagogue with their parents on holy days, but in the past the family joined the small congregation for *Shabbat* worship only rarely. Now, however, the entire family began regular Saturday worship.

The morning of *Shabbat* was unlike other mornings. *Abba* and *Imma* remained secluded in their bedroom until late in the morning. *Yeshua* could sometimes hear low talking and sweet laughter punctuating the mysterious silence of the parental bedroom. He knew that *Abba* and *Imma* were awake even when there was deep silence because he could not hear *Yosef*'s snoring. He often wondered what his parents were doing on the special morning of *Shabbat*. He sensed that somehow it was both joyful and sacred. It was another one of those *Kabbalistic* things that adults knew about.

The children were encouraged to sleep late and allowed to play in the immediate area outside until they were called in for a special breakfast. *Imma* did not prepare food, but laid out dishes left over from the evening *Shabbat* dinner. It was a morning Thanksgiving meal made of succulent morsels from the weekly Thanksgiving feast. Prayers and psalms were intoned. *Yosef* sometimes read from the Scrolls, and other times spoke about the Way of Adonai.

Then it was time for the entire family to dress in their finest clothing and walk to the Synagogue. Even though *Yosef* was relatively wealthy and highly respected in the community, he made a point every week of seating himself and his family humbly in back or middle areas of the floor. Many times, however, he was asked to read a Torah portion by the *Chazzan*. On those occasions he was invited to come forward to occupy a seat of honor next to Eleazar—an invitation that would be impious to refuse. *Yeshua* remained with his family and took his father's vacated seat, as the eldest son was expected to do.

After worship everyone gathered on the porch to share treats saved by the women from *Shabbat* feasts. These included salted fish, sweet breads, dates, and other seasonal fruits. Many of the men lingered far into the afternoon discussing Torah, politics, and the latest gossip while the women and children returned home. However, the boys being instructed for *Bar Mitzva* were invited by Eleazar back into the Synagogue, where they practiced reading and intoning Hebrew Torah and studied *Targumim* and the interpretation of Torah.

At the Synagogue *Yeshua* and *Yakob* were part of a group of eleven boys, most of whom were dull-witted, and none of whom knew how to read. *Yeshua* and *Yakob* were called upon to individually assist other boys most of the time. At first this was interesting, but soon it became drudgery. Eleazar sympathized with their situation, but expected them to conscientiously assist the other boys, no matter how slow and dull the task. So while the brothers did not particularly look forward to *Shabbat* school, they understood it as a responsibility that they must take seriously.

However, the week-day sessions with Eleazar were entirely different. The boys were in their own home, there were no other students, and Eleazar made good on his promise to teach them about anything they could form into a question. *Yeshua* and *Yakob* soon lost their shyness in the presence of Eleazar, who treated them with the affection of an uncle.

"Rabboni, what do *Abba* and *Imma* do privately on *Shabbat* morning?" asked *Yeshua*.

"They enact the *Kabbalistic* mysteries of Adonai and Matronit," was the answer.

"What are these mysteries?" asked *Yakob*.

"They are not taught to young boys or even young men, but only to certain observant married men and women." Eleazar smiled. "Perhaps you will one day be worthy to practice these mysteries."

"Who is Matronit?" asked *Yeshua*.

"Who is Adonai?" Eleazar asked.

When their questions were met only with more questions, there would be no more answers. The knowledge was not yet to be given. But for many years *Yeshua* pondered that question: "Who is Adonai?"

For a year both boys learned not only Torah and Targum, but the *Kabbalistic* or oral teachings of the Elders. These were the deeper teachings that had been developed in the schools of the prophets and assimilated in Babylon through the School of Daniel. There were also mystical practices of the *Merkabah* or ascent to the Throne of God, but they were not open to *Yeshua* and *Yakob*. Yet they were able to learn a little about them through questions and hints.

"How did Enoch, Elijah, and Isaiah ascend to the Throne, while Moses was allowed only to see the lower parts?" asked *Yeshua*.

"I will tell you *why*, but not *how*, if you wish to hear," was the reply.

The boys nodded eagerly, pleased that they had managed to get any kind of answer about the deep mysteries.

"Moses had spilled human blood onto the Earth. He had led armies of conquest. He had glorified himself with the power of Adonai at Mamre for his own political purposes. Therefore no matter how great a leader he might have been, he had stained and obscured his interior purity. Without the highest purity of heart, it is not possible to see God or operate the *berakoth* of sacred Priesthood. That is why Aaron, not Moses, served as the High Priest of El Elyon. But even Aaron was not pure enough to speak with God, and after many generations his Priesthood was brought to an end."

After a silence *Yakob* asked, "We know that the Romans have installed a false High Priest in the Temple. What is the true Priesthood? From whom does it descend?"

Eleazar closed his eyes, drew a long breath, and began to rock forward and backward as though he were praying. After a time he opened his eyes and said, "The Essenes and all the *Hasidim* teach that the true and ancient Priesthood of El Elyon descends from Melchizedek, who lives and guides all true Israelites from the Throne of God. Many of those who practice purity feel that the true High Priesthood was established for us many years ago through Zadok, the Righteous One. But there is not a clear lineage. I myself feel that Messiah will return true Priesthood to Israel."

"When will Messiah come?" asked *Yeshua*.

"The *Bar-Enash* will come in the *razim* of Heaven," as the Prophet Daniel foretold.

"Who is the *Bar-Enash*?"

"Maybe not a Who, but a What," was Eleazar's mysterious reply.

"Then *what* is the Son of Mankind?" was *Yeshua*'s eager question.

"What is a *Bar Mitzva*?" Eleazar shot back. But this time *Yeshua* was not to be put off with questions for answers.

"It is a Son of the Covenant, so a *Bar-Enash* is a Son of Mankind."

"Who is included in *Bar*?"

Yeshua thought for a moment. "All Israel, male and female, through the circumcision and ceremonies of men. Are you saying that *Bar* includes both men and women?"

"You have answered well beyond your years, *Yeshe*, so I will tell you the *Kabbalah* of Daniel's vision," Eleazar replied. "The Son of Humanity is a New Humanity that will arise, both male and female. This New Humanity will overthrow the beasts who oppress all people. It will establish new government that will cause justice to roll like thunder, even as the Prophet Amos said. The rule of Romans and all their kind will end. The lion will lie in peace with the lamb, which is to say, the strong will no longer oppress the weak. Divine knowledge and holy visions will manifest to every person. The Divine *Malkuth* of Heaven will appear on Earth."

"Is this the coming of *Messiah Ben David*, who will destroy the Romans in battle?" *Yakob* asked.

Eleazar answered with only a smile.

"Our time has ended. Let us begin the prayers."

******* ******* ******* *******

After a year of studies, *Yeshua* was made a *Bar Mitzva* and the private tutorial ended. *Yakob* continued *Shabbat* School until he came of age.

This began a new phase in the spiritual education of *Yeshua*, for he was now a Son of the Covenant and was ready to begin his Apprenticeship as a Mason under the tutelage of *Yosef* and Lodge Zerubbabel. First, however, he and his whole family would make a pilgrimage to the Temple in Jerusalem, as was traditional in the Lodge for a first-born *Bar Mitzva*.

Chapter Five: PILGRIMAGE TO THE TEMPLE

Master *Yosef*'s family had grown over the years. He had added rooms to his home to accommodate his four sons and two daughters. *Yeshe* and *Yakob* now had three brothers—*Yosef, Shimone*, and Jehuda. They shared a room as infants and toddlers. The two girls, *Shalome* and *Miriam*, shared another room adjacent to the area where *Yeshe* and *Yakob* slept.

The *Pesach* pilgrimage to Jerusalem was a difficult trip. The two youngest boys had to be carried or supported while seated upon a donkey. The girls were able to keep up by walking, but they often lagged behind talking or wandering too far from the family. *Yeshe* and *Yakob* had to constantly watch over the girls while their parents managed the toddlers.

A great deal of responsibility for the girls was placed directly upon *Yeshe*, as he was now a Son of the Covenant and therefore a young man of Israel. He disliked having to always shepherd his little sisters, and when he was alone with them he teased them or told them frightening stories to make them obedient. *Yakob* joined in, and sometimes *Shalome* was reduced to tears. But when their mother approached, the boys became very nurturing and solicitous of her feelings, and thus disguised their pranks.

They traveled under the hot sun in company with a growing throng of pilgrims, some of whom were relatives who doted upon the younger children and congratulated *Yeshe* on becoming a *Bar Mitzvah*. During daytime the sounds of flute, drum, and song competed along the dusty road with gay conversation and laughter. In the cool evening campsites dotted the hills with dancing and storytelling until, one by one, they fell silent, the fires burned low, and the exhausted pilgrims slept.

On the final day of the journey, *Yeshe* could see City of David and its gleaming walls rising in the distance like a beacon. As the pilgrims approached, they grew silent. Caravans from other roads streamed together like tributaries forming to converge at the great city gates. Jerusalem loomed like an ocean, swallowing awe-stricken rivers of humanity. Soon all the pilgrims began singing the traditional Psalms of Ascent accompanied by flutes and tambourines. The multitude of voices echoed word and melody in hypnotic, disjointed oscillation as the Psalms were taken up by crowds at a distance.

Once inside the massive city gate, the sounds of song ended and *Yeshe* was overcome with a late afternoon hubbub of sight, sound, and smell—Roman soldiers barking commands, singers, dancers, merchants hawking their wares, beggars seeking alms, the colorful silks of the rich contrasting with the dusty woolens of the pilgrims. But most impressive of all—the gilded Temple of Solomon with its veritable mountain of huge stone steps and seas of Rabbis, Priests, and Levites.

Yosef paused to marvel at the detailed stonework and carpentry.

"My sons, look and remember. This is the finest work of the best architects and craftsmen in the world." He paused again. "Many of them are sons of Abraham. My brothers still work on the great Temple, and they oversaw the building of the great staircase that lies before you. Look and remember, my sons."

What seemed like hundreds of whitened stone steps led from platform to platform, each step large enough for scores of people to sit or lie upon. In fact, groups of bearded men sat together at different levels of the great stairway talking, arguing, gesticulating.

"Who are these men, *Abba*?" asked *Shalome*.

"They are the Rabbis of the Pharisees. They are teachers of Torah and tradition."

"Why are they sitting like an army on the great staircase?" was *Yakob*'s question.

"Because the Temple Priests of the Sadducees often try to stop people like us from our birthright, which is free access to the Temple of Solomon. The Rabbis of the Pharisees take up vigil here to ensure that pilgrims like us can climb the steps to Solomon's Porch and offer sacrifice. They hold a share of power in the Sanhedrin of Jerusalem, and they have made themselves keepers of the Gate of Solomon."

"But *Abba*, there are many gates and huge doors covered with gold—how do they open such doors?" asked *Shalome*.

Yosef laughed.

"Little one, the Gate of Solomon is not a huge arch or a door, as you see here. It means the religious discipline that leads back to the *Pardes*, the Garden of Eden. The Pharisees hold to all of our sacred writings and traditions. The Sadducees do not."

"Then, are we Pharisees?" asked *Yeshe*.

Yosef paused, then answered, "We are true Pharisees, but we are not of their party."

"Where do we go? Where do your brothers live?" *Yeshe* again asked.

"We go to the Guild hall and wait for sunset," he replied. "That is the arrangement."

"Where is the Guild hall? Do your brothers live in a Guild hall?" *Yakob* wanted to know. *Yosef* pointed to a distant hill smothered with crowded structures of all kinds.

They pressed through the moving throngs until they could no longer see the Temple, but seemed lost in a maze of streets and alleys lined by the ever-present merchants with their stalls. *Yeshe* wondered how his father knew where to go. The city was so huge, so cluttered. But within an hour they paused before a small, well-kept synagogue and knocked at the door.

"Who knocks?" was the muffled response.

"A son of Zerubbabel," answered *Yosef*.

The door was flung open and three bearded men stood beaming. "Welcome, *Mar Yosef*! And this must be our new *Bar Mitzvah*! *Shalom, shalom*!" They nodded enthusiastically at *Yeshe* who, somewhat taken aback, answered, "*Shalom*."

As they all entered the hall, *Yosef* introduced his wife and family to the men. It was clear now to *Yeshe* that these were not his uncles, but his father's Masonic brothers. He now understood what *Yosef* meant when he had said that one day, when *Yeshe* became an Apprentice, he would have "brothers" in many cities.

"Follow *Shimone* to his father's house. There you will have lodging and celebrate *Pesach* with us. We have already made all arrangements for you and your family, *Mar Yosef*."

As they followed *Shimone* to the place designated for them, the sun disappeared behind the fortress-like walls of Jerusalem and the streets emptied. *Shimone* spoke quietly to *Yosef* about details of *Pesach* and interpretation of the Writings, hanging on his every word and opinion. *Yeshe* was surprised and pleased to sense that the Jerusalem brothers held his father in high esteem, even beyond his status as a Guild Master.

   *******   *******   *******   *******

Early next morning *Yeshe* and his father retraced their steps to the Temple Mount. There were few people out and about, so the journey through streets and alleys was swift. This time *Yeshe* was able to recognize buildings he had passed by so slowly in yesterday's crowds. He used the orientation of the sun in the East to gain his bearings. *Yosef* also pointed out landmarks for him as they walked.

"If you are ever separated from me, you must find your way back to the house of *Shimone*'s father. I will look for you there," his father said. "See how the sun moves from East to West wall as the day passes. In the morning, the shadows point West, but in the evening they point East. See how the Temple Mount is positioned where the sun rises. When we come to Solomon's Porch, I will point to the hill where *Shimone*'s father lives. You will see the streets we have traveled, and I will point out the way back."

Yeshe nodded and made careful observations as they approached Solomon's Porch, where again he saw groups of Rabbis and other pious men gathered into groups for discussion. Some of the groups were very large, with one man speaking to many, while some consisted of only two or three hotly debating. Finally, made breathless by the strenuous ascent of the mammoth staircase, they reached the huge courtyard surrounded by walls and pillars within the Temple precincts, *Yeshe* was surprised to see several merchants setting up stalls to sell sacrificial birds and other animals. The huge altar of sacrifice, encrusted with the blood of countless animals, occupied its central position in the restricted area beyond the Temple pillars.

"Are we going to offer blood sacrifice, Father?" *Yeshe* asked in amazement. *Yosef* and Eliezar had said many times that the blood of animals was not pleasing to the Divine One.

"It is the custom for a *Bar Mitzvah* to offer blood sacrifice here in Jerusalem, but it is not our way. Instead, we will offer the true sacrifice of prayer and thanksgiving. You will pray, and I will listen to your prayers to be certain you make a correct approach to Yah, my Son. We will stand in the place of prayer toward the East and recite Psalms and Odes to prepare your heart, and then you will spontaneously offer your oblations and thanksgiving. But look now. See where we have traveled. Upon that hill is the house of *Shimone*'s father."

Yeshe nodded, then followed *Yosef* to the Eastern wall.

Wordlessly they stood together, slightly bowing and rocking with arms extended upward in orant position. *Yosef* began to hum and repeatedly intone in the familiar nasal style, "Yee-aaah-oooh-waay-eee." Soon he was leading *Yeshe* in the Psalm where David petitions forgiveness for the sins of his childhood. Then silence.

Yeshe, for the first time, felt a deep remorse for the way he had constantly teased his sisters. Men didn't treat little girls this way, and now he was a man of Israel. He felt deep shame for this and other behaviors of his past. His voice broke and trailed off as he began to intone, "Forgive me..." He took a deep breath and tried again, "forgive me for the stupid and childish things I have done, Holy One. I shall not do them again."

After a silence, he closed his eyes and began to intone, "*Baruch Attah Adonai, Eloheinu Melek Ha-Olam.*" His heart was bursting with new and powerful spiritual feelings that words could not express. He began to quietly intone a wordless melody that seemed to come forth from his heart. The melody began repetitiously, then developed into a plaintive, wordless prayer ascending with deep feeling and intensity.

"Lai, lai-lai-lai, nai..."

His voice was intense, powerful, shamanic. *Yosef* found himself irresistably drawn upward into his son's experience. He joined his voice with *Yeshe*'s, following his lead, as tears stained both their cheeks. The babble of the growing Temple crowds faded and they shared a divine joy.

They walked for some time in silence, when finally *Yosef* asked, "*Yeshua*, where did you learn to sing *niggunim*?

Yeshe was surprised. His father had never called him by his formal name. He had always been "*Yeshe*" or "my son."

"*Abba*, I do not know what *niggunim* might be."

"The Holy One, Blessed be He, has revealed them to you, *Yeshua*. Listen to His Voice. He is our true *Abba*."

Yosef said nothing more, but in his heart he was overjoyed. *Yeshua* was becoming a man of the *Ruach Ha-Qodesh*. With no human instruction, he had spontaneously intoned a *Kabbalistic niggun*, whose form and structure was given by the *Shekinah* only to great prophets and mystics. Even as a musician tunes a stringed instrument in order to perform psaltery, or as David tuned his lyre to bring the healing powers of Heaven to the diseased soul of King Saul, *Hochmah* was attuning *Yeshua* for deep and intimate instruction.

        *******   *******   *******   *******

The next morning was the Day of Preparation. *Yeshua* was allowed to find his own way to the Temple to observe the sacrificing of the Paschal lambs by the Temple Priests. However, he was admonished to return while the sun was still high in the sky. As he followed the landmarks leading to the Temple, he rehearsed the return route. Finally he approached the large steps leading to the sacred precincts.

As he ascended the steps, the din of human and animal voices grew louder until it was like thunder. Finally reaching the highest step, he stepped into a sea of pilgrims with their sacrificial sheep in endless lines leading through the inner pillars to the main altar at the center of the Courtyard. Blades of the Priests flashed swiftly, each animal's throat deftly sliced in a mass ritual. Blood gushed like fountains over the altar.

Yeshua pushed his way to the far wall where he could climb for a larger view. More people, more sheep, than he could ever count wended their way to the butchers at the altar. He was sickened by the strong odor of fresh blood and covered his nose.

He had never seen such a slaughter. In Nazareth, sheep were killed and butchered only for major feasts—one at a time. Through the heated air currents he saw something else slowly rising from the altar like a mist. It was the vital force of each animal being released. The sheep had not only life, but *nepheshim*, like people. He fell momentarily into a trance as he watched. Suddenly he was jostled back to physical reality by a man chasing a runaway lamb, and he began to look more closely at the Temple precincts.

Again, *Yeshua* had never seen such a wealth of gold, silver, and precious stones. These had been lavished upon the Second Temple not only by Herod and the Sadducees, but by contributions taken from all of Israel. He was dazzled by the rich clothing of the Temple Priests who strutted back and forth shouting orders to Levites. But most of all he marveled at the vestments of the High Priest Annas, who was just now being carried in procession upon his throne by slaves like a wealthy Roman. Even though he was not a holy man like Aaron or Moses, but a despised collaborator of the Romans appointed by the Tetrarch, he was accorded a show of respect from all present.

In stark contrast to the wealthy men of the Jewish Temple establishment were the modestly attired pilgrims standing in long lines to purchase sacrificial birds, or to have their lambs slaughtered *kosher* for *Pesach* according to levitical laws of purity. They were like the people of *Yeshua*'s village, some of them poor *amme-ha-eretz* making a one-time pilgrimage with the little money they had saved for many years, others pious Pharisees whose journey was supported by their synagogue. Only a few seemed to be as wealthy as *Mar Yosef*. But here in Jerusalem what seemed to be wealth in a Galilean village was no more than a lesser grade of poverty!

As he contemplated the sights and sounds of Solomon's Porch, *Yeshua* realized that in Jerusalem, Jewish wealth was dependent upon collaboration with the occupying Romans, and that this wealth was a betrayal of Jewish ways. He remembered overhearing that some of the Sadducees had undergone surgery to restore their foreskins so they could play naked in the Greek gymnasiums without revealing the sign of the Jewish Covenant.

But what about *Mar Yosef*? He was hired as a Mason to construct Roman buildings in Galilee. Was this a betrayal of the Covenant? No, *Abba Yosef* was the most righteous of men. Even those of the synagogue in Nazareth who were envious of him never implied that he was a Roman collaborator. Yet he, too, would probably show respect for the High Priest—not out of fear or convention, but out of respect for his sacred office.

Yeshua sat upon one of the large steps close to three men who were criticizing the High Priest. They were Pharisees.

"Annas places his own comfort and finery above the Torah. He keeps Greek and Nubian servants," one was saying.

"Yes, and how does he pay for all this? With Temple offerings from righteous men!"

After a pause, the third man spoke slowly and deliberately.

"More than that, my cousin. He is supported by bloody Herod and the Roman officials for his influence in the Sanhedrin, and probably for betraying the secrets of the righteous ones. He is the eyes and ears of Herod. He is the abomination seen by the Prophet Daniel."

Yeshua closed his eyes. They were right. The High Priest Annas was, indeed, a great abomination standing in the Temple, even within the Holy of Holies, to pronounce the Divine Name on the Day of Atonement—indeed a great and obscene abomination, and perhaps the one seen in the visions of the night by Daniel.

His attention returned to the clamor of the sacrificial altar, which was barely visible through the crowds of officials carrying out the rites of mass paschal sacrifice—one animal after the next in quick and skillful succession. How right Eliezar was about animal sacrifice. It could not possibly please the Divine One. It was not at all sacred, but mere butchery. Why pretend otherwise? It was meat for a feast, with the best part for the Priests and the burnt fat ascending skyward for the *elilim*. This was a smoky perfume to stimulate the stomach, not the heart or the soul.

Massive gilded stones, precious gems, silken finery—how incongruous it seemed when mixed with the blood of animals, burning meat, and the strutting self-importance of Roman collaborators masquerading as righteous men!

Yeshua hesitated, then turned his back on the entire scene. The sun was not yet high in the sky, but now he wanted to be back with his parents. The Divine Spirit did not rest upon this place. He pushed his way down the great steps and began the circuitous route back to the home of *Shimone*'s father.

When he finally entered the house, he found his mother working with the other women and older children to prepare the Passover meal. The house had been swept, cleaned, and sprinkled with water as a purification. A small bowl of special *mikveh* water had been set aside for ritual hand-cleansings before and during the recitations of *Pesach*. The air was heavy with fragrances of special holiday foods. Truly, the Divine Spirit *did* rest upon this place!

*******   *******   *******   *******

Yosef's visit with his Guild brothers was extended for several days beyond *Pesach*. Most of the pilgrims had left Jerusalem. *Yeshua* and *Yakob* were allowed to explore the neighborhood with some of the boys they had met, while the girls stayed near the house with their mother.

Yeshua could not stop thinking and dreaming about the Temple of Solomon. He felt strongly moved to return, as though being drawn by an invisible force. But it was totally out of the question with his mother.

"But *Imma*, I will not get lost. I know the way there and back, and I've done it by myself!"

"No, *Yeshe*." She still called him *Yeshe*, even though *Yosef* now used his given name, *Yeshua*. "There are thieves, murderers, and people who steal children and sell them into slavery. Jerusalem is a dangerous place for a boy without his parents. You may not go."

Yeshua knew that his father, by himself, would allow him to visit the Temple alone, but he was away on business with the brothers every day. He also knew that with his mother feeling so strongly, *Yosef* would not give permission even if asked in the morning before he left.

As each day passed, *Yeshua* knew that any opportunity he would have to see the Temple again was being lost. It would be many years before he could come to Jerusalem by himself. So on the last day before *Yosef* planned to begin the return journey, *Yeshua* ditched the boys and made his way to the Temple alone.

"Listen to His Voice. He is our true *Abba*," *Yosef* had said.

"Yes, if the Holy One of Israel is our true Father, then I shall obey the voice of his calling," *Yeshua* whispered as he walked.

When he finally arrived at the great staircase, the crowds were gone. However, there was a group of Rabbis sitting and keeping vigil on the highest steps leading into the Courtyard. As he ascended the stairs, he found himself more winded than before. He needed to stop and rest midway. As he sat, one of the men called down to him.

"Boy, you cannot come up here. Only Sons of the Covenant may approach."

Yeshua stood proudly and said, "I am a *Bar Mitvah*, and I made my offering here with my father just last week."

"Well then," the same man said, "come up here and tell us what you know. Can you sing *Berashit*?"

With new vigor, *Yeshua* clambered up the steps and stood before them.

"*Berashit bera Elohim eth ha-shamayim veth ha-aretz...*" he began, then carefully and correctly intoned the entire first chapter of *Berashit* or Genesis while the Rabbis pulled on their beards and nodded their approval.

"Who is your teacher, my son?" asked one of the men.

"My father *Yosef* of Nazareth and Eliezar the Essene," he replied. The men looked at each other in amazement.

"So they teach Torah in Galilee?" All the Rabbis laughed.

"Torah in the language of the angels, Targum in our human language, and the Prophets and the Writings," *Yeshua* answered respectfully. Now the men were intrigued.

"So you know the Writings and the Prophets. Do you know this: 'At that hour the Son of Man was named before the Lord of Spirits?'"

Yeshua closed his eyes, took a deep breath and finished the phrase from the Prophet Enoch: "And his name was the Head of Days."

The men looked at each other, then the Rabbi who had first called to *Yeshua* motioned for him to sit down with them. *Yeshua* hesitated. He had never been invited to sit with the men. Then he slowly took his place on the stone step.

"And he will be a light to all the nations," he continued.

"What do you know of Messiah?" asked the man who had invited him to sit.

Yeshua again closed his eyes. All the Scriptures he had ever seen, heard, or sung that could be attributed to Messiah seemed to swoop down from heaven and alight upon him like exotic birds.

"I know that Messiah cannot be David's son," he declared matter-of-factly, anticipating the incredulous response.

After a silence, he continued. "David speaks through a Psalm and says, 'Adonai said to my Master, Sit down at my Right Hand.'" If Messiah is David's son, why does he call him 'my Master?'"

This was amazing. *Yeshua*, a young boy from Galilee, was asking the kind of rhetorical question that only teachers used—and an excellent one at that! The Rabbis were speechless for a moment. No one had ever adduced this Psalm as a proof for the Messiah Ben-*Yosef*. Finally one of them produced another Scripture that could be construed to counter *Yeshua*'s example and provide evidence for the Messiah Ben-David. But immediately *Yeshua* responded with a grammatical observation that would change the meaning.

Soon some of the Priests and Levites were drawn to the spectacle of a young Bar Mitvah from the provinces holding his own in traditional theological debate with well-schooled Rabbis. They stood peering down from the Courtyard in rapt attention as the afternoon passed.

Suddenly from the lower platform of the staircase came a mother's cry, "*Yeshe*! *Yeshe*! You were forbidden to come here! How could you do this to your mother?"

She was followed by a group of boys who waved wildly at *Yeshua*. As they scrambled up the awkward stairs, Master *Yosef* appeared from even farther behind, standing sternly with arms folded near the great arch.

The Rabbis all stood up as *Yakob*, finally reaching the top steps, threw himself on *Yeshua*'s neck and hugged him fervently.

"Daughter of Israel, who is your son's teacher? I want him for my own student!" said one of the men, saluting and smiling. *Yosef* began ascending the stairs, still silent.

"You have a remarkable son. He was holding his own in disputation like a trained Rabbi! And you, sir—you are this boy's father? He tells us that you are his teacher—you and the Essene Eliezar. We are all very impressed with your student!"

By now *Yosef*'s grim countenance began to crack. He smiled and continued the ascent. *Miriam* was greeted by *Yeshua*, who started down the stairs to meet her. The other boys had stopped a few steps below and stood watching for what might be an entertaining beating by the approaching *Yosef*. But no such luck. He enclosed both *Yeshua* and *Miriam* with his cloak while she sobbed, then turned to the Rabbis above.

"Yes, he is a remarkable student, and more than that. But he is also a young man who has disobeyed his mother, and we will have to take him from you now," he said, fixing his eyes upon *Yeshua*. But the young man didn't look guiltily at his feet. Instead, he smiled at his father.

Yosef said, "*Yeshua*, why did you disobey?"

Yeshua answered, "I must obey the Voice of my true Father's calling."

Yosef paused, then slowly replied, "Yes, my son, you must."

Chapter Six: THE BROTHERHOOD

"What is your desire?"

"I desire to be an adopted Son of Zerubbabel."

"What is your parentage?"

"I am a Son of the Covenant through the blood of *Yosef* of Nazareth."

"Who is your true Father?"

"My true Father is *Yod He Vav He*."

"Intone His Name."

"Eeee-ahhh-ohhh-wahhh-ayyy-eeee."

"What is the meaning of the *Yod*?"

The interrogation and memorized answers continued as *Yeshua* stood blindfolded, naked chest exposed, and wearing only one sandal. This represented the moral blindness, ignorance, and spiritual poverty of the candidate for initiation. A noose hung loosely about his neck, representing his willingness to be led and instructed by the Brothers.

Before being blindfolded and led by cabletow into what he knew was the Guild hall, he had been seated in a room filled with Hebrew letters and various symbols. He was told to contemplate what he saw and await further instruction. The wait seemed interminable.

Yeshua had been preparing for initiation as an Apprentice to the Brotherhood of Zerubbabel for a full year. Now, as he answered the Apprentice's Catechism flawlessly, his father stood solemnly outside the circle of interrogators, filled with pride for his first-born.

Yosef was Grand Master of the Nazarene Guild. He had trained most of the others now conducting the initiation of his son, just as his father had trained him. But it was Guild tradition that a son could not be interrogated or initiated by his own father, so he stood in the background while the ancient drama proceeded.

Yeshua had been quick to grasp the details of the *Kabbalah* of Preparation. His mind had a natural affinity for the subtleties of Kabbalistic interpretation. These concerned first of all the basic moral teachings of the Prophets, and then their extension into mystical allegories based on principles of exegesis. In addition, the tools of stone-masonry, wood craftsmanship, and their basic processes were related to moral qualities through symbols of the Hebrew alphabet.

The goal of the Apprentice was to become *tam* or morally upright by consciously designing, sculpting, and reforming his internal character. This was done through morning prayers for attunement with the guidance of *Hochmah* followed by evening contemplation on the words and deeds of the day.

It was not good to force changes to the character. The unskilled Apprentice tries to hew stone with one mighty blow and, instead, cracks it apart. Rather, one improves and refines character by simply observing himself and his actions without blame, but with the goal of understanding the operations of his own *nefesh*. Then, by applying the motivation of the good *yetzer*, new and positive processes would develop. This was compared in the *Kabbalah* of Zerubbabel to the skilled Apprentice, who carefully examines the stone before deciding where to position the tools and what force to give. Always it was better to work slowly and with deliberation with stone or wood, and with the *nefesh* of oneself or others.

This and a thousand other teachings constituted the *Kabbalah* of Preparation, which was moral and self-reformative in nature, and thus based mainly upon the writings that were transmitted through the schools of the Prophets.

After initiation as an Apprentice, *Yeshua* would next be instructed in the *Kabbalah* leading to the grade of Journeyman. He would serve an Apprenticeship of three years. During this time he would serve a Master in all of his projects, compensated only by food and lodging, and study *Kabbalah* from sunrise to sunset on *Shabbat*. These studies were more advanced, involving geometry, mathematics, astrology, and the fundamentals of metallurgy. *Yeshua* would be known to the Guild as an Apprentice of the Magi. Here he would develop the basic mathematical skills necessary for advancing to the second degree of Journeyman or Assistant to the Master, for which increasing levels of salary were paid.

This, too, could be completed in as few as three years by extremely talented Journeyman Guildsmen. However, the Masters would not approve an Assistant for advancement into their elite society of free and independent contractors until he had demonstrated the character and abilities of an experienced Master Guildsman. Many Journeyman who lacked the mathematical skills they had been given opportunity to learn never advanced, but continued as well-paid Assistants to the Masters. Some few were finally advanced after many years of work, but only a small number had ever been advanced to the third degree of initiation after only three years. Master *Yosef* was one of these, and he fully expected his first-born son to exhibit the same genius.

Yeshua had been told very little about the advanced *Kabbalah* leading to installation as an independent Master. He knew that the process would require many years and that he would be a grown man before being given the opportunity for advancement as a Master. But his impression was that the advanced *Kabbalah* had to do with something called *yetzirah* or "formation," the first chapter of *Berashit*, and invocation of angels for spiritual instruction.

"Come into the Light!" the interrogator commanded, and with a snap the blindfold was removed. *Yeshua* blinked as his eyes adjusted to the scene. He was surrounded by Master Guildsmen with mallets raised as though to strike him dead. He was pushed to a kneeling position before a low altar upon which was placed a scroll of the Torah and three candles. The rest of the hall was dark and he could not see his father's face.

"You must take an oath of allegiance to the Brotherhood of Zerubbabel. If you violate this oath, these mallets will crush your skull and your lifeless body will be thrown into the sea. If you are not willing to take this oath, you will be escorted from this hall and never allowed entrance again, but you will not be under oath or liable for punishment. Now you must discriminate between the Way of Life and the Way of Death. Do you choose to take this oath in the presence of the Sacred Torah of Israel?"

Without hesitation he answered, "I choose to take the oath."

"Place your right hand on my thigh," ordered the interrogator. He placed his right hand on *Yeshua*'s one unbended knee in the ancient gesture for an *amana* or good-faith covenant between two rulers.

"Repeat my words," the interrogator began.

The Oath of Initiation was the only oath required by the Brotherhood. In it the initiand pledged to uphold all of the teachings transmitted to him in the *Kabbalah* of Zerubbabel, but to never reveal their source or any other information about the rituals, teachings, activities, secret signs of recognition, and other hidden communication signs of the

Brotherhood on pain of demission and death. This protected not only the secrets of the trade, but the lives of Brothers in foreign or hostile cities.

Yeshua never broke his oath or revealed secrets of the Brotherhood. The moral and spiritual teachings he received through the *Kabbalah* of Zerubbabel would mentor him from boyhood to manhood and help him to create within his own *nefesh* the noble and refined characteristics exemplified by all great *tammim*.

      *******   *******   *******   *******

Yeshua's life was forever changed. As his father's Apprentice, he arose early on Sunday morning, the first day of the week, packed rations of bread, fish, cheese, and water, and made the long treck with *Yosef* and his two Assistants to Sepphoris. There they worked Monday through Thursday. On Friday morning they returned home to Nazareth for evening *Shabbat* dinner. On Saturdays he rose with the sun for a full day of mathematical studies with *Yosef* and his two Assistants, Asa and Shlomo. They were still struggling with basic mathematics, although they had fulfilled the three years study for Journeyman and therefore been advanced into the next degree.

Both of *Yosef*'s Assistants mentored *Yeshua* kindly both in class and on the job. After a few months of *Shabbat* study, however, it became a *quid pro quo* where the men offered *Yeshua* detailed instruction with the craft in exchange for tutoring in mathematics and astrology, in which he excelled.

"You have a strong son!" shouted Asa. "Look what he has done with the stone in just one morning."

Yosef stood up and stretched his back. There was that pain again, running from his chest to his left hip. He took a few deep breaths while the pain subsided, then walked slowly to the West foundation of the new courtyard where *Yeshua* was working.

"Did you do all of this yourself, my son?" he asked. Truly he was amazed. *Yeshua* was growing quickly and now nearly as tall as his father. A juvenile beard had recently made its appearance on his strong, angular face, and his arms had sprouted bold sinews that rippled as he worked.

"No, Master," he replied. He no longer called *Yosef* "Abba," but "Master," as was befitting an Apprentice. "Asa helped me."

"Well, Asa is over there working now. What did he do?"

"He showed me how to start working with this kind of stone, Master, and he finished the first one."

Yosef chuckled to himself. *Yeshua* was practicing the strict honesty required by the *Kabbalah*. But in fact, he had done a prodigious amount of work in a short time and finished all the stones well.

"*Yeshua*, you have done very well. But please learn one more thing. It is not good to wear out your body when you work. Now you are young and feel invincible. But you will make yourself old before your time if you work this way. Develop the habit of resting between each finished stone and appreciating what you have produced."

Yeshua cast his eyes down. *Yosef* stretched out his hand and caressed the young man's head in a blessing.

"Don't worry, my son. I did the same thing when I was young. But learned to slow down and take pleasure in the work itself—not merely the production. That is why I am still strong. Remember, quality and perfection are the most important things—not speed and quantity."

Yeshua looked up at his father and smiled. He remembered what *Imma* had said about gardening—that the reward was in doing the work itself, without attachment to a harvest or a future result. She had said that we can't change the past, and we can't know what the future might bring, so we must work in the present, which is where the *Shekinah* always dwells.

"I know that you are right, *Abba*—I mean, Master. Thank you."

As sunset approached, *Yeshua* and the men walked across the wealthy city to their rented quarters with tools slung over their backs. The tables and stalls in the Roman-style market place were empty, but they had arranged with their landlord for him to purchase nuts, figs, dried fish, and other foods on their behalf.

The landlord, Eliud, was a wealthy Jewish merchant who, like *Yosef*, was deeply religious and devoted to the *Kabbalah* of Zerubbabel. He was a member of the Synagogue of the Babylonians which, unlike the conservative Synagogue of the Gophnites from Judea, was rooted in the mystical School of the Prophet Daniel. *Yeshua* knew that his father's Masonic tradition derived from Babylonian Masonry, but he was surprised to learn that the *Kabbalah* of his Guild came from the same sources.

"And that is not all," Eliud smiled as he reclined with them at his ornate dinner table. "The numerological *Kabbalah* of the alphabet is known to the Greek Guildsmen as well. However, it refers to their own alphabet, and it derives from the Master Pythagoras, who taught them many of the same sciences used in your Guild."

"Then *Hochmah* speaks to gentiles?" asked *Yeshua* in astonishment.

"But She is known as Sophia, Wisdom," replied *Yosef*. "The Holy One of Israel is the Ruler of all humanity, and He guides them all through their own prophets, which the Greeks call philosophers."

"Then, do we sit at the feet of gentiles to study Torah?" *Yeshua* asked, still somewhat offended at the idea.

"Ah!" chimed in Shlomo. "But the gentiles do not have the Torah!"

"Even so," responded *Yosef*, "they have received great treasuries of the Divine *Razim*. We ourselves learned higher Masonry from the Babylonians, and even today we have a large community of our people living in Babylon. There is much we can learn from the gentiles."

Yeshua pondered. "But perhaps they gained their knowledge from the fallen angels and demons."

"Then so have we," answered Eliud.

"*Yeshua*, are the Divine *Razim* good or evil?" asked *Yosef* pointedly.

"They are good."

"Then how can they come to us through an evil source?" he continued.

That night *Yeshua* pondered deeply before falling asleep. There were many factions, many opinions in Israel. The Gophnites, Essenes, and Judean Rabbis emphasized the literal fall of men and angels, but the Babylonians allegorized it. The Torah did not describe a fall of angels, but the Prophet Enoch told of it in detail. Yet *Yosef*, who was devoted to the scrolls of Enoch that tell how fallen angels gave knowledge of the sciences and arts to mankind—his father *Yosef* clearly felt that the *Razim* did not come through an evil source.

Perhaps that is because the angels are part of Divine Creation. They are good, whether fallen or not, whether in rebellion or not, because they are emanations of the Divine One. Therefore human beings must be good, whether fallen or not. But does that mean the evil *yetzerim* are good? What is the difference between Divine inspiration and the mediation of angels? Is *Hochmah* in some sense "fallen?"

******* ******* ******* *******

The *Shabbat* studies were divided into Practical *Kabbalah* and Moral *Kabbalah*—more of one and less of the other, depending upon the day. But this day was devoted entirely to Moral *Kabbalah*.

"Please read to us from this part of the Scroll of the Testament of Reuben," instructed

Yosef, pointing out the section.

Yeshua had never before seen this scroll, so he asked, "What is this Testament?"

"This is the wisdom of the Twelve Patriarchs. It is in twelve scrolls."

"How has it come to us?" asked *Yeshua*.

"It has come by means of the overshadowing of a wise man by *Hochmah*. He had attuned himself like a harp to the psaltery of Heaven. The *yechidah* of each Patriarch was allowed to speak through the overshadowing of *Hochmah*. The wise man wrote down what his soul heard. It is not perfect hearing, because even the purest of the *Chassidim* are imperfect. But it is well worth reading aloud."

Yeshua suddenly remembered what he had pondered about the fallen angels. They did not speak directly to men. Those who heard their teachings must have done so through the mediation, the overshadowing, of *Hochmah*. They must have also been wise and pure *Chassidim* to receive such teachings. Perhaps "fallen" was just a way of saying the rebellious angels had trapped themselves into the lower '*Olamim* of Asiah—the physical world of mankind.

He began to read.

"Seven spirits are appointed against man, and they are the leaders in the works of youth. And seven other spirits are given to him at his creation, that through them should be done every righteous work of humanity.

"The first is the *Ruach ha-Hayyim*, the Spirit of Life, with which the constitution of humanity is created.

"The second is the Spirit of Vision, through which ariseth desire for good or for ill.

"The third is the Spirit of Hearing, through which cometh teaching, for good or for ill.

"The fourth is the Spirit of Smell, through which discriminations are given to draw in breath and spirit.

"The fifth is the Spirit of Speech, through which cometh knowledge, for good or for ill.

"The sixth is the Spirit of Touch and Taste, through which cometh the eating of meats and drinks, by which strength is produced, for food is the foundation of strength.

"The seventh is the Spirit of Procreation and Sexual Intercourse, through which love and pleasure enter, for good or for ill. Wherefore it is the last in order of creation, and the first in that of youth, because it can be bloated with ignorance and lead youth as a blind man to the pit, and as a beast to a precipice.

"Besides all these, there is an eighth Spirit of Trance, through which can be brought about the sleep of nature or the Image of Divine Death, which is holy meditation."

Yosef indicated that he should pause.

"Each of these seven spirits is influenced by both good and evil *yetzerim*. You know that the good *yetzer* is the impulse of the heart that the *tammim* learn to follow. The evil *yetzer* is the impulse of the heart that the unwise and undisciplined habitually follow. But now we look more deeply into the *Tzelem*."

The *Tzelem*, *Yeshua* recalled from the Hebrew of *Berashit*, is the emanated Image of God, which projected like a shadow into matter and is the foundation of the human soul.

"How does Adonai create a human soul?" asked *Yosef*. Before *Yeshua* could make a reply, he went on. "The *Elohim* said..." Then he asked, "What are the *Elohim*?"

Asa replied, "They are the Voices emanating from Adonai at the beginning of any creation."

"The *Elohim* said," *Yosef* continued, "let us make *Adam* in our *Tzelem*, after our *Damoth*." Now *Yosef* looked expectantly at *Yeshua*.

Yeshua picked up the thread of *Kabbalistic* interpretation and said, "*Adam*, humanity, and *damah*, blood-likeness, are both based on *dam*, blood."

"What does this imply?" asked *Yosef*, looking at Shlomo.

"I don't know," he drawled in puzzlement. "Oh! I see! The *Elohim* will form mankind in their own *damoth*, out of their own blood!"

"That is right," said *Yosef*. "The Magi of Babylon tell a similar story of *Adam*, the first man. Now do we see why he is called *A-dam*. Mankind is the blood-likeness of the *Elohim*. Mankind is a blood-child of the Most High, and it is his destiny to create like the *Elohim*."

After a pause, *Yosef* went on.

"But there are two stories of the formation of mankind, one in the first chapter of *Berashit*, and one in the second. The second says, '"Yod-He-Vav-He formed mankind of earth from the ground and breathed into his nostrils a *Ruach Ha-Hayyim*, and mankind became a living being.' Now, who can remember the word for 'formed'?"

Yeshua answered immediately. "That is the word *yetzer*."

"Yes," replied *Yosef*. "But have you ever noticed that here, in this one place in the Torah, the word is spelled *yyetzer*? What have the sages signified by the two initial yods?"

"Two formations? Two creations?" answered Asa.

"No, but two elements in Divine formation of the human constitution," replied *Yosef*.

"I see!" cried *Yeshua*. "That is why the *Ruach Ha-Hayyim* and all the other seven spirits appointed to mankind are influenced by two *yetzerim*—one good, and one evil. Does this mean that Yod-He-Vav-He put both good and evil formations into the heart of mankind?"

"That is right. Can a man walk with only one leg? How can a man choose between the Way of Life and the Way of Death if there is only one Way? Haven't you heard, 'Behold, I set two Ways before you—the Way of Life and the Way of Death?' Yes, it is Adonai who formed evil as well as good. Why? So that mankind can grow and perfect itself by discrimination in action. And that, my Brothers, is the essence of the Moral *Kabbalah* of Zerubbabel." *Yosef* arched his eyebrows and everyone nodded.

"Now, continue the reading, *Yeshua*."

Yeshua found the place in the scroll and began to read.

"With these Spirits are mingled the spirits of error.

First, the spirit of fornication is seated in the nature and in the senses. The second is the spirit of insatiable dissatisfaction; it is in the belly and genitals. The third is the spirit of fighting; it is in the liver, gall, and solar plexus. Fourth is the spirit of insincerity, obsequiousness, and untrustworthiness, that through outward show one may appear to be good and moral; it is in the heart. Fifth is the spirit of pride and arrogance in speech and action; it is in the throat. Sixth is the spirit of lying, deception, jealousy, and concealment from kindred and friends; it is in the forehead between the eyes. Seventh is the spirit of injustice, which offends against life and brings about thefts, rapacious cruelties, and other violence to satisfy perverse desires, for injustice works with the other spirits by taking and possessing.

"And with all of these the spirit of sleep is joined, which is that of error, fantasy, and insensibility to all but one's own concerns; it lies above the crown of the head.

"And so perisheth every young man, darkening his mind from the truth, not understanding the Torah of God, and disobeying the admonitions of his fathers, as befell me also in my youth.

"And now my children, love the truth, and it will preserve you; hear the words of Reuben your father."

After a silence, *Yosef* commented, "You see, the lower spirits actually take up residence in our flesh. Great powers of healing and redemption that can be exercised by those who know where these perverse spirits dwell in human bodies. I am not a healer, but perhaps some day you will meet a holy man who understands these things. But for yourselves, you will know them and feel them operating in their places in your own bodies, and perhaps now you will understand better how to control them."

Asa raised a finger, then spoke. "Master, you have never taught us this part of the *Kabbalah*. Why do you teach it now?"

Yosef smiled. "It is not I who teach. It is you who *learn*."

The next morning was a working day. *Yosef* motioned for *Yeshua* to leave his work and follow him.

"Take this staff, my Son."

He handed the young man an ornately carved walking stick very similar to his own. It had been made from dense oak heart—too tall and heavy for most travelers. The staff was stout and perfectly straight with an oversized rounded flair at top and bottom.

Yeshua was overjoyed and kissed his father's hand as he gratefully took the staff.

"Now I will teach you how to defend yourself from attackers. First, how to stand. Hold the staff in your left hand and point it at this stone."

Yeshua aimed the staff at a large red stone.

"No. Like this."

With a lightning-fast motion *Yosef* jumped into a crouching stance, right foot back and left foot forward, simultaneously whipping the staff from right to left hand. His right hand held the upper part of the stick, while his left balanced the middle in a strong grip. The rounded flair at the bottom was now aimed at the stone. He gripped the middle of the staff in his left hand, with the right hand closest to him controlling jabs or punches, much like a modern billiard stick.

"You must do this in the blink of an eye, or you may lose your weapon. Try again."

The young man practiced under his father's critical gaze until *Yosef* nodded his approval.

"Now, whenever you have to do this, intone in your mind the Psalm of the great warrior David, '*Ee-ah-oh-way-ee tzudi,* teach my fingers and hands to fight.' Practice now, but aloud so I can hear."

Again *Yeshua* went through the exercise over and over until his father once again approved.

"Now you are ready to bash heads, my Son. Let me show you how."

Yosef took the staff, whipped into position with the thick foot of the weapon pointed at the red stone.

"This is defense position. If you do this well, most single attackers will flee.

"But sometimes you have to fight two or more. Then you'll have to bash at least one head. If they don't back down immediately, you must not waste time or words. You must strike like a snake—before there is time to think. You must pick your easiest target at the very beginning when there are two or more so you don't waste time thinking. If defense position doesn't get immediate results, do this."

In a flash he grasped the thick top of the staff with his right hand and made a powerful jab at the stone. It shattered.

"I didn't know that wood could break stone!" marveled *Yeshua*.

"Normally it can't," replied *Yosef*. "But three kinds of skill make it possible. First, the staff must be jabbed or punched in an exacting straight line. That way the blow comes through the entire body of the stick from head to foot. If the aim is bad, the blow will glance and the staff may break."

Yosef handed the head of the staff to his son and held up the foot.

"Look along the line from head to foot. See how straight and heavy it is? Most walking sticks cannot be used this way because they are light and crooked."

Yosef took the staff back and posed in the defense position.

"Now second, the jab must be done in a flash. If you learn how to punch fast, you don't need to worry about force. Don't try to punch hard. Just punch fast as lightning. And third, when your staff contacts the target, do not follow through like this. Watch what happens if you do."

He aimed at another rock, but this time pushed through the punch. The rock did not shatter. It merely flew away.

"You see, my Son, the skill is to stop the staff the instant it makes contact, like this."

He walked over the the rock that had been moved several yards by his blow. With one quick motion, he shattered it.

"This is the hardest thing to learn. Don't follow through, don't pull back. Just stop the staff when it makes contact. Come, try. Do this many times until you get the feel. And then never stop practicing. Keep up the skill. Believe me, my Son, you will need it when you least expect it."

From that moment, the staff his father had given him never left *Yeshua's* side.

Chapter Seven: SEPPHORIS

Yeshua grew to manhood living and working in the great Roman-Jewish cosmopolitan center of Sepphoris. The Guild often held evening *chaburah* meals in a room at the Synagogue of Babylon. Here Master *Yosef* led prayer and psalms, with formal *kiddush* cups before and after the meal, as was usually done on *Shabbat*. However, these special religious gatherings were done on week-nights because the workmen would return home on weekends for *Shabbat*.

Yeshua was often asked to read from the scrolls. Several of them were written in Aramaic, the late dialect of Hebrew spoken by both Galilean and Babylonian Jews. Foremost of these were the scrolls from the School of the Prophet Daniel in Babylon.

The Visions of Daniel concerned the coming of the Messianic Age, when the powers of unjust and corrupt imperial gentile thrones—seen as carnivorous beasts and their offspring—would end. The Powers of Heaven under the Archangel Michael would defeat Shaitan's demonic armies, who held the Earth and humanity under their sway. The Ancient of Days would set up a new kind of government that the Prophet saw as ruled by an archetypal and humane Governor—the *Bar-Enash,* Son of Man, or Offspring of Mankind. This New Humanity would be the inevitable fruit of the holy lives of countless prophets, sages, and martyrs for righteousness who sanctify the Earth and mankind with the works of the *tammim*.

"I ascended unto the Throne during the night, and behold! In the hidden things of Heaven there came one like a Son of Humanity, and he approached the Ancient of Days, and was presented before him. And to him was given dominion and glory and *Malkuth*, that all peoples, nations, and tongues should serve him.

"His dominion is an everlasting dominion that shall not pass away; and his *Malkuth* is one that shall never be destroyed."

Yosef solemnly handed the scroll to Asa, who returned it to the archive.

"What do you say?" he asked.

Eliud, who was a regular guest of the Guild *chaburah*, was first to speak.

"The *Bar-Enash* is *Messiah ben-Yosef*, who is to come. He will teach all the nations."

"Where do you find authority for that?" asked Asa.

"Is it not written by the Prophet Isaiah, 'My House shall be called a House of Prayer for all the gentiles,' and, 'the gentiles shall come to your Light?' We who have lived in Babylon among the gentiles know that the Light is for all mankind, and that our work is to show forth that Light."

"What about the Romans?" snorted Asa.

After a silence, Shlomo observed, "There are good and bad Romans, just as there are good and bad Jews."

Yeshua had remained silent until bidden to speak, as was the Guild custom with Apprentices. But now Eliakim, a Jewish Babylonian Master Mason overseeing a major Roman project, motioned to him and asked, "What are the thoughts of your heart, *Yeshua*?"

"I do not know any gentiles, so I have no understanding of them," he smiled.

    *******   *******   *******   *******

It was the time of the Roman *Lupercalia* and all work had been suspended on the building projects. This had taken *Yosef* by surprise. Although he had spent many years in Sepphoris, he still didn't understand the Roman calendar and its Holy Days.

Rather than lose the time, *Yosef* had left *Yeshua* in Sepphoris to keep his eye on their partially completed private bath project while he taveled with Asa and Shlomo to Capernaum for carpentry repairs on a boat.

"Would you like to see how the Romans celebrate the birth of their founders?" asked Eliud. *Yeshua* nodded approval and followed him out into the narrow paved street.

"In the City of Rome, there is a cave on the Palatine Hill called the Lupercal. It is said that the twins Romulus and Remus were suckled and protected there by a mother wolf."

"Where was their real mother?" asked *Yeshua*.

"She was a prophetess, a Vestal Virgin, who was pledged to the Goddess of the Heart named Vesta and forbidden to marry. But Mars, the Roman Aries, was infatuated with her beauty and came upon her by night. She became pregnant with twins. But her uncle, who had overthrown her father's rule, feared the boys would try to regain the throne. So he stole the babies, placed them into a basket of reeds, and released them into the flooded Tiber River."

"Something like Moses?" asked *Yeshua* incredulously.

"The twins were rescued by the she-wolf, who took care of them in the cave."

"But the City seems to have its name from Romulus, not Remus. Why is that?" *Yeshua* asked.

"Well, later they were discovered by the new king's shepherd, who raised them. They became warrior-bandits and were finally caught by the king and brought up for punishment. But the new king was the father of their true mother, who after their birth had overthrown his evil brother, and recognized them as his grandsons. So they were freed and each decided to build his own city near the cave where the she-wolf raised them. But they argued, fought, and Romulus killed Remus. The city he founded was called Rome, after his name."

Just then there was a commotion farther down the street. An old Roman aristocrat clad only in a loincloth was whipping a group of women with thin, white cords. The women knelt before him and thanked him for the lashing.

"What is that?" asked *Yeshua*.

"That man is a Priest of the Lupercalia. He has sacrificed goats and dogs, then smeared the blood of sacrifice onto the foreheads of young Roman men, then wiped it off again, signifying the powers of blood for procreation and manhood. Then he made a whip out of strips of skin from the sacrificed animals for the women, who believe that it makes them fertile."

After a moment of thought, *Yeshua* observed, "These are strange customs. The gentiles are, indeed, in need of Light. This idea that a god would impregnate a chaste woman is especially strange."

"Yes," replied Eliud, "but the Greeks have many of these stories. Even the great philosopher Plato, they say, was not born from ordinary human intercourse, but through a visitation of the God Zeus to his mother in the form of a serpent." Eliud continued, "To the Greeks, every outstanding man is a demigod conceived by a human mother through intercourse with a god."

Yeshua looked up for a moment, then said, "In the Scroll of Noah, when his father Lamech saw how Light radiated from his newborn, child he was afraid that his wife had been impregnated by one of the fallen angels. He said, 'I have begotten a strange son, different from and unlike mankind.' So his father Methuselah ascended in consciousness to Enoch to seek an explanation, who told him, 'Make known to thy son Lamech that he who has been born is in truth his own son, and call his name Noah.'

"So you see, even though great prophets and spiritual leaders are born among mankind, they arise from *human* parentage, and not from angels and gods. That is our tradition in Israel, and I think it is correct. For why else would the Ancient of Days invest all dominion and *Malkuth* unto one like a Son of Mankind if humanity were unworthy of it?"

"Well spoken, *Yeshua*. But it is also true that there is much to learn from the gentiles, for the *Ruach Ha-Qodesh* has taught them many divine things under other names, like *Agathos Daemon, Sophia,* and the Muse. Perhaps one day you will learn prophetic *dabarim* from wise gentiles," laughed Eliud.

"Why not today?" retorted *Yeshua*.

"You want to meet a wise Egyptian?" countered Eliud, rising to the challenge.

"Yes, today! Now!" *Yeshua* pointed his forefinger upward like an Apprentice eager to speak.

"Then, follow me to the market place, where you shall hear the preaching of Ariston."

Previously, *Yeshua* had visited the market place only after it had closed, but now as the two men approached he saw crowds of revelers and more merchant stalls than he had ever seen before. They pushed their way through dancing women in various costumery and makeup to honor the great she-wolf of Rome—even one with men on both arms pretending to suckle at her breasts. The rhythm of tambourines, lutes, and the sacred seistron seemed to come from every direction.

Finally Eliud pulled *Yeshua*'s cloak and pointed.

"There, see that man on the steps to the palace? He is Ariston."

Standing elevated above the crowd and intoning in a hypnotic, highly inflected cant was a tall, handsome man attired like a Greek, but with a small golden breastplate like those worn by Egyptian Priests when they sung morning prayers and ablutions at the Temple of Isis. As they approached, *Yeshua* could hear his closing words. He spoke excellent Aramaic.

"The sleep of the body will become an awakening of the soul, the closing of your eyes a beginning of true vision, your silent meditation pregnant with the Good, and your words the instruments of divine wisdom. And you will become God-inspired, God-minded, and attuned to the Spirit of Truth."

As he sat down, two young men laughed, spat at him, and walked away. But another young man who appeared to be Jewish stood respectfully next to him, as was the custom for students in the presence of a teacher, and began asking questions. Eliud and *Yeshua* drew closer to listen.

"*Didaskolos*, do you know the teachings of Pythagoras?"

"I know them well, for he learned them in Egypt!" smiled Ariston

"Did he learn *Sige*, the Great Silence, in Egypt?" asked the young man.

"I see that you know something of the inner teachings, my young friend," was the reply.

"It is not unlike the approach to the *Merkabah*, I am told," the young man went on.

"There are many names and many ways," Ariston said almost in a whisper, "but the *Nous* of the *Authentia* is One," he replied.

Yeshua stepped close to the men and spoke, "*Shema Yisrael, Adonai Echad.* Do you know what this means?" he challenged.

"Indeed, young man, I know what this means. 'Hear, all ye who struggle for Divine *Gnosis*, The Master of the Universe is One, and ye are all One with Him.'"

Yeshua was surprised and pleased. Not only did Ariston know the translation of the Shema, but he had interpreted it with deep Kabbalistic understanding. The word "Israel" means "He who Struggles with God," the name given to *Yakob* after wrestling all night with the Angel of God. And he had interpreted "God is One" to mean "One with all Beings and All Humanity," which are His emanations.

"*Rav,* I must agree with your interpretation," was all *Yeshua* could say.

"*Didaskolos,* may we have the pleasure of your company for dinner tonight?" asked Eliud, with a slight shrug calling attention to the young *Yeshua*.

"I am engaged tonight, but would be honored to come tomorrow evening," Ariston replied, smiling at *Yeshua*.

"Then tomorrow evening when the market place closes, and you know my home, dear friend." Eliud again tugged slightly on *Yeshua*'s robe to indicate that it was time to leave. They stepped backward respectfully, then turned to walk away in silence.

As they reached Eliud's door, *Yeshua* stopped and remarked, "You are right, Eliud. There are wise gentiles. Perhaps I shall hear not only *dabarim* but even *Kabbalah* from this man, who seems to know Hebrew so well."

*******   *******   *******   *******

They reclined after the sumptuous meal Eliud had provided and settled into philosophical conversation.

"Do you think that remarkable men are produced only by intercourse between a god and a human woman?" asked *Yeshua*.

Ariston frowned. "No, that is a foolish superstition. It separates humanity from our divine origins and diminishes us. Greek myths have misled even the great philosophers like Platon, who wrongly applied wisdom from Timaeus, one of our Priests, to support his concept of a *Demiourgos*, a Creator God totally separate and transcendent from humanity."

"But the Judean Temple Priests teach that man is dust and Adonai is eternal," interjected Eliud.

"Yes, but the Pharisaic *Chassidim* teach that those who make themselves Sons and Daughters of the Most High with deeds of righteousness will gain eternal life," countered Ariston.

"But do they gain it, or regain it?" remarked *Yeshua* thoughtfully.

"A good point!" declared Ariston. "For the Rabbis, divine life is gained by developing and fulfilling the divine image within the soul. For the Hermetic saint, divine life already exists, like the royal pedigree of a prince, but it sleeps. It must be reawakened. It is not developed and fulfilled by acts of righteousness, but through *Gnosis*."

"But then divine life has no connection to morality and righteousness," objected *Yeshua*.

"Not so," answered Ariston. "Our human ideas of right and wrong, sinner and saint, are flawed by the sleep of ignorance in which we all participate to some degree, no matter how enlightened. Look at your Pharisees. How do they regard the Galileans or the Samaritans? Do they recognize the Image of God in them, or do they consider them to be inferior sinners unworthy of eternal life?"

After a pause, he continued.

"How do they justify their own righteousness—with human laws of purity and sacrifice? Do you think the blood of two doves reconciles theft or other sins?"

Yeshua nodded. "Yes, as it is written Adonai says, 'My ways are not your ways, and my thoughts are not your thoughts.' What men call righteousness is often what Adonai calls unrighteousness."

"So how can human ideas of good works truly awaken the soul?" asked Ariston. "No, it is Divine Knowledge that awakens the soul. Tell us what has awakened your soul, young man, for I perceive that you are a man of Spirit."

Yeshua was momentarily at a loss for words. Then he slowly began to speak.

"My Father, my Mother, my teachers, and perhaps most of all, the divine *dabarim* of the scrolls—and of course, my dreams and experiences of the Divine World."

"But have not works of righteousness also awakened you?" Eliud asked.

"Yes, especially the works of my Father, Master *Yosef*, and other righteous ones. But also the works of unrighteousness, like the finery of the Temple and the riches of the High Priest Annas—they have also awakened my soul," *Yeshua* answered.

"And I could say the same," replied Eliud. "There exists an absolute righteousness and unrighteousness, but great discrimination and awareness—like that of the Prophets—is required to perceive it. As the proverb says, 'Seeing, we do not see; and hearing, we do not hear.' Then what is it that teaches us to truly see and hear?"

The conversation turned to the Hermetic *Gnosis* taught by Ariston. He described the Egyptian emanations from pure Godhead that finally produced the world of matter and said, "So you see, the main difference between your *Kabbalah* and our *Gnosis* is that we use different names. It is names and homonyms that confuse and separate all religions. You will find the same *Gnosis* in India and Persia. If you travel to the Western lands you will find it among the Gauls and Brittons as well, and if you go beyond Nubia you will also find the *Gnosis*. Even the Greek Pythagoreans have the *Gnosis*. But it must be awakened, and how do we awaken it?" Ariston looked expectantly at *Yeshua*.

"So that is why you stand in the market place and sing your philosopher's stories," concluded *Yeshua*.

"And that is why your Prophets stood before the ancient temples of the Omri and delivered their *dabarim* publicly," nodded Ariston.

"Why do you care whether others awaken?" asked Eliud. "Isn't most of your *Gnosis* transmitted in secret?"

"The *Gnosis* awakens love and unity. How can I hoard the *Gnosis*? The world is in poverty and I have the greatest of all riches. How can I withhold such treasure from my brothers and sisters in need?"

Yeshua was deeply impressed with Ariston's spiritual purity and profundity. Indeed, here was a gentile saint as great as any known in Israel. Eliud was right. There was much to learn from the gentiles.

"Would you withhold your treasures from us?" asked *Yeshua*.

"Ours is a way of deep study—a Priestly study of mathematics, astrology, physics, alchemy, and all of the arts and sciences. It cannot be transmitted without decades of study—far more detailed than your *Kabbalah* of Zerubbabel. To learn the Work requires a lifetime of commitment. But yes, I can tell you about our Work."

Ariston then explained that all that manifests in form is divine emanation and therefore good, that we have forgotten our divine origins, and that we "remember" who we are by studying nature, for nature is a reflection of Divine Reality. There is no separation between man and God, Who extends his Grace to mankind through a hierarchy of worlds and beings, with our lowest world enclosed in seven planetary spheres through which each soul must descend at incarnation, where it receives the imprint of the astral *ethos* or what is known in Hebrew as the *nefesh*. At death it is able to ascend beyond the seven rulers of *Heimarmene* if, and only if, during incarnate life the soul has followed what the Jews call the good *yetzer* and if it knowns itself as an androgynous child and heir of God Most High, whom the Egyptian name as the *Authentia*. He said that the sciences are not evil arts of fallen angels, but divine gifts of the Divine Mother, whom the Egyptians name as Isis, through the thrice-great High Priest Hermes Trismegistos, and that wise people can use the subtle currents and forces of nature for the benefit of humanity if they master these sciences.

Then he said, "Always remember this *synthema* of the Great Work: 'As Above, so Below.'"

"This means that Adonai is revealed in His Works, and that He is always present in all that manifests in form," said Eliud. "This is also the teaching of the Magi."

Later that evening, *Yeshua* was unable to sleep, so he sat upright in contemplation. His *yechidah* seemed to speak to him wordlessly. He felt extremely restless in a most pleasant and spiritual way.

He thought deeply about the legend of the Lupercalia. If the gentiles had wisdom, there must be a Kabbalistic meaning behind the legend. Perhaps it was an allegorical myth.

Twin brothers, one good and one evil—this is like the twin natures in mankind, the good and evil *yetzerim*. Half divine and half human—this could be compared to the understanding of the Rabbis that the soul of each person was a harmony of both a mortal *nefesh* and an immortal *yechidah*. Saved from the flood and nurtured by a she-wolf—this could be understood as the human soul imprisoned in flesh and served by the animal nature. Found and raised by the King's shepherd—supported and raised by human parents. Developing as bandit warriors and finally captured by the king's police—the fall into the blind ways of the world. Recognition of kinship by the King and liberation to build their own city—the *tikkun* or restoration of the soul as Divine Heir. The final defeat and killing of Remus—a final triumph over the evil *yetzer*.

Yes, the potential for Kabbalistic higher understanding was there, but was it understood? Was it taught? No. There was hidden Light in the myth, but it remained invisible to those who celebrated the Lupercalia. Instead, as a literal legend it transmitted only a bizarre and immoral example of fratricide.

It seemed to *Yeshua* that only a few gentiles could truly understand the spiritual allegories of their own myths and legends. For most people they did not stimulate growth of the soul, but moral and spiritual ignorance.

When he finally was able to sleep, he dreamed again of *Eliahu ha-Nabi*.

******* ******* ******* *******

Ariston did not return to Sepphoris for two years. By this time *Yeshua* had been advanced to the degree of Journeyman and was learning the architectural arts of the Master Mason. He was also studying the advanced *Kabbalah* of Zerubbabel. *Yeshua* spent many wonderful evenings in philosophical conversation with Eliud and Ariston.

After advancement to Journeyman, *Yeshua* had been astonished to find that his teacher of the *Kabbalah* of Zerubbabel would be not *Yosef*, but *Rav Tzadok*, who was *Chazzan* of the Synagogue of the Babylonians.

"My son, he knows far more than I do. I teach other Journeyman this *Kabbalah*, but my decision as your Master is for you to study with Tzadok in Sepphoris. You will return home with me for *Shabbat* for three weeks, but on the fourth you will remain with Eliud in Sepphoris for your *Shabbat* seder studies with *Rav Tzadok*. He will instruct you privately on those days."

Yeshua was very pleased with this arrangement. Finally he would have a private teacher.

Over the years of weekly absence from his home, the relationship with his brother *Yakob* had become strained. As they each grew into manhood, they differed in their ideas.

Yakob had not been taken as an Apprentice into his father's Guild—this was reserved only for first-born sons. Instead he was hired as a shepherd by a close friend of *Yosef* with a contract to begin developing his own flock on his sixteenth birthday. He had no experience of the cosmopolitan world of Sepphoris or the spiritual ideas of gentiles. He had not studied the *Kabbalah*, and knew only what *Yosef* read and said at the *Shabbat* seder.

But *Yakob* had become deeply religious like his father, and he was—as his father often said—"a true Israelite." He devoted time to daily prayer. Most significantly, he was the only person in Nazareth able to develop a close friendship with the Galilean recluse and prophet known as *Rav Micah*.

Micah lived alone in the hills and came into Nazareth on the first day of the week to trade goat's cheese for other staples. He was a Nazirite who had never cut his hair, never touched a woman, and spent much of the time in silent divine communion and prayer. His custom was to sit on a large stone in the market place and wait until a small crowd had gathered, then deliver his teachings about Messiah. He quoted from Torah, Prophets, and the other Writings to prove that Messiah was soon to come and deliver Israel from Roman rule—even in this lifetime. He believed that Messiah would arise out of the sea and slay all the enemies of righteousness with the sword of his tongue.

The first time he laid eyes on *Yakob*, he motioned him to approach. *Yakob* was terrified, but came forward. Micah squinted at him through his fiery, piercing eyes and said, "If you hold fast to the truth in your heart, Adonai will make you His prophet." He then invited *Yakob* to sit next to him like another *Rav* while his hearers remained standing. *Yakob* sat, and sat again with *Rav Micah* every week thereafter.

What *Rav Micah* had said was buzzed all over Nazareth. People treated *Yakob* with respect, and his employer raised his wages. He found himself fighting spiritual pride. His reaction was to withdraw and keep silence.

Often his lack of communication was taken for arrogance, and his family members found him difficult to understand. To his mother and sisters, he seemed to lack warmth. To his brothers, and eventually even his father, he seemed overly self-preoccupied.

"Brother, why do you not speak to us?" *Yeshua* asked when they retired to their childhood room on *Shabbat* Eve. "People say that *Rav Micah* has gone to your head."

Yakob shook his head sadly and said nothing. Both young men lay down.

"I don't believe them," said *Yeshua* turning and smiling. *Yakob* gratefully returned the smile and grasped his brother's shoulder in reassurance.

"Brother, you know I cannot teach you the *Kabbalah*. I have taken an oath of secrecy," *Yeshua* lamented.

"*Yeshe*," whispered *Yakob*, "I have a teacher."

*******   *******   *******   *******

That Sunday morning *Yeshua* took his young brothers *Shimone*, *Yosef*, and Yehuda to the market place.

"Will we see *Yakob*?" piped Yehuda over and over.

"Yes, yes, yes!" repeated *Yosef*.

"We will also see and hear *Rav Micah*," matter-of-factly remarked *Shimone*, who was the sophisticated elder of the three. He was already studying for his *Bar Mitzvah* with Eleazar at *Shabbat* School.

There was a large crowd gathered around *Rav Micah*, and seated next to him was *Yakob*.

"'Behold, the Holy One, Blessed be He, will come with His holy myriads to execute justice for all, and to convict all the ungodly of all their deeds of ungodliness which they have committed ungodly, and all the ungodliness they have uttered against Him.'

"And who is this Holy One? He is the one to whom all dominion and power is given, the Anointed One. All the great prophets tell us of his coming—Daniel, Enoch, Micah, Zechariah. And I, Micah, tell you this—his coming is not far off. How will he find you when he comes? Will you be among the ungodly, or will you prepare your hearts and lives for him?"

Micah stared sternly at his hearers, confronting them with his questions and the demand for spiritual renewal.

"What should we do, *Rav*?" asked one of the young men. *Yeshua* marveled. It was the same bully that he had once humbled and humiliated! But now he seemed very different. Could *Rav Micah*'s preaching have helped make such a difference?

"Listen to the Prophet Amos, who said, 'Take away from me the noise of your songs…but let justice roll down like waters, and righteousness like an ever-flowing stream.'

"Do you think your circumcision or blood-sacrifice at Herod's Temple makes you righteous before Adonai. No! Circumcise your heart, young man! Offer the sacrifice of prayer and *berakuth*. Adonai knows the heart and the intention. Purify your heart, and then you will purify your words and deeds. Only this can prepare you for the Day of Adonai and His Messiah."

It was a simple message, but one that deeply impressed the simple people of Nazareth. He did not call for warfare against the Romans, but for spiritual revival—the same profoundly personal and moral renewal that the Prophets had demanded. *Yeshua* listened attentively to him, watched how he moved and inflected his words, and felt very close to this strange ascetic.

Now he understood why his brother *Yakob* was so devoted to *Rav Micah*, for the Spirit of the Prophets truly rested upon him. He rejoiced that his brother had an authentic teacher.

*******   *******   *******   *******

In no way did *Rav Tzadok* resemble *Rav Micah*. He was short, well-dressed, with a long but well-combed beard. He loved good food, was married to a beautiful woman, and had a large family. He imported goods from Persia, many of which were displayed in the Synagogue of the Babylonians, and he had a large personal library that he kept in his office at the Synagogue.

Yet, as *Yeshua* soon discovered, like Micah he was truly a holy man and a saint. And beyond that, he was also a wise man—a Hebrew sage.

"You have learned to work with the Seven Spirits to achieve moral purity, but now you will learn something about the Eighth Spirit—the *Ruach ha-Maat*."

"But Master, it was taught to me as the *Ruach ha-Mot*, the Spirit of Death, which rules both the sleep of nature and the *yetzer* of sacred death," *Yeshua* replied. "What is *Maat*?"

"This is an Egyptian word, my son. It was brought from Egypt by Moses, who learned how to work with the *Ruach ha-Maat* from his teacher Jethro, the Priest of Midian, who learned from *Melchizedek*, the High Priest of *El Elyon*."

"What does *Maat* mean?" asked *Yeshua*.

"It is not a simple meaning. It was the name of the Egyptian Goddess of Moral Justice and Spiritual Perfection, as well as these qualities of the upright heart. After death, the soul was brought before *Maat* to determine its purity. She symbolically weighed the heart against a feather. If the heart was pure, it would have no weight and be lifted up. Then the soul would be allowed to re-ascend to its divine origins. But if not, then the soul would pass through many harrowings and purgations. Finally it would return to reincarnate and again experience life in flesh, where it could continue the process of purification."

"This sounds very much like what the Egyptian sage Ariston tells me," remarked *Yeshua*.

"Remember this, my son. Our *Kabbalah* has four traditions—the Prophets of Palestine, the Babylonian schools, the Greek-speaking *Diaspora*, and Egypt. Only the Jews of Babylon have all these traditions. They are unknown to the Judean Rabbis and Temple Priests of Jerusalem, yet they were known to the prophetic Priesthood of Isaiah before the Captivity, when they were carried to Babylon. The Egyptian and Edomite are the most ancient of our Wisdom traditions, and it is from Egypt and Midian that Moses learned the *razim* concerning death and mystic ascent."

For many years *Rav Tzadok* taught *Yeshua* the advanced *Kabbalah* of Zerubbabel. He showed *Yeshua* translations of ancient scrolls of Egypt and Edom where many of the Psalms attributed to David and Proverbs attributed to Solomon could be found in their more ancient forms. He introduced him to the arts of the Magi, the mystic sleep of Pythagoras, and the Work of Formation or *Yetzirah*. But most advanced was the operation of the *Ruach ha-Maat*, the mystic ascent into the Heavens.

"This knowledge cannot be taught; it can only be learned from experience," said *Rav Tzadok* one evening after an ornate *Shabbat* seder at his beautiful home.

"Then how can it be learned?" asked *Yeshua*.

""I will explain the details of its operation. Someday, perhaps many years hence, you will meet a Rider of the Chariot who will transmit power to you for the Work of the *Merkabah*," he answered. "What I can give you is like a map to a strange land. But you must make the journey yourself."

"Have you made this journey?"

Rav Tzadok put his hands together, looked upward, then spoke softly.

"I have never succeeded. I haven't achieved the purity of Daniel, Jeremiah, and Isaiah. But I comfort myself with the knowledge that even Moses lacked the purity to see God face to face. Perhaps one day..." his voice trailed off into silence. Then suddenly he stared at *Yeshua*'s face.

"My son. We purify ourselves through many lives of service. Some of us are born with great purity that we may, or may not, perfect during our lifetimes. You are such a person. If you grow to full manhood and perfect your purity, you will be able to do what I have not yet achieved.

"But not now. You are too young and undeveloped. Dreams, yes. Visions, yes. But the Work of the Chariot—absolutely not! I shall give you the map, but before you can attempt the journey you must have the guidance of a *Ba'al Shem Tov* who is a master of the *Merkabah*. There is no such person in Sepphoris, and you are far too undeveloped for the Work. If you attempt it on your own, you will go insane. Promise me that if I teach you the operation, you will not attempt it without the guidance of a true *Rav*."

Yeshua looked deeply into *Rav Tzadok's* eyes and answered, "I promise, not by a sworn oath or in the Name of Adonai, but in the Name of my own Heart."

Chapter Eight: THE DEATH OF *YOSEF*

Two men—bearded, powerfully built, broad forehead, noble angular profile. One young and vital, bronzed by the relentless sun, strengthened by years of physical labor; the other old and failing, spent and weakened to the point of death. One almost a mirror image of the other, but separated by a span of more than two generations—almost like grandfather and grandson.

Yeshua had known for some time that his father's health was failing, but nothing could prepare him for what he now felt. Death seemed to be an impenetrable stone wall like the mighty structure surrounding the Temple in Jerusalem, but designed by the Grand Architect of the *'Olamim* and artfully wrought by his mighty *Malachim--Michael* at His right hand, and *Gabriel* at His left. But if there was Justice at the right Pillar, there must also be Mercy at the left. The *Kabbalah* taught the continuity of consciousness for the righteous after death.

Miriam kneeled at *Yosef*'s left hand, *Yeshua* at his right, with all of his children and closest associates of the Brotherhood standing close. But it was to *Yeshua* only that he spoke.

"Remove my sandals."

Yeshua unstrapped his father's unique sandals and began to wash his feet, just as he used to do when he was an Apprentice. The heavily-constructed sandals were the envy of all the other masters. They were strapped with heavy thongs made of ox leather. To protect the foot from falling stone, here was a thick pad of leather that extended from the reinforced front of the sandal back across the top of the foot. The heavy straps threaded through the pad, which was marked with gashes from accidents that could have been far more injurious without the protective pad.

The old man tried unsuccessfully to raise himself on one elbow, then sank back down.

"*Abba*, don't exhaust yourself," *Yeshua* pleaded. He couldn't stop the tears that leaked from his brimming eyes, but he controlled his voice as he swallowed against the painful lump in his throat. *Miriam* and her daughters sobbed silently.

"Take my sandals. I want you to have them." His voice was weak and strained.

Yeshua nodded.

"Put them on your feet." *Yeshua* hesitated, then removed his sandals and strapped them onto his feet while everyone watched in a silent hush.

When this was done, *Yosef* slowly and painfully raised his right index finger and spoke again.

"My Son, the order of separation…is exactly the reverse of the order…of formation," *Yosef* again whispered as he lay struggling for breath.

"Tell me, my Son…the order of death."

Yeshua drew a deep breath, then spoke in measured words.

"When the *ruach* departs on the last breath, the *nefesh* separates from flesh…" he choked back his tears…"and after forty days the divine portion separates from the *nefesh* and returns to its Divine Source, *neshemah*." He paused.

"Yes?" *Yosef* asked, just as he always had asked as a teacher, requiring a further response from his student.

"But *neshemah* returns, riding the winds of *ruach,* for a new formation in the World of *Yetzirah*. In that *'Olam*, the *Elohim* form a new *nefesh* from the invisible elements; they form it in the womb of a woman, and it is born a new child in this World of *Malkuth*."

"Yes? And what…about your *Abba Yosef*?"

Yeshua and his brothers could no longer stifle their tears. After a few deep breaths *Yeshua* composed himself again and answered.

"My *Abba Yosef*…" he breathed deeply again…"my human father as I know him…his *nefesh* will dissolve back into…the visible and invisible elements; but his mighty spirit will always live and will return to this *'Olam*."

"Who is your true *Abba*?" *Yosef* seemed to gain strength. His eyes burned like coals.

"*Adonai, Ha-Shem*…is our true Father…and the Spirit of our Master of the *'Olamim* lives as a spark, and as an image, and as His Holy Bride in the divine *yechidah* of each one," *Yeshua* answered. He felt a feeling of strengthening and a sudden glimmer of what might be joy in his heart.

The two men locked their eyes in an embrace of deepest spiritual love.

Time passed, but the old man's eyes did not close. *Miriam* fell upon her husband's breast and sobbed openly, while her daughters tried to comfort her.

Yeshua knew that *Yosef* had consciously allowed himself to begin the process of death, as it was taught in the advanced *Kabbalah* of Zerubbabel, and that his eyes would have to be closed for him. He reached forward tenderly and closed first the old man's left eyelid, then his right. There was still a relaxed smile on the old Master's bearded face.

Then, *Yeshua* became aware of a slight glow or radiance that seemed to emerge above the crown of his father's head, linger, then slowly expand and disperse in all directions until its presence could no longer be detected. He calmly looked back at his brothers, but it was clear that they had seen nothing—except for *Yakob*.

The two brothers had not been close for many years, but Jakob came forward, smiled, and embraced *Yeshua*. They held each other with eyes closed. *Yeshua* realized that of all his brothers, *Yakob* was the one who truly understood divine things.

******* ******* ******* *******

Many years ago *Yosef* had carved his own burial chamber into the soft rock of the Brotherhood Garden of Eternity. It occupied a central position among the smaller cliff-hewn *kukhin* that surrounded the oasis-like spring with its small fig and pomegranate orchard. Within the tomb he had carved two pedestals—one on the right for himself, and one on the left for *Miriam*. Four large, carefully hewn stones were to be used for sealing the tomb in such a way that it could later be reopened for *Miriam*'s interment.

Yosef had provided well for *Miriam*. He had left her income-producing property in both Nazareth and Capernaum to be managed for her by sons *Shimone* and *Yosef* as well as a large herd of livestock to be managed by *Yakob*. His daughters were all expected to marry, and he had accumulated generous dowries for each of them. *Yeshua*, as firstborn, would make his own way as a Journeyman in the Brotherhood and eventually take his place as a Master.

Master *Yosef* had also provided for his funerary memorial in the Brotherhood—an *Ahavah* or Love Feast to be celebrated after his entombment and annually thereafter on the anniversary of his death. *Yeshua*, as firstborn son, would preside, as he also would at the Brotherhood rites of mourning.

The procession, with mourners preceeding and casket following in the Galilean tradition, slowly climbed the hot, stony trail leading into the hidden garden. In attendance were members of *Yosef*'s family from all over Galilee, associates from the Brotherhood, and friends like Eliud and *Rav*s Eleazar, Tzadok, and even Micah, whose hermitage was not far away from the Garden of Eternity. No one spoke.

When they arrived at the spring, *Yeshua* motioned for the mourners to sit. They began to intone the first of the fifteen Psalms of *Aliyah* or Ascent that would be sung on *Yosef*'s behalf over the coming seven weeks.

"In my distress I called upon Eee-ahh-ohh-way-eee and He answered me…"

The *Kabbalah* taught that the deceased remained close to his physical body, earthbound with a thousand invisible ties from which he would slowly become disentangled by keeping his attention focused upon the Light of *Adonai*. His friends and family must both release him from these ties, and help him to release them for himself. The fifteen Psalms of Ascent had been arranged into a special order long ago by sages, and their meaning and use for funerary rites had been taught in Galilean synagogues for many generations. However the deeper Kabbalistic meanings, which derived from ancient Priestly Egyptian and Zoroastrian teachings, were not known to any but the Brotherhood, which presided over the death rites for their member families.

The first three Psalms of *Aliyah* were intoned at the time of physical death. They provided a current of prayer and intention that assisted the deceased to look up and away from the grief and sorrows of Earth, and to aspire in consciousness for release and return to the Higher Worlds.

Two of the Brothers readied the stones while four others lifted *Yosef*'s casket into the tomb and placed it on the right-hand pedestal. The mourners intoned the second Psalm of *Aliyah*:

"I will lift up mine eyes unto the high places, from whence cometh my help."

Then *Yeshua* assisted the Brothers with the four large stones to permanently seal the tomb, after which he led the mourners in the third Psalm of Ascension:

"Let us ascend to the House of Eee—ahh—ohh—way—eee."

The *Kabbalah* of Zerubbabel taught that now the *neshemah* of *Yosef*, like the bones of the Patriarch *Yosef*-Asaf, would be carried by the *Ruach Ha-Kodesh* across a great sea to journey in the vast wilderness, then finally come to rest in the Promised Land. It would experience three stages comprising six weeks: Crossing the Sea; Wandering in the Wilderness; and Approaching the Promised Land. For each of these, his *neshemah* would be assisted by four consecutive Psalms of *Aliyah* sung by those devoted to him.

The first stage, Crossing the Sea, had begun with sacred entombment. It would require three days and two nights. The second, Wandering in the Wilderness, would require forty days and forty nights. The third was only one night—Approaching the Promised Land—and it ended the period of mourning.

The mourners returned to the house of *Miriam* for the first memorial Love Feast. The *Ahava* had been prepared by neighbors hired to do the cooking, serving, and clean-up. It was elegantly set out in the courtyard with tables and couches for the family and honored guests. *Yakob* took his place next to *Yeshua* at *Miriam*'s right.

"Brother," *Yakob* said quietly, "we must help bring the bones of Asaph to his home."

Yeshua was amazed. *Yakob* had intuitively developed a basic Kabbalistic understanding without instruction. He grasped the deeper meanings of the Psalms of *Aliyah*—how and why they were used.

"Dear Brother, you are a man of deep understanding. Even though we will be separated for these coming many weeks, we will be united in assisting the *ruach* of our father. Do you know the order?"

"Please tell me," *Yakob* answered.

Yeshua hesitated for a moment. Would he break his vows by clarifying the Kabbalistic practice of *Aliyah*? But he knew in a flash that if *Yakob* had already understood the basics, it was by the guidance of the *Ruach Ha-Kodesh*. She was the source of all divine *Kabbalah*. If She had revealed it to *Yakob*, did he not have a responsibility to clarify so that *Yakob* could participate in the practice for the sake of his father?

Quietly and privately, *Yeshua* explained the order, times, and usage of the Psalms to his brother *Yakob*. He was overheard by Master Jehuda of Jaffa.

Yeshua had asked *Rav* Eleazar to provide the oration. He began by reading from the Scroll of the Wisdom of Solomon.

"The souls of the righteous are in the hand of *Yah* and no torment will ever touch them. In the eyes of the foolish they seem to have died, and their departure was thought to be an affliction, and their going from us to be their destruction; but they are in a state of *shalom*.

"For though in the sight of men they were punished, their hope is full of immortality. Having been disciplined a little, they will receive great good, because *Yah* tested them and found them worthy of himself; like gold in the furnace he tried them, and like a sacrificial burnt offering he accepted them.

"At the time of their return to flesh in the Messianic Age, they will shine forth, and will run like sparks through the stubble. They will govern nations and rule over peoples, and *Adonai* will reign over them in the World to Come."

He sighed deeply and handed the scroll to *Shimone*.

"We each knew this great man only in part. We saw him only with our own eyes, understood him only with our own hearts. But I tell you, the Divine Image still shines through him as a blazing flame for those with eyes to see, and the *Ruach Ha-Qodesh* still dwells in his heart as in a holy temple.

"*Yosef*—*Yosef*, my dear friend. We know that you are present here to witness our devotion, so we will not offend you with flattery. But *Yosef*, besides you, I have never known a man so filled with so great a measure of *hesed* and *geburah*—such a sublime balance of divine mercy and justice. You are truly among the greatest souls of the righteous ones.

"Let us all commune with the great *ruach* of Master *Yosef* and feel his presence in our hearts."

He raised the first Cup of Blessing, recited the *Beraka*, adding, "and Who has formed such a great soul as *Mar Yosef* of Nazareth." The Cup was passed first to *Miriam*, then *Yeshua*, then to brothers and sisters, and finally to all the guests.

Rav Eleazar then offered the *Beraka* over the bread, adding the same words, and *Miriam* distributed the bread to all in the same traditional order.

Yeshua raised his arms and began the formal banquet with the invitation, "Let us feast in the memory of Master *Yosef*." Soon quiet conversation turned to laughter and good spirits.

******* ******* ******* *******

Master Yehuda of Jaffa had been a business competitor of *Yosef*, but as a member of the Brotherhood he had maintained cordial relations. He did not have *Yosef*'s unusual spiritual qualities or his natural affinity for deep Kabbalistic understanding. But he saw himself as a righteous and upright servant of God and defender of the Brotherhood.

When he overheard *Yeshua* explaining details of the Kabbalistic use of the Psalms of *Aliyeh* to *Yakob* at the Love Feast, he had been scandalized—shaken from head to toe. This was a blatant violation of the Brotherhood Oath, and one that troubled him every waking moment. Out of respect for the seven-week mourning period for Master *Yosef*, he held his tongue. But a few days after the fifteenth *Aliyeh* had been sung, he traveled to Sepphoris and called an emergency meeting of Brotherhood Guild Masters.

"*Yeshua ben-Yosef* has broken the Oath of Secrecy," he announced in a solemn voice. The other Masters demanded to know what he had said, to whom, when, and how Yehuda knew these things.

"This is the testimony of only one witness," said Master *Shimone*, who was now *Yeshua*'s Master and protector. "It is not legally binding."

"Then let us bring the Journeyman *Yeshua ben-Yosef* before our Council to see how he answers this charge," suggested Jehuda. "Let us require him to answer on oath."

Early the next morning *Shimone* spoke to *Yeshua* as they walked to their project.

"My son, the Council requires you to meet with them tonight. You have been charged with oath-breaking."

The words struck *Yeshua* like a blow on the back of the head. He stopped in shock and looked at *Shimone*.

"Who makes this charge?"

"It is Master Jehuda of Jaffa. I cannot tell you anything more." *Shimone* looked searchingly into *Yeshua*'s eyes. "But I cannot believe that you have broken the Oath of Secrecy."

Immediately *Yeshua* remembered the Love Feast and grasped the situation. Master Jehuda must have overheard his private conversation with *Yakob*.

They walked slowly to the project. All *Yeshua* could think about until that evening was the charges. Was he truly an oath-breaker? Had what he told *Yakob* been wrong? He sat in meditation and prayer during each of his work breaks and searched his soul for the answers. He could not eat that day and did not join his friends for supper. But he realized that there was no point in preparing a speech or defence. This was in the hands of God, and he must try to keep himself attuned to divine guidance.

"*Yeshua ben-Yosef*, we have summoned you here to answer charges of oath-breaking. We now ask your accuser to formally make his charges."

Master Jehuda stood and quietly repeated what he had witnessed at the *Ahavah* for Master *Yosef*. After he finished speaking there was silence. The Master of the Council looked at Jesus as *Yosef* often had and made the simple, familiar demand, "Yes?"

"Masters of the Brotherhood," *Yeshua* began, "my brother *Yakob* is a righteous man with deep spiritual discernment. At the *Ahavah* for our father, he interpreted for me the return of Asaph's bones to the Promised Land through the Sea and the Wilderness. He was taught these things by the *Ruach Ha-Kodesh*—not by *Rav Micah*. I reasoned that if the Divine Spirit had revealed these things to *Yakob*, and if he then sought a clear understanding of how to use the Psalms of Ascent, how could I not obey the Spirit in teaching him?"

Master *Shimone* raised a finger and was granted the floor.

"My Brothers, do we not learn in the *Kabbalah* that obedience to *Hochmah* is primary?"

Jehuda raised a finger and was recognized.

"Obedience to *Hochmah* does not include breaking the Oath of Secrecy, in my opinion."

"How do you answer?" asked the Master of the Council, fixing *Yeshua* with eyes piercing from beneath whitened brows.

"Masters, I knew that it was *Hochmah* that urged me to impart this knowledge because I, like my father *Yosef*, have always striven to hear and know Her Voice."

There was silence. All of the Masters knew *Yeshua* to be an honorable and disciplined Journeyman—a righteous young man with perfect integrity.

Jehuda did not wait for permission to speak, but blurted, "But the Oath takes precedence!"

Immediately it was clear that all sentiment in the Council shifted on behalf of *Yeshua*. Nothing was said, but everyone—including Jehuda—realized without doubt that no human oath can take precedence over the obligation to obey Divine Spirit. After a silence the Master of the Council spoke.

"Brothers, escort *Yeshua ben-Yosef* from this room so that we may take our vote."

Yeshua was led into the adjoining room, and within a few moments invited to re-enter the Council room.

"*Yeshua ben-Yosef*, it is our opinion that you have not violated the Oath of Secrecy. You may be excused."

From that moment on, *Yeshua* had a bitter enemy in the Council of Masters. Yehuda of Jaffa regarded him as an oath-breaker unworthy of the Brotherhood, and one whom God would punish—especially for the humiliation he had inflicted upon the righteous Brother Jehuda. He would bide his time, spy upon the audacious Journeyman, and bring other witnesses against him when *Shimone* nominated his protégé for advancement to the degree of Master.

And from that moment on, *Yeshua* would know the sting of many enemies—antagonists that every man of charisma and integrity must churn up in his wake. For the mantle of *Yosef* fell upon *Yeshua*—the mantle of leadership that generates jealousy or loyalty, and no middle way. *Yeshua* would become an outspoken controversial man among the Brotherhood.

******* ******* ******* *******

"An oath is a crutch for a lame man," *Yeshua* remarked to *Shimone*. "A righteous man has no need of an oath. He speaks his heart, and he keeps his word. His 'yes' means yes, and his 'no' means no. He does not need to swear in the name anything external, or under pain of any penalty, because he always speaks and acts in the name of his own heart."

Shimone sat back from the rough project drawing he had made in the sand, thought for a moment, then replied, "But that is quite a different thing from making and breaking an oath—or even the appearance of breaking it. You were very lucky to be judged righteous in the Council."

"No, *Shimone*. The Council was righteous to judge righteously, and not merely based on appearances."

After a moment, *Yeshua* continued.

"Remember how often the prophets acted under the impulse of Divine Spirit, then later understood the meaning of their action? Jeremiah was inspired to buy a linen waistcloth, but not dip it into water. Then he was inspired to take it to the Euphrates River and hide it in a cleft rock, wait many days, then dig it up to find that it was rotten."

"I have never heard that *dabar*," said *Shimone*, "but if you tell me, it must be so."

"Then, after doing these things, Jeremiah understood their Kabbalistic meaning and was able to deliver his prophecy. You see, the *Ruach Ha-Qodesh* sometimes inspires us to act, then we later understand that act. This was so when I instructed *Yakob* about the *Aliyah*. Should I have been fearful of the censure of men, or should I have followed the direction of Spirit?"

Shimone smiled teasingly. "Then, you are a prophet like Jeremiah?"

"Remember what *Rav Tzadok* said at the seder—'Ye are all prophets of *El Elyon*.'" *Yeshua* smiled back.

"But surely it is not good to act without thought or intention," objected *Shimone*.

"The prophet acts with the thought and intention of *Adonai*, not of himself. But too often people are puppets in the hands of dark spiritual forces if they act without thought and clear intention in their hearts. Only when one is clear and pure can he discern the difference.

"I had purified myself with much prayer and fasting after the death of my father. What is more, my brother *Yakob* had done the same. That is why he had begun to understand the *Kabbalah* of the *Aliyeh*. And my father *Yosef* was worthy of an *Aliyeh* by sons as well as Brothers. All that is why *Adonai* moved me to impart the *Aliyeh* to *Yakob*."

Shimone nodded in agreement and returned to his work.

His new protégé was quite a piece of work, but would the Council of Masters allow him to advance? Jehuda was on a campaign to discredit *Yeshua* and was calling in all the political favors owed him by others. If *Shimone* were to propose an advancement to the degree of Master, there would not be enough support at this time—and possibly never. He loved *Yeshua*, but perhaps it would be better for him to transfer to another jurisdiction—far beyond the influence of Jehuda.

That evening *Shimone* spoke with *Rav Tzadok*.

"My dearest Journeyman and best assistant is unfairly opposed by several influential Masters who work in Sepphoris. He can never be advanced in this jurisdiction. Where can we send him?"

Tzadok arched his eyebrows. He recognized the description of *Yeshua* and replied, "But he is my best student. I could not bear to lose him."

Then after a moment of thought, "He should go to my community in Babylon."

"What? Babylon! That is *too* far away!" *Shimone* objected.

"Yes, but *Yeshua* is much more than a Brother of the Guild. He is a man of Spirit. He needs to learn from the Sages. In Babylon he can advance to the degree of Master Architect under the instruction of far greater Masters than we have in your Guild. Then he can return with higher Guild authorities than anyone in Palestine, and would never again be successfully challenged by any enemies. He would be a Grand Master and Architect," said Tzadok with a finality that seemed very credible to *Shimone*. "And he would be deeply in your debt," Tzadok added slyly.

"Yes, he does have the talent, the intelligence, and as you say, the Spirit of *Adonai*. But I am afraid he would become a Priest of the Magi!" laughed *Shimone*. "Then you would never see him again, either."

"*Yeshua* is a true man of Israel. He will return," replied Tzadok.

"Shall I make this proposal to him?" asked *Shimone*.

Rav Tzadok looked into *Shimone*'s eyes. "You are his Master, appointed by *Mar Yosef*? Then you don't propose—you command, and he will obey."

He had never commanded *Yeshua* to do anything. The young man's father had used all his influence to have *Shimone* advanced. What is more, *Shimone* owed *Yeshua* even as much because the young man had tutored and prepared him for the exams he was finally able to pass. How could he use his rank to command him, to force him to leave home and family?

Tzadok continued to fix *Shimone* with his eyes. "You command, and he will obey."

"As God wills," *Shimone* sighed in resignation.

Chapter Nine: JOURNEY TO BABYLON

At first, *Yeshua* had resisted *Shimone*'s proposal, but he knew that his Master had the right to command, and then he'd be faced with the imperative to obey. But something else finally dissolved his resistance. Every night for a week he dreamed about taveling or being in Babylon with the Jewish community. On *Shabbat* Eve he realized that it was more than *Shimone* urging him—it was *Hochmah*. He must go to Babylon.

It had been a tearful parting with his family, but *Yeshua* could see that all was well with *Miriam* and her daughters. His brothers responsibly oversaw the family wealth and property, and they were devoted to their mother.

"I have heard that you got into trouble for teaching me the *Aliyah*," *Yakob* said privately. "What you did was right, my brother, and I thank you for the teaching. It has opened up much more for me."

Yeshua was deeply moved. Perhaps *Yakob* understood more than anyone else. He grasped *Yakob*'s shoulder and looked into his brother's eyes.

"Every week at the *Shabbat* seder, remember me, *Yakob*, and I shall remember you. When I return, tell me if God has given you any visions, and I will tell you the same. From now on, I will take no oaths of secrecy. All that is given to me shall be given to you."

Many years later, when his *talmidim* would ask who would be their teacher after his death, *Mar Yeshua* would say, "You shall go to *Yakob* the Righteous, for whose sake Heaven and Earth were formed."

Even later, the authenticity and sanctity of *Yakob* the *Tzadik* would be so highly regarded by everyone that even the High Priest Ananias would be forced to allow him to assume his Temple role on the Day of Atonement—to enter the Holy of Holies, intone the Divine Name, and purify the land on behalf of the people. When finally the jealous Priests threw the elderly saint over the wall of the Temple and and hired a fuller to beat out his brains with a mallet, the deepest teachings of *Mar Yeshua* –some of them acquired during the sojourn in Babylon—would be lost with him.

*******   *******   *******   *******

The flat top of Mt. Arbel towered menacingly over Magdala as the caravan made its way South over the *Via Maris* toward Judea. *Yeshua* kept watch, for this was the Valley of the Robbers where travelers were often attacked by zealots or other thieves.

"Look at those caves," said Mordechai, pointing to an area high on the cliffs. "That is where Herod slaughtered the freedom fighters sixty years ago when he took over the Galilee. They had hidden themselves in caves halfway down the sheer cliff, but Herod lowered his butchers on ropes and baskets—three to a basket. Our kinsmen were each alone in the small caves, so Herod's soldiers were able to kill them one by one, then throw their bodies off the cliff."

"Yes," replied *Yeshua*. "I sense that the Earth is drenched with human blood in this place. I can almost smell it."

Mordechai was a merchant from Magdala, known as *Magdal Nunaiya*, the Fish Tower. It was a large fishing port on the Sea of Galilee where *Yosef* and *Yeshua* had often worked. The fishermen would sell to them directly off the boats because they were respected Guildsmen. The two men cleaned and salted their fish and, on their return trip to Nazareth, always brought as much home as they could carry.

But Mordechai didn't deal in fish. He traded perfume, precious stones, and oils on behalf of the wealthy Essene community located in the desert near the Dead Sea in Judea. That would be the first destination of the small caravan.

After this they would undertake the long journey to Damascus on the Eastern side of the Jordan River, where Mordechai would acquire unique glassware pieces produced by Jewish craftsmen. Then they would pass through the dangerous city of Palmyra and enter the ancient Persian lands now ruled by the Parthians. From there they would cross the Orontes and Euphrates Rivers for the final Southern journey to Seleucia and Babylon.

"When I return, I shall be a rich man, and I shall marry my wonderful *Miriam*," Mordechai had told *Yeshua*. But the journey was long and dangerous. Caravans were often attacked by large bands of raiders because they carried great wealth. Mordechai's Essene investors had also bought interests in two other caravans transporting other kinds of goods. They would make a lot of money even if only one of them survived the journey.

There was safety in numbers for caravan merchants. When they finally crossed the Euphrates they would be joined by endless caravans from the Royal Road. But until then, they would face danger in their lonely sojourn through the Judean wilderness.

Mordechai had hired *Yeshua* as a caravan guard specifically because he was taller and stronger than most Jewish men. Even better, like most Journeymen Masons he was skilled with staff and mallet, and he was known to fear no man. The fact that *Yeshua* would remain in Babylon was not an issue. He could always find other strong Jewish men there who would work their way West for a pilgrimage to Jerusalem.

"Perhaps some day I will meet your wonderful *Miriam*," remarked *Yeshua*.

"That is most likely, my friend, because both of us have many close relatives in Babylon."

Yeshua reflected that the name Mordechai is not Hebrew, but Babylonian.

"So that is how you developed your trade as a merchant?" he asked.

Mordechai laughed. "My whole family are merchants, except for one famous Rabbi. And we are all descendants of King David."

"Who is the Rabbi?" asked *Yeshua*.

"None other than Rabbi Hillel," he answered casually.

Yeshua was impressed. "Did you ever study with him?"

"No!" Mordechai laughed even more heartily. "He is an outcast in Babylon, but a great man in Palestine."

"Why an outcast?"

"Because his parents did not support his religious vocation. They wanted him to be a merchant. He finally made his pilgrimage to Jerusalem and worked as a wood-cutter to support himself. That is why he said, 'If I am not for myself, who is for me?'"

Yeshua smiled. "Yes, but he added, 'If I am *only* for myself, then what am I?' And most important, he said, 'If not now, when?' signifying that all things exist in this moment."

"Hah!" declared Mordechai. "Who needs a Rabbi when you've got a Stone Mason? Are you sure you're not a Master Mason?"

*******   *******   *******   *******

They arrived at *Khirbet Qumran* in the evening. The guard at the watchtower signaled that the holy meal was in progress and no one could meet with them until the next morning, so they set up camp. This might have seemed to be a complicated process with thirty men and twelve camels, but after a signal from Mordechai indicating a sheltered location, everything was quickly put into order—one fire for servants, another for guards and merchants, baskets of food, and many pallets for sleep were laid out. As the sun set, the murmur of conversation and song fell away. Finally the dark, moonless, endless sky came ablaze with stars.

That night *Yeshua* dreamed of being with the Prophet Eliahu, who seemed to be telling him many things. But when he awoke at sunrise, all that remained was the sensation of having been in the presence of a great one.

"They do not allow us to enter the compound," said Mordechai. "They will call me to the gate and there I will bargain with them for flasks of oils and perfumes, for incense, and for pearls or other gemstones. But truly, they do not bargain. They set their price and either I will agree or not. It is that simple."

"But how can you travel this far without knowing the outcome?"

Mordechai shrugged. "Because their price has always been fair. I can always do business with them, and their goods are highly valued everywhere."

By early morning the business was transacted, the camels loaded, and the journey to Jericho had begun. Mordechai planned to acquire balsam and meet his second caravan. This would transport high-grade Jewish pitch or asphalt taken from the floor of the Dead Sea and follow them to Babylon. It would be used to repair the famous Hanging Gardens, which no longer had its local supply. *Yeshua*, as an experienced builder, would be in charge of this second caravan and its delivery to the Masons in Babylon.

As they descended into what the Bedouins called the Great *Wadi*, the Winter Palace of Herod could be seen from a long distance away with its theater, hippodrome, and luxurious baths. They followed the Roman road to a central plaza where all caravans were required to check in with Roman sentries. After a brief search and payment of fees, they were waved on to a staging area where new caravans were forming. Most would turn toward the Mediterranean to travel what the Romans called the *Via Maris*, Way of the Sea. Only Mordechai's group would turn East to take the treacherous switchbacks into so-called Arabia, where they would travel along the high mountain road of ancient Moab to Philadelphia, and thence to Damascus.

A burly man—Jewish, but wearing the caravan garb of a Bedouin—stared silently at *Yeshua*. Then he knelt, knocked his right hand onto the ground three times, stood up, and waited expectantly. Could he be a Brother?

"Who knocks?" asked *Yeshua*.

"A son of Zerubbabel," he answered in a deep Galilean drawl.

They clasped right hands, each holding the other's forearm, in the sign of recognition, and both men smiled broadly.

"Brother, if you want to return to Jericho, there will be a great building project that will require many years."

Yeshua was silent for a moment. "What is it?"

"Herod wants to build something that will make Caesar jealous."

"He wants to expand this?" asked *Yeshua*, nodding toward the Winter Palace.

"No. Look across the valley—over there. That's where he wants to build. And he will have it rival the palaces of Caesar."

Yeshua smiled and said, "You must be the foreman of my new caravan."

"Ah!" he nodded. "And you must be the Son of Zerubbabel who will deliver the pitch and work with the Babylonian Masons to repair the Hanging Gardens."

"Is that what I'm supposed to do?" asked *Yeshua* in surprise?

"If you want the job," Mordechai announced from behind him.

Yeshua turned to see a smiling Mordechai reeking of balsam.

"Yes, I'll take it," replied *Yeshua*, feeling a sudden surge of happiness. Now he would enter Babylon as a Son of Zerubbabel—not a common laborer.

That evening *Yeshua* ate a fine meal with Mordechai and his new friend and Brother, Zeb. After too much wine and a deep sleep, they assembled the new, larger caravan of camels and donkeys.

Yeshua gave Zeb specific instructions about the pitch-pots that he translated for the Bedouin drivers. The pots were to be covered with blankets at all times, but no lids, so the pitch could soften and harden day and night without obstruction. The pitch-pots were to always be kept upright. If a pack animal died, then the men themselves would have to carry the pots. This way he ensured that the animals would be well fed, watered, and not driven too hard.

It was a hot and tortuous journey out of the Great Wadi, over the switchbacks, and onto the *Via Regis*—the King's Highway. But now they could see all of Israel, even to the Sea. *Yeshua* had never been on such a high mountain, nor had he ever seen such a view. At night his dreams were filled with wonderful music and spiritual inspiration.

As they traveled farther to the leeward side of the mountains and approached the city known as Philadelphia, their expansive view was lost. This was the city of the Ammonites.

"If we set up tents here, we'll have all those Egyptian Bedouins visiting, and you know what that means," said Mordechai.

"What?" asked *Yeshua*.

"It means we'll have to offer hospitality and serve them beer," he grimaced. "If we don't, they might turn on us if we're attacked. But if we do, they are honor-bound to defend us with their lives."

"I'll get the tents set up, and you can go into the city and buy beer," *Yeshua* returned, not skipping a beat.

That evening the tents were joined together into one large tabernacle. It was lighted with many small fires and boiling pots. A yeasty aroma of still-fermenting beer permeated the dusky air attracting groups of Arabic Bedouins, who arrived smiling, bowing, and offering sweets. Soon a large crowd was sitting around Mordechai with many lively conversations.

As each small jar of beer was served, the guest bowed and said, "Once," or "Twice" or "Thrice." This was to keep count of the jars. A fourth jar was considered to be gluttonous and an insult to the host, as would be refusing the first jar. Stopping after one, two, or three was not only part of the ritual, but quite practical, as *Yeshua* discovered when after three jars he finally lay down in a groggy stupor.

The next morning they prepared to enter Philadelphia and pay the Roman road fees.

"When we travel South to Petra, we cannot travel through the territory of any sheik or do business with him until we have done the beer ritual, and then he has provided a meal. After that we conclude our business, but only if we show great appreciation for the meal. It is all custom," sighed Mordechai, "and without custom, there can be no trade."

Yeshua nodded, his eyes still propped open against his will. He had never felt so tired!

The journey North from Philadelphia to Gerasa was restful and pleasant. The Beq'ah Valley was sprinkled with small farms and villages. After two days they arrived at the gates of Gerasa in the area also known as Gilead. It was a well-sheltered location near forests and trees. Many caravans passed North on the King's Highway carrying incense, silk, and other exotics that had been brought to the Near East by way of the long, hard, desert route from Persia via Petra.

Here Mordechai traded some of the perfumes from Qumran for amphoras of wine—some of which he and his friends would enjoy, but most of which he would sell in other cities.

After a short but pleasant rest, the caravan pushed again toward Damascus. Soon, however, the terrain changed from lush to rocky and volcanic. There were several volcanoes in this region and huge black lava fields. There was now, more than ever before, real danger of attack by bandits. The entire area had been able to resist Roman control, and each village hidden in the rocks was a potential a hideout and haven for professional caravan thieves.

"It is prudent for us to take a little side-trip," announced Mordechai. "I have business associates in Bosra who will protect us, and there I can sell wine and perfume."

"Why not just cross the rocks and go straight through without paying fees?" asked Zeb.

"First, we don't have to pay fees at Bosra, and second we'd be ambushed and left for dead up there!" replied Mordechai. "Many caravans have been lost there. It's better to take the long way."

After a day in Bosra, the caravan headed North again. Now Mount Hermon was visible—the guidepost pointing to Damascus. As they skirted the mountain they found themselves descending into the lush, green valley of the Barada River. Finally they arrived at the gates of Damascus.

"After we do business and pay fees, we will rest in Jobar," said Mordechai.

"What is Jobar? Asked Zeb.

"It is a Jewish city with a synagogue," replied *Yeshua*. "I know some of the Brothers who worked on the projects."

The next day was *Shabbat*. The three Jewish men attended the new synagogue and were invited to supper.

"Will you go to Dura Europas?" asked one of their new friends. "We have a community there."

"No," replied Mordechai. "We will take the desert route from Tadmor to Circesium."

"Well…we hope you have influence with the Palmyrans. They are the only ones who can offer you safe passage."

After supper *Yeshua* asked Mordechai why he chose the dangerous route this time, when he had taken the more prudent detour through Bosra.

"Danger is a matter of degree," he answered matter-of-factly. *Yeshua* was silent, but he had an unshakable premonition of disaster.

******* ******* ******* *******

After four days of travel, Tadmor, the City of Palms, suddenly appeared as a gleaming jewel as the caravan surmounted a rocky peak in the endless desert foothills. It was nearly dusk, and the sounds of revelry wafted in and out through the shifting breezes. This was the last source of water and safety before turning East toward Circesium and access to fords across the Euphrates River. Thus the streets of the city were frenetic with musicians, dancers, prostitutes, and other purveyors of food and pleasure to the caravaners.

Yeshua was weary and fell asleep almost immediately upon setting up camp. But Mordechai, Zeb, and most of the Bedouin camel drivers reveled through the night.

The next morning *Yeshua* awakened to a sleeping city. He walked to the famous Efqa Spring, where the waters migrate from the mountains in a long, cool aquifer. It was surrounded by the towering date palms that gave the city its name. There were also pomegranate trees with much fruit. He broke his fast in luxury by the bubbling waters.

By noon it had become too hot for anything but rest in the shade. The city was coming to life again, but people moved slowly. Mordechai took *Yeshua* with him for a meeting with Palmyran chiefs. Through them the caravan would secure the services of a guide and several armed guards to lead them through the many days' journey to the Euphrates and Circesium.

After obligatory rituals of hospitality and beer, a business arrangement was made with the host. Mordechai offered payment in a silken pouch, which was accepted, and the two men took their leave.

"I don't trust these people," *Yeshua* confided after a long silence.

"We don't have any choice," was the reply. "Sometimes I get good protection, other times the guards desert us two days out!"

"Then we should be certain we have the loyalty of our Bedouins and some good weapons," *Yeshua* remarked forcefully, "and we should offer weapons as gifts to the Bedouins."

"Bandits won't attack the Bedouins—they may be cousins! And most Bedouins won't do any serious fighting with bandits. If we give them weapons, they might turn them against us," was Mordechai's reply.

"Then," *Yeshua* insisted, "let's get some good weapons for ourselves."

Mordechai agreed, and soon they returned from the small bazaar that had appeared next to Efqa Spring with sturdy Roman spears and daggers.

"What is this?" growled Zeb, who had just awakened when they returned. "You got guards, didn't you?"

"*Yeshua* thinks we need more protection, so keep these things close to you day and night," was Mordechai's answer.

That night Mordechai provided beer, music, and girls to all his Bedouins, being careful to loudly praise them for their loyalty. *Yeshua* also reminded them that his part of the caravan carried only pitch-pots, which were of no use to anyone except the builders at Babylon.

They began their journey toward the Euphrates River late the next afternoon. They could have been ready by noon if they wanted to antagonize the Beduoins by forcing them to arise early, but it was better to leave later as the day cooled and travel late into the evening. They now had a guide who know the terrain and best camping spots even in the dark.

The first night was spent on a windy, rocky hill. Two sentries alternated the watch. It was quite cold and uncomfortable, so everyone was ready to push on right after sunrise. The guide told them to prepare for a mid-day stopover next to cool caves, where they could water the animals and rest from the heat. *Yeshua* felt uneasy. He wasn't sure why.

At high noon there were no caves. The donkeys were panting for water. Men and animals had slowed to a listless pace in the unrelenting desert heat. Mordechai walked to the rear of the caravan for a conference with *Yeshua* while Zeb took his place at the head.

"The guide took our guards and rode ahead. He said it was to scout for bandits and find the caves, but I'm worried."

Yeshua suddenly knew. He was filled with vital force and took command of the situation.

"We will be attacked at any moment! Get your weapons, get Zeb, and pull the caravan into tight formation for defense."

Mordechai didn't waste words. He ran back to Zeb barking out orders. As the caravan regrouped, he handed weapons to three of his most trusted Bedouins. They took up a position on the left flank, while Zeb and Mordechai took front and right. *Yeshua* remained toward the rear.

Suddenly from the East, where the guide and guards had gone, they heard the clatter of horses. Eight armed horsemen appeared over the next ridge riding hard with scimitars drawn. They were not the guards that had been hired for protection. They were bandits that had been tipped off by the guide, who had drawn the guards away to leave the caravan defenseless.

As the horsemen galloped along both sides of the caravan, they aimed long, powerful blows against each of the armed resisters. The first blow nearly severed Zeb's left forearm and he fell writhing onto the rocks. Mordechai pierced one of the bandits directly through the stomach with his spear, which broke as the mortally wounded man fell from his horse, leaving Mordechai with only a Roman dagger. He quickly grabbed another spear while the next horseman wheeled out of his way to avoid his comrade's fate.

Yeshua's spear wasn't needed at the rear. The bandits seemed to know that the pitch-pots were of no value, and they had focused on Mordechai's part of the caravan. *Yeshua* rushed forward to protect Zeb. One of the bandits was making a run for the wounded man and leaning low to the side with scimitar raised for a final blow. *Yeshua* stood directly in his path with spear extended. The man pulled back up into riding position and reigned in his horse to avoid the spear. But *Yeshua* ran forward, launching his spear with deadly force. The horseman tried to duck, but it pierced his ribs right at the heart. *Yeshua* yanked the spear from his flailing body. Blood spurted through the broken rib that protruded where the spear had been yanked out. The bandit fell unconscious onto his horse's neck. The animal spooked and ran away carrying the dying man with it.

Now the three Bedouins stood shoulder to shoulder with spears raised against the bandits. One of them threw a dagger against an oncoming horseman and it caught him in the thigh. He reeled in agony and turned his horse around. Two of the other bandits trotted over to assist him, then regrouped with the other three. One of them yelled something and spit towards the caravan. Then all six rode away toward the South.

Falling to his knees, *Yeshua* uncovered Zeb's partially severed arm. He tied it to stop the bleeding with cloth torn from his own clothing. Then he and Mordechai carried their friend to the shady side of the caravan and lay his on his back. One of the Bedouins brought water, and another offered drugs for the pain. *Yeshua* swabbed Zeb's forehead with a wet cloth, then stood up, breathed deeply, and knelt again.

"My friend, can you feel with your fingers?" he whispered.

After a moment, "No, I have no feeling," Zeb muttered.

Yeshua felt himself slipping into a different state of consciousness. His breathing became shallow and he could hear a kind of chanting and singing, "Eliahu…Eliahu ha Nabi." Was he becoming faint from the heat and shock of battle?

Then he called out, "Bring me balsam and oil." He waited until they were brought, then anointed his left hand with balsam, and his right hand with olive oil. Next he laid his hands so that his right palm was on the nape of Zeb's neck, and his left palm on Zeb's crown. Then he began to sing a *niggun* beginning with, "Eeeee…aaah…oh…way…" then "Lai..lailai..nai…"

The Beduoins were transfixed by this demonstration of Jewish healing. By now all of them had gathered to watch, while Mordechai had stood up with his eyes fixed on *Yeshua*.

When *Yeshua* was finished, Zeb had relaxed into a deep and healing sleep.

"We must make a camp here." Mordechai spoke slowly, then more animatedly as he barked out directions for the Bedouins. To the three men who had helped defend the caravan, however, he spoke more softly.

"These weapons you used to defend us are now yours. They are my gift of appreciation to you. And tonight you shall have double portions of wine."

The dead bandit's horse had returned, so the Bedouins tied the body of his master to the horse and sent it running home toward the South.

Yeshua remained in the tent with Zeb while he slept. As it became cooler in the late afternoon, he again heard the sound of hoofbeats. This time, however, he felt no anxiety. They were the guards returning.

The guide had deserted them. He had led them far from the caravan, then left promising to return shortly. When they realized he was not returning, one of the men took over as leader. He knew the trade route as well as the guide, and he feared that the caravan had been massacred. If so, he and his companions might have faced serious reprisals from the Palmyran chiefs. They were all relieved to see that the caravan had been able to protect itself.

"Then you will be our guide to Circesium," said Mordechai to the man through his interpreter. All the guards nodded.

All night long *Yeshua* lay next to Zeb supplying water and other needs, slipping in and out of sleep. Late into the night, he fell into a deep sleep. Suddenly he awakened in his sleep. He knew that his body was still sleeping, but his spirit was wide awake. He could see Zeb's tortured body, both outside and inside. In this state he prayed.

"*Amen, Amen, Amen,* I seek your help and power, O' *Ruach Ha-Kodesh, Hochmah,* Guide of all who seek to walk your Way. I seek it not for myself, but for my friend Zeb. Send upon him your power of healing, that he may mend and recover his life."

As he prayed, he was lifted up into a holy white radiance that began to glimmer golden and violet. He saw Zeb illuminated in this light and his slashed forearm bathed in a violet light so powerful and palpable that it seemed like a kind of oil. Then he heard a voice speaking.

"Ignite the flame of his fidelity to walk the Divine Way. Then he will have power to heal himself."

"How can I do that?" *Yeshua* wondered.

"He will take from the flame of your own Heart," was the answer. Then came deep sleep.

Yeshua was awakened at daybreak by Zeb's insistent request, "Food! Some food, please!"

"Why such a hurry?" he asked.

Zeb bellowed, "My stomach is very hungry!"

Yeshua looked closely at his friend. He looked stronger.

"I'll bring you fruit and bread right now."

Zeb was able to sit up for his food. He devoured dates, pomegranate, and a small loaf of bread. Soon after he stood up and walked by himself to the sheltered latrine.

"Let's put him up on a camel litter," suggested Mordechai. Cargo was rearranged and soon Zeb was enthroned at the rear of the caravan with water and shade like a Bedouin sheik. *Yeshua* walked alongside and the two men talked.

"What do you know about religion, Zeb?"

"*Shabbat*, Pesach…all the stuff," he answered.

Yeshua remembered what the voice had said about Zeb's power to heal himself: "He will take from the flame of your own Heart." So he began to remind Zeb of his previous spiritual education as a Son of Zerubbabel.

"What do you know of the *Kabbalah* of Zerubbabel?" he asked.

"Well, we were taught some things…but the Master didn't really know much…" was his hesitant answer.

"Then I will teach you," said *Yeshua*.

For the next several days he expounded the deep teachings of Brotherhood spirituality to Zeb, who never stopped asking questions. Each day Zeb grew stronger, and finally when they reached the Euphrates River, he had begun to find sensation in the fingers of his left hand, which he could now open and close.

******* ******* ******* *******

Circesium was the last outpost of Caesar's empire. At this time of the year in this location, it was possible to ford the River as it was never more than hip-deep. The Romans had built the city to collect caravan fees for the crossing. Once a caravan had reconnoitered onto the Eastern bank of the River, it was in Parthian territory.

"Why not take the Western bank?" Zeb asked.

"Because we would soon find ourselves between huge cliffs and a raging river with no place to ford it. The only way to Babylon and Seleucia is along the Eastern bank, where there are fields and water" Mordechai replied.

"This was the path our Abba Abram followed from Ur before the Holy One, Blessed be He, changed his name to Abraham," remarked *Yeshua*.

"And the path our people followed into Babylonian captivity," commented Zeb.

"So now it's the path our pitch-pots will take to help repair their Hanging Gardens," Mordechai reminded them. "Let's go deal with the Romans and get across the River."

There was a wide road on the East bank with many places to stop for rest and camp. This was the first time *Yeshua* or Zeb had ever been outside of the Roman Empire. Instead of Roman soldiers, there were now Parthian guard stations to collect fees. They were far more hospitable than the Romans. All in all, the journey Southeast to Babylon was easy and pleasant.

Finally the gates of massive Babylon began to loom in the distance. The city itself was no longer a governmental center. Long ago many of the inhabitants have moved to Seleucia somewhat East on the Tigris River. It was built by the descendants of Seleucus, one of the generals of Alexander the Great. This family had ruled for centuries before Parthian conquest.

Babylon was still a giant. Surrounded by massive fortress walls like those around parts of Jerusalem, it occupied a space larger than one man could walk around in a whole day. There were nine gates, each leading out on a road connecting another city. The city was built on both sides of the Euphrates River, which flowed through it with overhanging gates for security. At the Northwest gate, from which the caravan approached, there were palaces, temples, military fortifications, and the famous Hanging Garden itself.

The Gardens were built on a structure that resembled a small mountain overlooking the River. As the caravan passed by the huge structure, *Yeshua* noted that it seemed to be built on a series of overlapping cubical walls made of fired earthen bricks and asphalt to keep the water from dissolving the bricks—this is what the Jewish pitch would be used to repair. These vaulted terraces were filled, at least at the top, with soil supporting all kinds of trees and exotic flora.

There was a huge straight staircase—much longer than the one at the Jerusalem Temple. It extended from River level almost to the top of the artificial mountain. Alongside it were ranks of water engines on pullied cables reaching down to the river. Scores of workers were pulling the cables to haul the attached buckets of water up from the river. As they reached their various destinations, they tripped over to spill their precious load into one of the terraces, where it would run along low aquaducts to collect in pools for watering.

Now they approached the processional way, where ancient Persian rulers marched triumphantly hauling captured rulers and princes on cabletows. At the far end to the left was the Ishtar Gate and Temple of Ishtar, while the imposing Temple of Marduk loomed to the right.

"You'll be happy to know that there is a synagogue here," remarked Mordechai cheerily to *Yeshua*, "and not just a lot of Babylonian temples."

"Will we see it on this route?" asked Zeb.

"No, it's not in the Old City. We will stay with our own people tomorrow," he replied. "And I believe you have a letter of introduction to *Rav Tzadok*'s people?" Mordechai raised his eyebrows and looked at *Yeshua*.

"Yes, but first I must fulfill my obligation to you, and I will not leave Zeb until he is fully recovered. So show me my employer."

"In due time," replied Mordechai. "First I want you to meet my people."

Chapter Ten: THE FELLOWSHIP OF DANIEL

After paying fees, the cargo from the lead caravan was unloaded and the animals tethered. Mordechai met privately with a group of Jewish merchants, who quickly turned his goods into gold. Soon after, he and *Yeshua* paraded the second part of the caravan down the wide main street to a storage area adjacent to the Hanging Gardens. Part of it was a Guild temple of stone masons.

Yeshua knocked loudly on the huge wooden door three times. Silence. He knocked again louder.

"Who knocks?" It was the voice of a young woman! *Yeshua* was dumbfounded. How could a woman be in the Brotherhood temple? She spoke in the same Aramaic dialect as his own people in Galilee.

"A Son of Zerubbabel," he answered. More silence. Then finally the door opened to reveal the face of an old Jewish man.

"Are you the Brother from Galilee?" he asked.

"I am." *Yeshua* presented the sealed letter from *Rav Tzadok*. There was a pause.

Suddenly the door was flung wide open. The old man grasped *Yeshua's* right hand in the sign of recognition, then hugged him joyfully.

"I am Azariah, Master of this temple, and you are the disciple of *Rav Tzadok*!" The old man excitedly pulled *Yeshua* into the room, and Mordechai followed.

"Mordechai! It is good to see you, old friend! So you have survived another journey—good! Now tell us, is this young Galilean everything *Rav* says? Is he a saint and a Samson, and does he know more than most Master Masons?"

For the first time *Yeshua* saw the young woman standing in the outer court of the assembly room, where guest Brothers were normally allowed. Her beauty was beathtaking. He blushed and felt extremely awkward.

"Oh, no. He is a shlump—a useless know-nothing. I had to carry him all the way from Judea!" Now the young woman began to giggle, and *Yeshua* blushed crimson. "But he's your problem now."

Recovering quickly, *Yeshua* bowed politely to the old man and his daughter and said, "Master, I am just a poor shlump, but I have come to serve at your pleasure."

Now the young woman fell into fits of laughter, and the old man smiled.

"Good. You have humility and poise. Welcome, *Yeshua*. You will stay at my home and oversee my workers at the Garden."

"May I ask a question, Master?" The old man nodded affirmatively. "Who is this lovely woman, and why is she in a temple of the Brotherhood?"

"She is my daughter, Shoshana. I have no son, so I have taught her everything. She cannot be initiated, but in our lodge the Brothers have decided to permit her to serve as my personal assistant and secretary. She knows everything—mathematics, astronomy, and the advanced *Kabbalah* of Zerubbabel. And she knows them better than most men."

Now it was Shoshana's turn to blush.

"Aha!" replied *Yeshua*. "Then she is not a shlump!"

Everybody laughed. She and *Yeshua* exchanged furtive glances.

What was that fragrance? The sacred *Shushan*, the Lily of the Divine Mother.

How amazing! Was it perfume, or just Shoshana? The fragrance seemed contradictory—a divine sweetness like the breath of angels combined with a voluptuousness that took his breath away. How could these two seeming opposites compose one fragrance? Yet there she was—Shoshana, the conjoining of Heaven and Earth.

Yeshua felt his heart coming into another kind of Babylonian Captivity—a very wonderful kind of captivity. He knew…what? Something glorious? Something tragic? No time to examine his feelings.

"We are the Jewish builders, so it is our privilege to do the work nobody else wants," Azariah smiled sardonically. "The Garden architecture is terrible. It was designed as a present for a king's wife who was used to verdant hills and garden greenery—not the hard-pan plains of Babylon. So he built this monstrosity next to the river and imported all kinds of plants. His Masons created water hoists that have to be worked everyday or the plants die. But the whole thing is made of baked clay, so it wasn't long before they found that the water was dissolving their little mountain! So the Jewish Masons were ordered to fix the problem! All we could do was smear asphalt in the seams, then keep adding asphalt as it hardened and cracked after many years. So it's a constant problem of maintenance, and we have to keep replacing old bricks with new as well."

Yeshua raised his eyebrows and slowly spoke, "So…my job is to oversee workers? But I am a Journeyman, not a Master."

"No Master wants the job, so it's yours!" Azariah answered cheerfully. "And if you do well," he gazed into *Yeshua's* eyes, "I will sponsor you for initiation as a Master."

"Thank you, Master," the young man replied.

******* ******* ******* *******

Yeshua enjoyed a farewell *Shabbat* meal with Mordechai at the home of Azariah, where he was to remain as a guest until he could rent suitable quarters. He was amazed when Shoshana offered the *Kiddush* cup—an honor always reserved for the man of the house.

Her mother had died during Shoshana's birth. She was raised by her Aunt *Miriam*, who came to live with Azariah and assumed the role of mother. When Shoshana was ten years old, *Miriam* had married a wealthy mechant and moved with him to the Galilee. Shoshana inherited the matriarchal role, overseeing kitchen, marketing, and housekeeping for her aging father. Now she exercised more authority than any young woman *Yeshua* had ever known.

Whenever she glanced in his direction, he averted his eyes. He was learning things about women he had never known. Shoshana was a woman who could read Scripture, who knew *Kabbalah*, who seemed in every way his spiritual equal. He didn't realize it yet, but he was smitten to the core with a new kind of love that few men ever experience.

"You will want to continue your studies?" Azariah asked rhetorically.

"Will you teach me, Master?"

"No, no!" Azariah laughed. "*Rav Tzadok* wants you to study with the Rabbis of our synagogue—specifically with *Rav Shealtiel*. You have already exceeded the knowledge held by the Brotherhood through the *Kabbalah* of Zerubbabel. Now you must prepare for admission into the Messianic Fellowship of Daniel."

"I have never heard of this," *Yeshua* remarked.

"You are not supposed to know about it. This is the secret school of the Prophet Daniel which was maintained by his disciples, and his disciples' disciples, down to the present time—many generations. Only a few highly developed souls are invited to prepare for admission. *Rav Tzadok* is one of the secret prophets of the fellowship, and he has nominated you for admission."

"How do you know this?" asked *Yeshua*.

"He wrote it with his own hand in the sealed document you delivered to me. If you had unsealed it, you would not have been worthy, and I would never have told you about the Fellowship. But even if you had broken the wax seal, it would have been impossible for you to read his message. It is written in the astral script of the Magi."

Azariah opened the letter and showed everyone the magical script of the heavens. It seemed undecipherable.

"Each character represents a constellation or asterism visible in the night sky. It correlates to a Hebrew letter. Each letter is closed on all ends with a circle representing a star, and each star is the power of an angel. The first thing you will learn is to read this script." Azariah leaned back and fell silent.

Yeshua wondered if Shoshana was a member of the Fellowship. She gazed at him, then lowered her eyes. The subtle interaction did not escape her father's notice.

"You will not know who the other members of the Fellowship are until you have passed the trials and been initiated."

Trials? Initiation? These were strange and unfamiliar concepts for *Yeshua*.

"I am afraid we can say no more."

Mordechai sipped the last dregs of wine and stood up.

"I must get back to my Bedouins. Tomorrow morning we move on to Seleucia for more business and the long journey North to the Silk Road."

Shoshana stood and bowed, then asked, "Will you give greetings to Aunt *Miriam* for us when you go to Magdala?"

"Of course," he replied. "She always asks for news of you and your father. I will tell her also about *Yeshua* and what a great help he will be to your father." He looked at *Yeshua* with a twinkle in his eye. "And what a poor shlump he is."

"Oh, stop!" cried Shoshana with a fleeting glance at *Yeshua*. They all laughed.

******* ******* ******* *******

Azariah was technically *Yeshua's* Master or superior, but he was old and frail. Long hours in the hot sun were not allowed by his own superior—Shoshana. So for all practical purposes, *Yeshua* was the Master of Garden maintenance.

He had found a room not far from Azariah and Shoshana. He was able to take meals in the assembly room of the Brotherhood temple, which became his headquarters, and was gladly accepted by the other members of the lodge, none of whom wanted his job. Rather than meeting with the Brotherhood Guild for *Shabbat*, however, he joined Azariah and Shoshana privately in their home. On Saturdays he attended the large and beautifully appointed Babylonian Synagogue in company with Azariah and Shoshana.

Zeb had made amazing progress. He was able to use his left hand well enough to grasp and hold tools. Now that *Yeshua* had become Overseer of Maintenance for the Hanging Gardens, Zeb had a job identifying and reporting weak areas in the walls. *Yeshua* was appointed to exercise the same authority as a Master Mason, which included hiring and firing, and Zeb was his first new hire.

"I felt power and force coming into me when he laid his hands on my head and intoned," Zeb told Shoshana. "He gave me back my life. He could have been hacked to pieces trying to defend me, but he took no thought for his own safety. He protected me and then healed me. You don't know what a great man you have with you."

Shoshana said nothing, but she did know.

She had never cared for the many suitors who sat next to her in synagogue and tried to stir her affections. Many young men desired her, but she shunned them. Her father was upset by her behavior.

"How will you ever get a husband?" he asked. "You must treat men with cordiality even if you don't want to marry them."

No, she had never cared for other young men. But now she was burning with love for *Yeshua*. She found every excuse to deliver him messages from her father. If a day passed that she didn't see *Yeshua*, her heart ached. She yearned for his presence. Her life was just a series of intermissions between *Shabbat* supper, synagogue, and other excuses to see *Yeshua*.

As for him, he was thoroughly and hopelessly smitten. He could lose himself only in physical labor, so he impressed his workers by joining in their labors just to make the days pass. But he knew nothing about courtship conventions, and he was too shy, too loyal to Azariah, to make any advances to Shoshana. Yet he knew in his heart that she loved him. When he was alone he was aware of the slight but voluptuous fragrance of lily that she always wore. Her thoughts were always with him, he knew.

On Saturdays *Yeshua* studied in small groups with *Rav Shealtiel* in the library of the Brotherhood Synagogue. He was indoctrinated into the ideals and traditions of the Brotherhood, their commentaries on the Messianic prophecies of Daniel, and teachings about the *Messiah Ben Yosef*. He met several of the members, who taught classes. Some of them were gentile Persians who were members of the Magican Priesthood. With them he studied astronomy, horoscopy, and the Alphabet of the Stars. Soon he had distinguished himself by his intuitive brilliance in the Magican sciences.

"The sciences are easy for you to comprehend and use. You have the soul of a High Priest and a Magus," he was told by *Rav Shealtiel*. "You have the mind of a Pythagorean."

"Perhaps that is because I am trained in architecture and building," replied *Yeshua*.

"No, it is beyond that. You know far more than a Free Master of your Guild."

"I am not yet a Master of my Guild, but all that I know was taught to me by my Father *Yosef*, who was a Free Master."

"Yes?" mused *Rav Shealtiel*. "He must have been a great man."

"He was the best of men, and now the greatest of souls." *Yeshua* pointed to his feet. "And I proudly wear his sandals."

"There is a great deal that can be inherited through the soles of the feet—even the foundations of understanding. Yet what I have seen in you comes not through man, but directly from Divine Spirit.

"You were sent to us by *Rav Tzadok*, who was a great and discerning soul. Just last night he appeared to me in a dream and pointed to you. He wants me to observe you more carefully. I am not certain what this means, but I feel that it is very good. We may want to advance you into a higher level of training—one that is not normally given as preparation for regular initiation."

Yeshua felt a thrill of anticipation, but *Rav Shealtiel* motioned that the session had ended. The young man bowed and left the synagogue.

One evening at *Shabbat* supper there was a guest—an old man perhaps the age of Azariah, but in much better health. Both Azariah and Shoshana paid him great deference. Before the first cup, introductions were made.

"*Mar Belteshazzar*, here is *Yeshua*, the disciple of *Rav Tzadok*."

Mar? He was addressed as a Master—even more than a *Rav* or Great One. *Yeshua* bowed deeply.

"Are you ready to begin a higher level of preparation?" the old man asked.

"If it pleases you, Master."

"No. If it pleases the Divine Spirit. And it does," he replied. "It has been your blessing to be taught by a great man—one who discerns and knows. He has sent you to us, and we are honored to receive you for deep training in discernment and knowledge."

The old man closed his eyes.

"And the Spirit of God says, heretofore, you have grown and developed through discursive means—words, Scripture, teachings. Now you will learn mastery through non-discursive means. You will tame ferocious spirits and the five elements by commanding them silently within."

He opened his eyes and pierced *Yeshua* with his gaze.

"And you will succeed or die. Are you ready for that?"

"Yes," *Yeshua* replied.

Shoshana gasped. "But Father, if he takes the Way of Mastery, he could die!"

In the potent silence that followed, all pretence was gone. The old men knew what had never been spoken—that *Yeshua* and Shoshana were deeply in love.

"And if he lives," Azariah said in measured words, fixing his eyes upon *Yeshua*..."If he lives, you shall be his bride."

Shoshana and *Yeshua* recoiled in stunned silence, then slowly turned to each other and locked eyes. Their hearts were bursting, but neither could speak a word. Finally...

"I shall live, if only to take this woman as my wife," whispered *Yeshua*. Shoshana fell joyfully into his arms. Then almost as quickly she looked fiercely at her father.

"Why does he have to take the Way of Mastery? None of us have ever done so!"

Azariah put his finger to her lips.

"Silence, my Dearest. The Holy One, Blessed be He, has sent us this man. This is his destiny. But we will prepare him fully. He will not fail."

Shoshana grew more agitated. "Father, if he dies, I too shall die, by my own hand!"

Yeshua drew her back to his embrace and held her while she sobbed.

"Hear me, my Bride. Look at me." She turned her face toward him.

"I feel in my heart that the Divine Spirit speaks through *Mar Belteshazzar*. She also speaks to my heart and urges me to take this path, whatever it might be. Tell me, Beloved, what do you feel in your heart?"

Yeshua continued to hold Shoshana while she slowly closed her eyes. Finally she took a deep breath and said, "I feel only love for you, my Darling. But I know that death cannot separate us, and we will share eternity together."

Mar Belteshazzar raised the Kiddush Cup and intoned, "*Baruch Attah, Adonai, Melek Ha-Olam,* Who guides and strengthens us by his Spirit of Holiness, and delivers us from the test, and has given us the fruit of the vine that we may sit with Messiah and experience the marriage of Heaven and Earth, and the divine conjunctions within our own souls, and the reunion of *Yechid* and *Yechidah. Amen, amen, amen.*"

As *Yeshua* tasted the wine, he knew that his soul had found itself in Shoshana—*Yechid* and *Yechidah*.

That evening he wrote a letter to his Mother announcing the betrothal. It would be carried by one of the tradesmen to Damascus, where it would be given to another caravaner who would pass near Nazareth. The likelihood that it would be received was very low, but nevertheless he wrote and paid a large sum for the delivery.

******* ******* ******* *******

"Choose."

Twenty-two goblets were spread out before him. *Yeshua* picked one towards the center.

"Drink."

It was bitter vinegar. He spat it out.

"Choose."

He hesitated.

"Don't hesitate. Choose."

He took the goblet next to it and drank. It, too, was vinegar.

"Choose."

"But I need a moment to think…"

"No!" *Mar Belteshazzar* said firmly. "Don't think. Choose."

He picked another goblet from the left. It was sweet wine.

"Don't drink it—just spit it out. Now choose."

And so it went in the evenings after work, day after day. By the second week *Yeshua* was becoming very accurate. He nearly always chose the sweet wine and refused the vinegar.

At the end of this training, *Mar Belteshazzar* asked, "How did you learn to choose correctly?"

Without hesitation *Yeshua* replied, "Not by thinking, but by knowing in a flash. If I pause, my mind comes in and I'm lost."

In the next training there were again twenty-two goblets, but only one contained sweet wine.

"Choose."

Without hesitation *Yeshua* reached and drank—vinegar!

"Choose."

Again, vinegar.

Yeshua tasted sixteen goblets of vinegar before finding the wine.

After two more evenings of this, *Yeshua* changed his approach.

"Choose."

He closed his eyes and let his hand pass over the goblets until he could sense sweetness, then took and drank. It was the wine!

"Well, you have won the game!" observed *Mar Belteshazzar*. "What have you learned?"

"I can make my mind still and my soul will seek," he replied.

"Why do we make you taste bitter and sweet?"

"Because…if it all were, as you say, just a game with no consequences for pain or pleasure, I could not learn. Learning comes by the rewards and punishments of trial and error. It can't just be mental. It has to have physical consequences," mused *Yeshua*.

"Yes, my Son. Here you have the benefit of repetition, but in life you often have only one chance. If it comes to you in a flash, and you *know*, then act. This happens in battle. But other choices require time and careful attunement. Learn to discriminate these kinds of situations."

The same training was repeated every night for two more weeks. The game was not always over on the first try, but *Yeshua* learned to find the sweet wine in no more than two or three tries.

"Tonight, the consequences become more serious. Twenty-one of these goblets have honey mixed with an herb that will burn your mouth like fire; the other one is pure honey. You must dip your finger into the one goblet that has only sweet honey and lick it. If you fail, you must continue until you find the sweet cup. Now, choose."

Yeshua closed his eyes and was still for a very long time. He seemed not to be breathing. Then he slowly extended his left hand as though it were a sensitive antenna. His eyes opened, his hand moved, stopped over one goblet, then moved decisively to the next. He dipped and tasted. Then he smiled. The game was over.

"Good," *Mar Belteshazzar* smiled back at him. "Do you need any more practice with this?"

"I think this has been enough," was the answer.

"Then you are ready to learn the alphabet of the Magi and interpret the Urim and the Thummim," said *Mar Belteshazzar*. "We will begin this study on *Shabbat*."

*******   *******   *******   *******

Now that his evenings after work were free, *Yeshua* spent them always with Shoshana at her father's home. Azariah retired early to give them privacy.

"Did you find the sweet wine?" Shoshana slyly asked.

"How do you know about that?" *Yeshua* demanded in surprise.

"Because I only had to practice for a week," she replied. "I believe it took you twice that time—at least."

Yeshua had suspected that Shoshana was a member of the Fellowship, but had kept this to himself. Now she had chosen to reveal herself.

"How long did it take you with the honey and pepper?" he asked.

"That wasn't part of my training," she replied. "They are training you much more rigorously. Eventually it will become very dangerous. No one in this generation has received the training you will get, and only *Mar Belteshazzar* is qualified to train you."

"Has he succeeded in the Way of Mastery?"

A silence. Then, "No. He chose not to undertake the Ordeals. That is why I fear for you, my Darling. He cannot train you for the ordeals. All he can do is prepare you to train yourself."

"These, then, must be the ordeals of the Prophet Daniel and his disciples—is that right?" persisted *Yeshua*.

"I—I am bound by oath not to speak."

"But if I already know…" The implication reminded *Yeshua* of what he had learned about oaths and oath-breaking. Did Shoshana understand these things?

"Yes," she hesitated. "The furnace and the beasts."

She did understand. So that is what the Spirit meant when She spoke through *Mar Belteshazzar* and said, "You will tame ferocious spirits and the five elements by commanding them silently within." *Yeshua* would eventually have to survive many hours in a furnace, and in the lair of hungry lions.

"But the legend says that angels protected them from flames and beasts," objected *Yeshua* half-teasingly.

"The angels are powers of God, and those powers live within you to be summoned as needed. You have been formed in the Image and Likeness of God," she replied.

"But you are my angel," murmured *Yeshua*. "Will you protect me from the furnace and the beasts?" again, teasingly.

"Always, Darling. And you are my angel. You must always be with me and protect me, too."

Shoshana's eyes became moist and *Yeshua* was deeply moved by feelings he could not decipher. They clung to each other in silence.

******* ******* ******* *******

Yeshua now began his night training. This was under the supervision of Master Azariah. By now it was clear that both Azariah and Shoshana were initiates of the Fellowship, but *Yeshua* was not allowed to speak of it with them.

For the first part of the training, *Yeshua* slept at the home of Azariah. The routine was always the same. After leaving his work at the Gardens, *Yeshua* made a stop at his rented room, where he exhaled a warm, moist breath upon his bed pallet. Then he walked to Azariah's home for supper. After supper he was accompanied by Azariah to the upper room, which served as his temporary sleeping room. There he was guided into sleep by Azariah's hypnotic chanting.

Each night his goal was to awaken out of his body and travel consciously to his rented sleeping room. There Shoshana had placed objects he was to identify—different ones each night. Sleeping posture was important. He was taught to sleep on his back with hands folded over the center of his chest, which was known as the "Heart," even though it was not quite the same location as his physical heart. His right palm rested upon his left hand. To keep his hands in this position, his elbows were propped up from either side with pillows. Azariah called this the Posture of Daniel.

As Azariah intoned one of the Psalms of Ascent, *Yeshua* envisioned himself as a being of golden light centered in his Heart. As he began rhythmic breathing—seven heartbeats slow, shallow inhale, seven heartbeats exhale—he drew himself upwards. He envisioned a climb upwards with each inhale, and a resting in the higher place with each exhale. When he had reached a position between his eyes, he allowed his breathing to become normal, clearly envisioned his rented room and his purpose, then allowed himself to fall asleep.

The first several nights he awakened the next morning with no memories. When questioned about the objects in his rented room, however, he immediately responded with mostly correct answers.

"It is much like the first work with *Mar Belteshazzar*," he told Shoshana. "The answer comes in a flash without thought. But if I hesitate, the mind comes in with all kinds of suggestions and I am lost."

"You're pretty good, for a man," Shoshana teased. "But you know, this is women's work. Don't get too good at it. I don't want you to become effeminate before we get married!"

"Actually, that is true," commented Azariah. "The male Priests teach their Priestesses these skills, and then push them into madness or early death with their demands for performance. But we are not trying to make you into a temple psychic. Rather, this training is necessary before you can develop the skill of Joseph and Daniel, who interpreted and received prophetic dreams. And it will not make you effeminate. Shoshana, you of all people should not want to plant that seed in his mind."

"You are right, Abba. Things said in jest too often become hidden suggestions." She took *Yeshua's* hands, looked into his eyes, and said, "You are a big, tall, strong, beautiful man, and you will always be."

Yeshua smiled and said, "Seeds can be planted without words, and they can be removed without words."

"Tell us more," requested Azariah, interested to hear what this amazing young man might already know.

"Seeds are constantly sown—some good, some bad. They are not merely words, but acts, gestures, intentions, thoughts, and even more subtle energies. They exist in *Yetzirah*, the World of Formation. We can germinate and cultivate them in two ways—knowing, and not knowing. But most people do not see or hear them because their attention is fixed upon the outer manifestation of this world, *Asiah*. They do not examine their own motives and intentions. All too often they cultivate, multiply, and cast forth bad fruit. The problem is not what we know and recognize—it is what we don't know, don't see, don't recognize. Until we make ourselves aware, we are like open fields accepting all seeds indiscriminately."

"Hmm," Azariah pondered. "And what is the source of the bad seeds?"

"It was inherent in the Shattering of the Vessels. If there is to be divine birth, the waters must break, replied *Yeshua*.

Shoshana interrupted to continue the thought.

"If we had only a right foot, we could not walk. We need left and right—the two. We also cannot experience ecstasy without agony, joy without suffering, love without hate. Without dark forces to test and try us, we cannot grow into spiritual adulthood, and certainly not into divine mastery."

"Yes…" Azariah paused. "And are you prepared to know and experience the evil as well as the good?"

A sudden chill seemed to arise from nowhere. Nothing more was said.

That night *Yeshua* became fully awake while he slept. He found himself floating over the pallet in his rented room. There, laying on the bed itself, was Shoshana. She was sleeping in the same position he was using. He reached out to touch her, but she was like a phantom without physical substance. His hand seemed to pass through her.

Suddenly Shoshana smiled and opened her eyes. She spoke, but nothing was audible. Yet a force seemed to push him toward the wall as he floated. She pointed to her eyes, beckoning him to gaze into them. He drifted closer and looked. Now he found himself able to hear Shoshana say, "I love you, *Yeshua*."

He tried to speak an answer, but again some force pushed him back to the wall. He drew near again, looked into her eyes, and thought, "I love you too, Dear Shoshana."

She smiled, then faded and disappeared from the room.

An instant later *Yeshua* found himself back in the upper room of Azariah's home. His physical body still lay in the prescribed sleeping position. He wanted to know where Shoshana was. Had he communicated with her physical or subtle body? He had never been in Shoshana's room, but he knew where it was. He floated through the floor into the central room of Azariah's home, then through the wall of Shoshana's room.

Again he saw her in the Posture of Daniel, but this time she did not smile or seem to awaken. As he floated gazing at her beauty, a strong force jerked him up through the ceiling and back into his own sleeping body. He awakened to see the dark, star-studded sky through the open side of his room.

He stood up and looked out at Babylon. All was dark and still. There were no lights—just a sense of clarity. The city was sleeping, and the psychic atmosphere was clear. This was the time when deep spiritual contemplation could be done without the clangor of human noise—both physical and subtle.

He sat on a pillow near the edge of the roof under the stars, pulled up his knees with both arms, and dropped his head between his knees. This was the posture of the Prophet Elijah on Mt. Carmel. He allowed his breathing to become shallow and infrequent, as *Rav Tzadok* had taught him. Thought melted away as he focused on evoking the Holy, Limitless White Light.

That morning, when asked what he had seen in his rented room, *Yeshua* described seeing his beloved on the pallet.

"Shoshana, what were you doing," asked Azariah.

"Abba, I forget to bring the figs and pomegranate to *Yeshua's* room yesterday, so I put myself there instead," was her cheery reply.

"Do you remember what we did," asked *Yeshua*.

"Yes. I told you that I love you, and you told me the same," she smiled.

Azariah was upset.

"Shoshana, you know this is forbidden. He is still a neophyte. And now you have imprinted your *nephesh* with *Yeshua's* breath, which he left for himself on the pallet."

"But Abba, he is to be my husband," she objected.

"If he lives," he answered.

"Whether he lives in a body or not, he will be my husband in the Eternal *'Olam* of the Messiah," she said matter-of-factly.

"Yes I will," *Yeshua* added.

"Then it is so. But do you understand what has been done? Her link to you is now so strong, you may be unable to continue in the training without her cooperation."

"I welcome this," replied *Yeshua*. "I trust Shoshana implicitly. She will be with me in all my trials."

"So be it," said Azariah with a shrug of resignation.

"So might it be, and so it is," pledged Shoshana.

Yeshua realized that she had just used the oath form of the Brotherhood of Zerubbabel, which she had no way of knowing. She had spoken his mind for him in his own terms.

There was such fidelity and finality in her declaration that all fell silent.

*******   *******   *******   *******

Mar Belteshazzar pointed to a lone date palm next to the river.

"This being has *ruach* and *nephesh*, just like you. It is very old and wise, and it speaks a language most people cannot comprehend. It is very close to the Throne of God. If you can make it your friend, it will teach you many things," the old man said.

"How do I commune with such a being?" asked *Yeshua*.

"You have said it—you commune. That is, you make yourself one with it. Then, if it chooses to take you within its being, you will become that tree and you will know what it knows. This communion requires concentration and time to achieve, but one day, when you have made the elements of nature into friends and allies, you will achieve it in a flash. Now sit here facing the tree about arms' length away with your palms upward on your knees."

Yeshua complied.

"First you will approach the being with your male form. Do this by stopping your left nostril with your left forefinger and breathing slowly through your right nostril. Envision your Heart-self flowing outward, approaching this being, and seeing it closer and closer, until you are floating onto its bark. Now you are very small. Examine the details of what you see. Now enlarge and begin to merge with this being from the outside."

He waited for a moment.

"Now remove your left hand and stop up your right nostril with right forefinger. Breath only through the left nostril. Admire and appreciate the beauty of this being. Allow yourself to smell and taste its fragrance, feel its texture. Take time. Slowly."

Yeshua began to have physical sensations. Soon he could small, taste, and feel. The image of the palm bark grew palpable.

"Now expand and become aware of the entire being. View it from top, then from side, then from bottom. See its roots, then examine its leaves."

After more time.

"Now remove your finger from your nostril and slowly inhale through both nostrils. Inhale this entire being. Take it inside yourself and become this being. Put it on like a robe and be what it is. When you exhale, end with mouth closed and say 'Hum.'"

A few minutes later.

"Close your eyes and feel this being. Know this being. Stay with this being. Rest with this being for a long time."

Ordinary time no longer existed for *Yeshua*. He was in a timeless state of well-being. Sun above, earth below, water flowing—not just in the river, but inside himself. He felt enveloped in a dynamic kind of strength. Paradise. The Ancient of Days.

When *Yeshua* came back into himself the sun had set. *Mar Belteshazzar* was no longer present. The entire *Shabbat* afternoon had passed, but he had no memory of time.

This phase of the training was in addition to exercises he now did while sleeping. Its focus was upon connecting the inner universe with its counterparts in the outer universe. There were two heavens—day heaven, and night heaven. They corresponded to what people knew as wakening and dreaming, but were actually the same heaven. It was necessary to find the correspondences, but they were different for each person. *Mar Belteshazzar* could only give general pointers and allegorical teachings.

Yeshua awakened several times each night—sometimes physically, sometimes within a dream while his body still slept. Each awakening was a point of recollection and analysis. What was I dreaming? What did it mean? By morning he was able to recollect everything he had experienced during the entire night.

The first connections were made with the coming day. Often parts of his dreams foreshadowed experiences he would have during the coming day or week. The correlations were often quite symbolic—not literal—but with practice he was able to understand the language of the night heaven enough to expect what to most people would come as surprise.

"Thank you for the figs and dates," *Yeshua* smiled as he took Shoshana's hands.

"Good. Now, how many?" she retorted.

"So it is figs and dates?" he asked.

"Yes. How many?" she persisted.

"Well, you took them from a large pot…you picked them out carefully…perhaps fifteen? He asked.

"You're not supposed to ask; you're supposed to know," she replied.

He took a deep breath. He hadn't counted them in the basket he'd found lying on the road to Sepphoris in his dream. Was there something in his memory that would give him a clue? In the dream his mother had referred to the Gates of Babylon.

"Nine!" he cried triumphantly.

She spilled out the contents of her purse. Four figs and five dates.

"You're pretty good!" she laughed. "But I already ate one of the figs."

"No, you ate two figs and one date," he said flatly.

"Oh, you're *too* good!" she crooned petulantly.

The *Shabbat* sessions with *Mar Belteshazzar* always brought them to the river.

"It is not just plants and animals that are alive and have souls," he said. "It is everything. All things are emanations of the Holy One, Blessed be He. Air, water, earth, fire, and the ether—all these are roots of soul. God emanates as fire, as the Chaldaean sages have said. God manifested to Moses as fire. Within each of our souls, at the center is fire. It is to that Divine Reality that we now turn our attention."

They sat at the banks of the river with feet dangling into the cooling current.

"But Master, this is water," *Yeshua* observed, knowing that in order to stimulate the flow of knowledge he must ask questions.

"No, my Son. It is fire. It is cold, wet fire. And this," he said, picking up a handful of earth, "is fire. It is cold, dry fire."

"Then what is fire?" was the next question.

"What we call fire is not the true fire. It is hot, dry fire."

Yeshua paused, then remarked, "The true fire must then be what you call ether."

"That is the first form of fire. It is invisible and permeates all reality. It is the first emanation of *Ain Soph Aur*, the Limitless Light. It contains the qualities of hot, cold, moist, and dry, but its greatest quality is divinity. It is the fire worshipped by the Magi."

"How can we know this fire," asked *Yeshua*.

"You already know it. It is in your Heart. You should ask, How can I make a friend and ally of this fire?"

Yeshua was silent for a moment, so *Mar Belteshazzar* continued.

"You cannot stand in the Presence of this fire, so you must make allies of its elemental manifestations—what we call air, earth, fire, water. In the lower worlds they derive from the four Kerubim who continually surround the Throne of God, each with four faces: human, lion, ox, eagle. The Seraphim, Ophanim, and angelic orders derive from their powers. The Seraphim are fire serpents that are evoked in magical operations like those of Moses. They are allied with the staff you may one day use. But first you must make alliance with these four elements: air, earth, fire, water."

"How is this done?" asked *Yeshua*.

"I cannot tell you. You must sit with each of them, call upon them, tell them you are a Son of the Most High. Appreciate them, enjoy them, laugh with them—each one at a time. Only you can find the way. When you succeed, they will never harm you, but always protect you. That is how you will prepare for the Ordeals of Daniel."

Yeshua pierced the old man with his eyes and asked, "And what of the one who succeeds with the Ordeals of Daniel?"

Mar Belteshazzar returned his gaze and replied in measured words, "He...will be...a great prophet and a teacher of Israel. The signs of his birth were seen many years ago by the Magian astrologers."

Yeshua was stung with powerful feelings.

"And you think I may be this prophet?"

Mar Belteshazzar sighed. "I think God sows the seeds for many judges and prophets, but few of them flower and bear fruit. I know that you are one of these, but I do not know whether you will ripen."

"It is no accident that Azariah has offered Shoshana for my bride, with the condition that I am successful in the Ordeals of Daniel—is it?"

"No, my Son. But do not think that he is merely using your love for Shoshana. He trusts with all his heart that you will succeed. He loves you as a son—and so do I. You are the one that we were never able to raise up from among our own people. God has cultivated you like a strong vine and sent you to us from the Galilee."

Yeshua was dumbfounded. He felt a weight of intense responsibility far beyond anything he had ever imagined. Who were these Babylonian Jews? Would he agree to all this if there were no Shoshana?

"I know there are many questions, my Son. I believe that your Beloved can be of great assistance to help you discover alliances with the elements. From now on, merely attend our *Shabbat* discussions at the synagogue. During the *Pesach* Full Moon you are to become an initiate of the Fellowship. Then the other members will reveal themselves to you—for otherwise we remain anonymous. Take all the time you need—perhaps many years. When you are ready for the Ordeals, you will tell us."

******* ******* ******* *******

Moonlight illuminated every street and alley of the temple district. It was the first full moon after the spring equinox—the Festival of *Pesach* or Passover for the Jewish people of Babylon. But how different it was from Jerusalem!

In spite of the fact that they had been settled in Babylon many centuries longer than its Parthian rulers, the people of the Jewish quarter were foreigners in a strange land. Passover was not a city-wide celebration, but a private affair between the people and their synagogue. Most private of all was a special Passover meal that would be eaten by the Fellowship of Daniel. What appeared to be the large home of a wealthy Jewish merchant was now revealed to be a secret synagogue.

Yeshua was led into the main assembly room by Shoshana. At the Western end, directed toward Jerusalem, was a beautifully crafted arched wall with seven-branched menorah and doors behind which the Torah scroll was kept. But there were also many other compartments on either side of the arch. Hundreds, perhaps thousands, of manuscripts were stored in this library. Many chairs and desks had been moved to the perimeter of the room, which obviously served as a hidden scriptorium.

"Where will we eat the Passover?" asked *Yeshua*.

"You must wait here until called, Darling. We will eat the Passover in another area after you have been initiated," Shoshana replied, then glided out of the room.

Yeshua examined some of the manuscripts that had been left out. Most of them were in Greek, which he could not fluently translate. Finally he found one in Aramaic. It was a different version of the *Testaments of the Twelve Patriarch* than he had known in Galilee—full of scribal glosses and with much more text than he had known. Most of the added paragraphs were prophecies of the Messiah.

Suddenly he became aware of Shoshana's presence. He turned, but could see her nowhere. She seemed to be beckoning him to walk through the curtained door through which she had disappeared. She had told him to wait until called. She hadn't said that she would return for him.

"She is calling me, so I shall come."

He opened the curtains and saw nothing but darkness. He began to step forward, then hesitated. Feeling carefully, he realized that this was a staircase that descended into some kind of subterranean area. This was part of his initiation. Quite different than the Brotherhood of Zerubbabel, where one was led in blindfolded by cabletow.

As he descended the stairs, he felt the floor at his elbows, then tunnel walls. By extending his arms, he was able to keep his balance and descend safely. He counted steps—twenty-two in all, the number of the alphabet. At the bottom step there seemed to be nothing but solid iron walls ahead and to the sides. Without hesitation he reached to the bottom of the right wall, found a handle, and pushed.

The heavy iron door creaked outward on a hinge from the top, and *Yeshua* stepped into what appeared to be dank cellar with clay walls and dim lighting coming from above. The door fell back into place with a loud clang and locked. There was no way to pull it back in.

He surveyed the large cell into which he had been locked. To the left was an empty cage for large animals. Inside the cage was another iron door. This one had a handle on the inside. It was the only way out of the cell.

"Probably for the Ordeals," he mused.

He squeezed between the bars of the cage and walked to the iron door. Again, the handle allowed him to push it out, and he squeezed through. Now he had entered another large cage, but there was a heavy door leading from the cage out into another dim clay cellar. This time the gate opened easily. The low cellar became a tunnel to the left, which *Yeshua* followed with keen interest. This was obviously the location of the Ordeals of Daniel. There must be some kind of large furnace in the next area.

The tunnel widened into another low cellar and there, on the right, was a huge metal smelting furnace. It was made of ceramic and clay, shaped like a great beehive, and had another huge iron door—this one hinged on the right side. In the dim light, *Yeshua* could see an Aramaic inscription on the door: *Shadrach, Meshach, Abednego*.

He pulled back the two sets of iron bolts that secured the door shut, then pulled it open. The inside of the furnace was visible because a large chimney admitted light from overhead. The floor was brick. Halfway to the rear was a semi-wall that contained elements for the fire. It had been used recently, probably for firing pottery that would have stood on the floor nearest the door—and where *Yeshua* would be placed bound hand and foot for the Ordeal.

He slowly pushed the door closed and locked the bolts. To the left was a staircase leading upward. As he entered the tunnel into which the stairs were hewn, he could see light from a trap door on the ceiling. This would be the floor of the synagogue.

The door wouldn't budge, so he knocked. No response. He knocked again, louder. The bolts on top rattled, and the door was lifted up. *Yeshua* ascended the final steps to see Shoshana, Azariah, *Mar Belteshazzar*, and several other people, including Zeb.

He stood for a moment as the members of the Fellowship smiled silently. Shoshana was the only woman among them. The rest were prosperous merchants whom he recognized from synagogue, the elder *Hazzan* of the synagogue, the two men who have tutored him, and Zeb.

Mar Belteshazzar stepped forward and took his hands.

"Welcome into the Fellowship of Daniel. You heard the call and did all things well."

He turned to the others and said, "Now let us show this remarkable young man a true *Pesach*!"

Shoshana hung by her father' side, resisting her impulse to fly into *Yeshua's* arms, and followed the group into another room, from which they ascended steps into a large upper room that was partially open to the air, but well shaded from the setting sun to the West.

After the first part of the *seder* when the feast had begun, *Yeshua* spoke to Zeb.

"Why were you in Jericho?"

Zeb said, "I was hired to protect you."

"By *Rav Tzadok*?" was the question.

"Yes. He arranged many things for you. He is a senior member of the Fellowship. But it looks like I needed you to protect me, instead!" he laughed.

"Then you do not plan to return to Jericho to work for Herod?" *Yeshua* asked.

"I shall remain here with you and the Fellowship."

"Then, let me ask one more thing. Why did you lead me to believe that you had little spiritual knowledge?"

Zeb looked down, then returned his gaze.

"I really have very little spiritual knowledge. My training in the Fellowship has been in the preparatory work—like what you have done, but to a much lower degree. It qualified me for initiation. I will be joining the School of Daniel when you do—next *Shabbat*."

Yeshua looked at *Mar Belteshazzar*.

"Master, what is the School of Daniel?"

The old man paused, put down his wine glass, and cleared his throat.

"The Prophet Daniel was taught in the spirit by the Patriarch Joseph. *Mar Daniel* had many disciples. It was they who first committed his acts and visions to writing. In turn, these disciples elected successors whom they brought into the Fellowship and trained in the prophetic arts. Many of them became saints who received visions and interpretations of their own. These were added as interpretation to the Daniel scrolls.

"But they also learned from the Magian Priests, taking from their tradition what was useful—astronomy, architecture, alchemical and medical arts—and integrating this knowledge into the prophetic arts originally transmitted through Daniel from the spirit of Abba Joseph.

"Over many generations the Fellowship gathered prophetic writings from other schools of Jewish wisdom. Many of these were brought to us by merchants who had been initiated. Our predecessors learned to speak and translate Greek, since many of the revelations came from the Diaspora. You are familiar with some of the scrolls we possess.

"By the time of the Parthian conquest, the School of Daniel had became a fellowship of scholars—not prophets. So the next generation of disciples worked to revive many of the traditional Priestly and divinatory arts of the First Temple. These were my teachers. They built this synagogue and designed the chambers beneath it to simulate the holy Ordeals of Daniel and his disciples. However, none of them was able to demonstrate mastery in the Ordeals, and two of them died horribly. I was elected to lead the school after them.

But I have not had courage to attempt the Ordeal because I know that I would fail, and there would be no worthy successor. So we study and wait."

The entire table had fallen silent.

Azariah said, "We think you will become the worthy one."

All the others nodded.

Yeshua looked around the table. He saw the earnest faces of seventeen devotees turned expectantly toward him.

"Teach me everything you know, and the *Ruach Ha-Qodesh* will teach me all else that is necessary."

Shoshana closed her eyes and took a deep breath of resignation.

Chapter Eleven: COMMUNION WITH ANGELS AND ELEMENTALS

Since his arm healed, Zeb had been assuming more of *Yeshua's* physical labor at the Gardens. He had been promoted to the rank of Foreman. The workers respected him.

"*Yeshua*, you need more time for study and training. Let me assume responsibility for the morning shift, and you keep this time to yourself. "

The arrangement was made, but only on *Yeshua's* condition that Zeb accept compensation out of his own wages. This left *Yeshua* with clear mornings each day. He undertook training like an athlete preparing for a contest.

Each day he arose before sunrise, devoting himself to prayer and meditation. Then he undertook the Jubilee Walk taught by *Mar Belteshazzar* through the river gate and into a wilderness beyond the city. This way of walking coordinated footsteps, the inhaling of vital *Shemesh*, and the exhaling of *Barukot* or Divine Blessing into nature and humanity. The walking was done bare-headed in seven series of seven steps plus one, or fifty steps, then repeated. It filled his etheric bodies with energy and resistance to the dark spirits of disease.

He had chosen a special place on the riverbank. He had established communion with each of the trees and large bushes where he stood or sat for prayer, as well as the species of birds, fish, and insects that inhabited the area. He knew that the human soul was a harmony of more primitive animal and plant souls, and these were harmonies of the four elements subsisting in the mother fire—the ether, which was also symbolized Kabbalistically as air. In order to restore his friendship and alliance with the four elements, he would first have to establish communion with them.

"*Eeee—aaah—oooh—wayeee*," he intoned at first aloud, then silently in the ether. "Spirit of Holiness, Mother of Wisdom, Teacher of Disciples; I beseech You to show me how to make communion with the elements."

He sat in the posture of Elijah, head between his knees, until he could no longer hear the musical sounds of the river water, no longer hear the song of the birds. Finally he received an inspiration.

"*Eeee—aaah—oooh—wayeee*," he silently intoned. Then he stood facing the risen sun.

"*Kerubim* of the Throne, I beseech You; Face of the Waters, Eagle of the Air, Lion of the Fire, Ox of the Earth. I am a Son of *El Elyon*, a Child of Heaven. I call upon you from my Heart to establish communion, friendship, and alliance between me and all your elemental emanations." Silence. Nature seemed to hold its breath.

"*Eeee—aaah—oooh—wayeee*, he intoned for a third time, then extended his right hand.

"I am a Son of *El Elyon*, a Child of Heaven. I beseech You, *Micha-el*, Angel of Messiah, Ruler of the Divine Gates, Sovereign of Angels, Right Hand of the Almighty One; lead me with safety into the realms of the *Kerubim* and their emanations. Give me protection to commune with Fire, Wind, Wave, and Earth."

He extended his left hand.

"I beseech You, *Rapha-el*, Angel of Divine Healing, Restoration, and Strengthening; Give me power to restore and repair all relationships that have been broken and damaged between humanity and the Divine Elements. Give me power to purify and heal them, that I may offer blessing to them."

He brought his hands together and bowed deeply.

"I beseech you, *Ori-el,* Angel of Holy Light, Scatterer of Darkness, Illuminator of Souls; Give me power over the *qlippoth, elilim,* and other dark forces that try to control Fire, Wind, Wave, and Earth so that I may earn their trust, friendship, and alliance. Give me power over demons of all kinds."

Then he spread his hands far apart and turned sunwise toward Jerusalem and the West.

"I beseech you, *Gabri-el,* Angel-Messenger of God, Proclaimer of Prophecy, Revealer of Apocalypse; Give me the power of second sight, true dreaming, instant knowledge, prophecy, and interpretation through the elemental manifestations of Fire, Wind, Wave, and Earth. Let all nature stand as Sacred Scripture for me to read and understand."

"*Eeee—aaah—oooh—wayeee,*" he intoned aloud.

"*Baruch Attah, Elohenu, Ruach Ha-Kodesh, Kerubim, Malachim.* I beseech You, Almighty *Abba,* Almighty *Imma*—for the sake of Israel and all humanity, make me worthy for your work."

After he had completed prayers, he sat again in the posture of Elijah. But this time he listened to the songs of water, birds, and insects. He emptied his mind of thoughts and filled it with the sounds of nature. After a long time, he heard *Rav Tzadok*'s voice repeating the Kabbalistic proverb he had often recited.

"Study Nature, my Son, and She will make an obesience unto you, and she will reveal her secrets unto you."

He opened his eyes, sat up, and marveled at the beauty all around him—sights, sounds, fragrances, textures. This would be the way—not by retreating from nature into his prayers and meditations, but by interacting and playing with elemental nature. By speaking to it silently, for its consciousness was etheric and psychic. By touching and enjoying physical matter. By respecting, protecting, and healing nature. By these means he would earn the trust of the elements.

On *Shabbat* he spoke with *Mar Belteshazzar* about his discoveries.

"Yes, the many species of nature each have particular kinds of soul and consciousness. We have names for their spirits, but our names mean nothing to them. They address each other in the psychic and etheric worlds, and we can address them only by using the same means. Words, speech, and language are only the external husks of true communication, which is telepathic. Plants and animals understand and respond to your feelings—not your words. Joy, fear, light, darkness are real to them. Even so, there are greater spirits of the elements themselves who respond in the same ways.

"You must learn to earn the friendship of hungry lions, so establish your communion with animals. But far more difficult, you must earn the friendship of hungry fire in the smelting oven."

Yeshua was silent for a moment, then spoke.

"What is the soul of hungry fire?"

Mar Belteshazzar folded his hands and looked.

"My Son, it is the same spirit that controls the hungry lion, and the same spirit that was ablaze in the burning bush of Moses. It is the *Seraph,* which is the Fire Serpent of God."

"But for Moses," *Yeshua* replied, "the fire was not hot. It did not consume the bush."

"Oh, it was hot, my Son! It was very hungry! But it did not consume, and it did not burn, and it did not destroy."

"In the Daniel scroll," *Yeshua* paused for a moment, then continued, "we are told that there was a fourth person in the oven with the three disciples—an angel, who held back the flames for them."

"That was not an angel," replied the old man. "That was *Mar Daniel.*"

Yeshua remembered what Shoshana had said: "The angels are powers of God, and those powers live within you to be summoned as needed. You have been formed in the Image and Likeness of God."

"Then I need more than communion with the elements, or even with the angels of *Yetzirah*," *Yeshua* responded decisively. "I need communion and alliance with the Archangels of *El Elyon* who reside in *Briah*."

The old man was silent again. Finally he stood up and walked to a scroll cabinet on the right wall. He removed the scrolls from the cabinet and reached farther inside. There was another compartment. It had not been opened for some time, and he had to ask for *Yeshua's* help pulling it open from its frozen position.

"This is the Magian commentary on the *Aliyah of Enoch*."

Yeshua was puzzled.

"Is this the ascent to the Throne, or the ascent after death? I know only the Galilean Enoch scroll."

"They are one and the same, my Son. In the Palestinian scroll, Enoch ascends in a dream—a vision of the night, like Daniel. But this scroll is a commentary on the final Initiation of a *Rav* who is worthy to make the Ascent himself. It was dictated by *Mar Daniel*.

"You see, *Mar Daniel* was taught by two great spirits, Abba Joseph and Abba Enoch. He devised a form of initiation to prepare a worthy successor to make the Ascent to the Throne of God. It was by means of an etheric body of *Shemesh* fire that can ascend through the heavens by means of an interior *Merkabah* or Chariot Throne of the Sun.

"*Mar Daniel* did not name a successor. Three disciples performed the Initiation, and two attempted the Ascent. The first went insane, the second died during the ascent, and the third, a Magian Priest who had sat at Daniel's feet as a disciple, performed the Initiation and added commentary, but did not attempt the Ascent. Since those days, the scroll has remained hidden."

Yeshua remarked, "We learned our astronomical science from the Magian Priests. Is that why he was qualified to make the commentary?"

"That, and also the fact that he was a saint—the greatest disciple of *Mar Daniel*. He was circumcised and became a Jew. When he died, his body did not decompose. It radiated a soft light and sweet fragrance for seven days. Many came to view his body, Persians as well as Jews. The phenomenon helped to perpetuate royal protection for the Jewish community in Babylon after Daniel's generation had passed."

Mar Belteshazzar handed the scroll to *Yeshua*. It was written in Greek with Aramaic commentaries added throughout. *Yeshua* had learned to slowly translate a little Greek while in Sepphoris. To aid him, there was a scroll showing Aramaic—Greek word correspondences in the library.

"If you want communion with the Archangels, this and Divine *Hochmah* will be your guide."

Later that evening *Yeshua* described his experiences to Shoshana.

"Master has told me that you, above all, can help me to communicate with the elements of nature. This is not ascetic work, but another kind of aspiration and striving that I don't know anything about. Can you be with me and teach me about nature during the mornings?"

"What will be my reward?" she teased.

"Hugs and kisses and undying love."

"Agreed," she laughed, kissing his hand.

*******   *******   *******   *******

"Feel the water, taste it, let it run all over your hand. You men are too fussy about getting messy," said Shoshana, sprinkling and splashing *Yeshua* with the cool river water.

"Hold it in your hands and let it drip down your arms. Tell it how beautiful it is, and how you love it."

Yeshua obediently complied.

"Play in it and sprinkle me with it. This is a love *mikveh*," she sung. Continuing to sing she said, "We share our love with you, dear water. Thank you for cleansing us with your cool moisture, and you must thank us for blessing you with our eternal love."

After playing in the river, the two walked back to the Garden, drying in the warm, hot air.

"Thank you, warm and friendly air. Receive our friend the water and take it where you will," Shoshana sang.

"Why do you always sing to the elements?" asked *Yeshua*.

"Because that is the best way to communicate with elementals, elementaries, and angels," she declared. "When we make a song-voice, we lift ourselves out of our normal ways of seeing, and we can communicate with nature."

They ascended the long staircase to the upper portions of the Garden. Shoshana pulled *Yeshua* aside to one of the terraces that had just been watered.

"What do you see?" she asked.

"Mist rising from the earth where it has just been watered."

"Do you know this is a very special water? This is the water that rises into the heavens. If you play with it, the mist will draw you upward in your dreams tonight."

They lay on their backs watching and feeling the rising of the mists as they dissolved into the air. Then they watched and felt the clouds as they dissolved and reappeared in the vast Southern sky.

"Water we see you, then you disappear, then you return in another form…" Shoshana chanted quietly.

The next day they played and communicated with earth in its many forms.

"Touch my breast, Darling."

He caressed her soft, warm breast beneath her robe.

"Yes, I see. This is also a form of earth—*adamah*. From earth we have been formed, and to earth our bodies will return, no matter how sweet and how lovely. But your breast emanates from something more sweet and lovely without your soul, my Love. Long after your body is dust, you will still have beautiful breasts, and lips…" He kissed her.

"Hey! Excuse me, but aren't you back on duty?"

It was Zeb.

Yeshua pulled himself up, offered Shoshona his hand, and the two shook potting soil from their clothing.

"Studying the elements with my teacher, *Rava* Shoshona," he joked. "May I introduce you to *Rava* Shoshona?"

"I should have such a teacher," commented Zeb wryly.

******* ******* ******* *******

As summer merged into fall, the weather cooled. Some mornings were too hot or windy for walking, and so the two lovers spent their time with Azariah talking of marriage.

You are very sweet, my Daughter, but I insist. You must not live here with me. You must have your own home. That is the *Torah*.

"And you, *Yeshua*, if it were possible, you should have one entire year to enjoy your wife without having to work. That is the ancient tradition of the Jubilees. Then, perhaps, I will become a grandfather, eh?"

Yeshua knew that he could not leave his work for a year, but since Azariah was his Guild Master and the royally commissioned supervisor of Garden maintenance, he would be able to continue on a reduced schedule—perhaps working only in the afternoons. But he needed more money if would be able to purchase any property, and he would need time to build or rebuild a suitable dwelling for Shoshana.

He leaned forward and asked, "Master Azariah, if I succeed with the Ordeals, will you loan me money to purchase land?"

"My Son, if you succeed in the Ordeals, I and all the Fellowship will give you such a wedding gift that you will be able to purchase a fine, large home. That is a pledge."

Every *Shabbat* supper at Azariah's home was enlived by one or two guests from the Fellowship. In this way *Yeshua* became better acquainted with the membership, and they learned first-hand why *Mar Belteshazzar* had privately proclaimed to each of them that this young man would one day succeed him as Master.

The gathering was also an opportunity for *Yeshua* to absorb more of the *Kabbalah* of Daniel than there was time to teach in Saturday Fellowship lessons. The Friday night Fellowship *Shabbat seder* was quite different than what *Yeshua* had known in Galilee.

The meal itself was a mystery ritual—an enactment of the future Marriage Banquet of Messiah in the 'Olam Ha-Ba* or World to Come, which exists eternally in the Divine Aeon of Atziluth. The Banquet was an allegory of the marriage of heaven and earth, of the spiritual ripening of all humanity. The New Humanity was to manifest in this Aeon of Becoming known as *Asiah,* but the time and place of its manifestation was hidden in the *razim*, clouds, or "mysteries" of Heaven.

Azariah presided over these mysteries like a Priest. He wore not the robes of a Levite, but raiment similar to those of a Jewish Temple Priest. They were covered with symbols taken from the *Kabbalah* of Daniel.

Mar Daniel had been shown in visions obtained through the *Merkabah* Ascent that the brutal empires of Earth based upon war, slavery, and despotic rule would one day come to an end. They were allegorized in his visions as various kinds of sub-human beasts. Messiah, whom Daniel saw as "one like unto a son of mankind," meaning a human being as opposed to a beast, would be given power and authority from *El Elyon* to rule the Earth with justice and peace. He was known as the *Bar-Enash,* the Scion or Offspring of Humanity—a New Humanity.

Satan, known as *Sathaniel* and *Shaitan*, whom the Greeks knew as *Diabolos* the accuser or enemy of humanity, had tried to overthrow the Divine Order. He and his lawless compatriots were sorely defeated by the Archangel Michael and his Hosts and banned from Heaven. Some say they fell onto the Earth, but *Mar Daniel* taught that they were summoned and invited by lawless men seduced by their power and knowledge. They enslaved those who summoned them, then proceded to invisibly inhabit and enslave the world of humanity through greed, envy, lust for power and possessions. The kingdoms of the beasts seen by Daniel were part of the infernal hierarchy that invisibly rules the world through its human puppets. Satan is the Prince of this world, and his archons and their minions pull the strings for all who make themselves puppets—all who forsake the guidance of the good *yetzer* of the heart for that of the evil *yetzer*, thinking to gain advantage for themselves.

When the time is ripe, Messiah will engage the battle with Satan here on Earth. The dark forces will be driven down into the deep netherworlds, where they will be imprisoned to serve out the term of their punishment. There they will experience the same trials and agonies that human beings have brought upon themselves. One day they will emerge purified by Fire and take part in a universal *tikkun* or restoration, but only after the New Humanity has appeared and carried out the Messianic work of redemption.

A small gong was sounded, and all those reclining about the table sat upright. Azariah raised the first *Kiddush* cup with both hands like a Priestly sacrifice, looked heavenward, and prayed aloud.

"We return unto Thee, Our Master and Lord of the Universe, the Blessing that Thou hast poured forth upon all beings—symbolically through, for, and by means of the fruit of the vine."

The Cup was passed sunwise to each participant, who took a sip with closed eyes.

Then he held up a whole piece of leavened bread in the same manner, lifted his eyes to Heaven, and prayed aloud.

"We return unto Thee, Our Master and Lord of All, the Blessing that Thou hast scattered everywhere and to all—symbolically through, for, and by means of the fruit of the Earth."

He broke the bread into two pieces, broke off a small portion of one for himself, and passed the rest of that piece anti-sunwise or counterclockwise around the table. Each person broke off a small portion, passed it on, and consumed the bread with eyes closed.

Then Azariah lifted up the other half of the loaf and prayed.

"In Thy Grace and Blessing, we participate in Thy Messianic Wedding Banquet, its joys and its mysteries. We sit at Thy table in communion with Thee and Thy Wisdom."

The other half of the loaf was passed sunwise and all partook. After a moment of silence, the guests smiled, relaxed back into the reclining position, and began to talk as the *Shabbat* banquet was delivered to the table.

What a banquet it was! Meat, fish, and fowl, with exotic fruits and vegetables—some of them served as sauces or condiments—in several courses. Wine was served to each person as well as sweet fermented milk and juice beverages.

This was no ordinary, gluttonous feast. It was a sacred meal. Sacred, but not solemn. In joy and gratitude each person appreciated, complimented, and discussed the remarkable delicacies that had been prepared. At other times conversation focused on Messianic interpretation of prophetic revelation. It was a religious service, a round-table discussion, a forum for inspiration of the *Ruach Ha-Qodesh*, and an occasion of joy and harmony for everyone.

Shoshana understood the sacred dimension of food. She designed a menu and presentation that transcended mere gourmet sensibilities. She worked expertly in her kitchen with hired cooks to integrate herbs, spices, nuts, meats, and fruits into a manifestation of ecstasy—an experience of all the elements brought into their most pleasing and nutritious expression. The eyes loved it; the nose loved it; the mouth loved it; the stomach loved it; every cell in the body loved it. It was not merely a pleasure feast, but a true love feast.

Before the desserts were brought, the small gong again sounded. Everyone sat upright, and Azariah recited *Kiddush* with the second Cup, which was again passed, but this time anti-sunwise. When the Cup had returned to Azariah, he began intoning one of the Odes of Solomon, which he read from a scroll. All the guests repeated what he intoned antiphonally, verse by verse.

"The *Ruach Ha-Kodesh* opened the Father's Raiment, and mingled the milk from the Father's two breasts."

After sacred song and chanting, the desserts were summoned. People relaxed back into their reclining positions and finished the evening with sweets, conversation, and sleepy goodbyes as each retired to home or bed.

*******   *******   *******   *******

They sat contemplatively on the East bank of the Euphrates. The sun was rising behind them and causing a heavy mist to lift and hang suspended over the quiet waters. As the rosy rays of *Shemesh* diffused and reflected back through the shifting mists, *Yeshua* felt agitated. Something or someone was calling him.

Shoshana seemed to have fallen into a trance. She sat cross-legged with rigid spine, palms resting on her knees, and a relaxed, almost featureless face.

Faces seemed to form and dissolve in the rosy mists above the river. *Yeshua* felt his Heart call out, "Spirits of Water and Air, I am watching, listening. Deliver the burden of your message."

Immediately he saw the face of *Rav Tzadok* forming deep inside the rosy, glowing mists. His Heart leaped with deep feelings—joy, pain, recognition, knowing. His beloved teacher had died.

Just as the realization came, Shoshana began to speak. Her voice was deep, like a man. She began haltingly, then became fluent.

"My...Son...my greatest disciple...I have a lesson to teach you."

"Master, have you died?" *Yeshua's* voice was a hoarse whisper.

"I have left my *basar*-body behind, and now I move freely in an invisible *ruach*-spirit, my *nephesh*-body." He paused, as he always did when he invited his students to ask questions.

"Master," *Yeshua* asked, "where are you?" He lept to his feet to stand in respect for his old teacher.

"I am anywhere I desire to be in *Malkuth* of *Asiah*. I can float through walls or instantly be anywhere my mind can conceive." Another pause for questions.

"Do you breath or eat?"

"I have no need of food or breath. I am breath. But there is a rhythm—something like breath or heartbeat—that sustains my consciousness. I do not sleep, but I dream. When I finally choose to fall asleep, I will die the Second Death."

Yeshua remembered the *Kabbalah* he had been taught about dying. It is a slow process—two nights and three days. A normal person remains unconscious or may dream. The seven spirits within the *basar* of flesh gather at a point in the body where the person has centered his life focus. For most people this is at gut-level above the stomach, the Spirit of Conscious Knowledge.. But for saints and masters they gather in the Heart—the Spirit of Sincerity and Devotion. The seven spirits re-unite into a seed that exits the *basar* or flesh as a kind of mist.

The person then re-awakens in his *nephesh*-body, where he lives as a spirit, unfettered by physical boundaries. The *nephesh* retains its human form, features, sex, and personality. It can see, hear, and in some cases communicate with the living. But the *nephesh* is still a projection of the spiritual soul or *neshemah*, which is neither male nor female. The *nephesh* is merely an outer garment, a reflection of the personality developed in physical life. After forty days, it grows weary and falls asleep. This is the Second Death. Now the *nephesh* will decay and dissolve back into the invisible etheric currents from which is was formed, and the person—no longer wearing the mask of personality—exists in his *neshemah* or spiritual soul.

Most people dream in this state and prepare for later incarnation, but some attain the *qimah*, where they re-awaken into the World of *Yetzirah*. Now they are like angels. They work in harmony with the *Ruach Ha-Qodesh* to guide spiritually sensitive disciples in dreams, inspiritaions, and through other telepathic means.

"You will attain the *qimah*," *Yeshua* announced firmly. "And you have no need to remain in this state."

"Yes, I know I shall attain the *qimah*. Even now I communicate with the Blessed Ones who have guided me. But I still have much to resolve before I depart."

"What are these things?" asked *Yeshua*.

"My students mourn my death. They walk through the funerary rituals I have prescribed, but their hearts are heavy. I must enlighten their understanding and guide them through their grief. Otherwise, I would generate *hub* that I should have to repay in another lifetime in flesh.

"I told you that we generate *hub* with every activity or inactivity we choose to manifest in life's responsibilities to other souls—human and non-human. The ones we have sinned against can choose whether or not to hold us to the consequences of these debts. But only the Holy One, Blessed be He, can release us from their consequences. He releases us only if we release all others from the the consequences of their offenses against us. If I were to leave my disciples now without guidance, it would be like a father abandoning his children. One day, you will have many disciples. You must not leave them without a *p'raqlita* to guide and strengthen their spirit."

"Master, I shall always remember your words," pledged *Yeshua*.

"One more word, my Son. You will know when your time comes to die. But before that time, *nothing can harm you!* Do you understand?"

Tears welled up in *Yeshua's* eyes. His dear teacher confirmed what he already knew—that he would master the Ordeals of Daniel and live to marry Shoshana. He nodded and bowed.

Shoshana began to slump forward unconscious. *Yeshua* knelt down to hold her in his arms and she regained consciousness.

"I must have fallen asleep…" She began to cough. "Oh…my throat feels so strained! I must have taken in some bad air from the river."

Yeshua held her tightly for a long time, then looked into her eyes.

"We received a message from my teacher, *Rav Tzadok*. He spoke with me through the elements of air and water, and through your mouth."

Shoshana's eyes widened.

"Oh." A pause. "It is not good for me to submit myself to spirits."

"It was good this time," smiled *Yeshua*. "And it was necessary."

After describing what had happened, Shoshona said thoughtfully, "Yes, I believe with all my heart that you will succeed in the Ordeals—and then we shall be married!" She brightened.

That evening *Yeshua* spoke with both Azariah and *Mar Belteshazzar* about the death of *Rav Tzadok*.

"Often the elementals will play with you, creating illusions that are not true. Also, we do not recommend that our people allow themselves to come under trance. That is making oneself into a puppet for whatever spiritual opportunist might appear," solemnly warned Azariah.

"No, this was not an illusion," replied *Yeshua*. "You will have confirmation of his death…next spring."

Chapter Twelve: THE ORDEALS OF DANIEL

"This is our Brother, Stephanos. We have asked him to instruct you in the ways of descent."

Stephanos seemed to be an intelligent and educated young man, but much younger than *Yeshua*.

"Descent?" *Yeshua* showed his amazement.

"Yes, my Son," replied *Mar Belteshazzar*. "We refer to the Portal of Divine Presence as *Aliyah*, an ascent. But we do not float into the sky! The Presence is within, not without. It is just as well to understand it as a *descent* into the Divine Heart. What posture did Elijah take when he listened to the voices of Heaven?"

Without hesitation *Yeshua* answered, "Head between his knees. I have done this same thing many times."

"Yes, and you have drawn close to the Holy One. You have withdrawn into the *Yetzer Ha-Tov*, the Divine Heart. When you make the *Aliyah* of Enoch to the *Merkabah* Throne of the Most High, you will use the same method, but you will have to find your own way. Stephanos will teach you his tradition of descent into the Divine Underworld. You will learn much that you can apply to find your own way."

Bowing respectfully to Stephanos, *Yeshua* replied, "I have heard of the ways of Pythagoras from Ariston, the Egyptian Hermetic. Are you a Lord of the Lair?"

Stephanos was pleased at the title. He smiled and said, "Not I, but my grandfather. He was a great *Pholarchos*. He taught me many things about the sacred journey, but he never guided me through it. The Mysteries of Holy Pythagoras are all but dead now."

"Are you a Jew?" asked *Yeshua*.

"Yes, and a descendant of Zerubbabel, like you," he answered.

Yeshua was amazed. "Then we must be second or third cousins," he observed. "But your name is Greek."

"My family adopted the Greek language and customs many generations ago. We keep our religion, but we have also learned many things from the Greeks. YAHWEH is the God of all people—not just the Jews. He has given a share of his Wisdom to all people, and especially to the Greeks and their prophets, who are called philosophers. The greatest of these was Pythagoras. His disciples developed the highest arts of mathematics, architecture, design of machines and weaponry, metallurgy, alchemy, and glassmaking. Their wisdom is still used by the Essenes in distillation of perfumes. Do you know that the *Kabbalah* of *Yetzirah* was developed by Jewish Pythagoreans in Babylon?"

Yeshua felt a bit overwhelmed by all this. He looked helplessly at *Mar Belteshazzar*, who merely smiled and nodded approval.

"I...I realize that the *Kabbalah* of Zerubbabel came from our ancestors in Babylon, and that it was the Persians who taught us our masonic skills, but the Greeks, too?"

"My Son, it is we, the Jews, who are the *Israel* that "spiritually strives" and prepares all humanity for the coming of *Messiah*. But the *Ruach Ha-Qodesh* and divine wisdom are given to holy prophets and philosophers of all nations. To deny the source of gentile wisdom is to deny the Holy Spirit. We must have the humility and discretion to learn from the *Ruah Ha-Qodesh*, whether She enlightens us through Jews or gentiles."

After a silence, *Yeshua* laughed.

"So the same *Kabbalah* of *Yetzirah* that I have studied here in Babylon derives from the Greeks?"

Stephanos was quick to reply.

"No, it derives from our Hebrew alphabet and mathematics, and it was revealed many generations ago through the Jewish saints. But many of them studied mathematics and alphanumerics in the school of Pythagoras, adapting what they learned to Jewish understanding. These men were our ancestors—both yours and mine."

"Then, I am ready to learn from you Stephanos, my cousin!"

Turning to the old man, he raised his eyebrows and promised, "And I shall adapt it to my own understanding."

He paused, then again turned to Stephanos. "Am I to address you as master?"

"No, no!" laughed *Mar Belteshazzar*. "Stephanos is a student, like you. But he has knowledge of an important tradition that will be of use to you when you study the *Aliyah of Enoch*. He will not formally instruct you, but he will impart what he knows in conversation."

For the next week *Yeshua* and Shoshana spent their mornings with Stephanos. What he was able to tell of the tradition of the *Pholarchoi* was fascinating and, indeed, helped shape *Yeshua's* understanding of how he might make the *Merkabah* ascent.

"In the days of Pythagoras, the deepest spiritual mysteries of the Greeks were *chthonic*, that is, involved communication and inspiration from the Divine Underworld. Their experience of the One God came through nature and the Earth, whom they called *Demeter*. Deep under the Earth was the court of the Divine King *Hades*, also named *Pluto* for the "Wealth" that he bestowed up humanity from out of the Earth—metals, fruits, and other treasure.

"His Queen, *Persephone*, was the Greek perception of the *Ruach Ha-Qodesh*. It was She, the *Kore* or Eternal Maiden, who mediated arts, sciences, agriculture, music, and all the treasures of culture to humanity through chosen prophets. She was also the source of divination, communication with dead ancestors, and prediction of future events. Wise men and women, called philosophers, sought her counsel and presence.

"But She was accessible only to those who had been spiritually reborn as *kouroi* or divine humans. Pythagoras taught the mysteries of divine rebirth. When the ground for them had been prepared within a disciple, he or she was presented to the Pythagorean Priest known as the *Pholarchos*. He would guide the disciple through the perilous descent into the Divine Underworld into the Presence of the *Kore*. Once She had accepted the disciple, She completed the Mysteries of Rebirth.

"The *Pholarchos* was a Greek title meaning Master of the Lair, because the method for descent into the Divine Underworld was like the hibernation of a lion in a lair. The disciple was brought into an hypnotic trance-like sleep in a sacred cave by the *Pholarchos*. The descent took three days and two nights to accomplish, during which the disciple's sleeping body needed protection. The *Pholarchos* not only guarded the body, but communicated psychically with the disciple's *nephesh*, which the Greeks called a *psyche*. He guided it through the many perils, gateways, and portals of the descent, and then the return journey. He used a kind of flute with harmonic intoning and chanting to keep communication with the soul.

"This process was called *exsomatosis*, or traveling out of the body. It was literally a form of death. The process was the same as death, but under skillful guidance and control. When the soul returned, it had been purified by divine contact, and the body had been made healthy, young, and strong through divine incubation.

"Although the process was described as a descent into the Divine Underworld, the later Pythagorean alchemists purified plant and stone extracts through a method similar to *exsomatosis*, but which was described as an ascent. It was called the spagyric work.

"Why an ascent? Because the descent into the Divine Underworld was a journey within what Pythagoras called the microcosm, or internal universe mapped within the structure of the soul. But only human beings had a soul that was "in the Image of God"—a true microcosm. This is because the human soul is the final development and aggregation of mineral, vegetable, and animal souls that the particular *neshemah* (or "monad") had experienced through aeons of *metempsychosis* or transmigrations of the soul. Thus when Body, Soul, and Spirit are alchemically separated in a stone or plant, the Spirit journeys to its source in the Hyperion beyond the harmonies of planets and fixed stars, then is pulled back down into purified Body and Soul to be recombined in a spagyrically purified form.

"From the Pythagorean perspective, then, the *Aliyah* to the Chariot-Throne of God would be a descent into the Divine Underworld. It could be accomplished by using the techniques of the *Pholarchos*."

Stephanos ended his dissertation.

"But the Riders of the Chariot have never been guided by a human," observed Shoshana. "They were in seclusion, alone, and guided by angels."

"Perhaps that is not the issue," remarked *Yeshua*. "It is not a matter of who guides, but of how the guiding is received."

"What do you mean?" asked Stephanos.

"It's like teaching and learning. The teacher can explain and explain, but unless the student is a learner, there can be no learning," said *Yeshua*. "There must be ears to hear, and eyes to see."

"Yes, I remember that Grandfather told me of failures—disciples who were thoroughly prepared, but then unable to make the descent. They would fall out of trance into sleep and remember nothing."

"Besides all these, there is an Eighth Spirit of sleep, through which is brought about the trance of nature and the *yetzer* of death," *Yeshua* recited.

"What is that?" asked Stephanos.

"It is from the Testament of Reuben, where he describes the Seven Spirits within the constitution of the soul. But this is an Eighth—above the crown of the head. And he also says, 'And with all these,' by which he refers to the evil forms of the Seven Spirits, 'the Spirit of Sleep is joined, which is that of error and fantasy.'"

"Yes," continued *Yeshua*, "the danger is in falling away from the 'trance of nature' which is a holy kind of sleep that associates with the *Yetzer Ha-Tov*. When one falls away, he drifts into normal human sleep."

"Do you know how to do that?" asked Shoshana.

"Yes, and I think I can maintain it if I will it so," replied *Yeshua*.

*******   *******   *******   *******

Yeshua had carefully studied the Magian commentary on the Greek translation of the *Aliyah of Enoch*. It was a map of the Ten Heavens. The First Heaven contains the treasuries of rain, dew, wind, and snow overseen by their angels. Clouds float in a vast, clear sea. A mighty angel rules over the stars and their courses. Its permission must be gained to enter this world and ascend beyond. This is Malkuth of the lowest World of *Asiah*.

The Second Heaven is a place of darkness and purgatory, where *nepheshim* of evil men and angels suffer for a time so that they may be purified. Fallen angels who had followed Satan and the Grigori in their rebellion against God are imprisoned here and guarded by powerful dark angels. *Sathani-el* and his princes however, occupy the Fifth Heaven. In order to pass into and through the Second Heaven, it is necessary to die, or to achieve the trance of death through the Eighth Spirit above the crown of the head.

The Third Heaven contains both *Gehenna* and Paradise. Eden is in the South, but *Gehenna* or the place of purification is in the North. The Paradise or *Pardes* of Eden is a lush and fragrant garden into which the *neshemah* of good people come to rest and dream after the Second Death. Great souls may temporarily depart their bodies and ascend through trance into Paradise, where they might be instructed by other great souls. This is also the way of ascent to the *Merkabah* Throne of God.

But *Gehenna* is for purification of a soul or *neshema* that has been stained by bad works and accumulated *hub* of the *nephesh*. Before it can enter into its rest in the *Pardes*, it must be purified by the fire of Spirit like gold being separated from the dross of its ore. The human *nephesh* that has polluted itself so badly that it cannot ascend through the Second Heaven refuses to die the Second Death and tries to maintain its existence by sucking vital force from living, incarnate beings. It becomes part of the *qlippoth* or subtle dark forces opposing humanity—an evil spirit that must be exorcized from its host. When it has lost its power to remain among the undead, the *neshemah* withdraws completely and allows the *nephesh* to burn, decay, and decompose into the lesser souls of animals, plants, and minerals from which it was formed. It is like an imperfect pot that is cast back into the slurry so that another, more harmonious vessel might be formed. In this way the *neshama* of even the most evil of men will eventually withdraw into the Second Death and sojourn for the necessary time in *Gehenna* until it can sleep in the *Pardes* awaiting reincarnation. Thus each new child comes into birth pure, but also burdened with the *hub* it has created in previous lives.

The Fourth Heaven is portal to the World of *Yetzirah*, which opens into *Tiphareth* through *Kether* of *Asiah*. It is the habitation of the living spirits of *Shemesh* and *Keseh*—Sun and Moon. *Shemesh* serves God accompanied by great wheels of stars, angels, with giant Phoenixes and the Chalkydri, who are great fire dragons with feet and tail of a lion and the head of a crocodile. *Keseh* has hosts of armed troops praising God with cymbals and flutes. They move from East to West and rule the four seasons.

The Fifth Heaven is filled with Satan and his fallen princes—the Grigori and the Nephilim. They are jealous of humanity because it will one day rule them. To pass through their realm requires aid from on High. Some sages taught that their ruler *Ialdabaoth* ignorantly considered himself to be the Demiurge of Creation because he forgot his own origins from Mother-Father *Barbelo,* the First Emanation of the *Abba*.

The Sixth Heaven is portal to the World of *Briah*, which opens into *Tiphareth* through *Kether* of *Yetzirah*. It is the realm of Archangels and the ultimate abode for the *neshemah* of every human being. Here there are six Phoenixes, six Kerubim, and six Seraphim continually singing and praising the Holy One in the world above them. The one who ascends through this Heaven must have total purity of soul.

The Seventh Heaven consists of great light and hosts of archangelic and other beings of Divine Light. They are called the Ionit Stations of Light, ever worshipping the Holy One. Only one whose *neshemah* is fully illuminated by the sacred marriage of *yechid* and *yechida* can pass through this Heaven.

These masculine and feminine monadic rays of every Divine Being were separated from each other at the beginning of the monadic journey into matter. They each emanate seven souls—all of the same essential being—through mineral, vegetable, animal, and finally human kingdoms. Over cycles of incarnation the seven resolve into two—one incarnate while the other is awakened in the *qimah* out of body. The main guide of an advanced disciple will be his own discarnate soulmate. For a man, female; for a woman, male. When they are both ready for their last and final incarnation, they will incarnate within a few years of each other, find each other, and conjoin in the most sublime form of human love. When one dies, there is no separation. The other is fully present waiting to receive him or her in death, which becomes a sacred and eternal marriage. Then they enter into the Eighth Heaven, which the Greeks know as the Ogdoad, where they exist reunited as one Divine Being. Slowly they rise into the Ninth and Tenth Heavens and sit at the Throne of God.

The Eighth Heaven is portal to the World of *Atziluth*, which opens into *Tiphareth* through *Kether* of *Briah*, or the Seventh Heaven. It is known as *Muzaloth*, the place of the stellar constellations. Only one who has known his Soulmate is able to enter and ascend, and he must be guided by an Archangel.

The Ninth Heaven is known as *Kuchavim*, the Zodiacal Houses. Its splendor is so great that only the purest of souls can exist here, and he must be guided by an Archangel.

The Tenth Heaven is *Aravoth*, the Throne and Court of Almighty God. It is to this state that Enoch was brought by the Archangel Michael. This is the direct Divine Presence of *El Elyon*. It is here that prophets receive the Divine Message of God to deliver to mankind.

After the Ascent, the Descent must be made. If not done correctly, the disciple will die or be held in a state of suspension, unable to return to his body.

Yeshua had decided to make the *Aliyah* of *Enoch* in order to gain the friendship and alliance of Archangels. He could not do it the first time alone. He would need an assistant to intone the liturgy and guard his body—for this was a dangerous out-of-body trance that could result in death or insanity.

Only one person could guide him properly through this. It would have to be Shoshana.

"If I am to succeed in the Ordeals, I must have the friendship of Archangels," he told her. "Therefore I have decided to make the *Merkabah* Ascent. Only you can serve as my guide and protector. Will you agree?"

"Yes, my Beloved. But remember, the Ascent is also a Descent deep into your own Heart, and the Archangels exist within the Image of God that is your own soul. You will evoke them from within yourself."

"This is true," answered *Yeshua*, "but the process is different for men and women. I am more successful at communing with other beings when I breath through my right nostril, approach, and enter into them. You are more successful when you breath through the left nostril and draw them into yourself. It is easier for me to bring my Heart up into my spiritual eye, but easier for you to descend with your spiritual eye into your Heart. I am *Yechid*, you are *Yechida*. Together we are One Divine Being, but for now we are two. That is why I must make the Ascent, and you must guide me and merge with me in your Heart to hold us together in sacred union."

"Beloved, if there is any interruption, we could both be harmed."

"Then we must do this after Babylon sleeps, and in a place no one can find."

For the next two weeks as the moon waxed full, Shoshana and *Yeshua* practiced the form of holy sleep induced by the Pythagorean *Pholarchoi*. With the tender voice of love, Shoshana sung *Yeshua* into a trance. As he had requested, she then called upon the Prophet Daniel to prepare and guide her beloved into the Heavens. After this they both slept—he in Azariah's upper room, and she in her own room.

After the first night, Azariah asked *Yeshua* what he had experienced.

"I felt myself leaving the flesh and floating as in a waking sleep. But I did not look down at my body. I was ascending, floating upward like a boat. All around me, like living water, was the voice of my beloved. Soon I had no sense of my *nephesh*-body. I was just a head with eyes, nose, ears, mouth, ever floating upward.

"Soon everything became very still. Then out of a great silence I heard many voices singing—*Eliahu Ha-Nabi*. I have heard this many times since I was a child. I felt the presence of a Great One nearby. I could not see him, but it seemed to me that he was the Prophet Elijah."

Shoshana broke in excitedly.

"I, too, had a dream of Elijah! He with with both of us, and we were his students. But I can't remember anything he said. Only that he was fiery and wise."

"But what happened next?" Azariah persisted.

"The light of dawn began to break and I slowly descended into my *nephesh*-body, and then sunk backwards into my body of flesh," he replied.

Azariah thought for a moment, then asked, "When have you heard this singing about the Prophet Elijah before in your life?"

"Perhaps," *Yeshua* hesitated…"when I was a very young child. I used to awaken from a horrible dream when the moon was full. I was a young man. My parents were dead, and I lived with my grandfather. He hated me—I don't know why—and demanded that I be stoned to death for insubordination. I begged for my life, but the stones came as I crouched, breaking my bones." He shuddered.

Azariah gasped, then regained his composure.

"There is a story…I have heard a story…" he began slowly. "It was *haggadah* that was told of the Prophet Elijah."

Yeshua leaned forward.

"The *hasidim* who lived in the caves below Damascus used to say that when Elijah was a young man, he ran away from home to join the prophets of their community. He was caught, accused, and stoned according to the old law. The people of his village left his body to be eaten by buzzards in the desert, but the brothers found him. They used their arts to revive him. They nursed him to health, adopted him as one of their own, and trained him in their wisdom."

Yeshua was silent, but his eyes were moist.

"My Son, Elijah is your Teacher. He guides and protects you on behalf of the *Ruach Ha-Qodesh*."

Yeshua nodded, awestricken. Shoshana draped her arms around him and covered his neck with kisses. She, too, was weeping for astonishment and joy.

"My Son, this knowledge is good. It is very good for the holy work that you will do on behalf of Israel."

That night *Yeshua* again practiced the first part of the ascent. This time he could hear the voice of Elijah, but he could not see him. He said, "Be still. Seek for the Light, and you will know." *Yeshua* spent the night in a deep form of meditation that was suffused in holy, white Light.

After seven nights of practice, *Yeshua* found himself able to speak to Elijah. He spoke not with his mouth, but through his mind.

"Abba, why can I not see you? He asked.

"Does Elisha speak?" was the tender answer. *Yeshua* felt himself hurled violently back into his sleeping body. He awakened and could not sleep for the rest of the night.

"Why does he call me Elisha?" he asked over and over.

The next night soon after Shoshona had left, *Yeshua* was unable to maintain his concentration and fell into fits of dreaming. Scenes of patriarchs and prophets passed before him. He was Abel being murdered by his brother. He was Joseph accused by Potiphar's wife. He was Aaron, speaking to Israel on behalf of the stuttering Moses. He was Judith beheading Holofernes. He was King David betraying Uriah. He was Amos denouncing the immorality of Israel. He was Elisha holding the mantle of Elijah. He was Daniel protecting his disciples from the fires of Nebuchadnezzar's furnace.

"Last night I drifted into dreams," he confided disconsolately to Shoshana.

"What did you dream?" she asked. He told her.

"Those were not mere dreams, my beloved," she stated forcefully. "Those were visions transmitted to you by your Teacher to tell you about your previous lives in Israel."

Yeshua was silent, but he took her words to heart.

That night, he was able to make the ascent as he had before. In the presence of Elijah he asked again, "Abba, why can I not see you?"

"Does Elisha speak?" was again the answer.

Yeshua felt himself blowing about like sand in a windstorm. He felt hot, then cold, then hot again. He couldn't maintain this state of being, so he chose to sink downward, where he found himself floating in his *nephesh*-body over the sleeping Shoshona. He saw her *nephesh*-body floating alongside him, so he sent her a greeting. The eyes of her *nephesh*-body opened and she saw him floating next to her.

She smiled and thought, "My darling! I was having such a bad dream. I was being blown like a leaf through fire and ice."

"Yes, my love," he returned. "We were."

It was the final night for the practice. *Yeshua* promised himself that he would ask his question once again and hold the universe still for an answer.

After the ascent, *Yeshua* sought for Elijah, but he was not present. "I seek Elijah," he projected powerfully through the billowing Light. No response. "I seek Elijah, my Teacher," he again projected with great might. Still no answer.

"*Abba*, why can I not see you?" he projected with power and force. "Why? Why""

Suddenly he felt the presence of his Teacher—fiery and wise.

"Does...?"

"Yes, he does!" shot *Yeshua* without waiting for the question.

Visions opened up within him. A cave not far from the Dead Sea. Below, a small city carved into the limestone. A man dressed in white cotton robes. One of the Brothers, but unique, non-conforming, prone to isolation, wiser and more fiery than anyone *Yeshua* had ever seen in flesh.

The man sat in the posture of Elijah, head between knees. He was ascending in his *nephesh*-body. But there was something more—another body, a vehicle, a golden Chariot made of the substance of his etheric body. It formed from a golden ether that exuded from his Heart—the center of his invisible bodies. A silver cord from head to head, a golden bowl from Heart to Heart. He was chanting, intoning. The bowl became like a whirlwind that was forming into a Chariot with wildly spinning wheels.

The man looked toward *Yeshua* and said something, pointing to the Chariot.

Suddenly *Yeshua* knew. This man was Elijah, his Teacher. But he was living in flesh, on Earth, not far from the Essene complex at Qumran. That is why *Yeshua* could never see him. He was living far above in his *neshemah*, which had emanated far below into a flesh incarnation. Elijah was not living as an ascended angel. He was an angel manifest in flesh!

Now *Yeshua* could see the details of the man's *Merkabah* ascent. He did not ascend naked and unprotected, but in a divine vehicle—an image of the Divine Chariot-Throne itself. And now the Chariot seemed to become alive and conscious, with eyes, with wheels within wheels.

Elijah, or whatever his name might now be, pointed again and stepped into the Chariot. He began to ride the Chariot in his *nephesh*-body, with left palm over his Heart and right hand pointed out and up. He intoned, and the Chariot ascended into the clouds. Now the man's *nephesh*-body vanished and he appeared as a vortex of flame burning within the speeding Chariot, which disappeared into the sky—into the First Heaven.

Yeshua now understood how the *Aliyah* of the *Merkabah* was done. He had been shown by his Teacher, Elijah.

*******   *******   *******   *******

After consultation with *Mar Belteshazzar*, it was decided to use the subterranean cell designed for the Ordeals at the Fellowship synagogue. The building itself would be guarded by Zeb, the concealed iron doors to the cell locked from the inside, and Shoshana would hold the only keys to the doors.

"It will be the Fall Equinox tomorrow night and a Full Moon," Azariah said. "I think this is the best time."

"Yes," *Yeshua* agreed. "Shoshona, Zeb, and I will fast and spend the day in prayer. Then we will make preparations in the underground chambers when the Moon appears at sunset. We will make the *Aliyah* after the city becomes quiet while the Moon is ascending towards the Zenith."

That day *Yeshua* showed Shoshana how to work with him. She would help him ascend in trance with the power of her canting voice. But then, instead of leaving, she would remain with his sleeping body and hold her palms one finger-length from the soles of his naked feet, supporting and participating in his journey through the eternal power of their love.

He would not sit with head between knees to connect crown and sole of feet. That would not be necessary because *yechid* and *yechida* were together in flesh. Instead head and feet of the one *neshemah* whose emanations they were would conjoin into a flowing cycle of *ruach*—head, Heart, feet, hands, Heart, head. Shoshana would participate in his journey through her own visions of the night.

While the Moon ascended in the East, Zeb took up his post at the doorway of the Brotherhood synagogue. Shoshana locked the doors leading to the subterranean chamber of the lions. Protected within the cage, the two lovers kissed and prepared themselves for spiritual labor.

First, Shoshana intoned psalms of *Aliyah*, her voice rising and falling in perfect intonation, lush with the ripeness of love. *Yeshua* coordinated breath and heartbeat. He willed his consciousness to ascend through the crown of his head. This was unlike projection, where he exited through the point between his eyebrows. Briefly he passed through a stage of unconsciousness, then awakened into a sacred trance in the Eighth Spirit, floating in his *nephesh*-body. Shoshana had learned to recognize the signs of trance, so she began to intone the Sacred Name: *Eee—yah—ohh—way—eee, Eee—yah—ohh—way—eee...*

Yeshua placed his left palm over his *nephesh*-Heart and pointed his right forefinger at the Heart of his sleeping body. He joined Shoshana intoning *Ha-Shem*: *Eee—yah—ohh—way—eee, Eee—yah—ohh—way—eee...* But his voice was deep, like thunder, and it was joined by many more deep voices. Shoshana had a sense of these many voices as she intoned.

Outside at the door of the synagogue, Zeb thought he heard thunder for just a moment. He stood and looked up at the clear sky filled with the light of the rising Moon. No clouds. No lightning. He shrugged and sat down again.

Shoshana's eyes were closed, but she felt extremely alert. Subtle lights of different colors seemed to form and fade in the periphery of her consciousness, but *Yeshua* was embroiled in a maelstrom of fiery forces.

From the Heart of his being he was summoning forth more than merely etheric substance. Fiery nectars bubbled forth like water from a fierce and fathomless spring. He formed and directed them with his right hand as he intoned *Ha-Shem*. But the forces also shaped themselves into form, flowing through the *'Olam* of *Yetzirah*.

Now Shoshana began the recitation of *Bereshit*. "In the beginning, the *Elohim* created the Heavens and the Earth... As she slowly chanted each occurrence of the Divine Name *Elohim* as it arose in the Genesis text, *Yeshua* engraved the forms of fiery Hebrew letters and *Sephiroth* attributed to each of the thirty-two positions in the *Kabbalah* of *Yetzirah*. He imprinted the Seven Doubles with the seven Planets, the Twelve Elementals with the twelve parts of the Zodiac, and the Three Mothers with the three firmaments—the *Shin* of Fire, the *Mem* of Water, and the *Aleph* of Air mediating between the two. He wove them together as *netivot*, hidden paths connecting the Ten *Sephiroth*, and he engraved the Four Kerubim, the Six Directions, and set the wheels within wheels into fiery motion until they whirled wildly.

Shoshana finished her recitation, her eyes still closed. She visualized the perfect Image of God, the little *'Olam* of *'Olamim* which Stephanos had described as the Pythagorean Microcosm—the little Divine Universe within each human soul. She visualized it in the form of ten perfectly symmetrical *sephiroth*, all bound together in the original Divine Unity of emanation. She knew that her beloved had kabbalistically constructed the perfect soul of mankind before its fall into the lower worlds. He had repaired their human soul and created a new pattern that would lead them into the *Tikkun*—the Divine Return.

"My beloved," she silently projected, "you have created our wedding vessel."

Yeshua lowered his right arm and ceased his work for the moment. He stood in awe of what Shoshana and he had created. This golden vehicle superficially resembled the chariot-throne of an Assyrian warrior king. But it was constantly fluid, at the same time fiery and crystalline, always changing shape and dimensions like a watery reflection. Through the brilliance he saw multiple pairs of eyes. Many holy living creatures momentarily appeared then withdrew back into the flame about the Chariot. As he watched, stars, planets, and constellations formed and dissolved into the whirling wheels.

Shoshana began to recite from the vision of Ezekiel: "And above the firmament that was over their heads was the likeness of a Throne of sapphire gemstone, and upon the likeness of the Throne was the likeness of a man sitting upon it…" She grew silent.

Yeshua surmounted the Chariot Throne, placed his left palm over his *nephesh* Heart, raised his right arm, and pointed upward. All form melted away as he rose. His *nephesh*-body melted away. He became a flame: at his head *Yod*, at his chest and arms *He*, at his spine and trunk *Vav*, and at his hips and legs *He*. He and the Chariot pierced the first hidden world—Malkuth of Asiah, the First Heaven—then hovered before a gigantic being, the angelic ruler of this realm.

"Who desires passage?" boomed a voice like a volcano.

"*Eee—yah—ohh—way—eee*," intoned *Yeshua*. His voice was even more powerful.

The angel bowed in obesience and *Yeshua* resumed the ascent. He passed through the dark regions of the Second Heaven, then pierced into the *Pardes* Paradise of the Third Heaven.

"My Son, you have died!"

Yeshua saw a golden light forming into the face of his Father *Yosef*. He continually sensed the presence of his Father after his death, but his Heart lept with joy to hear his voice.

"Father, I have experienced the form of death, but I continue to live in the flesh."

"My Son, you have an appearance unlike any of the great ones in Paradise. Have you become a Rider of the Chariot?"

"For the sake of Israel—yes, Father."

"Then we will add our voices, prayers, blessings to support your holy work, my dear Son."

"Thank you, Father," he projected, bowing in respect.

"Do not tarry in this place, my Son. You must continue." *Yeshua* saw many more golden lights gathering.

Then he heard *Yosef* leading them in a psalm of *Aliyah*: "I was joyful when they said to me, 'Let us go into the House of *Eee—yah—ohh—way—eee*. Our feet shall stand within thy gates."

Yeshua again raised his right hand and the living Chariot resumed its ascent. He left the World of *Asiah* and entered the World of *Yetzirah*, where he passed through all the glories of *Shemesh* and *Keseh*, the divine spirits who appear to humanity as Sun and Moon. Here were hosts of angels praising God. They drew near to *Yeshua* and their leader spoke.

"The Fifth Heaven is the realm of Sathaniel and his archrebels. You will need assistance from on high to pass safely through their regions. We have heard the prayers and blessings of the saints in Paradise who have sent forth powerful petitions for your help. We, therefore, will send you forth with praise and blazes of Divine Fire, and we will make petition to the Archangels for your protection and help."

Yeshua bowed in gratitude and continued the ascent. As the Fifth Heaven began to form and appear, he saw gigantic beings. They were a Brotherhood of Darkness, highly organized, each being a powerful ruler in his own right—but a ruler of dark forces. A glaring, brassy kind of light seemed to flicker and emanate from each of them, like flames from a dying campfire whipped by the wind at night. They hated humanity, whom they desired to corrupt, ruin, and finally destroy from the inside out. They were the guides and teachers of all that was evil on Earth.

Suddenly there appeared beside *Yeshua* in the Chariot a golden flame.

A voice said, "You can make yourself invisible to them and pass through their realm. You must become an anonymous, unknown one—no one worthy of notice. This is how a woman makes herself inconspicuous to evil men. Assume the cloak of anonymity. You are an Unknown Adept—invisible to the world of darkness. Keep this cloak here and on Earth as long as possible."

The being disappeared.

After taking thought, *Yeshua* engraved a cloak of mirrors all about him. Not a cloak of darkness, not a cloak of invisibility, but a cloak of mirrors. He would be seen, but not noticed, because they would see only themselves reflected. Any impulses unleashed at him would reflect back to their source if he were discovered.

In this way he passed through the archontic realms of Sathaniel and emerged safely into *Kether* of *Yetzirah*, Portal into the World of *Briah*—the World of Archangelic Beings. This was the goal of his quest, to make alliances with Archangels for the Ordeals of Daniel.

But in the Sixth Heaven there was a ring-pass-not. Only beings who were fully *tammim*, saints of God with total purity of Heart, could ascend through this realm into the *Tiphareth* or Heart of the Archangelic World of *Briah*.

Yeshua had pondered over this many times. He did not know whether he was pure of Heart or a saint of God, but he did know that Shoshana was his soul-mate, his *yechidah*. The Magian commentary to the *Aliyah of Enoch* declared that one who had found his soul-mate in flesh could ascend through the Eighth Heaven with the guidance of an Archangel. If, then, he had found his true soul-mate, he must have the same purity of Heart that Shoshana possessed. This thought gave him courage to attempt further ascent.

A giant archangelic being of fire appeared before him. It was neither male nor female, but had some characteristics of both. It spoke not in a human normal voice, but intoned with a sound somewhat between a bell and a trumpet.

"Only the pure of Heart can enter this World. This is a World of Fire. You must be all and completely one pure flame to exist among the Ionit Stations of Light."

Yeshua placed both hands on his Heart and slowly unfolded them outward. A brilliant flame of white fire blazed forth. The cloak of mirrors dissolved. All outer form dissolved. The Chariot dissolved. He became one continuous, pure flame.

He knew that communication with angelic beings was by thought projected through intoning, so he held a thought and produced a long, gentle tone: "I seek archangelic assistance on Earth. I seek an archangelic friend, guide, and ally for the sake of Israel and all humanity."

Lights of all colors and hues blazed around him. Sounds of angelic choirs resounded in praise to *El Elyon*, God Most High. Then there was a hush. A human voice began to speak through projection into *Yeshua's* mind—a voice that he knew. The *Neshemah* of *Elijah* addressed him in and said:

"My Son, you have done everything well. But you cannot proceed beyond this place until *Yechid* and *Yechidah* have been joined in eternal marriage."

Then another human voice resounded in his mind—that of Shoshana.

"The angels are powers of God, and those powers live within you to be summoned as needed. You have been formed in the Image and Likeness of God."

Yeshua projected a question.

"Abba, how should I summon aid from the Archangels so that I can succeed in the Ordeals of Daniel?"

Light of all colors blazed forth anew and the glorious visage of the Archangel Auriel appeared. In a voice like a trumpet he projected this message:

"I am within you. Messiah is within you. Call upon Messiah to send me. Messiah will send me."

Then the blazing fires parted and *Yeshua* saw a vision of the Ancient One seated upon His Throne. Eyes and sacred living things surrounded him. But kneeling before him was one in human form, but androgynous like the angels. This was the *Bar-Enash*, the New Humanity.

The Ancient One anointed his head with golden oil, spoke in a voice like thunder, and said:

"Unto you I give all power and authority on Earth and in the Heavens. The works that I do, you shall do. Through time, turmoil, and sacrifice you shall enter into the human world—one soul at a time."

Then the Ancient One stood up, pointed his right hand directly at *Yeshua*, and said:

"You shall become the first-born of a New Humanity. Behold the Wedding Banquet."

Yeshua saw himself and Shoshana seated with a host of beings at a great table overflowing with meat, drink, bread, and fruit of all kinds. The two lovers radiated light from around their heads. Their light merged and grew brighter until it became one flame that resembled the *Merkabah*-Chariot that had carried him through the lower Heavens. It was punctuated with ten symmetrically spaced lights—the Ten *Sephiroth* of the pre-fallen state. Now he could see himself and Shoshana as one being, one great *neshemah*, ever ascending from glory to glory.

"My Son," came the human voice of *Elijah*, "do you understand?"

Before *Yeshua* could formulate an answer, he felt himself descending at such a great speed through the lower worlds that he could make out no details. He descended though light and darkness until he found himself standing in the *Merkabah*-Chariot. He saw that he was coming into form in his *nephesh*-body. Then he stood floating next to his sleeping flesh-body with Shoshana still holding her palms next to the naked soles of his feet. The *Merkabah*-Chariot grew fluid and melted back into the Heart of his etheric body.

He floated above his flesh-body and sunk back into it, awakening as from sleep. Shoshana also began to stir. She took several deep breaths, then opened her eyes and smiled at him.

"Have we succeeded?" she asked.

"I think so, my love," he answered with his eyes still closed. "I think so."

*******   *******   *******   *******

Yeshua decided that he wished to attempt the Ordeals of Daniel on the New Moon of the Equinox—two weeks from his *Merkabah Aliyah*. Zeb had purchased a wild lioness that had been trapped in her lair late in the winter and kept in a cage in Seleucia. He was warned that the animal was extremely dangerous, and that raw meat should be thrown into the cage.

The beast was now secured in the double cage of the subterranean chamber at the Brotherhood synagogue. She was allowed to move from one cage to the other through a bolted iron door so that each area could be cleaned and the lion dung harvested for sale. The dung was spagyrically purified by Magian alchemists to produce a potent aphrodisiac and restorer of virility in old age. Sales of the dung more than paid the animal's price.

She despised her human captors, even Zeb, who fed her daily. When he brought food for her, he dropped it into the unoccupied cage, then release the connecting door from outside. Even so, he always came with his own spear and an armed assistant.

Yeshua was treated like a sacrificial king by the Brotherhood. He was furloughed off his job, given whatever he asked, and looked upon with great awe. According to his wishes, no one spoke about the lioness or any of the other preparations being made in the furnace chamber. He spent his days privately in the company of Shoshana, with occasional visits from Zeb, Azariah, and *Mar Belteshazzar*.

Shoshana never expressed doubts or fears. She was, in fact, supremely confident that *Yeshua* was the long-expected one who would prove himself and assume leadership of the Brotherhood.

"My beloved, I now understand what you meant when you said the angels are powers inscribed within us."

Shoshana smiled and said, "But we lost our communication with any but the rebel angels when we were cast out of the *Pardes* and took on coats of skin—this flesh. The angels are not inscribed within this coat of flesh, but within the Divine *Yetzer* as an Image of God in our Heart. We have both the Divine Image and the fallen image inscribed within us."

Yeshua continued the thought.

"Humanity cannot return to the *Pardes* because an angel with a flaming sword guards the portal against impure souls. Thus we cannot communicate with the angelic worlds as we would with human beings, and we cannot find them within our flesh. But…"

Yeshua held out his two hands and extended all ten fingers.

"Ten fingers, ten *Sephiroth*," Shoshana observed.

"Yes, and each finger is connected to the *netivot* subtle pathways, as well as palms of hands, soles of feet, eyes, nostrils, breath, voice. All these connect to the Seven Spirits and the Eighth above the head. And your *netivot* and mine are connected in the *neshemah* spirit that emanated us."

"So becoming *tam* and perfectly upright is something that can be done only from the inside out through the *netivot* and subtle channels. It is the intention before the action that governs whether and how we might restore ourselves in the *tikkun*," she added.

"Even more, no *yechid* or *yechidah* can complete this work in isolation from its unity in the *neshemah*. We don't have a *neshemah*; the *neshemah* has us. We are its emanations. Only by completing our spiritual unity can I act for both of us in the Ordeals. When I can co-exist with you in our fully restored Divine *Yetzer*, then together we can walk with the angels and gain cooperation of the elementals."

"Yes, I know," she whispered. "But what does that mean?"

"I heard you say something very important during the first part off the *Aliyah*. When I evoked the *Merkabah*-Chariot out of my own Heart, you said, 'You have created our wedding vessel.' Do you remember?"

She nodded.

"You have not asked, and I have not told you what I saw in the *Aliyah*. But now I tell you that I saw the Ancient One sitting on the Throne of Glory. He shined the Divine Face upon me and spoke to me"

Shoshana's eyes widened and she sat upright.

"The Messiah was anointed before me and I was shown his wedding banquet. But the Bride and Groom were you and I seated at a banquet table with hosts of living creatures. It was our spiritual wedding. We merged into one being. This was our sacred union of *yechid* and *yechidah*. We became one being in the *Neshemah*—no more man and woman, no more male and female, but androgynous like the Messiah."

Shoshana slowly said, "Do you remember when you asked me to help you in the Ordeals? I thought you were joking. But now we both see that this cannot be done in separation from each other."

Yeshua looked lovingly into her eyes.

"When I undergo the night of Ordeal, you must sit undisturbed in the upper chamber of your home where I have slept. You must bring yourself into trance through the Eighth Spirit and project your *nephesh* to me. Your father must guard your privacy. Together as one being we will act to preserve my body from harm."

"I understand, Beloved."

*******   *******   *******   *******

On the evening of the New Moon *Yeshua* walked to the Brotherhood synagogue accompanied by Zeb and Stephanos. Azariah stayed home with Shoshana, and *Mar Belteshazzar* worked with others to prepare the conditions for the Ordeal.

First, *Yeshua* was to be locked into the empty cage of the lioness who had not been fed for three days. A pulley was rigged that would allow one of the Brothers to lift the iron gate separating the cages so that she could have free acces to *Yeshua*. No one would remain in the underground chamber to witness what happened because none of the Brothers wished to see *Yeshua* killed and eaten. He would be left with the beast until midnight. Then *Mar Belteshazzar* would descend into the chamber to see the result.

If *Yeshua* survived under these conditions, he would then be given an hour to rest while the furnace was stoked. He would then walk into the part of the furnace where pots were fired and metals melted. He would remain there until the fires subsided enough for *Mar Belteshazzar* to enter and see the result. That would be about two hours.

All the Brothers hugged *Yeshua* before he descended the stairs into the lion's chamber. *Mar Belteshazzar* kissed him and locked him into the empty cage. Nothing was said by either man. The last thing *Mar Belteshazzar* saw before he ascended the steps out of the chamber was the brave young man sitting on the earthen floor facing the gate where the snarling lioness stalked back and forth.

When the door leading into the chamber had been made fast, he signaled on of the Brothers to hoist the pulley.

In the dim lamplight that illuminated the chamber, *Yeshua* watched the iron gate creak slowly up. He watched the lioness stalking and backing away impatiently as the gate lifted into her cage. She was expecting food.

On the first floor, the Brothers head the gate creak to a halt. It was fully open. Then they heard a horrible, deep growl that literally shook the floor.

"Oy, he is a dead man!" cried Zeb in shock as tears filled his eyes. "This is murder that we have done!" He fell to the floor utterly despairing.

Mar Belteshazzar said nothing, but held up his right hand to signify silence. Everyone listened. There was no sound.

"He would not cry out if his body was slashed in two pieces," mourned Stephanos. "He is the best of men...the best of men."

"My Brothers, if *Yeshua* is dead, we can do nothing to help him. If not, then we must honor his request not to interfere with the Ordeals. Let us retire to our own homes and return at midnight to see the result."

Zeb tore his garment in grief and rage.

"No, Master. I shall stay here and guide his soul if he has been killed. But I shall not leave him, dead or alive."

Mar Belteshazzar gently took him by the arm, pierced his eyes, and quietly said, "You will not disturb the chamber or open the door until we return."

"No, Master. I will honor the agreement." He sank down again onto the floor.

Yeshua felt absolutely no fear of the lioness. He did not fear death. He could endure any pain. When the gate opened and the lioness challenged him with her awe-inspiring roar, he merely smiled. When she leaned back on her haunches as though to pounce and make and end of him, he raised his eyebrows, focused his eyes at a point between her eyes, and created a will from his solar plexus for her to sit back on her haunches. He projected this through a gentle, low intoning of *Ha-Shem*.

The lioness sat somewhat confused, shifting back and forth on her front paws. Now *Yeshua* became aware of Shoshana's presence floating above him to his right. He thought, "We are first going to remove her hunger. She has not eaten for several days."

From Shoshana a guiding suggestion: "I have eaten to my fill. My stomach is full. I am sleepy."

Yeshua projected this suggestion through sound using both solar plexus and throat: "Ah...oh...mm; ah...oh...mm..."

The lioness stopped shifting her feet and slowly lay down with head on paws. *Yeshua* stopped intoning.

"When she awakens, we must make her into a pet," he thought. "Meanwhile, let us commune and merge in spirit, my Darling."

Soon the lioness was snoring. *Yechid* and *Yechida* sat together in meditative bliss.

In her room, Shoshana had experienced difficulty in coming into trance. She realized that negative forces and suggestions were troubling her in subtle ways, so she stood and forcefully banished them. After this, she was able to bring herself into a trance in which she visualized exiting her flesh through the crown of the head. Soon she was visualizing herself with *Yeshua* in the chamber. In her vision, however, it was not dimly lit, but full of light.

As she became aware of the chamber in her *nephesh*-body, she saw that *Yeshua* had already held the lioness back on her haunches. She had perceived *Yeshua's* idea about removing her hunger. She translated this into a suggestion. *Yeshua* immediately took the idea and projected it. Together they temporarily subdued the lioness. But more would have to be done when the big cat awakened.

"She is very beautiful," thought *Yeshua*. "I will order that she be released back into the wild. While she sleeps, let us merge with her and form a communion of *netivot* so that she will become our pet."

Together they performed a communion with the soul of the sleeping lioness—*Yeshua* by projection and Shoshana by merging. They loved and appreciated the noble animal. They experienced her consciousness and lay with her in their *nephesh*-bodies.

Late at night the lioness began to stir. She lifted her head from her paws and shook herself awake. Seeing *Yeshua*, she slowly ambled over to him, sniffed, then lay down beside him. He stroked her chin and she nuzzled his legs. Then he saw the shackle-bands that had been locked onto her back legs so that humans could drag her against her will. Gently her rubbed her legs where they had chafed, found the spring bands, and unlocked them. He let them drop to the floor as each leg was freed.

The lioness licked her wounded hind legs for some time, then turned her head to *Yeshua* and licked his face.

At that moment the door into the chamber began to creak open. Light from large lamps cut into the cages as *Mar Belteshazzar* slowly descended the stairs.

The lioness started, but *Yeshua* and Shoshana told her telepathically, "You are safe with us. Lie quietly. We love you. We will return you to your home away from humans."

When he saw *Yeshua* with the lioness snuggled against him like a close pet, *Mar Belteshazzar* remained silent, but his Heart was overflowing with joy. He stood in wonder and awe at the sight.

Yeshua and Shoshana told their pet to return to the other cage. The lioness reluctantly obliged by raising up to her feet, shaking her head, then ambling back through the portal. *Mar Belteshazzar* signaled for the iron gate to be closed, and it slowly creaked back into place.

Yeshua slowly stood up and shook the dust from his robe. He felt just like the lioness.

Without a word, *Mar Belteshazzar* opened the iron leading from the chamber into the cage where *Yeshua* had been imprisoned, and the young man exited.

At this point *Mar Belteshazzar* could not contain his glee. Running ahead of *Yeshua* up the stairs he cried, "Brothers, come and see what *Yeshua* has done! Come! See for yourselves!"

Zeb reached down the stairway and grabbed *Yeshua*, pulling him up and into his rough embrace. He could not speak, and tears rolled from his eyes.

After greetings and congratulations from all, *Yeshua* requested that he have the next hour to himself before undertaking the furnace. He lay on a pallet in the library and closed his eyes. "Wake me when the fire is hot," he said.

"And," he opened his eyes, sat up, speaking firmly, "let Zeb guard this door. I want no disturbance while I sleep."

A few minutes later *Yeshua* had projected into his *nephesh*-body and was able to communicate with Shoshana.

"My body needs sleep," he said. "Please watch over me and the progress with the furnace. When the furnace is nearly ready, awaken me so that I can prepare."

He floated over his flesh body and soon slept in his *nephesh*-body. Shoshana watched the particles of vital force transmitted to his etheric and flesh bodies through the medium of his *nephesh*. They shimmered like globules of pure water or sparks from a camp fire as his bodies were refreshed and healed in sleep.

She placed her right palm over his etheric solar plexus and left palm over her Heart to increase vital force, then remained in that posture for some time. Then she disconnected and sped through the floor into the underground furnace. The Brothers were still stoking it with pitch, wood, and coal. They approached the stoking hatch, thrust in fuel with averted faces, then quickly stepped back The iron walls were starting to glow red-hot. No human being could survive in that heat.

She returned to *Yeshua* and awakened him in his *nephesh*.

"The furnace is very hot. You must enter it naked so that your robe will not immediately catch fire and burn your skin. You have *netivot* to your flesh body, but not to your robe."

Yeshua nodded agreement.

"When I stand naked before the furnace, we must merge. You look into my eyes, and I will visualize your eyes. Then I will call upon Messiah to evoke the Archangel Auriel from within our *Yetzer Ha-Tov* to protect my flesh from fire and heat. Now, I sense that the Brothers are approaching, but they are disputing whether to proceed. Zeb's Heart is full of doubt."

Yeshua stood up and found a rejected copy of a small manuscript that was to be destroyed. Then he removed his robe and walked naked through the door with the manuscript in his hand. Zeb was holding back Stephanos with a raised hand, commanding silence. His back was turned to *Yeshua*.

"He needs more rest. Can't you wait a while more?"

"No, Zeb. I am ready for the Ordeal," answered *Yeshua*. Zeb spun around, then relaxed.

After a silence, Zeb answered, "As you wish, *Ravi*."

"I am not yet Master of the Brotherhood," answered *Yeshua*.

"I believe that you will be in another hour," answered Zeb.

Yeshua bowed. "But perhaps I will be a very naked Master?"

This broke the tension and they all laughed.

"It is good that Shoshana is not here," joked Zeb.

Yeshua smiled to himself and began the descent into the furnace chamber. As he appeared on the stairs, *Mar Belteshazzar* and three Brothers greeted him.

"Very good! I see that you know how to work with fire," he remarked admiringly.

Yeshua held his right forefinger to his lips. Everyone became silent.

"Please be still and keep silence while I prepare, then you may all remain and watch," he said quietly.

He stood naked before the open furnace gate. Fire blazed. The heat outside the gate was unbearable.

He tossed the manuscript through the gate onto the floor where pots were fired. It immediately burst into flame and was consumed, leaving only a pile of smoldering ash.

All the Brothers gasped.

Yeshua stepped back and crossed his arms over his Heart—left over right—in the *nacham* posture. This signified submission of the personal self to the high self or *neshemah* and Divine Will. He closed his eyes of flesh and visualized Shoshana's clear, brown eyes before him. He felt his Heart bursting with love and appreciation for her. The merging was accomplished.

Then he placed both palms over his Heart—again left under right. With eyes still closed he began to intone *Ha-Shem*: "*Eeee-yaaah-oooh-way-eeee; Eeee-yaaah-oooh-way-eeee; Eeee-yaaah-oooh-way-eeee.*"

He intoned three times while sending forth this prayer:

"I evoke Thee, *Mashiah ben-Yosef*, anointed *Bar-Enash*, Thou Who art to come and manifest in Earth soul by soul, Thou Who shalt create and steward the new Heavens and the new Earth, Thou for Whom all power and authority art appointed—send Thine Archangel Auriel to protect my flesh in this Ordeal, for the sake of all Israel."

Suddenly the chamber grew unbearably hot. The Brother saw hot, white light radiating from *Yeshua's* naked skin. Light and fire blazed through the chamber. The men cried out in fear. *Mar Belteshazzar* pointed to the escape door, and they all scrambled up the stairs for their lives.

Even beyond the escape door the heat was so intense that the Brothers were forced to close it.

"*Yeshua* was not burned," cried out Zeb joyfully. "He is more than human—he is a god!"

"No," replied *Mar Belteshazzar*. "He is a great saint of God—greater, I think, than *Mar Daniel*. For *Daniel* was able to summon an angel to protect his three disciples in the king's furnace, but *Yeshua* will be able to withstand the furnace in his own naked flesh. If he had merely extinguished the flames through control of elementals, that would have been enough. But we have seen him become a greater flame that the fire itself. My Brothers, you have seen with your own eyes what many great saints and prophets have longed to see—a true Master greater that Solomon and Moses."

Shoshana was aware of being in a place of great light and bliss. She knew that all was well with *Yeshua* because she was one with him. Other than that, she remained in trance.

Yeshua opened his eyes. He was one brilliant flame. But like the burning bush of Moses, he was not consumed. He stepped forward through the gate into the furnace. The temperature was pleasant—not hot, not cool. He bent down and scooped up the ashes of the burnt manuscript.

Just then the escape door opened. *Mar Belteshazzar* peered down the stairs. The chamber was no longer unbearably hot because the source of that heat—*Yeshua*—had entered the pottery firing chamber of the furnace. He motioned for the Brothers to follow him down. They all moved tentatively down the stairs into the chamber.

Yeshua's naked body appeared to glow like molten metal. He lifted himself over the firing wall into the roaring flames. Now his body appeared to be a white-hot flame. He walked back and forth within the blazing fire, then stepped over the firing wall back into the pottery area. Now his body looked like molten metal.

Mar Belteshazzar cried, "There is no need to continue the Ordeal! You have succeeded. But please allow us to leave the chamber before you come out."

With that all the men climbed the stairs and again shut the escape door.

Yeshua heard nothing that *Mar Belteshazzar* had said. He was in union with Shoshana in their *neshemah* of the Seventh Heaven. His fiery body stood in *orant* prayer posture in the midst of the flames, for he had returned to the bowels of the furnace. The flames around him were red, blue, and yellow, but his naked body was a great white flame as he stood in wordless prayer and praise. He remained in that posture as though in trance for many hours.

The Brothers continued to look in on the miracle every half hour until the fuel was exhausted and the furnace was cool. Pre-dawn light arose in the Eastern sky when they finally descended the stairs.

Yeshua was standing in *nacham* posture on the floor of the chamber outside the empty furnace. He was facing West toward Jerusalem with his eyes closed in wordless prayers of thanksgiving. When the Brothers appeared he said simply through closed eyes, "You are safe now."

He opened his eyes and bowed respectfully to *Mar Belteshazzar*, Zeb, Stephanos, and the others, still in *nacham* posture. Zeb moved close to touch him.

"No!" warned *Yeshua*. The men stepped back.

"Please bring me my robe and sandals," he asked. Zeb jumped to comply, and a moment later *Yeshua* was no longer naked, and they all climbed the stairs and assembled in the library as the sun rose.

"I am famished," said *Yeshua*. "I shall go to the home of Azariah. But before that, I want you all to ponder something. Stephanos, when you saw me naked you joked and said, 'It is good that Shoshana isn't here.' But I tell you, Shoshana was here with me all night, and without her I would have been unable to succeed in the Ordeals."

The men looked at each other questioningly.

"Was this some kind of trick?" asked one of them.

"No," replied *Yeshua*. "I will tell you about that and many other things later. My main motivation for succeeding in the Ordeals, and the only reason I agreed to them, was to win the right to marry Shoshana. I leave you with this information to see what each of you might understand."

Mar Belteshazzar pulled on his beard and said, "My Brothers, there was no trickery. I am anxious to learn what this great man has to teach, and you should be as well. On the next *Shabbat* supper, we must all gather here for the Initiation. Afterwards I shall announce that *Yeshua* will be my successor."

All the men smiled and nodded in agreement. *Yeshua* took his leave, dragged himself to Azariah's home, and called for Shoshana.

She was standing at the upper threshold still in bedclothes. Sleepy-eyed Azariah appeared at the entrance to his room. Shoshana rushed down the steps and pulled him to the couch in joyful embrace, while Azariah raised his hands in the Orant posture and silently praised God.

All three spent the day at home snacking, napping, and recuperating from the Ordeals—for all of them had been drained by the experience.

Yeshua was released from work with pay for the rest of the week.

On *Shabbat* eve all members of the Brotherhood gathered at a huge wood-hewn table in a room never before seen by *Yeshua*. He recognized several men from the Synagogue of Babylon. Azariah sat next to Shoshana—the only woman present. All were attired in white linen tunics.

Yeshua had been seated outside the table. He had been told to wear only his normal garments, but to remove his sandals at the door. Everyone else had done the same. He had been cautioned not to speak or even smile in recognition, so he simply observed.

Mar Belteshazzar was seated on an elaborately carved cedar Throne. It had images of *Kerubim* on each side. He stood and raised his right index finger to his lips. Instantly the hubbub of conversation stopped. Raising a polished golden Chalice inlaid with precious stones, he began to intone the *Kiddush* praise. He was joined by the voices of all in unison. The Chalice was passed sun-wise around the table so that each person could partake, but not to *Yeshua*.

Next he elevated a large loaf of leavened bread on a silver platter embossed with multicolored ceramic and glass. As he began to intone the *Kiddush* he was joined by all voices. He broke the loaf, took a portion, and passed it anti-sunwise around the table so that all but *Yeshua* could partake.

When this part was over, *Mar Belteshazzar* motioned to Zeb, who left the table and approach *Yeshua*. Taking his right hand, he led him to the front of the table facing the Master. There he was asked to stand while all other sat, including *Mar Belteshazzar*, who now spoke from his Throne.

"Are you worthy to join the Wedding Banquet of *Messiah*?"

"It is my hope to become worthy," was his memorized response.

"Do you possess a proper garment?"

"My garment is the radiant light of my *neshemah*," he replied.

"Let this light shine," was *Mar Belteshazzar's* command. One of the Brothers took a white linen tunic that was hanging on the wall, held it to his Heart, and passed it to the next Brother. The ritual was repeated around the table until the garment was handed to *Mar Belteshazzar*. He motioned for *Yeshua* to kneel, kissed the seamless tunic, and drew it down over *Yeshua's* head. Zeb assisted with the arms. Then he stood up, took *Yeshua's* right hand, and raised him back to a standing position.

"May you become one of the Standing Ones," he recited, then added, "And I believe that you already are, my Son. Welcome to the Brotherhood."

As *Yeshua* looked at those around the table, they all stood in silence.

"Brothers—and Sister—this man has done what I could not do, and what no Master of this Brotherhood has ever been able to do. He has successfully passed the Ordeals of Daniel. By now you have all heard testimony from eye-witnesses. Please pay your respect to *Mar Yeshua*, my successor as Master of this venerable Brotherhood."

Every member bowed deeply. *Yeshua* bowed in return.

"Would you honor us with a teaching, Master?" asked *Mar Belteshazzar*. He stepped away from the Throne, led *Yeshua* to it and seated him upon it. Zeb brought the old man a large-backed chair from the altar in the West and he seated himself. Everyone else remained standing, as was the custom, including Shoshana and Azariah.

Yeshua sat for a long time with his head bowed, then drew a deep breath and began to speak.

"My Brothers, I told those of you that witnessed the Ordeals that I was not alone. Has any of you understood what I meant?"

After a silence, Stephanos replied, "You were with Shoshana, but not in this flesh."

Yeshua nodded.

"You and your intended Bride are somehow united as *yechid* and *yechidah*." Stephanos continued. "When we look, we see two persons. But somehow you are one being."

"That is correct," replied *Yeshua*. "And this is the meaning of the Messianic Wedding Banquet that we merely ceremonialize here. None of us can become whole and *shalem* by ourselves. The Archangels and all beings of the higher Heavens neither marry nor are given in marriages, because Divine Union has already been accomplished within them. It is the sacred interior marriage of *yechid* and *yechidah* that creates the true garment of *Or*, the Divine Light of God. When this is accomplished in the Heavens, it can manifest on Earth and in flesh. For me and my Beloved, this has already occurred in the Heavens. Soon it will be repeated on Earth. I would request that our wedding, the feast, and our seclusion, be done here in the Synagogue of the Brotherhood."

Everyone smiled and nodded. *Yeshua* continued.

"Listen to me. When Eve was taken out of Adam's body and formed into a woman, she was not meant merely to be a servant to Adam. She was formed by the *Elohim* as a twin, partner, and equal to him. What is more, without her union, Adam became incomplete. The *Elohim* formed Adam and the *Pardes* as a crowning achievement, then went one step further to form Eve. So who is the greater—Adam or Eve? Adam because he was the source, or Eve because she was the final and most beautiful achievement? When a man finds his Eve, then he must leave the home of his father and make a new home with his wife. It is the same in Spirit. *Yechid* cannot become *shalem* in isolation from *Yechidah*. Even more, without Shoshana's teaching, cooperation, and active participation, I could not have succeeded in the Ordeals."

Rav Shealtiel raised his finger.

"Then, Master, does this mean that we are to reverence Shoshana as we do you?"

"Indeed it does," replied *Yeshua*, raising his eyebrows and looking around the table.

"Is she, then, to share the role of Master of this Brotherhood?" asked one of the other Brothers.

Shoshana cleared her throat and spoke.

"No, Brothers. You may reverence me as a Sister and as the Master's wife. But I do command this one thing—*that you reverence your own wives even as Yeshua reverences me.*"

After a pause, *Rav Shealtiel* again spoke.

"I offer my obesience to all that has been proposed," and turning to Shoshana he bowed deeply. One by one all the other Brothers did likewise. Finally *Yeshua* and *Mar Belteshazzar* rose from their chairs and bowed deeply to Shoshana, who returned the bow in sacred *nacham* posture to all.

Yeshua turned to *Mar Belteshazzar* and whispered, then the old man made this announcement.

"*Mar Yeshua* wishes to sit with his bethrothed and her father, and wants me to take my position on the Throne of Daniel."

Several of the Brothers said, "Yes, that is good."

Yeshua held up his finger and spoke.

"I shall not assume this Throne until our beloved Master has no breath left in his body!"

Everyone smiled and nodded. *Mar Belteshazzar* had trained all of them and was well beloved.

"But you will teach those who wish to hear you on Saturdays in the library?" asked *Rav Shealtiel.* "I am anxious to hear the *razim* you can impart."

"I, too," joined Stephanos. Many others voiced the same desire.

"Then we begin tomorrow afternoon in the library," answered *Yeshua*.

Chapter Thirteen: SHOSHANA

"Hold still!" Shoshana demanded. *Yeshua* shifted his feet.

"It is harder to be still while you take these measurements than to sit all night in a cave," he mumbled.

"You will love your wedding garment," she countered.

Shoshana planned to weave a simple outer tunic of pure white linen for *Yeshua*. The linen would be brought from Palestine, where it was loomed for sacred purposes. She would weave it from one whole piece. It would be seamless—a requirement for Priestly robes.

"You know that the tunic of the High Priest, and all his garments, are symbols of *Or*, Divine Light. Your wedding tunic will glow like the moon and stars—whiter than snow on the Northern mountains. Now hold still if you want a good fit," she laughed. "My Aunt *Miriam* will bring the finest linen when she arrives next week. I don't want to make a mess of it."

Shoshana's Aunt *Miriam* was the youngest sister of Azariah. She had cared for Shoshana after the death of Azariah's wife. She was the only mother Shoshana had ever known. Now she lived as a wealthy widow in Magdala.

"This is the woman Mordechai loves," said *Yeshua*.

"Yes, and this is the woman who taught me to be a woman," whispered Shoshana playfully in his ear.

"Does she return his love?" he asked.

"I...don't know. But you can be certain Mordechai will be back in Babylon for our wedding. He and his clients do business with her all the time, and he knows she plans to be here for the wedding."

Yeshua felt a sudden pang of anguish. He didn't know why. This did not escape Shoshana, who looked at him intently.

"Did you know that *Miriam* was trained by *Rav Tzadok*?" she asked.

"What?" *Yeshua* knew of no female disciples.

"He trained her secretly. She knows as much as any Initiate of the Brotherhood, but she was never initiated. I am the only woman ever formally initiated."

"Do any of the Brothers know about her?" *Yeshua* asked.

"Only Father," she replied. "And he has promised to never reveal it."

"When I assume leadership of the Brotherhood—ow!"

"Sorry, Dear."

"I shall make it possible to initiate any qualified disciple—male or female."

"You won't get far with that, Beloved. You can tame beasts and walk through fire with many credible witnesses, but initiation for women will never be tolerated. You will destroy the Brotherhood if you try. Even if *Mar Daniel* himself appeared before all of the Brothers and commanded that women be admitted, they would consider it to be an illusory apparition of *Shaitan*! Maybe when *Messiah* appears on Earth, it will be different," she sighed.

Yeshua frowned.

"Now, I am done. You can sit down," Shoshana announced.

"I am looking forward to meeting the woman who taught you the wonderful secrets of womanhood," he said, falling onto a couch and smiling with a twinkle in his eye.

"You can look, but not touch," shot back Shoshana. "She is a very beautiful woman."

Yeshua had sent several letters to his Mother but never received a reply. He knew that despite his exorbitant delivery fees, she had not received them. There was no way to communicate with his family as Shoshana did with the wealthy *Miriam*, who had business covenants with all the major tradement and caravans. His only way to contact the family would be to make the journey himself, and this was simply not possible. These facts weighed heavily on his mind.

That night at dinner Azariah said, "Almost a year ago when you first arrived, I promised that if you did well, I would nominate you for advancement to Free Master in the Guild. *Yeshua*, you have done more than well, and I have nominated you for advancement to Master. There was unanimous agreement among the Masters, and you are to be promoted at a *Shabbat* ceremony in the Guild hall this Friday."

Yeshua was overwhelmed with gratitude.

"Thank you, Master."

"You needn't call me that any more, my Son. From now on, please call me Azariah."

Shoshana rushed to the kitchen and returned with a platter of delicacies usually reserved for *Shabbat*.

"Congratulations, my husband-to-be! And soon you can call me wife!" She hugged him and kissed his neck in a way that sent thrills up his spine.

Women were not usually allowed in the Guild hall, and never at a Guild meeting. But Shoshana was an exception. She was well known to all the stone masons, and especially to the Free Masters. She was welcomed into the hall and allowed to observe from the visitor's seat.

The *Shabbat* ceremonies were administered by Azariah. After recitations and prayers, *Yeshua* was asked to rise before the assembled eleven Guild Masters and take oaths of honor. There were no oaths of secrecy nor threats of punishment, as there had been in earlier degrees. However, he was tested on signs of recognition, which would be necessary to verify his status to other Masters of the Guild when he traveled to foreign regions. Finally he was invested with symbolic architectural tools of his trade as a Master and a white leathern apron to be worn only at Guild meetings. As Azariah tied the apron onto *Yeshua*'s waist, tears came briefly to the old man's eyes.

When done, he stood and presented *Yeshua* to the Masters.

"Tonight a terrible wrong has been made right. Our Brother *Yeshua* was denied advancement to the office of Free Master by jealous Guildsmen after the death of his father, the great *Yosef* of Nazareth. But we have come to know and marvel at his skill. Today he is more accomplished than any of the Masons of Galilee, and it is with great pleasure that we acknowledge and certify his office as a Free Master."

With this the banquet began. It had been prepared by men who brought their wives' contributions to the hall. Shoshana tried not to make faces as she sampled some of the offerings. *Yeshua* knew which things Shoshana had made, and he eagerly indulged himself in her food.

Yeshua and Shoshana started the short walk home, leaving Azariah back at the hall to reminisce with old friends. Suddenly Zeb appeared and caught up with them.

"Master…" he began.

"Please my friend, call me *Yeshua*. I will not be Master of the Brotherhood for many years, I hope."

"*Yeshua*…I have some bad news."

The walking came to a halt.

"Mordechai…"

"He's dead!" cried *Yeshua* in sudden realization. "How did it happen?"

"He was murdered in his sleep somewhere along the Silk Road three weeks ago. He and several other caravaners were butchered. No one knows who did it. Some of the Seleucian guards searching the roads came into Babylon this afternoon. That is how I heard."

Yeshua bowed his head and became very still, as though listening. Shoshana joined him. Then he looked at Zeb.

"Thank you, my friend. We shall arrange a private *ahavah* for all who knew him."

The two lovers walked on in silence. Finally Shoshana spoke.

"Aunt *Miriam* will arrive next month for our wedding."

Yeshua had been thinking the same thing.

"Mordechai had planned to meet her in Damascus with a caravan, according to his last message," he said.

"We must try to help Mordechai and *Miriam*, and we must begin tonight," said Shoshana with conviction.

"You have the Heart connection to lead the visitation with *Miriam*, and I am best to lead with Mordechai. We will speak to her in a dream, and we will strengthen Mordechai in his death process," *Yeshua* answered. "We will appear in your form to *Miriam*, and in my form with Mordechai."

That night they projected *nepheshim* and traveled instantly to *Miriam*. She floating above her flesh in sleep, but surrounded with dark entities.

"These are the *elilim* of bad dreams," *Yeshua* observed in a thought projected to Shoshana. "I shall dissolve them."

The lovers approached *Miriam* as a sphere of blazing light and the *elilim* vanished into the shadows.

"How can we keep them away from her?" thought Shoshana, examining the series of tunnel-like entry points used by the *elilim* to penetrate *Miriam*'s subtle sheaths.

"Let us repair the openings," thought *Yeshua*. "We shall cause them to heal by touching and intoning."

Momentarily the subtle wounds were repairing themselves and *Miriam*'s breathing became shallow and relaxed.

"You must awaken her *nephesh* and communicate with her," thought *Yeshua*.

Shoshana kissed her Aunt's forehead and her etheric eyes began to open. Shoshana touched *Miriam*'s *nephesh-heart* with her right hand, placed her left hand upon *Miriam*'s forehead, and held silent. She communicated what had happened to Mordechai in a flash, then pulled away. *Miriam*'s *nephesh* began to churn wildly in the space about her body until finally it flew up and out of the ceiling connected by the silvery cord that extended from behind her sleeping body.

"She will lead us to Mordechai," thought *Yeshua*. He and Shoshana followed the cord. It led them to the *nephesh* of Mordechai, which floated in a posture of deep separation and mourning directly above *Miriam*'s roof. It was covered in a black cloak. *Miriam*'s *nephesh* hovered agitatedly around the dead man's apparition, but neither were able to see or communicate with each other. Both were in states of great isolation.

"I shall try to penetrate Mordechai's self-imposed isolation," thought *Yeshua*. While Shoshana invisibly soothed *Miriam* by intoning and touching, *Yeshua* approached closer to Mordechai. Then he seemed to become very small and disappeared into the black cloak.

"You are merging with a dead man. Is that safe?" thought Shoshana.

Before she could panic, however, the cloak seemed to dissolve and *Yeshua* was revealed standing and trying to communicate with Mordechai, who had now risen up from his posture of mourning. *Yeshua* projected a thought.

"I have been murdered in my sleep."

Mordechai held completely still, controlling himself, and asked,"What has happened to me? I was having such a bad dream. It was as though I had been murdered in my sleep."

He was thinking to himself. He could not perceive the presence of anyone.

Yeshua produced another thought.

"*Yeshua* can help me."

Mordechai spoke slowly to himself: "Like the day *Yeshua* saved Zeb…bandits trying to kill me…*Yeshua* can help me…where is *Yeshua*?"

"*Yeshua* is here with me."

"Where am I? Is *Yeshua* here?"

Shoshana had an inspiration.

"Tell him that *Yeshua* is speaking to him." *Yeshua* immediately projected the thought.

"I…I think I hear *Yeshua* speaking."

"His voice is saying, 'Turn your face upward and seek for the Light of Heaven'," projected *Yeshua*.

Mordechai turned his face upward. Now *Yeshua* projected a powerful seed thought.

"When I turn my face upward, I prepare for my *aliyah* to Paradise. When I turn my face downward, I send comfort to those who love me."

Yeshua repeated this projected thought rhythmically, then began to intone it repeatedly. He was joined by Shoshana. Together they drove the suggestion into Mordechai's consciousness.

Miriam's *nephesh*-body had retracted through the ceiling and was again floating serenely over her sleeping form.

"We have done what we can do," thought *Yeshua*. "Let us return to our own places, my Love."

Instantly they were each floating above their physical bodies and sinking into sleep.

The next day was Saturday. *Yeshua* had promised to begin teaching at the Synagogue of the Brothers. After a leisurely breakfast, he walked with Shoshana and Azariah to the private synagogue and its hidden scriptorium. Already many of the Brothers had begun to assemble, including *Rav Shealtiel* and *Rav Belteshazzar*.

Yeshua seated himself. Everyone else stood.

"I want you all to sit with me. It is traditional and respectful to stand. But if you do, your feet will start complaining, and soon they will become more real than the teaching. Besides, should we make our revered Masters of the Brotherhood stand?" he said, bowing towards *Shealtiel* and *Belteshazzar*. "Please, sit down."

With great relief, everyone found a seat.

"Master, will you reveal to us your visions of the night?" Stephanos asked.

"Will you tell us about your *Merkabah* journey into the Heavens?" was Zeb's question.

Rav Shealtiel rose to his feet in objection.

"Brothers, Brothers! Have you learned nothing I taught you all these years? A prophet speaks only what Heaven gives him to speak. He cannot reveal everything he has seen. Would you tell people the intimate details of lovemaking with your wife? Show some sense and respect."

Then he sat down shaking his head and muttering to himself.

Yeshua cleared his throat.

"My Brothers, I do have words to give you. But do you have ears to hear them?"

He paused. Zeb and Stephanos looked down at their laps.

"Today we must try to understand something more about *Messiah*. We all know that *Mar Daniel* was shown the many kingdoms and rulership of men. They were like beasts. One usurped the other. Our school has produced many commentaries on their histories identifying one with the Persians, another with the Romans. We have tried to decipher the future by interpreting these allegories. But it is a fruitless task, for the mysteries of Heaven are not revealed in this way.

"The important part of *Mar Daniel's* vision is this: 'I saw one like unto a Son of Man.' The *Bar-Enash* is the New Adam of a coming humanity. He is both male and female, like the Archangels. He is the collective *neshama* of a new humanity who will not be ruled by beasts on the Earth, but by justice.

He paused and searched the face of each person. Finally *Rav Belteshazzar* raised a finger and asked, "How will that happen?"

Yeshua closed his eyes and spoke in measured words. "*Messiah* comes onto the Earth one soul at a time. He suffers in human flesh and sanctifies the Earth with his sacrifice."

Belteshazzar responded, "We know that he does not come like the *Messiah Ben David* of the Zealots—a conquering warrior who subjects all nations to Israel..." His voice trailed into a perplexed silence.

"No." replied *Yeshua*, "The *Bar-Enash* is the future fruit and *Neshemah* of a New Humanity, androgynous like an archangel or one who has achieved the *qimah*—not merely a human being with gender. *Messiah* comes through the conjunctions and marriages within our own souls, and with the return in flesh of all the prophets of Israel—yes, and even the prophets and righteous ones of the gentiles."

"And with the return of Elijah," remarked *Shealtiel*.

"When will this occur?" asked Zeb.

"I..." *Yeshua* hesitated. "I feel that Elijah has returned and even now walks the Earth."

The Brothers sat in stunned silence.

"The season of the Beast is coming to an end. We have entered into a time that will bring great tribulation for humanity. This has been brought about by humanity itself—not by Heaven. The coming trials will be like labor pains for the *Messiah*. After untold ages of suffering and self-purification, mankind will begin to bring itself to birth as a New Humanity.

"When the *'Olam ha-Ba* has fully arrived, all will see the Divine *Malkuth* on Earth. There will be many *Messiahs*, many prophets, many righteous ones on Earth. The Earth itself will be renewed and restored. Men and women will walk as equal souls in partnership. Things that seem impossible and miraculous will come to pass every day. Everyone will have the finest foods. Figs will grow to the size of a man's head. People will travel from Jerusalem to Babylon in the time it takes to walk from here to your homes."

Yeshua opened his eyes and again let his gaze pass over every face. Then he said sternly, "*Messiah* cannot come until each one of us prepares his way. Each one who is able must purify himself daily, send out prayers for the sanctification of the land and the people, develop the heights and depths of his own soul, and assist other souls. Each of us must shine the Light of Heaven into the darkness of our human world. We must overcome the evil archons and all their works. We must liberate first ourselves, and then others, from bondage to their service. We must become fully what Heaven has formed us to be."

Yeshua fell silent.

The Brothers were deeply impressed with what they had heard—not because much of it was different and more detailed than what the old men had taught them, but because there was a power and force to the words of *Yeshua* that planted them like germinating seeds into their Hearts.

"These are the words of Life," said *Rav Shealtiel*. "They are living things, like the alphabet of Heaven. Long have I studied, but now I begin to know."

Stephanos turned to Zeb and whispered, "He knows much more than he tells."

Zeb smiled and nodded. "He is much more than he appears."

Azariah raised a finger.

"Then, does *Messiah* somehow dwell within each of us?"

"Did you dwell within Abraham's loins?" was the reply.

Rav Shealtiel interjected, "My Brother Azariah, the *razim* of Heaven are perhaps not so easy to understand. I am sure that *Mar Yeshua* will have many things to tell us on another day, but as for now the fountain ceases to flow. Let us give him back to his Beloved and move on to other studies for the day."

All the Brothers stood, bowed, and silently moved out of the library. Shoshana stood looking at *Yeshua* with love, then walked over to where he sat.

"My Love, you feel very warm—almost fevered," she remarked, laying a hand to his neck.

"Yes," he answered hesitantly. "I have never sat as a teacher before. I was brought up into a state of bubbling, like boiling water. Yet I felt very calm. The words flowed from my mouth without thought."

"You were prophesying," she observed. "You spoke of the future. Do you remember what you said?"

"Oh, yes. It is etched into my Heart. It is what I *know*," he replied.

"Do you know what I'm making for supper?" she asked teasingly.

"Do you want to surprise me?" he smiled. "Then I won't look for it in my Heart. If it starts to pop up, I'll look away."

******* ******* ******* *******

"Master, I mean *Yeshua*!" cried Zeb from far below. "Shoshana has come for you!"

Yeshua lept down the huge brick steps of the Hanging Gardens to the plaza below.

"Darling, guess what?" cried Shoshana.

Yeshua looked into his Heart. An impression returned from the death of Mordechai a month ago. Suddenly he knew and replied, "Aunt *Miriam* has arrived?"

"Yes! She is at our home now. And she brought us precious and exquisite linens for our wedding clothes! You must come home now. Father commands it!"

Leaving Zeb in charge, *Yeshua* walked quickly with Shoshana to Azariah's house. In the street facing his gateway stood a donkey loaded with goods tended by a young Persian boy. The gate opened and a striking woman wearing simple white robes called to the boy, "Bring the large bundle—no, that one," she pointed.

Looking up, she saw the lovers.

"Ah, Shoshana, so this is your *Yeshua*!" She held the gate for the boy and waited for the two to catch up to her.

Yeshua bowed.

"Well, young man, I hope you know what a treasure you will have for a wife." *Miriam* smiled, but she probed him with her eyes seeking his response.

"Aunt *Miriam*, don't try to test my husband," laughed Shoshana.

But *Yeshua* smiled, pierced *Miriam*'s eyes with his own, and replied, "Dear Lady, I do know what a treasure I shall have for a wife."

Miriam paused, then responded warmly, "Yes, I believe you do."

"May I help with your things?" *Yeshua* asked. "It looks a bit much for your porter." Bowing again, he strode over to the donkey and began to help the beleaguered boy release the carefully balanced burdens.

"Your *Yeshua* is quite a man," whispered *Miriam*. "It was good you waited."

"Aunt Mirian, he is more than a man," was Shoshana's whispered reply. "He has survived the Trials of Daniel and taken *Belteshazzar's* position as Teacher of the Brotherhood."

Miriam drew a stunned breath and dropped a small spice urn. It shattered upon the stony ground. Both women knelt to retrieve what had spilled, but *Miriam* continued to stare first at Shoshana, then *Yeshua*.

"He wants to bring you into the Brotherhood. It would be a disaster," whispered Shoshana. "We will talk privately later."

******* ******* ******* *******

Shemesh burned low in the Western horizon when all members of the Brotherhood gathered in the courtyard garden. A sliver of Mother *Keseh*, invisible to all but most keen eyed, shone dimly above and to the left of the sun.

Mar Belteshazzar stood leading call and respose, intoning verses from the Song of Songs, while Shoshana and *Yeshua* sat on florid wedding thrones smiling into each other's eyes. He wore the white, seamless Priestly garment that Shoshana had designed for him. She wore a simple white robe. The richness of Miriam's alto voice added mysterious sweetness to the male voices of the Brotherhood, like honey poured over sesame cakes.

Azariah motioned for attention.

"The betrothal has been accomplished, the *Ketubah* has been made, the bride-price has been paid, and now the groom must offer gifts to the bride. If she accepts them, they will drink of the Cup of the Covenant to sanctify their union."

Yeshua motioned to Zeb, who handed him a simple golden ring and an exotic bracelet studded with precious stones that only queens could have possessed. Everyone was amazed—especially Shoshana. Had *Yeshua* robbed the King's treasury? How could he offer such a gift?

Yeshua looked into Shoshana's eyes and asked,

"Would you accept either of these gifts from me, Shoshana?"

"If you will adorn me with them, darling," she replied in a hushed voice.

"Which do you prefer, if I were to give you only one?" he asked.

Without hesitation she reached forward, slipped the simple ring onto her finger, and kissed it. Then *Yeshua* draped the royal bracelet over her other wrist.

"It is the gift of *Miriam*," he whispered. Shoshana's eyes darted to her aunt's face, her mouth open in wonder. "She gave it to me, and I have given to you," he added with a smile. "I don't think she intended for me to wear it!"

Azariah stepped forward. In his hands was a huge golden chalice filled with the finest wine. The chalice was studded with precious stones and skillfully cast representations of grapevines and pomegranates.

"And this is also for you, from my dear and very wealthy sister!" he exclaimed.

Yeshua sipped first from the fragrant wine, then passed the Cup of the Covenant to his betrothed. She sipped from his eyes as she drank from the Cup, signifying final agreement to the *Ketubah* and full sanctification of the marriage. She passed the chalice back to *Yeshua*.

"My Brothers and Sister," he declared, "there is far too much wine for us to drink, and since it is such fine wine, and the traditions have been fulfilled, let us all share in this Cup!" He motioned from his throne for Zeb to take the chalice first to *Miriam*. The other Brothers averted their eyes from her stunning beauty as she sipped. Then Zeb passed the chalice frist to Azariah, then the elders, then all of the Brothers.

The sun was sinking beneath the Western horizon to reveal a silvery crescent of the New Moon. Shoshana retired to her father's house with *Miriam* for for the bridal *mikveh*, and

Yeshua walked to their new home followed by Zeb, Arariah, the elders, and many of the Brothers. Here he would complete preparations for the bridal procession.

"In ancient times, men actually kidnapped their wives from neighboring clans," remarked Stephanos. "We Greeks tell legends of the stealing of Persephone and of the seven Samothracian women."

"Even in those days, I think that much was prearranged, just as it is now," *Belteshazzar* replied thoughtfully. "Yet even in these days the bride does not know the hour when her husband will come to take her home. She awaits nervously with friends and servants, lamps kept lighted, for the procession to her new home. *Mar Yeshua*, does she know much about her new home?"

"Ha!" he exclaimed. "She designed and furnished every inch of space, inside and out. She knows the whole house!"

Everyone laughed.

"Except for one thing…"

"And what is that?" asked Zeb.

Yeshua smiled slyly, bit his tongue, and said nothing.

"Oho! cried Stephanos. "The bed! The bed!"

Yeshua blushed and everyone hooted in glee. He stopped and looked at them all with eyebrows arched. Immediately the teasing ended.

"My friends, there is one tradition I will not keep. I will not come out of the house while you keep your merry vigil to show you the wedding tokens. What God has created between husband and wife is not for public show. So go to your homes after the procession. However, at the end of the seven days you may assemble at our new home and I will give legal testimony that we have established a true marriage of our flesh as well as our souls."

After a brief silence, *Belteshazzar* cleared his throat and announced, "Yes, this is the proper way to respect the sanctity of marriage. I agree."

All the Brothers nodded their agreement.

Yeshua indicated for all to stand outside his new home while he entered. He quickly lighted the lampsticks seasoned with fragranced oils, checked the supplies of dried fruits, grains, water, wine, and cheeses for the coming week-long seclusion, then returned to the company outside.

"Master, are you going to take your bride so quickly? Let her wait while we drink and tell stories. This is the tradition of the bridegroom."

Yeshua motioned for silence so he could answer the Brother.

"This is another tradition I shall not observe," he said firmly. "Come, let us take my bride."

Amid groaning and complaining, the men followed *Yeshua* to Azariah's home. As they approached, Zeb shouted joyfully, "Behold! The Bridegroom comes!"

Immediately *Miriam* and several of her servants appeared at the courtyard holding torches, which were lighted from the oil lamp in her hand. Several of the Brothers took the torches and assembled for the procession.

Azariah came forward with a royal *merkabah* or throne chariot drawn by four young boys, which was placed toward the rear of the procession. People in the nearby homes shouted encouragement from their doorways while *Yeshua* entered Azariah's courtyard and opened the front door.

There, in the brilliant light of a hundred lamps, stood his bride. She took his breath away, adorned in the finest robe and garments—dressed as a queen with bracelets, necklaces, and a crown. For a moment he couldn't speak.

"Take her," whispered *Miriam*, who had followed him into the house.

"I don't want to ruin her garments by picking her up," he whispered back.

"But this is the moment for which they were made," answered *Miriam*. "Pick her up!"

Yeshua approached Shoshana hesitantly, kneeled before her on one knee, and held out his arms.

"May I carry you to the chariot? It is traditional," he spoke in a hoarse whisper.

"Yes, my darling!" she whispered with a deep excitement, and lay herself carefully into his powerful arms. He stood up holding his queen and turned toward the doorway. Many faces that had been pressed together to watch faded quickly back to allow the King of the Night to pass with his kidnapped Queen.

In a moment they stood together in the golden chariot as it floated homeward surrounded by a sea of torches.

While the silvery crescent of Queen *Keseh* slipped behind the Western horizon in a lover's embrace with King *Shemesh*, the new bride and groom entered their nuptial chamber and sealed the door for seven nights and days of bliss and seclusion.

Chapter Fourteen: THE CURSE

"What are you thinking, my love?"

Yeshua reclined before the *Shabbat* table and sought for words. Then taking Shoshana's hand, he spoke.

"I remember *Shabbat* evening at my home when I was a child and my father was alive. *Abba* and *Imma* always retired early, but I never heard my father snore. In the morning they remained secluded for a long time after we were all awake and I heard *Imma* laughing."

"Of course," Shoshana smiled. "At *Shabbat*, *Adonai* and *Matronit* make love. Without that the world would cease to exist."

"*Adonai* and *Matronit* never get old or die, but we do. How was your father able to live without his beloved wife? And at *Shabbat*, what did he do?"

Shoshana was silent for a moment.

"My mother died in childbirth, so I never saw her with my father. I knew only Aunt *Miriam*. But I do remember that on *Shabbat* eve, father left me always with *Miriam* and secluded himself. I think that he somehow communed with my mother's soul."

Yeshua looked questioningly into Shoshana's eyes.

"He no longer secludes himself, does he? At least, not for the many times I have shared the meal with him. Yet he has never remarried. I wonder why?"

"Perhaps you should ask him," she replied. "I don't know."

Yeshua drew her close to him and whispered, "I don't know how I could live without you beside me—and I don't mean a bodiless spirit, but as a woman of flesh and blood."

Shoshana put her finger to his lips, but he gently removed her hand and spoke again.

"I know that we must all grow old and die. I know that there will be a time when one of us will no longer be present in flesh. I can't bear it. I don't have the strength."

She felt his heart bursting with grief, though there were no tears or sobs.

"Darling, stop! Nothing can ever separate us—certainly not a little thing like death! We shall always be with each other, and if one of us remains behind in flesh, it will be only for a little while."

Yeshua felt a small, warm flame kindling within the foreboding that flooded his heart.

"Yes, my love. Nothing shall ever separate us."

*******   *******   *******   *******

Miriam had departed for Magdala before *Yeshua* was able to propose her initiation to the Brotherhood. He knew that Shoshana had urged *Miriam* to leave before he could meet with the Brothers, but he did not resist. It was, after all, still their year of the marriage Jubilee. However, *Miriam* had promised to deliver a letter to his Mother and family in Nazareth letting them know of his circumstances. He knew that *Miriam* would deliver the letter without fail, and this relieved his mind.

Yeshua continued to work his short week, which allowed him to spend a great deal of time with Shoshana, planning and expanding the construction of their modest home.

Weeks passed into months, and far sooner than he and his bride would have liked, *Yeshua* was obliged to return to fulltime work. The new pattern of absence created pressures that resulted in occasional hurt feelings and lovers spats. Both Shoshana and *Yeshua* began to learn the ways of true marriage in a world far more complex than the dream life of romantic lovers.

Yeshua continued to teach the Brotherhood of Daniel, but his insistence upon the spiritual equality of women and men began to inspire an opposing faction among the Brothers. It was represented by one of the elders named *Rav Ubar* who had not witnessed *Yeshua's* success in the Trials of Daniel.

"We did not see the miracles that *Rav Belteshazzar* and the other friends of *Yeshua* have claimed for him, but we do know doctrinal errors when they proceed from the mouth of one unworthy and untrained. Brothers, this succession of leadership came without our full knowledge and consent. We must take action."

Yeshua finally understood why Shoshana had insisted that he not propose to initiate *Miriam*. Yet whether he did or not, opposition was certain to grow.

"Why can't I bring together people in unity?" he asked Shoshana. "They are just like the Brothers who accused me of oath-breaking in the Guild after my father's death."

Shoshana took his hands and looked into his eyes for a long time, then spoke to him in measured tones.

"It will always be like this for you, my love. You will confront them with the Way of Life, but many will choose the Way of Death, thinking they do God's Will. Their hearts have been blinded by the glare of false human doctrine and the glamor of their own ambition."

Azariah urged *Yeshua* to privately demonstrate miracles for *Rav Ubar*, but he refused.

"Even if I did so, he would come to doubt his senses and turn against me. No, he and his faction don't need miracles, but *emunah*—fidelity to keep faith with the Spirit within that knows and recognizes spiritual truth. They lack faith. It is a covenant that they must build within their hearts. I cannot do it for them."

"Then you must expel them from the Brotherhood," cried *Rav Belteshazzar*.

Yeshua paused, then said, "No. But I shall offer *Rav Ubar* the right to dispute with me before the assembly of the Brothers."

The following Saturday every member of the Brotherhood gathered at the Synagogue of Daniel for the disputation. Brothers sat around the long table while others stood in the remaining spaces. *Yeshua* presided at the head of the table with close friends and elders. He held up his hands and quieted the assembly.

"My Brothers and dearest Sister, today we must hear the grievances of *Rav Ubar* and the Brothers who support him."

Ubar immediately stood and began to speak.

"Brothers, all of the prophets, kings, and judges of Israel have been men. Adam was created first, and Eve from his rib. The proper position of women is to assist their husbands and raise their children. All Scripture verifies these facts. It has never been traditional for a woman to sit with men to study the Divine Mysteries, and it should not be allowed in this Brotherhood!" He abruptly sat down.

"Does anyone wish to dispute to what *Rav Ubar* has said?" asked *Yeshua*.

Stephanos rose hesitantly from his seat.

"Brothers and elders, I am a young man and a Greek, but by divine grace I have been accepted and initiated into this Brotherhood. Let us examine what our elder *Rav Ubar* has said.

"First, he tells us that all the prophets, kings, and judges of Israel have been men. While it is true that most of them were men, there were also great women among them. Was not Deborah a warrior who defeated our enemies? Did not Judith do what no man could accomplish? She cut off the head of Holofernes and saved Israel by her own hand, like David. What is more, there have been many women prophetesses of Israel, although mostly among the Diaspora. We know them as the Sybils, and we revere their utterances. So we must recognize, as our Master *Yeshua* so strongly affirms, that Heaven acts and speaks through great women of Israel."

Stephanos paused while a tide of whispers flowed around the room.

"Second, my Brothers, it is not true that Adam was created first. He was not created, but divinely generated, and he was made *last*, on the Sixth Day, as the crowning achievement of Divine emanation. But Adam was both male and female, like the angels, until the Blessed One divided him and produced from his heart—not his rib—the first women Eve. So in fact, Eve was the final perfection of mankind."

Ubar jumped to his feet.

"But it was she who was seduced by the Serpent and caused the downfall of Adam! That is why we have lost Paradise, and that is why she must bear children in pain and agony." He looked around while others nodded their heads.

Shoshana stood up. Everyone was stunned. Even though she was an initiate, she had never before claimed her right to speak before the Brotherhood. *Yeshua* held up his hands and demanded attention.

"My Sister, what do you say?" He felt his heart pounding and took several deep breaths.

"Brothers, we do not live in ancient times. This is the beginning of the Age of the Messiah foreseen by Daniel. We must listen to the Spirit of *Hochmah* and learn from Her. Let me correct my Brother Stephanos. It is not true that Eve was the final perfection of mankind. The Blessed One generated Adam as Mankind, the Father-Mother of all men and women. But he merely separated Adam into two parts. The man we call Adam derived from the wisdom of his mind, while the woman we call Eve derived from the wisdom of the heart. So men and women are different—not one subordinate to the other, but both equal brothers and sisters. The sin of Eve was also the sin of Adam, who was forced to work among the briars and thickets and wear a coat of skins. You all know that means both Adam and Eve were expelled from the Third Heaven of Paradise and incarnated in flesh to labor on this Earth.

"Yes, we women suffer in childbirth, but so do all children—male or female—and so does Messiah suffer in the Birthpangs of the New Humanity. And it is also true that men suffer grievously in their lives, labor, and warfare—often, I think, more grievously than women in childbirth."

Many of the Brothers nodded vigorously.

"So if we are brothers and sisters in the sufferings of life, we must be Brothers and Sisters in the *gnosis* of life," she concluded and took her seat.

It began slowly—one rap, then another joining in, until finally the great majority of the Brothers were smiling and rapping their knuckles upon table, floor, or wall. This was the sign of strong approval used in the Brotherhood. *Ubar* and those sitting with him looked around and grimaced. They had lost—for now.

Yeshua's heart swelled with love and pride for his Shoshana. He drew another deep breath and raised his hands for silence.

"My Brothers, you are growing in the true teachings of Messiah. You are hearing the *Bat Kol* speaking in your True Heart.

"There is a great woman, trained, initiated, and made worthy by *Rav Tzadok*. I had wanted to bring her into the Brotherhood, but my wife arranged for her to return to Palestine before I could make the proposal. Shoshana does not want to force women upon the Brotherhood if it will result in disunity. We all respect *Rav Ubar* and those who disagree, but there must come a day when another worthy Sister will appear."

Yeshua looked upon *Ubar* and asked, "Elder Brother, do you accept my wife Shoshana as a true Sister of the Brotherhood? She has been trained, tested, and formally initiated just as you have, and she has tested with greater abilities than any of the Brothers. Do you accept her as a true Sister of the Brotherhood?"

This was a clever move. If *Ubar* answered in the affirmative, that would open the door to other women initiates. If he answered in the negative, he would have admitted disloyalty to the Master of the Brotherhood of Daniel, for Shoshana was his wife and had been pledged loyalty by all of the Brothers. If he showed disloyalty, *Yeshua* would then have the right to demit him from the order.

Rav Ubar stood silent, then turned and left the room. No one else followed.

"We will await Brother *Ubar's* reply," announced *Yeshua*. "And now let us have some refreshment and continue our studies."

Shoshana privately drew him aside and said, "Why did you antagonize *Ubar*? He is a powerful *magos*. I am afraid of what he might try to do."

Yeshua assured her that he would speak with *Ubar* and assuage his feelings. But as time passed, his attempts to speak with *Ubar* were frustrated. Eventually he stopped trying.

*******   *******   *******   *******

Azariah's hand lay gently upon Shoshana's slightly protruding belly.

"Will you bring us a grandson or a granddaughter?" he asked. "You can see and know many things. What do you see, my daughter?"

Shoshana closed her eyes, then opened them.

"I see many, many girls!" she shot back.

"No you don't," he replied.

"But you want boys, not girls—right *Abba*?" she teased.

Stung with the realization that what she said was true, Azariah blushed.

"And what about you, my love?" she asked *Yeshua*. "Do you want a son?"

Yeshua smiled, then replied, "Whether girl or boy, the child will become worthy of initiation into the Brotherhood even younger than you did, my sweet love!"

Beneath the banter Azariah was aware of an ominous feeling. Shoshana's mother had died in bringing her to birth, and Shoshana had a deep fear of dying in childbirth.

Lately Shoshana had a recurring dream in which she sickened and died far short of full term, the baby was born dead, and *Yeshua* killed himself to be with her in death. She had not told him or her father of this, but they sensed her anxiety.

That night *Yeshua* lay sleepless. Something was wrong. He scanned the psychic space around their bedroom for intrusion but could find none. Yet—something was wrong. He prayed for God to show him what was wrong, but when he was finally able to sleep, his dreams seemed to reveal nothing.

That morning he confronted Shoshana.

"What is wrong, my darling? I know that something is wrong."

Shoshana averted her eyes. "All will be well," she said.

He gently took her hands and again asked, "Darling, what is wrong?"

She took a deep breath and told him all her fears and nightmares.

"It is only that which we don't speak, don't recognize, and don't allow ourselves to see that can harm us," he said. "Now that there is another soul being formed your womb, I can't see into your soul the way I used to. Something interferes."

"I know,"she replied. "I can no longer see as I used to. Something has dimmed my psychic sight, and I can no longer travel in my *nephesh* as I used to do with you. I am afraid…"

"You are vulnerable, and we are both blind to danger. Something is happening—someone is trying to harm us. We are both losing our powers while the new soul is forming in your womb. What can we do for protection?" *Yeshua* asked.

"You cannot make the Ascent and neither of us can see or hear clearly in the invisible worlds. You must go to *Mar Belteshazzar* to seek help," Shoshana urged.

That afternoon *Yeshua* sat with *Mar Belteshazzar* at the Synagogue of Daniel to discuss the problem.

"There are many powerful Priests and magi in Babylon," the old man remarked. "Many are for hire. You need to identify both the sorcerer and the patron before you can counter their influence. But because of Shoshana's pregnancy and your unique communion with her, your powers are temporarily diminished. How can you identify your enemies if you cannot track them?"

"I know who my enemy is," replied *Yeshua*.

"You mean *Rav Ubar*?"

"With very little question," *Yeshua* snapped back.

"But you must be absolutely certain."

"That's the problem. It's like defending yourself blind without knowing who, when, where," shrugged *Yeshua*. "That's why I need your help. I need to be certain before I act."

"What can I do?" asked *Belteshazzar*.

"Tell *Ubar* that you have become sympathetic to his views about women and that you are disillusioned about me. Tell him what he wants to hear, then listen deeply to what he says about me and Shoshana and how he says it. When you can sense the venom in his heart, tell him you want to lay a curse upon me. Ask him for the name of a sorcerer."

Mar Belteshazzar shuddered. "It goes against every moral instinct."

"You must learn to deceive those who deceive others," replied *Yeshua*. "Remember *Yakob*'s deceit of Laban after Laban's treachery. But there is much more at stake here than a flock of sheep! You must do it for my sake, Shoshana's sake, and for the Brotherhood."

Belteshazzar closed his eyes and remained silent for a moment. Then he turned his face to *Yeshua* and spoke with great resolve.

"I shall begin today."

That night as they prepared for sleep, *Yeshua* invoked the Archangel *Michael* to guard Shoshana's *nephesh* from the evil suggestion that was being propelled into her heart. For the first time in many weeks she slept well and awakened refreshed.

However, with each new day she became weaker. Her legs and feet began to swell, and often her face flushed a crimson red, and she became too dizzy and nauseated to stand.

A week passed with no report from *Mar Belteshazzar*. Although Shoshana had experienced no nightmares, *Yeshua* knew that she was sinking into greater danger. He went again to see *Belteshazzar*.

"He has made it very difficult for me to meet with him," the old man reported. "Something always seems to interfere. I think that he must be working with a powerful sorcerer."

"Then we must find a more powerful one," *Yeshua* replied. "How can we find one?"

"I have never had any dealings with such people, but possibly Stephanos can help us," the elder Brother suggested.

"Your experience confirms my feelings about *Ubar*. I, too, was met by interference when I tried to see him. The problem is that I cannot stop the curse by dealing only with him, and only he knows who is working the curse. I shall go to Stephanos."

With that *Yeshua* walked directly to the Stephanos' home, but the young man was not there. He was beginning to feel lost and powerless. It was not he, but Shoshana, who was in danger, yet he had no use of his powers—powers that he had always depended upon to lead him by the most direct paths. He could not consult his heart, so he was dependent upon his mind to lead him. It proved to be a poor guide for matters like this.

That evening he took up a position next to Shoshana, but on the floor. He sat up with hands on his ankles and head bowed between his knees, as the Prophet Elizah had done on Mount Carmel. He called upon Elijah to show him the nature of the danger that he perceived.

Eventually he fell into a trance. When he awakened, he could hear Elijah's voice still echoing in his mind.

"The curse was predetermined when Shoshana was born. It is *Sarpasapa*, the Curse of the Serpent. The pitiful efforts of evil men to harm you never had any power. Their evil magical works were mere ripples from the great and tragic tide that now engulfs you. It was the Ruler of this evil age that carefully laid this snare for you both.

"Your love for each other is the instrument of this curse. If you had never met, the curse could not have been activated. If you had never loved, the curse could not be activated.

"Go to a great Magian Astrologer to understand what you now face. But there is no remedy. It is too late, my Son."

Yeshua arose early and knocked at the door of the Temple of the Magi. There was no answer, so he persisted by trying to find another place of entry. Finally he was recognized by the gardener, who supervised plant maintenance at the Hanging Gardens.

"How can I find a Magus Astrologer?"

"They are easier to find during the evening. Now, in the morning light, they are sleeping," the gardener answered.

Suddenly an old man appeared from a hidden entry to the Temple. He walked toward them.

"That is *Shamash-Nasir*, the Teacher," whispered the gardener.

"Sit with me, young man," said the Teacher pointing to the hidden entry. *Yeshua* followed him inside to a study filled with manuscripts and astronomical tools. The old Teacher motioned for him to sit.

"I was told in a dream that you would come this morning. My wish is only to serve you, young Master. Tell me the date and time in question."

Yeshua knew the exact date, time, and place of Shoshona's birth because it was written below an image of her mother that she kept in their bedroom.

"This will require time. Please sit quietly while I do the calculations," the Teacher said.

Yeshua sat in contemplation while the old man worked. Suddenly he realized that Shoshana's birth information was kept in one place other than their bedroom. It was part of the Brotherhood records, where it could have been accessible by *Ubar*.

Slowly a vision of knowledge formed in his contemplative mind. *Ubar* recording the birth information for Shoshana, handing it to a sorcerer, the sorcerer doing calculations, then writing glyphs on a brass plate while making incantations.

"I have it now," the old man droned, "and it has a serious problem."

"Is it something called a Curse of the Serpent?" asked *Yeshua*.

"Yes. How did you know that? But the horoscope is extremely complex. This is the horoscope of a very great and talented soul. Nothing can stop her as long as she does not take a husband or become pregnant with child. But if she does, then the child will kill her and die. See the fifth house, the seventh, the sixth. See the yoga formed by *Ishtar* and *Rahu*. This is the most deadly form of a *Sarpasapa*. I have never seen it so exact."

"Is there a remedy?" asked *Yeshua*.

"Propitiation of *Ishtar* through worship and sacrifice to the Goddess here in the Temple on given days and hours—or possibly to the Serpent *Rahu-Ketu*. Unless…"

"Unless what?" the young Master shot back.

"Unless…someone skilled in evil magic has so inflamed the Serpent *Rahu-Ketu* that he is even now poisoning her blood. Then there would not be propitious time for the remedy to be established. Today the Serpent wheels backwards into the lunar mansion that can bring sudden death."

"Does this mean that the entry point for a black magician would be the child forming in the womb—not the mother?" asked *Yeshua*.

"Yes, that would be the Fifth House," was the old man's answer.

Sudden revelations raced through *Yeshua's* mind. That was why Shoshana could be relieved of her nightmares, but not from her increasing sickness. As the fetus grew, the sickness grew.

"If the fetus were removed, would it stop the Curse?" asked *Yeshua*.

"Probably so," was the answer.

"I thank you deeply," said *Yeshua* as he rose to leave. "We are Jewish. I don't know how we could propitiate any of these deities."

"You have the *Teli* and the Archangels—it could be done by careful correlation, my Son."

As *Yeshua* ran home to Shoshana, he tried to see himself propitiating astral deities. Could there be correlations? Or could the fetus be removed?

He entered the courtyard out of breath and saw Azariah at the door.

"She is in your bed," answered Azariah before *Yeshua* called for her.

"What is wrong?" the young man asked.

"She is having pains," he replied.

"But she is not due for another six months." *Yeshua* spoke softly to himself.

He entered the bedroom, which she had asked to be darkened with curtains. She lay half asleep, curled up around her belly. *Yeshua* felt her hands. They were clammy.

"What is it, my love?" he asked gently.

Shoshana moved her head toward him with her eyes shut.

"I am afraid…that I am having some bad pain," she gasped.

"May I pull the covers down?" he asked. She nodded.

Her feet and legs were incredibly swollen and purple, as though she had been stung by wasps. He lay his hands upon them. They were burning hot.

"Azariah, Azariah!" he shouted. "Get a physician immediately!"

He covered her legs with sheets cooled in water and began to intone with hands upon the soles of her feet to awaken her own bodily resources for healing and balance. She moaned.

Finally Azariah arrived with a physician.

"This is *Sin-Nasir*. He has left another patient to see Shoshana," the old man explained breathlessly.

The physician carefully examined Shoshana's legs and questioned her for symptoms. Then he motioned for the two men to consult with him outside of the bedroom.

"This is a condition that can be remedied only by removal of the child from the womb. It is called the Demon that Strangles. If the child is not removed, she will swell and strangle inside of herself and die," he advised in a matter-of-fact voice.

"What…is the procedure?" asked *Yeshua*. "Is it dangerous?"

"I must reach inside of her womb and bring the child out with tongs. This will kill the child, but it may save the mother," the physician answered.

"But how dangerous?" snapped *Yeshua*.

"Sometimes a woman lives, and sometimes she doesn't," he answered. "But if the procedure is not done, she always dies in terrible pain."

"How much time do we have to make a decision?" asked Azariah.

"With her symptoms, she may have a seizure and die tonight," was his answer.

Yeshua fell on the floor and tore his garment. Azariah was unable to move or speak.

"I must also warn you that there will be better chance of success with your wife if the procedure is done immediately. Waiting will be fatal," warned *Sin-Nasir* in a stern voice. "I left my other patient behind when Azariah told me her symptoms because waiting is always fatal."

Yeshua tried to search his heart for guidance, but none was forthcoming. He felt completely lost and abandoned by Heaven.

"Then as her father, I authorize the procedure to be done as soon as possible," cried Azariah.

"Do you agree?" asked the physician, laying his hand on *Yeshua's* trembling shoulder.

"Yes…yes," the broken young man whispered. "As soon as possible."

Sin-Nasir immediately left to make arrangements for the surgery.

Yeshua kept vigil by Shoshana's bedside, held her hand, and gave her remedies for pain that Azariah had procured from the physician. She was becoming increasingly uncomfortable, slowly turning one way then the other with the waves of pain that flowed through her body. Her breathing became a kind of panting.

He was Master of the Brotherhood of Daniel, of the elements, of the animals. But where was his mastery now? Even masters could not cure the incurable, or raise the dead. He called silently to the Almight One for power to help, for strengthening Shoshana, for success in the medical procedure. That seemed all he could really do. His heart was breaking.

Sin-Nasir arrived after sunset with a woman assistant.

"I shall have to ask everyone to leave the room," he ordered. "Especially you, young man."

Azariah, took *Yeshua's* arm and led him outside to the courtyard. The young man did not resist.

Suddenly they heard horrible screaming, then silence. *Yeshua* lept forward and burst into the bedroom. Shoshana lay limp and white on the sheet with a great quantity of blood staining her thighs and legs. In his tongs the doctor held a bloody piece of flesh that was once a fetus. The woman assistant was reaching into Shoshana's womb for parts that might not have come out. But Shoshana lay unconscious, her mouth open and her eyes squeezed shut.

"Please leave the room!" the physician roared.

Yeshua couldn't move. He stood paralyzed, his mouth open and his eyes frozen open. He sensed Shoshana's *nephesh* for the first time in months, and he knew that she was entering inevitably into death.

Azariah dragged *Yeshua* again from the room. Within minutes *Sin-Nasir* and his assistant emerged from the room whispering to each other. The assistant immediately left without a word. Shoshana was unconscious and dying.

"I wish to sit with my wife while she dies," said *Yeshua* in a soft and defeated voice.

"Yes," was the physician's reply. "I am so very sorry." He bowed and left.

Yeshua knelt by Shoshana's bedside, looked heavenward, then placed his left hand over his heart and right hand over her heart. He summoned his vital force and sent it surging into Shoshana's solar plexus. But she did not awaken. Her brain was already dead. Instead, he became more and more drained. He wished to die with her, and he continued to pour his diminishing vital force willingly into Shoshana's empty body.

Azariah sat next to *Yeshua* until finally the young man slumped to the floor as though dead. Then he put his head into his hands, separated *nephesh* from flesh, and quietly began the procedure that would consciously create his own death.

Much later, after the lamp had burned low, Stephanos and *Belteshazzar* burst into the room.

"Look, they have all died!" cried Stephanos.

Belteshazzar held up his hand for calm. Azariah's body had fallen to the floor alongside *Yeshua*. Slowly he touched Azariah's mouth.

"Azariah has died. He has no breath and no warmth."

Then he knelt next to *Yeshua* and touched his mouth.

"There is no breath, but the lips are still warm. Quick, turn him onto his back," he commanded. "Transmit vital force into his heart."

Stephanos acted quickly.

Belteshazzar examined Shoshana's cold body. Then he cried aloud and slumped onto the floor.

"No one can bring her back! The cord has been severed," he wailed, tearing at his garment. "The evil ones have triumphed."

"Not completely," whispered Stephanos. He stood up and pointed to *Yeshua*. The young man had started to breathe.

******* ******* ******* *******

Yeshua did not speak to anyone.

He buried the corpses of Shoshana and Azariah privately in the Brotherhood cemetery, doing all the labor himself. Over his wife's tomb he hung their wedding canopy and adorned it with unripe fruits, as was the custom for a dead bride. He entombed her bloodied sheets and their half-formed child with her, as both blood and unborn fetus were considered to be parts of her body.

Yeshua sat by the tomb in prayer day and night for seven days. Consuming only enough food and water to maintain life, he felt Shoshana agonizing in her *nephesh* until the third day, when she awakened in complete separation from the flesh of her corpse. She was no longer in pain.

He felt her merging with him, smiling and kissing his forehead. He could sense her in the subtle fragrance of lilies that pervaded the environment as she drew near—night or day. But each time he sensed her presence, he realized that he would never again feel, touch, and know her in the way he always had. Then he found himself overwhelmed by a sea of grief.

Grieving made it still impossible for him to rise out of his body in his own *nephesh* to be with her. Moreover, he knew that in about six weeks she would die the Second Death, leave her *nephesh*-body behind to dissolve back into its elements, and ascend in the *neshama*-spirit. How then would he have any way of knowing or recognizing her?

At the end of this week he sat with *Mar Belteshazzar*, Zeb, and Stephanos at the Brotherhood table.

"I renounce my office as Master in the presence of you three witnesses, whose testimony will not be doubted."

After a silence, Stephanos asked, "Will you take vengeance?"

Yeshua sighed deeply.

"Justice belongs to God," was his reply.

There was another awkward silence, then *Yeshua* said, "Tomorrow I leave Babylon."

"Where will you go, Master? Let me come with you," begged Zeb.

"Beloved Brothers, please understand that my wish is to be alone. I have learned that I know nothing. I must devote the rest of my life to seeking God's Way and reuniting with my Beloved."

There was nothing more to be said.

At the next sunrise he departed Babylon along the Eastern river road from which he had come. He took only his staff, sandals, blanket, and purse. Carefully folded deep in his purse he carried the seamless white garment that Shoshona had made for him. He vowed to wear it again only when he had found his God and his *Yechida*.

Chapter Fifteen: THE WANDERER

It was not his plan to wander toward the East. His only goal was to be in the wilderness far from the human vibration so that he could devote himself to communion in the *nephesh* with Shoshana. Her time would be only about forty days, then she must undergo the Second Death.

Yeshua slept on high ground in protected areas that could not be reached by occasional caravans so that he could project his *nephesh* to be with Shoshana. He transmitted what he knew about the causes of her death and their separation, and she helped him to gain better understanding of what they had experienced. They did not speak in words, but instant transmissions of *manda*, or what the Greek called *gnosis*.

Shoshana did not want to die the Second Death. She would rather exist as a sidereal *nephesh*-soul in her human identity and remain with *Yeshua* until he died. She could be kept alive in the *nephesh* through occult means, but they both knew that would sever their carefully constructed communion with *neshama*-spirit and destroy all the spiritual work that they had been destined to accomplish.

As the end of the forty-day period approached, they made a pact. Shoshana would manifest her spirit to *Yeshua* through the fragrance of the lily, and *Yeshua* would seek to better know the Way of the Messiah. Shoshana—no longer Shoshana, but *Yechida*—would remain ever with him in spirit. He would be able to feel her presence and know her counsels. Then one day, when she could see him fully prepared, she would inspire him to again teach the Way of the Messiah.

The Full Moon rose in the East making the wilderness seem almost like a winter morning. The call of birds and other animals punctuated what would have otherwise been a dark and silent night when *Yeshua* lay down for what he knew would be his last communion with Shoshana. At the Second Death, the *nephesh*-soul or human personality begins to disintegrate just as the physical body does at death. It releases the higher monadic principles and the animating spirit returns to its *neshama*, where it resides in the Third Heaven of Paradise until born again into flesh, or slowly ascends to the Eighth Heaven, where it dwells with other ascended Masters at the *Merkabah*-Throne of God.

Once it has experienced the Second Death, the spirit-soul is no longer male or female. It no longer has personality, nationality, a human language. It becomes like the angels and can speak to those in flesh only in the modality of angels—through sacred impulses, symbols, dreams, memories, inspirations. Thus it was now that *Yeshua* truly must lose Shoshana as he had known her, and learn to recognize and commune with her divine eternal spirit.

A profound sadness and sense of loss enveloped the young Master as he began the process of separation. He soon became aware of Shoshana in a seated posture at his right side. She signified to him that she would always be at his right hand. Then she placed her head in her own hands and closed her eyes. As she and her father had learned from the Brotherhood, this was the procedure for conscious death through severance of the vital link.

Slowly he became aware that her beautiful *nephesh*-body was becoming transparent. It was dissolving back into the sidereal elements of which it had been composed. He etched the memory of her physical beauty into his physical mind, especially of her face. For it was by visualizing the face of the final incarnation that one could draw near to an ascended one, the Brotherhood had taught.

Finally all that remained for *Yeshua* was his constructed mental image of Shoshana's face. But as he gazed upon it, he was suddenly enveloped in the finest fragrance of lily.

With tears in his eyes, he returned to his body and remained in vigil until the Full Moon sunk beneath the Western horizon and a new morning dawned in the East.

A few nights later *Yeshua* saw Shoshana in a dream. She was pointing toward the rising moon illuminating a large, snow-capped mountain. When he awakened, he remembered the word *Meros* or *Meru*. He decided that he must find that mountain.

******* ******* ******* *******

By day, he continued to wander South and Eastward following the small trade routes from village to village. There were many small emporia or Parthian trading stations where he was able to purchase food and other supplies, but his purse was nearly empty when he walked the great valley leading to the ruins of Persepolis. He found himself beyond the land of the Parthians and now pasing through the Indo-Parthian territories ruled by King Gondophares. An occasional Jewish trading caravan provided him with information, but the only common language for large emporia was Greek.

He had learned to communicate in Greek while working with his father in Sepphoris. Most of the language he had acquired served the needs of a stone mason working for foreigners—little grammar, but many useful words for food, money, shelter.

As he gazed at the palatial ruins of Darius' empire, which had later been sacked by the armies of Alexander the Great, he saw the patterns of Persian architecture so familiar from his life in Babylon. The ruins were desolate and uninhabited. But clearly they had been quarried for other local projects. The main road led East. He needed work to earn money, so he continued Eastward. Perhaps he could find the projects for which Persepolis had been stripped and get temporary employment.

In the distant North great mountains were always visible. No road led far into these mountains, but *Yeshua* was told that there were roads to the South that led to the sea. However he continued on the main trade route East. Often he was forced to travel by night because the days were becoming unbearably hot.

Early one morning after a long walk, *Yeshua* arrived at a trading village where he found several men laying stonework on the main plaza. Their work was of poor quality. He tried to speak with them in Greek, but they did not understand his words. One of them pointed to a stone dwelling, so *Yeshua* approached the home hoping to find an official who spoke Greek. When he arrived at the doorpost, he was greeted by a young boy.

"*Eimi teknon* (I am a stonemason)," he said in Greek. "*Ou pater sou* (where is your father)?"

The boy smiled and motioned for *Yeshua* to wait. He entered the home and soon retuned with a man who looked and dressed distinctly Greek. He hailed *Yeshua* in the accustomed way and asked (in Greek), "Are you a stonemason?"

Yeshua nodded and bowed slightly.

"Do you see what our workmen are trying to do in the *agora*?" he asked.

Yeshua grimaced, shook his head, and said, "They need my help."

"Can you tell them how do do it?"

"Cannot speak their language, but can show them," *Yeshua* answered.

Clearly there were no stonemasons anywhere in the vicinity. His expertise was worth good wages.

"I can pay you double what I pay the workers," the man offered.

Yeshua shook his head. "No; four times," he said, holding up four fingers. "Try me one day. Then you will know. I am a Master Mason."

The man arched his eyebrows. "A Master?" Then why are you traveling alone and on foot?" he asked.

"I travel from Babylon to the East," he answered.

"To what city?" was the question.

"To a mountain called *Meros* or *Meru*," he answered.

"Ah, the birthplace of Dionysos!" the man replied. "Then you will go the Nysa, the City of Alexander. This is a very long journey."

"What is the way there?" asked *Yeshua*.

The man thought for a moment.

"First, you must go East to the great river called the Indus. This is a journey of many months. Then you must take the Northern route toward the source of the river. This is also a very long journey. When you see mountains to the West and North, there is a great road to the West. Ask the way to Peucelaotis and Alexandria. Beyond Peucelaotis on the road to Alexandria you will come to another large river. There a road turns North. That is the road that leads to Nysa and Mount Meros."

Yeshua bowed in gratitude.

The man continued, "There is much work for a Master Mason in the valley nearby. The King employs many workers to build temples for his god Buddha."

"I have not heard of this god," replied *Yeshua*.

"If you journey East, you will hear much about this god," smiled the man.

Yeshua worked for two weeks with the peasant laborers. He showed them how to smooth the stones that had been carried from Persepolis so they would fit together, then how to make a mortar to seal the cracks so it would not rot.

All of the merchants were grateful because heavy carts could now pass through the paved plaza without damage. When he was ready to resume his journey, several merchants gave him gifts for dried fruit and meats, in addition to what he purchased for himself.

On the advice of his employer, he also purchased a pack animal—an unusually gentle donkey. This allowed him to carry many blankets, most of which he could trade for food, but some of which would be necessary for the increasingly cold nights. For a fee he was able to join a small caravan for protection from bandits. One of the caravaners spoke Greek, so he had a source of information.

The donkey had been raised by children. They had named her Artabanus as a joke—that was the name of the Parthian King. His employer had advised him not to speak it in front of the wrong people. *Yeshua* decided the animal needed a new name.

He sat with the donkey when the caravan stopped for the animals to drink, speaking to her in soothing tones, shading her head from the hot sun, and feeding her special grains.

Unlike the others, he also unburdened his donkey when they rested at an oasis, then reburdened him when they were preparing to get underway. He slept with the little donkey at night.

"What would you like to be called?" he often asked the animal with his inner voice. After three days, he began to form a picture in his mind of a mountain with three peaks when he spoke to the animal. He knew this was Mount Meros.

One morning as they awakened on the rising sun he asked the donkey, "May I call you Meros?"

The animal stood up and brayed loudly.

"Then that will be your name!" declared *Yeshua*.

From that time forward the donkey always responded to the name Meros.

Ever since the night of Shoshana's final departure, *Yeshua's* thoughts and dreams continually evoked memories of their life together. He knew that he was participating in her process of reintegration after death, and that he himself was reintegrating with her.

Although he could no longer feel her presence as he used to when they were physically separated, he had an awareness of her at all times. He was always in silent dialogue with her, sharing thoughts and experiences. Sometimes he found himself speaking aloud to her. Since no one in the caravan understood Aramaic, and the other were engaged in their own conversations, his eccentricity went unnoticed.

It was not that he heard her voice. Rather, their minds were joined such has his thoughts were her thoughts. The only times she manifested as separate from him were in dreams. Sometimes they were memories, sometimes they seemed to be flying together as though projecting in the *nephesh*, and on rare occasions she appeared from a long distance away and pointed to something—as she had on the Full Moon of her Second Death. When he remembered the vivid image of her standing and pointing, ideas and words seemed to bubble forth from inside his heart. This is how he had heard the phrase "Mount Meros," and this is why it had become the object of his wandering.

Now, however, on the long trek East he sometimes awakened from a seemingly deep and dreamless sleep with the memory of Shoshana standing and pointing. Once it was a warning about bandits laying in wait. *Yeshua* was able to prepare the caravaners for defence so that the bandits, seeing them alert and armed to the teeth, turned and fled. He gained the reputation of a seer among the other men, who now bowed to him out of respect.

On another occasion Shoshana warned him about bad water from a spring. When he told the Greek-speaking caravaner not to stop at the oasis because the water was bad, there was no hesitation. The entire caravan agreed to move on without any questions.

Yeshua realized that his love for Shoshana was more than healing—it was empowering. As he contemplated his life, he realized that in spite of his innate spiritual talent, it was only by finding Shoshana that he had begun to exercise true mastery. The same was true for her. It was their spiritual marriage that caused them to ripen.

This marriage was actually a reunion of *Yechid* and *Yechida*. They were two souls, but one *Neshama*. They were what in Babylonian *Kabbalah* was known as "the Twins." Every soul is connected to every other soul—human, animal, vegetable, and mineral. But every soul in manifestation is connected closely or more distantly to another soul, like pieces of a puzzle. Some are contiguous, others separated by one, two, or more levels of distance.

He imagined that as three-dimensional. The contiguous parts are soul families. But at a deeper level, each piece of the puzzle has also two parts. They were joined at the beginning of God's emanating, but widely separated in manifestation of the *Sephiroth*. In the "breaking of the Vessels" the Holy One established Paths and Worlds that are designed for the growth, evolution, and reintegration of souls.

Ultimately each soul emanates from its *Neshama*, but the *Neshama* can manifest and develop many souls through the paths of mineral, vegetable, animal, and human. Even though complex human souls are both masculine and feminine, like the angels, they incarnate only as males or females separated by gender. It is only human souls that contain the complete Divine Image or *Yezer*, for it is only the human soul that has evolved through all the lesser kingdoms of life and contains the Path of *Aliyah* to *Neshama*. They hold in their hearts the *malkuthim* or interior universes of the *Malkuth* of God. Each soul must become a master of its own *malkuth*.

The Twins are *Yechid* and *Yechida*. Normally they never manifest together in flesh, but one remains unmanifest as a guide to the other—which may or may not attune to its guidance in life. But when *Neshama*, after many aeons of incarnation, has developed and united all of its psychic elements into two Great Souls, then it is possible that the Twins might manifest together in flesh, as *Yeshua* and Shoshana had done.

Were they to find each other on Earth, there must always be terrible obstacles designed by the dark forces to destroy their union. Otherwise, the Prince of this world and his Beasts would lose their powers on Earth and the Age of the Messiah would come. So one of the Twins might be young and the other old, one royal and the other peasant, one Roman and another Parthian. Their love could not survive long in flesh. In the case of *Yeshua* and Shoshana, she was marked at birth by a sidereal trap that would cause their love to produce a deadly poison.

But the Prince of this world rules only through illusion. His *Malkuth* is not designed to last forever, but to bring forth the ripening of human souls. The Evil Ruler of this world has power only through the immaturity of human souls who follow the *Yetzer Ha-Ra*, the Evil Impulse. *Adonai* leads Leviathon by a hook through his nose. The *Malkuth* of Heaven is spread out upon the Earth, but men do not see it. *Adonai* transforms the evil of this world into good, just as a mother comforts and nurtures a child after he has hurt himself. One day the child will mature, master his interior world, and inherit the Divine Sovereignty.

In many months of contemplation *Yeshua* began to understand the Divine Way—not merely in theory, but in practice. He found that all the powers that had developed in his soul when he dwelt with Shoshana were still there. Even after death they continued to be reunited, and there could never be any separation. At the highest level of being, they were One with each other, and One with God.

In this new relationship, Shoshana was *Yechida*. She was his special manifestation of the *Ruach Ha-Qodesh* and the *Bat Kol*. She was *Hochmah*, Wisdom, or what the Greeks called Sophia and *Agathos Daimon*.

He often remembered the words of *Yeshua* Ben Sirach that his father had expounded to him. But he remembered as Ben Sirach had given—not with the esoteric gender reversal that *Yosef* had done—because this was a different application, and one that enlightened his understanding:

"At first She will lead him by tortuous paths, filling him with craven fears. Her discipline will be a torment to him, and Her decrees a hard test, until she fully trusts Him.

"But then She will come straight back to him again and bring great joy, and reveal Her secrets unto him."

He knew that when he finally reached Mount Meros, after much struggle and effort, She would guide and teach him through his beloved *Yechida*.

******* ******* ******* *******

"*Potamos Indus!*" shouted *Yeshua's* Greek friend from the top of a ridge. He pointed straight ahead over the hill where the road was leading.

The caravan continued its measured pace to the crest of the hill, then stopped. Everyone pushed forward to see the grand panorama that unfolded before them.

A long, green valley dotted with villages and punctuated with many roads spread out far toward the Eastern horizon where, barely visible as a silvery ribbon, flowed the sacred Indus River.

Yeshua closed his eyes and offered thanks to the Holy One.

His Greek friend stood beside him and pointed to the Northwest.

"Here is your road. It is the main road from that village North to the land of Ashoka, where you will find your mountain. You must join another caravan in that village, for it is the starting point for the journey North."

That afternoon they entered the village emporium and traded most of their goods. *Yeshua* replaced many of his blankets that remained with a bounty of fresh and dried foods, then lay down with the caravan for several days of rest and refreshment.

Within a week he had planned to join another caravan going North. This time three of the men spoke Greek, and one was a Jew who spoke Aramaic. *Ehud* was Babylonian and was pleased to hear that *Yeshua* had lived there. He planned to turn East where *Yeshua* would turn West so that he could join the spice trade. Until then he would carry salt-dried ocean fish Northward.

"It is a light cargo, and you can eat it. You put your cargo into food and get a higher value for it. Ocean fish are in great demand upriver. Come with me to trade for it tomorrow."

The next day *Yeshua* traded most of the remaining blankets for dried ocean fish.

The new caravan moved slowly up the Northern river road, which seemed to host a new village at every turn. Most of them, however, were not emporia, and the villagers were poor. There would be no trading for two weeks.

The Indus Valley was far more lush and green than any land *Yeshua* had ever seen.

"What is that structure?" asked the young master, pointing to a carefully maintained but small temple.

"That is called a *stupa*. In it the Buddhists bury relics of their saints," answered *Ehud*.

"What is a Buddhist?" asked *Yeshua*.

Ehud laughed.

"A very good question! I know nothing of their religion except that it is new. The old religion sems to be a superstitious combination of magic and various festivals, many of them tied to this river. This new religion has been adopted in the Land of Asoka to the North—where your mountain is. However, there is a city on the mountain established by the Great Alexander where many Greeks and Parthians live, and where the ancient religion of Babylon is mixed with the religion of the Greeks. But in the great valley below there is the Land of Asoka, which is full of *stupas* and temples to the Buddha."

"Is the Buddha a god?" asked *Yeshua*.

Ehud paused for a moment, consulted with another caravaner in Greek, then returned with the answer.

"No. He was the son of a king who renounced his wealth and became a prophet of some kind. At his death he became a protector of his devotees. His teachings are handed down by disciples who wander, like us. They are poor and do not work, but depend upon villagers to put food into their begging bowls."

"Then, they are religious beggars?" asked *Yeshua* with a slight tone of indignation.

"Well, you have to see them for yourself. They are not like beggars on the streets of Babylon. They are considered to be holy men, and it is a blessing for you to offer them food."

"It is their corpses that are put into these *stupas*?" asked *Yeshua*.

"No! Have you not seen the way they treat their dead? They burn their bodies and resolve them to ashes and calcined bones. That is what they put into the *stupas*."

"Hmm!" remarked *Yeshua*.

"I'll tell you more. You know that the Parthians also do not bury their dead, but put the corpses out in trees and on mountains for the birds to devour. Then they collect the bones and place them into stone rooms. In the new religion they especially revere the bones of their holy men, so in the Land of Asoka, they continue to feed human flesh to the birds, but they place the bones of holy men into their *stupas*."

"This seems quite barbaric," remarked *Yeshua*.

"I'll tell you something," replied *Ehud*. "The people in this river valley are not at all barbaric. In fact, they are the kindest and most gentle people I have ever seen—much more than any Jews. I would rather dwell among them than among the cut-throats of Babylon."

Yeshua was quite amazed by what *Ehud* had told him. He began to observe the people of the many villages and take note of their customs. What *Ehud* had said was true. They were gentle, kind, and generous.

Most amazing, there were no bandits on the Northern road. Just farms, orchards, fishing villages. There was no evidence of armed forces of any sort. But again, they were completely vulnerable to conquest by arms. They had no means of defense.

When the caravan made its first stopover at a major emporium, the only cut-throats were other traders. Local people were simple and fair. Whatever they offered in trade was usually quite reasonable.

At the emporium, *Yeshua* met another Greek man. He lived locally and spoke the language fluently. Moreover, he was a member of the new religion of the Buddha.

Yeshua asked, "What are the teachings of Buddha?"

The man laughed.

"You can study them all your life and still not know them all," he said. "But Lord Buddha teaches us a path to *moksha*, which is liberation from the dark forces that rule this world."

"That is not unlike the goal of *Kabbalah*," thought the young master. Then aloud he asked, "By what means does one attain liberation from the self-bondage of evil?"

"By righteous living, thinking, intentions," was the answer.

"But I thought Buddha was a god who liberated mankind," said *Yeshua*.

"No, it is the Teaching of the Buddha that has the power of liberation if understood and implemented," replied the man.

"This is like the Teaching of the prophets," thought *Yeshua*. Then aloud, "So Buddha is a prophet or, as you might say, a philosopher?"

"Yes, but he has renounced his liberation to help all other sentient beings achieve liberation. He is what we call the Bodhisattva. He is present with us now, and he is guiding this conversation," answered the man.

"What do we have in ourselves that can liberate us?" asked *Yeshua*. He was now very intrigued.

"All sentient beings have the Buddha nature. It must be awakened."

Just then *Yeshua* heard *Ehud* calling him back to the caravan for the next leg of their journey.

"Thank you for helping me to understand," smiled *Yeshua* and took his leave.

*******   *******   *******   *******

After a month the caravan broke into two sections—one headed East, and one West. *Yeshua* said a warm farewell to *Ehud*, who hoped they might meet someday in Babylon.

Shaking his head, *Yeshua* told him that he did not know where he would be in the future, but that if he returned to the West, his journey would take him on the trading route to Palestine—not back to Babylon.

"Then goodbye, friend. May the Holy One shine his face upon you," declared *Elud*.

"And may you also be blessed," *Yeshua* replied with a wave of his hand.

The road took them slowly up along a smaller river valley into foothills. These finally led into a broad and fertile river plain that stretched toward the West as far as the eye could see.

They reached the emporium of Peucelaotis after two weeks. *Yeshua* found that many people were speaking a simple form of Greek that he could interpret enough to communicate. He also found that his dried ocean fish were considered to be prize delicacies. He traded half of what he had for food and other necessities, as he was growing sick of eating fish.

After a weekend on rest, the caravan moved West.

Two weeks later they reached a large river spilling down from mountains to the North. A main road led upward out of the valley along the river. This was *Yeshua's* landmark. He and his donkey parted from the caravan the next morning and began the long journey into the mountains that loomed in the North.

"Now you are my only friend, and I am yours," *Yeshua* said softly to Meros. "We are going to the mountain in whose honor you are named. Soon we shall see if it is worthy of this honor."

Reaching Eastward from the Northern range of mountains, a series of foothills curved outward and forward. The river valley rose gently, so a day's journey was not strenuous.

Toughened from months of travel on foot, *Yeshua* found himself strong and lithe as the mountain rose before him.

After three weeks the wanderers arrived at a high plain overlooked the river valley, which was now too small and brambled for a road. Upon this plain was a fortified Greek city—Nysa—which they entered by means of a gate facing Northeast toward a gently sloping mountain covered with agricultural plateaus. Mostly hidden by foothills, but clearly visible, *Yeshua* could see three peaks. It was Mount Meros.

Chapter Sixteen: THE WAY OF THE BUDDHA

Eimi Teknon Archon.

"I am a Master builder." These were the magic words that opened the mountain sanctuary to *Yeshua*. For the Temple of Dionysos was in disrepair and no one but the Priest and his assistants were allowed access.

In a dream, Shoshana had pointed to the Temple. When *Yeshua* made the early morning climb through man-made terraces of cultivated plots and wild, rock-strewn olive groves, the gate was locked. He sat with his little donkey to gather his thoughts when a small procession approached. It was the Priest and devotees.

The Priest stopped and stared, so *Yeshua* used the magic words. Immediately the Priest smiled and welcomed him.

"You have come to oversee the repairs!" he declared.

Yeshua repeated his Greek phrase slowly, trying to understand it, but the Priest took that as, "Yes, I have come to oversee the repairs."

"My prayers have been answered!" joyfully replied the Priest. "Please enter and wait in the sacred grove with your beast while we perform our matins. Then I will show you all that needs repair."

The gate swung open to reveal a beautifully tended grove of olive and laurel. *Yeshua* remembered that the laurel was sacred to the Greeks, and that small groves of it were planted in some of the temples of Sepphoris.

He unburdened his animal friend, sat down on a stone, and gave him a little grain. Then he closed his eyes and whispered sardonically to Shoshana, "So you have brought me here to repair a pagan shrine?"

Suddenly he was overwhelmed with the fragrance of lilies permeating the air. He opened his eyes in astonishment. He had not experienced such a tangible manifestation of Shoshana's presence since her death. Standing up, he examined the grove for lilies or any kind of flower. There were none, yet the fragrance had now become overpowering.

Then he sensed the ripple of Shoshana's laughter.

"Very well," he said aloud, "I shall take the job."

He sat again upon the stone and closed his eyes in communion with his beloved. He felt supremely at peace and time seemed to stand still. Then a sudden interruption.

"Are you a Buddhist?" asked the Priest in surprise, finding the Master builder in a sitting posture with eyes closed.

"*Eimi Judaios*," was the proud reply. "I am a Jew."

"Good, because it is not lawful for us to hire the *Indiaoi*. They claim our Temple to be that of *Vishnu*, one of their ancient gods. But the Great Alexander reconsecrated the sacred mountain and its Temple precincts for Dionysos many generations ago, for this is the sacred mountain *Meros* from which the Savior came to mankind.

"Come, I will show you everything."

With that began *Yeshua's* residency as Master builder and restorer of the Temple of Dionysos on the sacred Mount Meros. He was given a small hut with a spring located in a grove of wild olive trees below the Temple precincts. His animal friend spent most of her days grazing among the rocks, called upon for burden only occasionally when supplies had to be brought in from the *agora* at Nysa.

Yeshua was given charge over three workmen who were citizens of Nysa. One specialized in woodcraft, another in bronze, and the third in stone masonry.

The stone mason, a Parthian with the Greek name of Andronikos, was suspicious of *Yeshua's* credentials, so extended his hand for the pass grip of an apprentice, which *Yeshua* returned correctly. Andronikos scowled.

"Now, the grip of an *Archos*?" *Yeshua* asked for the grip of the Master.

The young man smiled, shrugged his shoulders, and bowed deeply. He was only an apprentice. From that moment on, he was devoted to *Yeshua*. The two became friends.

Restoration of the Temple went slowly. Part of the stonework was very ancient and had partially decomposed. It had to be replaced with the right color and grain. That meant quarry work and creating smooth stones from rough *ebenim*. A new apprentice had to be initiated and trained. Andronikos enthusiastically recommended his only son.

On the first day of the week *Yeshua* formally initiated young Gregorios in the Sanctuary of the Temple by special permission of the Priest, and the excited boy began his apprenticeship.

*******   *******   *******   *******

"*Abba…Abba*; why am I here? What am I to learn? I seek only your Way and the coming of Messiah."

Yeshua often awakened at night and prayed for guidance. On this particular night, however, he found himself unable to return to sleep. Finally he put on his sandals and made his way through the wild olive grove.It was pitch dark—the kind of darkness that can be experienced only deep in the wilderness on a clear, moonless night.

The *Keseh* had wheeled below the Western horizon many hours ago with *Shemesh*. It was the time of the New Moon, and the sky was filled with blazing starlight. Embedded in the black void of the sky were myriad points of light—mostly stars, but a few planets. *Yeshua* could distinguish the Great Lights of the angels of *Yetzirah* guarding the Royal Road of Shemesh, as well as the myriad other beings of light who populated the Divine Sky. The air was so still that none of the lights sparkled or twinkled, but each lay like a jewel embedded by a master craftsman. Each star seemed to cast rays of slightly different color, from red to blue. *Yeshua* could even make out mysterious fuzzy star-clouds toward the North when he slightly averted his eyes.

"O' Father of Lights, show me Thy Way," he whispered, gazing at the four bright stars that formed the Head of the Serpent. "What is my purpose here?"

He lay on his back and continued to gaze at the wonders of God until the Morning Star arose in the East, heralding the approach of a new day. Then he returned to his hut and slept in a deep and dreamless state.

That afternoon Gregorios and Andronikos were trying to dislodge a large boulder when another above it fell and crushed the boy, killing him instantly. The grieving father strapped the boy's body to a pack-donkey to take him back to Nysa.

When *Yeshua* saw the man and his son, he realized immediately what had happened and ran to the main road.

"Are you certain he is dead?" he asked Andronikos.

"There is no breath and his heart does not beat," he answered slowly. "And it has been an hour since he died."

Yeshua lay his left hand upon the boy's chest, motioned for silence, and closed his eyes. His interior sight revealed that the silver cord had not been broken. Then he felt himself moved with a powerful compassion. A hot energy seemed to sear his loins, solar plexus, rising into his heart.

"He is not dead," he declared in a resonant voice that Andronikos had never heard from anyone before. "Lay him on his back."

The grieving father, hoping for any kind of a miracle, unstrapped his son's body and laid it lovingly on the Earth.

Yeshua fell to his knees, cupped his left palm over his heart, lay his right palm upon the young boys heart, and intoned, "E-e-e-ya-a-a-ho-o-o-wa-a-ay." He felt power flowing from his heart. He intoned again and again, until he was able to feel the young man's heart beating faintly. Then he lifted the young boy's head, breathed onto his face, and commanded in a loud voice, "Gregorios, awaken!"

The boy's eyes fluttered and Andronikos uttered a joyful cry. "*Iakos, Iakos! Dionysos!*"

Georgios sucked in a shallow breath, then another, and finally a deep breath. His eyes opened and he whispered, "I have broken my arm, Father. I am sorry."

Yeshua felt the boy's arm. It was not broken, but badly crushed.

"Take your son home. You may both have two weeks to recuperate," he spoke softly. "Then come back. We have much to do."

The two men returned to Nysa.

Within a day, pilgrims from the city had begun to arrive. News of the great miracle performed by the god Dionysos through his Prophet, *Yeshua*, had spread through the entire city of Nysa. Merchants who heard the story would take it with them down to the Cophen Valley, both Eastward to the Indus and Westward toward the Parthian Stations on the spice routes to the Mediterranean.

The Priest of Dionysos accosted *Yeshua* in the Temple sanctuary.

"What is this miracle? You have raised a young man from the dead! Are you a *Theios Aner* (Divine Man)?"

Yeshua remained silent because he didn't know what a *Theios Aner* might be, and the last time he slowly repeated the Priest's speech to decipher it, he had been misunderstood.

The Priest fell to his knees and cried, "This is the greatest miracle that has happened at this Temple! Look!" he pointed through the gate, "Look at the people! They wish to be healed by Dionysos. Go to the gate and do something!"

Yeshua stepped hesitantly toward the gate. Immediately throngs of people—old, young, sick, and well—surged forward and began to pound on the gate. "*Iakos! Iakos!*" they began to chant in one voice.

Suddenly the Priest appeared and held up his hands for silence. The crowd quieted down.

"Citizens, it is true that Dionysos has performed a great miracle on these Temple grounds. Today the Temple Sanctuary is being renovated. There will be many miracles here. But today," he quieted the crowd one more time,"today there will be no miracles. You must return in four weeks on the day sacred to Dionysos."

Many cries and groans went up from the crowd. Women cried loudly for the Priest to make an exception in their case, but he shook his head and motioned for them to leave.

When everything had quieted down that afternoon, the Priest tried to question *Yeshua* about details of the miracle. But the young Master merely held up his hand and shook his head.

"Great one," the Priest pleaded,"can we have the Sanctuary ready in to weeks?

Yeshua smiled and nodded in the affirmative.

******* ******* ******* *******

A few days later *Yeshua* experienced another dreamless sleep, but as he awakened he clearly saw Shoshana pointing down the mountain toward a huge Buddhist *stupa*. As he contemplated the vision, his hut was filled with the scent of lilies. He realized that he was being advised to leave the small city-state of Nysa and find work as a Master builder in the Land of Asoka.

"But I cannot speak their language," he protested aloud. "How can I communicate with anyone?"

Nevertheless, when the Sanctuary work was completed, he resigned his position with the Temple. He recommended that Andronikos take his place.

As he began the trek with his burdened pet donkey, he realized how differently he appeared to the Hellenistic culture of the area. He had a full beard that slightly parted, long hair, and simple robe and staff. He looked like a foreign trader to some, like a Jew to those better acquainted with the world. But as he passed other people on the descent from Nysa, he was aware of stares and the whispered phrase, *Theios Aner*. Apparently people thought he was some kind of Greek prophet.

Finally he reached the Great High Road or *Uttarâpatha*, as it was known locally, and turned West towards Gandara, an area known to the Greeks as Parapamisos, and the city dominating it as Peucelaotis, or *Pushkalâvatî*, the City of Lotus Flowers. There were many caravans traveling his way, usually within hailing distance of each other, so there was no need to join one. The road was a veritable highway of commerce and virtually free of bandits.

He was not surprised to find many caravaners who spoke Greek, but was amazed to find that Greek was a major language of the entire region. Yet the prevailing religion was that of the Buddha, which was forbidden in the city of Nysa.

Along the road he saw many rock paintings and an occasional *stupa*. None of these little temples were very large or resembled what he had been shown in the vision. He stopped from time to time to examine the architecture of a *stupa*, which was quite different from anything he had ever seen.

The temple was basically a circle contained within a square. There were gilded wooden gates at the four directions with a large Southeastern gate, and a foundation burial mound with carved clay brick-stones surrounding several tiers. Stairs led to a kind of balcony surrounding the mound on which pilgrims or monks circumambulated in the anti-sunwise direction. There were carvings in the ornate lintels and wooden architraves above each gate that seemed to show events or legends in the life of the Buddha.

Yeshua tied his donkey and followed pilgrims into the temple grounds. He could now see that there was a ground-level walking path made of stone that was also circumambulated, but in a sunwise direction. The entrance to this path came from any of the gates, but there was a stone-paved area with columns holding a shade roof devoted to arriving pilgrims.

There seemed to be no Priest or other official to take money from devotees, but there were many beggars. They did not grasp at passersby, but remained silent in meditation holding out a bowl for rice. These must be monks, too, thought *Yeshua*.

Finally he arrived at the large City of Lotus Flowers, and it was well named. Innumerable ponds of water stood alongside the main street, each filled with lily pads sprouting exotic lotus flowers. As he approached the *agora*, he could hear a man's voice speaking Greek but using the word "Buddha" many times. *Yeshua* drew his animal with him to hear what he could of the Buddhist sermon being delivered in Greek. But the words flew by so fast that he couldn't put them together. Many of them were not Greek words, but seemed to be the language of the Indus River Valley.

When the sermon was over and the small gathering of hearers had left, *Yeshua* approached the man. He was a monk.

Yeshua bowed with palms held together in the Eastern way, but not held above his head to indicate submission or lower class, and addressed the monk with his magic phrase.

"*Eimi teknon Archon.*"

The monk smiled and returned the gesture.

"*Boulo mathein...Buddha*," a halting phrase attempting to convey that he wished to learn about Buddhism.

The monk, who was fluent in Greek, understood him to be requesting to become his disciple.

"What is your language?" he asked.

"*Eimi Judaios*," he replied—"I am a Jew."

"Aha! Then you must speak Greek!" replied the monk.

No, *Yeshua* protested, he spoke only a little Greek. He spoke the language of the Chaldeans (Aramaic).

"Good!" replied the monk. "Then I will take you to the monk *Nutesh* who speaks your language well."

Yeshua understood what was said and agreed to follow him to the monastery.

They climbed a steep path into the rocky foothills on the Northern side of the city. It was a trek of more than two hours, but long before the sun set *Yeshua* saw the pillars, caves, and *stupa* of the monastery coming into view. It was perched on a plateau overlooking the city. Before they entered by the Southeastern gate, the monk pointed to a rocky point covered by brush.

"When you defecate, do it there. It will be aged and used in the garden."

They were greeted by several young men in monk's robes who did not speak but smiled and bowed profusely. *Yeshua* returned their gestures. He tied and unburdened his donkey in a place indicated by his friend, then followed him to one of the caves that had been carved into the side of a hill that rose to the North. There, sitting in a posture of meditation, was the aged monk who would teach him.

His guide put a finger to his lips to indicate silence, then motioned for them both to sit and meditate. Here they remained until the sun had set. Finally *Nutesh* began to move and stretch, then he arose and left the cave for a moment, returning with a lighted oil lamp.

After a few words in Greek, *Yeshua's* guide stood, bowed, and departed, leaving him with *Nutesh*.

"My name is *Yeshua*," he offered in his native Aramaic. "Do you speak my language?"

The old man coughed and cleared his voice. Apparently he did not do much talking.

"Yes…my Son."

There was a pause. Clearly he did not wish to say anything more than necessary.

"I wish to learn about the Buddha," declared *Yeshua*.

The old man smiled, grew pensive, then asked, "Do you…speak Greek?"

"I can read Greek, but I cannot understand the language very well when it is spoken," he answered.

"Ahh," the old monk said pensively. "Then…you shall study…the Edicts of Asoka."

"What are they?" asked *Yeshua*.

"The great King Asoka…brought Buddhism to this land…many generations ago," he explained in slow and painful phrases. "He inscribed…summaries of the ethical Teachings…on stones…in many locations…to…correct the morals and superstitions of the people. He…caused them to be inscribed…in both his native language…and in Greek…because much of the population…speaks only Greek."

He smiled and said nothing more. This much speaking had evidently been a great effort for him.

"Where will I find these stones with the Edicts in Greek?" asked the young Master.

"The others…" he paused, pointing toward the common gathering place for the monks, "they will show you." A pause, and then he said, "Eat and sleep here." The old man indicated a dark corner of the cave.

Yeshua stood, bowed in the Eastern way, and walked out into the moonlight to find his donkey. After caring for the animal's needs, he returned to the cave with a blanket. The aged monk smiled and extinguished the lamp when the young Master had spread his blanket.

That night, as he lay sleeping, he dreamed of gemstones—both in the rough, and faceted. Jewels fit for the Breastplate of Aaron. He interpreted that to be an excellent sign pointing to the value of Buddhism, and he awakened feeling excitement.

When the sky began to lighten and hour before the sun would rise, everyone was awake. All the monks gathered in the main plaza between gate and caves for chanting and prayer. *Yeshua* sat with them but did not know the words, so he closed his eyes and intoned with them wordlessly.

After this *Yeshua* approached the monk who had brought him and asked, "Where can I find the Edicts of Asoka?"

"You must follow the main road West from the City of Lotus Flowers for three days. Then you will see the Edicts carved in stones by the Great Stupa," he replied.

After breaking his fast, *Yeshua* burdened his donkey and began the three-day trek.

*******   *******   *******   *******

The sun mercilessly baked the waterless landscape—rocky, dusty hardpan with only a few scrubby bushes. The water carried in canteens had slowly evaporated, and by the third day they had no water. Eventually they were forced to stop and take shelter from the sun under blankets *Yeshua* had rigged to rocks and shrubs. The poor little donkey was faint and panting. She would die of dehydration unless she had water.

Yeshua had been communing with the local elemental spirits. Now he called upon them in the *nephesh*.

"Come to us, spirits of air and water, clouds, vapors; come from the sea, from the snowy mountain tops. Winds, gather your clouds of moisture and bring them here. Cause life-sustaining rain to fall upon us."

In this way he worked, drawing all the forces of the elementals to him, then merging with them in the *nephesh* until, indeed, he *was* the moisture of the air. He *was* the life-sustaining clouds of water that floated in the heavens.

Then, in a physical voice vibrating with power, he sounded and intoned the Divine Name over and over. Soon the skies were filled with dark, cooling clouds. Lightning thundered from cloud to cloud. Then heavy drops of rain began to fall in torrents. Murky rivulets flooded down the hills.

The young Master gave thanks and filled his canteens with the clearest water that he could find in standing pools. He applied the cool, rain-soaked blankets to his donkey's head and belly, gently speaking words of encouragement to her as she gratefully sipped the water from his cupped hands. As the rain continued to fall, *Yeshua* turned his face heavenward and allowed the droplets to fill his mouth, drenching his hair and beard.

The scene had not gone unobserved. High on a rocky hill, also reveling in the blessed rainfall, was a *Bon* Priest. He had been sitting under an ornately decorated ritual parasol attempting to bring water from the sky for many days without result. Thus he watched in amazement while the dusty-robed stranger chanted and summoned the clouds within the space of less than half and hour.

Jian-Chi stood and collapsed the parasol, then picked his way down the rocky slope toward *Yeshua*. He had no fear because he was a master of evil spirits. He was determined to learn from this foreign *Bon-Po* with the donkey who had demonstrated such power and skill.

"Ho," he smiled and bowed deeply.

Yeshua had watched his progress down the hill as the sky cleared and the clouds dissipated. He was already standing, so returned his bow.

Jian-Chi quickly found that the Master did not speak his language, so pointed to his head with the forefingers of both hands in a gesture which *Yeshua* instantly understood. He was saying, "Let us communicate by telepathic means." This man was an adept.

Yeshua repeated the gesture and invited his guest to sit with him. They would use a combination of gesture and sound to send thoughts, for as the cloud rides upon the wind, and the rider upon the horse, so do our thoughts travel by coarser means—of which human language is only one modality.

"Master, will you teach me to bring the rain as you just now did, without ritual?" was the request.

"Yes, but first you must tell me this: What is the purpose of your ritual?" asked *Yeshua*.

"To force the local spirits by means of more powerful spirit allies with whom we have established covenants. We cannot command the local spirits, but they are subject to our powerful spirit allies."

"What are your covenants with the powerful spirits?"

"We offer them sacrifice and feed them with sweet goat milk and the best parts of the meat. We also honor them with an altar consecrated in the blood of young goats."

"And to whom are these greater spirits subject?"

"There are no greater spirits—only the Tao."

"What is Tao? Is it Spirit? Does it have a Voice?" the Master continued to probe.

"No one knows," was the response after a short delay.

"If you want to develop my skills, you will have to know what you call the Tao," indicated *Yeshua*, drawing a clockwise circle in the sand.

"But that is…impossible," thought *Jian-Chi*.

"Do you want to know the Tao?" asked the Master. "Then you must show me to the place of the rock Edicts of Asoka. There I will help you to know the Tao."

Jian-Chi prostrated himself three times.

"First you must show me to good water," the Master smiled, pointing to the muddy water canteens. He stood up, bowed, and indicated that the Bon Priest should also stand.

Jian-Chi wordlessly led *Yeshua* and Meros up the Northern slopes to a plateau. He pointed to what had been a small man-made lake or reservoir before the recent draught. The foliage surrounding it was brown and fruitless. But now it was overflowing with churning water that spilled into it from canals that had been long ago scraped into the hillsides. At the center of the lake was a shrine with images of deities.

They walked to a small pool into which the overflowing lake spilled. A hardened dam decorated with *swastika* symbols allowed only the clean top-water to fall into the pool after a heavy downpour, while sediment slowly settled into the rest of the lake.

While Meros drank, the two men filled their canteens and jars with living water from Heaven. Then they stepped into the lake, not only for cleansing of body and clothing, but to receive the blessings of the living water.

*******   *******   *******   *******

After a night's rest at the sacred lake, they began the trek to the rock-engraven Edicts of Asoka. Meros obligingly carried the Priest's large parasol, which they opened when they rested during the hottest part of the day.

Finally a large, hemispherical hill came into view. It was strewn with boulders. As they approached, *Yeshua* began to make out inscriptions. They were hammered into fourteen large boulders positioned so that they circled the the hill on two levels—each with a walking path—quite similar to the structure of a *stupa*. There were two versions on each stone. The first was in an alphabet and language unknown to *Yeshua*, but beneath it was a translation into the common or koine Greek spoken throughout the territory of Gandara. Altogether, there were fourteen such Edicts.

Yeshua had promised to introduce *Jian-Chi* to the highest spiritual Reality, which he called Tao. He wasn't quite sure how he would do that, but he planned to undertake the project at night, after reading the inscriptions. He indicated this to the Priest, who bowed and lay down to rest beneath his parasol.

As *Yeshua* began the work of translation from Greek, but without any library scroll to help him.

The First Edict declared the traditional killing of any living beings, especially of animals for ritual sacrifice, to be against *Dhamma*, which seemed to be something like Divine Torah. Some was still allowed, but with the hope that eventually it, too, would cease.

Yeshua was impressed. This was a good law.

In the Second Edict, the King declared that he had dug public wells and planted fruit trees to make life better for the population, and that he was importing and making available medical herbs for all people and animals of his kingdom to benefit the common health. Later Edicts made it clear that he was promoting the work of physicians to replace the superstitious and expensive rituals of the magicians. Was he speaking against the Priests like the one who had led him here?

The Third Edict had a powerful section: "Respect for mother and father is good, generosity to friends, acquaintances, relatives, Brahmans and ascetics is good, not killing living beings is good, moderation in spending and moderation in saving is good." It seemed to be a necessary moral teaching for a population who did not necessarily support these virtues.

The Fourth Edict said this:

"In the past, for many hundreds of years, killing or harming living beings and improper behavior towards relatives, and improper behavior towards Brahmans and ascetics has increased. But now due to the beloved of the gods, king Piyadasi's *Dhamma* practice, the sound of the [war] drum has been replaced by the sound of the dhamma. The sighting of heavenly vehicles, auspicious elephants, bodies of fire and other divine sightings has not happened for many hundreds of years. But now because the beloved of the gods, king Piyadasi promotes restraint in the killing and harming of living beings, proper behavior towards relatives, Brahmans and ascetics, and respect for mother, father and elders, such sightings have increased."

A *Dhamma* practice seemed to be not just something spoken, but true ethical action in life.

The Fifth Edict declared that it is hard, at first, to do good, but always easy to do evil. It declared that the King had appointed spiritual administrators called *Dhamma Mahamatras* to not only instruct, but to inspect how prisoners were kept, to ensure that individual circumstances would be dealt with justly and those falsely imprisoned or under extreme hardship be released. Prisoners were all to be unfettered.

The Sixth Edict was a stunning exemplar of true Philosopher Kingship that actively and dynamically took responsibility for aspect of stewardship:

"In the past, state business was not transacted nor were reports delivered to the king at all hours. But now I have given this order, that at any time, whether I am eating, in the women's quarters, the bed chamber, the chariot, the palanquin, in the park or wherever, reporters are to be posted with instructions to report to me the affairs of the people so that I might attend to these affairs wherever I am. And whatever I orally order in connection with donations or proclamations, or when urgent business presses itself on the Mahamatras, if disagreement or debate arises in the Council, then it must be reported to me immediately. This is what I have ordered. I am never content with exerting myself or with dispatching business. Truly, I consider the welfare of all to be my duty, and the root of this is exertion and the prompt dispatch of business. There is no better work than promoting the welfare of all the people and whatever efforts I am making is to repay the debt I owe to all beings to assure their happiness in this life, and attain heaven in the next.

"Therefore this *Dhamma* edict has been written to last long and that my sons, grandsons and great-grandsons might act in conformity with it for the welfare of the world. However, this is difficult to do without great exertion."

What a contrast to Palestine and Roman rule!

The Seventh Edict declared that the practice of all religions was allowed, but that anyone who was lacking in "self-control, purity of heart, gratitude and firm devotion," would not be considered worthy.

The Eighth Edict stated that in the past, kings indulged themselves in selfish sport and hunting, but that this King instead visited and consulted with saints, and that he spent his travels dispensing gold to the needy.

The Ninth Edict could have been a proclamation made by the prophet Amos. It declared:

"In times of sickness, for the marriage of sons and daughters, at the birth of children, before embarking on a journey, on these and other occasions, people perform various ceremonies. Women in particular perform many vulgar and worthless ceremonies. These types of ceremonies can be performed by all means, but they bear little fruit."

Here he definitely refered to the kinds of ceremonies that the Priest who guided him here would do for money.

"What does bear great fruit, however, is the ceremony of the *dhamma*. This involves proper behavior towards servants and employees, respect for teachers, restraint towards living beings, and generosity towards ascetics and Brahmans. These and other things constitute the ceremony of the *Dhamma*."

Now he refers to *Dhamma* as a ceremony—which it apparently is not, *Yeshua* realized. He must be speaking in the way that the prophets spoke, for example, of the true circumcision—which is of the heart, not the flesh. Or the true sacrifices, which are not of animal flesh, but of praise and thanksgiving. He is taking the ancient traditions to a new and spiritual level by referring to *Dhamma* as a ceremony or form of ritual. This is truly enlightened, thought the young Master.

So this is the Teaching of the Buddha, and it is very good!

"Therefore a father, a son, a brother, a master, a friend, a companion, and even a neighbor should say: 'This is good, this is the ceremony that should be performed until its purpose is fulfilled, this I shall do.' Other ceremonies are of doubtful fruit, for they may achieve their purpose, or they may not, and even if they do, it is only in this world.

"But the ceremony of the *Dhamma* is timeless. Even if it does not achieve its purpose in this world, it produces great merit in the next, whereas if it does achieve its purpose in this world, one gets great merit both here and there through the ceremony of the *Dhamma*."

Now the King recognizes that even if the practice of justice and righteousness does not seem to be effective in this world, it gains great merit in the Divine World.

As he translated the rest of the Edicts, *Yeshua* was especially struck by the Twelfth, which declared that all religions should be honored.

"But the beloved of the gods, king Piyadasi, does not value gifts and honors as much as he values this—that there should be growth in the essentials of all religions. Growth in essentials can be done in different ways, but all of them have as their root restraint in speech, that is, not praising one's own religion, or condemning the religion of others without good cause. And if there is cause for criticism, it should be done in a mild way.

"But it is better to honor other religions for this reason. By so doing, one's own religion benefits, and so do other religions, while doing otherwise harms one's own religion and the religions of others. Whoever praises his own religion, due to excessive devotion, and condemns others with the thought 'Let me glorify my own religion,' only harms his own religion. Therefore contact between religions is good. One should listen to and respect the doctrines professed by others.

"The beloved of the gods, king Piyadasi, desires that all should be well-learned in the good doctrines of other religions."

This ran quite counter to what was taught in the religion of Moses, thought *Yeshua*. Yet he had found it to be true. He had learned much from the Magi, the prophet of Hermes Trismegistos, and the Babylonian school of Daniel—which was not accepted in Judea, but only in the Galilee. If different Rabbis could argue different opinions, why not different Priesthoods, cultures, and religions?

Now he understood why Shoshana pointed to the great *stupa*. Divine Wisdom had left Her Teachings among many tribes and peoples. The *Ruach-Ha-Qodesh* was now laying upon him a new discipline—to learn from the wisdom of the great prophet of the East known as the Buddha.

******* ******* ******* *******

The two men silently ascended the dome-shaped hill to the top as twilight faded into night. There had been no pilgrims. They were in total solitude.

Yeshua sat on a blanket and touched his forefingers to his forehead, signifying that the Priest must establish telepathic communication. They sat facing the darkened Eastern horizon with eyes closed.

"Where do your spirit allies dwell?" asked *Yeshua*.

"In the World of Sun and Moon."

"We shall ascend into the World of Sun and Moon," thought *Yeshua*, "and you shall glimpse the Worlds beyond that, and you shall see how great is the Tao."

"How can I gain admittance?"

"Come forth out of your flesh-body and I shall lead you."

"Then I must protect my flesh-body from evil ones and attackers," the Priest thought.

Yeshua observed from the *nephesh*. The Priest's etheric aura began to condense and take the shape of a hideous lion-man with brilliant flames darting from his eyes, head, and hands. It shrunk into a tiny light that remained above his forehead like a sentinel.

"What is this?" flashed through *Yeshua's* astral mind.

"This is my terrifying aspect—my Fierce Guardian," was the reply. "I have created it out of my own substance. It is what the demons and evil spirits see when I approach. They flee because they know that if I demand their names, they will be forced to tell me, and then I can command them to do whatever I wish. I dissolve them in sea water whenever I find them possessing animals or humans."

"Then you have something to teach me, too," thought *Yeshua*.

"You show me the Tao, and I will show you anything you want," promised the adept of *Bon-Po*.

"Listen to my voice as I construct the Chariot that we will ride."

The astral forms of the two adepts finally were enclosed in the *Merkabah* vehicle and they ascended through the First Heaven, where they were allowed to pass, and through the Third Heaven.

"Now you are entering the World of Formation, where the great Tao can be seen only through *Shemesh*, the Sun. Tell me what you see," said *Yeshua*.

"I see…great fire dragons with feet and tail of a lion and the head of a crocodile."

"These are the Chalkydri. What do you hear?"

"They are…intoning and singing praises."

"To Whom do they sing?"

"I can't see…; they seem to be made of both fire and water."

"This is the primordial substance of all matter—the energy of Formation. Let us approach the Chalkydri."

"But…we will be destroyed by the fire!"

"You must come with me if you wish to know the Tao."

"Master, I cannot stand in the flame. I am not worthy. I will be destroyed."

It was true. The Priest had a degree of mastery over lesser forces in the World of Assiah, but he was totally unprepared for higher ascent.

"Where are your spirit allies?"

"I do not know. They are not here."

They descended into the First Heaven.

"What do you see?" asked *Yeshua*.

"Gods who oversee rain, wind, snow."

"Some of these are your allies. Call their names."

He did so, and immediately giant beings appeared before them. *Jian-Chi* communicated with them telepathically.

They told him that he had been tricked by playful nature spirits into offering them vital force from human devotions and animal sacrifices. All his altars and blood were not serving the angelic beings who oversaw the elementals of weather. Rather, they were serving the dark local spirits and creating even more powerful negative forces in the land. They told him that their work was to serve the Great Spirit of all worlds. They did not command the local spirits, who were merely free-willed inhabitants of the land. When he saw results in the weather from his ceremonies, it was merely because the local spirits had collaborated to continue the play. Otherwise, without blood sacrifices how would they vitalize themselves? They would merely come to the ends of their natural lives and dissolve back into their sources.

Jian-Chi asked if the Great Spirit was also known as the Tao. They answered yes.

Then he asked them if they knew where to find the Tao. They replied that She was closer than a heartbeat and more distant than a star. He asked if they knew the Tao, and they replied that we are all known by the Tao, and when we recognize what it is to be known by Her, then we will know Her.

Suddenly the two riders of the Chariot found themselves being pulled down toward their flesh-bodies, which were surrounded by a host of raven-like creatures being held at bay by *Jian-Chi's* Fierce Guardian.

"Destroy!"

The command had barely risen to the Priest's astral throat when the Fierce Guardian expelled multiples of himself in a stream of breath through his mouth—one for each evil spirit. Each of these, in turn, burnt the demons with fire that issued from their mouths. All that remained of the creatures were wisps of black smoke and ashes that quickly dissipated. Then the multiples flowed back into the nostrils of the fierce guardian, for whom the entire operation had been no more than an exhalation followed by an inhalation. Then the guardian himself dissolved back into the etheric aura of the Priest's sleeping body.

"I want one of those!" thought *Yeshua* in great admiration.

"You already have all the materials. You merely need to build them," answered *Jian-Chi*.

"How?"

"Begin on a New Moon. To prepare, you form a complete and detailed vision of the Guardian with all Its powers. You will build this form out of your own Double."

"This Double is the large being of energy that invisibly envelops the flesh-body when it is alive?"

"Yes."

The lesson in shamanic exorcism continued for some time until *Yeshua* understood the exact process. It would create what was essentially an etheric being that would react automatically without necessity of conscious thought like an invisible organ against psychic danger. It could also be sent forth to protect or exorcize others, and it could trace, track down, and destroy even the most subtle form of psychic attacker.

The skills of the *Bon-po* made sense to *Yeshua*. They were a coarse but clever development of things he had begun to master in Babylon. But they went far beyond what he had learned there, especially in the area of demon possession and exorcism.

When *Yeshua* had extracted all he needed from the mind of the Priest, it was *Jian-Chi's* turn to receive instruction.

"How do you call the rain?" inquired the *Bon-po* Priest.

"I make my alliances directly with the elemental spirits. I do not force or compel them. Rather, I make them my friends. I call rain through friendship and cooperation with the elementals."

"How do you establish these friendships?"

"The elemental spirits of any location are not static beings. Like us, many of them choose to grow on a spiritual path. The wisest of these know that in their future spiritual transmigrations, they can be part of a human soul—which is the greatest of all incarnations because it contains the All. Therefore they desire to gain merit for their future incarnations by serving the needs of a human soul who strives to maintain attunement with the Tao."

"So simple! So honest! No tricks!" marveled *Jian-Chi*.

"Everything is that way. All knowledge can be found in the Pure Heart."

"No ceremonies, no rituals…but I heard you chanting to bring the rain."

"If I give you the Word of Power, you must promise to use it according to the Edicts of the great King Asoka."

"Buddhism has been the enemy of *Bon-po*. How can I join forces with the enemy?" thought the Priest.

"There is no enemy, but within our own Hearts. Are you ready to awaken?"

"The Buddhists are fools. They are simple and sweet, but they do not know how to protect themselves from the attack of humans or evil spirits. They laugh at our rituals and traditions, but their religion does not prevent them from being sickened and slaughtered by evil ones. No, I cannot accept Buddhism."

With that the Priest snapped back into his body and began to awaken. *Yeshua* lingered for a moment, knowing that communication would be very difficult in the flesh-body, then sank back into his own flesh.

Morning twilight heralded the new day. The two men made their way to the base of Asoka's mound, bowed, and parted company.

Chapter Seventeen: THE *STUPA*

It had been many months since *Yeshua* had returned to the little monastery outside the City of Lotus Flowers. He meditated and practiced with *Nutesh* in the old man's cave. Now that he had the responsibility of a disciple, *Nutesh* had chosen to no longer maintain silence. He had become fluent in speech, just as he had been many years ago before undertaking the life of a Buddhist monk.

His wife had died childless, but he had enjoyed many years of a prosperous and happy marriage with her in Ctesiphon, where he had established a thriving business importing gem stones. After her death, he sold the business, donated most of the proceeds to the poor, and traveled by boat to the Indus River. There, being fluent in Greek, he studied Buddhism with Greek-speaking monks. He undertook a pilgrimage to Gandara and dwelt in *Takkasilâ,* which had a large Greek-speaking Buddhist population and was known to them as Sirkap. From there he took Buddhist vows, wandered to the City of Lotus Flowers, and joined the brothers of the monastery there.

Yeshua explained that he was a pious Jew, but that he agreed with Asoka's *Dhamma* that recommended that we should understand and honor other religions. He told him that he had received special guidance from his highest spiritual sources that he should study Buddhism and work as a Master builder to construct a great *stupa*.

Nutesh became very fond of *Yeshua* and taught him daily from the Buddhist Scripture that he had studied. He guided the young Master through the morning and evening group practices and *kirtan* of the monks, translating each word of the sacred chants so he could understand what he was singing. The day was divided into meditation, prayer, and work, with each monk taking his turn to do necessary menial tasks. *Yeshua* especially enjoyed working in the vegetable garden.

After winter had passed, *Nutesh* told him privately, "The monastery has received a large contribution to build a *stupa*. It will contain relics from the Buddha that have been saved from another *stupa* in an uninhabited area that has rotted away for lack of maintenance. Would you be willing to serve as the Master builder?"

Yeshua was stunned. The vision was coming into manifestation.

"To whom do I report?" he asked, forgetting even to answer in the affirmative.

"To me," was the matter-of-fact answer.

"Ah, I see...so you didn't give away all of your jewels when you swore the vows of poverty?" he teased.

"Yes, and no. You see, the jewels are kept in this cave in a wooden casket of cedar. I dedicated them to the Buddha when I joined the monastery. Everyone in the brotherhood knows where I buried them thirteen years ago—everyone except you."

Yeshua marveled at the integrity of the brothers, for any one of them could have taken them and become a rich householder.

Yeshua suddenly remembered his dream of jewels during his first night in the cave almost a year ago.

"I know where they are buried," he announced with a twinkle in his eye. "Right under the place you gave me for a bed."

"That is correct. In fact, the very place where you rest your head. Would you please unearth the cedar casket?"

Feeling carefully with both hands, *Yeshua* found a smooth but hard surface without pebbles. Using a sharp rock, he began to excavate. After a few minutes the rock scratched wood. More digging, and he could begin to see the outline of a small strongbox. Finally after much more effort, he drew the little casket from the ground and presented it to the old monk.

"It must be opened with a tool," he said. "I sealed it with iron bands."

Yeshua ran to the garden and found an iron plow blade. The other monks watched him, then joined him in a procession back to the cave of *Nutesh*. They broke silence when they saw the old man with the casket on his lap. Everyone began to excitedly tell the story of the jewels.

With his powerful shoulders, *Yeshua* applied a force to the iron bands using the plow as a wedge. Suddenly the bands burst apart. He handed the box to *Nutesh*.

The old man held up each stone to the light, examining it critically. There were too many to count, but *Yeshua* could see that they represented a true fortune. They would finance a very great structure, indeed!

Nutesh addressed the monks in Greek.

"My Brothers, we shall build a great *stupa* to honor relics of the Buddha. This will be larger and more beautiful than any others in Gandara. Many people will make pilgrimage and our little brotherhood will grow.

"Our friend *Issa,* my disciple from Babylon and Judea, is a *teknon Archon*, a Master builder. He will work under my direction as the head architect of this project.

"Our first job is to find a translator who is fluent in Chaldean and can communicate the orders of *Issa* to all the workmen."

Thus *Yeshua* became chief architect for the Great *Stupa* of *Pushkalâvatî*, the City of Lotus Flowers.

Land was purchased that summer. *Yeshua* specified a large, boulder-strewn mound in the foothills Northwest of the city that he had noticed on his journey to the rock Edicts. It was downslope from a quarry to the North, and near to a field that had proven to contain a proper proportions of sand and clay for baking durable bricks. It was not far from the city and accessible from a main Gandaran trade route. It would attract many pilgrims.

By fall, *Yeshua* had hired a translator—Ariston. The true name was *Aristun*, but he had modified it to the Greek form many years ago to facilitate business. He was not a Buddhist, but an older man retired from caravaning the trade routes—like *Nutesh* a native of Ctesiphon. He did not read, but he was verbally fluent in Chaldaean, Greek, and various local dialects. Best of all, he was pleasant company and a loyal friend.

The Master builder traveled with Ariston to several *stupas*, including the grand *stupa* at Sirkap, where he took notes and sketched dimensional scales. He observed what kinds of construction were most successful for the balconies and what configuration of base stones served best for a durable foundation. With the help of Ariston, who was also an astute judge of character, he hired several artisans who worked in wood joinery, carpentry, wood carving, and bronze casting. But good stone masons were either already employed at major sites, or unemployed because they lacked skills or good character. *Yeshua* finally decided he would train ten of the monks who would volunteer to become apprentices.

Iron tools and equipment were purchased or commissioned in the City of Lotus Flowers along with arrangements for food, water, and housing.

Since the stone foundations had to be properly quarried, smoothed, and laid before any of the other work could go forward, the Master builder spent most of the next spring supervising the quarry. The foundation work stopped during the hottest part of the summer, then resumed after the fall harvests.

Yeshua was inspired by the design of the Great *Stupa* in Sirkap, even though it was modeled somewhat after a Corinthian temple by Greek-speaking architects. One important improvement they had made was to build a stone dome, rather than using a rough natural mound into which they dug and fortified tunnels.

Under this dome they built a small but beautiful sanctuary. It was not furnished for Priests offering animal sacrifice, but for silent meditation and divine communion. It was open to all of the public—Buddhist or not. The charred bones of Buddhist saints were deposited in a reliquary positioned under a central altar.

Yeshua's design for the great *stupa* of the City of Lotus Flowers incorporated just such a sanctuary, but much larger. His main engineering problem would be building a durable stone dome. His solution for the dome was to raise high circular walls that could help support two levels of terraces for circumambulation, then nest carefully hewn stones on a shallow slant to create the domed roof.

Roman masonic *collegia* had developed their design for rock domes after many failures. *Yeshua* had hewn proper dome stones for the Roman Masters in Sepphoris and participated in raising them, so he knew the techniques. But success hinged upon the skill of his apprentices. After another year, after building the circular wall, they would be seasoned.

Yeshua shared a small house in the City of Lotus Flowers with *Nutesh* and Ariston. As the sun set each *Shabbat* eve, the Master builder offered the *Kiddush* cup for all three. But instead of wine, it was filled with water. Instead of bread, they shared barley and salted *ghee*. They became as eager to learn about the religion of the Messiah as their Jewish friend was to study Buddhist principles.

On Saturdays work on the *stupa* was suspended out of respect for the religion of the Master builder, so *Yeshua* and *Nutesh* spent the day discussing their two traditions while Ariston listened and questioned. They discovered innumerable parallels and similarities between the two religions—both in their purest forms, and in their corrupted forms.

******* ******* ******* *******

During the quarrying for the circular wall, one of the monks was seriously hurt in an accident. *Yeshua* brought in a Buddhist physician and also worked secretly to help the young man heal. Not long after, another apprentice grew ill. He could not stop vomiting and became extremely weak. This time the physician recommended that they find a *Bon-po* exorcist.

Yeshua remembered what the *Bon* Priest had said—that Buddhists were gentle and kind, but they could not defend themselves against the attacks of violent humans or evil spirits. He also realized that, if these were psychic attacks, they were directed against him personally. The apprentices were the key to building the great *stupa*. Without nine or ten trained and healthy apprentices, the project would languish.

That night the Master builder ventured out of his flesh-body in the *nephesh* to inspect the quarry site and his monk apprentices while they slept. He found nothing out of the ordinary, but decided to continue keeping watch.

Next week the thin crescent of a New Moon was visible following the sun into the Western horizon. *Yeshua* began the procedures he had learned from the *Bon-po* Priest to construct a Fierce Guardian from his etheric aura. He modified them with other procedures he knew to be superior to those used by the *Bon-po*. When the Full Moon could be seen rising in the East as the sun set in the West, he completed his operation. He was now prepared to provide psychic protection for all of his workmen.

A few days later the young Master walked among his apprentices as they quarried rock for the circular wall. As he approached, one of the men fell to the ground and appeared to be having a seizure.

"Tell me your name," commanded *Yeshua*.

One of the other apprentices said, "We all know his name."

Again, the young Master commanded the evil spirit to tell its name.

In a deep and strange voice, the obsessed monk-apprentice answered, "*Azabaal*."

"He is possessed!" cried the others.

"No, he is obsessed," whispered *Yeshua*.

"*Azabaal*, why do you trouble this young man?" he demanded in a loud voice.

After a pause, the answer was returned in the same deep voice: "I have been bound by a powerful magician and forced to ruin your apprentices."

"*Azabaal*, where did he find you?"

"At the site where my flesh had been eaten by the large, black birds."

In desert areas like those of Parthia, bodies were not buried, but left for birds to devour so that the bones could be removed to a clan ossuary. *Azabaal* was the *nephesh* of a dead man who had been captured and bound to the Earth to serve a magician.

"*Azabaal*, I shall release you from your bond, for I am more powerful than your magician. But first you must return to the one who sent you and deceive him into thinking you have been successful. If you succeed, I shall set you free."

"Master, I shall do as you command."

"*Azabaal*, I adjure you, release this young man and never trouble my apprentices again," sternly warned *Yeshua*.

Immediately the young apprentice stopped rolling on the ground, opened his eyes, and said, "Why is everyone looking at me?"

A sign of relief went up for the crowd of workmen.

"My Brothers, you will not be troubled again by evil spirits," declared *Yeshua*.

That evening *Nutesh* asked why he had said the young man was not possessed, but obsessed.

Yeshua answered, "Possession requires a long time. The evil spirits enter at first through here (he pointed to the nape of the neck and the ears). They enter through the Spirit of Pride, which is the hidden back entrance to the Spirit of Teaching and Hearing. They can cause distractions, accidents, and bad thoughts that won't go away—like insects buzzing around the head. This is obsession. It is easier to relieve.

"Once established behind the Spirit at the throat, however, they finally gain control of the entire *nephesh* through the Spirit of Disputation (he pointed to the solar plexus). This activates the *Yetzer-Ha-Ra* in the Heart through the Spirit of Guile. That constitutes possession, and it is much harder to relieve. Once the entities are removed, it may take a full year of recuperation in a clean and sacred place before the victim is no longer easily vulnerable to obsession. The portals to invasion heal slowly, once they have been allowed to open by the victim. Until the victim has beome strong and whole, the evil entities are able to return easily and progress to possession in a short time."

Ariston asked, "Is there no other way to protect one who has been cleansed of possession? A year is a long time."

Yeshua thought for a moment, then replied.

"If the victim had developed true *emunah*, he could be sealed with the *Ruach Ha-Qodesh*. Then as long as sanctity was kept, he or she would be invulnerable to obsession or possession. But if the victim follows the destructive impulses of the *Yetzer Ha-Ra* with his Heart, the Spirit will depart from him and leave him vulnerable again."

Again Ariston inquired, "What is true *emunah*?"

"You know what faith is. True faithfulness to Divine love and justice is fulfilled through intentions and deeds, not just words. If a victim has faithfulness, then he will remain faithful after release from bondage to the evil ones."

"Can a saint become possessed?" asked Ariston.

"I suppose that the most powerful of evil forces could overwhelm even a *tzadik* who did not maintain sanctity. Then, when that saint was freed from bondage, he or she could immediately be filled with the Holy Spirit and thereby protected—at least as long as the *halakah* of sanctification and holiness were faithfully kept."

That night *Yeshua* tracked *Azabaal* in the *nephesh* to find who was controlling the spirit. He was amazed to find that the magician who was trying to destroy his apprentices was none other than *Jian-Chi,* the very *Bon-po* Priest he had tried to help! Hatred of Buddhism, which had taken over his people and his land, was his motivation for stopping construction of the *stupa*.

After a moment of thought, *Yeshua* broke the bondage that had been placed upon *Azabaal's* soul, and the released *nephesh* immediately began to dissolve into the Second Death—the true release that the young Master had promised.

Yeshua knew that when the *Bon-po* Priest next attempted to call up *Azabaal*, and no spirit appeared to ruffle the water of his black bowl, he would realize that he had been cheated. He would then mount a new effort against the *stupa* project. The young Master would have to take stronger action to neutralize the evil work of *Jian-Chi*.

He returned to his flesh-body and prayed for guidance. Then he sank into sleep.

When he awakened in the morning, he could smell the fragrance of lilies. He knew that the guidance had been given. It would simply require time for the *Manda* or Divine Guidance to descend into the lower *yetzirah* of his conscious mind. With that realization, he fed and watered his donkey, then walked to the construction site.

******* ******* ******* *******

Three weeks passed with no more trouble at the construction site. The moon had waxed full. Lunar *keseh* permeated the warm spring night.

Yeshua sat upright in the chamber at the center of the *stupa*. He had sealed the entrance to the inner dome that was designed to house the sanctuary. His body was protected from any danger of intrusion into the chamber while he carried out his mission. But this would be more than simple projection of the *nephesh*. With the assistance of Shoshana, he would contact *Jian-Chi* from above—from the high regions of his *neshama*. They would establish a seed of *Manda* linking *nephesh* and *neshama* that would slowly take form in the *'Olam of Yetzirah*. The *Bon-po* Priest would experience it as Divine Illumination.

The seed of *Manda* would not act like hypnotic suggestion implanted in his lower mind. That would be the kind of mind-control used by inferior spirits. It was not lawful for a Brother to use such a mechanism, for it resulted in bondage—not liberation.

Rather, the seed would simply allow *Jian-Chi* to see Buddhism in a clear light, without the influence of prejudice and mental distraction. Since Buddhism is a vessel for Divine influences, the Heart of the *Bon-po* would receive these influences. This would stimulate the *Yetzer Ha-Tov* which would then present good impulses regarding Buddhism to counter the evil ones.

To prepare the ground for the seed, *Yeshua* would have to liberate *Jian-Chi* from the evil forces that had obsessed him about Buddhism and influenced his attack on the *stupa*. However, this work would have to come after the initial operation in the *neshama*.

To be effective, a liberator must descend into the lower realms from the higher—not the other way around. There is much danger in any attempt to ascend from the lower into the higher without the *merkabah* vehicle, and that vehicle cannot be built in the context of exorcistic battle with inferior spirits of the lower realms.

Thus *Yeshua* would first need to make a conscious ascent that could put him into clear telepathic contact with Shoshana—something he had never before attempted and, indeed, had not thought possible. This would mean retaining full consciousness in the flesh while making the ascent. But this idea had come to him in the fragrance of Shoshana's lilies. He knew that, with her help, he could make the ascent and remain conscious.

But how to do this?

A solitary oil lamp provided stark illumination. He extinguished the wick with his fingers. The chamber dissolved into ink-black darkness. He noted with satisfaction that the roof of the mound had been laid so well that not even one crack admitted the bright light of the full moon. When his work was done, he would have to grope for the iron handle of the wooden door that he had positioned himself to face.

Yeshua sat upright as he had learned to do at the Buddhist monastery—spine perpendicular to the Earth, foot touching foot, hand touching hand, so that there were no currents of duality across his limbs. His body now formed a single, unified central column. Now he made his ears into a single Ear by listening deeper and deeper within. He made his eyes into a single Eye by focusing his attention not on the place his eyes of flesh looked downward in the blind darkness, but above and deep into his forehead.

He breathed slowly and regularly, pacing one slow breath in for every five heartbeats, then one slow breath out for another five. After some time he lengthened it to six, then to seven. His breaths became very shallow, but he was fully awake in his body. When his legs or neck complained, he adjusted them very slightly without loosing his breathing rhythm.

After a long time he realized that he was hearing different voices and sounds of praise—sometimes the deep OM of the monastic brothers, at others the tone of a flute, and even others the voice of a *Rav* intoning the "lai, lai" of *niggunim*. Golden light seemed to be descending from above his head. Glowing clouds formed and dissolved into a violet shimmer. But he knew they were only the illusory fire and lightning of Elijah. The sounds grew louder until they seemed like a dull roar, but he knew that they were only the illusory thunder of Elijah. As he realized these things, all grew dark and silent for a long time.

Then, a still, small voice.

"Lift up your eyes, my Darling." It was like the echo of a voice—something that had been spoken and was now remembered a split second after.

The fragrance of lilies.

Yeshua turned his eyes upward with lids still closed.

"Open your Eye and behold my face."

He opened his lids. It was pitch black, but the inner light remained as long as he focused his attention from that Eye. Then gradually the image of Shoshana's face as he had known her in life emerged from what seemed an infinite distance behind his head, or perhaps from a tiny droplet of light suspended before him, expanding to take form where his eyes were focused. Her face glowed in golden light as she smiled upon him.

He continued to breathe with his Heart, which glowed with gratitude and joy, and to listen with his Ear. It was a delicate balance of consciousness, but he was beginning to master the technique. The wide smile that stretched across his bearded face seemed to empower the balance.

A very long time passed as he developed his balance and basked in Shoshana's light. He felt no grief, no yearning—just pure bliss.

Yeshua closed his eyes and Shoshana's face still glowed before him. They kissed and drew breath from each other. She breathed into his mouth, and he into hers, as he continued the rhythmic inhale and exhale. As her face slowly withdrew from his, a golden seed of light hung suspended between their lips. Slowly it sank downward and out of sight into the depths.

"I am always with you, Darling. My angels minister to you always."

Her soft voice echoed inside his head.

Now he opened his eyes and turned them downward. Very slowly, very gently, he slid into a reclining posture. Foot touch foot, hand touching hand, he continued his coordination of breaths and heartbeats—one for every seven.

Now he began to slow the breaths—one to eight, one to nine. As his body and brain entered into sleep, his *nephesh* awakened. He became aware of the silver cord as his subtle body rocked back and forth over his flesh like a boat at anchor, then suddenly shot like an arrow toward the Western horizon, to *Jian-Chi.*

He looked down at the sleeping body of the *Bon-po*, whose subtle body floated unconscious above his bed. Yes, at the nape of his neck there was something like a sleeping monkey clinging to *Jian-Chi's* vital centers.

Yeshua called to it like a carnival master.

"Your name!" he commanded. The startled entity awakened.

"Your name," he repeated more gently.

"I have no name. I am still being formed by the Heart of my master, the *Bon-po* Priest."

Jian-Chi had not been obsessed by dark entities—that was good. Perhaps his faith had kept him from that in spite of his exposure to them through his arts. Rather, he had unknowingly created his own obsession.

"Then I shall give you a name," replied *Yeshua*. "Your name is *Raqa*, for you are an *elil* of nothingness. Now you must return to the roots from which you came."

He touched the little beast and immediately it dissolved into a black smoke and dissipated.

Just over the crown of the *Bon-po's* head he could perceive a golden glow. The seed had found its mark. How would *Jian-Chi* integrate the Divine influence?

Yeshua carefully inspected the wound that had been left by the little beast as it sucked nourishment from the vital forces at the nape of the neck. He spat upon it and sealed many of the broken fibrillae, but it would remain an opening for other dark forces until *Jian-Chi* had strengthened himself with acts of righteousness.

Looking into the man's Heart, *Yeshua* saw a confused complex of good and evil impulses that had been woven together. For *Jian-Chi,* Buddhism was the source of political and religious injustice that had disempowered his people when Asoka forced the new religion upon them. The result was a Heart that sought to create justice by commiting acts of injustice against Buddhists. *Jian-Chi* was obsessed with zeal for what seemed to him the redress of injustice.

Well, the exorcism would stop the *Bon* Priest's attacks for now. But had there been enough *emunah* in his life to protect him from further entities? Would he change his Heart toward Buddhism? These were not questions that *Yeshua* could answer. The fruit would tell whether or not the tree was good.

Yeshua returned to his sleeping body in the chamber of the *stupa*. When he awakened later that morning, he could see that there were chinks of light. These he carefully marked before leaving so that his apprentices could mend them.

*******   *******   *******   *******

The Great *Stupa* of *Pushkalâvatî* entered its final stages of construction two years later. There had been no further attacks by the *Bon* Priest and all had gone well since then. The *stupa* had become a marvel that attracted pilgrims far and wide. They could not yet enter the sanctuary chamber, but walls, walkways, water supply, and outer gardens were in place.

The monks made a monthly pilgrimage to circumambulate the *stupa*. They made heroic efforts not to be bursting with pride but, as *Nutesh* confided to Ariston, "I am afraid we have all fallen somewhat short of our vows of humility."

Yeshua did not have that problem, due in large part to the fact that he was a perfectionist. With every visit he found flaws that required mending. He would not authorize the finishing of the inner chamber until everything else had been completed to his satisfaction. However, he had authorized the opening of the grounds for pilgrims once the garden had taken root and the water supply was in place.

Once Ariston asked him point blank, "Master, when will you complete and open the sanctuary? The money for this project is running short."

Yeshua replied, "Before the *stupa* can be formally consecrated and opened, there is something that must occur. I do not know what it is, but when I get the sign, we will procede with all speed to complete the inner chamber. Meanwhile, I have reserved all the funds needed to finish the sanctuary."

Ariston threw up his hands and walked away.

It was now fall. Work had stopped for the hot summer months and would soon resume. Soon after, the pilgrims would begin to appear again in even greater numbers.

Yeshua awakened with the fragrance of lilies. He remembered nothing from his sleep, but he knew that something significant was about to occur. He had an urge to make the hot, dry, and very unpleasant trip to the *stupa*. He didn't know why. The grounds would be silent and vacant. But he loaded water onto his donkey and made the trek while the sun was still low.

As he approached the *stupa*, he saw a lone figure slowly circumambulating the three-level steps that surrounded the central mound. By the time *Yeshua* had arrived at the gate, the man had completed his ritual and was sitting in a meditation posture in the shade of the garden.

The young Master tied his donkey under a shaded structure designed for pilgrims and their animals, brought water for the animal, and then strolled into the garden. The pilgrim looked up, startled to see anyone in the vicinity. Their eyes met.

The pilgrim was *Jian-Chi*.

Yeshua stopped short to asses the situation, but the *Bon* Priest lept forward with a beaming smile on his face, then threw himself in joyful prostration at the young Master's feet.

They could not speak each other's language, so when *Yeshua* took his hands and raised him up he pointed to a place in the garden shade where they could sit and write in the sand.

Jian-Chi pointed to himself and said, "Buddhist."

Yeshua's eyes widened. He raised his hands and leaned his neck forward in a posture of asking. The *Bon-po* drew Greek letters in the sand: A-S-O-K-A. He had studied Buddhist principles of Edicts of Asoka inscribed in rocks in many locations throughout Gandara, sometimes in both Greek and the local language.

Then *Jian-Chi* pointed to *Yeshua* and asked, "Buddhist?"

Yeshua found himself at a loss for words. Was he a Buddhist? No, he was a Jew. But he found Buddhist principles to be very much like those of the Jewish prophets, and he found the Buddhist people to be the kindest he had ever known. Was he a Buddhist?

Yeshua pointed to the *stupa*, then to himself, then drew a picture of the temple in the sand and again pointed to himself. He spoke the Greek words he knew, hoping that the Priest might understand them: *Eimi Teknon Archon.*

Jian-Chi's eyes widened and he slowly repeated, *Teknon Archon.* He understood. Then he fell to his knees and again prostrated himself before *Yeshua*, this time with tears and sobs. The young Master undertood that the *Bon-po* was very distressed to find that his friend, whom he had always loved since they first encountered each other, was the man whose work he had tried to destroy using black magic.

Yeshua laid his right hand upon the young man's head and placed his left hand upon his own Heart. The two remained in this posture for some time until *Jian-Chi* no longer sobbed. He knew that *Yeshua* was a great Master—greater than he himself. He realized why his attempts to stop the *stupa* were not successful, and that *Yeshua* probably knew more about all this than he had thought. He also realized that *Yeshua* truly held no grudge, but sincerely forgave his rash actions. And he was filled with a peace and gratitude that overflowed from his Heart.

Again *Yeshua* raised him up and looked wordlessly into his eyes with great compassion. He knew that *Jian-Chi* was, indeed, a true *tzadik* who had lost his way in the service of what he had perceived as justice. Now he had found his way. The seed of Divine influence had fallen into the fertile garden of the *Bon-po's* Heart and borne fruit. He had self-healed the vulnerability to obsession by dark forces that he had self-created.

They meditated silently together in the garden until the sun was low in the Western sky. Then *Yeshua* pointed to *Jian-Chi*, to himself, then to the hills of the North and asked in his best Greek, "Buddhist academy?" The Priest nodded enthusiastically, so they loaded the donkey and began trekking toward the Buddhist monastery where the old saint *Nutesh* lived.

They arrived late at night and camped outside the monastery, then entered the next morning. After greetings by all the monks, *Yeshua* brought *Jian-Chi* to the cave of *Nutesh* and explained the young Priest's conversion to Buddhism.

"We have several monks who speak his language," *Nutesh* advised. "He can visit as long as he wants to be here. If he wants to become a Brother, we can consider that, too."

Nutesh called out in another language, and soon a young Brother appeared. He spoke the native language of *Jian-Chi*, and within minutes the two were engrossed in long conversation.

"You will be happy to hear that I am ready to finish the inner chamber and prepare for the formal consecration and opening," *Yeshua* announced to the old saint. *Nutesh* was overjoyed. He took the young Master's right hand and kissed it. The young brother stopped talking to *Jian-Chi* and listened attentively.

"But I have one condition," continued *Yeshua*.

"Anything you want!" the old man joyfully replied.

"You and your monks have to promise to remain humble," he drawled with an imitation Hindi accent.

Everyone laughed, even *Jian-Chi*, who didn't have a clue about what was so funny. But he was amazed to find a Buddhist monk who could speak his language and was bursting with happiness.

When *Yeshua* returned to the City of Lotus Flowers late that afternoon, *Jian-Chi* remained at the monastery.

Chapter Eighteen: EGYPT AND THE *THERAPEUTAI*

Many years had passed since *Yeshua* wandered heartbroken into the Eastern desert. Slowly his Heart had mended. He felt no separation from his beloved Shoshana. He also had no desire to have sexual contact with any other woman. What many religious ascetics found difficult was natural for him. He was full and lacking nothing—no emotional need for life with a woman, and no desire to have children.

But with the completion of the Great *Stupa*, he now felt a deep responsibility to visit his Mother and family. He would come not to live in Nazareth or return to the work of a Master Builder—indeed, he knew that his enemies in the local Guild would refuse to honor his status as a Master—but to seek *Hochmah* and the Will of the *Abba*.

He awakened often with an echo of the voice of the *Ruach Ha-Qodesh,* speaking sometimes in Shoshana's dulcet tones, other times in the masculine whisper he had come to identify with Elijah. Heaven was urging him on to Egypt.

Yeshua had accumulated a small fortune for his work on the *stupa*. Most of this was kept for him by *Nutesh*, with just enough for his basic needs being paid out regularly. At the Consecration of the Sanctuary by Buddhist Priests, *Nutesh* had presented him with a large purse filled with Bactrian gold coins.

It was more than sheer coincidence that an Aramaic-speaking Babylonian merchant from Sirkap was present for the Consecration. He was an admirer of the Greco-Roman style used in the Great *Stupa* at Sirkap, which had strongly influenced the design of *Yeshua*. After the ceremonies he rushed to the young Master's side with a business proposition. Would he design and build a home for him in Sirkap?

"Ah, it is nice to hear my language spoken," replied *Yeshua*. "But I intend to depart for Egypt as soon as I can find a way to get there."

The merchant thought for a moment, then looked up slyly and said, "The best way is to sail from Karachi. My Nabataean partners have already arrived with the seasonal monsoon, but they cannot make the return journey until the season changes and the wind blows from the East. That will be many months.

"Come, stay with me in Sirkap and build me a new home. I will pay you very well. Then we will travel by caravan down the Indus through the territory of Sindh to deliver my goods to my partners in Karachi. From there you can depart for Egypt on one of the ships."

Yeshua was silent while he measured the man's character.

"Okay, I'll make the deal even sweeter. During my last trip through Bactria, I was able to purchase a large amount of highest-quality *lapis lazuli*. I'll let you invest in a portion of it. You will triple your investment even if one or two ships go down."

Nutesh was sitting nearby in the garden and had heard everything.

"I shall consult with my friend and employer for a moment, then give you my answer," replied *Yeshua*.

Nutesh rose from his seat and approached the two men smiling.

"*Ratah…Ratah*? Is that you? I didn't know you were living in Sirkap!" he said warmly.

"By my Life, I didn't recognize you either, *Nutesh!*" replied the merchant.

"*Yeshua,* Dear *Yeshua.* So you are determined to go to Egypt! I am afraid that I've grown attached to you. Now you have found another vice to add to my pride—my attachment to your company. How we will miss you!" declared the old man.

"Then, you vouch for this man's character?" laughed *Yeshua.* "Yes, he seems quite genuine to me—for a merchant!"

They all laughed.

"Well, we were friends as youths, but I can't vouch for how he's turned out," *Nutesh* teased. "However, anyone who wants to be present for hours and hours of Buddhist Temple Consecration certainly demonstrates endurance."

Ratah spent the next days and nights with *Yeshua, Nutesh,* and Ariston at their home in the City of Lotus Flowers while the young Master made preparations.

His sweet little donkey Meros had aged. *Yeshua* did not want to use her as a beast of burden any more, so *Nutesh* brought her back with him to the monastery where she would live out the rest of her life as a pet. *Ratah* had a small caravan of strong camels to bring *Yeshua's* few possessions across the Valley to Sirkap.

Yeshua left one skilled monk in charge of *stupa* maintenance, brought four others with him who had agreed to work, and embarked with *Ratah* and his caravaners upon the long road to Sirkap.

******* ******* ******* *******

The weeks went by quickly as the young Master and his men devoted their full attention to *Ratah's* new estate.

Sirkap lived up to its name, "City of Stones." Beautiful examples of Greco-Roman architecture had been erected in this metropolis of trade. It was clear why *Ratah* wanted his own impressive estate—not only for comfort and show, but also as a place to host business clients.

Yeshua was able to find stone masons trained in the cutting of proper Corinthian pediments and columns, since most of the city's architecture was based on Greco-Roman themes. Consequently he was able to lay the foundations and walls with his monks while local masons cut the more exotic stone. Within a few months the structure was ready for indoor carpentry and his job was done.

Their arrangement was that instead of the large builder's fee expected at the end of the work, *Yeshua* would be given the equivalent in valuable goods-in-trade that he would deliver to *Ratah's* Egyptian merchant partners. Half of the sale would be for *Yeshua* and half for the Nabataean captain whose fleet would deliver him there.

Ratah was very pleased with the work. He had provided room and board for *Yeshua* and his men for minimal fees, which were deducted from daily salaries. Now it was time for the Brothers to return to their monastery, and *Ratah* to begin the trek South down the Indus River with *Yeshua* and the caravan.

"How do you know your partners will wait for you at Karachi?" the young man asked as they made the turn onto the Indus Valley road. "What if the monsoon comes early?"

Ratah laughed.

"Without my incenses, spices, and precious stones, they lose money. They have to wait for us."

He paused for a moment, then became somber.

"Now I want to tell you more about the Nabataean traders. Most of them are out for money. Don't turn your back on them. Hide your purse and sleep with a big knife. They have no allegiance to you, and I'll have no way of knowing whether you survive the voyage.

"Very often we lose one or two ships. That's why we use the smaller *dhows*. Even if you send a letter to me on one of their ships when they return next season, how do I know it's from you? They could have slit your throat and thrown you into the ocean. Remember, they are also pirates."

"Well, is there anything good about sailing with the Nabataeans?" asked *Yeshua*.

"It gets you to Egypt, if that's what you want," replied the merchant. "Or at least it gives you a good chance, if you are smart and blessed by Heaven."

Yeshua was silent.

They arrived exhausted at Karachi two weeks later. The Nabataean ships were in port and already loading goods.

Ratah introduced *Yeshua* to the fleet captain, who looked more like a short, squat pirate king.

"This is my son *Yeshua*," he lied in Koine Greek. "He is traveling to Alexandria with my goods and will be received by merchants in the city. He will get you the best price for everything, especially the *lapis*. Keep him safe. If he falls into the Sea, pull him out again. I charge you personally with his safety, and I will confirm next year by caravan delivery with my merchants in Alexandria that all was done correctly. You are my partner, yes?"

The captain smiled broadly and bowed.

"Then you want to remain being my partner, yes?"

He bowed again. Then reaching up to *Yeshua's* broad shoulder he called out to some of his crew.

"*Huios Ratahou…Akouei, Huios Ratahou!*" The men laughed. *Yeshua* towered over both *Ratah* and the captain. It was clear to anyone that he was not remotely related to *Ratah*. The sailors replied, "Nai, nai…," but their "yes" did not mean "yes."

Yeshua chose his sleeping space carefully in the captain's larger *dhow*. The stern area was covered with a flat wooden roof with sides that provided protection from wind and rain. He positioned himself against rear and side walls to minimize possible angles of attack. He was bigger and stronger than the swarthy Nabataean crew members, but an attack from two or more could be deadly.

The *dhow* was unlike the Roman Triremes and Quadriremes he had seen from a great distance on the Mediterranean. There was a large rudder, no ranks of oars, and a huge sail mounted askew on a mast. The mast and boom were held in place by a system of ropes that the crew had worked long hours to repair while in port. If they were to fail in a strong wind, the entire mast could come down.

Yeshua had brought water and provisions for three weeks, but the journey to the Red Sea would take longer. He planned to re-provision at *Cane,* the Nabataean colony on the other side of the Persian Gulf, but knew that he might have to depend upon the ship's large water supply that was carefully rationed each day to the sailors.

For the first few days out he kept to himself. He was not expected to work as a sailor, but he took note of everything the crew members did. The captain was friendly but did not offer food when the crew was fed.

For many days the voyage was uneventful. The hot sun beat upon the parched deck, which the crew washed from time to time with sea water to keep the planks swollen and tight. The salt water also preserved wood from rot. The monsoon winds blew steadily from the East, moving the flotilla of boats Westward toward the red skies of the setting sun. The wind slackened at night but continued to move the fleet.

Then one morning the sun rose in the East obscured by roiling clouds. They approached rapidly during the morning. The sky darkened, the wind began to howl, and sailors rushed to double their lines and lower the angle of the sail. The captain barked orders and the other boats closed in to be available for mutual rescue work when the storm hit. The waves grew larger and the little ships rocked up and down in what were becoming small mountains of water, each seeming to disappear then reappear.

Suddenly the sky grew as black as night, the wind gusted crazily from all directions, and a torrent of rain seemed to drown the boat. The other boats disappeared into the chaotic storm. Many of the sailors were paralyzed with nausea and simply clutched onto anything they could for stability. Black seawater repeatedly rose like a monster over the bow and crashed down onto the deck. The captain lashed himself to the large steering rudder, working every second to keep the boat's stern to wind and waves.

Yeshua controlled his nausea. He crawled inch by inch to the mast and pulled himself upright. The captain motioned for him to lay down, but the young master stood erect to his full height. He held onto the mast with his left arm and raised his right to the Easterly storm winds.

Now he intoned with such power and resonance that its vibration could be felt and heard even over the tumult.

"Ee-ah-oh-way-ee!" he repeated over and over.

The wind began to slacken. The rain drizzled to a stop. A great opening appeared in the black clouds overhead. As the disk of the sun appeared, the howling of the wind diminished to the normal sound of the trade wind. The huge, chaotic waves began to resume their normal orderly swell as they passed quickly beneath the *dhow*.

Captain and sailors watched dumbfounded by this display of what were assumed to be powers only of gods—not of men. Then the captain realized that without full sail, he was not able to control the rudder and quickly barked orders. *Yeshua* stepped away from the mast and looked for the other boats. They had all survived the storm. Then he sat on the deck next to the captain while the little ship was brought underway.

The rest of the voyage to *Cane* was uneventful, except that now *Yeshua* was paid great deference by everyone and offered rations when the crew was fed. When the fleet passed the wide bay that formed the Persian Gulf, the captain pointed and explained in Greek that the regions near Babylon were a week's sail North. *Yeshua* realized that he had no desire to return to the place that had given him the happiest days of his life, even if it were possible.

The port of *Cane* was a Nabataean colony established to service trading ships in the Arabian Sea. It was prosperous but isolated—gleaming structures on a desolate shore. Large and small *dhows* dangled from temporary moorings as they bobbed in the gentle Easterly swells awaiting their turn at the dock. There cargo was traded, offloaded, and new cargo taken on for transport to the the Red Sea. It was not a time for shore leave, but food, water, and other rations were renewed with luxury items like dried figs, dates, and Egyptian beer for the sailors. The day was filled with intense activity and shouted greetings among brothers and cousins after the long sea journey.

Yeshua watched over *Ratah's* spices, mother-of-pearl, and *lapis lazuli*, which were not to be transferred. They were bound for a port at the far North of the Red Sea.

The next morning the fleet of *dhows* was again under way. After another week's sail they arrived at their next portage—a large island from which the shores of Egypt could be seen. This was a Nabataean pirate sanctuary safe from Roman patrols. Here precious frankincense was taken on board.

It had been gathered, dried, and wrapped in storage by native Bedouins after they collected resins from the rare desert plant that produced the sweet incense, which was highly prized by the Romans. For many years the Roman rulers of Egypt had tried to control the profitable frankincense trade. Roman quadriremes patrolled the Red Sea looking for the Nabataean *dhows* that ran cargoes of the illicit resin North to Bedouin caravan outposts. But the quadriremes could not catch or trap the fast little Nabataean ships, which were powered by reliable winds that pushed their sails faster than the oars of the Romans. Even if a *dhow* were trapped by failing wind, the Roman patrols could be bribed. In fact, the game of chasing *dhows* was played mainly for the prize of a bribe because merchants would not buy frankincense from Roman patrols.

As they began their run up the Red Sea, the captain passed the time entertaining *Yeshua* with stories of close calls with Roman patrols. His simple Koine Greek was limited by a short vocabulary that required attempts at Aramaic words or simply pantomime, but *Yeshua* found himself able to both understand and respond in Greek. His many years of travel away from home had sharpened his use of the common Hellenistic language of merchants.

Yeshua did not like the common Greek language. The Koine could express only simple ideas and stories suitable for traders in foreign lands. It would be impossible for a prophet or philosopher to communicate spiritual teaching in the language of pirates and businessmen. It was a blessing that he had been able to discuss divine realities in his own Aramaic language with brilliant philosophers like the Hermetic master Ariston, the Pythagorean Stephanos, the urbane Eliud, and of course his many Jewish masters. He would never have been able to grasp the subtle teachings of Buddhism if his dear friend *Nutish* had not spoken Aramaic.

The Red Sea was unbearably hot at midday and there was no wind. The fleet of *dhows*, which had now dwindled to only four ships as others headed for different destinations, rafted together to share rations and nap under reed shelters erected from stern to mast. When the wind returned, the men awakened, unrafted, and opened the sails wide.

In conversations with the captain, *Yeshua* learned that when they made port he would negotiate prices with *Ratah's* merchant partners. The goods would include both *Ratah's* and those given in payment to *Yeshua* by *Ratah*. Included in these negotiations would be his own transportation overland to the Nile River, where he would hire water transport to Alexandria, with its large Jewish colony. The captain offered advice about how to negotiate and what prices to offer. If one merchant would not pay his prices, he could simply wait for the next caravan. *Ratah* was in partnership with all of them.

The captain would receive half of whatever total price was negotiated. He would also ask *Yeshua* to write a short receipt for *Ratah* in Greek affirming that he had arrived safely in Egypt, and detailing what prices had been received for both his and *Ratah's* goods.

******* ******* ******* *******

They reached port at Clysma, an ancient mining area now used by Nabataean pirates for delivery of frankincense. No one was in sight—just flat salt marshes and desert.

Yeshua asked the captain when the caravans would arrive. He explained that they would come down from the North when their lookouts sighted the fleet. It could take a day or two.

After tieing their ships to mooring stakes, everyone debarked fully armed with swords and knives. They waded through murky water to a large mud-brick building that looked down upon the fleet. The late afternoon sun was still hot, but the building was relatively cool with small windows facing the bay and on the opposite wall.

Here on the cool earthen floor it was hard for *Yeshua* to keep his balance even while sitting. The floor seemed to bob and sway like the deck of a *dhow*. It would be a few days before he stopped feeling the sensation of being on a rocking boat day and night. But the smell of earth and the cool air helped him to realize how happy he was to be back on land. He tucked his purse under his head and joined the others in a welcome nap.

That night they made no fire because it would be seen by Bedouin raiders from the Eastern deserts. Instead they quietly ate dried fruit and drank Egyptian beer. Lookouts were posted and changed throughout the night.

In the cool morning light before the sun had risen, everyone was awake. Nanataean men had appeared from the North leading empty pack camels. They led them to the shore next to the earthen building and the captain offered the men hospitality. Everyone sat together outside next to the camels and indulged in a fine meal of dates, figs, and dried meats—but no beer. Then the captain ordered the sailors to help the camel men unload cargo and secure it to the pack animals. *Yeshua* carried much of his own cargo, which he tied to three camels.

Now began the journey North to rendezvous with Egyptian trading caravans. The captain assigned some heavily armed men to guard the *dhows* and others to accompany him and *Yeshua* to the meeting place, which was half a morning's journey.

Just as the sun had begun to bake the marshy landscape, which stretched like a valley to the East of the rocky footpath taken by the caravan, they reached an abandoned mining colony. Its broken-down huts provided shelter from the scorching heat, and there were large indoor supplies of fresh water kept in earthen pits for weary caravans. This was no oasis. Any ground water would have been brackish, for the Red Sea extended Northward in marsh plains all the way to the Mediterranean.

"When will the traders arrive?" asked *Yeshua*.

"They travel by night during this time of the year. Since they are not here today, they will probably arrive late tonight or tomorrow morning," answered the captain.

Again, early in the morning twilight the alert was given. The Egyptian caravans had begun to arrive. Everyone bolted into action. Guards took positions for possible defense, and the camels were strung together into a tight circle.

The first caravan settled into a group of huts about fifty yards away while the trader in charge walked halfway to *Yeshu's* camp and sat down, his arms spread in greeting. *Yeshua* and the captain strode smiling to the preordained place of negotiation and sat facing the trader.

Yeshua saw the *tzitzit* or special purple fringes dangling from a prayer shawl underneath the trader's rough outer wear.

"Ah!" he said in Greek, "are you a Son of Abraham?"

The trader bowed and smiled. Now *Yeshua* spoke in Aramaic.

"I am *Yeshua* of Nazareth, son of *Yosef,* and a Master Builder like my father."

The trader was overjoyed. He took *Yeshua's* hand and kissed it.

"I speak a little of the language of Israel, but—I am—an Alexandrian and Greek is my native language," he uttered in halting Aramaic.

"This is very good," whispered the captain to *Yeshua*. "You do the negotiations."

The Jewish trader drove a hard bargain, but so did *Yeshua*. The trader would sell to Alexandrian merchants, who would be required to pay large tariffs, and the frankincense would have to be sold at far below market rates to Roman smugglers. *Yeshua's* passage to Alexandria with the caravan was part of the negotiation as well.

Eventually, however, they came to agreement on everything—both *Ratah's* goods, which had been given in payment to *Yeshua,* and all the rest of the captain's cargo. *Yeshua* and the captain oversaw the inspection of goods by the Jewish trader and after final approval, while goods were being transfered, they received purses full of Roman coins.

Departure for Alexandria began in late afternoon as the land cooled. The Jewish caravan began its journey on a well-worn road leading West toward the setting sun. *Yeshua* walked with the trader and spoke in a mix of Greek and Aramaic.

"That place where your fleet landed, that is Clysma. Between there and this abandoned mining camp was where the Exodus of our people was done."

"But there is no Sea, only marshes," protested *Yeshua*.

"Oh, there will be a great Sea if you stop and wait. It comes in with big tides on the full moon, then recedes. *Moshe* knew this place and understood the tides. He brought us across the marshes when they were dry from a very low tide. When we had made the crossing, Pharaoh's armies were trapped in the Sea that rushed in. If you were a miner, you would know that when this happens, you can see great walls of water both to the South and to the North. When you see them, get up out of the marshes as fast as possible!" he laughed.

"How do you know these things?" asked *Yeshua*.

"My family used to work the mines many generations ago," he explained. "This story was told by the Jewish miners from oldest times."

The full moon rose in the East as the sun set over the Western horizon.

"What is that?" *Yeshua* asked, pointing to a huge dry ditch that sprawled across the desert.

"That was once a great canal. Many of our ancestors died digging it into the desert. It leads to the Nile," was the terse answer.

The caravan made its way Northwest under the light of the full moon. After many hours, when the moon stood at midheaven, they reached an oasis. After an hour's rest, the trader pointed to the top of a hill.

"Come. I will show you something you will not forget."

They climbed the sandy ridges until they stood high over the *wadis*. The trader pointed East. The dry marshland from which they had come was now a great gleaming ribbon of tidal water.

"That is the Sea of Reeds. It will be gone by morning, then return in the afternoon. But in a few days it will be completely dry until the next moon. That is where our people crossed with *Moshe*."

Yeshua was silent for a moment.

"Then, where is the holy Mount Sinai?" he asked.

"My grandfather told me that *Moshe* must have followed the Eastern banks of the Reed Sea to the North, guided by the stars. The holy Mountain is far to the North," was his answer.

*******   *******   *******   *******

After many nights of travel, they reached the sacred city of Memphis on the Nile River. There the caravan would offload its cargo to barges pushed by currents and poled by strong men North to Alexandria. *Yeshua* would travel with the trader on one of the barges. However, he was told that it usually required a few days for the bargemen to appear once news of a new caravan arrival was made known.

Yeshua knew that Memphis had been an ancient center of Egyptian Priesthood. Now, however, the Temple had fallen into ruins.

"Where are the Priests?" he asked.

"I have never seen them. It is said that their sacred precincts are hidden under the earth, but I don't know whether this is true."

Yeshua decided to devote his time there to searching for the sacred precincts. He began that evening when the gibbous moon rose. His strategy was to sit in silent vigil in the midst of the Temple ruins and listen, then perhaps find a protected niche and project his *nephesh* for psychic skrying.

For hours he heard nothing. Finally he found a non-descript cave-like opening in which his body would be safe while he explored in the *nephesh*. Laying back in a partially sitting posture, he began the process of projection. Soon he passed through his own tunnel of unconsciousness and awakened floating above his *basar* in the sidereal body.

He drifted into the earth below him and began to look for light. He found that the small opening where he had lain led to a long tunnel with many turns and false exits, then finally into a small cavern furnished with one decaying chair, next to which the rotting remains of two oil lamps lay on a mound of earth.

He saw wet, collapsed earth where there had once been another tunnel. But now all structures had fallen into ruin.

Clearly there were no longer Priests to carry on the ancient traditions of initiation. But what were these traditions?

A fragrance of lilies wafted into his consciousness. In a flash he remembered what Shoshana had told him about the mental and etheric substances that living humans leave behind like footprints. She termed this substance *mummia*. It is a permanent record that can never be erased.

She said, "The good and evil that people do cannot be changed. It leaves its clues relentlessly inscribed in the Mind of the *'Olam* like memories. We may try to balance past evils with good actions, but the consequences of our evil deeds always remain, like debts that can never be repaid."

"Yes," he had replied, "but there is a way to release ourselves from the consequences of those debts. Do you know what it is?"

"How can that be?" she asked.

He burned with inspiration and said, "Heaven releases us from the consequences of our moral debts to the extent that we release those who have harmed us."

"Then, we can be released from the power of our own sin by forgiving others?" she asked incredulously.

"No, I said that we can be released from the *consequences* of our sins by forgiving others. The consequence of sin is self-destruction. But this is also a consequence of bitterly hating those who have sinned against us. We destroy our own souls by our lack of forgiveness. That very attitude allows us to remain in bondage to the evil *yetzer*."

"Then, what does it mean to forgive? Is it to forget?"

"No, my Darling. As you said, the Mind of the *'Olam* never forgets. Rather it is to step into the shoes of the enemy, try to understand his pain and bondage even though he might not, and then release your hatred against him."

"Would you be able to do that if someone brutally murdered me, my Love?" Shoshona asked.

Yeshua was jolted by this vivid memory, which snapped him back into his sleeping body. For a moment he nearly awakened, then slowly floated free again.

Had he been able to forgive *Ubar* and his cronies, whose fear and hatred of Shoshana had empowered her death?

Again, the scent of lilies.

Well, at least he had not slaughtered them with his bare hands. He had abandoned Babylon. He had slowly recovered from the deepest of all possible spiritual wounds inflicted by the cruel ignorance of men, but it had required many years.

Yes, he had been able to release them. He felt no bitterness. He did not desire their destruction—only their liberation from human evil. Indeed, the Buddhists were right. The only way for all humanity is the way of liberation.

"That is the meaning of my name," thought *Yeshua*. "The *Ruach Ha-Qodesh* inspired my Father to give me this name. I shall be worthy of this name."

Now he greatly desired to explore the memories engraved in the ruined Cave of Initiation—to learn more about the ancient Priesthood of Orisis before he was merged by a later Priesthood with *Apis* to become the God *Serapis* of Alexandria.

He followed the collapsed tunnel. It was permeated with *mummia*. Flashes of young men crawling on hands and knees in utter darkness seeking for an entrance into the Divine Underworld of the night heavens. Many steps leading deeper into the Earth. Bright lamplight gleaming through a closed wooden door framed in bronze.

Now he could hear chanting—not in Greek, but in another ancient and seemingly semitic language. There were many "m's" and "r's"—almost a kind of mumbling. Sacred Egyptian rites.

He drifted through the door. There he became aware of the fleeting outlines of many Priests attired in white linen robes and seated on gilded thrones. Each wore a gilded black mask, but each was different, apparently signifying different deities. They all sat facing a large underground lake.

A natural cavern extended perhaps the length of 1000 cubits to a cliff from which fresh water flowed over small waterfalls. There must also have been a place for water to exit. Its source must have been ground water seeping from the Nile.

Each shaven-headed Priest wore a large golden breastplate that covered his solar plexus. It was tied in place by four gilded cords strapped around the back and waist. *Yeshua* could see that this served to shield them from negative subtle forces. It also made them extremely sensitive to other invisible entities.

They were watching a naked young man ritually bathing in the black waters. Now he ascended the marble steps onto the island. *Yeshua* followed.

There, lying on a bed of linen, was the dismembered corpse of an old man. The head was propped up in a ghastly display, barely visible in the dim light. The neophyte gasped and stepped back. Immediately the Priests began to intone a hymn. The grizzly scene grew brighter. *Yeshua* became aware of a Priest without a mask hidden from sight of the neophyte. He was manipulating a lamp and mirror from the oblique side of the island.

As the Priest directed more light upon the scene, it began to change. Colors began to emerge. The dismembered arms, legs, and head seemed to rejoin the body. The bearded face assumed flesh tones, grew younger, and its expression transformed from one of from pain to serenity. As the light grew stronger, what had seemed to be a grizzly murder scene took on the appearance of a gilded throne, florid with spring-like greenery. Finally, seated upon the throne was the impressive appearance of a youthful bearded god.

This must be an enactment of the *qimah* of the ancient god Osiris, realized *Yeshua*.

Abba Yosef had once made the cryptic remark that although Egypt had been a place of captivity for Israel, it was also a source great spiritual knowledge given to Israel through *Moshe*. Clearly the ancient Egyptians understood the *qimah* of the *tzadik*, realized *Yeshua*.

After this vision, the Priest hidden on the island stepped forth and, while a new hymn was sung, wrapped the neophyte in a white robe. Then he led him back to shore across a bridge obscured from view behind the island.

This was the High Priest. He wore no mask. His breastplate was large and ornate. As he stood with the new Initiate and began to speak to the other Priests, *Yeshua* was able to glimpse his face. In amazement, *Yeshua* saw his own face! He felt a thrill of energy.

The vision faded from view and *Yeshua* returned to his physical body.

On the following morning the Jewish trader asked if he had found any Priests.

"I think there are none living in this area," he replied.

******* ******* ******* *******

After the hot barge journey on the Nile, *Yeshua* was ready for the caravan that greeted them. There was a short leg overland to Alexandria where he could negotiate a sea fare to Caesarea, and from there the trader's *Via Maris* to Sepphoris and Nazareth. This, however, was not to be.

Just outside of Alexandria the caravan was attacked by bandits. They suddenly appeared from behind the ruins of a mud hut, running at top speed. There was no time to prepare for the onslaught. *Yeshua* had no weapon—not even a staff.

One of the bandits swung a large curved sword. Seeing the pouch of coins tied around *Yeshua's* neck, he lunged for the throat. *Yeshua* ducked the blade, but his left arm was slashed to the bone, gushing blood. With a lightning lunge, *Yeshua* grabbed the bandit's sword hand with his powerful right arm and squeezed it with a relentless power. The man's eyes grew fearful, then howled in pain as his wrist and fingers snapped. The sword dropped from his crushed hand. Immediately *Yeshua* gave the bandit's arm a powerful jerk that dislocated his shoulder. Then he released him and brandished the fallen sword in his right hand. The Bandit ran howling after his compatriots, who were already fleeing with their contraband, leaving several caravaners wounded or dying.

Yeshua quickly tied off his left arm with a strip of linen from his tunic. He was able to stauch the blood loss with this temporary tourniquet. He pulled down the head of one of the pack camels, who obediently dropped to both knees. Using the bandit's curved sword, he slashed the cargo from the animal's back, threw himself onto the camel, and tried to slow his beating heart.

"You will have to pay for the cargo!" yelled one of the caravaners in Greek. *Yeshua* threw him a large Roman coin. The man took the coin and nodded his assent.

"I will take you to the *Therapeutae*," he said. "They are better than physicians, and today they will be under the city doing public healings."

Pack animals were loaded with fallen cargo. Both slain and wounded men were thrown like sacks over the backs of camels whose cargo had been stolen. As the sun set, the caravan resumed its slow journey toward the gleaming walls of the City of Alexander.

At the merchant's gate, Roman tax collectors did a thorough inventory of goods, but allowed the wounded to walk into the city if they were able. *Yeshua* dismounted from his camel.

"Where are the *Therapeutae*?" he asked one of the Roman officials in Greek.

The man pointed to what appeared to be a large well or cistern.

"You will find them under the city," he replied.

At this point *Yeshua* felt too weak to ask more questions, so he stumbled to the cistern, not knowing what to expect. Steps led down into darkness. The gentle sound of flowing water echoed amost musically from below. He looked back at the man who had pointed the way, who nodded encouragement. So the young Master made his painful descent into the darkness.

He found himself in a seemingly endless tunnel. Dim light revealed a great trench with flowing water. On either side were paved walkways. As his eyes became used to the darkness, he saw the source of light some distance away. Making his way toward the light, he could hear a woman's voice. She was singing or chanting.

Marble arches appeared, beyond which lay a chamber which was the origin of the dim lamplight that had guided him. He was amazed to recognize what the woman's voice was chanting. It was a Psalm of Solomon in Aramaic.

As he finally stumbled into the chamber, he fell to his knees and began to faint. He was aware of several people in white robes rushing to his aid. Then he lost consciousness.

He awakened in the *nephesh.* Floating near the ceiling of the chamber, he saw two men and a woman attired in white linen robes tending to his fallen body. One bearded man carefully removed his tunic and examined the deep wound in his left upper arm, then slightly loosened the tourniquet *Yeshua* had made to staunch the bleeding. There was no doubt that the man was Jewish, for he wore the *tzitzit.* The old woman who supported his head and the young man who gently pulled his body onto a clean reed mat were also both Jewish. They spoke little, but always in Aramaic.

The old woman said, "He is a son of Abraham, big and strong. He will heal."

One of the men returned to the several patients who lay on mats near antechamber on the far side. It led to another cistern with stairs, but this one much larger and more ornate with marble steps and archways.

Now *Yeshua* saw something else that amazed him. The old woman healer poured olive oil onto her right hand, which she then laid upon his wound. Then she laid the palm of her left hand upon her heart, with fingers positioned in a special way, and began to quietly intone a wordless *niggun*. Moving close to his wound, he could see flesh and blood slowly knitting together. Within a few minutes she was able to remove the tourniquet while his body breathed regularly and peacefully.

"This one must be a master!" she whispered excitedly to the man who assisted her. "I've never seen anyone heal this fast. What do you think?"

The man closed his eyes, then murmered, "He is one of us. He has suffered greatly. We must bring him to the community."

Yeshua had lost much blood. His *nephesh* sank into his body and fell into an unconscious and healing sleep while the two *therapeutae* and the old *therapeuta* gently placed him on a litter.

******* ******* ******* *******

He awakened the next morning to find himself alone in a hermit cell, still lying on the litter that had brought him here. He felt his left arm. It was very warm and throbbed gently, but seemed to be in no danger of bleeding or becoming infected. When he tried to sit up, he grew faint for a moment, but propped himself upright to see more of his surroundings.

The cell was constructed of dried mud-brick. Outside he could hear the gentle lapping of ocean waves on sandy shores. A cool breeze wafted into the front entrance to the cell, which faced the shoreline, and exited through small holes in the opposite wall. It was a great relief from the Egyptian heat, but he was also extremely dehydrated. He needed water.

Next to his head was a large ceramic pot. It was filled with fresh water, and there was a dipping cup attached to it with a woven reed rope. Painfully he sat full upright to free his right arm, then slowly drank his fill of water.

In a few moments he realized that he was nearly faint with hunger. On the other side of the litter was a reed basket. He removed the top and was overjoyed to find figs, dates, and a fresh loaf of bread. Again, he slowly consumed only what he needed.

Now the sun had risen and its bright glare filled the outside world. He felt strong enough to drag himself to the entrance and look out. As his eyes became accustomed to the brightness, he saw a sparkling blue sea that stretched beyond the horizon in both directions. His hut was not far from the white sands of the beach.

He peered out of the entrance and saw many more huts just like his. However, they were built on a grassy plain above the shoreline. His must have been some kind of a guest hut.

The other huts were isolated and greatly separated from each other, unlike a village, but clearly belonged to a community of hermits. In the distance on a raised part of the plain he could see a very large brick building where they probably assembled.

He whispered a thanksgiving to God and leaned back into the hut. He felt too weak to stand, so he sat quietly in prayer and meditation. After a while his attention was drawn again to the wound. With eyes closed he felt his whole consciousness focused upon it.

He became aware of a powerful force of healing that was at work within him. It seemed to have the purple color of a deep bruise, but as he grew more aware, the color lightened to an almost clear violet. The force emanated from his Heart. This reminded him of what the old woman healer had done, and he was moved to place the palm of his left hand over his Heart.

Suddenly he felt power moving forth like water from his Heart and into his left arm. With his eyes closed he saw the violet energy flowing to his right hand and concentrated at his right palm and forefinger. He thought about the old woman again and remembered that she had placed her right palm upon his wound while her left palm and fingers rested on her Heart. He imitated the posture, placing his right palm directly over the wound.

Gentle warmth began to develop where his right palm touched the wound. It grew into a soothing heat—far more than mere contact would generate. He opened his eyes in surprise and looked. He could see nothing unusual, but the heat was definitely stimulating potent healing in his flesh. With closed eyes he sat in this healing posture until the sun was high in the sky. Then he lay back and slept.

He dreamt of angels ministering to him while Shoshana smiled and watched. He finally awakened when the light of the setting sun shone through his doorway to the West. He lay quietly for some time, and then a shadow moved between the entrance and the bright twilight following sunset. It was the old woman healer.

Yeshua leaned on his right elbow and drew himself up. The throbbing pain he expected in his left arm did not appear.

"Mother, I want to thank you..." he began. She knelt beside him and put her right forefinger to her lips, signifying that he should keep silence.

She brought her lamp close and motioned for him to bare his wounded arm. He was pleased to feel only slight pain as he withdrew it from his tunic.

After a brief inspection, she motioned for him to wait, then stepped outside the entrance. Momentarily the two men who had been with her earlier appeared at the doorway, then gathered around him with the old woman.

She held the lamp near *Yeshua's* wound so they could all inspect it. They all looked at each other and smiled. *Yeshua* indicated that he, too, wished to see. In the bright light of the oil lamp, all that remained of the gaping wound was a u-shaped scar. He touched it lightly. No pain! He pressed it more. It felt like an old bruise.

The old woman motioned to the young man who seemed to be her assistant. He reached outside the entrance and dragged in a large basket and earthen water jar with which he replenished the food and water that *Yeshua* had used.

She motioned for the men to leave and, taking *Yeshua's* right hand, kissed it tenderly and smiled. This was followed by a silent gesture with her right forefinger, touching first her Heart, then forehead, then extending it heavenward. Still smiling, she withdrew from the hut and left the young Master with a lighted earthen lamp.

Realizing that he was famished with hunger and thirst, *Yeshua* feasted on dried fruits and water. As he looked around for someplace to relieve his bowels, he noticed large covered earthen pots at the corner of the hut. They contained everything necessary for containment and sanitation. Furnishings were very modest, but they were designed to allow a monk to remain for long periods of time in his hut without need for leaving.

The young Master remained in his cell in prayer and meditation through most of the night. As the morning twilight appeared, he once again lay down and slept through most of the day.

Late that afternoon the old woman and her younger assistant appeared once again at his doorway to awaken him. This time, however, she spoke.

"We will welcome the Angels of *Shabbat* when the sun sets. Those who have not undergone Probation and taken the Vow are not normally permitted on our shores, and certainly not at our sacred gatherings. But we invite you to join us."

Yeshua rose to a sitting position. He was able to use both arms—no throbbing, no pain. He felt moved to place his right palm on his Heart, his left palm over his right, and bow in submission.

"Look, Sister Shoshana! He knows the *nacham!*" blurted out the assistant.

Yeshua's mouth dropped at the name of his beloved.

The old woman turned to her assistant with a finger to her lips signifying silence. He bowed and withdrew. She unrolled a reed mat that lay next to a wall, carefully brushed sand from it, and sat in silence smiling at the young Master.

As he looked into her eyes, he felt a kind of sweet happiness—strangely like the warmth that had generated healing for his wound. A slight fragrance of flowers wafted into the hut on an evening seabreeze. It was not the scent of lilies, but it was beautiful.

He realized that Sister Shoshana was inviting him to speak and ask questions.

"You don't bring other patients here. Why did you bring me here?" he asked.

"Because we recognized you as one of us," she said matter-of-factly, almost as his beloved would have said it.

"How?" he asked.

"It is *manda* of the Heart, which is remembered when seeing certain allegories that can be observed in life. In your case, it was your remarkable healing ability. The great physician must first be able to heal himself. You are a great healer."

"What you observed is God's gift to me," he answered. "I have evoked healing from others, like one who ignites other lamps from his own flame. But healing comes from God within one's own Heart."

"That is true, my Brother. What is your name?"

"I am *Yeshua* of Nazareth, son of *Yosef* the Master Builder and *Miriam*."

Sister Shoshana closed her eyes and went into a deep silence. After some time she drew a breath and spoke slowly and deliberately as though in trance.

"Yes…and your father has passed out of the body."

Another silence.

"Your mother…has recently learned that you married…your Beloved was slain by evil forces…you have wandered many years in the East…you are returning home. Is this true?" Her eyes remained closed.

Yeshua took a deep breath. Sister Shoshana was a prophetess.

"Yes, Sister. I am overjoyed to know that she has received my message."

"Your Beloved stands next to me now. She whispers to me in dulcet tones. She is…one of us, too. She wants you to learn from us."

Another pause.

"You have a great mission…It is God's Will that you tarry with us. You will know when it is time to leave us, and you will have our blessing and the spirit of our community always with you."

"What is this mission?" he asked.

The old woman did not hear his question. She was straining to hear something else.

"She says…her name is Shoshana!" she cried in sudden shock.

The old woman fell backwards as if dead. *Yeshua* cradled her in his arms. Her heart was beating hard and fast. He exhaled a warm, healing breath onto her face. She revived and opened her eyes.

"Rest a moment in my arms," he said, smiling. She took a breath. He could feel her Heart slowing to a normal pace. After a few minutes he sat her upright and withdrew his arms.

"Yes, my Brother. You are one of us."

"Where are we?" asked *Yeshua*.

"Our community is on the shore of Lake Mareotis, South of Alexandria," she replied. "It is not really a lake. It is the Mediterranean Sea. But no one sails here because it is isolated from the Sea by land and shallow mudflats impassable to ships. There is no wealth here, so we are not plagued by bandits, and there are no cities near the shores. Our community has grown on an elevated plain far from the putrid marshes and mudflats."

"What was the underground place where I found you in Alexandria?" he asked.

She smiled.

"That is the great underground canal that brings in the flood of fresh water from the Nile to replenish the city's cisterns. It extends all the way to the Great River. The canal fills on the spring flood, then retreats in the fall. Many parts of it have been constructed with marble arches and pavement, such as the special workman's area that we use."

The young Master still looked puzzled.

"You see, we go into the city on the day of the full moon and offer healing to anyone who comes to us. During the hot season we work underground and the people are brought down into an antechamber to escape the heat. There our assistants attend to the acute cases using many different methods. The chronic cases are brought to the master healers in the workman's area. You entered from the back way, but since you were in severe danger, we worked with you there."

"What is your way of life?" he asked.

"We remain unmarried and abstain from sexual intercourse. We develop our Divine powers and gifts for the good of humanity. We abstain from food from sunrise to sunset, and we praise God at both of these times. We seek the Vision of God alone in our oratories every night. And we take a sacred Vow to keep this way of life."

"How is one admitted to your community"" asked *Yeshua*.

Sister Shoshana smiled.

"You must come to the *Shabbat* Assembly. You will be nominated by me and the two Brothers who know you. The Master of the Synagogue will present you to the Brothers and Sisters as a Probationer and you will be questioned. Then you will be granted a plot of land upon which you will build your private cell and Oratory. You will learn all of our ways from an Elder to whom you will be attached by the Master. After three years you may be invited to take the Vow and sit among the Council."

Yeshua was silent. Then he spoke.

"I have no need of a Vow, but I do know that it is Divine Will for me to sojourn with your community."

"See, you have already begun to imitate our way of life! You sleep during the hot hours of the day and enter into Divine *mishqad* during the sacred hours of the Night Heavens to seek Divine Communion. Is this not so?" she asked.

"I am already committed to a very similar way of life," he said, "but I do not take vows. The practice that I have been taught by Mother Spirit is somewhat different. I am a Master Builder. My work is done during the day, and I sleep at night. Nevertheless, I often keep Vigil for part of the night."

"Then, come as a Probationer. You are free to live with us and learn our ways. Indeed, I perceive that you have a Mission in the world that is different from ours, yet you are one of us."

They arose and began the trek to the House of Life, as they called their Synagogue. The fiery sun seemed to cool as it approached the Western Sea. They walked along the hardened sand flats next to the shore to make the journey less arduous than it would have been in sand. Finally they turned inland and ascended to a grassy plain.

Many Sisters and Brothers were making their way to the large brick building, while others could be seen busily preparing food at an outside kiln. As they greeted each other, they used the same hand gesture that *Yeshua* had seen Sister Shoshana use—Heart, forehead, Heaven. As they approach the entrance to the Synagogue, *Yeshua* was greeted in this way by the man he recognized as Shoshona's elder assistant. He and the old woman returned the greeting.

When they entered the brick building, he saw that it was all one great room. There was no place for cooking. There was no need for an oven because the *Therapeutai* ate no meat. This was good, because the heat of an oven would have destroyed the cool environment of the earthen hall. A large table covered with a feast of fresh and dried fruits was in final stages of preparation before sunset. Brothers and Sisters were also bringing pots of milk, eggs, leavened bread baked in the sun, and hot lentils.

Shoshana led *Yeshua* to a special reed mat by the entrance to the Synagogue and asked him to sit in meditation until called. He sat and closed his eyes.

After a while all became quiet. There was a long silence. Suddenly three loud claps of one person's hands sounded and was answered by three claps from the assembly. A man spoke in Greek.

"We have an approved Postulant for Probation. He is recommended by Sister Shoshana, Brother Toma, and Brother Eleazar. He is admitted to our assembly and the Rite of Probation by demonstration of profound healing gifts.

"Brother *Yeshua*, please rise."

The young Postulant opened his eyes and stood up. He saw about forty members attired in white robes. The men were seated on one side of a great wooden table, women on the other. Each of them stared intently at *Yeshua* as he rose to the standing position. It was customary for disciples and servants to stand while their masters sat.

Sister Shoshana was seated next to the elderly Master of the Synagogue. Evidently she was most senior of the *Therapeutrides* and highly respected. All of the Brothers and Sisters sat with right hands tucked inside immaculate white robes, palms laid upon their Hearts. Their left hands were positioned palms up on their left thighs.

"Do you desire admission to our community as a Probationer?" was the Master's first stern question.

"I do," replied *Yeshua*.

"In what ways can you contribute to the life of our community?"

Without a pause, *Yeshua* answered in a halting Koine Greek, "I am a Master Builder and can assist with building and repair. I also have gold coins that I desire to donate to the community for its food, clothing, shelter, and other needs."

Sister Shoshana raised her left hand and was recognized with a respectful nod from the Master.

"*Abba*, I have seen that God has given this man more healing force than any of us. The most important work he can do for the community is the public clinic. His work will bring us many large free-will donations."

The Master returned his stern gaze to *Yeshua*.

"Then so be it. I hereby appoint you, Brother *Yeshua*, to serve as Mother Shoshana's apprentice and assistant for the public healing clinic."

Shoshana winced and whispered, "*Sister* Shoshana."

The Master's face, which until now was wooden and expressionless, crinkled into a warm smile. He spoke directly to *Yeshua*.

"*Imma* Shoshana is our Spiritual Mother. But she refuses any title of authority and insists upon being called Sister."

The old woman blushed.

"I would suggest," he continued, "that as her student, you honor her wish."

Yeshua smiled and made the hand gesture he had seen—Heart to forehead to Heaven.

The old Master sprung from his mat like a young deer, taking *Yeshua* by surprise. His face was old, but his body was young and powerful. Turning away from the Assembly, he faced the Torah Scroll. It was enshrined in a large wooden casket that had been opened for *Shabbat*. Shoshana took *Yeshua's* hand and led him to a position facing the Scroll, but directly behind the Master.

The old man raised his arms in the *orant* position and began to intone *Berashit*. The congregation of *Therapeutae* and *Therapeutrides* joined him. Although the melody was not the one he knew, *Yeshua* raised his arms and joined his voice with those of the community.

Now speaking in Hebrew, the old Master intoned: "Unto us a child is born." He turned to face *Yeshua* and placed his left hand on the crown of his head. The entire Assembly arose and stood with left hands extended toward the youthful Postulant.

All stood silently with eyes closed. The gentle lapping of Lake Mareotis faded as *Yeshua* became aware of many loving hands touching him. Each of the Brothers and Sisters drew a slow breath to receive an impression of his spirit and establish psychic communion. *Yeshua* also drew breath to form impressions—first, of the entire community, then of each Brother and Sister. The taste of purity formed in his mouth, then the scent of lilies on his palette. His Beloved One had drawn near.

After a long time, the old Master returned his hand to his side. *Yeshua* opened his eyes and found him smiling.

"Turn and greet your Brothers and Sisters, Brother *Yeshua*."

The new Initiand turned slowly to see the full Assembly standing and saluting—Heart, forehead, Heaven. He returned their warm greeting.

The Master of the Synagogue motioned for all to sit. Shoshana indicated that *Yeshua* should continue to stand and again face the Master. She and the old man returned to their mats.

"Brother *Yeshua*, you will be given land and materials to build your dwelling and your Oratory. You will be part of our community and sit with us at our Table in the House of Life. You will join the Assembly for worship and my own instruction every week on the Eve and afternoon of *Shabbat*. During the morning of *Shabbat* you will be instructed in our way of life by Sister Shoshana, Brother Toma, or Brother Eleazar. You will keep the night Vigil always, and you will assist with the work of the community two hours before sunset and until two hours after sunrise all the other days of the week. On the afternoon of the Full Moon, you will accompany Sister Shoshana and her assistants to the Great City, where you will provide healing service to all who ask."

Yeshua nodded.

"We keep silence at all times as far as possible. At sunset and sunrise we praise God, each in our own way—silently or with a voice. From two hours before sunset on *Shabbat* Eve until the completion of the Sacred Day at the following sunset, we break solitude to assemble, sing hymns of praise, teach, and learn. Approved visitors are admitted to the *Shabbat* Eve supper, but never to the *Shabbat* Feast of Praise."

Again the young Master nodded.

"Our goal is to abide in communion with Divine Sovereignty for the perfection of our souls. Under the Night Heavens we nourish the soul by seeking Holy Vision and Revelation. Under the hot skies of the Day Heavens we nourish the body with sleep. Under the cool skies of the Day Heavens we work to sustain the community. We fast under the Day Heavens and take food under the Night Heavens."

Yeshua indicated his understanding.

"Tonight you will join us at the Table. You must choose your own place at the Table. Bring up your mat and place it where you will."

Yeshua bowed.

"Please, do not bow in submission. Here you are a Brother. Even when you receive instruction, you will not stand. You will sit with your teachers. Instead, use our greeting."

Yeshua complied with the gesture—Heart, forehead, Heaven. Then he purposefully strode to the mat he had been given, rolled it into a bundle, and spread it out at the position of least honor—the farthest seat on the men's side of the table. The Brothers and Sisters smiled their approval of his humility.

As he was about to recline, Sister Shoshana raised her left hand and spoke in Aramaic.

"I wish to have Brother *Yeshua* at my side."

The Master of the Synagogue nodded his approval.

"Brother, come and take your place next to me. You shall serve me," she commanded in a stern voice that could not be refused, and that dispelled any illusion of favoritism that might have evoked jealousy among the Assembly.

Yeshua complied, but again before he could sit, she motioned him to continue standing and again spoke.

"Brother, do you know why we are known as the *Therapeutae*?"

"No, Sister Shoshana. I do not know," he answered.

"In Greek, the word means 'those who serve by attending to the sick.' It does not mean 'servants,' in the sense of house servants, but 'attendants to the sick.' We are not called physicians, and we are not paid for our service. Thus we are all a special kind of servant dedicated to the healing of ourselves and all who seek our aid. So we are servants, not physicians. Will you always remember that?"

Yeshua smiled.

"I shall never forget that, dear Sister."

She motioned for him to sit, and he joined everyone at the Table.

******* ******* ******* *******

Before *Shabbat* sunrise *Yeshua* was greeted at his hut by Brother Toma. Together they stood facing the East in *orant* posture. Toma demonstrated how to close the eyes and view the sun through a thin slit that admitted only a golden glow. Then he explained how to maximize health and vital force by coordinating heartbeats, breath, and subtly perceived motions of the *Ruach Ha-Shemesh*. The energizing effect was instantaneous and potent. Now *Yeshua* understood how the old Master retained such vigor.

Now they spontaneously sung praises to the Spirit of God behind the the sun. Toma began.

"*Baruch Attah Adonai*, Who sendeth illumination upon all souls. We return grace unto Thee for the Blessings of Thy Love, Which warmeth all beings and giveth Life to the All. May we each reflect Thy Love and Healing unto all beings."

He intoned softly but with great control and beauty, then fell silent. *Yeshua* felt a pulse of joy running up his spine to his throat, then he also began to intone praises. After this he, too, fell silent—still standing in the *orant* position.

After some time Toma crossed his arms over his Heart, left over right, and bowed reverently to the Reality behind the sun. *Yeshua* imitated the gesture.

Toma led the young Master along the shore to a path that turned inland. They ascended to a grassy plain dotted with monastic cells. Each was an isolated brick hut erected too far from others to form a village. But unlike the guest dwelling where *Yeshua* had recovered from his wound, they were built in two square sections. Each structure was aligned to the four directions, with the smaller section extending to the East.

"Here is where you will build your cell and Oratory," said Toma, pointing to an area farther inland. "You must find a site that is as far away from other cells as these two are from each other. When you do that, I will show you how to measure the dimensions." He motioned for *Yeshua* to walk ahead and find a proper site.

Pacing the distance between the two huts that Toma had indicated, *Yeshua* transferred that measurement to a point directly inland near a cluster of tall reeds. Pulling up two of them, he pushed one into the ground to mark the spot. Taking the other, he paced an equal distance inland from the second cell and marked that spot. Sighting along the two reeds, he examined available sites in both directions. Some were sandy, others had drainage ruts. Finally he fixed upon a site that was slightly elevated on a spot barren of grass.

He walked to the location and examined it. A flooring of sedimentary rock showed no evidence of erosion or other degradation. It was non-porous, so would drain any rainfall.

Pointing to the chosen site, he looked at Toma. The Brother nodded and motioned for him to follow.

After a brisk walk in the cool morning air, they arrived at Toma's cell.

"We measure dimensions from our own bodies. That is why each cell is slightly different in size. You are tall, so your dwelling must be larger than mine."

Toma handed *Yeshua* a carefully marked measuring reed and lay upon his sleeping mat.

"What is the measure from my feet to my head?" he asked.

The young Master measured and said, "About two and one third."

"Treble that for the Oratory walls. Go outside and measure them. Then see how the cell walls compare."

Yeshua did so. The measurements of the Oratory walls were exactly seven reeds in all three directions. He found that the cell walls extended four and two-thirds reeds farther in both directions from the outside Oratory wall—in other words, two of Toma's body lengths farther in each direction. Thus the cell walls measured seven body lengths in a square.

"How many body lengths is the total perimeter, including the Oratory?" asked Toma.

"Thirty-two," answered *Yeshua*.

"What does this number signify?" Toma asked.

"It is the number of times that the Elohim spoke when they brought forth the Heavens and the Earth," he answered.

"What is the perimeter of the Oratory?" was the next question.

"It is twelve body lengths, which is the number of the *'Olamim* that divide the Heavens," he answered.

"What else?"

"It is the number of the Single Letters that correpond to the Zodiac of the Persians," he answered.

"Aha, so you know the *Kabbalah*. Then, what is the number of body lengths for each wall of the cell?"

"Seven, which is the number of the Double Letters and the Chief Planetary Angels," he answered.

"From which direction do you enter the cell?"

"The entrance is contructed at the West wall, and it is also from this direction that one enters the Oratory."

"Good. Now, in what direction do we place our bodies for sleep?"

Yeshua observed the sleeping mat at the Southern side of the entrance to the Oratory. Feet would not point East—that would be impious.

"With head to the East, feet to the West," he answered.

"Yes, and you can also sleep with head to North for certain kinds of activities; but never to South or West."

"Yes," the young Master answered. "Head to South or West debilitates vital forces that one wishes to replenish during sleep."

"Excellent," replied Toma. "And why would we sleep with head to the North?"

"For sacred work in the *nephesh*," he answered.

"Can you do that?" asked Toma.

"Yes," replied *Yeshua*.

"Will you teach me?" was Toma's eager request.

"I am afraid it is a gift. I can teach you about it, but I can't help you to do it. It would be very dangerous."

"It is a gift, but one that you have earned through many lifetimes," observed Toma. "Now, to the Oratory. Where is the altar?"

"It is at the East wall, where there is a small window to observe the time when the sun is about to rise."

"Yes. And what direction will you face when you Vigil in your Oratory under the Night Heavens?"

"The East."

"But which side of the Oratory?"

"Does it matter?" asked *Yeshua*.

Toma laughed.

"Aha! I can finally teach you something. Yes, it matters. When the Moon rises, you sit on the side that shields you from Her light. From Spring to Fall equinoxes that will be the Northern side. Near the solstices however, if you have made your window too wide, Her light will shine in your face. So make your window tall and thin."

Yeshua nodded.

"The light of rising Sun and Moon," Toma continued, "should pass through the entrance into the Oratory and strike through another window that you will make at the center of your Western wall, where you can observe them setting. This, however, must be a wide and short window. Do you know why?"

Yeshua thought for a moment, then asked, "Is it so that the sunset can be viewed at all times of the year?"

"More than that," Toma replied. "It is made wide so that at all times of the year, and at all declinations of the sun, the light that comes before sunset will strike through into your cell. It will awaken you for worship and evening Vigil after your period of sleep during the hottest part of the day. But make that window short as well as wide, because you don't want to be awakened until sunset is near. Otherwise you will lose sleep."

"I see," said the young Master.

"Otherwise, raise your floor with sand so that water will flow around your cell when we get rain, and make a small cistern to collect rainwater. The very little rain we get is precious. Most of our fresh water must be packed in from the oasis where we purchase food from merchant caravans. You will need to purchase various kinds of pottery and woven reed mats for your cell and pay for their transport here. These supplies are stored next to the Synagogue"

"What are your customs, and do many of the Brothers and Sisters speak my language?"

"Most of us are Alexandrian Jews, so we speak Greek. Since we have learned Hebrew, we understand Aramaic. However only Mother Shoshana and I speak the language of Palestine and Babylon fluently."

Yeshua nodded.

"We arise at sunset and offer private worship. Some of us compose psalms, some intone wordlessly, and some sing silently. But all keep silence and peace, so that you will not hear the sounds of another Brother's praise. After the sun sets, we eat in private. Then we attend to any bodily needs so that we can Vigil for the night. Before sunrise we again take food and offer praise. Then we attend to our portion of the community work until the sun grows hot. Some transact business with the merchants to secure food and water for the community, others assist in building, maintenance, repair of clothings and mats—whatever task they have taken as their part. We do not speak during the week except whatever communication is absolutely necessary during the mornings. That is when you can bring whatever needs repair to the Synagogue. In your case, you will walk to the Synagogue and be available to help with construction and repairs once you have made your bricks, erected your own cell, and stocked it with the goods you require from our stores."

"When do we sleep, and when do we assemble?" asked *Yeshua*.

"We return to our cells when our work is done, usually before the sky grows hot. Then we sleep. We gather for the *Shabbat* feast before sunset on Friday, then for worship in the Assembly before sunrise on Saturday. It is time for the Gathering. Come with me.

"There we sing hymns and praise Heaven with both men's and women's choruses. You will learn the hymns by participating. Sometimes the Master introduces a new hymn that a Brother or Sister has composed. Then we sit for the Teaching of the Master, and for the Visions of Mother Shoshana. She enters into sacred trance and delivers discourse while the Master sits directly across from her. Both Masters are required for the discourse to flow. On the afternoon of the Full Moon, those who are healers accompany Mother into the Great City, where the healing clinic is offered after sunset. You will be among them."

Brother Toma arose, saluted, and led the way to the Synagogue. The sun was growing hot, but when they entered the large building it was cool.

The women were gathering on the South side of the banquet room, men on the North. All were facing East toward the Altar. Each person was wearing an immaculately white linen robe—apparently not normal daily clothing.

Realizing that his robe was dirty and wrinkled, he saluted Toma and returned to his guest hut. There he found the wedding robe that Shoshana had made for him. It was wrinkled but pristine, snow-white, and seamless, based on the design of the High Priestly robe.

With a lump in his throat, he removed all but his loin cloth and dropped the robe over his head.

As he approached the Synagogue, he heard the angelic voices of the women's chorus. They were singing in Greek from the Odes of Solomon.

"I love the Beloved and I myself love Him, and where His rest is, there also am I."

After another strophe, the men's chorus sung, "I have been united to Him, because the lover has found the Beloved."

Then the two choruses together, "Because I love Him that is the Son, I shall become a son."

Suddenly *Yeshua* remembered what his father had once told him:

"Our highest souls are female and destined to Holy Union as the Bride of Adonai. So in the future when you read this passage, you will identify Wisdom with Adonai and a *talmid* with *yechida,* his feminine high self, and say,

"At first He will lead her by tortuous paths, filling her with craven fears. His discipline will be a torment to her, and His decrees a hard test, until she fully trusts Him.

"But then He will come straight back to her again and bring great joy, and reveal His secrets unto her."

He could hear the voice of *Yosef* like an echo, and he realized that the old saint was present at this time in a very special way. This further confirmed his resolve to progress in the ways of the *Therapeutai*.

He found a mat and took his place at the far end of the men's chorus. For the first time since his years with Shoshana, he felt truly at home.

*******   *******   *******   *******

Yeshua became known as a great healer during his years with the community. His ability to awaken self-healing in those who were spiritually prepared for release from bondage increased proportionally to the great spiritual progress he achieved during the night Vigils.

But many of his nights were spent in Alexandria working as a healer, where he was soon recognized as a master physician. He was positioned in the workman's area of the underground canal, where the Brothers brought him only the most difficult cases.

One night an elderly Egyptian Priest was brought in on a litter. He was considered to be a great spiritual Master. Four disciples bore his weight, while several more stood outside quietly intoning prayers. *Yeshua* was told that the Priest had awakened with a paralyzed left leg. Nothing he or they could do was effective.

"He was shown in a vision that there is a great physician among the *Therapeutai* to whom he should be taken without delay. We were told that you are that man."

Yeshua knelt by the litter and looked silently into the Priest's eyes. He felt that he knew this man.

"Do you remember me?" he asked in Aramaic.

The Priest squinted and motioned for a lamp to be brought near.

"I have known so many people…yes! You are the bright young man who was introduced to me by Eliud in Sepphoris! We had many conversations."

Now *Yeshua* remembered. This was Ariston, the Prophet of Thrice-Greatest Hermes, whose teachings had deeply affected him many years ago.

"My dear friend!" he exclaimed, and embraced him with kisses.

"So now you are a great physician," mused Ariston, "and I have been sent here as your patient. What will you do with me?"

Yeshua smiled. "What will God do with you? We shall soon see."

He stood up and placed his right palm upon his heart. Then he held his left palm over the crown of Ariston's head and shut his eyes. All fell silent while he received impressions.

"There is an obstruction."

He washed his hand, then applied some olive oil. Laying both palms upon the crown of Ariston's head, he closed his eyes and began to intone "Ee-ah-oh-wah-eey…"

"I feel something in my leg now," commented Ariston. *Yeshua* continued intoning, then opened his eyes. Taking Ariston's hands, he said, "Now you can stand."

Ariston swung his legs over the side of the litter and, depending upon *Yeshua's* strong hands, pulled himself to a standing position.

"Let us walk together," suggested the young Master. He held one hand and put the other arm around Ariston's shoulder to steady him.

The Priest took one step, then another. Together they circumambulated in a sunwise direction and returned to the litter.

"You will need to do this many times each day, then rest," counseled *Yeshua*.

"You told me many deep things about our Jewish Kabbalah while you were in Sepphoris. Now I will tell ask you something about your Egyptian mysteries. What is the sacred tree that sheltered Osiris after his death?"

"That was the willow," answered Ariston.

"Why the willow?" asked *Yeshua*.

Ariston looked puzzled. "I don't know. Do you?"

"The bark of the willow has a special healing property that relieves pain, reintegrates body parts, and can help to dissolve blockages. That's why it was the remedy for the dismemberment of Osiris.

"Therefore you must do one other thing besides learning to walk again. You must make a tea of fresh, green willow bark and drink it twice a day until you can walk without any paralysis or obstruction. After that, it would be good to continue with a small infusion every morning."

"Thank you, and I thank the Godhead that is truly Real, and the Brothers who serve from the *Ogdoas*! But I have a request."

"Whatever seems right to you, my dear friend," replied the young Master.

"I feel that we have much to learn from each other. I request that you return with us to the Temple and Sacred Lake at Sais for the duration of my recovery."

Yeshua turned to Mother Shoshana with eyebrows raised and began to answer.

"I have work to do here with the Brothers…"

The old woman gently touched his shoulder to interrupt.

"Master Ariston, he will leave with you tonight."

Yeshua looked at her with questions in his eyes.

"My Son, do you not know that the Archpriest Ariston is the greatest Master in all Egypt? It is no accident that he has come here. The Almighty One gave him a vision that sent him to you. Disciples of the Thrice Greatest One might study all their lives hoping to be given the opportunity he now offers to you. You must go to Sais to serve as the Master's physician. He will refine your knowledge so that you can benefit many souls. You already have your staff and your purse, and now you have our blessing."

Ariston laughed.

"I think the old saint has overstated my importance. But you should follow her wise advice. I think we have much to learn from each other."

*******   *******   *******   *******

Sais was a religious center with a cosmopolitan population of Greek-speaking citizens. The older Temples in Memphis and Hieropolis were several days journey from Alexandria, which was now the ruling center of Egypt. Therefore the Ptolemaic royal families had rebuilt and greatly expanded what had once been only a minor Priestly center. Now Sais housed Priesthoods of Osiris, Thoth-Hermes, and other major temples important to Alexandrian administration of Lower, Middle, and Upper Egypt.

Priesthood was a training that began in childhood, when the most gifted and precocious were invited to leave their villages to live most of the year at the Temple. Priesthood study was not only a life-long career, it was the greatest and most desired path for any village child. It was the dream of every Egyptian parent that their child would be chosen, for that insured the financial future of the parents as well as the child.

Master Ariston had been not only the most brilliant child of his village, but the greatest among his peers at the Temple school. That is why he was appointed to rule as Archpriest of the Temple of Thoth-Hermes.

The Egyptian Thoth was Scribe of the Gods and Revealer of the sciences, arts, and mysteries of Isis. However, Thoth was understood in Hellenistic theology to be identical with the Greek Hermes. Thus the Temple was designated as that of Thoth-Hermes. It housed a great library with copies of all the Books of Thoth-Hermes, comprising architecture, astrology, medicine, and all of the Priestly arts.

Greeks attributed the Temple to Thrice-Greatest Hermes, or Hermes Trismegistos. Philosophers like Plato had made pilgrimages to Sais specifically to learn from the Priestly masters of Hermes Trismegitos.

The Priesthood itself was highly respected, comprising the most educated and cosmopolitan of Greek-speaking Egyptians. Many of them traveled to other religious centers, as Master Ariston had done in earlier days when *Yeshua* had met him in Sepphoris. The Temple scholars, for all their worldly ways, were more knowlegable in classical Heiroglyphic and Demotic Egyptian characters than Priests of other more traditional temples. Instead of specializing in one area like astrology or medicine, the Priests of Hermes Trismegistos were experts in all of the sacred sciences that had been revealed in ancient times by the legendary Thoth-Hermes.

But Master Ariston presided over a special section of Temple religion that was unlike anything found elsewhere. It was an initiatic mystery school open to all righteous souls—not just Priests. But unlike the *Therapeutai*, who appeared in public as healers and on rare occasions accepted new members into the monastery for three-year probation, the School of Hermes Trismegistos actually sent their Prophets into public forums. They told the story of Creation, of how Earth was formed in the sacred temple city of Hermopolis, and of the vision that Thoth-Hermes himself had received for the liberation of all humanity from *Heimarmene*—Ruler of this age and of the cosmic forces that imprison all souls in flesh. The Prophets of Thrice-Greatest Hermes taught that true vision can be attained by closing the eyes of flesh, opening the eye of the *Nous* or Higher Understanding, and attuning one's soul to the guidance of those Hermetic saints who have overcome flesh and now exist as ascended beings in the *Ogdoas*.

Some of those who heard the message turned their backs and walked away. But others—those for whom the message was meant—threw themselves at the feet of the Hermetic Prophets and begged for more instruction. These were organized into private academies of many disciples. They were required to study the sacred arts, sciences, and philosophy of Thoth-Hermes, which were translated into Greek and Coptic from the original Demotic Egyptian characters. These studies required decades of devoted perseverance.

During this time students experienced many stages of initiation. They were baptized in the waters of *Nous* from the *Krater* or sacred bowl and raised slowly through the cosmic spheres. The more advanced disciples were promoted into smaller groups with deep initiatic studies until finally the most advanced were taken into groups of two or three. Here they developed as Hermetic Prophets and undertook missionary travels, as Ariston had done.

After many years, when one of the Prophets showed proper signs, he or she was allowed to receive highest Initiation directly from the Master Ariston, who was known as Father Thoth-Hermes. In an all-night session high on a hill, or at the top of a pyramid, he played the role and transmitted the energy of Divine Hermes as Begetter of a new spiritual soul. With another Prophet sitting as Scribe, the detailed procedings of the Initiatic Rebirth was recorded as a formal certificate that would be kept in the House of Life. The disciple was reborn, his *Nous* was opened, and he learned to intone the ascent to the *Ogdoas*.

There he saw a vision of the Hermetic Brothers. They were called Brothers, but they were like the angels--neither male nor female, but androgynous and whole. These Hermetic saints were once incarnate men and women. But through divine *gnosis* they had overcome the evil rulers of this *'Olam*, the forces of Fate, what the Greeks called *Heimarmene* and some Jewish sages named as the Archons of *Yaldabaoth*. Through diligence and fidelity they had purified their souls from lust, greed, envy, and self-seeking. At the death of the body, they awakened into the eternal life of the Divine *'Olam*. Now they existed as spiritual saints who had ascended as spotless beings, as divine energies helping souls to grow into spiritual liberation.

Once Father Thoth-Hermes could psychically see the Vision of the Ogdoas within the soul of his disciple, he would be able to assist the Initiand to discover the Vision for himself. This was done by closing his eyes of flesh, intoning a special kind of divine praise, and seeing with the Nous—the true Single Eye of Spirit. Once the Initiand had seen the Vision of the Ogdoas and developed communion with the ascended saints, he was reborn in Divine Spirit as a High Initiate on his way to developing as an Hermetic Master. This was the final human initiation of the Mysteries of Hermes Trismegistos.

"I see that the decades of preparation and study required of our Initiands has already been completed within you," said the Master Ariston. "What you lack in knowledge of our sciences is more than fulfilled by the Divine Gnosis within you. It would be fitting that I transmit to you our highest initiation, for I perceive that you have a great spiritual mission to accomplish."

Yeshua was speechless. Could a Son of Abraham and the Prophets take initiation from a gentile?

"I need time and solitude to find an answer to your proposal," he finally answered.

That evening *Yeshua* retired to a small study adjacent to the Sanctuary of Hermes and sat with his head between his knees. After some time he became aware of the fragrance of lilies, then what seemed to be an echo of the sweet voice he had so loved on Earth. He found himself remembering his many days and nights of meditation in the Buddhist monastery. The thought came, "My Buddhist Brothers were gentiles, yet I learned many spiritual things of great value from them. And I was guided to them by my Beloved. How can I then refuse this great spiritual initiation that Master Ariston has been inspired to offer me? All of these experiences prepare me for what is to come."

He arose and went to his bed. That night he dreamed that he and Shoshana were climbing a steep, stony mountain. Finally they stood at the pinnacle viewing the plains below in serene joy. He awakened the next morning with that feeling of that joy still fresh in his heart.

After a careful examination of Ariston, *Yeshua* smiled. He bowed, thanked the Master for his offer of Highest Initiation, and accepted.

"The proper time is here, my Son. It is the Spring Equinox, the time of Initiation. That is why I was brought to you as a patient, and that is why I received the knowledge that you should be initiated.

"Tonight Father Thoth-Hermes shines brightly in the Scorpion, while *Ra* sits on his Throne in the first degree of *Krios*, the Ram. We must accomplish the Vision tonight before *Ra* leaves His Throne. Until then, you must fast and pray for the Blessing of the Almighty. However, you must take a little olive oil to prepare your body for the fiery forces—a dram now, another at noon, and the final one in place of the evening meal. Meanwhile, abide in the Temple of Thoth-Hermes and prepare your soul with prayer and self-examination."

Some time after the sun set, the Master Ariston appeared at the door of the Temple.

"Come with me to greet the rising of Father Thoth-Hermes," he said, pointing to the Eastern courtyard. They went together into the cool night air.

There above the Eastern horizon shone the brightest luminary in the sky, like a diamond on velvet. It was *Tzedeq*, the Ruler of the *Tzadikim*, also known to the Babylonians as *Neberu*.

"So that is Father Thoth-Hermes," silently mused *Yeshua*. "*Tzedeq* is the sign of Melchizedek, the King of Righteousness and Ruler of the Righteous Ones. It is this great Being that instructs and initiates the Egyptians. Thus it is Melchizedek who will give me the Birth that is from Above tonight."

After a moment of silence, the Master Ariston fixed *Yeshua* with his eyes, then spoke in a deep, unfamiliar voice.

"Go with my Archpriest. You will descend in seven steps to a cave under the Temple and purify your body in the Pool of Rebirth. Then you will be clothed in a white cotton tunic and ascend to the Temple in eight steps."

The Archpriest appeared seemingly out of nowhere and motioned for *Yeshua* to follow. A large cubic stone had been removed from a portion of the outer wall of the Temple. As *Yeshua* entered into the darkness he was met by another Priest wearing the black and gold mask of ibis-headed Thoth. The stone was pushed back into place and all became black as death.

Then a voice asked in the Greek language, "O *Atum*, why have I traveled to a deserted place? There is no water, there is no breeze of air. This place is deep, deep, dark, dark, having no limits or boundaries!"

Yeshua felt himself pulled down to his knees to descend the first step.

"Here, thou shalt live with thy heart at peace," answered the voice of the God.

The young Master crawled down another step.

"But here one cannot satisfy desire!" objected the first voice. "Here there is no food, no beer, no land or water. I see nothing, hear nothing. It is the death of all that I have known!"

A third step.

"True, but it is here that I have placed the powers of Mind instead of water, cool breezes, and the pleasures of love; and the peace and rebirth of the soul instead of bread and beer," was the answer.

Fourth step. Now *Yeshua* turned a corner and could barely make out a glow of torch-light somewhere ahead.

"And what," asked the first voice, "will be the span of my life?"

Another turn, another cold stone step.

"Thou shalt live for millions and myriads of years," replied the other, "yes, thy life shall last for millions of years!"

After descending the sixth step, *Yeshua* could smell and hear water. One final step and he was pulled to his feet by two Priests. They dropped a thick hoodwink over his head so that all remained dark, even though he knew that he was being led into a cavern that was torch-lit.

His clothing was removed, and in silence he was slowly submerged in cool water. Now the hoodwink was suddenly jerked from his head and his eyes overcome momentarily with brightness.

The Ibis-headed Priest motioned for him to submerge himself. He crouched down into the black pool until every hair on his head was submerged. He held his breath and rubbed himself as though bathing. When he finally burst up from the water and shook his black hair and beard, he opened his eyes.

On the other side of the pool was a stone staircase bordered in polished wood with gold inlay and brilliantly lit with torches at every step. He looked back at the Ibis-headed Priest, who silently pointed toward the steps. As he waded toward the steps, he was met by the other two Priests, who perfunctorily dried his body then clothed him in a seamless cotton robe.

With that he slowly ascended the eight steps to a wooden door. He pushed the door open and found himself standing in the sanctuary of the Temple. The Master Ariston was seated on a gilded throne facing him.

"My Brother, sit on this throne." Ariston pointed to another god-throne throne on his right side. *Yeshua* nodded and complied.

"I see in you evidence that you have often made the Ascent," said Ariston, closing his eyes.

"That is true," answered *Yeshua*. "Knowledge of the Ascent is found in the traditions of Isaiah, Elijah, Jeremiah, and Daniel. I learned to ride the Chariot in Babylon through the School of Daniel."

"But did you learn how to take another one with you on the Ascent?" asked Ariston.

Yeshua thought for a moment.

"I have made the Ascent with my Beloved in attendance, and I have communicated with her after death. But I have never taught another one to make the Ascent with me. How is this possible? The Masters do not teach each other. They must each learn the Ascent within themselves. It cannot be taught."

"That is true. *Gnosis* cannot be taught—it must be learned. But if you have a disciple who is very advanced in *gnosis*—one who has already developed internal communions and divine fire—you can ignite him by sharing your flame. Is it not so with healing?" asked Ariston.

"That is true. It is not the physician who heals the patient, but the patient who heals himself. The physician communicates energies of self-healing that he has developed within himself, and these ignite the same energies that lie dormant within the patient. The physician may use all kinds of remedies, but the patient cannot respond with healing if the physician does not have the powers already developed within himself. And those powers are gained by the physician through overcoming of sickness and suffering by unconquerable fidelity."

"Yes, my Son. And just as you have developed your own powers of self-healing through fidelity to the Divine Way, you have also developed communion with the higher worlds and the ability to make the Ascent."

"You have done the same, Father Hermes. Then why was it necessary for you to seek healing from the Therapeutai? Why did you not heal yourself?" asked *Yeshua*.

The Master was silent, then spoke.

"There are some forms of disease that one cannot heal through one's own powers—especially as we grow old. I tried to heal myself, but I could not. It was then I chose to seek help from the Therapeutai. But there is more to it than that. Father Thoth wanted to set you before my face. He wanted to bring you to the Temple for Highest Initiation. This is how He accomplished that goal. And behold, he made you my physician so that we might share our flames."

Yeshua declared, "But I already know how to make the Ascent."

"Yes, my Son. So it is now time for you to learn how to transmit the Ascent to worthy disciples."

Again *Yeshua* objected, "But I have no disciples."

Ariston smiled.

"You will have many disciples. I see them as a great throng within your heart. Yes, you will have many disciples of varying spiritual degree. I see one in particular—a woman—who will be your greatest disciple."

"That must be my wife, Shoshana," replied *Yeshua*.

"No, this is a woman who lives now in a body of flesh—one who will adore you as would a mother and a daughter. You will transmit the Ascent to her and to other great souls."

They both fell silent.

"My Son, on a New Moon when the night sky is lighted only by stars, you will lead the purest of your disciples to the top of a hill or mountain. From sunset to sunrise you will transmit the Mysteries of the Ascent. You will teach them to take counsel with the ascended Great Ones. Indeed, they will take counsel with you after your own death and bring the Divine Message to all the world. And you will live forever to guide those who are worthy."

Yeshua was momentarily stunned.

The Master Ariston extinguished the three lamps at his left hand that had illuminated the sanctuary and the Temple grew dark. Only one dim lamp continued to burn on the altar.

"And now I begin to receive Divine Spirit through the Great Power…Be still and wait in watchfulness for the manifestation of Spirit."

Ariston closed his eyes and grew silent. A long time passed as the two men settled into deep co-meditation. Their breathing grew shallow, their breaths infrequent. *Yeshua* was aware of silent hymns of praise emerging from his heart.

The Hermetic Master began to softly intone something quite different from what *Yeshua* had previously done with the vowels of the *Shem Tov*.

"*Aa-oh-eeee-oh-ayyyy-ooooh-aiiiiiii-oooooooh-aaaaaaaah-ooooooooooh-uuuuuuuuuuh-oooooooooooooooooooooooooooooooh*…Thou art the One Who exists eternally in Spirit. I sing praise to Thee in a divine state!"

Yeshua opened his eyes. The sanctuary of the Temple seemed to be filled with a golden luminescence emanating from above. From the darkened upper corner of the Temple a very large and disembodied face smiled down at him.

"Blessed Father Thoth, we thank you for your presence," intoned Ariston, "and we ask for your guidance. Show us what is fitting for *Mar Yeshua*."

Yeshua straightened his spine and sat at attention. It had been a long time since anyone had called him *Mar*, Aramaic for Master.

The face dissolved into a scene of five men sitting in a circle on a high hill. In the blackness of a moonless night they were enveloped by a luminous cloud. In the center of the circle sat *Yeshua*. He was conversing with the Prophet *Eliahu*. The other three men were afraid. The scene faded, leaving a slight golden glow.

The face of Thoth did not reappear.

After a time *Yeshua* became aware of a young bearded man standing before him. He wore the *tallit* and *tzitzit* of a Babylonian Jewish sage. As *Yeshua* examined the man's face he realized he was in the presence of *Mar Belteshazzar*. But not as he had known him in life—a frail old man. Instead, he appeared in his physical prime, yet with all the wisdom of age.

Yeshua stood with a sense of deep joy and bowed reverently to the man who had instructed him in the Way of Mastery. *Mar Belteshazzar* smiled and pointed toward the altar, where another man stood in the robes of Egyptian royalty. His body was also young, but his face was that of a bearded sage. He raised his staff and threw it to the floor, where it assumed the form of a living serpent. It returned to its master and wound itself around his body in a counter-clockwise fashion from the feet to the head, then positioned its own head with burning red eyes over that of the sage. Then the serpent spoke.

"The *Seraphim* of the Throne honor you, *Mar Yeshua*. The Holy *Kerubim* honor and support you along with the *Malachim* and all the Host. You are honored in all *'olamim* and in the *Malkuth* of the Heavens."

Suddenly *Yeshua* realized that he was looking upon the ascended Moses.

"This is the Egyptian Master *Mosis*, the royal patron of your people," said Ariston. "He was born of Pharaoh *Tutmosis'* daughter *Nefure* and her Hebrew lover. He was named *Senmut* by his mother and raised in the palace as Prince *Tutmosis II*. Under the tutelage of Priests who prepared him to be the successor of *Tutmosis I*, he mastered all the arts of Thoth. Later in life he became an advocate and defender of his Hebrew father's people. Political enemies of the Hebrews gained influence over *Tutmosis I*, falsely accused the Prince of murder, and he was exiled from Egypt. His grandmother later became Queen *Hatshepsut*, a woman Pharaoh of Egypt."

"You Egyptians know more about our greatest Prophet than we do?" mused *Yeshua*. "I desire to speak with him myself."

Ariston laughed and said, "That is why he is here."

Yeshua bowed low before the Prophet Moses and asked, "'O Great Giver of Torah and Light of Israel, is it true that you were born half Egyptian and half Hebrew?"

The serpent spoke on behalf of Moses.

"It is true. Many things that are written in Scripture have been twisted by the minds of the men who wrote it. When Moses was made a Priest of YAHWEH by Jethro in the land of the Midianites, he became a Prophet of *El Elyon*, the Most High God. He did not speak the language of the Hebrews with any fluency, and thus required an interpreter, but it is not true that he stuttered. It is true that he was sent by *El Elyon* to redeem Israel from Egyptian oppression. He trained his older half-brother *Aaron* to serve as a Priest of YAHWEH, and it was *Aaron* who spoke on his behalf to the Hebrews."

The Prophet motioned for *Yeshua* to stand. Then he himself spoke.

"*Yeshua*, do not grovel before me. Stand up. You are my Brother and my Successor. Do you not remember? Look into this mirror and see yourself."

The Prophet held a black obsidian mirror in his left hand and the dim lamp from the altar in the right hand. *Yeshua* looked at his reflection in the dark mirror. He saw the face of a powerful Hebrew warrior.

"Yes, I trusted you more than all others. You accompanied me halfway up Mount Zion when I received the *Torah*. You were faithful when all others were not. You were the only one of us worthy to lead the new generation across the Jordan into the Promised Land. You stained your hands with blood for the sake of Israel and sacrificed your right to attain the *qimah*. So once again you have returned to Earth for the sake of others. And once again you will be my successor."

Yeshua took a deep breath, then asked, "Why were you known as Moses instead of *Tutmosis*?"

"My Son, you know that only a Priest could intone the Holy Name of *El Elyon*. To all others the *Shem Tov* was unknown and unpronounceable. I dropped the first part of my name *Tutmosis*, which means "Son of Thoth," and changed it to *Mosis* with no Egyptian god-name, which means 'born of.' That is to say, my name means 'Son of the Unknown God Most High.'

"In legend and Scripture, I am called Moses, which means 'Drawn out from the Water.' But in truth, there was no massacre of Hebrew first-born, and I was not found in a basket of reeds like ancient King Sargon. I was born in the Palace and educated in the temples."

"Why do you appear to me as a man that I can touch and hear, but the Egyptian Thoth appeared only as a great face and communicated with visions and symbols?" asked *Yeshua*.

This time the serpent spoke.

"Moses lived as a real human being and attained the *qimah* when he left his body behind. Now he exists eternally in the Divine *'Olam* as the *malachim*, without gender or form.

"But Thoth is a god-form created by human minds from the lives and wisdom of many ancestors. If you were to ask Thoth this question, he would show you his many faces of those who became masters of wisdom on Earth, whether or not they attained the *qimah*. You would even see the face of Master Ariston. Great Thoth is a High Eggregore that continues to grow and develop. One day in the future, when mankind neglects the mysteries of Egypt and there are no Priests to mediate his wisdom, Thoth will sleep and perhaps die. But Moses cannot die and he will not return in a body of flesh. He lives in the *Malkuth* of the Heavens to assist other souls."

"*Eliahu* was assumed bodily into the *Malkuth*, where I have seen and communicated with him..." declared *Yeshua*.

"And yet he lives also in a body of flesh on this Earth." The serpent completed his statement. "Yes, he has returned to Earth, but he exists in both the Heavens and the Earth. That is because he has been sent by God Most High to fulfill the words given through the Prophet *Malachi*, 'Behold, I send you *Eliahu* the Prophet before the great and terrible Day of YAHWEH, and he shall turn the heart of the fathers to the children, and the heart of the children to the fathers, lest I come and smite the Earth with a curse.'

"*Eliahu* has been your Teacher, *Elisha*, and with Moses he continues to be your Teacher. But of the two, only *Eliahu* lives in a body of flesh on this Earth.

"You have found him in the Heavens, but now you must find him on Earth. He is the only one on Earth who can make you ready for the Mission, the Message, and the Great Work that has been ordained for you by God Most High. You will find him in your homeland."

With that Moses and the serpent faded and the Master Ariston began to intone, "We thank Thee, Lord Most High, for the guidance we have received. We send forth Thy Holy Blessing unto all beings, and especially unto the Master *Yeshua*, for the accomplishment of all Thy good works on Earth."

After a few minutes of silence, Ariston stood and lighted the Temple lamps from the single one that had remained on the altar. Then he sat and spoke.

"Master *Yeshua*, if you were one of my students, this would be the hour of your Spiritual Birth. We would inscribe the record of this sacred event and keep it in the House of Life. But you came to me already twice-born, and I chose not to have another Priest with us to record what transpired. Indeed, I have been blessed to learn as much as you have through this Ascent."

Yeshua nodded and said, "In the past I have created a fiery *Merkabah* Chariot and ridden through the many Heavens seeking divine counsel. But you have shown me that by making an internal Ascent, Heaven can manifest on Earth. By teaching those who are worthy of these Mysteries, they can ascend with me and take counsel from the Great Ones."

"Remember," cautioned Ariston, "all of the Seven Powerful Vowels are used to intone the Name of God Most High. We begin at the Heart in the center—aa—then move to the Root—oh—then to the Throat—ee—then back to the Root, then to the Single Eye—ay—then back to the Root, then to the Crown—ai—then back to the Root, then to the place of *Ra* where the Priest wears the protective golden shield—ah—then back to the Root, then to the place of Generation—uh—and finally to the Root. With each one we lengthen the time of the tone. In this way we thread all the Seven Spirits together and incarnate Heaven into Earth. Can you remember that?"

"These are the Seven Spirits of Truth appointed to the human soul at Creation spoken of by the *Testament of Reuben*. But there are also Seven Spirits of Error mingled with them," commented *Yeshua*.

"That is right. The unworthy can never make the Ascent simply by evoking these Spirits, because instead they will descend into illusion. Only the pure in heart will be able to communicate with the divine worlds," responded Ariston.

After another week, when *Yeshua* was certain of Ariston's successful recovery, he took his leave and returned to the community of the Therapeutai.

Chapter Nineteen: THE PROPHET *YOCHANAN*

At sunrise on a Saturday morning Shoshana appeared at the entrance of *Yeshua's* monastic cell and called from without.

"Brother, I would like to speak with you. May I enter?"

She sat on the guest mat, where she had spent many hours instructing him on techniques of healing.

"Brother *Yeshua*, you have said that you do not make oaths or vows. Have you reconsidered? It is now three years since you joined us. That is the length of time allotted for probation. Do you wish to take the Oath?"

Yeshua smiled. After a silence, he spoke tenderly.

"You are sending me away to find my mission among mankind—is this not so, Mother?"

Tears came to her eyes.

"It is not easy, my Son. I love you beyond the measure that any human being should be loved. It would make me unspeakably happy if you would remain."

The young master took her hands and kissed them. Tears came to his eyes also. He could not speak.

"The community wants you to have these," she said, offering him a neatly folded linen garment. It was the seamless wedding garment that his wife had made for him in Babylon. As he unfolded it, a large purse dropped heavily to the earth. It was filled with the very gold coins he had bestowed upon the community when he first arrived.

"You will need these things for your Mission, my Son. You must leave your community garments behind in the hut and depart this very morning. The Brothers will accompany you to the city."

Beginning with Brother Toma, all the monks had begun to silently assemble outside *Yeshua's* cell.

"Mother, I am ready to leave. But tell me, why must it be on this very morning?"

Shoshana smiled and pointed toward the Synagogue.

"This is the final day of your Probation, and the Master has decreed that it must be the day of your departure if you are not willing to take the Oath. It is best to travel in the cool of the morning and arrive at the city by daylight. At night, thieves and murderers roam the city streets."

With that, Shoshana bowed and exited the cell.

Yeshua removed his community garment, folded it carefully, and laid it upon the mat. With a mixture of joy and sorrow that brought many deep breaths, he donned the seamless robe of a Priest that had served as his wedding garment. It had been washed and restored by Mother Shoshana until it was almost immaculate. He gathered his few necessary possessions into the purse with the coins. With one long look at the cell that had nourished his spiritual life for three years, he took up his walking staff and joined the Brothers outside.

******* ******* ******* *******

Brother Toma and Brother Eleazar had accompanied *Yeshua* to the waterfront of Alexandria to find passage to Palestine. They would be returning to the community by night and were armed with stout walking sticks.

"There are no boats this morning, so let us find a place for Brother *Yeshua* to sleep tonight," suggested Eleazar.

"But we know a place…" began Toma.

"Of course! The man with the broken arm!" replied Eleazar. "He said if there was ever anything we needed, to come to his home. And he lives near the Temple of Isis, not far from the harbor and lighthouse."

Yeshua was lodged for the night with a very grateful man who had been beaten by thieves and healed through the work of the Brothers. His father owned a large square-sailed merchant ship that would return from its Mediterranean trade route in less than a week. He could arrange passage to Caesarea for *Yeshua.*

"It is not a Roman galley ship," remarked Toma.

"What is that?" asked *Yeshua*. He had been absent from his homeland for too many years to know how conditions had changed.

"The Romans take the strongest young prisoners from their jails and make them serve at the oars of huge boats filled with goods. These boats are heavy barges that do not rely upon the wind, but upon slave oarsmen. Their legs are chained to their benches, and they are allowed to sleep only when there is wind. Even their arms are chained together. Since they take direct routes across the Sea, often the men must row against wind and current."

"Do they earn an early release this way?" asked *Yeshua*.

Toma grimaced.

"They are promised an early release, but in truth most of them die onboard or soon after release because their bodies have been so severely abused."

"Are these prisoners murderers? What are their crimes?"

"Some are very dangerous men," replied Toma, "but these days many of the poor are imprisoned for petty crimes like stealing bread to feed their families. Others are falsely accused by personal enemies of being anti-Roman revolutionaries. Others are pulled out of debtors prisons to become oarsmen, and…"

Eleazar interrupted.

"You will not recognize Judea. It is far worse than when you left. There is no justice. Jews collaborate with Romans and falsely accuse their neighbors.

"The Roman galley ships are full of young Jewish men who have been imprisoned to prevent them from becoming part of secret zealot and *sicarii* operations. They have committed no crimes and are not even members of such groups, but the Romans put the biggest and strongest ones into prison. You are big and strong. If you had been born fifteen or twenty years later and grown up in Judea, you would be chained to an oar right now!"

"Yes, my Brother," said Toma. "When you return home, do not make enemies. Do not resist the Romans. Do not even speak against them. Your nation is bowed to the ground under Roman domination. You would be far better off to remain here with us."

Yeshua was sobered by this information. He asked many questions, and they shared what they knew. They knew that he was resolute in his determination to return home, so they provided him with as much information as they had about survival under Roman oppression in Palestine.

In five days the young Master found himself on a creaking wooden merchant ship. He soon discovered that the captain received highest deference from everyone, and that passengers were not allowed to spend time on the deck. That was because the captain's knowledge of his trade route was kept like a state secret. His personal charts and methods for using seasonal and diurnal winds that would drive the square-sailed rig toward its destination had been gained through experience on other ships and from other Captains willing to share or sell their knowledge.

After the ship wallowed for a day and a night with no wind, however, *Yeshua* approached the captain the next morning as he directed his professional oarsmen.

"I know a wind," he said.

The captain was displeased to see a passenger on deck, but he was intrigued.

"How can you know a wind? Are you a captain? Do you know these coasts?"

"Yes," *Yeshua* replied. "But you will have to change course to the West."

"No! We must move toward the coast to find wind," objected the captain.

"Yes, but there you will find contrary winds that will blow you back to Egypt," replied *Yeshua*. "If you make your way West, the winds blow in the opposite direction."

"How do you know?" challenged the captain.

Yeshua pointed East to the distant high clouds moving from the South over the coast.

"I will tell you a secret. The upper clouds are blown by winds that blow opposite from the lower winds. When you see the high clouds blown from the South, then there is wind blowing from the North over the coast. But the winds out at sea blow in the opposite direction to those over the coast. So we are likely to find winds blowing from the South farther out at sea—to the West."

The captain was very impressed by this information. He smiled.

"I think you may be right!"

He called to his helmsman, "Rudder starb'rd! Change course to make Easting." After some cursing and muttering from most of his crew, the order was obeyed.

By noon the large square sail had found reliable wind from the Southwest, the oarsmen were lounging on deck talking and joking, and the ship had resumed its progress toward Palestine.

For the rest of the voyage *Yeshua* spent his time on deck in conversation with the captain, where he learned even more about conditions in his homeland.

The approach to Caesarea was made from the North, where coastal winds and currents, with skillful use of oars, crabbed the ship into the glistening new harbor. It was early in the afternoon.

The journey from Herod the Great's man-made harbor to the village of Nazareth would be a trek of two days. *Yeshua* purchased new sandals and a water horn at the marketplace, then rested until the cool late afternoon. He decided to walk the stony roads alone with nothing but his staff for protection.

He set off on the Roman road to Megiddo, reaching the summit of the rocky hills late at night. A crescent moon had set soon after the sun, leaving a clear black sky studded with stars of many colors. He slept hidden in a split between boulders where he could not be seen by night travelers. He awakened before sunrise and performed his accustomed meditation. Then he began the descent to Nazareth.

From a long distance he could see the house of his father *Yosef*. It had been expanded to almost double its size, and the stone wall at the perimeter of the yard had been built up to create a large courtyard and gardens. There in the gardens he could see a women, but it was not his mother. As he approached, she stood up and stared at him.

"Is this not the home of Mary, wife of the Master *Yosef?*" he asked.

The woman stared for another moment, then shrieked, "*Yeshua!* It is you! Don't you know me? Of course not, how could you? I am your sister *Shalome!*"

She rushed to him and fell on him, covering him with kisses.

"*Yeshe! My Yeshe!*" cried a voice from the door. It was his mother *Miriam*. She ran forward and nearly stumbled before she reached him, but he caught her in his arms.

"Were my letters ever delivered?" he asked when he got a breath.

"Yes, my son. And another letter..." her eyes dropped, then she looked up again. "Another letter from the aunt of your bride telling us...all that happened." Tears of pain welled up in *Yeshua's* eyes, and he had to sit down. Suddenly he was feeling it all again—pain that choked his breath and made his heart falter. But he swallowed it down, and soon the pain had subsided.

"Nobody knew...where you were...until your letter came," *Shalome* whispered in halting phrases.

After a silence *Yeshua* asked about his brothers and sisters. Soon they moved out of the heat into the large family room, where they talked endlessly. Everyone was well, some had married, but *Yakob* had attached himself to a great prophet encamped on the Jordan River.

"He believes that this man is *Messiah*," said *Miriam*. "And many others also believe this and follow his teachings."

"They flock to him on *Shabbat*," *Shalome* continued. "He teaches them that the *Malkuth* of Heaven will appear on Earth, and that *Messiah* will arise from the line of David and lead Israel in Holy War against Herod and Caesar, with *Mikael* and all the angels at his side."

Yeshua paused, then asked, "And what is the name of this prophet?"

"His name is *Yochanan*. And he is called The One Who Makes *mikveh*, because he cleanses his followers in the waters of the Jordan," answered *Shalome*.

"But he is a thief who steals our children!" *Miriam* burst out with passion. "And they will probably be slaughtered in their delusions by Herod's army!"

Another silence, then *Yeshua* stood up and declared, "*Yakob* has always wanted to be the disciple of a great prophet, and that is why he follows this teacher. But I shall go to the encampment on the Jordan and try to bring my brother home to you."

"Thank you, son" sobbed *Miriam* as *Shalome* held her in her arms.

"But first you must rest," *Shalome* admonished. "Stay with us for a few days before you leave."

Yeshua rested at his father's house for several days. Then one morning, before the hot sun rose, he set out on the road South to find the encampment of *Yochanan*.

*******   *******   *******   *******

Yeshua walked for several days through Decapolis and Perea, asking along the way where he could find the encampment of *Yochanan* the Essene. He was told that the prophet moved between several encampments from the place where the Jordan River poured down from the Sea of Galilee all the way to its end in the Dead Sea East of Jerusalem. One encampment could be found on the Eastern bank near Bethany, another at Aenon near Salema.

After morning prayer, the young Master felt urged to walk to the region of Bethany. There was a dry ford upstream from the wild and often flooded area where the Jordan flattened out, and there he made his crossing to the Eastern bank. He was pleased to find a well-worn path leading South, which he followed. Late that afternoon he arrived at a place where the river widened and the current was slow. Muddy water stagnated in rocky pools abandoned by the River after the spring floods had passed, but the river itself was clean.

He sat on a stony embankment shaded by tall shrubs and gazed at the river. The rhythmic slapping of water against rock convinced his tired body to lie back and doze. When he awakened, the sun had set and the twilight air was cool. He stood up and had begun to look for firewood and a cave when he glimpsed the glow of a campfire from the East, just beyond the river channel. Gripping his walking stick, he climbed over rocks and brush until he could see the camp. Perhaps twenty men were standing in complete silence around a large fire. This was not a caravan route, so they were neither tradesmen nor bandits. Perhaps this was one of the encampments of *Yochanan*. He carefully approached.

As the sky darkened, *Yeshua* reached the perimeter of the camp. Suddenly a voice whispered "Stop!" and two men barred the way with their staves.

"Who are you and what do you want?" one of them demanded in a hoarse whisper.

"I am *Yeshua ben Josef*, from Nazareth. I am seeking my brother *Yakob*. Is this the encampment of the Prophet *Yochanan*?" he demanded in a loud voice, not intimidated in the least.

Several of the men standing at the fire turned and stared. While the two sentries hesitated, another man hurried over and came to their rescue. He fixed *Yeshua* with his eyes and said in a quiet voice, "Please whisper. We are at prayer."

Yeshua nodded in agreement and followed the man away from the camp to a small clearing in the brush that was illuminated by the rising full moon. The man motioned for him to sit.

"You have found the disciples of *Yochanan*, but *Yakob* is not here. He is with the Master. They will return tomorrow. We do not allow outsiders into our camp or at our meals. But since you are the brother of one of the great disciples, you may sleep near the fire when we have completed our prayers. Until then, please sit here, outside the circle, and remain absolutely silent. I will come to get you when it is the hour for sleep."

Yeshua considered for a moment, then nodded his assent. After the man left, he sat, opened his bag, and pulled out some figs. He stood to pray before eating, but before his heart could form words he heard a woman's voice singing, "El-i-a-hu, El-i-a-hu..." She seemed to be standing next to his right side. He opened his eyes and looked around, then realized that it was the voice of his beloved Shoshana. The singing faded.

He sat down again and pensively ate his meal of figs and bread. Then he stood again in prayer until the man came and motioned for him to lay down near the dying fire for protection against wild animals. That night he dreamt fitfully about Elijah, *Yosef*, and *Yakob*.

Everyone arose before sunrise for prayer. The fire was rekindled. The men stood motionless and nearly naked in the cold night air, wearing only garments woven from rough camel hair girded with cords of reed. *Yeshua* again moved to his clearing in the shrubs and stood in prayer.

As the sun rose, the disciples broke their silence, singing psalms while designated Brothers brought out a low table and prepared it with simple foods. The disciples sat around the table in order of seniority. Then the man who had spoken to *Yeshua* stood and led them in ritual songs and responses. *Yeshua* recognized some of these as Essene, for he had heard them as a child from his teacher Eleazar the Righteous.

Yeshua again sat alone outside the circle and ate his own food. When the Essene meal was over and the brothers dispersed to their various labors, the man returned to *Yeshua*.

"Your brother *Yakob* will probably arrive this afternoon with the Master and his other close disciples. They have instructed and baptized the righteous ones at a place on the river near Mt. Nebo. Now they will return for *Shabbat*. You can meet them on the road South of the camp. If you need water, we can offer you from our cistern."

Yeshua thanked the Brother and followed him to the cistern. Unlike the muddly holes left by the retreating river, the stone cistern had collected pure water from the rains of spring. It was covered with a large thatched mat and the water was clear and cool.

After taking his share of water, *Yeshua* saluted the man and quickly found the road South. He walked for several hours until the sun grew too hot, then found a shaded place down by the river to eat and rest.

No sooner had he settled down than he heard the sound of many footsteps on the road. He peered over the top of the bushes. Five men stumbled onward through the blazing sun without the benefit of cloaks or umbrellas. No caravan would be forcing its animals to bear their burdens on the hot noonday summer's sun, yet these men pushed themselves forward like slaves to a cruel master. The men were strong and muscular, but their faces were blackened by constant exposure to the elements. And a few of them looked barely conscious.

Yeshua quickly took up his staff and purse. Sprinting to the road he hailed the group of men.

"Is my brother *Yakob* among you?" he cried.

The men came to an exhausted halt.

"Who is asking?" the leader replied, raising his staff. His voice was powerful. Unlike the others, he was not exhausted, but almost radiant with vital force.

"It is *Yeshua ben Josef* of Nazareth who asks," he replied.

Immediately one of the four other exhausted men seemed to snap out of his semiconscious state, raised his arms, and shouted, "*Yeshe!* Is it really you?"

Yakob looked like a sun-baked desert bandit. He wore only a long camel hair shirt, reed girdle, and reed sandals. He was thinner, but much stronger, than *Yeshua* remembered.

"My brother!" he cried and rushed forward to cover him in kisses while the others looked on.

"All you Brothers, please—this is not the time to be out in the heat. I will show you to a cool and shady place down by the river. Let us rest and talk," *Yeshua* declared. His voice was firm and powerful like that of the leader. The men all looked toward the leader, whom it was evident must be the Prophet *Yochanan*.

"Yes, let us rest and talk," *Yochanan* replied. They all followed *Yeshua* to the place of rest. Finally *Yeshua* spoke.

"Master, I have heard that you are the *Meshiah*. Is that so?" The question stunned everyone, and there was silence for a moment.

Yochanan looked his questioner in the eyes.

"That is not true," he said simply. "But I declare His coming."

"The Zealots declare His coming, too," answered *Yeshua*.

"They are unclean, stained with blood. They cannot declare *Meshiah*," he replied.

"Are they wrong, but you are right?" asked *Yeshua*.

Yakob began to object to his brother's persistent and disrespectful line of questioning, but *Yochanan* raised his hand for silence.

"Yes," replied the grizzled prophet. "Would you like to know how that can be?"

"I would like to know that," replied *Yeshua*, "and I would like to know why my brother has left his mother and family to follow you."

"Then you must come to my encampment with us and learn everything."

Yeshua was at a loss for words. Finally he said, "But I am an outsider, excluded from prayer and meals. How will I learn anything?"

"You will learn if you wish," was the prophet's reply. "The choice is yours. My Brothers, let us resume our journey. *Yakob*, you may tarry with your brother."

With that *Yochanan* and his disciples arose, leaving *Yakob* with his older brother to talk.

"*Yeshe*, you do not realize that you were in the presence of a true prophet. His message is from God, and it is the truth."

"How can it be true when *Yochanan* proclaims the season of the *Meshiah*, but false when the Zealots proclaim it?" asked *Yeshua*.

"What kind of *Meshiah* do the Zealots proclaim, and what kind does the Master *Yochanan* proclaim?" countered *Yakob*. "Come with me and let your heart be the judge."

They talked until the day began to cool, then began the journey back to the prophet's encampment in Bethany-beyond-Jordan. The sun was setting when they finally arrived, and the Brothers were again at prayer. But they were greeted by *Yochanan* himself. The routine from the previous evening was repeated, and *Yeshua* invited to sleep near the fire.

*******   *******   *******   *******

The next morning after prayers and the Eucharistic meal, *Mar Yochanan* led the brothers to a kind of natural amphitheater to the West of a large, smooth rock formation.

"The Master invites you to join the brothers for instruction," whispered *Yakob*. "Please come."

The Master was standing upon the huge central stone while his disciples stood at respectful attention. *Yakob* and two others brushed away insects and lay down a reed mat. When he was seated, they unlatched his sandals, set a pot of water next to him, and returned to stand with the Brothers.

Yeshua stood outside the circle, but close enough to hear.

The Master stood and raised his hands in the *orant* position. The Brothers raised their hands to Heaven and closed their eyes.

"Blessed art Thou, Sovereign of All, Who offers us the means of purification to prepare us for Thine Advent upon Earth. May all Israel prepare for the coming of your Holy One. May each person straighten his path, make righteous his *halakah*, and cleanse his heart so that the Holy One can come forth into this *'olam*. Amen, amen, amen."

Mar Yochanan paused, opened his eyes, and sat. The Brothers remained in *orant* position with eyes closed.

Yeshua was impressed with their self-discipline, but even more with the prayer of *Yochanan*. As the prayer was offered, *Yeshua* felt a sudden upwelling of joy and gratitude in his heart. There was a subtle but divine energy that emanated from his mouth to the ears of his hearers, elevated them, and turned their hearts to Heaven. Clearly he did not proclaim himself as *Mashiah*. He was a prophet of God's *Malkuth*—perhaps a very great prophet.

"My Brothers, all Israel will not prepare for the coming of the *Bar-Enash*. The Jubilees have not been kept. The slaves have not been freed on the Jubilee, the land has not been allowed to lie untilled on the Jubilee, and forfeited property has not been returned. We live in a time of spiritual degradation. The *Torah* has been twisted to benefit the rich. Jerusalem has become a pit of vipers, and the Temple a nest of scorpions. Can the *Malkuth* arise in the midst of such impurity? Will *Mashiah* appear in the midst of Zealots and *sicarii* who stain the Earth with blood?"

Yakob turned back to look at his brother. *Mar Yochanan* had answered the paradox raised by *Yeshua's* challenging question.

"Well," thought *Yeshua*, "he does proclaim a different *Mashiah* than the Zealots, or perhaps a different means for the *Malkuth* to arise."

"Hear the Spirit of Holiness:

'The Jubilees shall pass by until Israel is cleansed from all guilt of fornication, and uncleanness, and pollution, and sin, and error; until Israel dwells with fidelity in the land. And there shall be no more a Satan or any evil spirit, and the land shall be clean from that time in this *'olam*.'"

He was quoting from the Book of Jubilees. *Yeshua* had read from it at home and heard it in Synagogue. But his Father *Yosef* had once remarked that it was untrue that the patriarchs could not have followed the *Torah* of Moses before it was written, as the book claimed. He said that the book rewrote the history of Israel to promote the rigid legalism of the Judaean Pharisees, and that it did not represent the Voice from Heaven, the true *Bat Kol*.

"Yes, the Jubilees have passed, but Israel has not kept them. Instead, it has embraced fornication and injustice. No, Israel has not become sanctified. Instead, it has grown foul and unclean. The land is filled with Satans and evil spirits—more than ever before.

"You expect the coming of the Holy One to defeat all the enemies and make Israel great? What did Amos say?

'The Day of the LORD will not be a Day of Light, but of Darkness—a Day of fear, horror, and pain.'

"It was so for Israel then, and it will be so for Israel now—unless…"

The Master paused. The Brothers opened their eyes.

"Unless we call forth, gather, and prepare the faithful remnant of Israel so that they might sanctify themselves and create a vessel suitable for the Advent of the King. My Brothers, here is what the Spirit of Holiness tells us to do. The *Bat Kol* says,

"Call my men into the wilderness. Recite their sins so that their hearts will return to God and submit to Heaven's Way. When they have fasted and taken the oath, cleanse them with *mikveh* in the living water of the River. Let them receive the *Ruach Ha-Qodesh* and the true circumcision of the heart. Then let them cross the Jordan once again into the Promised Land as newly-made Sons of the Covenant. By the power of Divine Spirit, they will remain faithful. When God's wrath purifies the *'olam*, they will be preserved. As the Jubilees pass, their children will see the true Promised Land arise—as in Heaven, so on Earth."

Yeshua felt he was afire with holy flames. He heard Shoshana singing "*Eliahu, Eliahu…*" The glowing eyes of *Mar Yochanan* pierced him to the core as he directed his gaze to *Yeshua*. In his heart the young master heard many voices chanting from the Priestly Blessing, *Panav Elekha vihuneka*, The Divine Face shines upon you.

All eyes opened. The Brothers turned to see why *Mar Yochanan* had stopped and was staring. All eyes were now upon *Yeshua*. He smiled and *Yochanan* smiled. Then the Prophet resumed his teaching and all eyes once again closed.

After the Brothers were dismissed, *Yakob* drew *Yeshua* aside.

"What happened? Why were you smiling? Do you now understand?"

Yeshua took a deep breath, then said, "I don't take oaths, but I am ready to receive the *mikveh* and follow the Prophet."

"You came here to take me home, didn't you?"

"Yes, but I will stay here with you to learn from this Prophet and send a message to *Imma* and *Shalome* to relieve their worries."

"*Yeshe*…I am very sorry about…your wife."

The two men stood in silence for a while. Then *Yakob* spoke.

"If you would become a follower of *Mar Yochanan*, you must observe certain laws of purity in food and life. If you would become a *talmid* and live with the Brothers, you must adopt strict *halakah* for prayer, food, and dress. That will require a period of probation. Beyond that, you may aspire to becoming one of the *zaddikim* like me. The discipline for this is very harsh."

"Yes, I have seen how he drives you in the hot sun without rest. And look at your knees—covered with callouses like a camel."

"That comes from many hours of prayer recitation for which we are taught to kneel."

"But prayer should come from the heart," objected *Yeshua*, "not in memorized recitations."

"True," answered *Yakob*, "but this is a discipline to purify the heart. The holy words, when repeated many times with great focus, uplift the heart and cleanse the land upon which we kneel. This is one kind of *mitzvah* that is recommended by the Prophet to hasten the sanctification of Israel. There are many others. This becomes the work of a *tzadik*. The other disciples keep the camp, gather food and water, prepare meals, and go into the cities to proclaim where and when to meet the Prophet. But we accompany and protect our Master, and we do constant prayer *mitzvoth* when we sit, stand, and walk. Even now I am reciting the Psalm of Ascents in my mind."

Yeshua considered for a moment.

"I shall be only a hearer, but I will prepare to receive the baptism. Mine is a discipleship of the heart, not of the flesh.

"There are many points upon which I do not agree with the Prophet. I have fasted and undergone great rigors, but only when I was told to do so by the *Ruach Ha-Qodesh*. Each time had its special purpose. To wear hair shirts and purposely irritate and inflame the body drives us out of the very world we wish to sanctify. Also, women belong to the Covenant as well as men. Even the Essenes accept women into their circles. And I do not agree that most of the people of Israel are corrupt. That is how the Pharisees of Jerusalem magnify themselves."

"The Prophet is not puffed up, and like you, he strongly opposes the self-righteousness of the Pharisees," objected *Yakob*. "And yet you still wish to be a hearer and to learn from the Prophet? How can that be if you disagree with so much of his teaching?"

"You will see," replied *Yeshua*. "When will the Prophet teach publically again?"

"Today he sends the *talmidim* into Bethany, where many of them have families. He will return to Bethany tomorrow to proclaim the *Malkuth* and take their oaths. Then his *talmidim* will baptize hearers in a spring that comes out of the rocks."

"Does he himself also baptize?" asked *Yeshua*.

"He baptizes only those who become *zaddikim*. I was first baptized by the *talmid* Andrew…"

"A Greek?" *Yeshua* interrupted.

"A Son of the Covenant with deep understanding," replied *Yakob*. "You will meet him today."

"So you were baptized a second time by the Prophet himself?"

Yakob smiled and nodded.

"But only after a full year working as a *talmid*."

Yeshua examined his younger brother for a moment.

"Do you not wish you had remained one of the *talmidim*? Your life now is so much more strict and harsh. I don't like to see you burned black like a dead shrub in the desert."

"But I prefer it," smiled *Yakob*.

"You are a Priest, not a Prophet," declared *Yeshua*. "Yes, you belong at prayer, but not memorized recitations and ascetic labors."

Yakob grew silent. He wanted the brother he had loved all his life to share the wonders that come through the Prophet. He wanted *Yeshua* to follow his path with the Prophet and become the greatest of all the *zaddikim*—for he knew that his brother was a great soul in Israel. But apparently this was not to be.

Later, when the afternoon sun was low, *Yeshua* walked down to the river with his *Yakob* and the *talmid* Andrew.

He was a lean, muscular man whom *Yeshua* found to be intelligent and sincere. He took time away from his brother's thriving fishing business when he heard *Yochanan* preach by the Sea of Galilee. He took the oath and *mikveh*, then on the same day requested probation to become a *talmid*. After only a month, the Prophet had accepted him as a disciple.

"How long have you followed the Prophet?" asked *Yeshua*.

"For over three years," Andrew replied.

"Why are you not one of the *zaddikim*?"

The question was blunt and *Yakob* raised his eyebrows.

"If the Prophet recognized you in less than a month, why are you not now one of the *zaddikim*, like *Yakob*?"

"*Yeshe*, he has never applied," whispered *Yakob*.

Yeshua continued to fix Andrew with his piercing eyes, demanding an answer.

"My friend," Andrew answered in measured words, "I do not wish to do the work of a *tzadik*. I prefer the life of a *talmid*."

"I love and deeply respect the Prophet, far more than either of you can know," *Yeshua* paused. "Yet I choose to be a baptized hearer only—neither disciple nor *tzadik*. Would you understand that?" asked *Yeshua*.

"Of course I would—very well I would!" Andrew exploded in laughter. "I am not an ascetic. When the New World comes, I hope to have a wife!"

Yeshua smiled and turned to his brother.

"Can you understood too, *Yakob*?"

"If that is right for you…then I must accept it too," was his flat reply.

******* ******* ******* *******

The next morning *Yeshua* joined the eight of the Brothers on the short journey to Bethany in Perea. They walked silently through stony desert toward the risen sun in the East. Before the heat of the day, they saw the walls and green oasis of Bethany standing upon a hill among the rocky red plains.

Everyone in Bethany knew *Yochanan*. He and his disciples had been given a large home for their use by a wealthy Essene, although most of their time was spent in travel or encampments. Several of the young men of Bethany had become *talmidim*. To some families *Yochanan* was a saint, to others he was a thief who stole able-bodied sons from their fathers and mothers.

"Five of these men will stay with their families, but two of them have been banned from their homes," he explained. "We will stay with them at the Brotherhood home tonight after we proclaim the *Basor* to the people."

"*Basor!*" exclaimed *Yeshua*. "Is *Yochanan* a King whose Queen has given birth to an heir, or who has anointed a successor, that you should proclaim a *basor*?"

Andrew again gave his hearty laugh.

"No, my friend. This is a *basor* of the Messenger of God, who comes to prepare the hearts of Israel for the advent of God's Sovereign Rule on Earth. We call it the *Basor* of the *Malkuth Ha-Shamayyim*."

"And who is the Divine Heir that has been born?"

"It is *Meshiah*, the *Bar-Enash* proclaimed by the Prophet Daniel. Do you know anything about the Prophet Daniel?" asked Andrew.

Mar Yeshua, Master of the Brotherhood of Daniel, smiled and shrugged his shoulders.

"Perhaps you could tell me more," he said.

"Well, *Mar Daniel* saw in a vision all the nations of the world as brutal beasts. He saw how they would rise in bloodshed and eventually fall. He saw that all humanity suffers under their rule, and that they are empowered and guided by evil Satans and fallen angels.

"Then he beheld the Throne of the Ancient of Days, and before it was brought one who was not in the form of a beast, but of a man born from woman. And to him he gave sovereignty over the entire *'olam* of this world. That is *Mashiah*, the *Bar-Enash*, the Anointed One of Israel.

"The Prophet *Yochanan* has been sent by Heaven to prepare Israel to receive the new King. He admonishes all Israel for its sin and apostasy from the Covenant, and returns the hearts of men to the Divine *Torah*. He has the Spirit of *Eliahu*. By serving him, we serve Heaven."

"You have spoken well," said *Yeshua*. "And I will tell you one more thing. *Yochanan* not only has the Spirit of Elijah—he *is* Elijah. Do you know that?"

Andrew nodded.

"How do you know that?" asked the Master *Yeshua*.

"Because...the Prophet Malachi said that God would send Elijah to restore holiness in Israel before the great and terrible Day of the LORD."

"Well said, Andrew. And if the LORD will send Elijah again in flesh, and *Yochanan* is doing the prophesied deeds of Elijah in our sight, and if we know in our hearts that *Yochanan* is truly a great Prophet, what can we conclude?" he pressed on.

"That the *Malkuth Ha-Shamayyim* will come upon us when faithfulness is restored in Israel. That is why we gather the people for the Prophet."

"What is fidelity, and what is holiness?" *Yeshua* asked. "Is it keeping the *Torah* of the Essenes, of the Pharisees, of the Sadducees?"

This was a sore point, for Israel was riddled with sects and opinions interpreting what constituted fidelity to the Covenant.

"None of these. *Yochanan* teaches the true *Torah* of the Prophets," declared Andrew.

"Do you mean the Torah that is inscribed upon the heart?" asked *Yeshua*. Then he intoned:

> 'The Spirit of the LORD is upon me, because he has anointed me to preach good news to the poor; He has sent me to proclaim release to the captives, and healing of sight to the blind; to liberate those who are oppressed; to proclaim the year of of LORD's acceptance, and the Day of His Vengeance.'

"So, you know the Prophets," answered Andrew. "Yes, that is the *Torah*, and that is also the *Basor*. You should become a *talmid*."

"I am already," replied *Yeshua*.

Andrew stared at him, then said, "Come with me. You can watch us proclaim the Prophet's gathering."

They walked to the central spring, which produced a green oasis that had been ringed by stones. As they filled their flasks with water, other *talmidim* began to arrive. Soon all seven were standing in a circle around the pool.

With one voice they intoned the Psalm *May God be gracious to us*. A few people walking in the streets took notice. Then they broke ranks and began to walk in pairs on streets laid out in the four directions. People came out to look at the men, who stopped every 70 paces and proclaimed, "The Prophet *Yochanan* will be at the spring tomorrow morning! The Prophet comes to Bethany tomorrow in the morning!"

After a while the *talmidim* returned to the oasis with several people tagging along. Some were family or friends engaging them in social conversation, but others were asking questions about things that *Yochanan* had said on his previous visit. Andrew was not a native of Bethany, so he sat with *Yeshua* on the large stones surrounding the pool.

"Where do you fish?" asked the Master.

"Far away to the North—Bethsaida, Capernaum. I return there during the best fishing season to help my brother *Shimone*. He is a wealthy man with a large boat and many employees. He is known in his city as as the captain. My brother loves *Yochanan* and is faithful to the *Basor*. He releases me to serve the Prophet and sometimes brings his men South to hear him preach when the fishing is bad."

Yochanan required his disciples to lead Spartan lives. Thus the home for the Brothers was cold and unkempt. *Yeshua* was invited to sleep on the dirty floor of the main room, but he preferred the courtyard, which had been purified by sun and wind.

Before day-break he heard Andrew and the two other Brothers intoning psalms, to which he added his voice from the courtyard. Then he ate the remaining bread and figs in his bag.

Soon after the sun rose, a woman came into the courtyard with baskets of food.

"Would you like to buy?" she asked.

"I would, thank you," he replied and quickly replenished his supplies.

She gathered her wares and turned to leave.

"Aren't you going to see if the Brothers want anything?" he asked.

"They never do," she answered and left.

Soon the babble of a large crowd began to fill the city. The Brothers emerged from the house, and they all made their way to the spring.

Yeshua counted twenty-six people standing near the pool, and more were arriving. Three other *talmidim* stood apart. *Yeshua* joined the throng while Andrew stood with the other disciples.

Suddenly there was a shout from the main road. The other four disciples were standing watch for their master's arrival. *Yochanan* strode swiftly into sight followed by his four *zaddikim*, including *Yakob*, and the four disciples falling into procession behind. As the

Prophet approached, the other four disciples who had stood apart now pushed their way through the thickening crowd to open a pathway for the procession.

For the first time, *Yeshua* realized that all eight of these *talmidim* were big, strong, and capable of protecting the Prophet's life if needed. That is why they had been chosen for these duties.

The Prophet was seated as before on a high rock. He raised his hands in the *orant* and sent forth a powerful, ringing prayer that left no one unmoved. It was not just the words that made such an impression. It was a divine power that carried the words like fresh horses speeding a chariot over smooth roads.

When he had finished he lowered his arms and indicated that the crowd had permission to sit. All the people made themselves comfortable, but the disciples remained standing. *Yeshua* also remained standing at the rear of the crowd.

"Men of Israel, who is your King? Is it Herod…or is it *Mashiah*?"

"It is *Mashiah*!" shouted the *talmidim* and *zaddikim* in one voice. The men in the crowd nodded their approval.

"What does the prophet say? Is it not this?"

> 'Prepare a triumphal road for *Adonai*! Make a straight highway in the desert"'

"What is this desert? Is it not the dead and stony garden that Israel has become? Is it not the barren orchard of Israel that no longer produces the fruits of justice, truth, and loving-kindness? Do you see righteousness? Do you see faithful devotion and prayer?

"The Romans have made Herod Antipas your King, but is he a righteous man? Is it righteous to take your brother's wife if your brother has not died? No! That is against God's *Torah*. But Herod has put away his own wife to marry Herodius, the wife of his brother, whom she divorced according to Roman law. I sent my messenger to Herod and warned him against this folly. But he has persisted, and now the so-called King of Galilee and Perea has dishonored God's *Torah*.

"Make a smooth highway in the desert…for whom? For Herod and Herodius?

"*Mashiah* cannot come into filth. The Divine *Malkuth* does not appear in the midst of a people who are unrighteous and impure.

"Do the rulers of the Sanhedrin and Priests of the Temple practice righteousness and purity? Look around you! Why has God allowed Roman soldiers into our cities? Is it not because so many of the Priests and teachers have become unrighteous? They are breeding like snakes in a pit.

The Prophet has warned us:

> 'The Day of the LORD will not be one of light, but of terrible darkness; not of joy, but of terrible wrath!'

"Terrible days are immediately ahead. Only a fool cannot see that. And only your fidelity will protect you from the wrath that must come. For there will be disasters, earthquakes, floods, wars—all manner of evil will come upon the Earth to cleanse it by trial and fire.

"Will the corrupt Priests and kings and teachers of Israel save us? Can anyone save Israel from utter ruin? Yes! And I will tell you who it is.

"It is *you*! My brothers and sisters, *you* are the true Israel. It is *you* who must prepare the Way of the LORD.

"How do you prepare His Way? By purifying your hearts and returning to the righteous ways of our fathers—one person at a time, one family at a time. By keeping faith with the Covenant of Israel here in Bethany and there in Bethsaida and yet again there in all the other cities of Israel, we will renew the Covenant. We need no Priests and kings.

"And what will happen? It is like the birth of a new child. First come pain and tears, but immediately afterwards—joy. These are the birth-pangs of God's *Mashiah*, Who will come forth on Earth and be sovereign. In that Day, as the Prophet Isaiah said, the wolf will dwell in peace with the lamb. There will be no more Satans in the land, no more poisonous serpents and scorpions to hurt the people. One fig tree will produce a thousand branches, and each branch a thousand figs.

"My brothers and sisters, it is only the effort of each soul that will save yourselves and Israel from the terrible days that are at hand. Here is what you must do. Come forward to the Brothers and make an oath that you will from henceforth be faithful to the Laws of God—to justice, truth, righteousness, and the traditions of Israel.

"Say it in your own words, or say nothing at all. But come forth to one of the *talmidim* and *zaddikim*. Stand before him and make your oath. Then he will cleanse you in the living waters."

Without exception, every person who had come to hear the Prophet stood up and came forward.

Including *Yeshua*.

He stood before his brother *Yakob*.

"I thought you didn't make oaths, *Yeshe*."

"I don't need to make an oath. You already know my love for God and the Covenant."

"Step into the water, Brother, and baptize yourself," he laughed.

The Prophet looked on. When *Yeshua* stepped out of the pool, he motioned for Andrew. A moment later the disciple came to *Yeshua*, who had positioned himelf on a rock in the sun to dry out.

"The Master wishes to speak with you," Andrew said.

Yeshua smiled at *Yochanan* seated on his reed mat high above the crowd, approached and kneeled, gave a salutation, and waited to hear what the Prophet would say.

Yochanan placed his hands on *Yeshua's* crown and closed his eyes. Finally he spoke.

"My Son, I think you are already a *tzadik*. And more."

He took his hands away.

"Tonight we celebrate the *Shabbat Seder* at the House of the Brothers. I want you to come and sit at my right."

Yeshua nodded his assent.

******* ******* ******* *******

As the sun hung red over the great rift to the West that formed the Jordan River, *Yeshua* entered the courtyard. It was guarded by two disciples. They knocked a special pattern at the main door, which swing open to reveal an entirely unexpected sight.

The room was swept clean. A skillfully carved cedar table had been placed in the center of the room. Clean reed mats indicated seating. Candles were at the ready in various locations and upon the table itself, which also supported large baskets and bowls of bread, fruit, and honey sweets. No one was reclining at the table, but two of the Brothers were at work to complete setting up the *Seder*.

Another door opened and the Brothers entered behind *Yochanan* and quietly took their seats. *Yakob* smiled at *Yeshua* as he took the position of honor to the right of the Prophet. The lowest position was left unoccupied for *Yeshua*.

The Prophet began the *Seder* with a psalm invoking the angels, then offered the first Cup of Blessing. As the liturgy progressed, *Yeshua* found that he did not know all the parts, which were probably Essene. But the Brothers participated fluently with call-and-response and intoned hymns. He participated where he could.

Then came the meal. The *talmidim* ate freely of all that was on the table, but *Yochanan* and his four *zaddikim* ate only from a separate basket. Their diet was restricted to food found only in the desert—the diet of a wilderness dwellers. His rations had grown sparse in the past few days, so *Yeshua* ate the meal of the talmidim with great appreciation.

There was no distinction of meats and sweets in the meal. When everyone was filled, *Yochanan* put up his hand to indicate silence, then began to speak.

"My Brothers, I have a Word for *Yakob ben-Yosef*."

All eyes turned to *Yakob*.

"The Spirit of Holiness says this: 'Beloved Son of Heaven, my Temple grows more impure each day. The lamp of righteousness has grown dim. The offerings are polluted with greed and injustice. For the sake of Israel, you must fulfill your duties in the Temple.'"

Yakob was disturbed by this message.

"But Master, we do not sacrifice animals and serve blood to the Holy One!"

"My Brother," *Yochanan* quietly replied, "you are not to serve at the altar in the courses scheduled for your lineage. You are to offer incense and pray daily for the awakening and cleansing of Israel. And you must do this in such a way that you are seen by many. This is far more important than smoothing the mat for me or unlatching my sandals.

"I have recognized you as a *Tzadik*. Now you must bring your holiness to the people of Jerusalem and the Temple.

"You must return to your Mother and family in Nazareth tomorrow. On the New Moon before the coming Passover, make your pilgrimage to Jerusalem. You will wear the outer garments of a Brother, as you now do, so that our people in Jerusalem will know you and provide for your food and shelter.

"But on the Passover you must discard these garments, cleanse your body in the *mikveh* of the *cohenim*, and don the white linen garment of Priesthood. You must continue thereafter in the life and dress of a Priest."

There was a stunned silence. *Yeshua* was taken aback even more than his brother. Had he not come originally to return his brother home? Had he not told him that his true vocation was that of a Priest? Now the Prophet was delivering this message in a way that *Yakob* could receive—but from a much greater perspective than anything *Yeshua* had imagined.

Yochanon lay his hand upon *Yakob's*.

"My Brother, I have seen a day when you will enter the Holy of Holies and perform the work of the High Priest for the atonement of all Israel."

The Brothers looked at each other and raised their eyebrows. The High Priest was a wealthy, corrupt Roman puppet despised by most of Israel. How could a holy man be appointed by the Sanhedrin and Roman rulers as a High Priest?

"Is it not so, *Yeshua*?" the Prophet asked, fixing his gaze upon the stranger reclining at the lowest place in the *Seder*.

"You have said it," he replied. "It will come to pass."

"My Brothers, I have a Word for you all.

He paused for a moment, took a deep breath, closed his eyes, and spoke.

"The *Ruach Ha-Qodesh* says this: 'What is a *Tzadik*, and what is righteousness? Does it consist in outer acts of *mitzvoth*, rigid observance of *Torah*, or pious words and prayers? If so, then the Pharisees are all *zaddikim*. But many of them are self-righteous pretenders. If so, then the Essenes are all *zaddikim*. But many of them are corrupt merchants seeking their own gain.

"Do you know that the *amme-ha-eretz*, whom you are privileged to cleanse with water, will enter into the *Malkuth Ha-Shamayyim* before many of those who are called *zaddikim*?

"Righteousness is not achieved through outer acts, but through inner fidelity. I have inscribed true *Torah* in the Temple of your hearts. Listen and watch, so that you may speak the words of the *Bat Kol*.

"Do you know that I send my angels to you in the appearance of strangers and foreigners?

"Who is the stranger in your midst? Watch, and listen."

All eyes turned to *Yeshua*.

The Prophet stopped speaking and opened his eyes. *Yakob* filled the final Cup of Blessing, and *Yochanan* completed the ritual.

That night *Yakob* slept in the courtyard next to his brother, as they had done all during childhood. The next day he departed for Nazareth.

During the heat of the day, *Yochanan* sent the Brothers to the River to bathe and rest in the shade. He instructed them to return to the encampment when the day cooled and prepare it for habitation. But he asked *Yeshua* to walk with him in the heat of the day to the encampment.

"If that is your desire, I will do so today," he replied. "But I do not agree with your tests and rigors. Why do you require them?"

The sun was very hot and the path filled with stone and dust, but the Prophet quickly strode with head uncovered.

He answered, "My father and mother died of old age before I had even been taught the *aleph-bet*. I can hardly remember them. I was raised by Essenes in the desert. They were very devoted to God, but impersonal. We were constantly tried and tested. They raised us to be *zaddikim* and warriors. Since mine is the lineage of Aaron, I was also trained in Priesthood—not for animal sacrifice, but for the sacred rites of the Essene community. But I preferred to be a warrior…"

He paused and caught his breath.

"So I was trained to run in the desert heat, which Roman soldiers cannot do. I was trained to survive in the cold of the desert night, when Roman soldiers sleep. I learned how to live and hide in the desert, and to eat what it provided. Finally I was in charge of training and commanded many fighters..."

"Let us stop a moment for rest and water," interrupted *Yeshua*. "I am a strong man trained in construction, but if I try to keep up this pace, I'll drop!"

The Prophet laughed and stood silently while *Yeshua* drank from his flask.

"But my friend, discipline of the body can bring us closer to the Spirit of Holiness," he remarked.

Yeshua caught his breath for moment, then said, "If suffering of the body brought us closer to God, then all the lepers of Judaea must be *zaddikim*."

"I see your point," *Yochanan* conceded. "But it is not my goal to torture the bodies of my disciples—merely to make them stronger for divine service."

"Well, I can tell you that my brother *Yakob* is not destined for the life of a prophet. He will never be able to perform the physical feats that you do. He never trained that way. He was raised by a loving father who taught him to be a man—not a Spartan warrior!"

Yochanan laughed heartily at the thought.

"We could have destroyed an entire Spartan phalanx!"

"How many were you?" asked *Yeshua*, glad to prolong the respite.

"We tried to have fifty good men at any time...no match for a Roman army of thousands, but our *zaddikim* said that God and His angels would fight on our side. They put their trust in a Messiah-ben-David who would descend from the skies and destroy the Romans. Deluded idiots! That's why I left the community. They never understood the *Malkuth Ha-Shamayyim* or the *Bar-Enash*."

"I know that you do not teach false ideas," remarked *Yeshua*. "I was trained in the Brotherhood of Daniel at Babylon."

"You would have made a good Essene warrior, *Yeshua*. You are bigger and stronger than most men," remarked *Yochanan*.

"If the Almighty One had wanted me to be a warrior, He would have made me one. But He made me a strong man of peace like you, *Yochanan*. Long after you are gone, you will be remembered for your words of truth—not for your feats of endurance in the desert."

They resumed walking briskly toward the encampment and continued their conversations. *Yeshua* found himself filled with energy, and the scorching sun no longer bothered him. The Prophet's presence somehow ignited him. He felt that he was blazing inside like the sun. The lingering clouds of pain and regret seemed to burn away. He was being cleansed by fire, and now the hot sun was becoming the healer of his physical body—not the destroyer of it.

As they neared the encampment *Yeshua* asked if *Yochanan* had ever known Eleazar the *Tzadik*. The Prophet stopped dead in his tracks.

"He was my teacher, my greatest human teacher. I loved him like a son loves his own father. But he left the community when I was young—probably for the same reasons I left. How did you know him?"

Yeshua smiled. "He was the *Chazzan* of the synagogue in Nazareth, and he taught me *Torah* for my *Bar-Mitzvah*."

"My Brother," began the Prophet (this was the first time he had called him a Brother), "there is much you are not telling me, is that not so?"

"Shall we speak of the Work of the Chariot?" asked *Yeshua*.

"Ah-h-h!" The Prophet stopped again and turned to *Yeshua*. "What do you know of the *Merkabah*?"

"My Teacher, have you not guided me through the Work? Have we not communicated many times in the Heavens?" asked *Yeshua*.

The Prophet squeezed his eyes shut.

"Yes…I know you. I wasn't sure before, but now I know you, my Brother."

He opened his eyes.

"Let us be silent and return to the camp."

At the next *Shabbat Seder*, the Prophet informed his disciples that *Yeshua* was a great *tzadik* from Babylon and henceforth would take his brother's place of honor at the table.

From that time forward, *Yeshua* and *Yochanan* spoke in long, private conversations. They discussed not only the Work of the Chariot, but their understanding of the Day of YHWH, exorcism, the Birth Pangs and Marriage Banquet of Messiah, sanctification, discipleship with the *Ruach Ha-Qodesh*, the *Bar-Enash*, the Suffering Servant, and the Messiah ben-Joseph.

They sat together many nights in the posture of Elijah to "watch" or meditate. *Yeshua* demonstrated the technique for the Ascent he had learned from the Master Ariston. On a moonless night they were able to evoke the Heavenly *Eliahu*, who appeared as another face above *Yeshua's* head and counseled *Yochanan* about his Mission.

It was after one of these nights that the Prophet said, "It is only a matter of time before *Jezebel* murders me."

"How can Jezebel kill *Eliahu*?" was the incredulous response of *Yeshua*. "What power does she have over you now?"

"She bought it with her own blood," he replied. "She accounted her suicide to my sin, put me into her debt, and I shall have to repay it before I can be free."

"Yes, we are like flies trapped in the web of Satan," mused *Yeshua*. "He spins tiny chains that grip us no matter what we do. The more action we take, the more we become entangled in his web. Then when we are so entangled that we cannot free ourselves, he sucks the life-blood from us until we are hollow shells."

Yochanan smiled and said, "Remember this—God gave Satan authority over Job's body, but not his soul. The ruler of this darkness can kill the body, but he cannot touch the soul. Many *zaddikim* will have their blood poured out upon the Earth before the rule of evil will end. Every righteous person will be tortured like Job, and every prophet will be martyred, until the sovereignty of the Son of Man has been firmly established on the Earth."

"The spider web reaches from generation to generation," mused *Yeshua*. "I have seen the cruel hand of *Eliahu's* father casting the first stone to kill him, and leaving him for dead. There is great sin and debt owing for that."

Yochanan looked up in surprise. "So you have seen this thing!" he exclaimed. "Where did you see this?"

"It was a recurring nightmare in my childhood. It was explained to me by the sages in Babylon."

Yochanan fell silent for a moment, then spoke.

"I was told that my father was a devoted Priest in the course of Abijah. He prayed and burned incense at the Temple, but his wife Elisabeth never bore children. When she was very old—beyond the age of childbearing—she was told by the *Bat Kol* that she would bear a child. I was conceived and born in their old age.

"I will tell you something that I have never revealed. My father Zachariah was the same soul as the father of *Eliahu*. He suffered much in his life, bound in the web of Satan, but when he died, his soul was free of debt."

"Yes, Satan had sucked him dry, and the debt was paid," said *Yeshua*. "Now tell me one other thing. Who is Jezebel?"

"She is Herodias, the new wife of Herod."

The Prophet paused, closed his eyes, then said, "My Brother, I have a Word for you.

"The *Ruach Ha-Qodesh* says this: You will all be martyred by Satan. But you must stand forth in this *'olam* and scatter the divine seeds as long as you can. *Eliahu's* hour will come soon, but yours will come later. *Yeshua* my Son, you must go unto all Israel and proclaim the *Basor*."

Yeshua drew a deep breath.

The Prophet opened his eyes and continued.

"There is not enough time. I cannot bring the Word to all Israel before my hour arrives. You must go forth and do as I am doing.

"And you must be wiser than I have been, my Brother. Do not provoke Herod or his successors. Keep out of their hands. Your *talmidim* will not protect you—only you can do that. But they can conceal you until you appear. And my Brother, I will teach you how to survive in the wilderness. The desert will be your greatest friend."

"How can I do this?" asked *Yeshua*. "I am a stranger now. I have no friends, and certainly no *talmidim*."

"You must go into the desert by yourself, eating and drinking only what it provides. And you must seek your answers from God.

"This week we baptize in the region of Judaea. Many will come. I shall publically recognize you as a *tzadik* by performing your *mikveh* before the witness of everyone. Then you must immediately go into the wilderness of Judaea to prepare for your mission."

*******   *******   *******   *******

Yeshua was amazed. Never had he seen so many people gathered in a desert place.

Entire Jewish families sat under tents and tarps awaiting the appearance of the Prophet. But there were also Jewish soldiers in the employ of the Romans, Essenes who had come down from their community, caravans and traders selling food and drink, and pious Pharisees from Jerusalem and outlying synagogues.

People were not here out of curiosity. They would not have their bodies cleansed in the *mikveh* of *Yochanan* unless they were prepared to make an oath of fidelity to the *Malkuth Ha-Shamayyim*. They were here out of commitment to the Advent of *Mashiah*.

But what did that mean to them? There were many doctrines, most of which expected the sudden appearance of the Warrior Messiah Ben-David with armies of angels and Jewish fighters to expel the Romans and establish a new nation of Israel.

Yochanan had told *Yeshua* that he could not change these illusions. Instead, his mission was to call Israel to submission, to turns the hearts of Israel back to God. The goal of his preaching was to make one idea absolutely clear—that Messiah could not come until the people of Israel had returned to the purity and sanctity of the Covenant. Thus he called Israel to restore personal sanctity in each person, and then to re-cross the Jordan into the new Promised Land as a restored and reformed Israel.

But today there were hecklers in the throng—Pharisaic *Torah* experts from Jerusalem who would try to discredit him before the people.

The crowd stood up as the Prophet stepped out of his tent. It was perched on the high ledge of the East bank of the River overlooking the rocky plain where people had encamped.

He held up his arms in the *orant* and the people followed suit. He gave forth a brief prayer, then opened his eyes and dropped his hands in a signal for people to sit.

His eyes blazed. He extended his right hand and pointed to a small group of Pharisees sitting smugly on portable couches while their servants stood by.

With a voice like thunder he demanded, "You brood of vipers! Who warned you to flee from the wrath that is to come?"

A shock crackled through the crowd. One of the Pharisees stood up to speak, but *Yochanan* walked toward him with hand still extended and thundered, "You are dry trees, pretenders to piety! Hear me! You must bear fruits that show true submission to God's *Malkuth*. You are puffed up with foolish pride, and not in any way prepared for this baptism! Don't say.'We are the true Sons of Abraham,' for I tell you God is raising up His true Sons from these common people you see here! The axe is laid to the fruitless trees. Every tree that does not bear the fruits of humility and purity will be cut down and thrown into the fire!"

The offended Pharisees threw up their hands and walked away with their servants scrambling to load their couches onto a recalcitrant camel.

"My friends, you are the true Israelites. You are striving to be righteous. You are seeking God with true hearts. You have come out into the desert to renew your Covenant with Heaven.

"You have seen the pretenders to righteousness. Now I will show you a true *tzadik*, and I shall bathe him myself in the *mikveh* of a *Tzadik*."

He motioned for *Yeshua* to accompany him to the baptismal pool, which had been cut from rocks on the bank near the ford on the River. The Brothers held *Yeshua's* outer garments while the two men descended into the deep pool. The Prophet placed his hands on the sides of *Yeshua's* head and looked to Heaven. Both men kneeled and dropped under the water, then broke the surface and reappeared.

The Prophet held his hands in the *orant* while *Yeshua* held his hands to his heart, and proclaimed in a loud voice, "My Brother, from this moment on, you are *Shalem*! You are a Son of the Most High!"

They climbed up out of the pool. Andrew assisted *Yeshua* to put on his garment. Then the new *Tzadik* sat while Andrew latched his sandals. He stood again and the Brother handed him his staff and bag.

Yeshua turned his face to the East and, looking neither to the left or the right, set off into the Judaean desert.

Chapter Twenty: NAZARETH

Yochanan had told him plainly, "You must immediately go into the wilderness of Judaea to prepare for your mission." *Yeshua* would need to seek guidance directly from God Himself, the Father of All. Therefore he remained in a state of constant prayer and contemplation.

As he wandered farther East into the wilderness, *Yeshua* considered the forty years that Israel sojourned in the desert before crossing the Jordan into the Promised Land. He pondered the fact that he had lived a life as another *Yeshua* who had been given the responsibility to succeed Moses and lead the new Israel into Canaan.

After their escape from Egypt, Israel's leaders turned away from God and became corrupt. If it were not for the intercession of Moses, all the people would have been destroyed in a plague. All but faithful *Yeshua*. Instead, the outraged Prophet ground their golden calves into dust, made the people drink it to release them from the bondage of idolatry, and ordered his Levites to slay the three thousand leaders. After that, Israel wandered forty years in the wilderness of Judaea until the rest of that corruptible generation had died.

All the men who came out of Egypt had been circumcised into the Covenant, but their surviving children had not. Now that all the offenders had died, God told Moses to command the people to take flint knives and circumcise the new generation of men as Sons of the Covenant. Then the aged Moses himself, who was the last living man to escape from Egypt, also died. Only then was Israel was finally allowed to cross the Jordan River into the Promised Land. They did so under the leadership of *Yeshua*, whom God appointed to be the successor of Moses.

In this day, the leadership of Israel had again become corrupt. *Yochanan* called the common people to a *mikveh* of Covenantal renewal and a recrossing of the Jordan into the Promised Land of God's *Malkuth*. *Yeshua* and the men in his family were of Priestly lineage, as was *Yochanan*. They all had the right to serve in their courses at the Temple in Jerusalem and to act as Priests for cleansing and other sacred acts. Therefore, using the desert survival skills that the Prophet *Yochanan* had taught him, *Yeshua* determined to offer Priestly prayer and fasting in the Judaean wilderness for forty days before recrossing the Jordan River into Israel.

He would listen for the guidance of Heaven. He would prepare himself to be a Son of the Renewed Covenant by seeking the true Messianic circumcision—what the prophets called the "circumcision of the heart." And he would offer his forty days of fasting in the wilderness—one day for each year that the Hebrews had wandered in the desert—as atonement and intercession for all Israel.

He also pondered another life he had lived as Elisha, disciple and successor of the Prophet Elijah. That is what the serpent of Moses had told him. Elijah had called him by the name Elisha once in a vision—long ago in Babylon. It was Elijah who had taught him in psychic visions how to make the Ascent in the *Merkabah*. Now he had found Elijah the Prophet, his Teacher, living on Earth as the Prophet *Yochanan*. They had made the Ascent together many times.

What did it all mean?

Yeshua followed the instructions of *Yochanan* about desert survival. He sheltered during the heat of the day and travelled by night. The Moon was full when he began his journey, so She would count his forty days. She would become new in fourteen days, then full in fourteen more, then new again in fourteen more days. When the Moon disappeared into the Sun for a second time, he would cross the Jordan River into the Land Of Promise.

At first the nights were bright as day, with Moon-shadows evoking strange shapes over the landscape. The constellations formed asterisms related to Hebrew letters that could be read by season for directions, as well as for divination. He lay often down at midnight to search for their message. But the Moon moved slowly out of the night heaven into the morning and day heaven, and the nights became black. Travel was no longer possible. Now he sat in prayer and contemplation beneath the divine lights for most of the night and did his travelling at dawn and dusk.

The temple of night was filled with the fiery eyes of the Divine Host—some burning white, others red, yellow, or blue. At the center shone the beacon of the *teli*, the eye of the pole-serpent. From here great Leviathon was hung by his nose as he coiled about the central egg of Creation that lay beneath the Throne of the Ancient of Days. It was as Ariston had said—nights like this in the presence of myriad Divine Spirits were appropriate to make the Ascent.

Yeshua was far away from the Jordan River, but he was able to find water in special places *Yochanan* had described. One was a small underground pool hidden at the base of a long stony slope. Other underground sources revealed themselves by the tiny green thistles they supported in cracks and fissures of great outcroppings. There was also a dry river where water could be found by digging in discolored concavities of sandy soil.

He made a tea of boiled thistles. They could then be eaten like a stew. When he came upon desert flowers he followed the bees to their hive. At night he could carefully remove some honeycombs. There were also many kinds of large insects and locusts that could be eaten, as well as water-hoarding cactuses.

As he walked on the night of the next full Moon, when he had wandered for twenty-eight days, he heard a voice whispering "*Yeshua…Yeshua.*" No one was visible, so he sat upon a stone, closed his eyes, and listened. He heard no more, but became aware of the presence of *Yochanan*. Images and impressions formed in his mind about the *mikveh* of a *Tzadik* with which *Yochanan* had publically honored him. He felt himself descending under the water with the Prophet and emerging cleansed.

He opened his eyes and softly spoke, "I thank you, my Teacher and my friend. I will keep faith with the *Basor* and carry on your work in Israel."

Over the next two weeks the night heaven grew dark as the Moon moved into the day heaven. *Yeshua* had turned his path West toward the Jordan and was retracing familiar ground. He realized that the wilderness was not a place of barrenness, but of spiritual regeneration. He would return here again to clarify his mind and commune with Heaven.

On his last night in the desert, with the campfires of human activity visible far away on the Western horizon and the black sky blazing with the divine fires of God, *Yeshua* remembered the legend of Zarathustra he learned in Babylon. He remembered the story of Buddha that he had been told in the monastery near the City of Lotus Flowers.

Both saints had retreated into a wilderness, where each was confronted by a form of *Shaitan*. The Evil Ruler of this world had tried to gain their allegiance by offering all the delights and riches of the world. They had both quoted Scripture and refused. Afterwards they received the ministration of angels.

"These things never happened," he thought to himself. "*Shaitan* does not appear to us. His strength lies in our ignorance of his influence and presence. It is the hidden scorpion that stings, not the one we can see and avoid.

"Zarathustra and Gautama had already renounced the illusions and vanities of human life. Prince Gautama left his palace behind at the very beginning of the quest, so how could *Shaitan* test him with riches and sensual delights many years later? It is more likely that he was tested with pride, like Moses. And it was not *Shaitan* who put him to the test, but he himself. It is not God who tests us. And in the final analysis, it is not *Shaitan*. It is we ourselves.

"*Shaitan* will attempt to lay hidden snares for my feet, but if he catches my eye he will retreat in terror. For the Father has given me the *Basor* of the liberation of my people from the bondage of *Shaitan*."

At this moment he understood clearly how to begin. He would teach the *Basor* of the God's *Malkuth* and demonstrate its reality by healing and releasing those in bondage to *Shaitan*.

With the next sunrise, he crossed the Jordan into the Land of Israel and set his face for his mother's house in Nazareth.

******* ******* ******* *******

"Thank you, my dear *Yeshe*, for bringing your brother home. But now he has gone to Jerusalem to serve in the Temple courses, and he is still a *talmid* of the false prophet *Yochanan*." His Mother wrung her hands in frustration.

"Mother," *Yeshua* lay his hands upon her shoulders and she became calm. "*Yochanan* is among the greatest of the Prophets."

"*Yeshe!*" cried *Shalome*. "Are you one of his disciples, too?"

Speaking slowly and deliberately, he looked into his Mother's eyes and said, "I have received the *mikveh* of *Yochanan*."

Miriam slipped from of his grasp and fell to the ground wailing inconsolably.

"My first-born son is insane! *Yeshe* and *Yakob* will be murdered by the Romans."

Yeshua knelt next to his Mother and again firmly grasped her trembling shoulders.

"*Imma*, I am not a zealot. I am not a soldier. *Yakob* and I are *cohenim* and *talmidim*. The Prophet does not teach armed resistance. He is not a threat to the Romans. He teaches righteousness and the renewal of our Covenant. He prepares us for the advent of the Age of the *Bar-Enash*—new Heavens, new Earth, new Humanity. An Age when *Shaitan* and his Beasts will no longer rule mankind.

"*Imma,* the Romans will not kill me."

Miriam became very still and pierced him with her eyes.

"Yes, my Son. The Romans will kill you."

In his heart he heard another voice—the whisper of his beloved Shoshana.

"*Yes, my Darling, my Love, my Heart and Soul. The Romans will kill you.*"

Still holding his Mother's shoulders, he bowed his head.

"Yes," he heard his Heart speak in the silence, "*the Romans will kill my Teacher Yochanan, and they will kill me. But not until I have done my sacred work on Earth. Until then, Heaven will protect me.*"

"*Imma,*" he heard his voice speaking aloud, "I shall be very careful. *Yakob* will serve in the Temple and the Romans will not dare to take him."

After a moment, *Miriam* allowed him to lift her back to her feet. She smiled through her tears and motioned for him to sit for a meal.

The next morning was *Shabbat*. As *Yeshua* entered the Synagogue of Nazareth with *Miriam* and *Shalome*, all eyes were upon him. The *Chazzan* approached them. He was very old, but *Yeshua* did not recognize him from his childhood days in Nazareth.

"This is your Son *Yeshua*?" he asked politely.

"Returned from Babylon," smiled *Miriam*.

"You wear the seamless garment of a *cohen*. We would be honored if you would read the *Nabi* portion for us today," he said, pointing to the *Torah* table. "Or have you forgotten your Hebrew after all those years of Aramaic among our Chaldaean families?"

Yeshua laughed.

"No, we always chanted in Hebrew, and I am quite ready to chant any portions you wish."

There were many whispers among the assembly as *Yeshua* took his place with the men of the synagogue. He recognized no one. They were all strangers. When he looked at them, they averted their faces and no one spoke to him.

He did overhear one whispered comment, however.

"He is the brother of *Yakob*." Several heads nodded.

When the time came to read from the Prophets, *Yeshua* strode to the *Torah* table, kissed the *tzitzit* of his prayer shawl, and looked straight ahead, instead of at the open part of the *Torah* scroll designed for today's reading.

In a clear and melodious voice he intoned from the latter part of the Prophet Isaiah:

"The Spirit of *Adonai Elohim* is upon me. For YAHWEH hath anointed me to proclaim His Good Message to the people of the land. He hath sent me to heal the brokenhearted, and to proclaim liberation to the captives, and the opening of the prison to those who are bound. He hath sent me to proclaim the acceptable Way of God and the coming of YAHWEH's justice upon the Earth. He hath sent me to strengthen and gladden those who mourn in Zion, and to take away from them the ashes of mourning, and to give them the oil of joy. He hath sent me to remove the rent garments of mourning for the spirit of heaviness and give them instead the spotless white garments of praise. He hath sent me that His people might be called trees of righteousness, and a new orchard planted by YAHWEH, that He might be glorified in the eyes of all."

He paused and looked at the startled assembly. Then he spoke.

"Today this Scripture is fulfilled in your sight and in your generation."

The old *Chazzan* was outraged. He stood up and declared, "This stranger is a Messianic fool. Don't listen to him. He will bring the Roman soldiers to burn our homes and kill our men and rape our women!"

A young man stood up and declared, "He is a zealot. He will bring disaster."

Shalome stood up and shouted, "No! My brother is not a zealot!"

Many people stood and walked nervously out of the synagogue, while some of the men stood and shook their fists.

One of them shouted, "He thinks he is a prophet, but he will bring only death to us!" Another said, "I want him out of my village." Yet another muttered, "He ought to be stoned." Glaring back at *Yeshua* and his family, they also departed the synagogue.

The old *Chazzan* moved protectively up to the *Torah* scroll and hastily removed it to the locked closet where it was stored.

Yeshua joined his mother and sister and returned to their home.

After a long silence, *Miriam* spoke.

"My Son, you must leave this village. Some of these men are collaborators. They will accuse you to the Romans. You can escape, but we can't. This is our home."

Yeshua was agonized. He hadn't understood until now how bad life was under Roman rule in the Galilee. If he chose to stay, his family could be harmed. If he left Nazareth, he could never come home except secretly and by night.

With tears in his eyes, he gathered his few possessions and prepared to leave. For where? He did not know.

"*Imma, Shalome,* I will send you messages, and sometimes I may be able to visit secretly or meet you in other villages. But for now, it is all in God's hands. I must leave you."

But when he came to his mother's gate, seven men approached him with large stones in their hands. For the first time he recognized some of those who had bullied *Yakob* as a child. They were intent upon sweet revenge. One of them threw a stone that glanced off *Yeshua's* purse but left a painful bruise. Anger rose in the Master's throat.

They expected him to run, but instead he strode quickly toward the men. They all threw stones, but few reached their mark. *Yeshua* was more powerful than any stone, and he was bigger and stronger than any of the men there. He raised his heavy staff, and as he reached the men they moved back in fear. With one blow he laid the first stone-thrower flat on his back with a broken jaw. The others dropped their stones and began to retreat.

He turned to them with staff held high in his left hand and eyes burning with power.

"I am leaving Nazareth, but if any of you dares to come near to my mother's home, or in any other way to threaten her, I shall return by night and kill you." He stretched out his right arm and pointed directly to each man, one by one. "Fear me. I might kill you now before I leave!"

With that, he pointed his staff like lightning and bashed two more men to the ground. All the others turned and ran for their lives.

Meanwhile, other men and women of the village had begun to gather on the road, including the elderly *Chazzan*. They had all witnessed the violence, which had erupted and come to its conclusion in only a few short minutes.

"*Yeshua!*" called out the *Chazzan*. "We mean you no harm. We did not send those ruffians against you. We know you are not a zealot. But we cannot allow Messianic teachings in Nazareth. Go to Capernaum. Go to the Eastern Galilee where the disciples of *Yochanan* have their homes. They will welcome you. But we are too close to Sepphoris—only a day's march for the Roman police. You cannot preach here."

Yeshua returned his staff to his right hand and knocked it once upon the ground. He looked at the *Chazzan* and the other men gathered with him.

"Brothers, protect my mother, or I shall have to return."

The men all nodded and the *Chazzan* spoke once more.

"Your mother and family are well-beloved in Nazareth. We will allow no harm to come to them, and these ruffians will not dare to try anything—not only for fear of you, but for fear of us."

Yeshua nodded and passed through the crowd. Soon he had begun the long trek on the stony road North that would lead to the Eastern Galilee.

*******   *******   *******   *******

As he walked the dusty road to Capernaum, the Master *Yeshua* had much time to ponder his rejection at Nazareth. Bits and pieces of information he had received from many sources about the conditions of his people under Roman oppression now, in the light of the impressions he had gained painfully in his mother's village, now began to come clear. Even though the Jerusalem collaborators and the Roman rulers did not dare to attack the Prophet *Yochanan,* still he retreated to desert encampments. Still he expected one day to be martyred, and the same for many of his *talmidim.*

"*Abba* Most Holy One, teach me Your Will and Way. Show me my work," was his constant prayer. With each step toward Capernaum, he asked to be shown. The Almighty One would be his only Teacher now.

In the mid-day heat of the second day, *Yeshua* found a cave to rest overlooking the Plain of Gennesaret. As he lay dozing, he had a vivid dream. It was a moonless night with brilliant stars overhead. The brightest of them descended from the night Heaven and came to rest in his outstretched palms. It became a tiny sacred flame that did not burn or consume, but blazed in his hands.

The *Ruach Ha-Qodesh* told him to spread that divine fire throughout the world until it was able to blaze everywhere on its own. But he had to protect it from the winds, nurture it, and feed it with more fuel.

Illuminated by starlight only, he had to find and collect many dry sticks, ignite them and kindle them to burning with his breath. Some sticks were dry enough to ignite, but most were damp and needed to dry next to the heat of the burning ones. Slowly and with great effort small fires were kindled in many places. More sticks dried and were able to burn. The fires made beautiful heat and light in the blackness of the night. Finally, other people came to help him in his work, and the landscape began to burn with many campfires.

As he continued his trek, now nearing the Sea of Galilee, he contemplated the meaning of his dream in the context of all that many great ones had told him about his spiritual mission—*Mar Belteshazzar*, Shoshana the *Therapeute*, the Hermetic Master Stephanos, the Prophet *Yochanan* who incarnated the Master Elijah. Soon ideas and patterns began to form in his mind. These finally produced a plan.

He would go to the fishing boats of Capernaum to seek out Andrew, his brother *Shimone*, and their friends who were sympathetic to *Yochanan's* teaching. They would bring him into their synagogues, where he would find others receptive to the *Basor*.

He would not only accept *talmidim* like other teachers of Israel, but he would know and recognize them when he first laid eyes upon them by means of his inner vision, and he would publically invite them to follow his *halakah*. In other words, rather than his disciples finding him, he would find them! He would walk with them, sit with them, eat with them—all the while teaching what the Spirit inspired according to the spiritual requirements of each one.

Instead of dwelling in one place, he would remain on the move, staying as a guest in different safe-houses. He would begin in Galilee, where many were receptive. His goal would be to kindle the divine fire of the *Basor* in the hearts of as many as possible before the rulers of this world could finally kill him. By that time the fires would be kindled, the seeds planted, and the *Basor* firmly established on Earth.

At this point in his life, the Master had spiritually outgrown all normal human desire for wife, home, family, or possessions. He had one desire only—to kindle the flame of *Bar-Enash*, the New Adam, whom the Almighty had already ordained to sit at His right hand of power and authority over all.

His beloved Shoshana was with him always. He did not fear anyone or anything. He knew that like *Yochanan* and all the prophets from Abel to Zechariah, and like the *Messiah Ben-Joseph*, the Anointed Offspring of Joseph, he would eventually be killed by the evil that rules in this *'olam*. But he also knew that the divine flame he would kindle had Heaven's power to transform mankind and awaken the Divine Sovereignty within their hearts.

Chapter Twenty-One: THE PROPHET *YESHUA*

Walking along the shore of the great inland sea, *Yeshua* saw the sun rise over the Eastern desert. It shown almost golden across a still, blue expanse of water. Birds flocked to the sea from clumps of trees, following the golden rays of the sun. A fishing village began to appear from the retreating shadows onshore.

He found a place where flat rocks protruded into the water and stepped out upon them. Bending low, he splashed water onto his face, then looked up again. Now across the water he could begin to make out fishermen onshore bringing carefully rigged nets onboard their dark wooden boats. Would Andrew be among the fishermen?

The village was half a day's walk on the stony path that followed the shoreline. All the while *Yeshua* could see the fleet of boats at work. They moved from one place to another, setting and dragging up their nets. It was a routine, moving from one known fish location to another, and all the boats remained within shouting distance of each other. Sometimes there was laughter and shouts of glee when nets were brought up, but other times silence or even cursing.

The sound of the men's voices travelled great distances over the water. *Yeshua* took note. A human voice carries over the water. A boat might be an excellent platform for a preacher. Everyone on shore would hear the words.

As the sun reached its zenith in the cloudless sky, the wind kicked up. It blew the boats farther offshore. The men simply guided their courses with large oars skulled from the aft section. They had no need to row. Now, however, their voices were inaudible. The Master noted that mid-day is not a good time to speak to people onshore from a boat.

He arrived at the village during the hottest part of the day, so he sought shelter at a large, green oasis on a hill overlooking the market place. He descended stone steps into the well and filled his water horn, then returned to rest under the same trees that were home to the birds he had seen flocking at dawn. As he looked out over the blue Sea of Galilee, he saw the birds bobbing unconcernedly on the waves, which had now begun to smooth out as the wind died away. Now again he could hear intermittent voices of the fishermen, but from much farther away. All the boats had erected various kinds of shelters and tents.

Fishermen, sea birds, and fishermen were all resting, so *Yeshua* closed his eyes and took a nap.

He awakened to the babbling of voices. Many laughing women were lined up with their water jars at the steps into the well. Some glanced furtively at him, then looked away. He stood up, brushed the dust from his clothing, and walked down the hill to the market place, where merchants and villagers were now beginning to gather.

Suddenly a woman ran screaming down the street.

"My little daughter! She has been bitten by a poisonous snake! Oh, help me! She will die!"

Several of the women hurried to her side as she fell to the ground tearing her hair. They pulled her to her feet, and she stumbled toward her house with everyone following, including *Yeshua*.

The child was lying unconscious at the gate of her home. Already her face was reddening, eyes bulging, and breathing nearly stopped.

"It is too late. There is nothing we can do for her," said an old woman. She seemed to be the medicine women of the village. "The poison has gone too far inside and we can't draw it out. She will die any minute."

The mother fell into the arms of her friends and fainted.

"She shall not die!" The strong words came out of the Master's mouth almost involuntarily.

Everyone turned to see the stranger who had made such a proclamation.

Yeshua motioned for the women to clear a space around the child and he knelt down next to her head. He placed his left hand on his heart, and his right hand upon the child's heart. He breathed a warm breath upon her face to strengthen the link between them. Then he intoned *Ha-Shem* slowly, ringing each vowel.

"*Talitha*, open your eyes," he commanded.

The little girl took a deep breath and painfully opened her eyes.

The Master cradled her in his powerful arms and stood up. He held her to his heart.

"She needs a cool bed and much water," he said to the mother, who now had recovered from her swoon and was staring at him with eyes full of amazement and hope.

In a few minutes *Yeshua* was able to lay her out on a soft bed. He soothed her fever with cool well-water and forced her to drink.

"*Imma,* it hurts so much!" the child moaned.

"*Talitha,* don't move your arms and legs. Just drink and breath," the Master commanded. Again he linked their hearts and intoned the Name of God. Then he laid his hands upon the child's head and appeared to be listening to something. Finally he removed his hands, stood up, and smiled.

"She will eat a meal with you tonight before the sun sets," he declared.

The old woman who was the only physician for the village knelt beside the little girl. She felt her forehead, hands, feet, and stomach.

"God be praised! I think the poison is gone. It must have been a very small snake."

Suddenly a man appeared at the door.

"Here is the snake," he declared. He held up a long boat hook. Still struggling was a huge poisonous snake that had been impaled in three places, strung like a giant fisherman's worm, and the head and teeth crushed.

"Look, my husband," cried the mother, "this physician has saved the life of our daughter!"

The man bowed deeply and said, "Sir, I am a poor fishermen. Today I was mending nets onshore and will not have a share in the catch until tonight, when the boats return. What fee can I offer you?"

The Master smiled and said, "My Brother, I do not charge a fee. It is God Who heals—not me. But I would ask a favor of you."

"Master, what can I do for you?" he replied.

"I am seeking two fishermen named Andrew and *Shimone*. Can you help me find them?"

"Master, that is too easy! They live in Bethsaida by Capernaum and fish here as well as in Lake Gennesaret. What is more, *Shimone* is very wealthy. He has the most beautiful home in Bethsaida, and the largest boat on the Sea! If you take the Eastern road to

Capernaum and Bethsaida, you will find *Shimone* easily. Look for his home. Look for his boat. And tell him that *Eli* sends his greetings!"

Suddenly the little girl struggled to a sitting position.

"*Abba*, I dreamed an angel! There is an angel in our house!"

Her mother, who had stood for her husband, quickly knelt by her daughter.

"The angel told you not to move, my darling! Lie down and be still for a while now."

The old medicine women bowed to the ground and held the feet of the Master.

"Master, I see now that you are not only a great physician, but a holy man. Tell me what we should do for the child when you depart."

She remained at his feet, but he raised her up and asked, "Do you have the willow bark?"

"Yes," she replied.

"Then make a strong tea and give it to her now. She is ready for it, and soon she will be ready to eat a meal."

It was mid-afternoon, and he wished to arrive in Capernaum before the sun set. So he took his leave, but only after *Eli* had stuffed a copious supply of dried fish into his purse.

As he walked the road East, he saw the fishing boats coming closer to shore. The winds had shifted and were now beginning to blow onshore, bringing the boats back with flukey gusts. If Andrew and *Shimone* were among them, they would be back to shore soon after he arrived at Capernaum.

As he entered the city, he saw that the wind had kicked up some large whitecaps. Most of the boats were within shouting distance of land. There was, however, one very large boat that was so heavy it would be coming in last. That must be *Shimone's* boat.

He found his way to the sandy place where the fishing boats were dragged onto the beach and staked. Several had already been pulled onshore, but the large boat appeared to be making for another destination. As the boat drew parallel to shore, he saw that it was both sculled and rowed toward a wooden wharf that had been designed as a special dock for it. Several men rowed the boat into place alongside the rickety structure, while two men jumped into the shallow water with ropes and guided it bow and stern. When the correct position had been achieved, they tied the ends of the little ship to stakes that were driven into the sand below and supported by ropes.

The captain of the boat was a large, muscular Galilean—every bit the size of *Yeshua*. He was simultaneously laughing and barking out orders to everyone by name. Then another man stepped off the boat onto the dock. It was Andrew.

Yeshua continued to stand onshore and watch without hailing Andrew. He looked again at the man who must be Andrew's brother *Shimone*. He felt something in his heart.

"You don't know it yet, but you *Shimone* will be my disciple," thought *Yeshua*.

At that moment two other fishermen appeared from another boat that had been pulled up on the beach close to *Shimone's* dock.

"Hey *Yakob, Yochanan!*" shouted Andrew. "What did you get?"

One of the men stopped and said, "More than we expected, but less than we wanted."

"I say they're still over at Bethsaida," boomed *Shimone*. "Why do I let my partners talk me into stink waters?"

Suddenly Andrew recognized *Yeshua*. He lept from the dock yelling, "*Yeshua! Yeshua!* Is it really you? My Brother, this man is the *tzadik* I told you about! *Yochanan* says he is a great prophet, and now he is here in the Galilee!"

Everyone turned to look at the Master. He smiled and stepped onto the dock.

"You are *Shimone?* Andrew has told me much about you. What's the matter? No fish?"

Shimone shrugged.

"Out all morning, all afternoon in the hot sun, back in the evening—practically nothing in anyone's nets. I say there are no fish here."

"I say there are plenty of fish, and you have been looking in the wrong places," smiled *Yeshua*.

Shimone nearly took offense, but controlled himself and said, "If you are such a great fisherman, show me where they are."

"Well, if I give you a big catch right now, will you give me a place to lay my head tonight?" was the Master's quick response.

Andrew tugged on his brother's tunic.

"Brother, he is a prophet. Listen to him."

Shimone nodded and motioned for his partners to come aboard and serve as crew for the challenge. *Yakob* and *Yochanan* immediately took the lines while *Yeshua* stepped into the boat with *Shimone* and Andrew. With several careful pushes the boat began to move offshore as *Yakob* and *Yochanan* jumped aboard to serve as oarsmen. *Shimone* took the sculling oar and guided the boat against wind and wave into the deeper water. *Yeshua* stood on the prow of the boat and made a silent prayer.

"*Abba-Imma*, I ask for your blessing. Show me where to cast the net," he asked in his heart. Then he looked intently at the roiling waters. His attention was caught by the seabirds, who no longer sat bobbing on the waves but were flying and diving.

"There," he cried. "See where the seabirds dive. That is where your fish will be. Cast you nets now and pass through that place."

Shimone realized the stranger could be right. Usually he cast his nets in places where underwater rocks formed deep-water reefs rich with large fish. It made sense that there would be little fish where the seabirds were diving, but no one wanted little fish.

"Sir, we don't want nets full of bait-fish," he protested.

"You will have large fish," promised *Yeshua*.

They rowed and sculled their net through the area designated by the Master and watched as it grew heavy, laden with a catch.

"It'll be nothing but small stuff," grunted *Yakob* as he pulled his oar.

"Bring it up," commanded *Yeshua*.

Oars and sculler were abandoned while four strong fishermen tried to lift the net high enough to see what was in it. They couldn't do it. It was too heavy, and if they had been able to bring it aboard, it would probably have swamped the boat.

"Make for shore," commanded *Shimone*. "We will have to drag it onto the beach."

The boat circled the net and was easily driven by wave, wind, and oar to a place on the sandy beach near the dock. The four fishermen jumped into the shallow water and hauled the net ashore.

It was filled with the biggest fish anyone had seen all year.

"Where is all the small stuff?" asked *Yakob* as he gasped for breath.

"It's in the big fishes' stomachs," replied *Yeshua,* who still stood on the prow of the boat. "The big ones will come up from the deep places to feed on small stuff in late afternoon when the onshore breeze starts to slacken. It is then that the seabirds become the fisherman's friend."

"Are you a fisherman, too?" asked Andrew. "I thought you were a stone mason."

"I am a fisher of men," replied the Master. "And you—Andrew, *Shimone, Yakob, Yochanan*—are today's catch."

Shimone had stood quietly observing this conversation. When the Master spoke these words, his strength seemed to leave him and he sat down on the beach in amazement. *Yeshua* slid from the prow of the boat into the shallow water and approached him.

"*Shimone*, do I have a bed to lay my head on tonight?" he asked.

"Master," he replied looking up at the prophet, "you have bed, meals, and anything you require from me."

Andrew laughed and said, "I should think so! This catch is the largest we have seen since I returned from the camps of the Prophet *Yochanan*. We could commission a new boat with the money we'll make from this!"

******* ******* ******* *******

That evening *Yeshua* sat at the *Shabbat Seder* with *Shimone*, Andrew, their business partners *Yakob* and *Yochanan*, and their father *Zebedee*. They were served by *Shimone's* wife and her mother. After the meal the women joined them to hear what the *tzadik Yeshua* would say.

"Brothers, have you understood the teaching of the Prophet *Yochanan*?" asked the Master. "Andrew, I know that you have, because you are a disciple. But what about you, *Shimone*? What do you say?"

His host was silent for a moment, then replied, "I have been sending money to help support the mission of the Prophet through my brother. Andrew teaches me and helps us all to understand.

"We have all made the *mikveh* of *Yochanan*. There is a place on the Jordan one day's journey from here where the Prophet encamps and teaches the people. But I am hungry to hear what you have to say. What did you mean when you said you are a fisher of men?"

Yeshua looked him directly in the eyes and said, "I have come to proclaim the *Basor* of the *Malkuth* of Heaven. I have come to cast the fire of Divine Knowledge upon the world, and I shall cause it to blaze in your hearts with my breath. And when it blazes in your hearts, the Almighty will also send you forth to proclaim it. And you will cause it to blaze in the hearts of others."

Andrew asked, "I know the *Basor* proclaimed by *Yochanan*. But what is the *Malkuth* of Heaven?"

The Master replied, "It is the sovereignty of God that is spread out upon the Earth, but men do not see it. It is the sovereignty of Messiah that is to come, and yet is already here."

"What is the evidence of this sovereignty?" asked *Zebedee*. "The only sovereignty I see is that of the Romans."

"What does the Prophet Isaiah say will be the evidence of the sovereignty of *Bar-Enash*?" asked *Yeshua*.

"Healing of the sick, opening the eyes of the blind and the ears of the deaf—power over the bondage of *Shaitan*," interrupted Andrew.

"These things are already coming upon you," remarked *Yeshua*.

"Yes they are!" exclaimed *Yochanan Ben-Zebedee*. "When we returned to shore this afternoon, we were met by the fisherman *Eli*. He had come to tell us that a great physician had brought his daughter back from death after being bitten by a huge poisonous snake—a physician who refused to take money, but wanted only to know where he might find Andrew and *Shimone*. Master, I realize now that you are the same man!"

Shimone marveled. "So you, Master, are not only the greatest fisherman I have ever known, but *tzadik*, prophet, physician? Tell us more. What is the *Malkuth* of Heaven like?"

Yeshua said, "You asked why I said I am a fisher of men, *Shimone*. So now I shall answer both of your questions. The *Malkuth* of God is like a wise fisherman who cast his net into the sea. He drew it up from the sea full of small fish. Among them he found one large good fish. The wise fisherman threw all the small fish back into the sea and chose the large fish without hesitation. Do you have ears to hear, *Shimone*?"

"Andrew, tell me what he means," begged *Shimone*.

"Brother, he is telling us why he sought us out. He is telling us that the Almighty chooses those who are ready for service and lets the others continue to grow that they, too, might have the opportunity to develop great souls for service," replied Andrew.

"So, you think I'm a big fish, Master?" chuckled *Shimone*.

"No, *Shimone*. I know that your brother Andrew is a big fish because I found him so at the encampment of the Prophet *Yochanan*. But I had a feeling that you might be one, too. So I came in search of both of you," was the reply.

"Well, am I a big fish?" *Shimone* asked again.

"Take me to your synagogue for tomorrow's assembly and we shall see," replied the Master.

*******   *******   *******   *******

The next day was *Shabbat*, so none of the fishing fleet was out on the Sea. As *Yeshua* entered the men's section of the synagogue with the others, there was a great cry. One of the men at the very front where he could not see anyone entering jumped up, fell on the floor, and shouted in a deep and unnatural voice, "Why are you here, *Yeshua* of Nazareth? What have we to do with you? Leave us in peace. Damned! You are all damned!" Then he fell into contortions, rolling from side to side.

The man's family had known that something was going wrong with him. They could not understand his irrational outbursts of profanity. But now it all came clear. The man was possessed by an evil spirit.

Yeshua stepped forward before the entire assembly and stood over the man, who was now writhing uncontrollably on the floor. He directed power with his right hand and pointed to the man.

"Be silent and come out of him now!" commanded the Master.

Suddenly the man's head jerked backwards and his body seemed to be thrown completely aside. Then he lay quietly panting, as though released from a terrible nightmare. *Yeshua* raised him up by both hands and looked him in the eyes. He placed his right hand upon the man's head and commanded, "Let no evil spirit ever take up residence in this habitation again!" Then he helped the man to his seat, and returned to his own place.

The assembly was stunned. After a long period of whispering among the people, the *Chazzan*, a devout Pharisee named *Mordecai*, approached *Shimone* and asked, "Who is this man? Is he a famous exorcist?"

Shimone smiled, shrugged his shoulders, and said, "Master, he is a *tzadik* declared so by the Prophet *Yochanan*, a physician who brings people back from the dead, a prophet who proclaims the *Basor*, and the best damned fisherman I've ever met. Now I guess he's also an exorcist!"

"Ah!" exclaimed the *Chazzan Mordecai*, who had himself received the Baptism of *Yochanan*.

Turning to the assembly, he proclaimed, "This is the physician who brought *Eli's* daughter back from death. He has been declared a *tzadik* by the Prophet *Yochanan*."

The people began to talk animatedly with each other, for the story of *Eli's* daughter had spread quickly among the fishermen and their families.

He bowed to *Yeshua* and said, "Master, would you be willing to teach us something of the *Basor*? Please lead the worship today and tell us the Word from on high."

How different this was from his reception at Nazareth!

The *Chazzan* led *Yeshua* to the *Torah* table, held up his hands for silence, then took his own seat among the assembly.

The Master began to sing a Psalm of Ascents, and the assembly joined in. Then he opened the scroll of the Prophets to Jeremiah and intoned:

"Behold, the days come, saith YAHWEH, that I will make a renewed covenant with the house of Israel, and with the house of Judah—not according to the covenant that I made with their fathers in the day that I took them by the hand to bring them out of the land of Egypt, which covenant they broke, although I was an husband unto them, saith YAHWEH. But this shall be the covenant that I will make with the house of Israel. After those days, saith YAHWEH, I will put my *Torah* in their inward parts, and write it in their hearts; and will be their God, and they shall be my people. And they shall teach no more every man his neighbour, and every man his brother, saying, Know YAHWEH. For they shall all know me, from the least of them unto the greatest of them, saith YAHWEH. For I will forgive their iniquity, and I will remember their sin no more."

Then he taught them.

"Men and women of Israel, the times spoken of by the Prophets have been fulfilled. The *Basor* of Messiah is being proclaimed by *Yochanan*. The *Malkuth* of Heaven is coming upon us. Make your submission to God, and be faithful to the Renewed Covenant."

With that, the Master returned to his seat.

The assembly began to question among themselves.

"What is the *Basor* proclaimed by *Yeshua*? How can we hear more? How do we make a *nacham* to God? Is it the *mikveh* of *Yochanan*?"

The *Chazzan* stood and held up his hands to calm the people. Then he asked the Master, "Where can we learn more?"

Yeshua stood and turned to *Shimone*.

"My Brother *Shimone*, after you have brought in your catch tomorrow afternoon, would you be willing to let me speak to the people from your boat?"

Shimone's response was immediate.

"I would be honored, Master. After the fishermen have finished sorting their catch, and when the sun is low over the western hills, we will cast off a little way offshore of the market beach. Many people can hear you then."

Yeshua nodded and remained standing for the closing prayers. But when the service ended, he found himself surrounded by a crowd that pushed their way between him and his friends.

"Master, would you come to our home for supper tomorrow?" asked one.

"Physician, my brother is very ill. He cannot arise from his bed. I am afraid he will die. Can you help?" begged another.

Shimone gently pushed the crowd back and loudly proclaimed, "The Master must retire for *Shabbat* prayers. You will see him tomorrow afternoon. Please go home."

But *Yeshua* said, "Thank you, *Shimone,* but before prayer I will see this man's sick brother."

The *Chazzan* was amazed and remarked, "But *Shammai* and the *Ravs* have declared that healing is a form of work that is forbidden on *Shabbat*. Do you intend to break Scripture?"

Yeshua raised his hands for attention and all fell silent.

"My Brother, there is no prohibition written in *Torah* or Prophets or any of the other Scriptures that forbids healing. You must listen to the opinion of *Rav Hillel*, not that of *Shammai.* Does Scripture forbid a man to pull an ox from a ditch, or to feed his animals, on *Shabbat*? If Scripture does not forbid us to serve the needs of animals on *Shabbat,* then surely it will not forbid us from serving the needs of our parents and brothers and children!

"Listen to me, all of you. *Shabbat* was created to serve mankind. Mankind was not created to serve *Shabbat!*"

With that he nodded to the man who had begged healing for his brother, and *Yeshua* accompanied him to his brother's home. All of the fishermen and many of the assembly followed at a distance to see what would happen.

They saw *Yeshua* enter the house, they heard him intoning, and some time later he emerged with the man and his brother, who was smiling and walking on his own.

They heard *Yeshua* tell the man's brother to drink plenty of water, breath deeply, stay out of the sun, and eat unspiced lentils.

From that day the fame of the Prophet and Miracle-Worker *Yeshua* spread throughout the Galilee.

******* ******* ******* *******

The Master sat with *Shimone,* Andrew, and several of the other fishermen to lead them in *Shabbat* prayers and psalms. However, *Shimone's* wife was beginning to be jealous of the attention given to the stranger. She pressed her husband to know how long *Yeshua* would be welcome to stay with them. Her mother, who lived with them, supported her daughter's concerns.

"How long, *Shimone*? One more night, a week? Soon we'll have crowds at our gate wanting to see him. Our lives will be disrupted. Set a day for him to leave, and make it soon."

The Master was aware of her ill feelings, so left at daybreak with the fishermen. He told *Shimone* that he would retreat into the wilderness and rejoin them in late afternoon.

Yochanan did not enter into the cities, but sent his disciples to announce the time and place of where the Prophet would appear, and to bring people for *mikveh* in the Jordan. *Yeshua,* however, planned to visit and revisit all the cities and villages of the Galilee. He would dwell among the people, not in the desert.

However, his brief experiences in Capernaum made him realize that he would need to find private wilderness retreats where he could cleanse himself from the dark webs of bondage that permeated the populated areas. Human needs were so great that he would be drained by them unless he could find regular spiritual refreshment and *shalom.*

With this in mind, he left the main road and began to trek through the stony wilderness of the Galilee. He knew it well, and by combining his childhood knowledge with the desert skills taught to him by *Yochanan,* he was able to find places that could provide food, water, and rest. And he was able to find his way back without getting hopelessly lost, as many wanderers had.

Yeshua had decided that all of his public work would be done in the wedding garment made for him by Shoshana—the seamless robe of a Priest. He had carefully removed it from his pack and aired it in the hot noon sun. Sitting in the shade next to it, he became aware of the fragrance of lilies and ascended into silent soul communion with his beloved. After the hottest part of the day had passed, he arose, sacramentally donned the clean, white robe, and fixed his prayer shawl over his head for protection from the sun.

He made his way to the shoreline where *Shimone's* boat was tethered. Already the nets were emptied, washed, and carefully repacked for the next day's fishing.

"Master, why are you are wearing the garment of a *cohen*?" asked *Yakob ben-Zebedee*.

"Because the proclamation of God must be made from the Temple, but the Temple has fallen under the control of Roman collaborators and false Priests," he answered. "Therefore I bring the Temple to the people."

The Master stepped onto the prow of the boat, and the men pushed off. Already all the fishermen and their families had gathered on the beach, and scores more people of the city.

Shimone sculled the big boat to a position a little way offshore and allowed it to stop and rock gently in the calm waters of the evening.

Yeshua bowed his head to the Father and Mother of All, then began to proclaim the *Basor* of Messiah in a loud voice that all could hear.

"Blessed are the downtrodden: for theirs will be the *Malkuth* of the heavens.

"Blessed are those who are persecuted for righteousness' sake: for theirs will be the *Malkuth* of the heavens.

"Blessed are they that mourn: for they shall be comforted.

"Blessed are the people of the land: for they shall inherit the land.

"Blessed are those who hunger and thirst after righteousness: for they shall be filled.

"Blessed are the merciful: for they shall obtain mercy.

"Blessed are the peacemakers: for they shall be called the children of God.

"Blessed are the pure in heart: for they shall attain a vision of God.

One of the fishermen on the beach called out, "When will the *Malkuth* of God appear on Earth?"

Yeshua said, "*Amen, amen,* I tell you, the *Malkuth* is already appearing on Earth. But it does not come in the way men expect, and it does not manifest where or when men might expect. But the signs of the *Malkuth* are appearing even now. And know this: The *Malkuth* of God is within your hearts, and you will bring it forth upon Earth through faithfulness and prayer. No evil power will be able to resist it."

Andrew asked, "How should we pray?"

Yeshua raised his arms in the orant prayer position and spoke in a loud voice.

"When you pray, don't be like the self-righteous, who love to stand in the synagogues and on street corners to be seen by men. *Amen,* I tell you, the only fruit of their prayer is self-glorification.

"But when you pray, enter into a private place. When you have shut the door, pray to your Father-Mother God Who dwells in the secret places of the heart. And your Father-Mother, Who can be known only in private, will bring forth the fruits of your prayer in public for all to see.

"But when you pray, don't repeat flowery praises, as the gentiles do. They think their prayers will be answered according to the number of words they use! You don't need to use many words, because the Father-Mother knows your needs before you ask.

"Instead of praying only for your personal needs, pray for the spiritual needs of all. Pray for 'us,' not just 'me.'

"Begin with a prayer for the coming of God's *Malkuth* in the hearts of men and on Earth, like this.

Our Abba Who art in the Heavens,

May Thy Way be hallowed in every heart,

May Thy Malkuth be made manifest in Earth,

And Thy Will be done in Earth,

As it is in the Heavens.

"Then pray for the spiritual needs of all.

Grant us today our spiritual bread of the Banquet of Messiah that is to come.

"Life is more than food and clothing. Blessed is the body that depends upon the soul, but woe to the soul that depends upon the body!

"You must seek your place at the Marriage Banquet of Messiah every day, and you must nourish your soul with the Bread of the Heavens. Without this, food and drink merely fatten the corpse. So pray and seek the communion of the Heavens every day.

"And here is another thing for which you should always pray.

Release us from the consequences of our debts,

In the same measure that we release our debtors.

"Listen well! If you release others from the consequences of their sins against you, then your Heavenly *Abba* will also release you from the consequences of your sins. But if you refuse to forgive, then you will remain in bondage to them.

"I will tell you a story. A debtor owed millions to a just and fair landlord—far beyond anything he could ever pay. When the debt came due, the man appeared before a magistrate.

"'Sir,' he pleaded, 'I cannot repay such a large debt. Have mercy upon me!'"

"The landlord had pity upon the debtor and commanded the magistrate to set him free. Immediately after, however, the debtor accosted a poor man who owed him ten or fifteen—a very small amount. The poor man begged for mercy, but with loud curses the landlord's debtor threatened to sue and have him thrown into prison if he could not pay immediately. Finally he took the sandals from the poor man's feet in settlement of the debt.

"The landlord's steward saw this and reported it to the landlord, who became very angry and said, "Drag this man back to court. I'll throw him into debtor's prison for the rest of his life!"

"Now do you see? The man had a great debt he could never repay, just as we owe far more *hub* than we could ever repay. The debtor begged for mercy, and he was released from the consequences of that debt—prison. The debt was not repaid, but he was freed from the consequences of an unpaid debt.

"What then did he do? Did he release the poor man from the consequences of his small debt? No. Instead he forced the poor man to endure all consequences of his debt, to the point of taking the sandals from his feet. So what will the just and fair landlord do? He will require immediate full payment from the debtor, which he cannot repay, and thus must suffer the consequence of default—debtor's prison.

"It is the same with man and the true *Torah* of the Heavens. If you want to be released from the harsher consequences of your own sins, you must do the same for others. This is not automatic. You must pray for the *Abba* to purify you from the web of *Shaitan*. And remember, this purification is subject to your forgiveness of others.

"But *Shaitan* always seeks occasion to bring *mishpat* and trial upon us. He revels in human pain and degradation. But I will tell you a secret. His power is rooted in our own hearts, and very few have mastered their own hearts. So we must also pray for the protection of our *Abba* in this way:

Do not abandon us to our tests,

But guide and deliver us from all evil.

One of the fisherman sitting with his wife onshore asked, "Do you accept *talmidim*?"

The Master answered, "Everyone who hears my words and puts them into practice is my disciple."

Shimone asked in a loud voice, "What shall we do, Master?"

Yeshua said, "Purify your hearts, submit to God, and keep faith with the Renewed Covenant."

The *Chazzan Mordecai* stood up and asked, "How do we make a submission to God, Master, and what is the way to make an acceptable *nacham*?"

Yeshua pointed to the East and said, "Purify your hearts. Make a *mikveh* in the Jordan. It is by crossing the Jordan like our ancestors that you find a new entrance into the Promised Land of the *Malkuth*. That is the beginning of acceptable *nacham,* and it is the way you receive circumcision in your heart to become Son or Daughter of the Renewed Covenant."

Shimone again asked, "Master, we have already made the *mikveh* of *Yochanan*, but we still don't know what to do." His brother and two partners nodded their agreement.

"*Shimone,*" proclaimed the Master, "I invite you to learn my *halakah* and become my *talmid. Yakob* and *Yochanan,* sons of *Zebedee,* I have chosen you to become my *talmidim.* Will you follow my instruction and serve the *Basor* of the *Malkuth* of God?"

The men bowed deeply in agreement.

"Andrew, you are already a *talmid* of *Yochanan.* Will you serve the *Basor* by assisting me with the new *talmidim?*"

"Master," he replied, also bowing deeply, "I am at your service."

Yeshua sent silent thanksgiving to God. He had suddenly acquired the service of four *talmidim* and the use of the largest fishing boat on the Sea!

After a moment, the same fisherman who had asked a previous question called out, "Master, we do not know when the Prophet *Yochanan* will come again. Will you help us to perform the *mikveh* in the Jordan?"

"Not I," answered the Master, "but my new *talmidim.* They have made the *mikveh* of *Yochanan* and I will instruct them further. They will tell you time and place after they have received instruction."

"But Master," the fisherman persisted, "if we are all your *talmidim* as you declared, then should we not also receive your instruction?"

Yeshua was very pleased with the question, and many of the people nodded in agreement.

"Brother," he called to the *Chazzan*, "may we meet at the synagogue on weekdays?"

All eyes were on the *Chazzan.*

"If that is the desire of my people, I grant permission."

A murmur of approval went up from the crowd, then *Shimone* and crew began to move the little ship back to its dock.

******* ******* ******* *******

News of *Yeshua's* fame reached Nazareth that week. When *Yeshua's* mother and sister learned of his fame, they feared that he would be arrested by the Herodians.

"He must be crazy to act this way," worried *Shalome*. "*Imma*, we must get *Yosef* and *Jehuda* and go to Capernaum. Perhaps they can persuade *Yeshua* to be more careful."

Miriam and her sons living in Nazareth accompanied by *Shalome* began the journey to Capernaum early next morning. They arrived hot, tired, and dusty the following evening. When they sought a room for the night, they were told that the innkeeper and many people were at the synagogue being instructed by the Master. But when they found the synagogue, they found only an old woman with a cane.

"They have all followed the Master to the house of *Shimone*. His wife's mother was dying of a fever, but the Master laid his hands upon her and healed her. Now she is devoted to him."

She pointed to a large home, perhaps the largest in the city. Crowds were standing inside and outside the open gate while *Yeshua*, wearing the spotless white of a *cohen*, sat on the porch and taught. At his side two women were serving him—mother and daughter—and seated next to him were his four new disciples.

Miriam pushed her way to the gate and said aloud to all who were nearby, "This man is my son. Please tell him that his mother and family are standing outside and want to see him immediately."

One of the men pushed his way through the crowd and delivered the message in a loud voice, "Master, your mother and brothers are standing outside!"

Yeshua stood, smiled, and with his arms extended in a blessing over the crowd said, "Who are my mother and my brothers? All of you who hear the Word of God and do it—you are my family!"

The crowd parted as he walked straightway to his mother, bowed, and hugged her.

"*Yeshe*, you must beware the Herodians!" blurted out *Shalome* before he could even greet her or his brothers.

"Yes, Brother," cried *Yosef*. "They will have you in prison or worse!"

"*Yosef, Shalome,* you must not worry," he said, placing his hands on *Miriam's* shoulders and looking directly into her eyes. "For the sake of the *Basor,* God has charged the Great Angel *Michael* to protect us all from Herod and *Shaitan.*"

Looking around, *Miriam* asked, "Who are all these people?"

"They are," he hesitated, then continued, "my *talmidim.*"

"You take married women as your disciples?" asked his brother *Yehuda* incredulously.

Yeshua again lifted his hands in blessing over the crowd and replied, "Yes, *Yehuda*. Even the children. They are all my disciples and my family in the *Malkuth* of Heaven."

"Then your mother will also be your disciple," declared *Miriam*.

"And I, too, Brother!" cried *Shalome*.

"That is good," answered the Master, "but you will not stand like these disciples. You will come to the porch and sit with me." With that he took both the women's hands and led them to the porch, where he made place for them to sit next to him.

Then he continued to teach.

"You have seen the Presence of God drive the *'elilim* of fever from this dear woman who now stands and serves us. What are the signs of the coming of *Mashiah*? What are the signs of the New Heaven and the New Earth? Are they not these things: release from the bondage of *Shaitan*, healing from all manner of disease?

"The Day of YAHWEH is at hand. Will it be a season of joy and light? Yes. Will it be a season of suffering and darkness? Yes.

"How can it be both of these things, as the Prophets have said? Because it is a season of birth.

"What is the *Basor* if not the proclamation of a new birth—a Divine Heir. It is the season of the birth of the *Bar-Enash*, the Son of Mankind, whom the Almighty will seat at His right hand of sovereignty. It is the time of the birth-pangs of Messiah. First comes suffering, then comes joy. And after that, many long seasons of growth and training for full sovereignty.

"Who is Messiah? Is he one man, a Son of the warrior David who will fight and free us from Roman domination? No. The *Torah* scholars of Judea are wrong. Their *Meshiah-Ben-David* will not be a warrior-king of Israel.

"*Amen, amen,* I say unto you, all who live by the sword will die by the sword. A warrior may free us from Roman oppression, but he cannot liberate us from the bondage of *Shaitan*. No matter how noble the warrior, warfare creates sin and injustice. The *Malkuth* of Heaven does not come through violence and bloodshed.

"Then who is Messiah? I tell you, he is the *Meshiah Ben-Yosef,* the man of peace and the *tzadik* beloved by God. He is the true *tzadik,* the suffering servant of YAHWEH, the prophet, the teacher. And therefore he leads no armies, commands no troops. Indeed, his blood is spilled upon the Earth every day. For some his blood pollutes the Earth and lays a curse upon it. But for you, my Brothers and Sisters, his blood sanctifies the Earth.

"It is by the sacrifice of every righteous life that the Jubilees pass and the Earth becomes sanctified.

"So who is Messiah? It is you! It is you who are the Coming One, my Brothers and Sisters. It is you who will one day sit at the right hand of the Almighty. It is you who are being birthed into the *Malkuth* of God on Earth.

"Therefore you must become *shalem*. You must all become *tzadikim* and saints of the Almighty.

He stopped speaking to drink some water served by *Shimone's* wife, who now looked adoringly at him. The healing of her mother had touched her heart deeply, and now she, too, was making herself a disciple.

The same fisherman who had asked so many questions earlier now pushed his way to the front of the crowd, bowed, and said, "Master, how do we make ourselves *shalem?* Shall we abandon our duties and go to the caves to practice austerities like the Essenes?"

The Master said, "Sit here by me, Philip."

The fisherman was amazed. How did he know my name?

"But sitting is for your close family," he objected.

"And it is for my invited *talmidim*," said the Master. "Philip, no disciple of mine will ever abandon his family. But he will often be required to be absent from home and labor to make many journeys with me. Can you do that?"

Without blinking an eye Philip replied, "Yes, Master."

"Then Philip, I invite you to become my *talmid* and learn my *halakah*," smiled the Master. "You will find that austerities are not what produce healing of the fallen soul, but sincerity, faithfulness, singlemindedness, perseverance, and lack of all guile."

"And that reminds me, Philip. Why is your friend *Nathaniel* not here? He is a man without guile and a true Israelite."

How did the Master would know these names? How did he know the character of *Nathaniel*? He had been at Capernaum and Bethsaida for only a few days. Everyone was amazed at this demonstration of psychic knowledge.

The *Chazzan*, who was still debating in his heart whether *Yeshua* was a pretender, shouted to *Shimone*, "Brother, did you tell this Master these men's names? Andrew, did you?"

They both shrugged, and *Yochanan Ben-Zebedee* answered, "I do not even know who *Nathaniel* might be!"

Yeshua continued, "Philip, bring *Nathaniel* to me tomorrow. Tell him that tonight I see him sitting beneath a fig tree, and I would accept a small gift of those ripe figs."

"Yes, Master," replied Philip.

"And tell him that I invite him to become my *talmid*," said *Yeshua*, to the amazement of all.

*******   *******   *******   *******

Shimone's wife had prepared a special room for *Yeshua*. She had invited him to stay in their home as often and as long as he wished. For the time being she also hosted *Miriam* and *Shalome*. The brothers had returned to Nazareth.

The Master now had six close *talmidim* whom he could rely upon to work with him in ministry, since *Nathaniel* had accepted his call. All of them were fishermen, so they had seasonal periods of no fishing when they would normally repair boats and nets. That season had arrived when *Yeshua* first appeared in Capernaum, and now they had time on their hands.

The captain *Shimone* had found a way to travel as a disciple during the fishing season while still earning income to support his large family. He would make extended fishing trips with Andrew and his partners to the villages that the Master planned to visit. His boat would be the speaking platform for *Yeshua* at all these small ports.

In this way, the twin villages of Capernaum and Bethsaida become the Master's base of operations, and the Galilee his major region for ministry.

The *Chazzan* of the synagogue at Capernaum had become a supporter and ally of *Yeshua's* mission. The Master gave him a seating place of honor when he taught, even though he could not be a travelling disciple, and he also was invited to hear the private instruction given to the six close *talmidim*—*Shimone, Nathaniel,* Philip, and the two sons of *Zebedee*—as well as Andrew who, although a disciple of *Yochanan*, was becoming a *de facto* disciple of *Yeshua*.

Much of the private instruction happened over meals served by *Shimone's* wife and mother-in-law, whom the Master invited to sit with the men after the meal.

"Master, you have promised the *mikveh* to many of your hearers in the city. You have said we will tell them time and place. What are we to say?" asked *Yakob Ben-Zebedee*.

Yeshua looked at Andrew. "Where is the place that *Yochanan* baptizes?" he asked.

"It is a day's journey on the Eastern road from here, Master. It is much closer to many other villages and cities on the Sea."

"In that case," mused *Yeshua*, "we will need to visit those areas and prepare them for *mikveh* as well. I would like to bring a letter of greeting and reference to the other synagogues from you, Brother," he said, nodding to the *Chazzan*. "That will open the doors for us.

"As for our hearers in Capernaum and Bethsaida, I shall announce to them tomorrow the time and place for *mikveh*. It will be done upon the day of the Full Moon before the Festival of Booths. We will plan to arrive at each new village or city on Thursday so that I can confirm preparations to speak in the synagogue on *Shabbat*. On Sunday I will speak from the boat, and on Monday and Tuesday teach in the synagogue. We will travel on Wednesday. How does that sound?" he asked.

All nodded in agreement.

"At each new place, Philip, *Nathaniel*, and the sons of *Zebedee* will enter before me to announce in the market place that I have come. Tell them that we will prepare all who wish for *mikveh* at the given time and place. *Shimone,* you will find the *Chazzan* and show him the letter so that I can be received to speak at the synagogue on *Shabbat*. Andrew, you will seek out your friends who have already received the Baptism of *Yochanan* to find lodging for us. Then everyone will return to me at the boat so we can go together to our lodgings."

"Who shall we say has come?" asked Philip.

"Tell them that *Yeshua* of Nazareth has come to proclaim the *Basor* of the *Malkuth-ha-Shammayim,*" he replied.

"I shall tell them that the Prophet *Yeshua* of Nazareth has come," replied Philip.

Yeshua was about to object to the title of Prophet, but Andrew interrupted.

"What about those who have already received the Baptism of *Yochanan?*" he asked.

"Tell them that they shall have private instruction from me at their homes if they provide us lodging," he replied.

That evening when *Yeshua* taught at the synagogue, *Shimone* announced the time and place designated for *mikveh*. The *Chazzan Mordecai* volunteered to travel with those who chose to make the journey when the time came. He knew the way to the place of *mikveh*, and would lead them to meet the Master and his *talmidim* at the appointed place on the Jordan River.

That evening the Master spoke about the meaning of discipleship.

"There are two kinds of hearers of the Word," said *Yeshua*. "Those who hear the teachings for discipleship and put them into practice, and those who hear but do not practice. Those who hear the Word and do it—they are my disciples. But if you hear the word and do not practice it, you are not my disciple.

"Hear this. A sower when out to scatter seed. Some of the seeds fell upon stony paths, and the birds ate them. A few others fell into the bushes and brambles, where they were choked out before they could grow. But most of the seed fell into good soil that had been prepared to receive them and they brought forth fruit—some one or two baskets, others five or ten, according to their powers.

"Have you prepared your heart to receive the Word? Have you crushed your clods of pride and ignorance? Have you nourished the field of your heart with prayer? Have you watered it with tears of remorse for your sins and compassion for the suffering of others? Ponder the sower and the field. You will understand much more than I have said tonight. Let those who have ears to hear, understand.

"Know that I have two kinds of disciples," he continued, "those who receive *mikveh* and serve the *Basor* by hosting me in their homes and synagogues, and these seated here with me whom I have appointed to perform the *mikveh* and accompany me on journeys to proclaim the *Basor*. I love both kinds of *talmidim* equally, and both receive private instruction in their homes.

"But the *talmidim* who travel with me are those who learn to practice my *halakah*. They leave their families for the sake of the *Basor,* and one day they will teach others. They are the *talmidim* who eat with me and I invite to sit close to me when I teach.

"And I tell you, my new *talmidim*," he said, looking at *Shimone* and the others seated next to him, "the time for training is much shorter than you think. You will not have gone out to all the cities of Israel before the *Malkuth* will begin to appear with great power. Then you will no longer be taught by me, but by the *Ruach Ha-Qodesh*. You will teach and Baptize many."

There was excited whispering among the assembly.

"He said the *Malkuth Ha-Shamayyim* will come very soon! He said Messiah will come very soon!"

But *Shimone* felt a great ache in his heart, for he alone had understood the meaning of what the Master had prophesied when he said, "Then you will no longer be taught by me."

Chapter Twenty-Two: THE MARTYRDOM OF YOCHANAN

Early in the morning, *Yeshua* and his disciples pushed the big boat out into the calm Sea of Galilee. *Shimone* stood on the prow with the Master pointing the direction toward the cities on the Western shores while Andrew took the sculling oar, which functioned as a rudder. The four other disciples manned the rowing oars.

By mid-day, the onshore breeze had become boisterous and cool. The upper clouds that had formed over the Sea were scudding quickly toward the South, and whitecaps blossomed in all directions. The big boat was being tossed around like a toy. Andrew and Philip were seasick and couldn't man their stations. The Master and the captain had been forced to move from the prow and sit on the small foredeck.

"Master," yelled *Shimone* over the screaming wind, "we are in danger of a capsize!"

They were too far from shore to make it safely to the beach. No fisherman would venture out in such conditions, but there had been no clouds when they set out. The windstorm seemed to blow from out of nowhere into a full-blown maelstrom.

The Master bowed his head for Heaven's help, carefully supported himself with his left hand and stood up facing the wind. He extended his right hand, extended his index finger, and intoned slowly in a loud voice, "Be still!"

The disciples stopped rowing and watched to see what would happen, while the Master continued to stand with right hand extended.

Suddenly they saw the wind line from the East, which had been moving in gusts over the water, start to disappear. The whitecaps sunk back into the Sea along a great line to the South, while the wind shadow dissipated North and toward the boat. The boiling waves around the boat melted into small chop and then smooth regular seas.

"Who is this man, that wind and waves obey his voice?" cried *Shimone*.

The Master sat down and smiled.

"He is *Yeshua* of Nazareth," he answered.

Andrew, who was recovering rapidly from his seasickness, raised his hand and said, "He is *Mar Yeshua,* the greatest Master of Israel."

From that time one, all the *talmidim* addressed him as *Mar Yeshua.*

The Master carried out his plans in each port. He was welcomed into the synagogues, and crowds thronged to hear his message delivered from *Shimone's* boat. He then instructed many people in the synagogues of each city during the evenings.

But something new was developing. As they approached each new port city, large crowds waved to them from shore. Word had spread from travelers that a great Master of Israel was coming by sea to cast out demons and heal the sick, and that he prophesied the immediate advent of Messiah. Many strong young men met the boat and helped the fishermen-disciples to drag it ashore. Others appeared with invitations for supper and lodging, as well as requests for healing. The *Chazzan* of each synagogue already knew of *Mar Yeshua* and required no letter of introduction.

"The fields are ripe for harvest," remarked the Master. "We need more harvesters."

In every city he was making many disciples, but he invited only certain men to become baptizing *talmidim*. They had to be willing to travel with him and learn his *halakah*. And they must have received the *mikveh* of *Yochanan*.

These he recognized in his heart and from dreams that he had received before entering a city. Their names were Bartholomew, Matthew, Thomas, *Yakob* the son of Alphaeus, Thaddaeus, and *Shimone* the Canaanite. All of these had been hearers of the Prophet *Yochanan,* and some had been his *talmidim.*

As the time for *mikveh* in the Jordan approached, the Master had chosen eleven close *talmidim* to perform baptism in addition to Andrew.

When Andrew asked why he had chosen so few close disciples, the Master replied, "Many are called, but few are chosen."

By this time, news of the Master had reached Judea, where there were many strict *Chasidim* known as Pharisees. They controlled most of the synagogues and the Sanhedrin in Jerusalem, practiced innumerable austerities, advocated a detailed repertoire of *mitzvoth*, and considered the Jews of Galilee to be rude country folk in need of extensive religious instruction.

While the synagogues of Galilee had assembled collections of prophetic, Messianic, and apocalyptic Scripture, the Judaean synagogues of the Pharisees emphasized levitical *Torah* and extensive interpretations of Scripture to guide the daily ritual of observant Jews in Jerusalem and the cities. The Galilean *Ravs* were Messianic mystics with family and trade connections to the large Jewish community in Babylon, but the Judaean *Ravs* carried on disputation about how the ancient Mosaic rules of Israel should be adapted to modern life. They had very little connection with Babylon.

Their interpretation of the Messianic texts was political. They expected the advent of the *Mashiah Ben-David* to lead Israel in a holy war of liberation. In these times many were secretly supporting Essene and Zealot guerilla actions against the Romans. However, they also made many accommodations to Roman rule because it was good for business. But they usually stopped short of actual collaboration with the Romans.

On the other hand, collaboration was the bread and butter of the *Zadokees* or Saducees, a small party of wealthy Jews controlling the Temple and the High Priesthood. The succession of the High Priest had been changed from lineage of *Aaron* to that of of *Zadok* after the Second Temple had been built. The High Priesthood, and thus control of the Temple, was a political appointment in the pocket of the Saducees, They were outright collaborators with Rome, and despised by most of the people.

News of *Yeshua* had also come to some of them in Jerusalem, but they were indifferent. They did not accept anything as Scripture except the five books of Moses. Prophecy, *qimah*, and Messianic fads did not interest them. If they wanted a healer, they could hire a Greek physician. If they wanted an exorcist, there were several Jewish experts in Solomonic magic that could be paid to operate their skills.

As *Mar Yeshua* moved Southward through the cities of the Western Galilee, Pharisaic *Ravs* and *talmidim* made the trek North to see for themselves what this man was doing. Was he another *Yochanan,* or something else?

By performing healings and exorcisms in the synagogues of the Galilee on *Shabbat*, the Master was breaking the *chasidic* interpretation of *Shabbat* law. In villages like Nazareth of the Northern Galilee, however, healing and exorcism were understood to be acts of God, exempt from all prohibitions. As they travelled North, the Pharisaic *Ravs* and their *talmidim* strictly warned the *Chazzan* of each synagogue not to receive *Yeshua*. Soon *Shimone* found that the synagogues were reluctant to host *Mar Yeshua*, so he began to arrange assemblies at private homes.

Most of the people were more interested in witnessing or experiencing the healings of the Master than in hearing the *Basor*. They descended upon the appointed assemblies in droves clamoring for healing. *Yeshua* therefore combined his proclamation of the *Basor* with the often spontaneous healings that occurred wherever he appeared. He instructed his *talmidim* to admit hearers in an orderly fashion and, since there were such large crowds, for everyone to sit so that he could see the face of each person. Instead of sitting, he often stood while all others sat.

When he was asked, "Are you a *talmid* of the *Abba Yochanan?*" he would answer, "I am a *talmid* of the *Abba* in Heaven and a *Bar-Enash* of His *Malkuth*. If you wish to become a *Bar-Enash* of His *Malkuth,* you must become not just a hearer, but a doer of the Word."

Among the hearers were hecklers of the Pharisees. Under the guise of innocent questions, they tried to best him in disputation.

"Master, why do your *talmidim* not fast, like those of *Yochanan*?" asked one, implying that *Yeshua* and his disciples loved food and wine more than devotion to God.

"Have you ever been to a wedding?" the Master responded, disarming the heckler with another question.

"Then you know that the friends of the Bridegroom feast and drink wine before the marriage while he celebrates with them. Then follow the procession to the Bride's home, the taking of the Bride, and then their seclusion in the Bridal Chamber. Then the conception of the Heir, and finally his birth pangs.

"Do you not know that the Age of Messiah is already appearing on Earth? Do you not know of the Marriage of Heaven and Earth? Do you not partake of the Messianic Banquet?"

He shut the mouths of hecklers with questions that they could not answer. If they said, "No, the *Malkuth* is not coming on Earth," then the people would be angered because they believed in the coming of Messiah. If they said, "Yes," then the Master would demand to know why they continued to fast and perform austerities.

"Then why do the *talmidim* of *Yochanan* fast and perform the austerities of the ancient prophets?" the Master continued, turning the question back on them.

They had no answer, because *Yochanan* did not follow the rituals and austerities of the *Chasidim*.

"I will tell you why," continued *Yeshua*. "It is because they are learning his *halakah*.

"*Amen, amen,* I say unto you, there is no prophet greater than *Yochanan*. It is he of whom it was prophesied that *Eliahu* would return to restore the love and purity of the Covenant, turning the hearts of the fathers to the sons, and the sons to the fathers.

"But *amen* I say unto you again, he who is least in the *Malkuth Ha-Shamayyim* is greater than *Yochanan*.

"Therefore make your *nacham* and be faithful to the *Basor-ha-Malkuth-ha-Shammayim*. Become my *talmidim,* follow my *halakah,* and be faithful to the Word that our *Abba* in the Heavens is sending forth into the world."

One of the *Ravs* asked, "Why do you admit impure people people and women into your teachings? If you are a prophet, surely you can see that there are sinners and prostitutes among this assembly!"

Mar Yeshua held up both hands and spoke to everyone.

"You all know that when a rich man gives a banquet in honor of his daughter's marriage, he invites all the wealthiest and most respected people in his city. If he is a righteous man, when the banquet is over he invites all his servants to bring in the poor of the city and share with them the food that remains.

"Once there was a righteous rich man who invited his friends for such a banquet. One of them sent his regrets saying, 'I have business in another city and must be absent.' Another said, 'I must visit my wife's family that day and cannot be present.' One by one, they all excused themselves for various personal reasons. So what did he do? He was angry and sent his servants to invite the *amme-ha-eretz* and beggars on the street. They all came and enjoyed the finest food and drink.

"*Amen, amen,* I tell you, the *Malkuth Ha-Shamayyim* is like this. Many of the wealthy and self-righteous of Israel have refused God's invitation to the Marriage Banquet of Messiah. Therefore He now invites the poor, the lame, and the the people of the land to share His bounty. And when Messiah appears, there will be wailing and gnashing of teeth among all those self-righteous ones who think they are God's only beloved."

The Pharisaic *Rav* left in a huff with two of his *talmidim*. But one remained and asked, "Are you saying that God accepts impurity in his holy places?"

The Master replied, "No. God desires purity, but it is not the purity of the Judean Pharisees that *Adonai* desires. You wash and shine the outside of your cups but leave the inside filthy. The most self-righteous of you take ludicrous measures to avoid levitical impurities, but do not keep the most basic forms of purity in the heart. I have seen your custom of straining your soup so that you might not accidentally eat one of the gnats that swarm around the table. But in straining at gnats, you swallow a camel!"

"A camel is far more unclean than an insect. What is this camel that you say we swallow?"

"It is the camel of self-righteousness that you feast upon," replied the Master. "Haven't you read the Scripture that says God requires first of all a clean heart and a humble spirit? How can there be humility in one who considers most of Israel to beneath his spiritual status?"

"Hear this. Two men went down to the Temple wall to pray. One was a wealthy Pharisee who was observant and always gave alms to the poor, but the other was a collaborator who collected taxes for the Romans and overcharged the people for his own benefit.

"The tax collector stood by the wall in great inner torment and whispered, "Forgive me, Lord, for I am a sinner and a cheat."

"The Pharisee stood by the wall and said, "I thank you, Lord, that I am not like that tax collector. I pay my tithe, perform *mitzvoth,* offer sacrifice at the Temple, and give to the poor."

"*Amen,* I tell you, that tax collector left his prayers reconciled with God, but the Pharisee's judgmental pride and self-righteousness offended God. *Adonai* desires the offerings of contrition and a humbled heart, not ritual and self-magnification. There are far heavier *mitzvoth* than the thousand burdens laid on their people by the *Ravs.*"

The *talmid* was being trained in Scripture by working as a scribe for his *Rav.*

"Then tell us, Master," he asked, "what are the weightiest commandents in your *halakah?*"

The *Ravs* had prioritized Scripture according to the parts that were heaviest, holiest, and most binding, which were those spoken from the mouth of God, down to the lightest and least binding in practice. The young *talmid* knew that *Mar Yeshua* had done the same, and he wanted to see where the Master's top priorities were for obedience to the Covenant.

"The holiest commandments are these two," replied *Yeshua.* 'You shall love YAHWEH your God with all your heart, all your mind, and all your spirit.'

"The second commandment is equal to it and supports it, for it tells us how to love God. It is this: 'You shall love your neighbor as yourself.'"

The Master turned to everyone and proclaimed, "You cannot love God if you do not love your neighbor."

The *talmid* asked, "Who is my neighbor?"

Yeshua raised his eyebrows, pointed to everyone in the assembly, and asked, "Who is created in the image and likeness of God?"

"All mankind," answered the young scribe.

"Then listen," said the Master, "A man travelled on the road through Samaria and was attacked by thieves. They beat him nearly to death, stole all his possessions, and even took his clothing and sandals. A *cohen* passed by him returning from his course in the Temple and in a great hurry to get home. But he crossed to the other side of the road and passed on without looking back. A Levite came upon the beaten man and, fearing to make himself unclean, avoided touching him and passed on.

"But a certain Samaritan, as he journeyed, came upon the man. When he saw him, he had compassion on him, kneeled down, bound up his wounds with his own clothing, and poured oil and wine into his wounds for healing. Then he set the suffering man onto his own donkey, carried him to an inn, and watched over him. When he departed the next morning, he gave money to the host and said, 'Take care of him. Whatever you need to spend beyond what I have given you, I will repay when I return.'"

The people crowding around the Master were very moved by the story.

Yeshua asked the young scribe, "Which now of these three do you think was neighbour unto the man who was attacked by thieves?"

The young *talmid* was astonished at this teaching, and answered, "The unclean Samaritan who showed mercy."

Yeshua fixed him with his eyes and said, "Now, you go and do likewise!"

The young Pharisee slowly rose, bowed, and departed deep in thought.

The Master smiled at the crowd and said, "It is not by ritual *mitzvoth* but acts of compassion and justice that we demonstrate true love of God. And remember this—love is rooted in the heart, not in the words of the mouth. Even thieves and prostitutes can fulfill these commandments without self-righteous ritual or babbling of prayers."

When he taught before the crowds, the Master answered all of the attacks of the Pharisees and *Ravs* brilliantly. It was proof that he spoke with the authority of the *Bat Kol* and the mouth of a prophet. No one could stand against his Word.

With that he would sit and motion to one of the sons of *Zebedee,* whose voices were strong as thunder. *Yakob* or *Yochanan* would stand and proclaim the time and place designated for *mikveh* in the Jordan and send the crowds home.

*******   *******   *******   *******

In the evenings *Yeshua* would liked to sit with disciples and hosts for a late supper. Often such a meal was a small banquet in honor of the Master.

It was his custom to offer three Eucharistic blessings over the wine. The first was followed by singing of prayers and psalms before the meal, the second included a blessing over the leavened bread that was then passed to everyone to start the meal itself, and the third was offered at the end of the meal, when sweets would be served and he would teach his *halakah* to everyone present.

These formalities were normally done in Israel only for the *Shabbat* supper, or augmented by extensive readings for the *Pesach* meal. But *Yeshua* taught that every meal was a ritual participation in the Heavenly Messianic Banquet in expectation of the marriage of Heaven and Earth and the coming of the *Bar-Enash*.

With everyone seated after the meal, including the women who served, he taught them his *halakah*.

"Hear me! If you wish to be my disciple and a true *Bar-Enash* and Heir of the *Malkuth*, hear me! Unless your fidelity to the Renewed Covenant exceeds the self-righteousness of the scribes and Pharisees, you cannot enter into the *Malkuth*.

"You have heard the great *Mitzvah*, 'You shall not commit murder.' And you know that whoever commits murder is in danger of divine *Mishpat*, to be totally cut off from the life of God's *'Olam*.

"But I tell you now that whoever among you disciples is angry with his brother without a cause, or despises him as a fool, or curses him, shall be in danger of divine *Mishpat*. For these are ways that men kill the spirits of others and commit murder in their hearts.

"If you approach the Altar of God, which is within your heart, and then remember that you have wronged your brother, first be reconciled to your brother. Then you can approach God with a clean heart.

"Always reconcile with any adversary quickly while time and opportunity remain, lest when you least expect it he delivers you to the judge, and the judge to the officer, and you be cast into prison. Do not allow the cursing heart of another to exact *Mishpat* upon you and deliver your soul into the bondage of *Shaitan*. Amen, amen, I tell you this. Nothing can deliver you from this debt until the last penny has been paid!

"You have heard the great *Mitzvah*, 'You shall not commit adultery.' But I tell you this. Whoever looks upon the wife or husband of another with the intention to fulfill lust has already committed adultery in the heart. Look deeply within, examine your motives, and choose to follow the urging of the good *yetzer*—not the entrapment of the evil *yetzer*.

"If your right eye causes you to sin, pluck it out and cast it from you! If your right hand causes you to sin, cut it off and cast it far from you! It is better for you to enter into the Life of the *'Olam* without an eye or a hand than to suffer the purifications of *Gehenna*. It is better to prune the rotten branches than to let disease infect the whole tree.

"The ancient customs decree that whoever wants to abandon his wife, let him stand before the community and say, 'I divorce you,' or write a public document of divorce.

"But I tell you this. Whoever divorces his wife for any reason other than her own proven adultery, commits grave adultery himself and makes her into an adulteress. For what can she do? He takes away the children and the dowry, no man will have her, and her only recourse is servitude and harlotry.

"The ancient customs decree that you must swear all your oaths by God's Name, and do not break them. But I say unto you, Swear not at all—neither by the Heavens, for within them is God's Throne, nor by Earth, for it is God's footstool, nor by Jerusalem, for it is the city of God. Do not swear by your own head, because even by deep meditation you cannot make one hair white or black.

"Rather, let whatever you say stand on its own integrity. Let your 'yes' mean yes, and your 'no' mean no. Swearing of oaths never brings anything but evil.

"The ancient customs decree that you must exact revenge, an eye for an eye, and a tooth for a tooth. But I say unto you, Do not fight offense with offense, and do not trade insult for insult. If someone slaps you on the right cheek, have the strength of character to seek reconciliation and turn unto him the left.

"If anyone sues you in court to take away your coat, let him have your cloak as well. Does your *Abba* in Heaven withhold his own even from thieves?

"And whoever compels you to walk a mile with him, walk two miles with him. Does your *Abba* in Heaven withhold his Presence from anyone who calls?

"Give cheerfully to whoever asks, and do not turn away from whoever would borrow from you. In all things, show forth the Way of God.

"The ancient customs decree that you must love your neighbour and hate your enemy. But I say unto you, Love your enemies. Bless those who curse you. Do good to those who hate you. Pray for those who abuse you. This is how you make yourselves worthy children of your *Abba* in Heaven.

"In all things, imitate God. For your *Abba* causes the sun to shine equally upon the good and the evil, and the rain to fall equally upon the just and the unjust.

"Listen to me. If you love only those who love you, what merit do you accumulate? Even the tax collectors and Roman collaborators love their own.

"And if you warmly greet only your own family, what merit do you accumulate? Even the tax collectors and collaborators greet their own.

"Understand that you must become *shalem*, even as your *Abba* in Heaven is *shalem*—compete, whole, perfect, and lacking nothing."

******* ******* ******* *******

The Master now had too many *talmidim* to travel by boat, so he would walk from city to village while *Shimone* and his friends moved the boat to the next port.

As he was travelling on the road with the new disciples, the Master was approach by a leper.

"Master, if you will, you can cure my leprosy."

Yeshua looked upon him with compassion, laid his right hand upon the man's head, and said, "I will. Be cleansed."

He did not use a physician's remedy or any kind of medicine. Instead, the Master spoke the prophet's Word, the *davar* that cannot be broken because the prophet speaks the *davrim* of God. *Yeshua* proclaimed him cleansed because it had already been decreed in the Heavens.

"What should I do?" asked the leper.

"What does *Torah* say? Look not to the left or the right, but go immediately to the *cohen*, wash and show him the proof of cleansing, then make the offerings required. But do not tell anyone about this or I'll be mobbed by lepers wanting to be healed," the Master sternly warned.

When the man did the cleansing *mikveh* required by Scripture, he and the Priest were amazed to see the many white, leprous spots wash away leaving healthy skin. He had been truly healed through the Word of the Prophet *Yeshua*.

The man was overjoyed. He excitedly told many others in his village what had happened, and the priest verified his story. The next few days multitudes of people with all kinds of diseases and infirmities took to the road to find the Master—not only from that village, but from others nearby where the story had spread in the market places.

Having been warned in a dream, *Yeshua* withdrew with his *talmidim* into the desert near the Jordan River.

"Only those whom God wills can seek and find me here," he told them.

For many days the disciples received small groups of men and women who had made pilgrimage into the desert to find the Master. They were admitted to his place of retreat and given healing and instruction. Several would later become disciples.

One evening as he ate with his disciples, the Master suddenly stopped talking and grasped his throat.

"What is it, Master?"

Silence, then tears welled up in his eyes. He suddenly knew that the Prophet *Yochanan* had been beheaded by Herod's bodyguards. He said nothing to the *talmidim*. Overcome with emotion, he excused himself and withdrew.

Before dawn the next morning, the Master and his entourage made for a small port on the Southern Sea to meet *Shimone* and the fishermen. The Full Moon before the Festival of Booths was approaching, and it was time for the *mikveh* in the Jordan River that *Yeshua* had announced throughout the Northern and Eastern Galilee. They would need to arrive early and restore the encampment of *Yochanan* for the event.

But when they met the boat, Andrew was in mourning. The Prophet *Yochanan* had been gruesomely murdered by Herod, he said, and his disciples were without leadership.

"He walked into the den of the Beast and openly rebuked Herod for his sins against *Torah* and for unlawfully marrying his brother's wife Herodias," Andrew sighed.

"Jezebel!" exclaimed the Master under his breath.

"She induced the old fox to have him beheaded as a public example," he continued. "She was told by her astrologers that by separating head from body, the Prophet's spiritual power would be dissipated."

"Rahu-Ketu. How wrong they were!" exclaimed *Yeshua*. "The power of the *Basor* cannot be stopped by the murder of a great *nabi*."

The Master stood and said, "Come, let us go to the encampment to prepare for *mikveh*. We shall do it in honor of Israel's greatest prophet."

"Master," warned Philip, "perhaps we ought to wait for a less dangerous time. Herod could send his troops to massacre everyone there."

Yeshua closed his eyes and entered into communion with the Heavens. A few minutes later he opened his eyes and spoke.

"Herod will not send his troops. But it will be a test of faithfulness for many who dare to come, and we will make many new *talmidim* who have hearts of lions. We shall procede as planned."

The disciples all nodded their agreement.

******* ******* ******* *******

Even *Mar Yeshua* was amazed at the multitudes whose pack animals and caravans kept arriving at the encampment—even more people than he had seen coming from Judea when he was baptized as a *tzadik* by *Yochanan*. Innumerable evening campfires illuminated the skies for miles away.

"I shall speak fom this ledge." *Yeshua* pointed to an outcropping high over the Eastern side of the river crossing.

"That is where *Yochanan* used to speak," remarked Andrew.

"Good," exclaimed the Master. "Where did you baptize?"

Andrew pointed to a series of shallow pools slightly downstream from the river crossing.

"I want them to be brought to the Eastern side in small groups by each baptizer. *Shimone*, you will lead your people to this pool," he said pointing, "Andrew to that pool…"

He continued to assign order and locations for each of his eleven baptizing disciples and Andrew, all of whom had previously received the *mikveh* of *Yochanan*.

"However, there will be certain men whom I shall baptize. They are learning my *halakah* and are fit to become baptizing disciples themselves. Many of them will journey with us after the New Year."

"We can't get everyone into boats," grumbled *Yakob Ben-Zebedee* with a trace of jealousy revealed in his voice.

"My Brother," smiled *Yeshua,* "the day will come when you will be glad for so many good men. They will journey with us on foot and open their homes to us for food and shelter. But they will not enter into your boats—only I will enter."

On the day of the Full Moon, the *talmidim* organized seating for hundreds of people on the Western beach of the Jordan. The Master stood on the high ledge protruding from the other side of the river and proclaimed,

"The Evil One has killed the body of *Yochanan,* but he cannot kill the great spirit that animated his body. He cannot silence the Voice of God, and he cannot stop the power of the *Basor-ha-Malkuth-ha-Shammayim.*

"Today you have come to purify your souls, circumcise your hearts, and enter into a Renewed Covenant in the eternal *Malkuth* of God.

"You each desire to become a *Bar-Enash* and fellow heir of the *Malkuth*. You each long for an end to the power of the Beast on Earth and in men's hearts. You each hunger and thirst for the life of God's *'Olam*, and for the Will and Way of God to appear on Earth in power.

"Today you pledge to become doers of the Word, not just hearers. Today you pledge to practice discipleship. Today you pledge to become stewards of the Heavens and co-workers with the angels. Today you pledge to help make manifest the New Heavens and the New Earth.

"Do I require you take an oath? No! Let your act of *mikveh* speak for your heart.

"Once you have washed in the Jordan and crossed into Israel, as did your ancestors, you are a new Israel. You have emerged from the waters of a new birth. The new *Bar-Enash* is born and will grow in your *nephesh*. The old Adam must wither away as you learn to follow the urgings of the *Yetzer Ha-Tov* in your heart.

"There are some here today that I shall invite to be my personal *talmidim*. The *Ruach Ha-Qodesh* will show you to me, and I shall call you forth. You all know what I require of my personal disciples. You are free to accept or reject.

"But I tell you this—once you have accepted, never turn back. For one who sets his hand to the plow and looks back is not fit for the *Malkuth*.

"And to all I say, resist your old ways. Do not take up with them again, like a dog returning to its own vomit.

"The path that leads to the Life of the *'Olam* is strenuous, and the Gate that opens to the *Pardes* of the *Malkuth* is narrow.

"Those who obey my call, I shall baptize with my own hands and instruct tonight when the Full Moon rises in the East. All others will be baptized by my disciples."

With that the ritual *mikveh* began.

Each of the disciples accompanied a small group over the crossing and led them to a pool. Lifting the left hand to Heaven and placing the right hand upon the head of each candidate, they gently pushed them under the water and raised them up again. Then they led each one to the river crossing. When the entire group had been baptized, the same disciple led them back across the Jordan to Israel and gathered a new group.

The Master sat at the Eastern side of the crossing on a portable throne that had been made for him by *Shimone* the Canaanite, who was a skilled carpenter. It could be disassembled into three parts, tied, and carried in a linen bag, but when fit together it formed a sturdy seat for the Master. It was used for hillside gatherings when everyone was allowed to sit at the Master's feet.

From time to time *Mar Yeshua* would point to a man making the river crossing East with his goup following a disciple. The man would be led to the Master, who stood and said, "I invite you to follow my *halakah*."

Every man he called dropped to his knees and accepted.

Then the Master would lead him to a special pool upstream of the crossing and perform the *mikveh*. In each case he made silent prayer, called out the man's name, and gave him a special secret name saying, "You are reborn into the *Malkuth,* and I name you *Michael,* beloved of God," or *Auriel,* Light of God, or *Ariel,* Lion of God, or other such names of angels.

As the day grew hot, the Master called for a rest. He was approach by *Shimone* and several of the other *talmidim.*

"Master, why have these new ones received secret names, but we have not?" they asked.

"My Brothers," he replied, "you have already been brought to birth in the *mikveh* of *Yochanan* under your own names and proven yourselves in service to Heaven. Your secret names will be revealed to you in dreams."

All the disciples were satisfied except *Shimone,* who did not return to sit with the others.

"Master," he said privately, "I did not understand what I was doing in the *mikveh* of *Yochanan*. He did not teach us of anything but submission to Heaven and *nacham* to God. Moreoever, he himself baptized only those of his disciples whom he declared to be *tzadikim*. The rest of us were baptized by his *talmidim*. In fact, I was baptized by my brother Andrew. But if I cannot be re-baptized by you, I wish to receive my secret name from your lips."

The Master thought for a moment, then called Andrew and his ten other baptizing disciples, who took their place at his feet.

"Brothers, *Shimone* wishes to receive his secret name from my lips, even though I advised him to receive it directly from Heaven. What do you think?"

Several opinions were expressed, but they all supported the Master's declaration that they should each receive their names from Heaven.

"So, what do you say, *Shimone*?" asked *Mar Yeshua*.

"I am cannot trust my impulses," he said. "But when I see your face, I see the face of God. There is nothing and no one in Heaven or Earth that I truly trust except you, Master."

With that *Shimone* took hold of the Master's feet and cried, "I beg you to give me my secret name."

Feeling deep emotion and overshadowed by the *Ruach-Ha-Qodesh,* The Master *Yeshua* placed both hands upon *Shimone's* bowed head, looked toward Heaven with closed eyes, and prophecied,

"Your name will be *Cephas* the Rock because you have the fidelity of the finest building stone. One day, my Brother, you will be the rock upon which all the others depend. And then you will no longer be unable to trust your impulses, but will receive the clear guidance of Divine Spirit. You will teach the *Basor* to all people—not just to Israel. You will lay hands upon the sick and cast out demons."

Opening his eyes and looking around at all the *talmidim,* he said, "My Brothers, the works that I do, you will all do one day—and even greater."

Then he stood, raised *Shimone* to a standing position, and said, "And you will henceforth be known unto all by the name *Cephas.*"

Later he would be known as *Petros*, the Greek word for Aramaic *Cephas* or Rock, when he revealed the Mysteries of God's Rule to Greek-speaking Jews and gentile hearers of the Word.

All the disciples were astonished, and before *Cephas* could say anything, the Master sat him down again and said, "Here is another thing for you to remember.

"Don't get too big-headed, Brother. I named you *Cephas* for another reason, too. It is because you are as thick-skulled and stubborn as a stone!"

Everyone laughed, even *Cephas.* For they knew that the Master had just served up an antidote for pride. Yet from then on everyone knew that the captain of the ship, who was older than all the other *talmidim,* was also one to whom leadership had been entrusted.

Andrew said, "Master, I wish to become your disciple and to receive my secret name from you, as *Shaitan* has now cut me off from discipleship to the Prophet *Yochanan.*"

"You are a great *talmid,* and I accept you," replied the Master.

Then all of the other ten disciples clamored to receive their secret names from his lips, so he relented and took them one by one and gave them all names of angels and archangels, who are the messengers of *El Elyon*. But he delivered no more prophesies to them.

That evening the Moon rose huge and ruddy in the East. From it seemed to emanate a mystic *ruach-ha-keseh* that one could almost taste, like the juice of a sweet, red pomegranate. No stars could be found in the sky because of the great brightness of the Moon. But the twinkling lights of many campfires dotting the Western bank of the Jordan made it seem as though the very stars of Heaven had come to Earth and taken up residence in the wilderness of Israel.

The Master gathered all of the new *talmidim* with his others at a separate encampment on the Eastern bank of the Jordan. There was now a total of over fifty men, most of them young and strong. Some of them had served as *talmidim* of *Yochanan*. Others had trained as Zealot guerilla fighters. Yet others were married Pharisees or Essenes who were were accustomed to austerities and religious commitment. They were householders who could provide not only food and shelter for return visits to their cities and villages, but secrecy and safe-houses when needed.

As they sat around the campfire at the feet of the Master, he pointed to the host of campfires that dotted the opposite shore of the Jordan.

"You see? The angels of God have descended into to this *'olam* to do battle with the powers and principalities that rule the Earth."

At that moment a blazing meteor shot across the sky from East to West.

"What was that?" asked Andrew.

"I saw *Shaitan* being cast down from his throne upon the Fifth Heaven by the Archangel *Michael*. Do you know what this means? Now he will rage like a roaring lion upon the Earth. He will send his minions to possess many souls, and he will spread violence and injustice upon the Earth. And this is but the beginning of new suffering for the saints."

One of the new *talmidim* asked, "How can this be the appearance of God's *Malkuth* upon the Earth?"

"Because it foreshadows the Birth Pangs of Messiah. There will be wars and famine and earthquakes. In the City of David, the Temple will be destroyed. Not one stone will be left in its place.

"When you see the abomination that makes desolation spoken of by the Prophet Daniel, which is the pollution of the Temple at Jerusalem by the Romans, then you must take your families and go out into the wilderness.

"It will be as in the days of Noah," he prophesied. "People will eat and drink and carry on their business, and then suddenly their world will come to an end. As in the time of Moses, suddenly one night the people of God will pack their belongings and make an exodus into the desert.

"Remember this and be forewarned! It will come to pass in your days!" he proclaimed.

"The *Malkuth Ha-Shamayyim* must appear first within your hearts before it can manifest on Earth. The *Bar-Enash* will come to birth in your hearts. The old world and the Old Adam must wither away in violence, injustice, and human suffering. One day the New Adam will sit upon a throne in your hearts at God's right hand of power.

"Are you surprised that you must face trial and suffering? Do you not know that all the prophets from Abel to Zechariah faced persecution, rejection, and martyrdom? Have you not understood the mertyrdom of *Yochanan?*

"How, then, shall the power of the *Malkuth* prevail on Earth unless it is stronger than the power of the Beast?

"*Amen,* I say unto you, your fidelity must be stronger than the evil forces of *Shaitan.* I have called you by the names of angels because you will fight and prevail against his forces in the power of Heaven. You will wield the sword of truth, and wear the breastplate of fidelity to the Way of God. You will be shod with the armor of my *halakah.*

"Tonight I give you authority over evil forces, to cast out demons with the power of God's *Malkuth* on Earth.

"I send you forth into all the villages of the Galilee. You must travel in pairs to protect yourselves.

"When you enter a city, do not go from door to door. Make one proclamation in the market place, as you have heard my other *talmidim* do. Then accept the hospitality of whoever offers it and stay at that house. People will bring to you the demoniacs and the sick, and you will cast out demons and proclaim the *Basor.*

"If no one offers you hospitality, then brush the dust of that city from your clothing to cleanse yourself of their lack of fidelity and depart. Do not waste the season in a field that is unripe for harvest."

With that he stood and motioned for all the *talmidim* to stand with him. Then he passed among them laying his hands upon the crown of their heads, all the while intoning the battle Psalm of David,

"*Baruch Ee-ahh-ohh-way-ee, tzudy,* teach my hands to make battle and my fingers to fight, in the Name of *Ee-ahh-ohh-way-ee.*"

Then he gave them all special teachings about techniques of exorcism and healing.

Several hours before morning, when the Full Moon hung low over the Western hills, the Master awakened from a dreamless sleep. He could hear the voice of the Prophet *Yochanan* echoing in his mind.

"The old fox is watching you. Leave the Southern Galilee and go to the regions of Samaria and Judaea."

In fact, when Herod and Herodias were told about the *mikveh* of *Yeshua,* they consulted their astrologers, who told them, "The body and head of *Yochanan* have been reunited in the Prophet *Yeshua.*"

Herod had dispatched spies into the Galilee to keep him informed about the activities, associates, and whereabouts of *Mar Yeshua.*

"The Judaean *Ravs* have tried to discredit you in the synagogues of Galilee," echoed the voice of *Yochanan,* " so you must boldly confront them in their cities of Judaea, and Jerusalem itself. They will not be able to withstand the Word of the *Bat Kol.*"

It was time to return to Capernaum to redeem his reputation, and to travel from there through Samaria to Judaea. That would also give him time to see his Mother and family in Nazareth.

The next morning, when all the caravans prepared to return to their villages, the Master asked *Shimone Cephas,* "Where was the *Chazzan Mordechai?* I saw only a few people from Capernaum and Bethsaida, and I never saw him."

Cephas replied that the few who had made their way from his home region had said that the *Chazzan* and most of his people had been persuaded by visiting *Ravs* of the Judaean Pharisees not to make the journey. Some, like the *Chazzan,* were afraid that Herod would send troops. Others had been convinced that *Yeshua* was a false prophet.

"All this was a plot by the Judean Pharisees to discredit you."

When he heard confirmation of what he had already sensed in his spirit, *Mar Yeshua* called his *talmidim* together once more and delivered a prophetic denunciation.

"Woe unto you you, Capernaum! For if the mighty works of the *Malkuth* that were done in you had been done in Sodom, it would have remained until this day!

"Woe unto you, Bethsaida! For if the mighty works of God that were done in you had been done in Tyre and Sidon, they would have repented long ago in sackcloth and ashes!

"But solemnly I say unto you, It shall be more tolerable for the land of Sodom in the final *Mishpat*, than for you in these days of woe that you have brought upon yourselves. For your fields will wither, and your waters become bereft of fish, and the caravans will no longer come to you."

Shimone Cephas and his partners were alarmed and dismayed.

"How can we make our living if the fish are gone?" asked Philip.

"It will not be long before you will have to drop your nets in other waters, my Brothers, for the Heavens will no longer bless your cities with abundance. But you are forewarned, so make your plans now. The *Bat Kol* has said this, and even my prayers cannot alter it."

After these days, *Shimone Cephas* and all the fishermen of his area were forced to go to the Eastern regions of the Sea to find fish. The cities of Bethsaida and Capernaum suffered many seasons of draught that ruined their agricultural economy and no longer attracted trading caravans.

Chapter Twenty-Three: *MIRIAM* OF *MAGDALA*

Mar Yeshua and his fishermen disciples began the long Sea journey Northward in *Shimone's* boat before the sun rose. This gave them calm water for rowing, then land breezes, when they could erect the sail. By noon the water was boisterous and the winds too strong, so they made for shelter near Migdal and waited for the winds to moderate into a consistent late-afternoon offshore breeze. Now they were able to make way to the area of Lake Gennesaret, where they could take shelter and sleep for most of the night. The next morning at sunrise they made for Capernaum and arrived about noon.

With the news of *Yeshua's* return, the *Chazzan Mordechai* came to the house of *Shimone Cephas* leading a small group of people. He wished to speak with the Master.

Bowing his head to the floor, he said, "*Mar Yeshua,* we did not make the long journey to the headwaters of the Jordan. When we heard about the killing of *Yochanan,* we feared that Herod's soldiers would massacre us. We did not know whether you would make the *mikveh* at such a dangerous time. So I advised my people to remain here until you returned. Even so, some of the young men did make the journey, and they have told us that you made the *mikveh* with multitudes of people.

"We are very ashamed that our fidelity was so weak. We ask what to do, and we beg for your mercy."

The Master was very moved.

"There will be other *Mikvehs,*" he answered.

Old *Zebedee*, father of the two disciples, knelt at *Yeshua's* feet and said, "Master, many of us are too old and infirm for such a journey to the Jordan. Since the waters of the Jordan flow from the Sea of Galilee, can we be baptized in the Sea?"

An old woman, mother of Philip, cried, "Master, we know that God is present when you are here. If you will, you can baptize us into Life even here in Capernaum."

The Master closed his eyes and went into silence for a long time. Then he smiled, opened his eyes, and spoke to everyone.

"You have been taught that *mikveh* can be made in any living waters that flow, or even with rainwater from the sky. Does the rain not fall upon the Sea? Then the Sea has living waters.

"Therefore I say this. You may receive this *mikveh* in any living waters."

Cephas raised his finger in a request to speak.

"The Master does not baptize—only his appointed *talmidim*. With the Master's permission, we will perform the *mikveh* at the place where living water from the river to the East flows into the Sea of Galilee.

"Master, will you approve, and will you be present?"

Yeshua nodded.

"Then we shall announce the time in the market place for all to hear," promised *Cephas*.

During the following days many sick and possessed were brought to the house of *Cephas*. *Yeshua* performed numerous powerful healings and exorcisms, and he proclaimed the *Basor* of the *Malkuth* daily. All who saw and heard him wished to be baptized.

On the following *Shabbat* after teaching in the synagogue, the Master and his disciples led a procession to the river. *Yeshua* stood and asked everyone else to sit.

"But Master, it is customary for the *Rav* to sit and his hearers to stand," objected *Yakob Ben-Zebedee*.

"Listen to me," cried *Yeshua* in a loud voice. "The Servant of God is a servant of mankind. You cannot be a Servant of God if you magnify yourself over others. I am standing in your service like a table-servant. I shall offer you the bread of God's Word. I am standing in your service like a midwife. I shall help you to bring the *Bar-Enash* to birth within your heart.

"Always remember that in the *Malkuth* of Heaven, we must all become like angels who serve and minister. That is what it means to become *tzadikim* and saints of *El Elyon*.

"When I depart from Capernaum, I will appoint Nathaniel to continue your instruction and baptize others. Later I will call Nathaniel and replace him with Philip. In this way the *Basor* will always dwell in Capernaum."

After many other teachings, he told the disciples to lead people one at a time into the river for *mikveh*.

******* ******* ******* *******

That week they departed by boat for Magdala, where *Yeshua* and his disciples would journey by road to Cana, Nazareth, and Nain. *Yeshua* was eager to learn what progress had been made by the many new disciples he had sent to these cities and the villages around them.

In Magdala, *Cephas* said, "I have heard of a wealthy widow whose reputation for piety is unmatched. Her husband died, leaving her a thriving business exporting dried fish. If the other *talmidim* have been here, she will know of you and shelter us for the night."

With that, the captain took off on foot with Andrew seeking the women.

The Master became aware of the fragrance of lilies. He felt Shoshana's presence and sat in blissful contemplation for the afternoon.

Later in the day *Yeshua* saw Andrew and *Cephas* running toward him. They were trying to keep up with a woman. She waved and called out, "*Yeshua! Yeshua!* Is it really you?"

Miriam! The Master's heart pounded in joy as he ran toward her. They collapsed into each other's arms and wept.

It was *Miriam* of Magdala, Shoshana's aunt who had raised her, and who had made the perilous journey to attend Shoshana's wedding in Babylon.

The disciples stood dumbfounded. How did the Master know this woman? Who was she?

But all the Master said was, "Follow me." He had eyes and ears for no one but *Miriam*. He never turned around to see if his disciples were coming, but walked slowly lost in conversation with the widow.

Her home was magnificent. It stood upon the top of a hill overlooking the city. Ornate stonework formed a walled courtyard with an arched gate. Heavy cedar double doors that opened inward were secured by a large outside lock. *Miriam* released the heavy iron inside bolts with a large key. They fell free with a solid clang, and the doors swung open.

She led *Yeshua* and his disciples into a fragrant herb garden with grape vines, fig trees, and a huge pomegranate bush heavy with fruit.

"Have we entered the *Pardes?*" joked Andrew.

"Yes," answered *Yeshua*. "And this gate is impossible for thieves to penetrate. You have protected yourself well, *Miriam.*"

After the death of her first husband, many suitors had pressed for marriage. She was wealthy and without a husband. But the man she truly loved, Mordechai the Trader, had died before she could remarry. Ever since that she had devoted herself to business, prayer, and spiritual practices she had learned as a Sister of the Brotherhood of Daniel.

Long after the fishermen lay sleeping in their comfortable beds, *Miriam* and *Yeshua* talked. She had always loved and respected him, but now as she understood who he was, and what he was doing, she found herself wanting to learn and practice his *halakah*.

"When will you teach again here in Magdala?" she asked.

"As soon as I find the two *talmidim* whom I sent this way, we will arrange time and place," he replied.

The next morning *Miriam* sent her maid to the market place while *Cephas* and the fishermen walked down the hill to check on the boat. The girl returned breathless with excitement.

"*Madame,* there were miracle-workers at the market place! They were proclaiming the *Basor* of God and healing sick people by anointing them with oil."

Miriam said, "Quickly, return to the market place and invite those men to stay here. They are disciples of *Mar Yeshua.*"

But the Master held up his hand and said, "*Miriam,* it is not good for you to host them. They will bring crowds of people to your home. You have no husband, and your only protection is the gate. Let others host them. We shall go together to wherever they receive hospitality, and I will teach my *halakah*. You can sit with the hearers."

Miriam agreed to this and sent her maid to find out who would host the disciples. She also carried a message to the *talmidim* that the Master and the other disciples would join them in the evening after supper.

When the sun was starting to sink behind the Western hills, *Yeshua* and all his company walked to the home of the dyer *Zechariah*, who was hosting the assembly and providing hospitality to the young *talmidim*. People had not yet started to arrive.

The *talmidim* were overjoyed to see the Master. They told him privately that *Zechariah's* small son was very sick and demon-possessed. However, they had not been able to cast the evil forces out of him.

Yeshua said, "These kinds of *elilim* are very hard to dislodge." He asked *Zechariah's* wife to bring the child into his presence.

She returned to the room with the screaming boy in tow. When he saw *Yeshua* he threw himself to the floor jerking wildly. His eyes bulged and and he foamed at the mouth. The Master kelt down and grasped the back of the child's neck with his right hand. With the left hand he rolled him on his side and held his palm tightly to the boy's stomach. Then he intoned *Ha Shem.*

The child immediately stopped kicking and became lucid. His mother wiped the foam from his mouth and cradled his head in her lap.

"This type can be cast out only by one who has attuned to Heaven with many years of acceptable prayer and the chosen fast of the Prophet Isaiah," said the Master.

"What is the fast of Isaiah?" asked one of the young disciples.

Yeshua took a deep breath and then quoted the Word of the Prophet Isaiah.

"Is this such a fast that I have chosen? A day for a man to afflict his soul? To bow down his head as a bulrush, and to spread sackcloth and ashes under him? Will you call this a fast, and an acceptable day to the LORD?

"Is not this the fast that I have chosen? To loose the bands of wickedness, to undo the heavy burdens, and to let the oppressed go free, and to break every yoke?

"Is it not to share your bread with the hungry and invite the poor and outcast out into your home? When you see one who is naked, that you cover him? And that you do not withdraw your love from your own family?"

Then he said, "If you remain faithful to the *Basor,* you will all become great exorcists. The *elilim* will cry out and flee when you approach.

"But know this. When an evil spirit is cast out of its house and wanders famished and without sustenance, it tries to return. Then it finds the house clean and swept, and the table set for a feast. So it invites seven more spirits more evil than itself to recapture that house. And the last state of that person is worse than the first."

"But Master, how is it that those you cleanse remain clean?" asked Andrew.

"When hear the *Basor* and accept it in their hearts, the *Ruach Ha-Qodesh* descends to dwell in the Temple of their body. As long as they remain faithful to the *Malkuth,* no evil spirit can enter them.

"But it is not so with a sensitive child whose gates have been broken down by the evil ones. His parents must protect him by their fidelity to the *Malkuth* for many years before his gates will be strong and the doors locked.

"And it is so also with grown men and women who have been foolish enough to open their gates to the *elilim.* But in this case, only their own faithfulness can protect them."

Then *Miriam,* who had watched and listened in amazement, said, "Master, I want to serve the *Basor* that you proclaim. From this day hence I choose the fast of the Prophet Isaiah."

Zechariah laughed and said, "*Miriam,* you already pray daily and serve the sick and outcast in the synagogue. What more can you do?"

"I can serve the Master," she said. "*Mar Yeshua,* I wish to accompany you on all your journeys, to makes arrangement for food and lodging, to keep your purse full, and to learn your *halakah.*"

Yakob Ben-Zebedee shot back, "You are asking to be a *talmid* like the men!"

Yeshua fixed him with his eyes and said, *"Yakob,* she is more than a disciple. She is a *tzadikah.* She may walk my *halakah* as far as she can.

"And remember this," he said to everyone present. "I have said that all who hear the Word of God and do it—*all*—are my family and my disciples. Whoever wishes to walk with us is welcome, man or woman."

The next morning *Cephas* spoke privately with *Yeshua.*

"Master, is it right for the newer *talmidim* to receive as much honor from you as the first ones? And especially for a woman? We have labored with you from the beginning to establish your ministry, but they are latecomers."

Mar Yeshua looked him in the eyes and said, "*Cephas,* I know that it does not seem just to you. But there are many things you cannot know about those who come to me later, and far too much for me to tell you about *Miriam.*

"The *Malkuth* is like like this. A landowner went out early in the morning to hire laborers for his vineyard. When he had agreed with the laborers upon a daily wage, he sent them into his vineyard. Then he went out about the third hour and saw others standing idle in the marketplace. So he said to them, 'Go labor in my vineyard, and whatever wage is fair I will give you.' Again he went out about the sixth and ninth hour, and did likewise.

"And again at even the eleventh hour he went out, found others standing idle, and said to them, 'Why are you standing here idle?' They answered, 'Because no one has hired us.' So again said, 'Go labor in my vineyard, and whatever wage is fair I will give you.'

"Now when the workday was over, the master of the vineyard told his steward, 'Call the laborers and give them their wages, beginning from the last and ending with the first.

"When those who were hired about the eleventh hour were paid, they received the full day's wage. But when the first came, they supposed that they should have received more, since they had worked all day. But they received the day's wage they had agreed upon.

"When they had received it, they murmured against the landowner saying, 'These last laborers have worked for only an hour, yet you have made them equal to us who bore the burden and heat of the day.'

"But he answered one of them and said, 'Friend, I do you no injustice. Did you not agree with me for day's wage? Take what you have earned and be satisfied. It is my generous decision to give unto the last laborers a full day's wage. Is it not just for me to do what I decide with my own money? Is your jealous eye evil simply because I am good?'

"Remember this, beloved *Cephas.* In the *Malkuth,* many of those who have been greatest will become least, and many of those who have been first will be last. And in the *'Olam* to come, the first shall be last, and the last shall be first, and a little child leads us all.

"I have been shown that I have not yet laid eyes upon some of my greatest *talmidim.*

"*Cephas,* The harvest truly is great, but the laborers are few. Do not be jealous, but pray to the Lord of the harvest that he would send forth more laborers into his fields. The Heavenly *Abba* will reward all equally."

The sons of *Zebedee* had overheard and understood the Master's story.

Yakob asked, "Then what might be our wages? We ask to sit with you at your right and left hands in the *Malkuth.*"

Yeshua replied, "In the Heavenly *Hekhaloth* there are many habitations. I shall go before you to prepare a place for each of you. But what that might be is not for me to say. It is for you to earn with your labor.

"But no one's wages will be greater that what you are already earning. For you will each sit upon thrones as wise elders guiding the Twelve Tribes of Israel."

Then he called the rest of his disciples to him and said, "You know that those whose lot is to rule over the Gentiles exercise lordship over them. And in turn their lords exercise authority over them. And so it is from king down to slave.

"But it must not be this way among you. Whoever would be accounted as great among you shall be your minister, and whoever of you will be the chiefest, shall be servant of all.

"For a *Bar-Enash* comes not to be ministered unto, but to minister, and to dedicate his life in service for many."

*******   *******   *******   *******

On the last night of their sojourn in Magdala it was the Dark of the Moon. *Yeshua* had been told by Shoshana in a dream that he was to initiate *Miriam* into the *Razim* of the Ascent. In the morning the words of Master Ariston echoed in his mind.

"I see one in particular—a woman—who will be your greatest disciple…one who will adore you as would a mother and a daughter. You will transmit the Ascent to her and to other great souls."

He did not reveal this to the men. He wanted to avoid creating an opening among them for the *elilim* to awaken the spirit of jealousy that always lurked at the forehead between the eyes, or the spirit of fighting that was seated in the liver and gall. They were already under strong attack by the forces of *Shaitan,* and it was all the Master could do to keep the Evil One from sifting them like sand.

None of the men were ready for such an initiation, and none of them would be able to stand in the fiery internal forces it would evoke. But Shoshana was right. *Miriam* could be initiated in the Mysteries of the *Malkuth-ha-Shammayim.*

After supper when the Sun was setting, *Mar Yeshua* told his *talmidim* that he would be performing a special *mikveh* to bring *Miriam* into the *Malkuth.* It would be done privately and under the stars with rainwater from the cistern on the roof. After that he would teach her all that the other disciples had heard.

Cephas said, "Master, women are not capable of retaining the Life of the *'Olam* while they live in flesh. They have only half a soul, and their nature is that of the Moon, to wax and wane. Their spirit is that of corruption and impermanence. How can you make her into a *talmid?*"

Yeshua replied, "*Shimone* Stone-Head and Stone-Heart, hear this. Neither are men capable of retaining the Life of the *'Olam* while they live in flesh. Neither the male nor the female is *shalem.* But I have planted in you all the Seed of the Word, that you might makes yourselves *shalem.*

"I shall plant within her heart the same Seed that has made you men whole, and hers shall become an eternal spirit like yours. What is more, every woman who makes herself *shalem* shall enter into the *Malkuth-Ha-Shammayim* while yet in her flesh.

"At midnight I shall perform a special cleansing of the Seven Spirits needed by a woman in order to become a *talmid.* After that it doesn't matter whether you call her brother or sister, because she will be your equal in the *Malkuth.*"

That night the Master initiated *Miriam* into the Mysteries of the *Malkuth-Ha-Shammayim.* He raised her in a *Merkabah* through purification of the four physical elements—Earth, Water, Air, and Fire. Next by means of the Seven Spirits of God's Image, he raised her through the Seven Heavens within her soul. Then he brought her into the Eighth Heaven, where she communed with the presence of Shoshona, and finally with her beloved *Mordechai,* her soul-mate. *Mordechai* also abode in the Eighth Heaven like Shoshana because he was chosen by *Metatron* to be reborn in flesh as a *Tzadik Nistar*—one of thirty-six incarnate Jewish saints whose lives uphold the world.

Finally *Miriam* was able to be raised into the Ninth Heaven unto the *Mekabah* Throne of Godhead and the *Hekhaloth* of the Mansions, where she spoke face to face with the ascended saints of Israel. Then they made the descent, and *Mar Yeshua* gave her the initiatic name of *Magdala,* "Tower of Strength."

The sons of *Zebedee* and others heard the Master intoning at midnight as he sometimes did in healing and exorcism.They heard seven separate intonations. Thus it was whispered among them that the Master had cast out seven evil spirits to make *Miriam* worthy of discipleship.

Those who later admired the devotion and good works of *Miriam Magdala* assumed that in order to have become such a great *tzadikah*, she must have been released from the bondage of much evil by the Master. So the word went out that *Mar Yeshua* had cast seven devils out of her. But that was not true. He had transmitted to her the highest initiation into the *Razim* that any saint could receive. She was able to receive it because she was already a great *tzadikah.*

The presence of *Miriam* among the close and accepted disciples of *Mar Yeshua* became a scandal to all the *Ravs* of the Pharisees. Women had never before been admitted as *talmidim* in Israel.

But *Yeshua* always said, "In the Heavens there is no male or female, and in the *Malkuth* there is no male or female. The *Bar-Enash* is the Son of Mankind. Just as *Adam Kadmon* contained Adam, Eve, and all of both sexes ever birthed into flesh, so the New Adam includes *Bat Enash,* the new Eve, and all the coming holy ones who will rebirth themselves into the Body of Messiah."

After those days in Magdala, other women were accepted as close disciples of *Yeshua.* *Miriam* became their leader, trained them, and served as their finest example. She came to be recognized everywhere as the greatest *tzadikah* among the women disciples of *Mar Yeshua*.

Chapter Twenty-Four: FIRST JOURNEY TO JERUSALEM

With *Miriam* seated on a donkey leading a small caravan and the other *talmidim* on foot, the Master set out for Cana. The two new disciples they found in Magdala had taken the roads leading to Cana earlier that week, where they expected to meet with another two disciples who had already began to proclaim the *Basor* to the small villages along these roads.

When he travelled, *Yeshua* wore normal clothing. Only when he taught and oversaw the *mikveh* did he wear the seamless linen of the *cohen*. What is more, in this caravan he walked alongside *Miriam*. With his large, muscular frame and powerful staff, he could be taken for her bodyguard. *Cephas* thought that it was wise for the Master to travel anonymously anywhere near Herod's summer palace at Sepphoris.

As they approach the first village, a group of young men came out to meet them.

"Is this the caravan of *Mar Yeshua?*" they asked.

Cephas, who walked at head of the caravan, responded with a question to find out what they wanted. He asked, "Who is *Mar Yeshua?*"

"He is the great Prophet of the *Basor,*" one of them responded. "Have you not heard of his works? His *talmidim* have taught us about the *Malkuth*. They have said that he will come and prepare us for the *mikveh* of *Yochanan*."

"How do you expect to make the *mikveh* so far from the Jordan?" asked the captain.

"We are prepared to follow him all the way to the Jordan River whenever he comes," the same man responded.

"This is his caravan, and we are his *talmidim*," responded *Cephas*. "We will take some rest in your village while you prepare for the journey. We plan to stay first in Cana, then take the small road that bypasses Sepphoris and stay again in Nazareth before we turn toward Tiberias and the Southern Sea.

"You will need to prepare for a two-week's journey if you wish to come," he added.

The same man who had spoken for the other young men said, "If you can stop for one night in our village, we will gather our wives and children and travel with you."

Yeshua was amazed at the zeal and *emunah* of these men. He called Philip to him and sent him to *Cephas* with this message for the young villagers.

"We will stay in your village this night."

The young men accompanied the caravan to their village, still not knowing that *Yeshua* was present.

"There is a good spring over there," one of them said, pointing to the bottom of a stony hill. "You can make camp and water your animals."

Yeshua walked up to the men and said, "Bring your sick and lame out to the oasis tonight after supper. The Master will be present."

The men were puzzled as to how the Master could appear. Was he travelling this way in another caravan? But they promised to inform the village.

In the cool of the evening as the Sun hung low over the hills, *Yeshua* ritually donned his seamless white garment and sat on the portable throne. *Cephas* and the other *talmidim* sat at his right hand except *Miriam*, whom he placed at his left. He led them in prayers and Psalms as the villagers began to assemble. Andrew gave them permission to sit, and to lay down the pallets upon which several sick people lay.

Some of the children stood shyly or played quietly near the spring. But one little boy was lame and sat leaning on his mother. His left foot was clubbed and turned in. He clutched a small walking stick.

Mar Yeshua raised his arms in a blessing and began to speak.

"The Spirit of God is here present with us now. The *Malkuth Ha-Shamayyim* is spread out upon the Earth, but men do not see it."

The young men who had greeted his caravan were amazed to realize that the rugged, dusty bodyguard was actually the Prophet himself.

"The Prophet Isaiah told us of the Age in which the Sovereignty of God would appear on Earth to purify it of all evil," *Yeshua* continued.

"He said, 'Then the eyes of the blind shall be opened, and the ears of the deaf shall be unstopped. Then shall the lame man leap as an hart, and the tongue of the dumb sing.'

"These are the signs of the appearance of the *Malkuth* of God on Earth, and of the advent of *Bar-Enash*, the new humanity whom the Ancient of Days has anointed as Messiah to rule at His right hand. *Amen, amen,* I say unto you, those days are here. You will see the evidence now."

He stood and motioned to his *talmidim.*

"Bring me your sick," he said. Immediately the disciples helped people carry their sick family members and place their pallets before the Master.

One by one *Mar Yeshua* cast out the *elilim* of disease. Fever subsided, weakness turned to strength, and most of the sick were able to stand up and leave their pallets.

Then *Miriam* tugged at his shoulder and pointed to the little lame boy leaning against his mother. *Yeshua* felt his heart fill with compassion. He sensed the fragrance of lilies and Shoshana's presence. In a dawning realization, he began to know that *Miriam* had been sent by Shoshana to heal the hidden places of his heart and reveal deepest compassion for others.

He had the heart of a lion, but now he realized that he also had the heart of a woman, and that without both he could not be *shalem.*

No tears came to his eyes, but he felt a powerful river of compassion flowing forth from his heart.

"Bring your son to me," he instructed the woman.

"But Master, nothing can help him. The foot is clubbed," she replied.

"Bring your son to me," he smiled and said again.

She stood up, pulled the child to standing, and he limped to the Master with his stick.

Yeshua sat the little boy down on his lap and said, "Would you like to run and play with the other children?"

"Oh, that's cruel," whispered the mother under her breath as she watched with tears in her eyes.

"Yes, Master!" cried the little boy.

"Then stand up and run to them," said *Yeshua,* setting the boy on his feet.

The child took one step, then another. Then he began to run and dance.

"What has happened to your foot?" cried the mother.

The little boy cried, "I don't know, *Imma*. But now I can walk and run without a stick!"

Some of the women rushed to the child and examined his foot. It was still clubbed, but it no longer turned inward. It pointed ahead like the other foot.

"*Imma*," said the Master to the mother, "his left foot will grow into a normal shape over the next few Moons. But even now he will be able to walk and run normally. Unbind the foot and throw away the stick. God has healed your son as a witness to His Presence on Earth. The bondage of the Evil One is broken."

Everyone in the village was astounded by this cure, for the little boy had been lame since birth. Even the *talmidim* were astonished, for they had never seen anything like this healing.

Yeshua turned to *Miriam* and looked deeply into her dark eyes. In them, he saw Shoshana's eyes. A miraculous golden light seemed to warm his chest.

He realized that Heaven had empowered his woman's heart for healing far beyond the authority over *elilim* that he projected with his lion's heart. And he knew now why Shoshana had wanted him to share the *Merkabah* Ascent with *Miriam*.

Through *Miriam,* who was almost the age of his mother, his link to the Spirit of Shoshana had become continual and palpable. The highest marriage of *yechid* and *yechidah* had become present and potent for him on Earth.

"Mother *Miriam* of Shoshana and Mother *Miriam* of *Yeshua*," he said to himself.

He suddenly realized how much he yearned to see his own *Imma Miriam* again in Nazareth.

******* ******* ******* *******

Cephas had arranged for the two young wandering disciples to stay with the village people to give further instruction. After that, they would join with young men of the village to lead all who wanted to make *mikveh* to the city of Tiberias on the Sea of Galilee. There they would meet the Master's caravan and any others for the walk to the headwaters of the Jordan.

Yeshua's caravan arrived at Cana hot and dry. Several of their water jugs had leaked and were empty. First stop was the oasis.

Cana was a city, not a village, with many Roman-style homes and paved roads. Andrew warned that it was filled with Roman collaborators. The safest place to speak would be at the Synagogue of the Doves, rather than in public.

Miriam accompanied *Cephas* to find the *Chazzan*.

He was a portly and prosperous merchant who was known as *Rav Ezra,* even though he had not received formal training under a Pharisaic master. He was found sitting at a small table in the market place keeping records of his latest shipment of goods.

"*Miriam*, dear lady, it is so good to see you again," he exclaimed as they approached. "Are you here on business?"

"Yes, *Ezra*. I am here on God's business," she replied demurely.

"We are all doing God's business," he laughed. "But what is special about your visit?"

She pointed to her caravan and replied, "We are travelling with *Mar Yeshua*. Have you heard of him?"

The merchant stood up.

"He is here? The Prophet is here? You must take me to him!"

"Sir, we must not make a public stir so close to the fox's nest," *Cephas* interjected. "We had hoped that you would give the Master leave to speak at the Synagogue of the Doves on *Shabbat*."

"Of course!" replied the *Chazzan*.

"How can we inform those not of your assembly who would want to attend?" asked *Miriam*. There were two other synagogues in Cana.

Rav Ezra thought for a moment, then said, "Aha! My nephew's wedding! Everyone will attend the wedding feast. Let the Master and his *talmidim* come tomorrow afternoon to the Synagogue of the Doves. I shall meet you all and show you the way to my brother's house. Wear your finest clothing. I shall introduce the Master and announce his visit to the synagogue."

Miriam paid everyone's lodging at an inn recommended by Ezra. During the day they mingled with the crowd at the market place and remained inconspicuous. Late that afternoon they met *Ezra* and walked to the wedding feast. The Master wore his seamless garment.

When they arrive at the gate of the large Roman-style mansion, they were amazed to see hundred of people attending. They were greeted by a servant who asked *Rav Ezra* the names of the guests. He motioned to a boy with a trumpet, who blew it three times for attention. The sound of talking ceased and all eyes were upon *Yeshua*.

"*Rav Ezra* with his guests *Miriam* of Magdala and *Mar Yeshua* of Nazareth and his *talmidim!*" he announced.

"Please blow the trumpet again," asked *Ezra*. The boy blew one long blast and *Ezra* held up his arms for silence.

"My friends, *Mar Yeshua* will speak and teach at the Synagogue of the Doves this Saturday. We invite you all to attend!"

Excited whispers melted into animated conversation as the Master was seated at a small throne that had been prepared for him. Finally everyone was invited to sit on cushions placed around huge banquet carpets that had been spread upon the ground Roman-style. There were too many people for the few tables that were set, but *Yeshua, Miriam, Ezra,* and the *talmidim* were all seated at one of them.

Rav Ezra was asked to offer the blessing cup, but he deferred to *Yeshua*.

"*Baruch Attah Adonai, Melek-ha-'Olam,* Who has given the fruit of the vine to cheer our hearts," he intoned, "and Whose sacred *Malkuth* is even now appearing on Earth, and Whose holy *Bar-Enash,* the *Mashiah* of Israel, is even now being born in the hearts of his people."

Many rumors had spread about the prophet-healer from Nazareth. But such a strange proclamation generated even more interest, and many resolved to attend the Synagogue of the Doves on *Shabbat*.

"My wandering disciples have not yet been to Cana," remarked *Yeshua* to *Miriam*. "The *Basor* has not been proclaimed here. It is good that I will speak in a private synagogue on Saturday. Perhaps Philip will remain in Cana when we leave and prepare people for *mikveh*."

Everything happened as he had suggested. Philip stayed in Cana to teach privately in the synagogue, with the arrangement that he would later lead a caravan of those ready for *mikveh*. They would meet the Master at an appointed time in Tiberias with the other caravans.

When *Yeshua* and *Miriam* departed with their company for Nazareth on Sunday, they took the high road that by-passed Sepphoris. It was not as safe from bandits as the main road, so *Cephas* and the others took up positions of defense on both sides, from front to back of the pack animals, and *Yeshua* continued to protect *Miriam*. On a few occasions they were watched by thieves, but no one dared to attack.

******* ******* ******* *******

"*Imma*, I want to travel with *Yeshe* to make the *mikveh*," declared *Shalome*.

Her mother was not surprised, but she was concerned about the danger from the Herodians.

She and *Miriam* of Magdala had taken to each other like sisters. She found the spiritual strength of the Magdalene to give her almost the same kind of comfort as had her husband *Yosef*.

"What do you say, *Miriam*?" she asked. "Am I too fearful for *Shalome*?"

The Magdalene smiled and chose her words carefully.

"Perhaps it is time that you and she both make the *mikveh*," she smiled diplomatically.

"He is my firstborn. I raised him from a child. It is hard for me to really understand just who and what he has become," she said helplessly.

"*Miriam*, tell us who and what he is," urged *Shalome*. "He is my brother, and yet to me he seems like one of the *Elohim*. What is he to you, *Miriam*?"

After a moment of thought, the Magdalene said, "You have no idea how like the *Elohim* he really is. He knows more than any man, feels more, is capable of more. He is more than a *tzadik*, more than a prophet. He is a *Bar-Enash* and a *Bar Elohim*. I will follow him until I die."

Miriam of Nazareth was amazed to hear such devotion to her son.

"Are you in love with him?" she blurted out.

"My Sister, listen to me. The man I love with my whole soul is dead. I gave up love with a husband long ago. I devoted myself to God. Now I see the Face of God in your son's face. I am devoted to him and to his holy work. I would die for him. But please believe me, there is no impurity of lust in my love for your son."

Shalome sighed and said, "Yes. That is how I feel now. It is the love of a sister."

"But what can be the love of a mother?" sighed *Miriam* of Nazareth. "I am torn between two faces I see in him—my son *Yeshe,* and a divine stranger who leads people to God."

The Magdelene raised her eyebrows, looked at both women, and said, "Maybe you should call him *Mar Yeshua* instead of his childhood name *Yeshe*. He has not called the people together or done any healings here. I think that is because you are trying to hold onto him as *Yeshe*."

"No, it's far more than that," remarked *Shalome*. "The *Chazzan* has not invited him back into the synagogue. The men who attacked him have suffered grievously with the wounds he inflicted on them. Many people are afraid of him, especially now that he has returned with a band of strong young *talmidim*. No one knows him or what to expect of him any more."

"I will tell him these things," said the Magdalene. "He will receive it better from me than from you."

She excused herself and walked to the encampment that had been set up for their caravan next to the small spring across the road.

"Andrew, where is the Master?" she asked.

"He is in prayer up there on the hill where he used to play as a boy," he replied. "I don't think he wants to see anyone right now."

"Then I shall wait at the bottom of the hill for him," she said.

After a while the Master made his way down the path and sat next to *Miriam*.

"I don't know what to do here," he said.

"I do, Master," she replied.

"Please tell me what you think," he responded.

"You beat some men very severely some time ago. They have suffered much from their wounds and have not recovered. You must seek them out and try to make them whole again."

"They were not whole to begin with," was the quick response—a bit too quick.

"Master, I have heard you say, 'Love your enemies, and do good to those who persecute you,'" she said softly.

After a moment of conflict he said, "Yes, you are right. And that is right. Why can't I do as I teach?"

Then he stood up as though as a man does after laying down a heavy burden, and he said, "*Shoshana* you are right. I mean *Miriam*. I shall do as you suggest. But I shall do this privately."

He took his staff and set out on the road to the market place alone. When he arrived, most of the merchants had taken down their stalls. Then he saw the worst of the ruffians, the man who had bullied *Yakob* as a boy and who had led the mob to stone *Yeshua*.

He was sitting on a small bench with his head bent grotesquely to the side from a poorly set fracture of the neck. *Yeshua* felt deep compassion and approached him.

When the man saw him, he jumped up as if to run away, but stumbled and fell.

"Master, have you come back to kill us in the night? We have done nothing to earn your wrath," he pleaded.

The few people who remained in the market place turned in horror to watch what would happen.

"No, my Brother," said *Yeshua*. "You have suffered long enough. I have come to heal you of your wound."

"I have heard that you have such powers," the man said, his voice shaking.

"God has given me such powers," the Master replied, kneeling down to the man, who had painfully propped himself up on one elbow. He helped the man to rise.

"Stand up as straight as you can," he commanded. "This is the staff that dealt you the blow. I want you to grasp it with both hands as I hold it straight up in front of you."

The man did as he was told. The Master placed his own left hand on the head of the staff and his right upon the man's crown.

"I am going to intone *Ha Shem,* and I want you to straighten your neck so that it lines up with my staff."

As he intoned, the man's neck slowly became straight.

The Master took back his staff, knocked it three times on the ground, and asked, "What do you feel?"

The man moved his head back and forth. "The pain is gone! My neck is straight! Thank you, and I thank God, for this healing!"

The people who saw this were astonished. "First he breaks his neck, and then he heals him."

The Master turned to the people and said, "Listen to me. This man has changed deeply in his heart since I left Nazareth. He has returned to God and renounced his cruel ways."

"That is true, Master," said one woman. "He now comes to synagogue every week, and he gives money to the poor."

"Bless you for healing me!" again cried the man, still amazed that he was no longer crooked.

"My Brother, it is your faithful *emunah* that has made you whole," said the Master. "Without fidelity, I cannot evoke the powers of healing in anyone. Remember this. It is your faith that has made you whole again."

Suddenly there were shouts from the opposite side of the market place. Another man whom *Yeshua* had wounded was running to meet them.

"Can you fix my jaw?" he begged. "It has been crooked ever since you struck me with that staff."

The Master looked at him carefully, then said, "No, it cannot be fixed. You are still the same person who tried to stone me. You have not kept faith with God."

The other man cursed and walked away.

"What you have said is also true, Master," remarked the same woman who had spoken before. "That man is evil. He steals from people. The man you healed does not associate with him any more, nor with the others who came out to stone you."

"What is your name," asked *Yeshua* of the man who had been healed.

"Master, it is *Micah,*" he replied.

"*Micah,* would you like to hear the Word of God?" asked the Master so that all could hear.

"Yes!"

"Then come to my camp tonight after supper— any of you and your friends who want to hear," he continued, turning to the crowd that had gathered, "and bring them to my camp when the sun is setting."

That evening most of the villagers turned out to hear *Mar Yeshua* proclaim the *Basor*. Even the *Chazzan* sat with the crowd. Many of the people did not attend synagogue except for high holy days, so he saw an opportunity to bring more people in by inviting *Yeshua* to speak on *Shabbat*. But the *Chazzan* wanted to hear whether the Master's Word might antagonize the Herodians.

When he heard *Yeshua* invite people to make *mikveh* in the Jordan River, he stood up, shrugged his shoulders, and left.

The Master's caravan departed the next morning for the villages on the road to Tiberias, but *Yakob Ben-Zebedee* stayed behind with *Miriam* of Nazareth to prepare people for *mikveh* and lead their caravan to Tiberias to meet the others.

******* ******* ******* *******

Most of the people of the Galilee had never heard the proclamations of the Prophet *Yochanan*. He dwelt in the Eastern wilderness of Northern Judaea and sent his disciples into the cities of that region. But everyone knew about his murder by Herod.

Legends about his successor *Mar Yeshua* had been spread all over Samaria and Judaea by merchants and trading caravans. Villages on the roads to the Sea of Galilee had already been visited by *Yeshua's* travelling *talmidim*. They had been welcomed into every village they entered. So as the next weeks passed, many people from the villages *Yeshua* visited on the way to Tiberias eagerly heard his Word and decided to make ready for *mikveh* in the Jordan.

As their caravan approached the gate of the city of Nain, they were forced to stop to make way for a funeral procession. *Miriam* asked one of the people who had died.

"It was the only son of the widow *Sarah.* He was a stone mason and fell from a cliff. Now she has no one to help her in her old age. It is very tragic."

Yeshua listened carefully to what was said. The pallet with the corpse of the dead man was carried by four of his friends. They were Guild masons bringing the body to the burial caves they had hewed from the side of a hill.

The Master was flooded with feelings of deep compassion for the widow and her son. He walked to the casket bearers and secretly gave the sign of a Master Mason. The four men stopped in their tracks. Then he examined the corpse. He could see a glow around the son's head and heart. The silver cord had not parted. He could be revived.

"Lay the pallet down on the road," he said firmly. The men complied.

Yeshua bent over and placed his right hand below the unconscious man's heart. He pushed the man's chest in and released it several times. There was a sucking sound as the chest expanded and the man began to take shallow breaths. His blue lips began to turn a pale pink.

Suddenly he coughed loudly and opened his eyes. The Masons who had carried his death pallet gasped in amazement.

"He is alive?" The widow pulled the black mourning shroud from her face and ran up to see what had happened.

"Sit up," whispered Master into the unconscious man's ear.

Painfully the man pulled himself up on his elbows.

"My son! You have come back to life!" cried his mother. She smothered him in kisses while everyone in the procession crowded around in amazement.

"Carry him home, give him figs and pomegranate juice to drink, and let him rest," ordered the Master.

That evening the whole city came out to hear the Prophet *Yeshua* proclaim the *Basor* at his encampment. Many more wanted to make the *mikveh,* so Andrew remained behind to prepare them. He was given the use of the synagogue every night, and would lead yet another caravan to Tiberias to rendezvous with the Master and the others.

In Tiberias there were many *talmidim* of *Yochanan.* They had heard many tales of *Yeshua's* miracles of the *Malkuth,* the most recent being his raising of the widows dead son in Nain.

"He is *Eliahu* returned to Israel," many said. "Did not *Eliahu* also raise the dead son of a widow? What could be a clearer sign than that?"

Others said, "He is the *Mashiah Ben-David.* He has come to bring in the Great *'Olam Ha-Mashiah* on Earth!"

Every synagogue in Tiberias had welcomed the Master's travelling *talmidim,* who had given their teachings, done exorcisms, and taken the road to Jerusalem to visit other cities and villages. They had just left and took with them the story of the raising of the widow's son in Nain.

Now every synagogue was open to *Mar Yeshua.* Hundreds of people from many villages of the Galilee had thronged into Tiberias. Every inn was full of caravan pilgrims planning to meet the Master and his *talmidim* for *mikveh* at the headwaters of the Jordan.

After final preparations, *Cephas* and Andrew brought all the caravans together in one place. They were joined by Philip, the sons of *Zebedee,* and the two new wandering *talmidim* they had found at Magdala. The master made them baptizing disciples, so that there would be eight men to oversee the *mikveh* pools. Since it was a long day's walk to the place of *mikveh* and most people were on foot, *Yeshua* planned to make several stops.

They finally arrived at the crossing of the Jordan below the headwaters where *Yeshua* had chosen his new disciples. Because the combined caravans consisted of many hundred of people, they were never in any danger from bandits. The encampment on the Jordan soon was covered with tents and campfires. The next night would bring the Full Moon, the second great ritual of *mikveh,* and many new *talmidim.*

******* ******* ******* *******

On the morning after *mikveh,* the Master found himself with more than twenty new *talmidim.* These needed much more instruction in *halakah*, so he did not send them out in pairs, but invited them to walk and learn from him on the road to Jerusalem.

When the combined caravans returned to the main road from the Jordan, *Yeshua* turned South toward Jerusalem and sent the rest of the caravans North to return to their villages. This included the pack animals and men accompanying his mother *Miriam.*

However, many of the people left their caravans to walk with him and hear his teachings for another day or two. They planned to meet with their families in Tiberias later and return home then. Among these was the Master's sister *Shalome,* who now joined *Miriam Magdala*, sometimes on foot, and sometimes seated upon a donkey.

As they approached the region of the Gadarenes, many people who had been hearers of *Yochanan* came out to the road to beg *Mar Yeshua* to visit Gadara on the Southern Sea. He agreed, so they made the detour.

As they approached the city, from the hills by the burial grounds they heard continual moaning and crying.

"He is a madman," one of the villagers explained. "He broke all the chains that bound him and threatened to kill us. Now he dwells among the tombs and slashes his body with sharp stones, as though trying to bleed out some kind of poison. He eats the offerings we make to the dead and goes about the hills raving. No man can restrain him, and everyone fears him."

Just then the madman appeared on a small hill by the Sea. He was naked except for a loincloth and yelling incoherently. When he saw the caravan he ran toward it. Then he stopped and fell at the feet of the Master.

"What have we to do with you, *Bar-Enash*?" cried the sound of many voices from within the man. "Have you come to destroy us?"

"Tell me your name!" commanded the Master.

"Our name is Legion, for many of us occupy this habitation," cried many voices in unison. Then they begged the Master not to force them into the wilderness where they could find neither man nor beast to sustain them.

"If we leave this habitation, how will we obtain vital *ruach*? We will die and decay," they cried.

The Master glanced at a small herd of wild boar feeding near a beach by the Sea. These animals were unclean to all Jews, and they were dangerous to humans.

Mar Yeshua pointed to the herd and said, "Go out of him now and enter into those swine!"

Immediately the man writhed in spasms, crying weakly in his own voice. Everyone in the caravan saw many of the wild boars leaping and stampeding into the water, then swimming back to shore.

The man finally lay still and became lucid. *Yeshua* took his hands and raised him onto his feet. He ordered his disciples to wash and cleanse his wounds. Then *Miriam* provided him with clothing and sandals.

"Walk with me," he said, "and I will fill you with a far greater Spirit than these *elilim*—a Spirit that will protect you from being seized and possessed by the evil ones."

All of this was witnessed by nearby village shepherds, who ran into town to tell what they had seen. Others returned with them and found the herd of large boars basking peacefully on the beach.

The caravan approach the village of Gadara with the madman at *Yeshua's* side still naked and bleeding from places where he had slashed himself. The villagers were afraid and begged *Yeshua* to leave the man outside.

"This man will remain with me until I release him to his family and friends," he declared.

Miriam gave money to *Yochanan Ben-Zebedee* and said, "Get this man sandals and clean garments to wear."

That evening the disciples asked the Master privately, "Why did you permit the *elilim* to take possession of the swine? Why did they run into the Sea? Where did the *elilim* go?"

He told them this.

"The *elilim* must always be destroyed. They are manifestations of the *qlippoth* or dark forces in the *'Olam ha-Yetzirah*. They were generated of necessity by God's shattering of the Vessels of Creation, which allowed for divine emanation into the *'Olam* and the *'olamim*. However, they must be dissolved back into their own elements, which can then make new combinations and marriages in the evolutions of time that will manifest as elementaries of light causing seeds to sprout, plants to grow, and healing in man and beast.

"The appearance of the *Malkuth* on Earth and in flesh eventually causes the *elilim* to die and dissolve, which they experience as being cut off from their hosts and falling asleep. If they are not separated from their hosts, they suck them dry until the host dies. Then its soul wanders in barren places, becoming like the *elilim* and seeking its own host to seize and inhabit.

"The *elilim* may possess both man and beast. They prefer human hosts because they desire the freedom and power of mankind.

"Why did I not simply force them out of the man? Because so many had taken up residence in him that the battle could have killed him. That's why I gave them an easy way out—the dangerous wild boars.

"They thought they would be able to inhabit the swine, attack humans, and find their way back into this man or someone else. Even though they knew that when they seize an animal, it jumps and lurches, they had no way of knowing the the animals were by the Sea. Animals always rush into salt water when attacked by an evil spirit because the *elilim* fear and avoid sea water.

"Salt water can actually dissolve the *elilim*. Use it as an antidote for any uncleanness. Always advise those whom you have cleansed to remain near the Sea. A grove of cedar is always a safe and clean environment for them. An incense of cedar and certain other woods will drive *elilim* from home or sanctuary. That is why the Temple has a great basin of sea water in imitation of the great sea that is said to surround the Throne of God. The High Priest will perform a cleansing of the Altar by the sprinkling of sea water for the same reason.

"So I gave them leave to attack the swine, who leapt and dashed into the Sea. The *elilim* were destroyed but the swine were cleansed.

"Does this answer your questions?" the Master asked.

The *talmidim* were overwhelmed. This was the first time the Master had ever given them true *razim*.

"What are the Vessels of Creation?" asked Philip.

"*Miriam* will explain some of these things to you," replied the Master.

Philip and the other men were astonished.

"How can a woman teach a man, and how can a woman know these things?" he asked.

Yakob added, "Why do you love her more than you love us?"

Yeshua answered, "I love you all equally with *Miriam*."

"Then why do you kiss her on the mouth, but you do not kiss us on the mouth?" asked Philip.

The Master smiled and asked, "Why can *Miriam,* who is a woman, teach you about the Vessels of Creation, but you, who are men, cannot teach her about the Vessels of Creation? I tell you, she did not receive this knowledge from me."

From that time on, *Miriam Magdala* was held in highest respect by *Mar Yeshua's* male *talmidim.*

Among the Gadarenes, all who wished had already made *mikveh* in the Jordan. Most had been hearers, and there were even a few *talmidim* of the Prophet *Yochanan* in the village.

Therefore that evening, the Master did not make arrangements for another *mikveh.* Instead, he invited the sick for healing and gave further teachings on the *Malkuth* and his *halakah.* Seated at his feet were the madman and his family, now lucid and normal. All the villagers marveled and their fidelity to the *Malkuth* was strengthened.

As they travelled into the regions of North of Judaea, it would be the same. His hearers had already received the *mikveh* of John. Now they needed to become hearers and doers of the Word, to learn and practice the Way of God in the *Malkuth.*

The Master was pleased to realize that his *talmidim* had brought *mikveh* to the people of the Galilee. *Yochanan* had been murdered before he could complete that work.

Yeshua had made good his promise to the Prophet, who had said, "There is not enough time for me to bring the Word to all Israel before my hour arrives. You must go forth and proclaim the *Basor.* Be wiser than I have been, my Brother. Do not provoke Herod or his collaborators, and keep out of their hands."

The caravan of *Yeshua* and *Miriam* traveled to the main road and turned South the next day. They were met by hundreds of people from surrounding villages bringing their sick and wanting to hear the Word of the Master.

"What shall we do, Master?" asked *Cephas.* "These people are hungry and they have no food. Shall we send them to one of the cities to buy something to eat?"

The Master told his disciples to seat people in rows on the Western hillside. Then he spoke to *Miriam.*

"What do we have in our supplies?" he asked her.

"Two large dried fish and five loaves is all we have until we get to the next village," she replied.

He closed his eyes and prayed silently for a moment, then said, "Give them to me, Sister, and I will show you something the *Rav* never taught you in Babylon."

She gave him one basket with the fish and another with the loaves. He walked to a high place on the Eastern hillside opposite the people and proclaimed in a loud voice, "We have fish and bread for everyone."

He held the baskets up to Heaven and intoned, "*Baruch Attah, Adonai Elohenu, Melek Ha-'Olam,* Who brings forth bread from the Earth and fish from the waters of the deep."

He called *Cephas* and Andrew, gave them each a basket, and said, "Pass among the people and let them each reach in and break off a portion."

It was later said that after everyone had eaten their fill, the two baskets were still heavy with fragments of fish and bread sufficient to feed the Master, his disciples, and all his company.

After the meal, *Mar Yeshua* began to instruct them in his *halakah*. The disciples had heard some of the *davrim* and *mashlim* many times, and yet each time the Master repeated them they seemed to understand them in a new and better way.

"Why call ye me *Mar* and *Rav*, but do not walk my *halakah*?

"The one who hears my teachings and puts them into practice is like a man who built a house. He dug deep and laid a foundation upon bedroack. When a flood arose, the stream beat violently upon that house but could not shake it, for it was founded upon bedrock.

"But the one who hears my teachings and does not put them into practice is like a man who built a house on sand with no foundation. When the flood came and the stream beat against it, the whole structure fell down and washed away.

"Take heed therefore that you put my teachings into practice. Whoever has fidelity to Heaven's Way, to him shall be given Heaven's treasure. Whoever does not have fidelity to Heaven's Way, to him shall be taken away even earthly the treasure he seems to possess.

"Be merciful, even as your Heavenly *Abba* is merciful unto all. He causes His rain to fall upon the just and the unjust equally, even as a father loves the disobedient child equally with the obedient one.

"Judge not, and ye shall not be judged, Condemn not, and ye shall not be condemned. Forgive, and you shall be forgiven.

"Give, and it shall be given unto you; good measure, pressed down, shaken together and running over, shall men give into your bosom. For with the same measure that you give, so shall you receive.

"Blessed are you when men hate you, and separate you from their company, and reproach you, and cast out your name as evil, for the sake of the *Bar-Enash*. Rejoice when that day comes and leap for joy.

"For behold, your throne in the *Malkuth* is secure. The forefathers of those who persecute you did even the same to the great prophets of old.

"Woe unto those who are addicted to riches! For you have no treasure in the *Malkuth*. Indeed, you have already received your reward. Where the heart is, there is your treasure. What have you stored up in the treasury of your heart? The good or the evil *yetzerim*?

"You cannot serve the God of Heaven and Mammon, the god of unrighteous riches. Can you ride two horses at the same time? You cannot serve two masters at once. Either you will love one and hate the other, or you will serve them both poorly. Serve the *Yetzer Ha-Tov*.

"Woe unto you that are bloated and satisfied with the world of the Beast! For you will go hungry in the *Malkuth*.

"Woe unto you that laugh and make merry in the world of the Beast! For you will mourn and weep in the *Malkuth*.

"Woe unto you when all men honor and speak well of you in the world of the Beast! For your forefathers gave no honor to the prophets of old. Yet they offered highest deference and itching ears to the false prophets. They will have no honor in the *Malkuth*.

"Why do you see the tiny speck that obscures your brother's vision, but remain blind to the log in your own eye? How can you say to your brother, 'Brother, let me remove the speck that is in your eye,' when you are oblivious to the log in your own eye?

"Listen, self-righteous one. First pull out the log from your own eye, and then you will see clearly to remove the tiny speck that is in your brother's eye. Can the blind lead the blind? Shall they not both fall into a ditch?

"Hear me. No *talmid* is above his master. But every *talmid* that makes himself *shalem* shall be equal to his master.

"A good tree does not bring forth rotten fruit, nor does a rotten tree bring forth good fruit. Moreover, every tree is known by its own fruit. For of thorns men do not gather figs, nor of a bramble bush do they harvest grapes.

"A good man brings forth good works out of the *Yetzer Ha-Tov* of his heart, but an evil man brings forth evil things out of the *Yetzer Ha-Ra*. For his mouth speaks and his life manifests out of the abundance or lack thereof in his heart.

"When you hear a spiritual teacher, measure him not just by his words, but by the fruits of his life and labor. Here is wisdom: By their fruits shall you know them.

"No one lights a candle and then hides it under a basket. Rather, he sets it on a candlestick for the illumination of all. In the same way, let the light of your good works shine silently and modestly, illuminating all, that the works themselves may glorify the *Malkuth* of God.

"Therefore be not like the Judean Pharisees, who like to blow trumpets on the streets to get attention when they give alms to the poor. They think to set an example for the rest of you. But I tell you in truth, their almsgiving is unclean before God.

"Be not like the self-righteous ones whose outer words and actions imitate piety, but whose hearts and motives are self-seeking and impure. They wash the outside of the cup to please the eyes of others. But they leave the inside filthy.

"Be not double-hearted and double-minded, saying one thing but intending something else. Learn to be single-souled. Make your 'yes' mean yes, and your 'no' mean no. Cast the spirit of guile completely out of your *nephesh*."

When he had finished and was about to give a blessing to the multitude, he was interrupted by a loud cry.

"Master, when will we enter into the *Malkuth ha-Shamayim?*"

"When you transform your two hands into the single Hand of God, and when you transform your two eyes into the single Eye of God, and when you transform your two feet into the single Walk of God's *Halakah*, then shall you enter the *Malkuth ha-Shamayim,*" replied the Master.

Then he gave the *Birkat Kohanim* and retired to his tent.

******* ******* ******* *******

The next day most of the people returned to their villages. *Yeshua* sent his sister *Shalome* back to Tiberias to join his mother. Now the Master's caravan was reduced to a few pack animals and his disciples.

"We will pass through Sychar, where the bones of the Patriarch Joseph are burried," *Yeshua* declared.

"That is a city of Samaria," remarked Andrew. "The Prophet *Yochanan* did not proclaim the *Basor* to Samaritans. Will you proclaim to the Samaritans?"

"We must honor the bones of Joseph," answered the Master. "His body was embalmed and entombed by the Egyptians. Then Moses carried them back to the land given to Joseph by *Yakob*, his Father Israel. This fulfilled the promise that had been made to Joseph. They are buried in a cave near Sychar, but no one knows where."

"But you are descended from the House of Judah and David," continued Andrew. "Why should you reverence the bones of Joseph, whose lineage has been lost?"

Yeshua motioned for all the *talmidim* to listen.

"What does it mean to say that the Anointed One is a Son of Joseph—not of David?" he asked. "Does it mean that the *Bar-Enash* is a certain man descended from Joseph?"

"No," replied Andrew. "*Yochanan* taught that the *Bar-Enash* could appear only after great suffering and tribulation. He called it the Birth Pains of Messiah. But he did not say where and when Messiah would come to birth, or in what manner. You tell us that Messiah and the *Malkuth* must appear first in our hearts and you show us the way to become *shalem*. So I do not think that the *Mashiah Ben-Yosef* is a certain man descended from Joseph."

"Good!" smiled the Master.

"Now Philip, when we say that a prophet is a son of righteousness, or that an evil man is a son of *Shaitan*, what do we mean?" he asked.

After a pause, the disciple answered thoughtfully, "We mean that the man is manifesting the spirit and works of a *tzadik,* or else of the Evil One."

"Then, what were the works of Joseph. Was he not the specially favored child of Israel's old age—the youngest? Have you heard me say that the last shall be first, and a little child shall lead us into the *Malkuth?*"

"Many times, Master," replied *Yakob*.

"So will it be with Messiah," declared *Yeshua*. "Was Joseph not an interpreter of dreams and a seer? Was he not one who knew the *Razim* of Heaven? So will it be with the Anointed One.

"Was Joseph not persecuted by his brothers? Did they not try to kill him? Did they not throw him into a pit, take away his glorious raiment, and sell him as a slave to the Egyptians? Was he not falsely accused of adultery by Potiphar's wife? Messiah also will suffer many things.

"Did the great Pharaoh not seat Joseph upon his right hand and give him the administration of his Sovereignty? And did Joseph not save Israel from destruction, forgive his brothers, rule justly, and bring mercy to all?

"So will it be with Messiah, and so we say he is a Son of Joseph—not of the warrior David. He is not the son of the magician and despot Solomon, but of the one who taught sacred sciences and divine *Razim* to the sons of the Patriarchs. He is the son of the Sages of Israel who knew the *Kabbalah* of God.

"The *Bar-Enash* is not one man, but he is the New Adam that God is forming in your heart. And some of us standing here will be among the first-born of the New Humanity.

"Amen, amen, I say unto you, there are some standing here among you who will not taste death before the *Malkuth Ha-Shamayyim* appears in great power.

"But do not say, 'Lo here!' Or, 'Lo there.' The *Malkuth* does not come by looking for it to appear, for it will be found within you and beyond your understanding.

"You have all been born of flesh and blood from the Old Adam. But now you must be born from above into the New Adam. The Anointed One is not born of flesh and blood, but of Spirit. Your birth *mikveh* will not be in water, but in fiery spiritual awakening."

When they approached Sychar in Samaria, the Master gave instruction that the caravan was to enter the city and make camp near *Yakob*'s well. He, however, would remain outside among the stony hills to pray and join them later.

As he walked into the hills, he saw an outcropping of rock. There was a stony path leading onto the back of the rock, which appeared to have been used as a lookout.

But *Yeshua* was more interested in the base of the outcropping, which was difficult to approach and overgrown with brambles. Clearing a way with his staff, he found a place to sit where erosion of rock had formed a hidden shelf.

Sitting with his head between his knees, he felt the presence of the great Patriarch Joseph. After a while he sat upright in the manner of the Brotherhood of Daniel and assumed the posture of *nacham*.

"Beloved One," he uttered aloud, "I have come to render honor to your ancient bones. I have come to honor the one who died a great sage in Egypt, whose embalmed remains were returned and planted like a seed in Israel. I have come to honor the root of the tree whose fruits were the Sages and Prophets of Israel. And I have come to honor the great Prophet Daniel, who stood in the spirit of Joseph and saved his people by interpreting the dreams of the King, and who revealed the advent of *Bar-Enash* coming into flesh in the *Razim* of Heaven."

He communed in this way for a long time, then made his way downhill over the rocks to take the road to Sychar and *Yakob*'s Well.

When he arrived at the well, he was thirsty. He had left his heavy water horn with the caravan. He had no cup to reach down into the well, but a woman soon came to fill a large water jug.

He sat on the stone that surrounded the well and asked her, "Sister, can I take a drink from your jug?"

She was surprised and answered, "How is it that a Jew asks for anything from a Samaritan?"

Yeshua smiled and said, "Ask of me and I shall give you an everflowing fountain of living water."

She mistook his words for a proposition and laughed, as she occasionally took a scarlet veil to mask her face and played the harlot for strangers.

"Sir, my well is deep. Do you have what is needed to draw water from it?"

Yeshua shook his head to indicated that he was not making a proposition, pointed to the Heavens, and replied, "Woman, after you drink the water from *Yakob*'s well, you shall thirst again. But if you drink from the fountain of living water that I shall give to you, you shall never thirst again."

"Then take," she said suggestively, offering the jug and bringing her face close to his while he drank.

"Now go find your husband and bring him to me, that I might offer him also the waters of life," he said.

"Sir, I have no husband," she replied with flirting eyes.

The Master stood up. He took her by the shoulders, looked deeply into her eyes, and sternly declared, "Woman, you have spoken the truth, for in fact you have had five husbands. Therefore the one whom you now call husband is not your husband!"

He released her and stepped back to keep a modest distance. She was astonished at his words and carefully set the jug on the ground.

"Sir, are you a prophet of God? No man in this city knows these things about me."

As she spoke, *Cephas* and Andrew appeared and said, "Master, we have set up the camp."

Yeshua said to the woman, "If you wish to drink of my living waters, come with your people tonight to my encampment after supper, and I shall give you to drink."

She hurried down the road with her jug just as *Miriam* and the rest of the disciples began to join them at *Yakob*'s Well.

"Master, you have decided to proclaim the *Basor* to the Samaritans?" asked Philip, his careful politeness betraying a mixture of amazement and disapproval.

"Yes," was his simple answer.

Meanwhile the Samaritan woman told everyone she knew about the Jewish prophet at the well, and how he had told her everything she had ever done in her entire life!

At sunset, a large crowd of people began to assemble at the Master's encampment, and he taught them. Many of them begged him to remain with them for a few more days and speak at their synagogue on *Shabbat*.

"But can a Jew attend the synagogue of a Samaritan?" asked *Cephas*. "Is this not against *Torah*?"

"Whose *Torah*?" responded the Master. "The *Torah* of the Jerusalem Pharisees?"

Then he addressed all of his *talmidim*.

"Listen. The hour is coming, and even now is, when God will no longer be worshipped only on the Mountain of Samaria or in Jerusalem.

Have you never heard the Word of the prophet Isaiah who said concerning the gentiles, 'Even them will I bring to my holy mountain and make them joyful in my house of prayer. For my house shall be called a house of prayer for all people.' And also, 'From one new moon to another, and from one *Shabbat* to another, all flesh shall come to worship before me, saith YAHWEH.'

"If he spoke these things concerning the gentiles, how can our ancient brethren the Samaritans be excluded from the *Malkuth*?

"The Word also says that the Jews of the diaspora in every land, even the Hellenists who have adopted the ways of the gentiles, shall be included in the *Malkuth*. Listen.

He closed his eyes and again began to quote Isaiah.

"'YAHWEH says this. I will also take of those scattered abroad for Priests and for Levites. For as the New Heavens and the New Earth, which I will make, shall remain before me, saith YAHWEH, so shall your seed and your name remain.'"

After a brief silence he opened his eyes, arched his eyebrows in the way he always did when he demanded full attention. Then with eyes that seemed to glow, he spoke slowly and deliberately.

"*Amen, amen,* I say unto you, the hour is coming, and even now is, when the true worshippers shall worship God not with ritual and animal sacrifice, but in spirit and in truth. For the *Abba* seeks such to worship him.

"God is Spirit: and those who worship God must worship in spirit and in truth."

After another silence, Andrew posed the question on the minds of all the *talmidim.*

"But how can these people make *mikveh?*"

"You, your brother, and the sons of *Zebedee* shall remain with them after I depart and teach them. When they have been prepared, lead them to a place on the Jordan where you baptized with *Yochanan*," replied the Master.

"You will be Master of the *mikveh,* Andrew, and you will stand in the place of the Prophet *Yochanan*. When you have baptized them, send the the Samaritans home and go directly to Jerusalem. You will find me at the Temple disputing with the *Ravs* of the Pharisees."

But *Cephas* had a further question.

"Master, if even the gentiles will enter the *Malkuth* of Heaven, will they also make *mikveh* and cross over the Jordan like our ancestors? Must they all become converts and be circumcised?"

The Master said, "What is that to you? Our mission is to Israel and Samaria—not to the gentiles," and he spoke no more. But *Cephas* pondered this question in his heart.

The next morning the caravan, less four disciples, made the long journey to Jericho. There the Master encamped outside of the market place and received many for teaching and healing after supper. Everyone who came had received the *mikveh* of *Yochanan*, and many wished to follow him into Jerusalem.

As the caravan left the gate of the city, a blind man sat begging on the side of the road. When he heard the name of the Master spoken, he cried out in a loud voice, "*Yeshua* of Nazareth, have mercy upon me!"

The Master asked who he was. One of the young men from Jericho answered, "That is Bartimaeus, son of Timothy. He has been blind since childhood."

Then he yelled, "Bartimaeus, do not beg from the Master—it is not honorable. Beg from the others."

But Bartimaeus cried all the louder, "*Yeshua* of Nazareth, have mercy upon me!"

The Master motioned for the caravan to stop, then asked that Bartimaeus be brought over to him.

"Be still, Bart. The Master has summoned you," said one of the blind man's friends, who helped him remove his cloak, stand, and walk to *Yeshua.*

"What mercy can I have upon you, Bartimaeus?" asked the Master.

"That I would regain my sight," he quickly responded.

"Let it be unto you according to your faithfulness," the Master said. "Will you walk with us to Jerusalem?"

"I will walk your way everywhere from this moment on," replied Bartimaeus.

Suddenly he tilted his head back, rubbed his eyes, then faced the sun.

"Master, I think I see the sun!"

"Take your eyes away from it and look at me," instructed *Yeshua*.

Bartinaeus did as he was told, then rubbed his eyes again.

"I see light and shadow!" he cried.

The Master asked *Miriam* for water and washed the man's face.

"Now close your eyes for a while and rest them," he advised.

"Walk with your friend and accompany us to Jerusalem," he said. "As you walk, open your eyes for a while, then rest them again, and you will recover your sight. But remember this," he said looking at everyone present, "it is this man's fidelity to God's Way that is making him whole."

By the time they were approaching Jerusalem, Bartimaeus was able to see the North Gate of the city and walk by himself. After they entered Jerusalem, Bartimaeus and his friend told his story many times in the market place, and word spread that the Prophet *Yeshua* had come.

Miriam had friends and business associates in the City of David, so she and Philip left the pack animals to secure lodgings.

The Master left the caravan in the hands of some of the men from Jericho and made his way to the Temple Mount and the Porch of Solomon. It was late in the afternoon, so the *Ravs* and devotees had left for supper. He had privacy and solitude for prayer until Philip came to show him to their lodgings.

As he was teaching the next morning at Solomon's Porch, Andrew, *Cephas,* and the sons of *Zebedee* joined their circle. They had returned from baptizing many of the Samaritans of Sychar and were overjoyed to tell *Yeshua* that over fifty men and women had made the *mikveh*.

They were overheard by the disciple of a Pharisaic *Rav,* who ran to his master and told him that disciples of *Yochanan* were teaching on the Temple Mount. The old *Rav* gathered others and approached *Yeshua's* circle to catch him in some error and make him look foolish.

"It is the Nazarene," one of them observed. "The one whom we sent emissaries to ban from the synagogues in the Galilee."

Seeing them sitting outside the circle, the Master began to provoke them.

"The *Ravs* of the Pharisees suppose themselves to sit in the seat of Moses with the authority to bind or release from the thousand *mitzvoth* of the *Torah.* They bind heavy burdens, most grievous to bear, laying them upon men's shoulders. And they will not lift a finger to lighten the burdens.

"But they are self-righteous and self-aggrandizing pretenders. They seek only to magnify themselves before others. All their works are done to be seen by men. They wear huge phylacteries and enlarge the borders of their garments and imagine they are superior in piety to all."

Many people, hearing the declamations of the prophet *Yeshua*, drew near to hear the disputation that must follow such blatant provocation.

"They love the uppermost rooms at feast and the chief seats in the synagogues. They love to be greeted as *tzadikim* in the market place, and to be called *Rav*, Great One, *Abba,* and *Mar,"* *Yeshua* continued.

"I tell you in truth, whoever exalts himself shall be abased in the *Malkuth.* But whoever humbles himself shall be exalted.

"You snakes, you generation of vipers, how will you escape the consequences of your sins? For you have laid waste the vineyards that *Adonai* has entrusted to your care and allowed them to fall into ruins. What will the Master of the Vineyard do? He will cast you out and raise up new stewards and vine-dressers.

"Who built this great Temple? Was it not Herod?" he asked the oldest *Rav,* pointing to the Court of the Gentiles.

He did not answer. The Roman-appointed ruling Tetrachy had tried to gain support of the Jews by expanding the Second Temple into a mammoth, ornate structure rivaling some of the greatest Roman temples of the Empire. It was Herod's wealth and his architects who had carried out the work just a few decades ago.

"*Amen* I tell you," declared the Master looking at the huge crowd that had gathered, "when the *Malkuth* appears in power, not one stone of this false Roman Temple will remain standing!"

The Pharisees whispered to each other, "He has spoken against the Temple. We will report this to Herod's administration. The Romans will bring this Galilean dog to trial for treason against the state."

They stood up as a group and turned their backs as a sign of disrespect. Then they hastened away.

That night at supper, *Cephas* said, "Master, it would be wise for us to journey to Bethany before sunrise. The Pharisees will accuse you before the Herodians and we will all be in prison by tomorrow night if we don't leave quickly."

The Master agreed. After brief and fitful sleep, they left the City of David by the South Gate.

Chapter Twenty-Five: INNER AND SECRET *HALAKAH*

The disciple *Yochanan* was the youngest among them, but he was quickly developing as a brilliant preacher and teacher. His older brother *Yakob* demonstrated the courage and devotion of *Cephas*. These *Boanerges* or Sons of Thunder—their initiatic names—had relatives at Bethany who had received the *mikveh* of *Yochanan* and kept faith with it.

These were Mary, Martha, and Lazarus. They would host the Master in Bethany, and they would provide a safe-house against spies of the Herodians. Here, the Master's teaching would be done privately—not in public. Invitations to hear him would be given out with discretion.

Most of the Jerusalem Pharisees had not made the *mikveh,* and they could not be trusted. Word had been put out by respected *Ravs* of the Sanhedrin at Jerusalem that *Yeshua* of Nazareth was a false prophet. Nevertheless there were some trustworthy Pharisees who had made the *mikveh* and were seeking the *Malkuth* of God.

It was *Yeshua's* custom to teach publically at sunset after supper, but in Bethany he was restricted to teaching in the home of Lazarus after supper. It was a large house, and seating could be extended into an open courtyard to accommodate thirty or forty people—no more—all of whom were eager to learn more of the *Malkuth Ha-Shamayyim.*

The Magdalene provided money to buy food at the market place. She often accompanied Mary of Bethany and talked with her. Mary and Martha served dutifully in the kitchen and ate separately from the men, but *Miriam Magdala* always sat for supper with the men. *Cephas* was seated at the right hand of the Master, and *Magdala* at the left.

After supper, when teaching time came, those who were invited would enter the gate and sit wherever they could find a place as close to the Master as possible. *Yeshua* and his *talmidim* remained seated at the table with their host Lazarus.

Mary and Martha were invited to sit in a special place close to their brother, but Martha always wanted to get the kitchen work done first before sitting down. On the first night of the teachings, Mary wanted to put the work off until after the teaching was done, and she insisted upon staying with *Miriam* and the men.

Martha called out to *Mar Yeshua* and complained, "Master, do you not care that my sister has left me to work alone? Please tell her to help me."

But he smiled and replied, "Dear, faithful Martha, do not be troubled. Mary has chosen to be a hearer, and she may become a disciple. You should do the same. Come sit here next to her. I shall excuse you both to leave and return to the kitchen if the time gets too late."

Both sisters became hearers of the teachings and joined *Miriam* as women disciples.

Indeed, teaching and questions often went late into the night. The male disciples had heard much of what was taught many times, but each time they understood it better. *Magdala,* however, already had perfect understanding and she was much older than the men. Often she would get very tired, fighting to keep her eyes open. Then the Master would put his arm around her, nestle her head upon his chest, and say, "You have my permission to lean upon me and sleep, Dear Mother."

Miriam Magdala had no children, but the Master called her Mother because she was like a wise mother to all the disciples. She often explained finer points of the Master's teaching to his other disciples, and she was accorded a unique position of love and respect among them.

The Master devoted the *Shabbat Seder* to teaching what he called inner *halakah* to his closest disciples. They were *Miriam, Cephas, Yakob, Yochanan,* and any others who were travelling with him. Now they included Lazarus, who was much beloved of the Master.

Often these were explanations of parables about the *Malkuth Ha-Shamayyim,* which he sometimes uttered in public along with other sayings that were hard to understand.

"Master, what did it mean when you said, 'Blessed is the lion which the man eats—and the lion shall become man. But accursed is the man whom the lion eats—for the lion shall become man?'" asked Philip.

"The lion is anger and the *Ruach Ha-Shaitan*, which rises up a man's throat from the liver. If he does not allow anger to rise higher than the throat, he can cast it down into the fires of the stomach and digest it with understanding. Then it returns to the elemental spirits from whence it was generated by the *Yetzer Ha-Tov* and becomes like food to strengthen the man.

"But if he allows anger to rise higher than the throat and become rage, and if he puts it into action by striking out against his brother—whether with words or fists, then the lion has eaten the man.

"You must not only control anger, but analyze and digest it. Always look within first before you take any action precipitously. Otherwise, how can you make yourselves *shalem*?"

"Master," asked *Yochanan*, "why do you say, 'Whoever does not hate his father and his mother cannot enter into the *Malkuth*?'"

He replied, "I said, 'Whoever does not hate his father and his mother shall not be able to become my disciple.' Now answer me, *Miriam,* do I hate my father and my mother?"

"Master, you love and honor your parents."

"Then *Yochanan,* what do I mean?"

"Perhaps that your love for God should be so great in comparison to the natural love you have for mother and father as to make human love seem like hate?"

"Not so!" laughed the Master. "Your love of God is seen in your love of humanity. Let me help you to remember the rest of my saying.

"I said, 'and whoever does not love his father and his mother cannot become my disciple.' Is this not a paradox? Who can explain it?"

Miriam said, "The seed of every child contains two *yezterim,* one of God, and one of the *qlippoth*. We call them the *Yetzer Ha-Tov* and the *Yetzer Ha-Ra*. That is because the Almighty One has set antagonistic dark forces within all His creations so that there can be birth, growth, and death.

"Therefore every child is generated from two kinds of parent—the Divine Image, and the infernal image. The Master's disciples must love the divine parent and hate the infernal parent."

The Master nodded approvingly while the others disciples, both male and female, sat in silent amazement at *Miriam's* wisdom.

Finally *Yochanan* said, "Master, you have spoken in many paradoxes. You said, 'If you fast, you will beget transgression for yourselves; if you pray, you shall be condemned;

and if you give alms, you shall cause harm to your soul.' I think I can explain these paradoxes."

"Let us hear what you think," said *Yeshua*.

"There are many kinds of fasting, many modes of prayer, and many ways of almsgiving," began the youngest of the disciples. "You are warning us against the ways of the self-righteous Jerusalem Pharisees."

"Well said!" replied the Master. "Then interpret this for us: 'It is not what goes into your mouth, but what comes out of it, that purifies or defiles.'"

"Master," replied *Yochanan*, "a person makes manifest in word and deed what is dominant in his heart, according to whether he follows good or evil *yetzerim*. Good words and deeds carried out in sincerity not only show the *Yetzer Ha-Tov* active in the heart, but give power to it and cause it to dominate. Therefore, good words and deeds can purify the heart, while bad ones defile it."

"But what about the laws of *kosher?*" asked the Master. "Can the foods we put into our mouth spiritually purify or defile our hearts? What do you think?" he asked *Cephas*.

"I am not a *Torah* expert," protested the captain. "But I do not think that unclean foods can defile the heart. I know many gentiles who eat swine, but they have good hearts."

Yochanan interjected, "But the intention and spirit with which food is taken can have an influence. When we eat with the Master and he offers the Blessing, we all sit in harmony regardless of what disputes we may have had during the day. The teaching he gives fills us like meat and drink, and we are all satisfied. What is more, anything we have for food tastes like a feast, even if it is only bread and dried fish. I truly feel like a guest at the Banquet of Messiah."

"Yes," answered *Yeshua*. "And you must partake of that Heavenly Banquet every day. Did I not say, 'Unless you keep the whole week as *Shabbat*, you shall not behold the *Abba*?' All times and all places are sacred because they emanate from the *Abba*."

"You also said, 'Unless you fast from this *'olam*, you shall not enter into the *Malkuth*,'" added *Miriam*. "That is why you said, 'Become passers-by.'"

"Indeed, to fast from injustice, greed, and cruelty is the only way to prepare yourselves for the Messianic Feast," remarked the Master.

"You know that foxes have dens and birds have nests, but the *Bar-Enash* has no home in this evil *'olam*. Do not attach yourselves to the things of this *'olam* that bind you to it. Keep *kihesh* like our wandering ancestors. Be unattached to things and places. Greed for money, possessions, and power is the root of all evil. Remember the Teacher, *Qoheleth*, who declared human thought and perception to be mere *hebel*--unreal and illusory, ever changing and insubstantial like a vapor. Thus *Adonai* revealed through Isaiah, "My thoughts are not your thoughts, neither are your ways my ways."

"Whoever has found this world has found a corpse; but he who knows this *'olam* to be a corpse, of him this world is not worthy."

"But know this: fruits, fish, herbs, rain, sun, stars and all things of Heaven and Earth that nourish and heal are not of this *'olam*. They are the gifts of our *Abba* and contain the *razim* of His angels. When we break bread from the Earth, we share the Bread of Heaven.

"As *Yochanan* said, it is the intention with which food is eaten that matters. While unclean and impure foods cannot defile the heart, they can harm the flesh. In the same way, foods eaten with blessing and thanksgiving can both nourish and sanctify the flesh."

"Master, tell us about death," requested Lazarus.

Yeshua said, "When the fruit is ripe, the reaper comes. If you strive to ripen the fruit of your soul, you also strive for death. Therefore the wise disciple does not fear death, which comes to the foolish like a thief in the night. Rather, he looks forward to it in joyful anticipation like a bride preparing for marriage.

"You will take off your garments of flesh and tread upon them unashamed like naked children at play. Then you will marvel at what great wealth has been clothed in such rags."

"Master, what if they kill you?" asked *Cephas*. "How can we know you then?"

"If you make yourselves one with the *Bar-Enash*, as I have done," he replied, "then I will be with you always. Look under the stone, and there you will find me. Cleave the wood, and there I am.

"I will not appear on the outside, but within. I shall be found in the *Malkuth* and in the interiors of all things. I will not be seen with these eyes of flesh, but the single eye of spirit."

Yochanan asked, "How can we purify our hearts so that we may be worthy of the vision of God?"

The Master replied, "Be faithful to the *Torah* of God that is inscribed in your heart. Follow the promptings of the *Yetzer Ha-Tov*. Put the Word you have received into practice."

"I have done all these things, and I know that they make us worthy to see God. But how do we actually see God?" asked the young man.

"I shall teach you all to make *mishqad*," answered the Master.

"Is that the watch of a lookout, who stands on a high tower or hill and keeps watch for bandits and caravans?" asked *Yochanan*.

"No. This is the watch of the wise men and prophets of Israel," answered the Master.

"We have never heard of such a thing," exclaimed Andrew.

"What did Moses do on the mountain? What did Elijah do when he heard the still, small voice? What did he do when he sat with his head between his legs and brought in clouds to end the draught?" asked the Master.

"We do not know," exclaimed the disciples.

Then the Master gave them detailed instruction about the *mishqad Ha-Malkuth*. He taught them how to prepare the body, how to sit, how to focus the mind upon the primordial *Aur* that will ever hide the *Tzelem* of God in seven veils. He taught them how to intone certain prayers and when, where, and how it is best to make the *mishqad* Vigil.

"The *Malkuth Ha-Shamayim* does not come by looking, but it does appear to those who have made themselves worthy in *Shaqad*," he said.

"From now on, if you wish to become *shalem*, you must always pray and make the silent Vigil."

The next evening was the dark of the Moon. It was a time when *Yeshua* would be able to make the *Merkabah* Ascent to take counsel with *Moshe* and *Eliahu*.

After some time in prayer, the Master decided to take *Cephas, Yakob,* and *Yochanan* with him to make midnight *mishqad* on a high hill. While none of them had the interior purity to safely make a *Merkabah* Ascent, he could raise them collectively into an experience of the higher *'olamim* of the Heavens. He would accomplish this by making the Ascent himself and carrying their spirits with him.

He told the men to wrap themselves in their prayer shawls, then sat them in a line facing East. It was the dark of the Moon and the Night Heaven was heavy with stars. He told them to close their eyes and visualize *Ha-Shem* in flaming black letters poised over their heads like a crown. With each inhalation through nostrils they were to draw fiery *ruach* from the letters down into their hair, and with each exhalation through the mouth to draw their hearts upward to meet the fiery *ruach.* They were to make their breaths increasingly shallow until it was as though they were sleeping.

"But," he cautioned them, "do not fall asleep. The *mishqad* must be done in wakeful *shalom.* If you catch yourself falling asleep, take deeper breaths and try again."

"You will see what you will see," he said.

He withdrew to a separate position higher on the hill and warned them strictly not to go to him or touch him.

After a long time the disciples felt a numbing cold descending upon them. It came so suddenly that they opened their eyes. At first it appeared that everything had been obscured in a freezing fog that was glowing with white light.

Then as their eyes adapted to the brightness they saw the Master sitting above them. His seamless Priestly garment seemed to be the source of the illumination. But then they began to make out the figures of two other men sitting and speaking with him. The brilliant white light emanated also from their garments, which were different from that of the Master. One of them wore the smooth robes of an Egypian Priest, the other the rough weave of a prophet.

The Egyptian was saying, "Do not return to Jerusalem until it is your time."

The Prophet agreed and said, "We can hold back the evil ones until *Pesach.* Then you must confront them on the Temple Mount and be prepared for great suffering and death."

The Master turned to his disciples and asked, "What of these men? Must they die too?"

The Egyptian said, "By no means! They must flee for their lives. If they do not save themselves, the work of the coming ones will be jeopardized."

The Master stood, bowed, and the two men faded into the cloud of light. Then the cloud itself slowly dissipated until only the sky and stars remained.

"Master, are those men or angels?" asked *Cephas,* standing and pulling *Yakob* up to face *Yeshua.*

"They are the great saints who guide our work and advise us," he replied. *"Yochanan,* you know who they are."

Yochanan, who was just now awakening from the vision, propped himself up. He blinked his eyes, then slowly answered, *"Moshe* and *Eliahu."*

Cephas cried out, "Master, this is a holy place, and God has revealed holy things here. We must put up three monuments to mark this place; one for Moses, one for Elijah, and one for you."

But the Master told them to keep strict secrecy about what they had seen, for that is the tradition of the Riders of the Chariot.

On the next evening, while it was still the dark of the Moon, the Master brought Lazarus alone with him to the same place at sunset. He required him to wear clean white linen. He instructed him extensively in the *mishqad Ha-Malkuth,* then at midnight began to transmit to him the *Razim* of *Malkuth Ha-Shamayim,* as he had for *Miriam.*

As the sun rose, they returned to the home of Lazarus.

*******   *******   *******   *******

After visiting Bethlehem and other villages of the area, *Yeshua* and his *talmidim* set North to bypass Jerusalem and take the road to Emmaus. From there they would visit the cities of Lydda and Arimathea, then take the main road through Samaria back to the Galilee.

In Emmaus, they were joined by many of the *talmidim* whom the Master had sent out to proclaim the *Basor* and do healings, exorcisms, and teachings. They had heard that the Master was in Judaea and wanted to walk with him to learn more of his *halakah.*

"Many of the other *talmidim* have completed their work and await you in Capernaum," he was told. "Some have returned to their homes to await your arrival."

Now, as the Master travelled from city to village, he was followed by large entourage of disciples and hearers. It was difficult to maintain secrecy, so he alternated between public teachings and private retreats into the Judaean wilderness.

In the city of Arimathea there were Pharisees named *Yosef* and his friend Nicodemus. They had received the *mikveh* of John and were seeking the *Malkuth. Yosef* was a student of the Greek as well as Jewish philosophers. He respected the wise advice inscribed upon the portal to the temple of the Oracle at Delphi. It was often repeated by the philosophers: *Gnothi Seautov,* which means "Know for Thyself." Thus in spite of the lies that had been spread about *Yeshua,* he wished to take the measure of this controversial prophet for himself.

He found *Mar Yeshua* seated after supper at the head of a table in the house of Levi, a despised tax collector who worked for the Romans. He was surrounded by male and female hearers whom *Yosef* did not know because they never attended synagogue. It was rumored that some of the women had been accepted as disciples.

A notorious prostitute was weeping and washing the Master's feet with her own tears, using her hair to wipe them clean. He said, "Your sins are forgiven."

Immediately *Yosef* was stung with righteous indignation. What *tzadik* would eat with publicans and sinners? What kind of prophet would not know that he was being touched by uncleanness worse even than that of a leper? And how could any person claim to offer forgiveness of sin?

Yeshua turned his face to *Yosef* and fixed him with his piercing eyes.

"Know this, Brother. The *Bar-Enash* has authority on Earth to forgive sins. Answer a question for me. A landowner had two debtors. One owed ten, the other ten thousand. He forgave both their debts. Which one will love him more?"

Yosef was rattled by the power and authority of this man, so his voice quavered when he answered, "The one who was forgiven the greater debt, I suppose."

"Behold the woman," said the Master, pointing to her as she wept and continued to wash his feet with her tears.

"She has sinned much and been forgiven much. Now look at her. She has far greater love and devotion than one who has sinned little and been forgiven little, like you."

Yosef nodded.

"A man had two sons. He asked them each to perform a difficult service for him. The older son said, 'Yes, Father. I shall do it.' But the younger was rebellious and said, 'No, I cannot do this.'

"The first son soon forgot his promise and never performed the service. But the second son felt remorseful about his answer, and he performed the service.'

"Tell me, which son did his father's will?"

Yosef began to see the Master's point. The eldest in line for the inheritance—like the many self-righteous religious people he saw in synagogue—gave lip service, but did not do his father's will. But the younger son—like the disinherited *amme-ha-eretz* who crowded around this strange prophet to hear his *Basor*—were rebellious against religion, but now were turning their hearts to God.

He replied, "The son who actually performed his service, even though it came after sin and rebellion, like this woman weeping at your feet."

The Master said, *"Yosef,* I invite you to become my *talmid* and walk my *halakah."*

"How did he know my name? How did he know the thoughts of my heart?" thought the *Yosef,* his mind racing. *"How can I, a Pharisee, become the disciple of a man hated by the chief Pharisees?"*

"Master," he finally replied, "may I hear your *halakah* before accepting or rejecting?"

Yeshua was pleased with his answer and motioned for him to sit next to *Yochanan* on his right.

"Ask, and I shall answer," he said to *Yochanan.*

"What is the *Malkuth Ha-Shamayim* like? To what can it be compared?" asked the young disciple.

"A wise merchant was seeking nacre stone, which is called mother-of-pearl, for his markets. One day he dug deeply into a likely plot of ground and discovered a vein of highest-quality mother-of-pearl. He sold all that he had and bought that land. He mined the nacre and became rich."

The Master looked at *Yosef* and said, "Can you explain what this means?"

Joseph thought for a moment, then said, "The *Malkuth* is not easy to find because it is hidden from the eyes of men. We must find the likely plot of ground..."

"And what is that?" persisted the Master.

Yochanan spoke up. "It is one's own heart."

The Master motioned for *Yosef* to continue his interpretation.

"Then, we must dig deeply into our own hearts to find the pearl," he said with a weak smile.

"And when you find it?"

Yosef hesitated, then replied, "We must sell all we own to purchase the plot that contains it—that means we must make all other things in our life secondary to...to..."

Yochanan again intervened. "To taking ownership of our own heart, which means making the sacrifices necessary to follow the *Yetzer Ha-Tov* and make our hearts, minds, and souls single and without guile."

"And by trading in that greatest of all interior merchandise, we are rewarded with the wealth of the *Malkuth*," said the Master.

Yosef was astounded. *"This man not only knows my name and can read the thoughts of my heart, but he is a master of the Kabbalah and knows the Razim of the Malkuth,"* he thought.

"To what else can we compare the *Malkuth*?" asked *Yeshua* rhetorically.

"A woman took a little leavening and hid it in some dough. She warmed it in her hands, and after a while it produced large loaves. Whoever has ears to hear, let him hear!"

The Pharisee *Yosef* found his mind whirling as he tried to interpret this saying. "She hid it—the *Malkuth* is hidden from profane eyes. She warmed it in her hands—that would mean actions, deeds. Or is the lump of dough like the heart? What are the large loaves?"

"Hear and understand," said the Master. "A woman was carrying a jar full of grain. While she was walking far from home the handle of the jar broke. She did not notice, and the grain streamed out behind her onto the road. When she got home, she found the jar empty."

Yosef tried to understand these *davrim,* but he realized that he had no basis for finding their meaning.

"Or again," said *Yeshua,* "a man had to fight a powerful warrior. So he drew his sword in his house and thrust it into the wall again and again to practice his mightiest blows. Then he went forth and slew the enemy."

"Does this mean there must be courageous struggle to gain the *Malkuth*?" thought *Josef.*

"Hear me. A shepherd had one hundred sheep. The largest one of them went astray. The shepherd left the ninety-nine and searched for the large one until he found it, for the large one was more precious to him than all the other ninety-nine. Whoever has ears to hear, let him understand."

By the end of the evening, *Yosef's* head was swimming. He didn't have "ears" to hear and understand. His heart told him that he must learn more from this man who had invited him to become a *talmid*—much more.

He spoke to Andrew and asked for a private meeting with the Master under the cover of darkness, so it wouldn't be seen or reported to other Pharisees of the city. The meeting was arranged for the following evening.

Nicodemus was a wealthy Pharisee, a highly trained *Rav,* and *Chazzan* of the synagogue in Arimathea. For the sake of his reputation among the Pharisees, he felt that he could not be seen in public with *Yeshua.* But after hearing all that *Josef* told about the Master, he insisted upon coming after sunset to the private meeting.

"Master," he said as he bowed low, "I have no doubt that you are sent by God. No one could perform such miracles and give such powerful teachings unless he were inspired by God. Will you please give me a Word?"

"Amen, amen, I say this: Unless you will be born from Above, you cannot see the *Malkuth* of God."

Nicodemus asked, "How can anyone be born when he is old? Can he enter back into his mother's womb and be born?"

Yosef whispered, "Nicodemus, he speaks in kabbalistic *davrim* and *mashlim*."

Mar Yeshua looked at him intently and continued, "Unless you purify yourself in the fire of spirit through the *halakah* of rebirth into the *Bar-Enash*, you cannot enter into the *Malkuth* of God. What is born of flesh is flesh, and what is born of Spirit is Spirit.

"Don't be amazed when I tell you that you must be born from Above in Spirit. When you see trees and grass moving, you have evidence of wind, which the Greeks call *pneuma*, but you can't see the wind. You don't know from whence it came and whither it goes. It is the same with one who has been born of fiery *Ruach* from Above. You don't understand whence she comes and whither she goes."

Nicodemus asked, "How can this be?"

The Master raised his eyebrows and said, "Are you a *Rav* of Israel and still don't understand these things? I speak of that which I have seen and experienced, yet you don't accept my witness. If I have told you simple things that worldly people have seen, and you do not understand them, how can I reveal the *Razim* of Heaven to you?

"No man of flesh can make the Ascent into Heaven if the *Bar-Enash* has not descended from Heaven and been born in him. And just as *Moshe* lifted up the serpent in the wilderness, so those have been born from Above must exalt the *Bar-Enash* within them. Whoever keeps faith with Him will inherit the Life of the *'Olam*."

Then *Yosef* asked, "How can we receive the *mikveh* and enter into the *Malkuth*?"

"First you must be prepared and purified in understanding. Then you must come to a place on the Jordan River on a date that I shall specify for the *mikveh* of *Yochanan*. But it cannot be done in secrecy. It must be done in the light of day, and you must declare and keep faith with the *Basor* in the view and knowledge of all," said the Master. "You must be like a city on a hill, in the plain view of all but well defended with strong walls.

"Then you must travel with me to learn and practice my *halakah*. Through this means, you will rebirth yourself as a *Bar-Enash*."

Rav Nicodemus thought for a moment, then responded, "Master, I invite you to speak at the synagogue on this coming *Shabbat*."

Then *Yosef* bowed and touched the Master's feet according to the Pharisaic custom of showing respect to a Master of Israel.

"*Mar Yeshua,* I accept the offer to become your *talmid*," he said with deep emotion in his voice, "and I invite you to stay with your disciples at my mansion whenever you come to Arimathea. All who wish to be hearers may come to my house after supper—including harlots and tax collectors."

Nicodemus was astonished.

"And I will make this announcement at the synagogue on *Shabbat*," continued *Yosef,* turning to look at Nicodemus.

"After you have heard the Master, you will become a disciple too."

Nicodemus bowed and touched *Yeshua's* feet. "I wish to hear more, Master."

The next evening he publically joined *Yosef* and all the hearers. On *Shabbat* the Master proclaimed the *Basor* to the synagogue and *Yosef* announced that *Yeshua* would be lodging at his home for the next week. All who would not be offended by sitting with the *amme-ha-eretz* were invited to attend the sunset teachings.

The next day the Master's entire entourage encamped within the gate of *Yosef's* mansion and occupied private rooms with servants. He made the decision to relocate there mainly for the sake of *Miriam,* who had silently endured far more discomfort in the encampment than her body was accustomed to bearing.

The evenings of the following week were spent in preparing people for *mikveh* on the coming Full Moon. However, during the afternoons before supper the Master received visitors and healed the sick.

One afternoon as he sat and taught a small group, several children were playing noisily at the open gate. One of them, a servant child about nine years old, stood alone listening to the Master.

Philip said to the other disciples, "Until a child becomes a *Bar Mitvah,* he does not have the Spirit of God and is subject to rule by demons. These noisy children are being used by the *elilim* to create a disturbance here."

But *Miriam* said, "That is a teaching of man, not of God."

The Master smiled and took the child who had been standing alone into his arms.

"Be careful that you do not dishonor a child," he declared, "because in the *Shamayyim* his angel always stands in the Presence of God and beholds the Divine Face. And woe to whoever abuses one of these little ones, for it would be better that a great stone were tied around his neck and he were cast into the sea.

"*Amen,* I say unto you, no one can enter the *Malkuth* unless he makes himself like this serving child. Whoever honors a little child, honors the *Malkuth Ha-Shamayam.* For of such is the *Malkuth.* Each of you is a royal *yeled,* a little child, in the *Malkuth.* You must apprentice and learn as a royal heir before you will be entrusted with Sovereignty—first a little, then more.

"In the *'Olam* of *Messiah,* a wise man full of years will sit at the feet of a little child to learn the *Razim* of Heaven. For the *Bar-Enash* descends from Above into the worlds of *Adam Kadmon* as a serving child."

Nicodemus asked, "What is true humility?"

Yeshua said, "Our *Abba* accepts the sacrifice of a contrite spirit and a humble heart, for in truth we are all but little serving children. Knowing this, the self-righteous ones imitate contrition and humility, but inwardly they are puffed up with pride.

"When one of them is invited to a feast, he does not take a prominent seat next to the host. Instead, he takes the lowest seat. Then the host will invite him sit at a position of higher honor and everyone will respect him. He knows that a foolish man will instead take a seat of honor, only to be asked to move to a lower one.

"But unlike that, true humility is not a social posture adopted for men to see. It is not an attitude of superiority to others, nor a fear that one is less worthy than others. Rather, it is a spiritual knowledge that we are all *yeledim,* little brothers and sisters equally beloved of our *Abba.* Then it doesn't matter what seat we take at the feast.

"When you can sit as comfortably with prostitutes as you can with *tzadikim,* and when you can see the Divine *Tzelem* in each one, then you will have awakened true humility. Why? Because in truth, there are no *tzadikim.* None of us is *shalem,* though we make it our constant goal.

"Now do you see why the *Basor* is proclaimed to the *amme-ha-aretz* equally with the righteous?"

Nicodemus again asked, "What does it mean to worship God in Spirit and in truth?"

"Listen to this," continued the Master.

"When the *Bar-Enash* makes his home on Earth and among humanity in his glory with all the holy angels, then he will sit upon the right hand of God. All souls will be gathered into his presence. Then he will separate them one from another, as a shepherd separates his sheep from the wild goats that sneak into the fold to drain the mothers' teats. He will set the sheep on his right hand, but the goats on the left.

"Then he will say to those on his right hand, 'Come, you who have earned the blessing of the Almighty. Inherit the sovereign power prepared for you from the foundation of the world. For I was hungry and you gave me meat. I was thirsty and you gave me drink. I was a stranger and you took me in. I was naked and you clothed me. I was sick and you strengthened me. I was in prison and you visited me.'

"Then the *tzadikim* will ask, 'Master, when did we see you hungry and feed you? Or thirsty and give you drink? When did we see you a stranger and take you in? Or naked and clothed you?

"The *Bar-Enash* will tell them this: '*Amen* I say unto you, Inasmuch as you have done it unto one of the least of these my brethren, you have done it unto me.'

"Then he will say to those on the left hand, 'Depart from me you self-accursed ones, and enter back into the fires of your *'olam,* where *Shaitan* and his minions are bound. For I was hungry and you gave me no meat. I was thirsty and you gave me no drink. I was a stranger and you did not take me in. I was naked and you did not clothe me. I was sick and you did not strengthen me. I was in prison and you turned your back on me.'

"Then the unrighteous will ask, 'Master, when did we see you hungry and feed you? Or thirsty and give you drink? When did we see you a stranger and take you in? Or naked and did not cover you?

"The *Bar-Enash* will tell them this: '*Amen* I say unto you, Inasmuch as you have not done it unto one of the least of these my brethren, you have not done it unto me.'

"And the righteous will receive their inheritance, but the unrighteous will be excluded from the *Malkuth Ha-Shamayim.*"

There was a sober silence, then *Yosef* remarked, "The righteousness of the *Malkuth* is not like that of the Pharisees. It does not consist in works of *mitzvoth* according to the traditions of men, but in works of compassion for every soul according to the ways of the *Abba.*"

Nicodemus added, "Then the *Bar-Enash* must be born spiritually in the heart of each one. Is that how he will judge the heart of each one?"

The Master was very pleased with this observation and he answered, "The *Bar-Enash* is not a judge. It is the heart of each one that judges. When the new *Adam* lives within the heart of humanity, the works of the old *Adam* will be known and rejected."

Then he asked, "Nicodemus, are you my *talmid*?"

He bent to the ground and touched *Yeshua's* sandals. "If you will accept an old Pharisaic *Rav,* I am."

Soon it was time to depart for Jericho, then to take the main road North to the Galilee. *Mar Yeshua* again assigned the work of baptism to Andrew and the same disciples who had baptized the Samaritans. However, he made a new pronouncement based on the fact that he had used rainwater from Heaven for *Miriam's* private *mikveh.*

"It is not necessary to make the long journey to the Jordan River for *mikveh.* Any living water that comes from the Heavens in the form of rain, melted snow, mountain streams, or flowing springs may be used.

"Why? Because God has said this:

'My thoughts are not your thoughts, neither are your ways my ways. For as the Heavens are higher than the Earth, so are my ways higher than your ways, and my thoughts than your thoughts.

'For as the rain and snow fall from heaven and do not return unfruitful, but water the soil and make it bring forth and bud, that it may give seed to the sower and bread to the eater, so shall it be with the *Davar* that goes forth out of my mouth. It shall not return unto me void, but it shall accomplish my will, and it shall prosper in the purpose wherefore I sent it.'

"This means that all waters are one, and from the same Heavenly source as the Jordan River. They will accomplish God's purpose in ways that are beyond our understanding. Therefore you may baptize these people in the mountain stream North of this city that flows from the hills to the sea."

Cephas asked, "Master, what if the water is not deep enough for them to go under?"

"Then let them kneel and you will pour it over their heads from a cup," he ruled.

In this way the disciples were able to baptize Pharisees, Samaritans, and others far from the Jordan River who had not received the *mikveh* of *Yochanan.*

Rav Nicodemus and *Yosef* were baptized and remained faithful as disciples. Because they were both wealthy and powerful men, they were able to stand together against the condemnation of the Judaean *Ravs.* Seeing their example, most of the members of the synagogue also became faithful to the *Basor,* and Arimathea became a safe Judaean city for the Master to revisit.

Chapter Twenty-Six: RETURN TO THE GALILEE

As they made the long jouney back to Magdala, they visited all the cities and some of the small villages on the road. In the cities they met the remaining *talmidim* that *Yeshua* sent ahead of him and, once they had left Judaea, gathered them for further instruction. This was done in public places and was open to all hearers. In every small village they distributed money for food and clothing to the poor that had been donated to support the Master's mission by the wealthier synagogues of Judea.

The disciples who preceded him had already done many healings and exorcisms, and they had introduced a great many people to the *Basor*. Nevertheless when word was spread about the Master's presence in any village, he was overwhelmed with requests for healing and the crowd pressed in to see him.

That evening he gave teachings on *amen,* faithfulness and perseverance in the Way of God. He held up a handful of very small, black mustard seeds from a nearby bush.

"The *Malkuth Ha-Shamayim* is like a tiny mustard seed. It is the least among all seeds, and yet see how great and powerful is the mustard bush. It begins from the tiniest of all seeds, yet grows into the greatest of all bushes.

"How does it do this? Through *emunah,* perseverance, keeping faith with the divine purpose that God has formed in its heart.

"This is how the *Malkuth* grows on Earth. It begins with the tiniest of seeds in the hearts of the faithful. And then, through their fidelity, it starts to sprout and grow.

"*Amen, amen* I tell you, if you keep the faith of a tiny mustard seed, you will say to the mountain of obstacles that hinders the growth of the *Malkuth,* 'Be moved,' and it will yield to you.

"You will say to a mighty sycamore that obscures the sunlight of the *Pardes*, 'Be cast into the sea,' and it will be plucked up and disappear into the waters.

A hearer asked, "What is faith like?"

Yeshua said, Hear this.

"There was a wealthy landowner who left his house and fields under the care of two stewards and their servants when he departed for a long journey. One of the stewards kept faith with his master's will. He was fair to the servants and kept the orchards and vineyards under his supervision properly dressed.

"But the other was not faithful. Eventually when much time had passed he said, 'The master will not return, all this is mine to do with as I will.' He began to beat and abuse the servants, spend the master's money, and allowed his vineyards to fall into disrepair.

"What will happen when the master returns? He will greatly reward the faithful steward, but severely punish the unfaithful steward and cast him out of his mansion.

"So it is with life in this *'olam.* The Master has entrusted us with His Will, which is justice, mercy, humility, and service to the needs of others. He will return at a time when we least expect, and then he will execute his just *Mishpat.*

"And he who is faithful in even the least things will be accounted faithful in great things. But those who are unjust in the least things will be accounted unjust in great things."

Another asked, "When and how will our souls be judged?"

The Master answered, "Hear the story of the rich man. His heart belonged to his possessions and worldly treasure. He built walls and gates to protect them and guarded them with his strongest servants so that no thieves could break in and steal.

"But one night he suddenly died. In his *nephesh* he peered into the *'Olam* of Life and was asked, "What gifts do you have to offer the Eternal One?

"He answered, 'All my treasure is on Earth, and I cannot bring it here.'

"Have you no treasure in Heaven?" he was asked. "That is the only acceptable offering to the Eternal One." But he had none, and his *neshama* was cast out of the eternal habitations into *Gehenna*.

"Thus we are judged by our own hearts in the mysteries of death. Spirit is fire and mind, and in *Gehenna* we each burn in the heavenly fires of self-examination until we have purified ourselves for sleep in the *shabbat* of the *Pardes*. Then *Metatron* awakens each *neshama* to return through the *gilgul* of rebirth in flesh. But those who have purified themselves in my *halakah* will never experience the sting of death. They will have liberated themselves from *gilgul*. They will achieve *qimah* and exist in the eternal habitations guiding human souls like the *malachim*."

"I tell you in truth, do not lay up for yourselves treasure on Earth, where rust and the worm devour them. Instead, lay up for yourselves treasure in Heaven that cannot rust and corrode. And the greatest treasure is this: faithfulness to the Way of God with good works. For faith without works is dead, and fidelity on the lips but not in the hands is no faith at all.

"Therefore I say unto you, "Be not worried about food, drink, and clothing. The true Life is more than meat, and the body more than garments.

"Consider the ravens. They neither sow nor reap, nor do they make storehouse or barns. Yet God provides their food. Then, how much more are you beloved by your *Abba* than the birds?

"Which of you by worrying and planning can increase his height by even a finger's breadth? If you are not able to even make yourself grow, which God does for you, then why worry about the rest?

"Consider the how the lilies grow. They do not work and spin garments, and yet I say unto you, that Solomon in all his glory was not arrayed like one of these. If God clothes the grass that lives for a while in the field and is cast into your ovens, how much more will he clothe you, even those of little faith? Have you not heard about *Mar Yosef* and his robe of many colors? When you enter *qimah* in the eternal habitations, you will receive a far more glorious robe.

"Do not make food, clothing, and possessions sovereign in your life like those who don't seek God. Heaven knows that you need them. But instead, seek to serve the sovereign ways of God, and all these things shall be added unto you."

Cephas said, "You have told us always to keep the *mishqad* and pray. Is this how we prepare for death?"

"Always keep *mishqad* and *tiphlah*. Be like servants who await the return of their master from a wedding. Be always prepared to receive the master, with your lights burning. When he knocks, they immediately open the gate.

"Blessed are those servants when the master comes and finds them keeping watch. *Amen* I say unto you, that he shall don a servant's robe, make them sit down to a feast, and will serve them with his own hands. Whether he comes early or late, if he finds them faithful, then blessed are those servants.

"What I say to you, I say to all: Pray always and keep *mishqad.*"

*******   *******   *******   *******

In Tiberias on the Sea of Galilee the Master saw Levi, the son of Alphaeus, sitting at a table and collecting taxes for the Romans. He was despised by the people in the city and accused of being a collaborator, but in reality he was not. He conducted his business honestly and, unknown to the people, secretly showed mercy on them by reducing their debts.

Yeshua motioned for his entourage to stop. He looked carefully at Levi, then said, "I invite you to be my *talmid* and follow my *halakah.*"

Levi stood up, bowed, and rolled up his accounts. He was ready to become a disciple.

The onlookers were amazed. One, a Pharisee, sought to test the Master.

"Is it lawful to pay tribute to the Romans?" he asked slyly. He knew that if *Yeshua* rendered a positive dictum, he would be hated by the people. But if he gave a negative dictum, the Pharisee could accuse him of playing false.

Yeshua said, "Show me a coin."

The Pharisee held one up.

"Whose image and superscription is that on the coin?" asked the Master.

"It is Caesar's," he replied.

"Then here is my dictum," stated the Master. "Render unto Caesar the things that are Caesar's, and unto God the things that are God's."

Everyone was amazed by the wisdom of his dictum. To refuse to pay tribute would bring on the repression of Roman troops, which no one wanted. But his answer indicated that paying tribute could be done without breaking *Torah.*

The Pharisee turned and walked away. However, two Saduccees were travelling North and had heard the dictum. They conspired to test him with a question that they thought would prove the Saduccaic argument against afterlife and the *qimah* based on the *Torah.*

"The Law of Moses says this:" one of them began, "If a man die, having no children, his brother shall marry his wife and raise up seed unto his brother.

"Now there were seven brothers and the first, when he had married a wife, died. Since he had no children, he left his wife unto his brother.

"The same thing happened with this brother, then the next, unto the seventh brother. Last of all, the woman died.

"Therefore in the *qimah,* whose wife of the seven brothers shall she be? For they all lawfully married her."

Yeshua laughed and said, "You are in much error, knowing neither the Scriptures nor the power of God! For in the *qimah* they neither marry nor are given in marriage, but are solitary and *shalem* like the angels of God in heaven.

"But concerning the *qimah* of the saints and the *tzadikim,* have you not read that which was spoken directly by the voice of God saying, 'I am the God of Abraham, and the God of Isaac, and the God of *Yakob*?' He is not the God of the dead, but of the living."

The people were glad to hear the Master shut the mouths of the Saduccees, who turned and walked away defeated.

That night Levi put on a feast for the Master and his disciples. After supper anyone who wished was invited to hear the Master.

Wishing to restore the reputation of Levi, he told this parable.

"There was a certain rich man who had a steward. However, the steward was accused of not collecting debts. So the master called him to make an account of his stewardship and was determined to cast him out.

"The steward said to himself, 'What can I do? The master will cast me out and I will have no food or habitation. I cannot work as a servant and I am too proud to beg.' Then he made a plan to gain the friendship of all the debtors so that when he was cast out of his house, they would receive him into their homes.

"He called each one of the debtors to him and said to one, 'How much do you owe?' The debtor replied, 'One hundred measures of oil.' The unjust steward said, 'Take the bill quickly and write down that you owe only fifty.'

"He did the same with all the master's debtors, releasing half of their debt to gain their friendship and collecting the other half for the master. When the master saw what the steward had collected, he did not cast him out but commended him because he had done wisely.

"Therefore the children of this world can show a wise example to the children of light. For good works of mercy, even if done for selfish motives, will speak out as witnesses for your defense in the *Mishpat* of the heart after death.

"Make yourselves friends in Heaven by means of the mammon of unrighteousness. When your righteousness is found lacking, your unjust works of mercy may find you a home in the *'Olam*."

Andrew asked, "Does this mean we can do *mitzvoth* with impure motives?"

"No," answered the Master. "But it is better to do good works with impure motives than to do none at all. No motives are pure and *shalem,* for the *Yetzer Ha-Ra* is never completely absent. But it is always better to give than to receive."

Now a wealthy young man who had inherited much property approached the Master. His name was Thomas because he was a twin *(toma).*

He asked, "Good Master, what shall I do to enter the Life of the *'Olam?*"

Yeshua answered, "Why do you call me good Master? There is only one who is good, and that is God."

Looking upon the man and seeing a soul ready for discipleship, he said, "Sell all that you have and give to the poor. Then come with us and follow my *halakah.*"

The young Thomas was amazed and disturbed with the idea of giving away his wealth, so he departed in much distress.

The Master said, "How hard it is for a rich man to enter the *Malkuth!*"

He pointed to the gate of the city. The rock pinnacles that formed the entrance were so narrow that before caravans could pass through, it was necessary to unpack all the goods that were slung over the camels and bulging out on their sides. For this reason the pinnacles were called the Needles.

"Amen, amen, I tell you this. It is easier for a fully-loaded camel to pass through the eye of the Needles than it is for a rich man to enter into the *Malkuth.* Yet with God, all things are possible."

The next day Thomas returned to *Yeshua* and said, "Master, I have given all my property and lands over to stewards to sell and divide among my servants and the poor of this city."

The Master said, "Sit here on my right hand next to *Cephas.* He has also sacrificed dearly of his substance for the sake of the *Malkuth.* See here on my left is *Miriam,* a wealthy widow of Magdala who dedicates her life and riches to the *Basor.* There are other married disciples in many cities who donate money for food, lodging, and distribution to the poor in villages who have no synagogue to assist them.

"You have chosen to dedicate your life to God, not Mammon. You have sacrificed the kind of wealth that most of my disciples never had and offered it to the poor. Therefore even though you are the least of my disciples in knowledge of the *Malkuth,* I give you this seat of honor, for you are among the greatest of them in sacrifice. I will teach you privately from time to time."

The Master found Thomas to be a brilliant disciple and eventually initiated him into the *Razim-ha-Malkuth Ha-Shamayyim.* Thomas never married, and for this reason was called *Thomas Asketes,* the Athlete or Ascetic. He later journeyed to the synagogues of the East to proclaim the *Basor.* On the coast of India, rigorous asceticism was considered to be the sign of a holy man, so Thomas and his teaching were revered by Buddhists and Hindus. When the Nestorian Monophysites were forced to leave Egypt by the Nicene Christians, they sailed to the coasts of India that had been visited by *Thomas Asketes* and found his tomb.

*******   *******   *******   *******

Yeshua wanted to visit his family in Nazareth, but disciples who had returned from the area warned that Herodian agents from Sepphoris had been there seeking information about him. He decided that it would be best to take the shore road directly to Magdala, where *Cephas* could ferry him to Capernaum.

They arrived in Magdala in the evening and left the pack animals in the village while the Master and disciples climbed the hill to *Miriam's* estate. It would be necessary for her to remain in Magdala for several weeks to oversee business and be certain her stewards were managing it properly. She also needed to recover from the journey, which had been hard on her.

In fact, everyone was in need of rest, so they had a luxurious stay of several days while garments were washed and supplies restocked for the land journey that most of the *talmidim* would make to Capernaum.

"You always eat like kings when you travel with me," laughed *Yeshua* as they sat at supper. "Everyone invites us to supper and puts on their best feast. I'm afraid you'll all grow fat."

"Not with all the walking," said Philip. "And in the earlier days there were many times when we had nothing but a few dried fish and stale loaves."

The Master smiled and said, "You all have become passers-by, but on many nights of the week you celebrate the marriage feast of Messiah, and every supper is a *Shabbat* meal."

Philip asked, "Master, why do you liken the *Bar-Enash* to a bridegroom?"

"Listen carefully," he replied. "The appearance of the *Malkuth* is a marriage of Heaven and Earth. God is present and dwells among mankind. Messiah, who is the *Bar-Enash*, is the bridegroom to every human soul, which is like a bride. While the New Adam must be born from Above and formed within the earthly heart of each one, he was present with our *Abba* before *Ha-Roshit,* the Beginning of all time, and stands with our *Abba* at *Ha-Acharit,* the end of all time. As we are brought to spiritual birth, our souls become joined to his spiritual body.

"The *Bar-Enash* is the New Adam. He is one single pre-existent spiritual being seated at the right hand of God, but we are many. God emanated all of the *'Olamim* for his sake, that is to say, for the sake of humanity becoming *shalem*. What is more, he is the Son and Heir of God who sits upon the throne of Sovereignty and rules the *Malkuth* from Heaven. But the Old Adam was *shalem* as a Single One who was divided into male and female, which is bridegroom and bride, *yechid* and *yechidah*. Because of this division, Adam and Eve were unable to remain in union and fell of the *Pardes* into incarnation—"coats of skin."

"The New Adam redeems the fallen soul of humanity, which is like a bride. Faithfulness to Heaven must be restored. Then the Bridegroom will come for the Bride, and they will become one body and one heart. The *Bar-Enash* is not our ancestor and progenitor, like the Old Adam. *Bar-Enash* exists in the Heavens and comes to us out of the divine future. He is like a child of God and humanity. That is why it was written, 'A little child shall lead them.' That is why I say, 'The last shall be first.'

"Therefore the coming of Messiah, which is the Marriage of Heaven and Earth, is brought about by a betrothal that is made in our hearts, and a marriage that is consummated in our souls. The soul of every disciple is the bride of *Bar-Enash* and must be joined in Spirit to the Body of Messiah."

Only a few of the disciples had heard deep Kabbalistic teachings from *Yeshua* about the Anointed One or "Christ" (as the Greeks would know him), since most had not been taught in the wisdom schools. So there was a long silence. Then Philip spoke again.

"We know that the *Ravs* are not allowed to discuss and interpret the Songs of Solomon until they have attained the age of fifty. There are great *razim* hidden in these songs we recite when a marriage is being consummated. But you have revealed mysteries to us that even the *Ravs* do not understand."

The Master said, "For those outside of our circle, I teach in parables and allegories. But for you, my close *talmidim,* I explain everything plainly.

"You must be the same. There are many lying in wait to snare you. For now, you must keep the *razim* hidden. Remember this: Do not cast your pearls to swine, lest they trample them underfoot and viciously attack you. Do not give the children's bread to the dogs. But to those who have entered into the *Malkuth,* you may reveal these things.

"Amen I say this unto you," replied the Master. "When the *Malkuth* appears on Earth in power, all the *razim* of Heaven will be revealed. What you have heard privately from me will be shouted from the housetops. They will see the *Bar-Enash* seated at the right hand of power and coming in the *razim* of Heaven. The veil of the Holy of Holies will be rent from top to bottom, and God will dwell on Earth with man."

"When will these things come to pass?" asked Levi, who had been given the name of Matthew by the Master.

"Of that time, no one knows but God. But I tell you this: The *Malkuth* of God is even now spread out upon the Earth, and men do not see it."

The day after *Shabbat* they departed for Capernaum—*Yeshua* and the fishermen in the captain's boat, and the others by a land route. *Cephas* was able to make landing without drawing a crowd, and the Master accompanied him and Andrew to his home.

The next morning the *Chazzan Mordechai* appeared at the gate and asked to speak with *Mar Yeshua*.

"The centurion Marcellus, who is sits in the court of the gentiles at our synagogue and has made many generous donations, is sick at heart because his servant Judah is dying. He begs for your help."

Judah was beloved to *Yeshua*. He was one of those who had been baptized on his last visit.

"Take me to him quickly," he ordered.

But as they approached Marcellus' house, friends of the centurion ran out to stop them on the road.

"Master," one of them said breathlessly, "the centurion Marcellus greets you in the Name of God, and he asks us to read you this message. 'Master, do not trouble yourself, for I am not worthy that you should enter under my roof. Moreover, I do not consider myself worthy to even stand on the road with you, so I have sent my friends in my place.

"'But speak the word only, and my servant shall be healed.'"

Yeshua was deeply moved. He turned to *Cephas* and the other disciples following him and said, "I have not seen this kind of humility and fidelity in all of Israel. Therefore I pray that I may speak in the *Kol Ha-Nabi* to command, 'Judah, be healed.' Then he motioned for his disciples to return to the house of *Cephas*.

At that very hour the fever left Judah and he was whole again.

The story of this miraculous healing was told in the market place, and soon there were many asking to see and hear the Master. For he had spoken the prophet's word, and God had made it good. It was arranged for a public teaching to be offered after the *Shabbat* supper on Friday at the home of *Cephas*. *Mar Yeshua* was asked about prayer.

"Master, you told us not to worry about the necessities of life for ourselves. But what about others? Can we pray for their needs?" asked the centurion's servant Judah.

"Yes, and you must," replied *Yeshua*.

"But often prayer doesn't seem to work," the servant continued. "I have been told that prayer is answered with what is needed, not what is wanted, and that we are not wise enough to understand the difference."

"That is true to a point," said the Master. "But listen to this. You have a friend who stops at your home while on a journey. It is past sunset and he is famished, but you have no bread to set before him. What can you do?"

"I would go to the home of another friend and ask for bread," answered Judah.

"Now, let us say your other friend has gone to bed for the night. When you stand outside his gate calling, he wakes up and says, 'Come back tomorrow.' So what do you do?"

"Well, I keep calling and explaining the need, and I keep on asking until he finally gets up and gives me the bread," he answered.

"That's right. Your other friend did not give you the bread because of the first friend's need, but because you persisted in asking. What is the word for perseverance?"

"It is *emunah,* faithfulness, faith," answered Judah.

"It is the same with asking God to relieve want and need in the world," said *Yeshua.* "If you would serve God, you must be his eyes and ears and hands. If you to pray for your own desires, it is just wind. But if you pray earnestly for the needs of others, then it becomes a test of your own fidelity, for you must persevere not only in prayer, but in the works of your own hands.

"The man in my story was seeking the means to assist another in need. If you persevere in that kind of asking, your prayers will be answered according to your desire. For that desire is of the *Yetzer Ha-Tov* and it is pure before God.

"So pray for the earthly needs of others, but for your own spiritual needs as well. Pray for the *Malkuth* and God's Way to appear on Earth. Pray for your spiritual bread of the *Malkuth.* Pray for deliverance from *Mishpat.* Pray for forgiveness from the consequences of your own offenses in the measure that you forgive others who have trespassed against you.

"Hear this! Persevere faithfully in asking, and you shall receive. Never cease seeking, and you shall find. Keep on knocking, and it shall be opened.

"If a son asks a father for bread, will he give him a stone? Or if he asks for fish, will he give him a poisonous snake? Or if he asks for an egg, will he give him a scorpion?

"Then if you, being evil, know how to give good gifts to your children, how much more shall your Heavenly *Abba* give to you when you ask unselfishly for spiritual things?"

After a silence, during which *Yeshua* took a cup of water, the *Chazzan* asked, "Does God answer prayer in this way to all, or just to those who have made the *mikveh?* What about people like the centurion Marcellus—uncircumcised gentiles, but God-fearers and lovers of our nation?"

The Master raised his eyebrows and said, "To those who have, will be given. To those who have not, even what little they have will be taken away."

"What is it that those who have, have?" asked *Mordechai.*

"Mercy, compassion, justice, humility, righteousness, fidelity—all the Ways of God in their heart and in their works," answered the Master.

"Then, why weren't the prayers of Marcellus for his servant Judah answered?" asked the *Chazzan.* "Marcellus has all the ways of God written in his heart, and he prayed unceasingly for the life of his servant. But Judah was on the verge of death before you came."

"That is true," replied *Yeshua.* "But were his prayers not answered?"

The Master pointed at Judah and asked again, "Were the prayers of Marcellus not answered?"

Everyone laughed.

Chapter Twenty-Seven: FINAL *PESACH* IN JERUSALEM

Mar Yeshua spent many days in solitary retreat outside the city of Capernaum, then returned to announce the next phase of his ministry. He gathered all his disciples after supper and told them his plans.

"After *Shabbat,* we will travel to Magdala. I shall go in the boat with the fishermen and the rest of you will take the land route. Philip, you will remain here to replace Nathaniel as the teacher for Capernaum and Bethsaida. Bartholomew and Micah, you will return to Nazareth to bring my mother and sister to Tiberias, where we will all meet on the New Moon. Bring any other disciples you find on the way, always leaving one in each city to remain as teacher.

"Remember this: I shall return to Galilee after *Pesach.*"

Cephas felt a powerful emotion in his heart when the Master said he would return after *Pesach.* It was a deep feeling of both dread and joy.

"In Magdala we will meet at *Miriam's* home, then make our way to Tiberias. On the Full Moon we will all meet at the fishing boats, where I will have landed with *Cephas, Miriam,* and the others in our group.

"We will provision for a long pilgrimage to Judaea, where we will return to Bethany through Arimathea."

He did not tell them that after this, they would go to Jerusalem for *Pesach.* They would all object to the danger he would face, and *Cephas* would oppose him all the way.

On Sunday morning, they began the journey. *Yeshua* and the fishermen arrived a day before the others and joined *Miriam* at her estate. She had recovered well from the first journey and was excited about making a second one.

"But this time you shall sail in the boat with us to Tiberias," insisted the Master. "Send a servant with well-provisioned pack donkeys to meet my disciples where the fishing boats land," he said.

When the others had arrived, rested, and provisioned at Magdala, they began the second leg of the journey to Tiberias, where *Yeshua* would join his mother and sister.

Again the boat arrived ahead of the land travelers, and it would be a few more days before the other disciples arrived with *Miriam* and *Shalome* of Nazareth. *Yeshua* met with large crowds at a synagogue. Again *Cephas* heard him announce, "Remember this: I shall return to Galilee after *Pesach.*"

That evening he met with three new *talmidim* whom he had called and accepted. After teaching them the *mishqad,* he led them out of the city to a high hill. That night he initiated them into the *Razim-ha-Malkuth Ha-Shamayyim* and gave them new names.

Finally *Miriam* and *Shalome* arrived from Nazareth. Then *Yeshua* called for a feast to be made for all who would travel South with him. This was funded by the Magdalene and served at a synagogue overlooking the Sea of Galilee.

Again he said, "Remember this: I shall return to Galilee after *Pesach.*"

As the large caravan of *Mar Yeshua* approached every city and village on the road South, multitudes gathered to welcome him. He bypassed some of the villages, but in every city with a synagogue he stayed for a few days, sometimes accepting new disciples into his entourage. He often gave private instruction to all the disciples, and sometimes offered public teachings in the synagogues.

In one city, the twelve-year-old daughter of Jairus, who was *Chazzan* of the synagogue, had become mortally ill during the night and was on the verge of death.

The *Rav* Jairus kneeled before *Yeshua* and begged, "Master, will you lay your holy hands upon my daughter that she might not die?"

Mar Yeshua agreed. He prepared himself with prayer, and began to follow the *Chazzan* to his home. His disciples protected him from physical contact by the crowd had started to form. They closed ranks on all sides.

There was a woman who had spent all she had on physicians to heal bleeding fibroids in her womb. Nothing had worked, and she was in danger of bleeding to death. She had prayed for many years to be free of this plague, to no avail. This woman was known in her city as a kindly saint who was faithful to the Covenant of Israel.

She stole up behind the Master while he was greeted by a horde of people seeking healing and blessings. She thought, *"If I can merely touch his garment, I shall be made whole."* Reaching stealthily through the phalanx of disciples that surrounded him, she touched the hem of *Yeshua's* garment and quickly withdrew her hand. Immediately she felt a warm river of bliss course through her body. She stood up and felt herself. The bleeding had stopped!

Yeshua stopped and turned around.

"I felt power flow out of me," he said. "Who touched me?"

Nathaniel replied, "You see this huge throng. How can we know who touched you?"

Then the Master called to the crowd, "Who touched me?"

With a mixture of joy and trepidation, the woman fell at his feet and said, "Master, I knew that if I could touch your garment, the bleeding that no one has been able to cure for twelve years would be healed. And now the flow has been stopped!"

He looked at her with compassion and said, "Your many years of faithfulness to God's Way has made you whole. Go in peace."

The Master knew that the key to healing was the power of faithfulness in one who was ill. He chose those to whom he offered healing based on the power of fidelity he discerned in them. There were tens of thousands of lepers in Palestine, but he facilitated healing for only a chosen few. He unlocked their powers of self-healing, like a flame lighting a lamp. But if their lamps had no oil and their wicks were not trimmed, he did not offer healing.

As they continued their walk to the house of Jairus, they were met by servants who said, "*Ravi*, it is no use. Your daughter died while you were seeking the Master."

Yeshua held up his hand for silence.

Then he took *Cephas, Yakob,* and *Yochanan* along with Jairus through the gate and into the house. Jairus led them to the room where the child was laid out on her bed. Her mother and the servants were wailing and weeping.

The Master said to them, "Why do you mourn? The chid is not dead. She is merely sleeping."

The mother screamed and scorned him, but he knelt by the child and took her limp left hand. Standing up and pulling, he commanded, *"Talithi, cumi!"* which means "Little girl, stand up!" in Aramaic.

The child sat upright and painfully rubbed her eyes. Then she took a deep breath and stood up. The mother fainted into the arms of a servant, and Jairus raised his hands in *orant* posture and cried his thanks to God.

Yeshua told the father, "Give her light food and drink, and let her rest as much as she wants." Then he sternly warned everyone present not to tell the crowd what had happened. He sent the Sons of Thunder outside to disperse the crowd, telling them to return with the other disciples to their encampment where he would meet them later. He and *Cephas* remained with the family of Jairus until the crowd had dispersed, then returned to the encampment by a path on the hills to avoid being seen.

"Master," asked the captain, "why are some healed and others not? And why was the woman healed by merely touching your garment?"

Mar Yeshua raised his eyebrows and asked, "How do you bear suffering, *Cephas*? One person is crushed by it. He makes himself into a spiritual dwarf wallowing in self pity. But another person smiles through his tears and grows into a spiritual giant. One person hardens his heart and is in danger of losing his soul, but another opens his heart to the suffering of others and loses himself in purifying compassion for all.

"This woman purified herself through suffering. She became a saint. The bonds of *Shaitan* were weak. She needed no prayer from me. She took my flame with her own hand and lit her own lamp. Her lamp was filled with the oil of love and fidelity. That is why I told her that her own faithfulness had healed her."

After a moment of reflection *Cephas* asked, "Then what about the child? She was neither saint nor sinner."

Yeshua smiled and said, "That is quite a different case. Why did I go to that child, and not to another?"

"Because she was the daughter of a *tzadik*?" *Cephas* ventured.

"Why did I choose you for discipleship, and not *Rav Mordechai*?" asked *Yeshua*. "The *Abba* showed you to me, and all those whom I have chosen. And it was our *Abba* who brought the daughter of Jairus to me.

"Remember this," he continued. "Many are called, but few are chosen.

"Only the Almighty One knows why. He is the one who brings you all unto my hand and into my heart. Do you understand?"

Cephas nodded, then repeated to himself, *"Many are called, but few are chosen."*

"The daughter of Jairus was not dead," explained the Master. "She was sleeping and may never have awakened, for the silver cord had parted. But the *Abba* showed me her light hovering over the body. The dead can hear the voice of a beloved one or a *Bar-Enash*. That is why even after one has died, those who love him will sit and offer prayer and comfort into his ears. I prayed to the *Abba* who showed me the little girl's light, and then I ordered her *nephesh* to return to her body.

"Learn this now," he continued. "The *Abba* shows me those whom I can help. Are there not thousands of lepers in Judaea? But how many have been cleansed—fifteen or sixteen? The *Abba* knows why one is cleansed and many others are not. I do not know. That is not my work. I am not a physician, but healing is a sign of the *Malkuth*. That is why the *Abba* now makes it manifest in this world, for the *Malkuth* is already appearing in power.

"The days will come when physicians will be able to heal all the world's lepers. Your children will learn to do all my marvellous works, and even greater things. The deepest mysteries of Heaven will be common knowledge.

"For the power of the *Malkuth* will grow and take root in this *'olam,* even as a mustard sprout grows into the largest of all shrubs and provides nesting places for the birds of Heaven. In those days a *Bar-Enash* will find many places to lay his head."

The Master revisited many Judaean cities and gave further instruction to his disciples and those who had received *mikveh*. As the time of Passover approached, *Yeshua* began to release his Judaean disciples to return to their cities and and celebrate with their families.

Only the Galilean disciples including *Miriam* of Magdala remained with him when they bypassed the Eastern Gate of Jerusalem and finally reached the hillsides of Bethany. The Master signaled for an early encampment and sent *Miriam* into the city with Philip and Nathaniel to tell Lazarus and his sisters that he would arrive the next day. They were to stay with Lazarus, and the rest of the caravan would arrive the next morning.

Late that afternoon he took his disciples onto a hilltop overlooking Jerusalem to the West, where the sun hung low in the sky. He sat with them in silent prayer for some time. Then he stood, raised his arms toward the City of David, and lamented in the *Kol Ha-Nabi*.

"O Jerusalem, Jerusalem! You killed the prophets and stoned those whom I sent to you! How often would I have gathered your children together, even as a hen gathers chicks under her wings, and you would not come! Behold! Your house will be desolate. Your Temple will be rubble."

Then he turned to his disciples and said, "When you see the abomination of desolation standing in the holy place, as prophesied by Daniel, then let those who be in Judaea flee to the mountains. Let them leave their homes and fields without turning back. And woe to those who are with child or give suck in those days. Pray that your flight be not in winter or on *Shabbat*. Let all those who have entered the *Malkuth* flee from Jerusalem, for there will be such tribulation in those days as have never been seen before. And if the Almighty had not shortened those days, no flesh would be saved. But for your sake, the days will be shortened.

"When the branch of a fig tree is yet tender and puts forth leaves, you know that summer is near. So likewise, when you see all these things come to pass, know that the *Bar-Enash* is being born within mankind.

"*Amen, amen,* I say unto you, This generation shall not pass away until all these things be fulfilled."

After a moment, the Master sat again. All was silent, then *Cephas* spoke.

"Master, you have warned us about the destruction that will come to Jerusalem and the Temple many times. But this time you spoke in the *Kol Ha-Nabi*. We have avoided Jerusalem, but now I think you mean to return there for *Pesach*. Is that wise? You have many powerful enemies in Jerusalem who want to kill you."

Yeshua asked, "Who do people say I am?"

Yakob replied, "Many say that you are the Prophet *Yochanan* returned from the dead."

Yochanan said, "Some say that you are *Eliahu* come to prepare Israel for Messiah."

Cephas raised his finger for attention and said, "We know who you are, Master. You are the Anointed One, the *Mashiah Ben-Joseph*, who brings *Bar-Enash* to birth in this *'Olam.*"

"*Shimone Cephas*, flesh and blood have not revealed this to you," answered the Master, "but the *Bar-Enash* has come to birth in your heart."

"Master," blurted *Yochanan*, "we know that Messiah *Ben-Yosef* must suffer and die like all great prophets and *tzadikim*. But are you going to walk into the jaws of the lion? Surely they will kill you in Jerusalem. And us too!"

Then *Cephas* and all the *talmidim* began to beg the Master not to go into Jerusalem for the Passover week.

Suddenly *Yeshua* shot up, waved his arms in anger, and shouted, "Get behind me, *Shaitan!*" Then he turned his back and began to walk away.

"He means to do it!" cried *Cephas*. "Then I shall go and die with him," he said in a resolute voice and began to follow his Master down the hill. The others sprung into action and also followed.

"Master, I will follow you to the death," cried *Cephas*.

Then the Master stopped and turned to his disciples.

"None of you will die. Take care that you don't, because if the foundation is laid waste, the house cannot be built. And you, *Cephas*, must deny me twice before the cock crows three times."

The next morning they brought the caravan into Bethany and met the others at the home of Lazarus, Mary, and Martha. Even though there was great joy at seeing friends and associates, the mood was somber. The two *Miriams* and *Yochanan* sat apart whispering, and *Cephas* did not tell his entertaining boat stories.

"Master, *Shimone* the Potter has prepared a great feast in your honor at his home for this evening. He will be very disappointed if we don't all attend," announced Lazarus.

"Then we shall all attend," answered *Mar Yeshua*.

Not everyone was in attendance that evening, however. Conspicuously absent were *Miriam* of Magdala and *Miriam* of Bethany.

Shimone was known as the Potter not because he made pots, but because he bought and sold pottery and fine ointments manufactured by the Essene community on the Dead Sea. He had the expansive and gregarious personality of a successful merchant, but this evening his mood was reflective and subdued.

"Master, we had hoped that you might honor us by eating the *Pesach* with us here in Bethany," he commented.

Yeshua smiled and said, "I must be about the work of my *Abba*, *Shimone*."

Midway through the feast the two absent women disciples appeared at the gate wearing black mourning veils. Mary of Bethany carried a small alabaster jar filled with precious ointments used for anointing the dead. All eyes were upon them as they entered the open courtyard where the feast was being served.

A hush fell over the gathering while the Magdalene knelt at the Master's feet. Mary of Bethany stood behind the Master and opened the jar. It contained a small fortune's worth of the finest anointing oils that *Shimone* the Potter had procured for her. He had mixed them according to the recipe for anointing a king found in the Book of the Exodus: "Take thou also unto thee principal spices, of pure myrrh five hundred shekels, and of sweet cinnamon half so much, even two hundred and fifty shekels, and of sweet calamus two hundred and fifty shekels, and of cassia five hundred shekels, after the shekel of the sanctuary, and of oil olive an hin. And thou shalt make it an oil of holy ointment, an ointment compound after the art of the apothecary: it shall be an holy anointing oil."

Mary of Bethany slowly and solemnly poured the oils onto the Master's head while the Magdalene intoned Psalms of the Messiah. Then she began to weep and intone songs of the Suffering Servant, and then traditional songs of mourning. Then the Magdalene took some of the oil in her hands and applied it to *Yeshua's* palms and feet.

He sat erect all the while, eyes closed and holding very still.

When the women had finished, *Shimone* the Zealot, who cared much for the poor and often distributed food among them from the Master's caravan, said, "Master, these expensive oils should have been sold and the proceeds given to the poor."

But *Yeshua* opened his eyes and answered, "*Shimone,* you have the poor with you always, and whenever you wish you can do good things for them. But I am with you yet only a little while. These sisters have done what the Spirit of God has told them to do. Let this honor they have shown me never be forgotten."

That evening the Master told all the disciples what he wanted them to do. Instead of entering the City of David by stealth and losing themselves in the anonymity of the crowd, the Sons of Thunder would stand outside the northern and eastern gates announcing *Mar Yeshua's* arrival to entering pilgrims. Then they would make the same announcement to those in the market place, asking all who had received the *mikveh* to assemble by the Eastern Gate Sunday morning. It was here by the Temple wall that pilgrims from the main Northern and Eastern roads converged as they completed their journey.

Mar Yeshua would approach the Gate from the Mount of Olives that next morning at the head of a Messianic procession followed by crowds of disciples and pilgrims. It was also known as the Beautiful Gate, and the Golden Gate. He would be seated upon a large, strong donkey according to the tradition of the anointed Kings of Israel, and as prophesied in the well-known Messianic visions of Isaiah and Zechariah.

"This will be the final opportunity for the rulers of the Sanhedrin to accept the *Basor-Ha-Malkuth Ha-Shamayyim,*" he explained. "They rejected the Prophet *Yochanan,* and now they want to betray me and hand me over to the Herodians. If I enter into the City as an Anointed One surrounded by hundreds of disciples, they will not be able to arrest me. There will be much disputation, and they may even yet submit to the Way of Heaven. But we shall see whether the tree has fruit or only a show of leaves."

The next morning he sent Philip and Andrew to the house of *Shimone* the Potter to find a strong young donkey that had been trained, but never used, for burden. He maintained a large stable of pack animals.

"Tell him that *Mar Yeshua* has need of it," he said. "Then meet us at the Mount of Olives, where we will find *Yakob, Yochanan,* and a large assembly of those who have received *mikveh.*"

When Philip and Andrew approached the Mount of Olives with *Shimone's* donkey, they were overjoyed to see a huge assembly of disciples from far and wide already assembled, many with pack animals. Scores of them had brought palm fronds to strew the road before the Master as they approached Jerusalem.

Yeshua was leading them in call-and-response Messianic Psalms while they awaited the special animal that was to carry the Master. But when Philip and Andrew appeared on the road with the donkey, all singing stopped and the entire crowd broke out in cheers.

The animal was led up and introduced to *Mar Yeshua*. He spoke softly to it, stroked it, and then allowed himself to be lifted onto its back by *Cephas* and Andrew. Again, everyone cheered. Then *Cephas* stood alongside to lead and guide the donkey while Andrew brought *Miriam* of Magdala and her donkey immediately behind to start forming the procession.

As the parade of hundreds reached the top of the road and began the long descent to the Eastern Gate, they saw hundreds of other disciples standing on the road crossing the Kidron Valley. They could hear the booming voice of *Yakob* giving directions. The Sons of Thunder had done their work!

When the multitudes in the Valley saw *Yeshua* seated on the donkey, they raised a great shout of "Hosanna!" It was picked up by the crowds in the procession and soon became a powerful chant that resonated from the eastern walls of the great City as the crowds merged. Pilgrims lay down their garments upon the road before the Master and waved palm fronds.

The Romans greeted military victors, who paraded through main city gates on horseback surrounded by armies, by lining the streets and waving palm fronds. But the *Mashiah Ben-Yosef* was not a military conqueror. He entered meekly and gently into Jerusalem by the Gate called Beautiful. He rode upon a donkey and was surrounded by chanting and cheering disciples.

Other pilgrims and bystanders asked, "Who is this man?"

"He is the Prophet *Yeshua* of Nazareth," they were told. "He declares the *Basor-Ha-Malkuth Ha-Shamayyim* like the Prophet John, and he says that the *Malkuth* is appearing on Earth."

Many of the City's most powerful politicians, both Pharisees and Saduccees, rushed to witness the strange event. Fear gripped them that the Herodians would interpret this as a Jewish conspiracy to overthrow them in a lightning-like coup to regain total control of Jerusalem. Indeed, many in the enthusiastic crowds were now calling for *Yeshua* to be carried into the Temple and anointed as King.

Several angry *Ravs* approached the Master and demanded, "How can you allow your *talmidim* to endanger the City and blaspheme the Temple this way?"

He dismounted the donkey and raised his hands for silence. The chanting of the multitudes faded and everyone waited to see what would happen.

He called for his staff and untied a small whip attached to the halter of *Miriam's* pack animal. Without a word he strode up the steps leading to the outer court of the Temple. The disciples and most of the crowd followed him.

"Will he be anointed as King?" many wondered.

But when they reached the large courtyard filled with caged birds, cattle, and other sacrificial animals for sale as blood offerings for the Priests, they heard the Master roar in the *Kol Ha-Nabi*, "I have said my House shall be a House of Prayer! But you have turned it into a den of thieves!"

With that he began violently overturning the tables of money-changers the merchants, threatening any resisters with his powerful staff. There was pandemonium and fear, for *Yeshua* was a tall and powerful man whose rage echoed like thunder from the walls. When he had cleared the court of merchants and Priests, he broke open all the reed cages and released the doves. Then he took the small whip and drove cattle, sheep, and goats down the steps through the crowd, which parted in haste, and out of the Temple precincts.

Finally he stood menacingly at the head of the steps barring entrance to the few who dared try returning the animals to the court. Calling for his disciples to keep guard, he motioned for the multitude to enter the court and sit while he taught them.

One of the Pharisaic *talmidim* sat with the *Ravs*, who continued to look for legal grounds to have *Yeshua* arrested by the Herodians.

He called out, "Our masters have trained and been authorized to teach by the Great Ones. They hold the authority of tradition and lineage. By what authority do you say and do such things?"

Yeshua countered, "By what authority came the *mikveh* of *Yochanan?*"

If the Pharisees attributed divine authority to *Yochanan,* the Master could ask why they did not receive the Baptism of John. If they denied it, then they would anger the many Jews standing near who had made the *mikveh* of John and awaited the coming of Messiah.

Hearing no answer, the Master said, "Then I shall not tell you by what authority I declare and do these things."

The Master stood up and glared at the *Ravs.*

"Woe unto you, *Ravs* and self-righteous interpreters of *Torah*! For you shut up the the Gates of the *Malkuth Ha-Shamayim.* You yourselves do not enter yourselves, and you prevent anyone seeking to enter.

"Woe unto you, self-righteous ones! For you devour widows' houses with severe tithes. You make pretense of long prayer to be seen in public, repeating memorized praise from the mouth, and not from the heart.

"Woe unto you, self-exalting Pharisees! For you journey many days to make one proselyte, and when he is made, you make him twice more a son of *Shaitan* than yourselves.

"Woe unto you, self-satisfied ones! For you pay ritual tithes of mint and anise and cummin, but have omitted the weightier matters of *Torah*, which are justice, mercy, and faithfulness to God's Way.

"Woe unto you, pretenders to piety! You are like white-washed sepulchers that appear to be beautiful from the outside, but inside are rank with dead men's bones and all uncleanness. You create an appearance of righteousness to men, but within you are unrighteous and impure.

"Woe unto you, self-righteous pretenders! You build the tombs of the prophets and garnish the sepulchres of the righteous saying, 'If we had been in the days of our fathers, we would not have been partakers with them in the blood of the prophets.' But in truth, you are the sons of those who murdered the prophets. You more than fill your forefathers shoes!"

One of the *Ravs* stood up and shouted, "You unlettered Galilean! We have Abraham for our Father and the coming Son of David for our King!"

"Is it so?" *Yeshua* asked. "Then tell me why you *Torah* experts say that Messiah is *Ben-David?* For in the Psalm, David says, '*YAHWEH* said to my Lord, Sit at my right hand, that I may bring your enemies into subjection at your feet.' If he is David's Lord, and Scripture cannot be broken, then how can he be his son?

"You are the unlettered ones, for you know only the Scriptures that seem to uphold your narrow traditions and beliefs."

Then the Master declared, "This is the final hour. The rulers of the Temple and the Sanhedrin did not submit to the *mikveh* of John. It was their forefathers who killed the prophets and brought disaster upon Israel. If they do not now submit to the Word of God, this Temple will be destroyed, Jerusalem will be razed, and Israel will suffer more horribly than it ever has before.

"I say to you, Shepherds of Israel, the times spoken of by the Prophets have been fulfilled. The *Basor* of Messiah has been proclaimed by *Yochanan*. I now proclaim once again to you: The *Malkuth* of Heaven is coming upon us. Make your submission to God, and be faithful to the Renewed Covenant.

"Will you do this?"

Some of the Priests stood up and nodded. Seeing this, the *Ravs* stood. turned their backs to *Yeshua* in the clearest sign of disrespect, and walked down the steps.

The Master continued to teach in the court until late afternoon, when people began to leave for supper. Then taking his staff and one hand and the bridle of *Shimone's* donkey in the other, he led his disciples back to the Golden Gate and to Bethany by way of Bethphage, where there were fig trees.

As the entourage came near one large tree, he called for a halt. He closely examined the leaves and branches. There were many large leaves, but not even one tiny fig.

He stood before the tree and pointed his right hand, forefinger extended, and said, "From now on, if you will be unfruitful, let no one ever eat of your fruit again."

As they walked silently back to Bethany, *Cephas* was puzzled.

"Brother, you always seem to understand things," he said to *Yochanan*. "Why did the Master curse a fig tree? That seems a bit spiteful."

"Captain," the young man responded, "he was searching for an omen—a sign. He did not curse the tree. He said, 'If you will not be fruitful,' then the tree would be accursed.

"Remember when he said that this was the final chance for the rulers of the Temple to submit to God's Way? He also said something like this: 'We will see if the tree is fruitful or nothing but leaves.'"

"Yes, I remember," said *Cephas*.

"Well Brother, it appears that the tree will probably not be fruitful. We will know for sure tomorrow."

Cephas thought for a moment, then said, "You mean, if we return to Jerusalem for *Pesach,* the tree will tell us whether or not we are liable to be arrested by the Herodians?"

"Yes. But I am ready to die with the Master," *Yochanan* declared.

"I remember what he said about that," *Cephas* countered. "He said none of us would die, and we should all make every effort to survive, if it comes to that, because the future of the *Malkuth* depends upon us."

Yeshua looked at them both and said, "What does the flock do when the shepherd is killed?"

Yochanan answered in one word. "Scatter."

"Why?" asked the Master.

"Because they are afraid?" asked *Cephas*.

"If they are sheep, yes. But if they are men sent by God, they scatter and disappear into the crowd so that they can live to carry on the work," said *Yeshua*.

"Remember this. The *Basor* is far more important than perceptions of honor and heroism. Your death-times will come. But you must use the time you have been given by God and not squander it.

"Did I run to Herod when he killed *Yochanan* and beg him to kill me, too? No. The Prophet told me to stay away from that fox as long as possible for the sake of the *Basor*. If I had not followed his wish, there would have been no *mikveh* in all of the Galilee or in Samaria. The fruit of the tree would have withered on the vine.

"So I tell you, be innocent and blameless as doves, but also be wise as serpents."

After two days of rest in Bethany, *Yeshua* and the male disciples walked to Jerusalem on Tuesday by way of Bethphage. When they came to the fig tree that the Master had cursed, they found it dry and withered.

Mar Yeshua stood for a long time staring at the tree. He wiped a tear from one eye, took a breath, and continued walking—never looking back. All the men knew what this meant.

"Master, look," cried Philip. "The Eastern Gate is now guarded by Roman soldiers."

"They don't want any more Messiah's coming through," observed Andrew. "Remember, the prophets declared that Messiah would enter the City through the Eastern Gate.

"We will enter by the Southern Gate," said *Yeshua*.

The Southern Gate was also known as the Gate of *mikveh* because there was a large bath cut into the rocks by the foot of the steps that could be filled with living water for ritual cleansing. There was also a large spring in the Southern City near the Gate known as the Pool of Siloam. It was called this because Siloam means "sent," and it was said that when the waters of the pool were rippled by wind, an angel of healing was present for all who could bathe in the pool at that time. The Hebrew word for angel is *malach*, which means a messenger that is sent from God.

As the Master entered Jerusalem a man who had been blind from birth sat by the dusty road begging alms from travelers.

Andrew asked, "Master, why was this man born blind? Was it because of his own sins, or the sins of his parents?"

The ancient doctrine of genetic sin declared that God visited punishment as a curse upon all the descendents of a sinner up to the tenth generation. Therefore this man's blindness at birth would indicate that he was suffering as a result of sins committed by parents or ancestors.

But the Prophet Ezekiel had declared the ancient doctrine of genetic sin to be obsolete. *Yeshua* had declared, "You have heard it said of old times...but I say unto you." In the same spirit Ezekiel had declared, "The soul that sins, it shall bear the consequences. The son shall not bear the iniquity of the father, neither shall the father bear the iniquity of the son. The righteousness of the righteous shall be upon him, and the wickedness of the wicked shall be upon him."

The Saduccees held to the doctrine of genetic sin, but the Pharisees held to the teaching of Ezekiel. The Kabbalistic *Ravs* of the Pharisees upheld the doctrine of *gilgul* or reincarnation. To them, therefore, this man's blindness at birth would indicate that he had sinned in a former lifetime and was now reaping the consequences of *hub*.

The Master smiled.

"Andrew, have you become a Judaean *Rav* that you now try to snare me?"

Andrew blushed. "I wanted to know whether sin is carried by one soul or by a family of souls."

The Master said, "Every soul carries its own debt, but families and whole societies—even mankind itself—carry different kinds of debt collectively. We can doom our children to many generations of suffering by iniquities we commit.

"Tell me this, Andrew. What was the sin of Job?"

Andrew paused, then answered, "He had committed no sin. He was a *tzadik*."

"Did he then suffer because of the sins of his ancestors?"

"Well," responded Andrew, "that is what some sages told him. But that was not true, as God reveals in the end."

"In fact," continued the Master, "he suffered because *Shaitan* wanted to test him, and God allowed it."

"Maybe it is not so good to be a *tzadik?*" Andrew joked.

"It is very good, but not in the eyes of the Prince of this *'olam*," *Yeshua* answered.

"The man was born blind not because of his own sins, or because of the sins of his ancestors. No one has the wisdom to look into the deep mysteries of the past to say this or that caused him to be born blind. Rather, we can look to the future and say, This man was born blind so that the glory of God can be revealed in his healing.

"Do you understand? Don't try to uncover blame from the past. That is why I said, 'Cover the nakedness of your brothers and sisters, and do not eat their flesh.'

"Rather, seek the remedy, which has its root in the future. For the *Bar-Enash* is revealed out of the future. The *'Olam* of God has its root in the future—not in the past.

"Now behold this afflicted one sitting in dark misery and begging at our feet. Who is my neighbor that I am commanded to love even as myself?"

Andrew remembered the teaching about the Samaritan and replied, "Whomever the *Abba* brings unto my hand."

Mar Yeshua nodded approvingly and said, "God has brought this one unto my hand. Therefore I must do the works of the One who sent me."

He spat into the dust, mixed it into a wet clay poultice with his hands, and anointed the eyes of the blind man with it.

"What is this?" the man asked, putting his hand to the poultice, "and who are you?"

"I am *Yeshua* of Nazareth. Now we are leading you to the Pool of Siloam."

When they reached the pool, there was no breeze and no one sat waiting for a breeze because it was approaching midday. The Master blew his breath upon the waters and said, "An angel stirs the waters. Let us help you bathe. Have you received the *mikveh* of *Yochanan?*"

"Master, I do not know what that might be," the blind man replied.

"Do you submit to the Word of God and His coming justice, mercy, and Sovereignty on Earth?" asked Andrew.

"I do!" cried the man.

"Then submerge yourself in the water and rub away the poultice from your eyes."

The man submerged once, then came up without the poultice.

"I can see many lights, but I don't know what they are," he said.

He submerged again.

"Now I see men as trees with roots in the Heavens, and they are walking!" he cried.

He submerged a third time.

"I am beginning to receive my sight!" he cried.

Philip took him by the hand, led him back to his family, and returned to the pool. Then *Cephas* and *Lazarus* went to the marketplace to meet the two Marys, who had entered by the Golden Gate and bought food for everyone. Finally they met in the shade of the Temple wall to eat.

After eating, the Master led his entourage to Solomon's Porch. As they sat near the box where people made offerings of money, they saw many rich people making large contributions. Finally an old widow came to the box and deposited two tiny coins.

The Master pointed to her and told his disciples, *"Amen,* I tell you, that old woman has given a finer offering than any of the rich. Those coins were the only money she had."

Then he sent *Miriam* to give the old widow a small purse of many coins and invite her to join them to hear his Word.

As he taught, the old woman blurted out, "Blessed is the mother who bore such a son, and blessed are the breasts that gave you suckle!"

But the Master replied, "Rather, blessed are those who hear the Word of God and do it."

Meanwhile the blind man who had received his sight was joyously proclaiming what *Yeshua* had done for him. The man was known by all the inhabitants of Jerusalem to have been blind since he was born. The word of his healing spread like wildfire, and soon the story was being told among the *Pesach* pilgrims as well.

Crowds wandered through the Temple precincts seeking the Prophet *Yeshua* of Nazareth. The circle of hearers quickly expanded until a huge multitude was assembled.

The Master told them a parable.

"A wealthy ruler planted a vineyard, set a hedge around it, dug a wine cellar, built a tower, and left it in the care of stewards and vine-dressers. Then he traveled to a far country.

"After a year he sent one of his servants to them to receive the owner's share of the wine. But the stewards beat him and sent him away with nothing. So again he sent another servant, but they stoned him and sent home away terribly wounded. Again and again the ruler sent servants, and some they beat, and others they killed. Finally he sent them his son and heir thinking that they would reverence him.

"But those stewards said, 'This is the heir. Come, let us murder him and the inheritance shall be ours.' They took him prisoner, beat him, killed him, and threw his body out of the vineyard.

"What do you think the ruler of this vineyard will do? He will come in wrath to destroy the stewards and the vine-dressers, and he will give the vineyard over into the care of others.

"*Amen, amen,* I say unto you, the rulers of this city have beaten and killed the servants of God. Now they have rejected His Sovereignty and His Heir, the *Bar-Enash.* They will beat and kill the *Meshiah Ben-Yosef.*

"What, then, will be the fate of Jerusalem and the Temple of Herod? I tell you, it will come to pass in your lifetime. The destruction will be so great that not one stone of the Temple will be left upon another. Never before has the City of David suffered what is soon to come.

"When you see the abomination of desolation in the Holy of Holies, as prophesied by Daniel, then flee to the desert. For the Birth Pangs of Messiah will have begun, and *Shaitan* will rage on Earth like a roaring lion.

"But keep faithful to the Divine Sovereignty of Heaven, for the *Malkuth* will appear on Earth. Many of you here will not taste death until you see the *Malkuth Ha-Shamayim* appearing on Earth in power."

******* ******* ******* *******

Some of the head Priests and disciples of the chief *Ravs* witnessed the Master's teaching. He had spoken against Herod's Temple and prophesied its destruction. That could be trumped up into a charge of treason. So they began the process of filing charges and recording the testimony of witnesses so that the Herodians could take legal action.

"We cannot arrest him by day," argued Annas, the retired High Priest. "There is too much danger of city-wide rioting. It must be done at night. Then he must be executed before sunset on Friday, when the *Shabbat* of *Pesach* begins. Indeed, it is a high holy day, for it is both the *Pesach* Full Moon and *Shabbat.* If we wait until after Saturday, he may escape."

"There are two charges—sedition and blasphemy," said Caiaphas, who was a Saduccee and the appointed High Priest. "He must be taken before the Sanhedrin on a charge of blasphemy. I have to be very careful how I preside because many of the things he has said against the Pharisees are also said by Saduccees and Roman officials! It is best if we can get two witnesses to agree and stick with a basic charge—blasphemy."

"Yes, but the Romans won't execute him for blasphemy," responded Annas. "The most important charge is sedition. That is why my witnesses have carefully recorded his threats about the destruction of the Temple.

"All you have to do, Caiaphas, is get through the council meeting with any sort of charge of blasphemy that both parties can agree upon. He calls himself a *Bar-Enash.* He led a procession into Jerusalem playing the part of Messiah. He committed acts of violence in the outer court of the Temple. Put that together and you'll get a charge of blasphemy."

Caiaphas looked to his counselor, then said, "Some of that ought to support a charge of sedition, too."

"For that, all we need are the proven violence against the merchants in the Temple, and witnesses to testify that he has threatened to destroy the Temple," replied Annas.

"What he actually said was that God would destroy the Temple," Caiaphas reminded him.

"Nothing that a bag of silver and a few witnesses can't remedy," chuckled the old man. "Pilate has pressure from Herod's Palace to get rid of this phony prophet. All we need to provide is an excuse and a plan to avoid rioting.

"Now, remember what I advised on getting the blasphemy charge—rend your garment!"

"Yes," answered Caiaphas. "Sudden, unexpected dramatics. Our tradition permits the High Priest to rend his robe when confronted with blasphemy. I'll lead the questioning about this *Bar-Enash* thing and get something out of his own mouth we can use for a charge of blasphemy. I'll have my seamstress cut a little place where I can rip the robe in one dramatic move. Then I'll call for a vote."

"Yes, and then send him over to the Romans immediately. If we work fast, we can have him dead Friday afternoon," Annas said. "Here is the order. First I'll have him arrested quietly at night with a contingent of Temple and Roman soldiers. They will bring him to me for a preliminary hearing, which I will do before sunrise. Then I'll send him to you. That means you need to have the Council assembled exactly at sunrise, since our law requires courts to operate during daylight. You'll have to get everyone there before sunrise."

"I can do that," replied Caiaphas. "This man has made a lot of people angry—Saducess and Pharisees!"

"Good. Then you must get a charge of blasphemy quickly. Don't allow issues of contention to be debated like *qimah*. Just bring up your witnesses, let people question him, then you take control. I'll write you a few leading questions that will put him into a snare if he answers. Then pick your moment, stand up outraged, rend your garment, and call for a vote—no further discussion."

By Tuesday evening all charges had been formally filed with accounts of witnesses—both true and perjured. All the enemies of the Master among the rulers of the Sanhedrin had been prepared for the Council meeting that was to assemble before sunrise on Friday. Other neutral members would be awakened and told of the trial at sunrise on Friday in the knowledge that most would choose not to attend on such short notice.

Finally, spies were hired to track *Yeshua's* every move so that he could not escape arrest on Thursday night.

*******   *******   *******   *******

Late Tuesday afternoon *Mar Yeshua* returned to Bethany with all of his disciples. He spent Wednesday night in private retreat in the Garden of Gethsemane.

About midnight the *Pesach* moon flooded the landscape with pale light. It was not a time to make the Ascent, and yet he deeply yearned to experience the presence of his Beloved. He sat with eyes closed and head between his knees trying to find some kind of contact with Shoshana. Finally he dozed dreamless for about an hour, then awakened. He could sense the faint fragrance of lilies. Then he began to hear faint echoes of Shoshana's voice—not words, but melodious inflections. As he closed his eyes again all these sensations became more palpable.

Images randomly appeared and faded before his closed eyes. He realized that Shoshana was communicating something important.

Finally an image of the lioness he had subdued during the Ordeals of Daniel stabilized in his mind. He remembered how he had felt no fear. The lioness was eating straw, not flesh. For a moment the strange scene seemed familiar, but then another image appeared beneath the ground where the lioness lay—that of the furnace where he had undergone the Ordeal. He remembered how he had invoked the *Mashiah Ben-Yosef* and the angel Auriel.

Now a fierce wolf appeared next to the lioness, but it lay with a gentle lamb. He remembered Isaiah's vision of the *Malkuth*: "The wolf also shall dwell with the lamb, and the leopard shall lie down with the kid; and the calf and the young lion and the fatling together; and a little child shall lead them."

All images except the lamb were engulfed in an evil darkness that rose up out of the Earth. The lamb was being led led to slaughter. He remembered Isaiah's vision of the *Meshiah Ben-Yosef:* "He was oppressed, and he was afflicted, yet he opened not his mouth: he is brought as a lamb to the slaughter, and as a sheep before her shearers is dumb, so he openeth not his mouth."

Suddenly this faded into an image of Shoshana covered with blood where the physician had tried to save her life by aborting the unborn child. He saw her pale, lifeless corpse as he laid it into a grave in the Brotherhood cemetery. He saw her serene face—so peaceful in spite of the horrors she had experienced when she died.

Something that had always been left unresolved suddenly seemed to settle in him like a great capstone when it was finally laid upon a skillfully prepared foundation. He finally understood why Shoshana had suffered and died so horribly. The serenity in her face showed that she had overcome the worst that *Shaitan* could do to flesh. She had purified her *nephesh* in the fires of ultimate testing.

He knew that he, too, was ready to overcome the final tortures that *Shaitan* had devised for him. He would die with peace on his lips and serenity engraved on his face.

It would be from this place, he realized, surrounded by the beauty and fragrance of Gethsemane Garden, that the Lamb of God would be led away to slaughter.

Late on Wednesday afternoon a servant arrived at the house of *Shimone* the Potter seeking *Yeshua*. He said that *Miriam* of Nazareth had come to Jerusalem with *Shalome* and his brother *Yakob,* and they wanted to eat the Passover with him on Friday.

Yakob Ha-Tzadik was now highly revered by householder disciples of the Prophet *Yochanan* in the City of David, as well as by many of the Temple Priests. Instead of serving in the levitical courses at the Temple, he had worn his Priestly garb and kept daily vigil on his knees, as the Prophet *Yochanan* had commanded him to do. From this he had developed huge callouses that resembled the knees of a camel, for unlike others he prayed on his knees, and he was known as the saint with camel knees.

In the mornings he would pray aloud for the redemption of Israel and the appearance of the *Malkuth,* kneeling in the public areas of the Temple precincts. In the afternoons he often taught on Solomon's Porch, but did not accept disciples. He was the most famous Jewish saint in Jerusalem. Disciples and hearers of the martyred Prophet *Yochanan* provided him food and lodging. He returned to Nazareth several times a year to help support his mother.

Until now, *Yakob Ha-Tzadik* had never been in Jerusalem or in Nazareth when *Mar Yeshua* visited. He had heard much about his brother's work, but kept faithful to his own assignment. Moreover, although he had great fame in Jerusalem, it was not known that he was the brother of *Yeshua*—only that he was a Priest whom *Yochanan* had declared to be a *Tzadik,* and that he kept the flame of the Prophet burning in Jerusalem.

Even though guestrooms were rented at a premium and usually unavailable to most pilgrims on *Pesach*, *Yakob Ha-Tzadik* had been offered a room to celebrate *Pesach* on Friday. The family wanted *Yeshua* and his disciples to join them.

The Master sent the servant back with this message: "It is better that you keep your distance from me and my *talmidim* while in Jerusalem. Know that I love you all with my deepest heart."

Because there were not enough rental rooms for pilgrims to celebrate *Pesach* on Friday, many of them rented rooms and celebrated on Thursday evening. Therefore Thursday morning the Master sent Philip and Nathaniel into Jerusalem with *Miriam* of Magdala to find an upper room where they might celebrate the Messianic Banquet on the evening before *Pesach*.

"Go to the well," he told them. "There, among all the women, you will find a manservant carrying a water pitcher. Follow him to his master's house. Find the master and tell him that *Yeshua* of Nazareth wishes to rent his upper guestroom for an early *Pesach* with his close disciples this evening. *Miriam* will oversee all preparations for the *Seder*."

His disciples did not ask how he knew about the man carrying water. They had been with him constantly in Jerusalem. He had made no special arrangements with anyone about a room. They had grown quite used to the Master's psychic foreknowledge and trusted it implicitly.

Yet they were still amazed when everything he said came to pass that day in Jerusalem. Indeed, the master of the house was found to be a devoted disciple of the Prophet *Yochanan*. He had heard all about the Prophet *Yeshua* and offered the room as a donation. He insisted that *Miriam* use his best table furnishings for the *Seder*.

On Thursday evening the Master sat at the *Seder* table with all his male disciples. *Miriam* served. She was seated at his left hand, *Cephas* at his right.

He offered the first *Kiddush* Cup of Blessing.

"*Baruch Attah Adonai, Melech Ha-'Olam, borei p'ri ha-gafen.*

"Let us all drink of this Cup. For this is the Blood of the New Covenant. The fellowship and joy that we share is the Life of the *'Olam*."

He led them in singing Messianic Psalms and then asked *Miriam* to pour out the second Cup of Blessing.

"*Baruch Attah Adonai, Melech Ha-'Olam, borei p'ri ha-gafen.*

"My dear Brothers and Sister, I shall not again drink the fruit of the vine until I drink it with you anew at the Marriage Feast of *Mashiah*."

Miriam wept. The heart of *Cephas* broke. All the disciples knew what this meant. As they passed the Cup, there it was difficult for anyone to drink more than a sip. It returned to the Master nearly full.

Mar Yeshua signaled for the first course of the meal to begin. *Miriam* brought a loaf of bread, a plate of lamb, and another of gravy to the table, placing the loaf before him, then sat. He elevated the loaf and began the Blessing over bread.

"*Baruch Attah Adonai, Melech Ha-'Olam, ha-motzi lechem min ha-eretz.*

"Behold!" he cried. "This is the Body of *Mashiah*, which is your Body. Remember this whenever you break bread together."

He tore off a piece of bread, then passed the loaf to *Miriam*.

They ate in silence, dipping bread into the gravy, until finally *Cephas* cleared his throat and asked, "Master, tell us what will happen."

Everyone stopped eating to hear the answer.

"Tonight we shall walk to Gethsemane Garden in the moonlight. We will meet Alpheus, the son of *Shimone* the Potter, whom I have prepared to receive *mikveh*. He will come to us in a white linen robe and carrying living water in a small jar. Nathaniel and Philip, you will administer the *mikveh*."

This reassured everyone and soon they were talking and laughing. After a final course of sweets and more singing, the Master lifted up the final Cup of Blessing.

"*Baruch Attah Adonai, Melech Ha-'Olam, borei p'ri ha-gafen*

"The wolf will lie down with the lamb, for behold! I create new heavens and a new earth; and the former things shall not be remembered, nor come into mind."

After they had all drained the Cup, the Master stood and motioned for them to remain sitting. He stood behind each one and, placing his palms upon the crown of the head, he intoned *Ha-Shem*.

Cupping his hands around the crown, he ordained them each as a *Rav*. He breathed upon the crown of the head of each one and said, "Receive the *Ruach Ha-Qodesh*. I give you power to teach Divine Law, to bind and to release from Scripture. Whatever *mitzvoth* you declare binding, it will be upheld as binding in Heaven; and whatever *mitzvoth* you release, it will be released in Heaven."

Then he took a basin of water and a towel. Kneeling before each one of his astonished disciples, he removed their sandals and washed their feet.

"Are you amazed that I play the role of your servant?" he asked. "Remember this: Whoever would be great among you must be a servant of all," he said. "Service is the sign of true leadership."

The disciples all pleased the Master by helping *Miriam* clean and wash up after the feast.

When all was finished *Mar Yeshua* stood and said, "When the hour of *Shaitan* arrives, you must scatter like sheep. Hide and save your lives if you wish to remain faithful to the *Malkuth*. Do not let them kill you! After that, I will meet you in Galilee."

The disciples wondered how he would meet them in Galilee. Was he planning an escape from almost certain death in Jerusalem?

"*Miriam,* you must return to Bethany with Judas and Simon. Tomorrow I want you to visit my mother and sister in Jerusalem.

"Now my Brothers, let us go to Gethsemane Garden."

The Master *Yeshua* led them out of the Beautiful Gate into the Kidron Valley. The *Pesach* full moon shone brightly over the eastern hills. Where the path divided, he sent *Miriam* with the other two disciples on the road to Bethany, then continued with the rest of the men up the dusty road to the Garden. As the approached the gate, the young Alpheus stepped out of the shadows. He was wearing the white linen robe of a Levite and carrying a small pot of water. He hailed them.

"Master, no one else is here. The *mikveh* will not be interrupted."

Yeshua felt a slight twinge, a kind of contraction in his heart that always indicated the presence of an enemy. But as he entered the Garden he could see that it was empty.

He led the disciples to the place where he had kept *mishqad* on the previous night and motioned for them to sit. Taking both hands of the young Chalphai , who stood before him with the brilliant moonlight illuminating both of their snow-white garments, the Master smiled a beheld him silently for a moment.

"My son, you spent many evenings with us as a hearer, but you had no opportunity to receive baptism. I promised you *mikveh* before Passover, so it shall be done at this very hour. But as soon as you have made the *mikveh,* you must immediately return to Bethany."

Turning to Nathaniel and Philip, he said, "Take Alpheus to the far corner of the Garden and procede with final instructions and baptism."

To the other he said, "Sit in *mishqad* and attune yourselves to Heaven while I withdraw for prayer."

As the Master knelt before a large olive tree and prayed, *Cephas* was overcome with a feeling of dread. He opened his eyes. Then he turned and looked back at the City of David.

Reflections of bright moonlight glimmered from the rooftop and walls of Jerusalem. Suddenly he saw bright objects glittering and moving quickly through the Kidron Valley. Swords! Roman soldiers were running silently up the road in two ranks. Behind them were the guards of the High Priest. They were coming for the Master!

Cephas jumped to his feet and quietly alerted his companions.

"We have to get him out of here!' he whispered fiercely. "Who has weapons? Is there anywhere we can run?"

But already the troops were approaching Gethsemane Gate. Nathaniel and Philip had discovered the impending attack and were trying to send young Alpheus out into the hills.

Only *Mar Yeshua* remained unmoved in silent prayer.

The troops burst into the Garden with swords drawn and staves poised.

"Where is *Yeshua?*" demanded the captain of the Temple High Priest.

Cephas and Andrew, who were both large and strong, stepped up to the captain.

"Why have you come here?" demanded *Cephas.*

"We have orders to arrest *Yeshua* of Nazareth on charges of blasphemy and high treason," shot back the captain.

Yeshua stood up. All eyes were upon him. He walked calmly to the captain.

"These are false charges," he said.

The captain pointed his sword threateningly at the Master. Instantly Andrew struck it out of his hand with a blow that nearly broke his wrist. *Cephas* grabbed the sword and aimed a blow that would have split his head, but he ducked. Instead, a severed ear flew into the air while the sword ricocheted off of his shoulder armor.

Each of the other disciples had already picked their opponents and were ready to fight and die. But before anyone could make a move, *Mar Yeshua* gripped *Cephas'* arm and loudly shouted, "Hold!"

Looking sternly at his men, the Master said, "Those who live by the sword shall die by the sword."

"You have no warrant for these men," he declared. Then turning to his disciples he commanded, "Scatter!"

After a second of hesitation, the disciples began to walk to the Gate. Some of the guards tried to grab *Cephas* and Andrew, but they knocked them backwards and made their escape. Another tried to grab Alpheus because he was small and an easy target in the moonlit white robe. But the boy slipped out of his garment and ran naked back to Bethany.

The soldiers led the Master out of the Gate in chains.

He was brought before Annas, who held a hearing in the dark of night. The Master remained silent when questioned. The retired High Priest quickly made the finding that *Yeshua* should be tried for blasphemy. Before the sun rose, the Master was sent before Caiaphas. He was still in chains.

The High Priest had been successful in assembling only those members of the Sanhedrin who hated *Yeshua*. They were anxious to return home for the rituals of *Pesach*. Two witnesses described the Master's violence at the Temple, and two others testified that he had threatened its imminent destruction. The Master spoke only once.

He said, "You will see the *Bar-Enash* seated at the right hand of *YAHWEH* and coming in the *razim* of Heaven." The Court returned a nearly unanimous vote convicting him of blasphemy.

As the sun appeared over the eastern hills, he was taken in chains to the palace of Pontius Pilate, the Roman Procurator. He saw the *talmidim* standing near the gate as he was led in. He shook his head to remind them not to interfere, but *Cephas* followed the procession inside.

He was immediately stopped by the Roman guard.

"Are you one of his disciples?" the guard demanded.

Cephas stopped in his tracks. If he said yes, then he might be arrested as well. That was what the Master had expressly forbidden.

A cock crowed.

"I am not worthy to be his disciple," he answered and turned to leave.

The guard held up his hand.

"Not so fast."

The cock crowed a second time.

"Your accent is Galilean. You must at least be a friend of the traitor. Do you know this man?" the guard demanded.

"No one knows this man, and I do not know this man—no, not at all!" angrily declared *Cephas,* pushing his way past the guard and leaving by the gate.

The cock crowed for the third time. *Cephas* had spoken the truth both times, but he had also denied him twice, just as *Mar Yeshua* had prophecied. Thus he kept faith with his Master's command.

Pilate was in no hurry to try *Yeshua* for treason. He lingered over his breakfast while the prisoner sat in chains. Meanwhile the Roman guards reviled the Master.

Finally *Yeshua* was dragged before the Procurator and the same four witnesses who had testified against him. Caiaphas himself appeared and read a long statement convicting the Master of blasphemy.

Then he said, "This man is a Galilean revolutionary. He has known Zealots and Sicarii among his disciples. He entered the City and declared himself to be the Messiah of David and King of the Jews. He has roused up all the people of Galilee and Judea, and now he tries to build his strength in Jerusalem. You know what that means."

Pilate rose from his chair and addressed the Master.

"You fools think that a rag-tag guerilla band can defeat a Roman army because you have angels on your side. Well, we have the God of the Jews, the Temple, and all the gods of the Empire on our side. You are the ninth false Messiah we have crushed in the last few years. Tell your followers that no Jewish King will ever defeat Rome!"

He angrily signed the execution order and told the captain of his guards to publically beat and mock *Yeshua* as a warning to other would-be Messiahs.

"And when you crucify him," he added, "post a sign in all three languages that says 'This is the King of the Jews.' Then make a mock crown of a thorn bush and shove it over his head."

Caiaphas added, "And get him up on the Place of the Skull quickly. His body will have to be taken down well before the sun sets, or we could have a major riot on our hands. It is against Jewish Law for the dead to remain unburied on *Shabbat.*"

The soldiers followed their orders with brutal obedience.

Meanwhile *Yosef* of Arimathea had arrived at the City to share the *Pesach* with *Yeshua's* family that night. But *Miriam* of Magdala had been told of the arrest by young Alpheus, who burst into his home breathless and naked in the late night. He grabbed another robe, ran out again, and awakened everyone at the home of Lazarus with shouting and wailing.

The two Marys and Lazarus rushed into Jerusalem with Alpheus and his father just as the sun rose. They awakened *Yosef* of Arimathea and the family of *Yeshua,* then went to find the disciples.

They found them standing on the street behind the Procurator's Palace, where the Master was being condemned to death.

"He has strictly commanded that we are to scatter. The appearance of the *Malkuth* depends upon our survival," said *Cephas.*

"What can we do?" cried *Miriam* of Nazareth.

Yakob and *Miriam* of Magdala held her up as she nearly swooned.

"*Imma,* he has always known that the Herodians would finally kill him."

Andrew knelt next to Mary of Nazareth, holding and kissing her hand.

"He wants us to be strong for him," he said. "He has told us to continue proclaiming the *Basor* and baptizing. We shall survive, and we shall do this."

"It is important that we scatter into small groups to avoid arrest," declared *Cephas.* "I was stopped by a Roman soldier looking for Galileans. Everyone, move away from here and stay in pairs. Don't speak to anyone.

"The Master will be led away on that road to Golgotha hill where he will be crucified. None of the men should approach—only the women. Otherwise they will know we are disciples."

Yosef of Arimathea raised his hand.

"If we don't take possession of his body, they will throw it to the birds and fires of *Gehenna* Valley. I have influence among the rulers of the Sanhedrin. I will get legal permission to have the body placed in a tomb that I have had hewn by local Masons for myself. I will warn the authorities that if they allow the Romans to desecrate the Master's body, all Jerusalem will rise up against them."

Cephas nodded his agreement and replied, "Get a document from the Romans that will allow the women to take possession of his body when it is brought down from the stake. Otherwise they will not be able to prevail against the soldiers."

Yosef left to make the arrangements, and everyone drifted apart.

Soon the gate of the Palace opened and a small contingent of Roman soldiers appeared. Stumbling behind them in chains was *Mar Yeshua*. He was bloodied, bruised, and nearly naked. His white robe was ripped and filthy. One of the soldiers carried a sign that said, "King of the Jews." Other carried tools and cross-piece for crucifixion. But the Master was forced to labor under the weight of the huge stake that would be used to lift him up.

The powerful man had been beaten nearly to death. He staggered under the weight of the stake, which was the size of a tree. The women wailed and closed their eyes. The disciples, now anonymous in the huge crowd that was being drawn to the scene, stood in prayer.

Two other criminals who had committed murder followed *Yeshua,* but they had not been beaten. The soldiers with them carried their stakes while the men walked in leg chains.

Normally executions of criminals brought large numbers of death-watchers who threw garbage and heaped scorn on the victims as they passed. But the few who tried to do this to the Master were quickly elbowed out of the way by a growing crowd who had awakened to hear that the Romans were executing the Prophet from Nazareth.

Because his wounds were so severe, *Yeshua* moved slowly and painfully. In exasperation one of the soldiers grabbed a husky man who was watching and forced him to carry the stake. Now the procession moved more quickly.

The crowd, including the family of *Yeshua,* followed closely as the procession entered the execution grounds. The disciples followed from a distance except for *Yakob,* the brother of the Master, who was so well-known in Jerusalem that he was in no danger of being arrested.

When the soldiers pounded nails into the wrists and feet of the two criminals, they screamed and yelled in pain. But when they nailed the Master to the cross, his face was passive and serene.

As he nailed the mocking sign to the top of the stake, one of the soldiers said, "This man is not like the others. Perhaps he really is a Jewish king."

"Then let us crown him King of the Jews!" roared a crude, burly solder, and he crushed a thorn bush onto the Master's head. Blood from the many small wounds on his scalp dripped down his forehead as they set the stake into its deep hole and raised him up to slowly suffocate.

When all three men had been crucified, the main contingent of troops returned to the palace, leaving only a few men to stand guard. Then the disciples were able to draw nearer.

With eyes still closed from the ordeal, the Master prayed aloud, "*Abba*, forgive them, for they know not what they do."

The Master opened his eyes. Seeing the youngest of his disciples, *Yochanan,* he called to *Miriam* of Magdala.

"Woman, behold your son. Son, behold your mother. Take care of my *Yochanan* and instruct him in the *razim*," he said haltingly in a weak and failing voice.

The mother of the Sons of Zebedee had died long ago, and their father did not have long to live. *Yeshua* foresaw that the older brother *Yakob* would soon be slain by the Herodians. He foresaw that *Yochanan,* like *Cephas,* would be one of his greatest *MeBasrim.*

As time passed and breath became harder to draw, he twisted and turned.

Then he tried to intone the Psalm of *Messiah Ben-Yosef.*

"*Eli, Eli, lama sabachthani.*" But his breath failed him.

Sometime later he took his last breath and said, "*Abba,* into Thy hands I commend my *neshama.*" Then he stopped moving and breathing.

The other two criminals had not died. They were still moaning and fighting death.

One of the soldiers said, "Let's get this done. Break their legs so they can't stand against the nails and keep breathing." The other soldier took a heavy club and bashed the lower limbs of both criminals. They each cried loudly, and in a few minutes were dead.

"You don't need to do the King because he's already dead. But let's be certain."

He pointed to the soldier who carried a spear.

"Longinus, push your spear between his ribs into his heart. If he is dead, we'll see water leaking out. If he isn't dead, he'll be dead after that!"

Longinus did as ordered, but he needed help. The big, burly soldier pushed with him. Suddenly a fountain of water spurted out of the Master's heart along with a thick flow of blood.

Miriam and *Yochanan,* who were now sitting very close to the cross, recoiled in horror. They scrambled back out of the way as the soldiers roughly jerked the vertical crucifixion stakes from their holes and laid the corpses flat.

Miriam ran to the soldier in charge and showed him the legal document that released *Yeshua's* body to her. He nodded and commanded one of his men to retrieve the iron nails piercing the Master's feet and hands.

Then Mary of Bethany helped *Miriam* and the mother of *Yeshua* lift his body to an upright position. *Yosef* of Arimathea rushed up with a clean shroud and headband to hold the mouth shut. *Yochanan* and the Master's brother *Yakob* came forward with a litter.

"There isn't time to properly wash the corpse for burial," sighed *Yosef.* "Let us get him to the tomb and see what we can do there. Try not to lose one drop of blood."

Miriam gently removed the thorn bush. The blood had dried on *Yeshua's* head and forehead. She replaced it with flower petals.

They spread the linen shroud on the litter and carefully laid the Master's corpse there on his back. *Miriam* tied the headband to keep the mouth closed, and they folded the other half of the shroud down over his head until his enture body was covered. Then the ends of the shroud were tied below his feet.

The two men hoisted the litter and, with the women following, began to make their way toward the cliff of tombs. It was late in the day and the sun was just a few fingers above the western hills. When they got to the tomb, it was nearly sunset, that is, the new day of *Shabbat*. Many of the other disciples had gathered there.

They lay the enshrouded corpse upon a stone shelf that had been hewn for the dead. The women had placed flowers that they found blooming on the way into and on top of the shroud. They had no proper burial ointments.

"On Sunday morning after *Shabbat,* you can come and properly prepare the corpse," said *Yosef.*

As the sun set, they rolled the large sealing stone into the opening of the tomb. It was so heavy that it required eight men to move into place. The tomb was secure.

That night *Miriam Magdala* was sick with grief, but she gathered as many of the disciples as she could find for the *Pesach* meal. *Cephas, Yosef,* Andrew, Philip, Nathaniel, and the Sons of Thunder joined Lazarus, the brother and sister of *Yeshua, Miriam* of Magdala. the other women disciples, *Shimone* and his son Alpheus, *Yeshua's* Uncle *Chalphai* and his young son *Shimone,* and their Jerusalem host for the traditional *Seder.* But most of the other *talmidim* had already departed in great sorrow for their homes in Galilee elsewhere.

Chalphai was Master of the *Seder.* He was the brother of *Yeshua's* father *Yosef.* Like *Yeshua* and *Yakob,* he carried not only Davidic and Levitical lineage, but that of Aaron. His young son *Shimone,* who was on pilgrimage to Jerusalem with his family in celebration of his *Bar Mitzvah,* was also an heir of Jewish royal Priesthood.

When the main course was brought, he raised his hand for attention and spoke with great solemnity.

"The blood of a *tzadik* atones for the sins of many. But the blood of the greatest of *tzadikim* atones for the sins of all Israel. What then of the blood of *Mashiah Ben-Yosef?* Surely you all know that our beloved Master *Yeshua* is the long-awaited *Mashiah.*

"Then as a Priest—indeed as one whose lineage qualifies me to serve as High Priest—I tell you this. The blood of *Mar Yeshua* attunes Heaven and Earth. He is the Lamb of God.

"Was he not sacrificed at the time of ritual sacrifice for this meat we have before us, and for all the lambs of *Pesach?*"

The young *Yochanan* raised his finger.

"And did he not walk straight into the jaws of the Beast? Did he not fearlessly confront *Shaitan* with full knowledge of the consequences? Then I say, he is not only the sacrifice that reconciles Heaven and Earth, but he is the one who offers that sacrifice—the true High Priest of God."

Miriam Magdala began to weep as she recognized the spiritual brilliance of the young disciple.

"Son, I am your mother now. I have many *razim* to teach you. But I can see also that you have many things to teach me."

Chapter Twenty-Eight: *QIMAH*

Utter and absolute darkness. No light. No water. No breeze of air. Deep…deep…dark…dark…having no limits or boundaries.

"*Abba,* where is this deserted place?" he asked in his heart.

Within himself he felt life, and that life became a light that shone in the darkness.

"Here, thou shalt live with thy heart at peace," answered the Voice of God. "It is here that I have placed the powers of *Manda* instead of water, cool breezes, and the pleasures of love; and the peace and rebirth of the soul instead of bread and beer."

He became aware of a lifeless corpse lying enshrouded in the abyss far below.

"And what will be the span of my life?"

Suddenly he realized that the corpse was his own flesh.

"Thou shalt live for millions and myriads of years," was the reply.

His light grew brilliant. He descended into the abyss, then into the corpse, which he tried to enter and wear like a garment. But it was cold and slippery. There was no way to put it on or contain it.

"My son, *Shaitan* shall not have your flesh or your bones to desecrate. I have raised you up. You are the first-born of the *Bar-Enash.* I shall build you and all who keep *emunah* into my Temple, which is the One Body of the New Sovereign Adam. You shall be Head of the Body and Cornerstone of the Temple. My *Ruach Ha-Qodesh* shall dwell in that Temple with you and all who keep *emunah.* You shall guide all those in flesh who seek the Birth from Above, and you shall purify them in the *mikveh* of spiritual fire."

"*Abba,* what is the *mikveh* of spiritual fire?"

His light became intense and blinding. The corpse began to glow and radiate. Like the burning bush of Moses, it made no heat, but it illuminated the tomb so that it seemed to be a furnace.

Suddenly the corpse flared and was consumed in a baptism of spiritual fire. It became pure light and disappeared from the physical world, leaving nothing but scorches etched into the shroud, which lay empty on the stone ledge where the corpse had been.

"My son, that is the *mikveh* your soul has desired."

"*Abba,* how shall I guide my *talmidim?*"

"You are not yet ascended, my son. You shall make yourself known to them in your *nephesh* through the power of *manda* and teach them during the forty days before your final *Aliyah.* You shall also walk among them unseen and unknown, as do my angels. You shall appear to them as a stranger, to be recognized only by those whose love of the *Malkuth* gives them eyes to see and ears to hear. Those who keep *emunah* will see and hear you. After that you must submit to the Second Death and make the Ascent. Then you will guide them in dreams and visions of pure Light. But only those who have purified their hearts will be able to receive and interpret them."

Mar Yeshua could make his *nephesh* dense and solid like physical matter, or weightless and invisible, because he could form his body by *manda* alone. He found that he could restrict his *nephesh* body to touching and moving physical matter, just as if he were in flesh, or expand it so that he disappeared from the eyes of flesh and passed through matter like a ghost. *Manda* is the cause of all physical form, but it is prior to physical manifestation. Thus the Master dwelt in a pure *nephesh ha-manda* during the forty days before dissolving his *nephesh* in the Second Death and making the final *Aliyah*.

He densified his *nephesh* and examined the shroud in his own light. There were bloodstains from his ordeal and scorch-marks showing not only his exterior corpse, but even interior bones. In Jewish *haggadah*, only Enoch, Moses, and Elijah had been assumed bodily into the Heavens leaving behind no trace of flesh or bone. *Yeshua* realized that now his *Abba* had given the same sign of bodily assumption for his death.

"I shall leave this winding cloth and head cloth for my *talmidim* so that they will have evidence of my *qimah*," he thought. "And I shall leave them neatly folded where my corpse disappeared into the fire of spirit."

He folded the cloths and laid them on the stone. Then dissolving the density of his *nephesh* body, he passed invisibly through the rock into the night outside.

"My family must be keeping *Pesach*," he thought. "I shall go to them without revealing myself."

Immediately he was standing next to the table where his mother Mary of Nazareth, *Miriam Magdala, Shalome, Yakob,* and many of his friends and disciples reclined. He smiled upon his dear Uncle *Chalphai*, who was known as Cleopas in his home village of Emmaus. He was *Yeshua's* eldest *talmid*.

An aura of thick blackness emanated from the assembly. Everyone was in deep mourning, yet trying to keep the *Pesach*. He read the heart of *Cephas* and found the captain repeating a phrase he had once used—"smile through tears…grow into a spiritual giant." Oh, yes. He had used those phrases when he taught him about the saint who healed herself by touching the hem of his garment.

Of all the disciples present, only the Magdalene seemed to sense something. Her moist eyes darted back and forth, then closed again.

The Master reached out and touched *Chalphai's* heart. Immediately the old man raised his hand and began to speak.

"The blood of a *tzadik* atones for the sins of many. But the blood of the greatest of *tzadikim* atones for the sins of all Israel. What then of the blood of *Mashiah Ben-Yosef*? Surely you all know that our beloved Master *Yeshua* is the long-awaited *Mashiah*."

"And so are all of you," the Master thought. "You, too, will pour out your souls even unto death, and you too will divide a portion with the Great Ones."

He decided to reveal himself first to *Miriam* when she would come Sunday morning with the other women to anoint his corpse.

Now he looked farther down into the black abyss. He saw *Sheol,* with its myriad lost human souls sleeping in their vile uncleanness and impurity.

Here was the *Gehenna* of the Old Adam, the *Tartaros* of the Greeks, the *Avitchi* of the Buddhists. The *nepheshim* of its inhabitants had dissolved at the Second Death, but their souls still lay unreconciled to Heaven and the Life of the *'Olam.* Their ignorance bound all incarnate human souls to the lower regions in unconscious service to *Shaitan,* condemning the Old Humanity to repeat the sins of the past in an unrelenting *gilgul* of rebirth and inability to achieve *qimah*. For the sake of the New Humanity, these ghosts must be purified, layed, and released into the light.

Suddenly he became aware of the fragrance of lilies. He sensed Shoshana's presence, then heard her voice ringing like a bell.

"It violates the traditions of men for you to heal on *Shabbat*," she playfully remarked. His heart lept with joy and he laughed.

His heart answered, "So let us violate the traditions of men, my Beloved!"

For the first time since her physical death he was able to take her hand. They were not One, for he had not yet ascended, but they were in palpable contact once again. He kissed her lips—not with passion, but with profound love. They were enveloped in brilliant golden light.

Then hand-in-hand, merged in the power of *Yechid* and *Yechidah*, they descended into the blackness of *Sheol* and walked among all those who slept—myriads and myriads. Their perfection and life-force shone like the light of a thousand suns. All of *Sheol* was ablaze with the golden spiritual fire of divine love that does not burn, but purifies, heals, and gives boundless joy.

Before the sun rose on Sunday morning, they ascended from the abyss. Like Orpheus redeeming Euridice from *Hades*, they were followed by the myriads that comprised the Old Humanity, now corporately reunited in the ancient eggregore of Adam and Eve. They led them into the Third Heaven of the *Pardes*.

When all had been accomplished, the Master again kissed his beloved one, then released her hand and watched her re-ascend. But now, unlike before, he felt her continual presence.

As the sun rose, he stood next to the great limestone plug that had been rolled by eight men to temporarily seal his tomb. The women planned to arrive early to anoint and re-wrap his corpse, for they had not been able to finish the work before *Shabbat* sunset. Then the great stone would be shaped by a stone mason, rolled, and fit into its permanent seal. That, at least, was their plan. But the Master had a different plan. He would unseal the tomb and reveal the sacred mystery of his *qimah*.

Densifiying his *nephesh,* he put his shoulder to the stone. He was able summon unlimited physical force. Thus the stone rolled easily to expose the entrance to the tomb.

In a little while *Miriam Magdala*, Mary mother of *Yeshua,* and *Shalome* met *Cephas* and the disciples at the foot of the road to the cliff of tombs. The women were dressed in black mourning robes and veils. Jewish tradition forbade the men from preparing bodies of the dead, and the Roman authorities were still looking for the Master's disciples. The men planned to stand at the bottom of the road while the women attended to the corpse.

"Who can roll the stone away and back again for us?" asked *Shalome*. "It took eight of you men to move it."

Cephas pointed to the garden surrounding the tombs and said, "Go and see if you can find a place to squeeze through between the stone and the cliff. If not, see if there are guards or gardeners who can help. If there are none, come back and we will have to risk discovery by moving the stone for you. But even so, Heaven may protect us."

The women approached the tomb, then gasped in shock. The stone had been rolled away and the entrance opened. When they warily looked inside, the tomb was empty.

The women ran back to the other disciples and cried, "They have stolen the Master's body out of the tomb and we don't know where they have taken him!"

Cephas grabbed *Yochanan* and ran to the tomb, leaving the others behind for safety. They found the tomb open with shroud and headcloth lying neatly folded and lying separately on the ledge where the disciples had placed the Master's corpse.

"Annas and Caiaphas must have had the body taken so it could be publically desecrated in *Gehenna*!" cried *Cephas*. "We must move quickly!"

The men passed the women as they ran back and said, "We must find the Master's corpse before it is desecrated!"

The weeping women re-entered the tomb. Flowers they had hastily placed in the winding cloth were scattered on the floor. *Miriam* picked up the shroud and headcloth. She placed them tenderly into a basket with the flowers and spices she had brought.

"Come back with us, *Miriam*. There is nothing more we can do," sobbed *Shalome*.

"I wish to remain here for a while," she answered in deep resignation. "You go on. I'll be back soon."

Mary of Nazareth and her daughter began the long walk to their host's home in Jerusalem.

As *Miriam* stood in prayer before the empty tomb with closed eyes, she became aware of a light. She opened her eyes. The tomb was no longer dark. It was as though a bright lamp were burning.

She stepped down into the tomb. The ledge where the Master's body had been placed was softly illuminated, but she could not see the source of the light. Then through her tears she made out the figures of two men, one at the head and one at the foot of the place where the Master's corpse had been laid.

Echoing in her head she heard a voice asking, "Dear woman, why do you weep?"

She spoke aloud and replied, "Because they have taken away our Master and we do not know where they have laid him."

Then she heard the rustling of sandals in the garden behind her. She turned and saw a man standing outside in the morning sunlight. He repeated what the others had asked, but this time audibly.

"Dear woman, why do you weep? Whom do you seek?"

She thought he might be the gardener. Stepping up out of the tomb, she took a deep breath and said, "Sir if you have removed our Master's body, tell me where you have laid him so that we can retrieve it. I am a wealthy widow and will pay you whatever you want."

The man smiled and called her by name.

"*Miriam!*"

Immediately she recognized the Master's voice.

"*Rabonni!*" she cried in great joy. She ran to him, but he held up his hand.

"Do not touch me, for I have not yet made the *Aliyah*. But go to our Brothers and Sisters. Tell them that I shall ascend to my *Abba* and your *Abba*, and to my God and your God. Remind them what I said: I shall go before you into Galilee."

Just as suddenly as he had appeared, the Master dissolved back into the invisible *Malkuth* that is spread out upon the Earth, but men do not see.

Miriam picked up the basket and ran in a joyous frenzy to find the others and tell them what she had seen and heard.

The most learned in Scripture of the *talmidim* who sat with many of the men that night at supper was *Yosef* of Arimathea. The doors were bolted because everyone was in hiding from the spies and guards of the High Priest.

"*Miriam* has told us that the Master's corpse has not been stolen, but that God has raised him up from death. I have found some places in Scripture that may indicate the *Mashiah* will be raised from death and bodily assumed into Heaven like Enoch and *Eliahu*. These hints seem to refer to the *Mashiah Ben-Yosef,* because it is he that is murdered by evil men, and thus he whom God would raise up from the dead.

"Here is one place in a Psalm of David: 'My life is safe. You will not abandon me to *Sheol*; you will not allow your faithful disciple to see *Shakkat*.'

"If the Master is the first-fruit of the tree of *Bar-Enash,* then a Kabbalistic understanding of the first-fruit command in Leviticus tells us that the sacrifice is to be waved or shown to YAHWEH on the day after *Shabbat*. That would be a Sunday morning, when *Miriam* was shown the risen Master.

"In this way we can find hints and types about the *qimah* of Messiah. But it is not prophesied plainly anywhere. None of us had any expectation of such a thing..."

Before he had finished speaking, everyone became aware of another person standing behind them in the locked room. All eyes turned upon the tall stanger. He strode to the head of the table and said, "*Shalom* be with you."

Instantly they recognized the Master's voice.

He showed them his pierced wrists and feet. Then he pulled his robe aside to reveal the deep wound between ribs piercing his heart.

As they watched spellbound, he dissolved back into the *Malkuth*.

Yakob, the brother of *Yeshua,* had not been present because he was with his mother and the women disciples that night. When he was told of this appearance, he swore, "I shall not eat bread until the Master shows himself to me!"

On the next day while *Yakob* was in prayer, he heard the Master's voice. Then he saw him standing in the shadow of the doorway.

"Bring a table and bread, my Brother," he smiled, stepping into the room. *Yakob's* astonishment quickly subsided into joy.

"Yes, my Brother!" he answered, then ran to another room to get table and bread. He was afraid that the appearance was just an illusion, and that *Yeshua* would disappear before he returned. But when he returned breathless carrying bread and table, the Master still stood smiling.

Then the Risen *Yeshua* took the bread, recited the *Berakah*, broke it, and gave it to *Yakob* saying, "My Brother, eat your bread. For this *Bar-Enash* has been raised by the *Abba* from among those who sleep, and you will join me in the *Malkuth* after false priests murder you not many years hence."

That same day as Chalphai was walking back to Emmaus with his young son *Shimone,* a stranger joined them. *Chalphai* had not been with the male disciples when the Master appeared because he, like *Yakob,* had been staying with the mother of *Yeshua* and the other women.

The stranger asked why they wore mourning garments.

"Have you not heard how the High Priest and Sanhedrin conspired with the Herodians to arrest and crucify *Yeshua* of Nazareth in Jerusalem last week?" replied the old man. "He was the greatest Master of Israel, the *Mashiah Ben-Yosef* sent by God to redeem Israel. Some women in their grief imagine that they have seen him risen from the dead, but all I know is that my dear nephew has been brutally beaten, crucified, and now his body stolen and desecrated."

But the stranger smiled and said, "You know that *Mashiah Ben-Yosef* must suffer and be killed by evil men. But what does prophecy say concerning his death? Have you read and understood the hints?"

Chalphai asked, "Are you a Brother? And are you a *Rav,* that you know Scripture so well?"

Then the stranger began to explain the many *razim* hidden in the prophets that pointed not only to the *qimah* of the *tzadikim,* but the special *qimah* and *Aliyah* of Messiah.

When they reached Emmaus, the stranger intended to go on. "There are many whom I have promised to meet in Galilee," he said. But they prevailed upon him to have supper with them at their home, and he agreed.

As he sat at meat with them, he took the loaf of bread and offered the Blessing. Then he broke it and gave it to them. Immediately their eyes were opened and they recognized the Risen Master. Then he vanished back into the *razim* of the invisible *Malkuth.*

After that the Risen Master appeared to numerous of his *talmidim* in the Galilee. During the coming weeks he revealed himself to well over five hundred Brothers and Sisters. After forty days he was no longer seen in his *nephesh* body, for he had ascended in the final *Aliyah*. But great souls who had purified their hearts, like the Master *Saul,* were blessed with true dreams and visions.

By then, however, the Messianic movement was scattered and spread far and wide. It could not be crushed by the Herodians.

******* ******* ******* *******

Mar Yeshua lives. He is a master and guide of all who seek him. He is a perfected soul and first-born of the New Humanity, which is the true Gate of Heaven to which all paths lead.

A PARAPHRASE OF *YESHUA'S BASOR* OR ETERNAL GOSPEL

The Old Mankind and the world of adolescent ignorance, injustice, and selfish exploitation that humanity created are coming to an end. A New Humanity is being brought to birth within the heart and soul of all people. We are coming of age as divine heirs and co-workers with Godhead to take responsibility for creation and stewardship—not only of ourselves and this Earth, but of the universe and all beings.

Submit your souls to the guidance of Heaven, dedicate your lives to the service of God and humanity, and keep faith with God's New and Sovereign Humanity.

The King James Version (for Comparison)

The time is fulfilled, and the Kingdom of God is at hand: repent ye, and believe the gospel.

THE PRAYER OF *YESHUA*

Translated and Paraphrased for Meaning

Lewis Keizer, M.Div., Ph.D.

Our eternal *Abba*,

Father-Mother of all,

Who art within and beyond our understanding;

May thy Way be hallowed in every heart,

And thine interior guidance be known in every soul,

And may thy spiritual sovereignty become fully realized,

In us and on Earth, as it is in the heavens,

> As above, so below;
>
> as within, so without;
>
> as in spirit, so in flesh.

Grant us this day our bread of the morrow;

And release us from the consequences of our sins, and of all sin,

As we forgive those who sin against us;

And do not abandon us unto our tests,

But deliver us from all evil, within and without.

For thine is the eternal sovereignty,

And the power, and the glory, always and ever.

Amen, Amen, Amen

AUTHOR'S COMMENTS

The spiritual influence of a Jewish prophet named *Yeshua* has endured for over two thousand years. Is it because Christianity, which bases its spiritual authority upon the claim that Jesus was its founder, has faithfully transmitted his teaching and spiritual power?

No!

By the time the Christian gospels were composed, the early churches were dominated by Greek-speaking gentiles who had only third-hand knowledge of the teachings and practices of *Yeshua*. They relied upon the earliest Christian writings—the Epistles of Paul. He had never met or studied with *Yeshua*. What little he knew of the Galilean Aramaic oral tradition transmitted by Apostles and disciples *Yeshua,* he combined with Judeans concepts from his rabbinical studies with the Pharisaic master Gamaliel to create what he called "my Gospel." Thus, rather than faithfully transmitting the teachings of *Mar Yeshua,* Greek-speaking gentile Christianity would transmit the theological doctrines of Paul.

Then in one of the great ironies of history, the later Christian Gospels spun *Yeshua's* prophetic indictment of the wealthy Jerusalem Temple Establishment into anti-semitic tirades against all Jews, who had supposedly rejected their own Messiah. Conflicts between Jewish and Pauline gentile churches came to a head after the siege of Jerusalem and destruction of the Temple after A.D. 70, when anti-semitism became politically shrewd. By A.D. 85, the Gospels of Matthew and Luke were produced to spin the orally-transmitted teachings of *Yeshua* into Pauline theology. Paul's revelation about the universalism and inclusiveness of *Yeshua's Basor* for all people was subverted to support the following exclusion: *Except Jews.* Later the exclusion would extend to pagans, heretics, Moslems, and all who refused to be baptized.

Gentile Christianity syncretized Pauline theology with Greek religious concepts from the worship of Isian, Mithraic, and other mysteries. This established the basis for an ascetic and devotional Christianity that would emerge in Western Catholicism and Eastern Orthodoxy. The context of Jewish mysticism necessary for a deep understanding of the teachings of *Yeshua* was lost. The *halakah* and spiritual practices he transmitted to his Apostles were misunderstood or kept secret. Sunday Christian Sabbath replaced Saturday Jewish *Shabbat.* Christians claimed themselves to be the True Israel and Jews to be unworthy heirs excluded from the divine covenant.

Faith (*emunah,* "perseverance, fidelity, faithfullness" to God's Way) was defined as credal belief, especially in the doctrine of the all-male Trinity of Father, Son, and Holy Ghost. Convoluted theological arguments were made for worshipping these three deities as faces of the One God.

How could monotheism devolve into tritheism? First, Jesus as Pauline and later Johannine Heavenly Redeemer was understood as the the genetic offspring of a Father God through miraculous birth. He had re-ascended to the Divine Throne from whence he had originated and where he now rules with God. So Christians had to recognize two *prosopoi* or "faces" of Godhead.

Beyond this, *Yeshua* strongly emphasized reverence for the Holy Spirit of Jewish wisdom tradition. The *Ruach Ha-Qodesh*, a Hebrew and Aramaic feminine in the language of Jesus—not a masculine—was a Kabbalistic representation of the Motherhood of God, who was understood as both a transcendant Father (as for example on *Yom Kippur)* and immanent Mother (as guide of the Jewish sages). It was She Who delivered prophetic messages to the community through the earliest Christian revelators.

But the *Ruach Ha-Qodesh* was given a hysterectomy to become the neuter *Pneuma Hagion* (Holy Spirit) in Greek New Tstament Christianity. In the ensuing centuries she got a wholesale sex-change operation to become the Latin masculine *Spiritus Sanctus,* as in Jerome's Vulgate translation. With this, the femininity and Motherhood of Godhead disappeared from Christianity to be replaced by a sterile patriarchal, and eventually ascetic, hierarchy.

If the Lord Jesus reverenced the *Spiritus Sanctus*, reasoned the gentile Christians, then the Holy Spirit had to be recognized as yet a third face of God the Father. These "faces" of Godhead could not be reconciled as they had been in mystic Judaism, which recognized the allegorical kabbalistic fatherhood and motherhood of the one *Abba* worshipped by the Jewish sages.

Along with this process of Godhead becoming the Three Guys, women were squeezed out of their original positions of authority in the early churches. By the fourth century *Miriam Magdala*, first among the women Apostles and possibly greatest among all Apostles, had been marginalized along with all other female Christian authority, and her identity conflated with an anonymous prostitute of gospel legend. Thus by the fourth century, Mary Magdalene had been demoted to the status of repentant whore.

My novel provides an antidote to this antifeministic poison and presents what seems likely about the Mary Magdalene of history—that she was a great saint, perhaps the closest disciple of Jesus, and about the age of his mother.

Preserved in the Pauline Epistles, Acts of the Apostles, and many other early Christian writings is the fact that *Yeshua* trained many female disciples. Some of them were highly respected and became itinerant Apostles like *Junio*. Fully a third of the earliest church leaders named by Paul are women—probably because church gatherings were often done private homes overseen by women until the first church building was designed in the fourth century.

Evidence from several sources indicates that *Yeshua* initiated his most talented disciples into the "Mysteries of the Sovereignty of the Heavens," the *Razim* that revealed the *Malkuth* or Invisible Sovereign Presence of God. This seems to have been an all-night, white-robed vigil on a mountain top done one-to-one with the Master himself like the highest teachings of *Merkabah* ascent that, according to Talmudic traditions, could be transmitted only on a one-to-one basis.

That modality is suggested by the *Secret Gospel of Mark* as described in a fragment of a letter from Clement of Alexandria, and by the content of the *Gospel of Mary (Magdalene)* which exists in Greek and Coptic fragments. The so-called Transfiguration event with three of the Master's closest disciples, known to us through Petrine tradition, was probably a lesser form of these *Razim*.

The ascent described in the *Gospel of Mary (Magdalene)* is modeled somewhat upon Jewish *Merkabah* ascent, but the Jewish Enochian structure is modified. The ten Heavens are amplified to include the three lower levels known to the chthonic mysteries of the Pythagorean *pholarchoi* plus a fourth that includes the seven planetary spheres of the Hermetic microcosm-macrocosm, apparently leading to an Ogdoad of ascended saints and an Ennead where the Mansion Hallways *(Hekhalot)* and Throne of God *(Merkabah)* were rooted. The cleansing ascent through the seven planetary *daimonia* like those of Trismegistos were probably misunderstood and used to marginalize *Miriam* of

Magdala as a sinner from whom "seven demons" were exorcized by *Yeshua*. This seems to have been part of the marginalization of women disciples that occurred in the earliest post-Apostolic period.

But to the contrary, much ancient Christian literature claims Mary to have been the favorite and "beloved" disciple of Jesus—too wide and varied in their sources to ignore. In some literature Mary Magdalene seems to have been jealously opposed by Peter *(Shimone)*. Could that have been because she was more spiritually talented and highly initiated than Peter, James, and John, who had experienced only the "Mount of Transfiguration" and were not favored by first contact with the Risen Jesus—as was Mary? Or was it because the churches claiming Apostolic lineage from Peter competed for primacy with those established in Asia Minor by Mary Magdalene and John?

There is no way to be certain, but in my novel the great Apostle *Shimone,* called *Cephas* (Greek *Petros* "Rock" or Peter) by *Yeshua,* is not portrayed as jealous or negative toward *Miriam Magdala.*

Peter, James, and John were recognized as three the greatest of the male Apostles. Peter was probably the oldest disciple other than Mary Magdalene and John the youngest. It was Peter, not Paul, who first initiated the adaptation of *Yeshua's* Messianic Judaism (Christianity) to include gentiles. The anti-Marionism of the later Petrine gentile churches (those who traced their Apostolic lineage to Peter) had nothing to do with the historical Apostle *Shimone Cephas* (Simon Peter).

The disciple John *(Yochanan)* was the younger brother of James. Both were the sons of *Zebedee. Yeshua* called them the Sons of Thunder because of their powerful proclamation of the *Basor. Boanerges* was probably the initiatic name he gave them. They and Peter were chosen by *Yeshua* to experience what Christianity understands as the Transfiguration, but was probably a lesser form of *Merkabah* Ascent.

This was the same John who accompanied Mary Magdalene to establish the Johannine churches in Asia Minor, and who was purposely conflated with "the disciple whom Jesus loved" (Mary) by the editors of the Fourth Gospel. Why? Because women were not allowed to teach in Jewish synagogues and late first-century gentile churches. The founder of their Apostolic lineage had to be portrayed as a male disciple. The Catholic scholar Raymond Brown theorizes that the feminine "she, her" references of the Forth Gospel were altered to "he, him" when the Johannine stories of the beloved disciple were finally written at the end of the century. He has tried to demonstrate that the "beloved disciple" of the Fourth Gospel was originally Mary—not John. The evidence has been expanded by twenty-first century women biblical scholars. This conclusion is based on sound evidence that is well worth studying.

Mary Magdalene's Apostolic lineage may have survived for a while in the Johannine churches of Asia Minor. A story from the Gospel of John, which was edited and compiled in Asia Minor, tells us that *Miriam Magdala* was given charge of the young disciple *Yochanan* and asked from the cross by *Yeshua* to assume the role of his mother. As opposed to the eleventh-century Golden Legend that tells of Mary Magdalene fleeing to Gaul, it is far more likely that she travelled with the Apostle John to Asia Minor, as recounted in the earliest Eastern Orthodox Christian hagiographies, where she died of old age before any of the other Apostles were martyred in the Neronian persecution of A.D. 64. That establishes her age as about the same as that of Mary of Nazareth, the Mother of Jesus. The tomb where the Mother of Jesus made her dormition (died) is still venerated in Orthodox religion, although it may in fact have been originally the death place of the Magdalene, who was a venerated Apostle long before theological legends of the Mother of God *(Theotokos)* and the liturgical veneration of the Virgin Mary developed. In any case, *Miriam Magdala* was probably John's mentor after the execution of *Yeshua* and a major source of Johannine theology.

According to a twentieth-century fabrication by Pierre Plantard, a French Nazi collaborator and occultist, the Merovingian dynasty of early medieval Europe was based on the bloodline of the alleged love-child of Jesus and Mary Magdalene. The Merovingians themselves never made such a claim. Their bloodline was supposed to have originated from the native Gallican gods, not from Jesus and Mary.

Plantard concocted a plan to succeed DeGaul as President of France. He would convince people that he was the descendant of Jesus Christ. Plantard inserted into various European private royal libraries information to provide evidence that he was a descendent of the bloodline of Jesus which he planned to reveal at the right time—which never came. Meanwhile he had leaked some of the forged information to a few journalists who took the bait. Michael Baigent, Richard Leigh, and Henry Lincoln, who were not scholars, produced a book entitled *Holy Blood, Holy Grail* which popularized the idea that Jesus and Mary Magdalene were lovers or spouses and produced a child whose bloodline was kept secret. This was supposedly at the root of the Holy Grail legends of medieval Europe. The love life of Jesus and Mary Magdalene became a twenty-first century urban legend spawning many other lucrative books by journalist and non-scholars, such as *The DaVinci Code*.

Why were people so receptive? Because Christianity deleted the Divine Feminine early on to be dominated by an ascetic male hierarchy whose marching order seems to be "if it feels good, it's bad; but if it feels bad, it's good." My fictional biography introduces readers to the original *Abba* Father-Mother Godhead of *Yeshua* and gives him a wife and soul-mate. Not Mary Magdalene, who was old enough to be his mother, but a remarkable woman of great spiritual talent who provides the Kabbalistically necessary *Yechidah* to his *Yechid*. I chose the Jewish name Shoshana.

It always seems to be the disciples of great spiritual teachers like *Miriam Magdala* and *Shimone* Peter who fight for status, not the masters themselves. The original Apostles were collegial, not hierarchical, although deference was always given to elders. Claims that Peter, or Mary, or John, or Thomas were the favorite of *Yeshua* are found only in the later literature of their Apostolic lineages. For example, the newly discovered *Gospel of Judas* portrays him as the favored and greatest disciple. The *Gospel of Thomas* represents Thomas as the greatest. The Gospel of John presents John as the greatest. The synoptic gospels (Mark, Matthew, Luke) claim Peter as the greatest.

Incidently, the portrayal of Judas as the betrayer of *Yeshua* is not found in the earliest Christian sources—the Pauline Epistles, the Q Source, and the *logia* preserved in the Aramaic core of the *Gospel of Thomas*. Paul makes one reference to "the night in which he was handed over for arrest," but no reference to Judas or to "betrayal," as Paul's description is incorrectly translated. It is in the anti-semitic Marcan Passion Narrative that the Judas legend first appears about A.D. 60.

Significantly, many details of the Passion Narrative (whether Marcan or pre-Marcan) are not derived from historical witness, but inserted to embellish the story to make it conform to Old Testament passages that were commonly accepted as Messianic prophecy. For example, the Roman soldiers casting lots to win *Yeshua's* garment is "in fulfillment" of Psalm 22.18 "they divide my garments among them, and for my raiment they cast lots." Bishop Spong's argument, which I accept, is that the Judas legend is an anti-semitic embellishment based on intertestamental stories about the betrayal and martyrdom of Jewish saints.

The name Judas means Jew. Let's see now, who was it that betrayed Jesus and is now an accursed race? Oh yes, the Jews! So where do you suppose the story of Jesus' betrayal by Judas ("Jew") crept into the legends that were written down in Mark and transferred into Matthew and Luke? (But significantly, not in John's Gospel, which disses Thomas instead because of Johannine competition against docetic doctrines attributed to the Syrian Thomasian gnostics.) The Judas betrayal legend originates in the conflict between gentile Christian churches and Messianic Jewish synagogues who followed *Yeshua* but refused to admit gentiles—the so-called Judaizers of the Book of Acts. The anti-semitic spin of the gentile New Testament takes the Petrine-Pauline inclusion of gentiles to a new level.

The legend of betrayal by Judas seems to have been introduced by Markan souces not deriving from Peter. It became a lynchpin of New Testament gospel anti-semitism. The New Testament gentile gospels have spun a nasty web of anti-semitic interpretation throughout their presentation of the parables of Jesus—parables that were originally directed against the small but powerful Judean ruling class and Temple Establishment in Jerusalem.

The recently discovered *Gospel of Judas* seems to be third-century Gnostic document based on Judas legends originating in Messianic Jewish Christianity to correct the anti-semitism of the three gospels of the gentile-corrupted Markan-Petrine traditions.

You will not find Judas represented as a betrayer in my novel because there is too much to indicate that his alleged betrayal was not historical. The Herodians and Jerusalem Establishment had been looking for an opportunity to kill *Yeshua* for a long time. They didn't need Judas. All they needed was a public act of blasphemy from *Yeshua*, which he supplied in shocking fashion during the Passover week by violently driving the money-changers out of the Temple. He knew exactly what he was doing and the consequences.

Yeshua probably named no successor, unless it were his brother *Yakob*, i.e. James the Just (as claimed in a fragment from the *Gospel of the Egyptians*), but simply said that Divine Spirit would strengthen and exhort his Apostles. John's Gospel designates this aspect of the "Holy Spirit" as the *Parakletos*, a Greek term for a function of the *Ruach-Ha-Qodesh* that was used in Aramaic for a legal counselor *p'raqlet*. The Roman successors of the Apostle Peter (Bishops) met in Synod to be guided as a group by the inspiration of the Holy Spirit. Whatever they agreed upon was considered to be inspired by the Spirit of God.

For nineteen centuries this remained the practice. Then in the mid-1800's the doctrine of Papal Infallibility was developed. The new Catholic dogma declared that only one Bishop transmits what is inspired by the Spirit of God—the Pope of Rome speaking from his throne. Opposition to that dogma resulted in events leading to the end of Roman monopoly over Apostolic Succession. Validly consecrated Bishops independent of Rome began a new era of *episcopi vagantes* founding the Old Catholic, Liberal Catholic, and the whole panoply of Apostolic lineages no longer subject to Rome. (See my free online book entitled *The Wandering Bishops: Apostles of a New Spirituality*, available at www.hometemple.org).

You should know that when the Apostles announced their decision to admit gentiles into the Church at their first Council of Jerusalem, thus opening the door to the development of gentile Christianity, they said "it seems good to us." The Greek root was *doxein*, which means "it appears to us." In later synods of Bishops, who were successors of the

Apostles, *doxein* became the Latin term *dogma*, which now means "totally infallible and correct doctrine." But Church doctrine never was infallible. Just ask Galileo or Darwin.

Male trinitarian theology, by the way, was the basis for the condemnation of the great saint and Bishop Arius. He adhered to the original adoptionaist views of Messianic Judaism (and probably the Gospel of Mark) that *Yeshua* was not a god, but a righteous man who achieved perfection and became what the Greeks called a *Theios Aner* or "divine human" like Apollonius of Tyana. He was therefore a pattern or template for all spiritually striving humanity, regardless of religion or culture—not a god like Zeus or Odin. This was probably based on *Yeshua's* Messianic and Kabbalistic teachings about becoming a *Bar-Enash,* as portrayed in my novel.

However, the trinitarian enemies of Arius, specifically Athanasius, spearheaded a movement to have him condemned at the first ecumenical councils along with other saints like Origen.

It was Arius' disciple Bishop Ulfilas and his followers who wandered far into Europe where they were regarded as spiritually powerful saints and healers. They established ecumenical relationships with Druid Priests that resulted in a syncretized native Celtic Christianity based on the so-called Arian heresy, which had a great deal more in common with the views of Jesus and the Jewish mystics than with the gentile Trinitarians. For that reason, Celtic Christianity was zealously suppressed by Rome and Bishop Alcuin in ninth and tenth centuries, when Catholic military power finally ruled Europe through the armies of Charlemagne.

But let us return to my original question. Why has *Yeshua's* influence persisted over two millennia? It certainly is not because Christianity faithfully transmitted his teachings. It did not. The historical teachings of *Yeshua* have become like brilliant gemstones wrenched from a royal diadem only to be shattered, dulled, and scattered among thieves.

Rather, I would maintain that his influence persists because he was, and is, a Master of masters. Our souls resonate to the Divine Way, which he brilliantly taught and exemplified, and which he engraved into the soul of humanity by his sacrificial life, death, and after-death manifestations not unlike those of Buddhas in *nirmanakaya* bodies. He lives and guides all who seek him as the first-born of a New Humanity, regardless of how church doctrines might have him.

Today scholars know more about him, his teachings, and his world than did the ancient writers of Christian scripture. This arcane academic knowledge is inaccessible to all but a few lay persons.

However, while we can never know much about the *Yeshua* of history, scholars have amassed a wealth of information that allows them to reconstruct the *historical influences, teachings and practices* of *Mar Yeshua*, the Master Jesus. Today we can begin to grasp the context and background of Jewish Messianic, Kabbalistic, and *Merkabah* mysticism out of which he taught. We can glimpse the influences apparent in his personal spiritual development. More important, we can begin to apply this understanding to our own spiritual growth.

The *Basor* or Gospel taught by the Master *Yeshua* was not a misguided apocalyptic expectation of sudden supernatural intervention to rectify a world ruled by evil. Rather, it was—and is—a timeless path of discipleship and spiritual growth that leads to the eventual manifestation of a new, spiritualized humanity and a sanctified Earth. Moreover, it can be experienced here and now by those who take this path.

His historical teaching of the appearance of the *Malkuth* of Heaven had more in common with the realized eschatology of John's Gospel than it did with the immediate apocalyptic expectation of the synoptic gospels and many of the early gentile churches addressed by the letters of Paul and interpreted by modern fundamentalists as the coming Rapture.

An end-of-the-world craze swept the Hellenistic world on both sides of the first century, and is preserved in non-Jewish sources like the *Dream of Scipio* and among the astrological papyri. Astrologers had no way to understand precession of the equinoxes, so they saw the world rolling off its zodiacal moorings. The *Aeon* of Aries was coming to an end, the *Aeon* of Pisces starting to emerge, and Great Pan was dead. Eschatological expectation was as common a modality of apocalyptic speculation among Greek, Romans, and Jews then as global warming is today. Everyone expected the end of the world.

And indeed, we mark the end of the ancient world with the incorrectly computed birth of Jesus the Christ, and the beginning of the medieval world. Daniel's Beasts of the ancient world seem as far removed from us as childhood nightmares, returning to haunt us only when civilizations regress into warfare and terrorism.

One of the reasons that gentile Christianity spread so rapidly was that it brought hope and humanism into the ancient barbarism. For example. it was the custom of the Romans to keep male children when they were born, but to expose females—leaving them to die on garbage heaps. This Roman form of abortion was, in fact, gross infanticide. The early Christians rescued these unwanted females babies and raised them as Christians, to give birth to even more Christians. The early theme of Christian redemption developed in this context, and so did the exponential growth of Christian devotees.

Today infanticide is properly regarded as homicide. But Christian ideologues have tried to represent legal first-term medical abortion as a modern form of infanticide which, unfortunate as it might be, is not at all the same thing. Many religious fundamentalists tacitly support psychotics spawned by anti-abortion rhetoric who murder abortion clinic doctors in the name of Jesus. They forget that nature itself generates numerous spontaneous abortions (acts of God?) for its own wise reasons.

They are quick to legislate against medical abortion, but what do they do about the misery of all the unwanted and neglected children born in our world because birth control and abortion services have been denied? Do they pick these children up and take them home, as the first Christians did? Or do they strain at the gnats of the Pharisees, pointing the finger of guilt at others while congratulating themselves on their supposed righteousness? I consider modern Christian fundamentalism to epitomize the Pharisaic attitudes so vigorously challenged by *Mar Yeshua*.

What I have written in my novel is historical fiction. But it is designed to transport a reader into the same world of Jewish Messianic and Kabbalistic mysticism that informed the historical teachings of the Master *Yeshua*—a world that was comprehensible to his original hearers and disciples, but that was lost to gentile Christianity.

I'd like to point out a few places where my fictional biography of Jesus differs from traditional accounts. According to my biography:

1. Jesus was the first of several children of *Miriam* and *Yosef*, conceived and born in the normal human way. Other scholars reason that some of the brothers and sisters of Jesus were from an earlier first marriage of *Yosef*. Specifically, they consider James to have been an older brother of Jesus, or simply the member of a secret Brotherhood with Jesus—anything to keep Mary a childless virgin! However, what little is implied in

literature and tradition about the early years of *Yeshua* makes him his father's apprentice—the role of the well-beloved first-born (Greek *monogenes*, wrongly translated from its Aramaic antecedent as "only-begotten"). Thus in my story, *Yeshua* is the first-born child.

2. *Yosef* was not a "carpenter." The Greek word in the gospels is *tekton*, which means a skilled craftsman—in this case, a stone mason who might occasionally work in wood. But in his Galilean location there were few trees, little wood, and much stone. *Yosef's* genealogy in Matthew's gospel traces his lineage from Zerubbabel, the builder of the Second Temple after the Babylonian Captivity. He was the founder of Jewish freemasonry, trained in Babylon by the masters of the Persian trade—i.e., the stone masons. As the first son, *Yeshua* would have followed his father's footsteps and been initiated through the conventional three Guild degrees into his father's Jewish Masonic brotherhood. The Hellenistic Guilds and Roman *collegia* were more than professional unions. They were spiritual associations with their own religious traditions and life-cycle ceremonies. *Yeshua's* earliest spiritual education would have come through father, mother, and a brotherhood Guild of Jewish stone masons.

3. The lineages of *Yosef* and *Miriam* transmitted ancient Jewish rights for Levitical and Priestly function. *Yakob* or James, the brother of Jesus who later was revered as the dynastic successor of *Yeshua* and unquestioned head of the Jerusalem disciples, exercised the function of the Temple High Priest in the Holy of Holies on the Day of Atonement in place of the politically appointed High Priest by popular fiat. He seems to at first have followed a spiritual path that was separate from, but complementary to, that of his brother *Yeshua*. In my novel he is a deeply respected ascetic *tzadik* trained by the Prophet *Yochanan* (John the Baptist). Both brothers could lawfully claim exercise of Jewish Priesthood. *Yeshua* wore the "seamless garment" of white linen required for Temple Priests.

4. *Yeshua's* first exposure to the excesses of Temple Judaism and class discrimination in Jerusalem would have come during a family Passover pilgrimage in conjunction with his *Bar Mitzva*, probably remembered in Luke's story of the precocious Jesus debating the Judean Rabbis.

5. *Yeshua's* first exposure to the Hellenistic world, its religious sects, and other religions would have occurred in the sophisticated culture of Sepphoris, the City of Herod not far from Nazareth, where he and his father would have worked as stone masons.

6. Galilean Judaism was characterized by (a.) the prophetic mysticism of charismatic healers, Rabbis, and hermits, (b.) the influence of dissident Jewish anti-Temple sects, (c.) home and synagogue worship, (d.) dynamic use of the Divine Name YHWH—as opposed to Judaean prohibitions against use of *Ha-Shem*, and (e.) Jewish saints like Honi the Drawer of Circles and Hanina, both Galilean miracle workers who were noted for using *Yeshua's* word for Godhead—*Abba*. Strong family ties existed between Jewish families in Babylon and their Galilean relatives, who were connected by trade routes through Damascus. These, considered in the light of *Yeshua's* Son-of-Man orientation to Messianic mysticism, suggest an historical connection with the Babylonian School of the Prophet Daniel.

7. *Yeshua* left the Galilee and lived elsewhere for many years (the "lost years"), as indicated by gospel accounts of his disastrous return home many years later. In our biography *Yeshua* travels to Babylon then in later years travels farther East, with a return by sea trade-route to Egypt, and finally home.

8. The unique sympathy and understanding for women that characterizes so much of the teachings of *Yeshua*, taken with the fact that he was the only *Rav* of his era that accepted female disciples (one exception: a Galilean Rabbi who secretly taught his daughter), clearly indicates he was not an ascetic hermit with no experience of women. I postulate that he loved, married, and lost his wife before becoming a wandering master and prophet, and that he had no children from this union. I further postulate a powerful psychic connection between *Yeshua* and the soul of his extraordinary wife that significantly enabled his ministry and ended any desire to remarry and become a householder.

9. So much of the language and so many of the sayings of *Yeshua* can be found centuries earlier in the intertestamental scripture (*Testaments of the Twelve Patriarchs, Wisdom of Jesus Ben-Sirach,* etc.) that it is clear he was deeply familiar with Hasidic wisdom and prophetic traditions native to the sophisticated Jewish community of Babylon, not Judea. He is also steeped in the apocalyptic teachings of the Messianic school of Daniel in Babylon. Although Babylon had lost influence to the new ruling city of Seleucia, there was a thriving Jewish community that had chosen to remain there since the days of the Captivity. They wrote the books of the Old Testament and the prophetic scripture used by *Yeshua* and the earliest disciples—Deutero- and Trito-Isaiah, Jeremiah, Ezekiel, Daniel, Enoch, and recorded the earliest Rabbinic traditions. The Babylonian Talmud formed much of the basis for the later Palestinian Talmud. I place *Yeshua* in Babylon for many of his lost years in the context of a Rabbinic school, synagogue, and the Babylonian Jewish wisdom school I call the Brotherhood of Daniel.

10. According to a saying remembered in the Gospels, *Yeshua* considered John the Baptist to be a reincarnation of Elijah, prophet of the Messiah. The Gospels try to distance Jesus from John the Baptist in many ways and to minimize the impact of John's prophetic ministry. Why? Because in his day John was considered to be a Messiah (and still is by the Mandaeans), thus was the greatest competitor of Jesus for the title of martyred *Messiah Ben-Yosef*. But the association of Jesus and John had been too close to deny, so John appears in the Gospels as the "forerunner" of Jesus. I postulate that the connection was far more profound than what the Gospels try to show. Instead of a dip into the River Jordan and immediately being driven into the Judean wilderness, I propose that Jesus developed a close association with the Prophet *Yochanan* upon his return to Palestine. After an intense discipleship, *Yeshua* returned to Nazareth to preach the *Basor* of the *Malkuth* according to his own experience and understanding. When John was beheaded by Herod, *Yeshua* became a target for Herodians, since many viewed *Yeshua* as the successor to John. He was forced to move from safe-house to safe-house in the Galilee to keep one step ahead of possible arrest. During this period his public mission developed from exorcism to healing and teaching. He was no longer identified as a disciple of the Baptist, and his unique Messianic teachings brought forth new core practices and *halakoth* for a Messianic discipleship that included both men and women. One of these was his Messianic interpretation of the *Shabbat Seder* that would eventually emerge as the Eucharist in gentile Christianity.

11. I have organized the public ministry of *Yeshua* into periods of time generally following the Marcan order found in the Synoptic Gospels. But the pericopes and stories in the synoptic narrations are laced together often without geographical sense and logical historical order. Even the context in which they are presented often differs in each (i.e. Sermon on the Mount in Matthew is Sermon on the Plain in Luke). So I have laced together my narrative in order and contexts showing how I think his ministry and teachings must have developed. For example, I put him among the Gadarenes as part of

a land journey rather than a boat journey, as Mark does. It could have been either. I think that the initial rejection at Nazareth was a catalyst that moved him to create his unique method of prophetic ministry, in which he actually called, picked, and invited disciples as he travelled, rather than the accepted practice of staying in one place and waiting for them to come to him. At first his emphasis was upon the *Basor* of the coming Messianic Age and ending of the rule of evil on Earth. His demonstration of the end of *Shaitan's* rule was by means of public exorcisms and healings—which in Jewish thought were two sides of the same coin and viewed as signs of God's presence on Earth. As he gathered more disciples and attracted huge crowds, he began to invite the women who served and hosted him in their homes to sit with the male disciples for extended teachings during and after the Messianic feasts and *Shabbat* meals over which he presided. Many of them began also to travel with his entourage, and they were accorded the status of disciples—something that no other master of Israel allowed. Soon he had developed an inner core of male and female advanced disciples who left their homes for extended periods and travelled with him. At this point he gave not only public preaching, but inner-circle teachings concerning the *Razim,* Secrets, or Mysteries of the *Malkuth*. Most of these were not recorded in the public Gospels that later appeared in the gentile churches, but probably made up much of the *Secret Gospel of Mark.* These inner teachings of *halakah* and the *Malkuth* seem to be the basis for many of the Gnosticized but very early *logia* preserved in the *Gospel of Thomas.* There is evidence that he transmitted not only teachings but forms of spiritual initiation to advanced disciples into these *Razim* (the Transfiguration, young man in white linen in *Secret Gospel,* Johannine Lazarus cycle appearing in several forms and sources, the Johannine Apostolic exsufflation, the Hermetic-like initiation of the *Gospel of Mary [Magdelene]*). My reconstruction of his ministry shows this order of evolution, as well as grouping the various parable and allegory themes into scenes of likely teaching contexts. In this way the reader can better grasp many of the concepts of his teaching—the absence and return of God, the *Messiah-Ben-Joseph,* the primacy of fidelity (faith), effective prayer, and so forth.

12. *Yeshua* used not only prophetic *davrim* and kabbalistic *mashlim,* incorrectly labeled as Greek logia and parables (which have quite different cultural functions), in his teaching, but often taught by asking questions with an implied answer in the rabbinic style, and also used extreme hyperbole. Undoubtedly some of this hyperbole can be attributed to the ways in which his *davrim* were transmitted and to the spin added by later writers to make them into Greek *logia*. But hyperbole was *Yeshua's* very semitic way of making a point. I have tried to paraphrase his hyperbole to promote understanding. For example, the New Testament gospels have him say, "Unless you hate your father and your mother, you cannot be my disciple." In the *Gospel of Thomas,* which preserves *logia* from the first-generation, pre-gospel time of the Q Source, this is presented as, "Unless you hate your father and your mother in my way, you cannot be my disciple; and unless you love your father and your mother in my way, you will not be able to become my disciple," adding the explanation, "for my mother bore me, but my true Mother gave me the Life." I think the *Thomas* version is more historical (without the added explanation, which has Gnostic and ascetic implications). When we put the saying back into its original context of Jewish wisdom tradition, we discover a truer way of presenting it, which I have done in Chapter Twenty-Four. The same holds true for other hyperbole. Incidently, biblical literalism bites the dust when it comes to dominical statements like, "You must hate your father and your mother!" The Master used extreme hyperbolic examples in all of his teaching, i.e. Pharisaic straining at gnats and swallowing a camel to keep ritual *kosher*. Camel meat was considered to be far more unclean than insects, so

Yeshua was criticizing them for making ritual *kosher* more important than love and mercy. He was not accusing them of eating camel-bone broth, as some literalists have ignorantly claimed. If you want to maintain biblical literalism translating the hyperbole of *Yeshua*, be prepared to hate your parents and all the rest!

13. How do I distinguish between probable historical acts of power and healing by *Yeshua*, and fictional legends? Let me give an example. The *semeion* or sign of turning water to wine at the wedding in Cana is described in John's Gospel. But the water-to-wine miracle was a trademark of Greek savior gods and appears in many of their legends previous to the time of *Yeshua*. It was a demonstration of Divine Presence in Dionysian, Mithraic, and other traditions. This legend seems to have been introduced by the gentile editors of the Fourth Gospel to indicate that *Yeshua* was a Heavenly redeemer. The water-to-wine miracle was a trick used by the charismatic Gnostic leader and *magos* known as *Markos* during his Eucharist to convince followers of his divine powers. So in my novel, *Yeshua* attends a wedding at Cana (which he may or may not have done), but nothing is said about turning water to wine. I did that just to tickle the tail of the fundamentalists—Wedding at Cana without turning water into wine? Blasphemous! Also, the Fourth Gospel seems to be a compilation of sermons about Jesus as the Christ and Heavenly Redeemer given by the Apostle John, who was probably under Mary Magdalene's tutelage when they went together to Asia Minor and established churches. In Johannine tradition, Jesus is made to sound like a megalomaniac with his "I am" pronouncements about his own divinity, when in fact they are either teachings of *Yeshua* about the *Bar-Enash* or "he is" Christological statements by the Apostle John and Mary Magdalene put into the mouth of *Yeshua*. They grossly contradict the more historical teachings of *Yeshua*, such as "Why do you call me good Master? The only good Master is God," clearly indicating that he did not preach himself as being God, as did Gnostic teachers like Simon Magus (*Megos?*) of themselves. The entire Fourth Gospel, though in many ways far more authentically semitic than the synoptics, seems to have functioned as a church-year lectionary. It begins with Jesus driving the money-changers out of the Temple and ends with post-Resurrection appearances glorifying the Johannite succession as opposed to the Petrine. This all takes place over the course of one year in such a way as to synchronize with the Jewish synagogue worship-year. In other words, it is a liturgical and Christological guide for worship over the church year. Historically, it is clear from the synoptic gospels that the cleansing of the Temple was the *final* provocation of the Temple Establishment done by Jesus at the *end* of his ministry—not at the beginning. They also indicate a two- to three-year ministry beginning with the *mikveh* of John the Baptist, and they have the ministry of *Yeshua* begin in the Galilee—not in Jerusalem. So I use the Johannine material carefully, and definitely not for historical order of the ministry. The Johannine sermons that I use are referenced to the *Bar-Enash* of Daniel, not specifically to Jesus. But I do find and use important themes of his historical teaching and spirit embedded in the Johannine narrative, and even make use of some of the Johannine *semeia* that ring true as authentic works of healing. I also make judicious use of *logia* of Jesus from the *Gospel of Thomas,* many of which preserve Gnosticized forms of the earliest "memoires" of the historical Apostles. If you look for Jesus walking on the water, you won't find it. It appears to be an early docetic legend, not unlike that of Jesus leaving no footprint when he walked. It was later attached to the original narrative about the stilling of the storm, which I consider to be historical based on the fact that control over weather phenomena is a well-documented shamanic technique. In Matthew it is given spin as a lesson about "faith," meaning gentile Greek *pistis*, "belief." Belief and doctrine were confused with historical teachings about Hebrew-Aramaic *emunah* "faithfulness" so that keeping faith with *Yeshua* was interpreted as believing in

(the Messiahship of) Jesus. Gentile Christianity competed with a multiplicity of Hellenistic saviour religions based on belief in the miracles of a god, so that is reflected in how the New Testament writers frame faith and miracle. Obviously *Yeshua* did not have to teach "belief" because all the Jews held the same beliefs. He did not teach doctrine, and certainly not doctrine about himself! But the gentile Christians had to start from scratch with teaching monotheism, Jewish Scripture, Christological interpretation of Jewish Messianism, etc. In that context it was, as modern fundamentalists have said, a battle of the minds. Belief in miraculous virgin birth and a host of other fictions totally unrelated to the teachings of the Master—which were no longer well understood anyway—dominated late first-century Greek Christian writings, coming to full flower in the second-century production of miraculous infancy narratives and other literature than was too outrageous to be included in later New Testament canon. But the idea of faith as belief, and that if one just believes hard enough, one can perform miracles and faith healings, entered Christianity that way. (If you believe in fairies, clap your hands, and Tinkerbell will be healed!) So whenever you find "faith" represented as "belief" by a gospel writer, it is not dominical. *Yeshua* taught faithfulness, not belief. He said that one cannot change even one hair his head by "taking thought."

14. No credible eyewitness reports of the trials of *Yeshua* before Annas, Caiaphas and the Sanhedrin, or Pilate exist—the New Testament stories notwithstanding. No one was there except *Yeshua* and his accusers. All we know is the probable sequence of events. I do not belabor them in this novel. The vicious humiliation and beating of the greatest of all Masters before his crucifixion is told best by the marks on his body, clearly visible on the Shroud of Turin which after much study I have agreed with other scholars is an authentic relic. I have chosen not to attempt a detailed account of the beatings and crucifixion. Untold millions of human beings have been brutalized by human beasts. But how many of them have taken these tortures with serene nobility? And how many have appeared after death? It is not the cross that we should dwell upon, but the *qimah*. The brutalization of the Master has been exploited by the producer of a well-known anti-Semitic movie which I have advised my students not to see or support. I do not dwell upon these things in this novel and neither did the Master, who chose to die quickly and is supposed to have said, "*Abba,* forgive them, for they know not what they do."

15. I consider the *qimah* or Resurrection of *Yeshua* and certain post-Resurrection appearances to his disciples for forty days to be historical fact, and I treat them as such. This does not mean I accept as anything but fictional the multiplicity of Redeemer appearances represented in the second-century explosion of Gnostic gospels. And it must be understood that the earliest reference to Resurrection (Paul) uses the Greek verb *ophthai,* "he was seen in a vision." The legend that Apollonius of Tyana "was seen in a vision" *(ophthai)* is an important parallel. The longer Marcan ending does not appear until it is added in the second century. Mark originally ended with the empty tomb—the sign of highest Jewish sainthood being bodily assumption that left no flesh or bones behind. However, deep study and experience with esoteric and paranormal phenomena of many cultures has shown me that *qimah* and after-death communication of saints—for example, through the medium of what Buddhists know as the *nirmanakaya* body—are not only possible but real. Scholars know that the crucifixion of a righteous prophet alone simply could not be the basis for the phenomenon of Christianity. What they like to cautiously describe as the "Resurrection event" and the ensuing "Holy Spirit" phenomena, however, were clearly the generating forces. Although Christianity as it developed did not transmit the *Basor* and teachings of *Yeshua,* it most certainly came into being as the result of powerful spiritual events that modern science has yet to understand. It is my opinion that some day the Shroud of Turin and Sudarion, whose

authenticity has been demonstrated by science, will be understood not only as historical relics of *Mar Yeshua,* but as demonstrations of new principles in a future Biophysics and Thanatology.

Christianity is not the religion of Jesus. It preaches its own gospel *about* Jesus rather than the *Basor* proclaimed *by Yeshua*. But I firmly maintain that the true and historical *Basor* of the Master *Yeshua* must be restored as the basic and highly relevant Christian message for this age.

Please look through the appended Hebrew-Aramaic glossary of terms used in this biography. Refer to it as necessary when you read the novel. It clarifies the concepts and terminology used by the Master.

******* ******* ******* *******

It is time for people to free their spirits from what Norman O. Brown called the "dead hand of the past," with its austere medievalisms. We need a *real* Jesus of flesh and blood, not a Gnostic redeemer myth. We need to grasp what he really taught and apply it to our lives and our world.

It is also time to reawaken our understanding of the feminine aspect of Godhead as known to *Yeshua* in the Kabbalistic mysteries he transmitted through the power of the *Ruach Ha-Qodesh* and Her women disciples and Apostles. For this reason, twenty-first century Christianity must reclaim its Kabbalistic and Magdalenic dimensions.

By understanding something about the process of his great achievement and the meaning of his teachings in their historical context, sincere Christians can finally undertake a truer discipleship with *Mar Yeshua*, the Master Jesus.

Most important, I hope this book might play a role in stimulating more high-quality research into the teachings of *Mar Yeshua*. Essential Christianity should be rooted in an understanding of the Master's *Basor* and *Halakah*. Unlike the Jesus of history, whose life can be known only as legend and fiction, we can do *much* to recover and expand our understanding of the historical teachings of Jesus.

It must be upon the bedrock of this foundation—not the sands of human of doctrine and dogma—that Christianity builds its temples of knowledge and practice.

GL0SSARY OF TERMS

LISTED APHABETICALLY BY ENGLISH TRANSLITERATION

Abba Father-Mother; respected elder; Father-Mother Godhead

Adam Collective Humanity resident in Atziluth, First Kabbalistic World

Adonai Lord, Master of the Universe

Ahavah Memorial love-feast, precursor of Greek Christian *Agape*

Aliyah Ascent of the Holy Mountain to the Altar of YHWH.

Aman Master architect, from same triliteral root as *Amen*.

Amen Liturgical-religious word used by *Yeshua* to mean "faithfully" or "in truth/fidelity"

Emunah Fidelity, faithfullness, trustworthiness.

Amme-ha-eretz "People of the land," the common Jewish people who were not observant practitioners of Rabbinically prescribed *mitvoth,* which were considered by *Yeshua* to be overburdened with the lesser commandments of men.

Asiah Fourth or mundane Kabbalistic emanation; physical universe.

Ba'al Shem Tov "Master of the Good Name," Jewish adept trained in the harmonic intoning of the Name of God YHWH; Jewish High Priest who enters the Holy of Holies and intones the Divine Name on the Day of Atonement.

Bar "Son" Aramaic

Ben "Son" Hebrew.

Bar-Enash "Son of Mankind, Son of Man, Child or Offspring of Humanity;" a self-designation of the later prophets. Daniel saw "one like unto a human being ("Son of Mankind") being given divine sovereignty over the world of the Beasts. This became a Messianic prophecy to later sages, and "one like unto a son of mankind" became the Messiah as Aramaic *Bar-Enash,* which in Hebrew was *Ben-Adam*. This is a key to understanding the *Basor* proclaimed by *Yochanan* and *Yeshua.* For *Yeshua* the "Son of Man" was the New Adam (cf. Paul) that was born "from Above" in the heart and spirit of those who could enter the new Age of God *(Malkuth)*. The *Malkuth* was appearing on Earth from the inside out and could not be seen merely by looking with the eyes of flesh. But gradually as the New Adam replaced the Old Adam, the Earth would be sancified, the power of *Shaitan* and his Beasts broken, and the "lion would lay down with the lamb." However this came only after the trials and Birth Pains of the Messiah. These were considered to last no longer than the life of a saint, when his/her soul (no gender) would achieve the *qimah* and dwell in the eternal habitations of God's *'Olam*. For this reason, many of the eschatological parables of *Yeshua* seem to make the apocalypse identical with death, which brings *Mishpat.* This is not "eternal" in the sense of "forever," as gentiles interpreted it. Rather it is "unto an *'olam*," meaning an intermediate state between incarnations for those who have not achieved the *qimah*, as found in various Kabbalistic texts. See *'Olam*.

Bar-Mitzvah "Son of the Covenant;" 13-year-old Jewish male who has been taught to read Torah and carry out the basic religious duties of a Jewish man.

Barukh Attah "Blessed art Thou; We return blessing unto Thee."

Berakoth Blessings, Divine *Metzloth* or subtle currents and influences.

berakuth Aramaic form.

Basar "flesh," body of flesh.

Basor Public announcement by messenger from king proclaiming birth of a son and royal heir to the throne.

Basor Ha-Malkuth Ha-Shamayyim Public Proclamation of the coming Sovereign Reign of Heaven; "Gospel of the Kingdom of Heaven."

MeBasor, MeBasrim(pl) Proclaimer of the *Basor;* an Apostle

Bat Kol "Daughter of the Voice;" the Word of God as uttered by sages. A lesser manifestation than the *Kol Ha-Nabi*, but holding great power. The Rabbis following the Council of Jamnia declared that the prophetic age had passed and even the greatest of the sages could henceforth speak only in the *Bat Kol*.

Berakah Hebrew or Aramain blessing; the blessing of God said before breaking bread

Berashit "In the beginning;" Book of Genesis.

Berashit bera Elohim eth ha-shamayim veth ha-aretz "In the beginning the Elohim formed the Heavens and the Earth."

Beth House.

Birkat Kohanim The Priestly Blessing

And God spoke to Moses, saying, "Speak to Aaron and his sons, saying, 'So shall you bless the Children of Israel – say to them:

May YAHWEH bless you and guard you – רברכ יהוה, וישמרו

May YAHWEH shine His countenance (Face) toward you and be gracious to you – ראי יהוה פניו אליו, ויחנן (For God to look upon you is the greatest of all blessings)

May YAHWEH lift up His countenance (Face) toward you and give you peace' – אשי יהוה פניו אליו, וישם לך שלום

They shall place My name (*Ha Shem*) upon the children of Israel, and I Myself shall bless them."

Bon-po A Priest of the ancient shamanic *Bon* religion that originally dominated Tibet, China, and Northern India.

Briah Beriah One of the four Kabbalistic Worlds or *'Olamim;* see Kabbalistic Worlds

Cabletow Rope used to lead captives, symbolically used in rites of initiation.

Chaburah Jewish religious fellowship or lay order.

Chazzan Master of a synagogue; later Rabbi.

Dabarim "Divine prophetic words and/or actions;" the *Dabar* of a prophet is considered to be the revealed Word of God.

Dam Blood, vital force, the life-force.

damah Bloodline (of humanity from A-dam in Kabbalistic interpretation

Damoth "Blood-likeness;" humanity is generated from deity in the same genetic way that human children are generated from human parents

Davrim See dabarim.

Day of Atonement *Yom Kippur*. During the week before *Rosh Hashanah*, the "head of the Year" or Jewish New Year in fall, the High Priest was purified in a five-fold baptism, ritual bathing, or *mikveh* and entered the Holy of Holies, where he intoned the Name of God (forbidden at all other times and to all other people) and sought release ("forgiveness") from the consequences of sin for all of Israel. In more ancient rites he magically conferred this burden upon a goat ("scapegoat") and released it into the Judean desert. Historians record that as the flames of rebellion began to rise in Jerusalem before the horrors of the seige predicted by Jesus, the people clamored for *Yakob* the *Tzadik* (James the Just), brother of Jesus, to take the role of the High Priest for the Day of Atonement in place of the Roman political appointee. The Romans assented, and the work was done by *Yakob*. However, he was thrown to his death from the great wall of the Temple soon afterwards by jealous Temple officials.

Demiourgos "Creator of the Universe" (Greek, Platonic, Gnostic).

Diaspora Jewish Dispersian into all nations (Hellenistic Greek term).

Didaskolos Spiritual Master or Teacher (Greek).

Divine Name, *Ha-Shem*; *See* YHWH

ebenim Rough, unhewn stones of high quality.

Eeee-yaaah-oooh-way-eeee Sacred and magical harmonic intonation of *Ha-Shem*, the Divine Name YHWH.

Eggregore A mental-astral form that is given life and animated by the imagination, devotion, and worship of incarnate human beings. Ancient gods are dormant or sleeping eggregores. Over time, an eggregore that is not enlivened with sacrifice or human thought will dissolve back into the elements from which it was constructed.

El Elyon "God the Highest," the Supreme One of the *Elohim*.

Eliahu Ha-Nabi The Prophet Elijah.

Elilim "Little nothings" (*elil* singular, cf. Greek *daimon* or "little god, evil spirit"); invisible dark forces, the *qlippoth* or negative energies released when God shatterered the vessels that prevented the primordial *sephiroth* from articulating, communicating, and forming a coherent universal whole. Symbolized today in Jewish marriage when bride and groom shatter a wine glass in a cloth to represent their union, which also releases negative forces between them that they will need to tame and resolve as their union grows into maturity.

Elohenu, Melek Ha-Olam "Our God, Ruler of the All."

Elohim Plural of *El*, "God;" one of the Names of God in the Old Testament indicating a more ancient concept of henotheism, or a Supreme God with multiple manifestations.

Essenes Messianic Jews living in separated desert communities. The Messianic teaching of John the Baptist show many affinities to Essene and other Jewish sectarian thought as revealed in the libray of Qumran (Dead Sea Scrolls). However, the Messianic teachings of Jesus are quite unlike that of the Essenes, who (along ith the Pharisees) would have considered him to be a "winebibber and a glutton", his *halakah* to be impious, and his saintly *Mashiah Ben-Joseph* (rather than the warlike *Ben-David*) to be unsupported by Scripture.

Ethos Greek "personality," astrally imprinted at conception or birth; analogous to Hebrew *nephesh*. Does not survive the Second Death, normally decomposing back into constituent elements, but in the case of extremely evil personalities can survive "earthbound" as parasitic *elilim* to possess human and animal souls until exorcised, when it decomposes for lack of vital force to keep it operating as a unified psychic organism.

gilgul "Cycles;" the kabbalistic teachings of reincarnation overseen by Metatron, who was Enoch in his earthly life.

Gnosis "Spiritual Knowing" (Greek) as opposed to belief. As Carl Jung said when asked about his religious beliefs: "I don't need to believe; I KNOW."

Ha-Acharit The ultimate end of all time

Ha-Roshit The ultimate beginning of all time

Hasidim Chasidim "Spiritually Pure and Righteous Ones," Jewish saints.

hebel Jewish wisdom term for human self-created illusions comparable to Sanskrit *maya* and Buddhist "appearances." Intensified by repetition *hebel, hebel* as in Ecclesiastes (inaccurately rendered "vanity, vanity" in English translations).

Heimarmene The anthropomorphized force of astrological destiny (Greek). Not unlike Gnostic Ialdabaoth.

hekel The Jewish Temple; palace or mansion.

Hochmah Wisdom, the feminine Presence of God, Divine Immanence in the Kabbalistic World of Asiah, the *Shekinah*; the strict Divine Mother (Greek *Sophia*), patroness of serious spiritual disciples, who first tests and tries them, and when they please Her, She guides, teaches, and reveals Her secrets to them. The Christian *Paraclete,* "Strengthener," or "Holy Spirit."

Hub, hubah, hayyab Spiritual debt, similar to Sanskrit *karma*.

Imma Mother; refers to aspect of God as Divine Mother.

Kabbalah Oral teachings of Jewish Messianic mysticism; *Merkabah* mysticism concerning Enochian ascent to the Chariot-Throne of God was most advanced form, not taught orally but "learned" through *Manda* or Gnosis. Practitioner was "taught by God" just as *Yeshua* said he learned from the *Abba* or Father-Mother of All.

Kabbalistic Worlds   *Atziluth* Archetypal World of *Adam Kadmon* where the coming *Bar-Enash* sits sovereign at the Right Hand of the Almighty; *Briah* Archangelic World ruling the angels of *Yetzirah,* the World of Formation, who create the patterns that will come forth in *Asiah,* the World of Physical Manifestation.

Keseh Subtle lunar *ruach* or spirit-breath.

kiddush Jewish cup of blessing for *Shabbat* or other religious celebrations.

kihesh Non-attachment to places and things of the world

Kol Ha-Nabi "The Voice of the Prophet." A prophet speaks the Word of God, which must come to pass. The prayer and words of a prophet are heard and honored by God. *Yeshua* called all of his disciples to be prophets, whose "yes" means yes and "no" means no. God will hear and honor whatever they ask. Cf. *Bat Kol.*

Kukhin Tombs hewn in limestone rock.

Lai, lai-lai-lai, nai Harmonic intoning in which the Seven Spirits (seven vowels addressing the seven Chakras [Sanskrit]) are stroked upward for ascent to the Divine World of Atziluth   See niggun(im)

Lupercalia   Roman festival; ancient Roman Church substituted St. Valentine's Day to separate the traditional celebration from the theme of lust.

M^eBasrim "Messengers of the *Basor*," Apostles.

Magos Latin *Magus.* Pejorative Greek term for a magician or black magician.

Manda Gnosis, spiritual knowledge of the Heart that cannot be taught, but must be learned by each soul. It is the only knowledge that can be accumulated, grown, and carried from lifetime to lifetime.

Malachim   Angels, literally "Messengers"

   Malach   Angel, Divine Messenger.

Malkuth Rulership, Sovereignty; not "kingdom." "Kingdom of God" is a mistranslation for the Aramic term meaning omnipresent Sovereignty of God--not a "king domain" or place.

   Manda Divine Knowledge, Gnosis.

      Manda d-Hiia Mandaean Holy Spirit, Divine teacher.

Matronit Lover-Wife Consort of God *Adonai* in kabbalistic tradition; God as Mother.

MeBrasrim See *Basor*

Melchizedek "King or Master of Righteousness;" mysterious High Priest of *El Elyon* who administers sacraments of bread and wine to Abraham; considered to be founder of all Divine Priesthood and of Christian Priesthood. When a Priest is Ordained in Apostolic Succession he is declared to be "a Priest forever, after the Order of Melchizedek."

Merkabah, Merkabah The Chariot-Throne of God. Ezekiel and other visionaries familiar with Near Eastern images in the Temple attributed this moving Throne of ancient warrior-kingship used to transport the King during battle to YHWH. Later was the microcosmic instrument of the Divine Image within the soul used by Jewish *Merkabah* mystics ("Riders of the Chariot") to make their Ascent through the Heavens to the Throne of God.

Messiah, Mashiah The Anointed One. Hebrew Priests, kings, and prophets were consecrated by means of oil poured over their heads; the *Bar-Enash* or Messiah was seen as consecrated in this way as supreme Priest, Prophet, and Sovereign of the New Heavens and New Earth, and of the entire Age of the *Malkuth.*

Messiah Ben-David Popular version of warrior-king in lineage from King David who would fight against the Romans, liberate Israel, and inaugurate the Messiac Age.

Messiah Ben-Yosef Prophetic and esoteric view of suffering Messiah who would die to redeem Israel and all mankind, and who would reveal the *razim* or mysteries of Heaven.

mikveh Purifying bath, hand-washing, or other immersion in "living" water.

mishqad A form of Jewish meditation known as a Watch or Vigil; done sitting, sometimes with head between knees or with eyes closed on dark nights. Root *shaqad* means keeping a sleepless (i.e. wakeful and alert) watch.

Nacham "Submission," wrongly brought into New Testament from teachings of Jesus as Greek *metanoia*, "repentance, change of heart;" this is also the basic meaning of *Islam.*

Nephesh, nefesh One word for the impermanent part of a soul, but meaning the personality. In the Kabbalistic thought of the Master's time, it was a double of the person in flesh, having the same sex, mind, and personality limitations. It was unique to each incarnation of a soul and could be sanctified and purified through spiritual practice during a lifetime. It probably derives from the concept of the Egyptian *Ka* and the Greek astrological *ethos* that could be contacted by Priests and mediums for a period of time after death. It is related to the medieval Paracelsian concept of astral or etheric body or personality-self used in astral projection and that survives the death of the flesh (First Death) for about forty days. It then dissolves back into its etheric elements, releasing the higher soul (Egyptian Ba) for rest until its next incarnation. The *nephesh* can experience purgation (Christian Hell and Purgatory), and it can remain "earthbound" for various reasons, avoiding the Second Death. In Kabbalistic thought, many cases of possession are understood to be caused by corrupt human *nepheshim* trying to retain form and consciousness. In certain types of exorcism *Yeshua* caused them to dissolve to release the higher human souls trapped in them. Their elementary forms then dissolved back into the World of Formation to re-emerge in positive transformation. *Nepheshim* (plural of *nephesh*).

Neshemah, neshama, Greek *augoeides*, Egyptian *sekhem*; the Divine Ray or Monad that projects lower psychic entities into human incarnation; resides in Seventh Heaven.

Netivoth "Paths" or etheric web connecting the Kabbalistic Seven Spirits of the human etheric consitution; related to Sanskrit *nadis* connecting *chakras*.

Niggun Sacred wordless chant that is intoned with harmonic-producing vowels; *niggunim* (plural form).

Nous of the *Authentia* Greek Hermetic designation for Godhead. *Nous* is Higher Mind of the philosophers; St. Paul said he would rather speak one word with his *Nous* than babble a thousand in so-called "tongues." True "speaking in tongues" is rational speech in a foreign language unknown to the speaker--a rare spiritual phenomenon, as at Pentecost in the Book of Acts. Irrational babbling falsely called "speaking in tongues" by Pentecostal Christians is not the speech of angels; it is a pre-literate phenomenon that can be stimulated from the lower brain cortex by electrical impulses, hypnotic voice or sound, hypnotic syggestion.

Nun The Hebrew letter N; symbolizes fish in *Kabbalah.*

'Olam (Greek *Aeon*) Kabbalistic term meaning Age, Aeon, Era, World. A state of existence. After death, human souls may dwell in an *'olam* of suffering (compared by *Yeshua* to Gehenna, a garbage dump in a valley outside of Jerusalem), or achieve the *qimah* and dwell in the *'Olam* of God. Although his teachings seem to be ambivalent about reincarnation and whether the Gehenna state is for purification, the garbage in Gehenna was regularly burned to purify it. That is why it was hot and emitted smoke. *Yeshua* seems to have had something like the Catholic doctrine of Purgatory in mind when he warned of punishment after death. The idea of a permanent Hell for Christians was taken over from Orphic myth in fifth and sixty centuries and added to the purgatorial concept. Earlier lovely punishments like the Flaming Lake of Pus were expected for the enemies of Christianity (third-century *Gospel of Nicodemus*).

'Olam Ha-Ba The invisible present and future Messianic Age of Divine Sovereignty on Earth in which the forces of injustice, disease, and bondage will have no place.

This *'olam* The current fallen world ruled by *Shaitan,* "the Prince of this World."

'Olamim The Four Kabbalistic Worlds or Ages: Atziluth, Briah, Yetzirah, Asiah

Pardes Paradise, Garden of Eden; place of rest for the righteous after death, located in the Third Heaven.

Pesach Passover.

Pythagoras Greek philosopher whose students became the scientists, mathematicians, engineers, and architects of ancient Greece. Associated with the chthonic mysteries of the *Pholarchoi* and the descent into the Divine Underworld by Parmenides, who brought the techniques to a Pythagorean Greek city, and Empedolcles, who established Air, Earth, Fire, and Water as the four physical elements.

qimah The Standing Forth or "Resurrection" after death of a Jewish saint. The ascended soul is neither male nor female, but *shalem* like all heavenly beings--a state often allegorized as androgynous "like the angels."

Qlippoth Dark forces released into all worlds like shards from shattered glass when the sephirotic vessels were broken by God so that they could communicate to create a unified Kosmos; dark forces and evil are necessary parts of Divine Emanation ("Creation") in Kabbalistic thought.

Quid pro quo "This for that;" both sides of a bargain.

Rab, Rav "Great One," Jewish Spiritual Master.

> *Rabbi* "My Great One;" later term for Jewish scholar and lawyer of Torah.

> *Rabboni* Aramaic for "My Master."

Razim Mysteries, Divine Secrets of Heaven; by extension, "clouds" of Heaven.

Ruach ha-Hayyim Spirit of Life.

Ruach Ha-Qodesh "Spirit of Holiness," the Holy Spirit (feminine); see *Hochmah*. Greek *Sophia*.

Shabbat Sabbath; often refers to the Friday evening *Shabbat* supper which begins celebration of the Seventh Day (Saturday); Jewish days counted from sunset to sunset, so *Shabbat* ends at sunset Saturday. Christian so-called Sabbath (Sunday) is derived from the ancient Eighth Day celebration of Messianic Jewish disciples of *Mar Yeshua*, based on his Sunday *qimah*, or so-called Resurrection. Christians were never released from keeping *Shabbat*--one of the Ten Commandments--by the synod of Peter, James, John, and others described in the Book of Acts, yet few if any modern Christian keep *Shabbat* in spite of their supposed adherence to the Covenantal Ten Commandments.

Shalom Peace, in the sense of perfection and wholeness. *Yeshua* counseled his disciples to become *shalem*, spiritually whole and full of integrity.

> *mishqad* Vigil, "Watch."

> Originally a lookout, night watchman; in Kabbalistic mysticism the Vigil was a divine meditation done under the Night Heaven or after sunset. In Christian tradition the Vigil came to be done only one night a year from the sunset of Holy Saturday to Easter sunrise.

Shaitan Satan, the fallen Prince of this *'olam* or world of human affairs. Originally a shining archangel of Heaven and (Greek) *Diabolos* (Devil), Accuser or prosecuting attorney in the Heavenly Court of *YAHWEH* who receives permission to test and break or prove the fidelity of saints like Job.

Shakkat Corruption of the body after death.

Shamayim "Heavens, high places" Refers to Day and Night Heavens or Skies.

There were two *shamayim* or heavens for the Hebrew mystics--day and night. The Night Heaven that appeared at sunset was equivalent to the Greek Divine Underworld--a sacred time and place for interior communion with the Divine *Malkuth Ha-Shamayyim,* The Sovereignty or "Kingdom" of Heaven.

Shekinah The "Glory" of God manifest in physical nature (feminine); the Motherhood of God; the Immanent Presence of God.

Shemesh The sun; solar breath.

Sicarii Political assassins who carried hidden knives and swords.

Sige Hermetic-Gnostic term of deep, profound, meditative silence; one of the Pleroma of Aeons.

Synthema Symbolic declaration made as part of initiation into the mysteries.

Talmid Disciple of the Jewish wisdom and mystery schools.

Tam Righteous, upright, pure.

tammim plural righteous ones.

Targum, Targumim (plural) Aramaic translations of Jewish sacred books.

Teli The constellation of the Pole Serpent in Kabbalistic astrology; the great *Seraph* or Fire Serpent guarding the *Merkabah* or Throne-Chariot of *YAHWEH*

tiphlah Intercessory prayer, prayer for the benefit of others and for all. This is the type of prayer that *Yeshua* emphasized in both the Lord's Prayer and in *mashlim* ("parables") about prayer

Tikkun Kabbalistic apocatastatic healing of the worlds, return to Divine Sovereignty

'*Tohu*' and '*vohu*' Primal chaos; linguistically Babylonian *Ti'amat,* slain by Marduk

Torah Jewish Law; the first five books of the Old Testament (Pentateuch).

T'raqlita Advocate (defense counsel) to oppose Shaitan (prosecuting attorney in the Court of Heaven); Strengthener, "Comforter" (Christian Paraclete).

Tzadik Rightous Person, Saint.

Tzelem The Divine Image of the Elohim, or of God; Latin *imago dei.*

Tzitzit Purple fringes on Jewish shawl died with precious substance from ocean periwinkles.

Yah Form of *YAHWEH* as specific name-function of deity.

Yechidah The feminine aspect of *neshemah,* the highest monadic soul.

yechidoth plural of yechidah.

Yechid and *Yechidah* The masculine and feminine aspects of the highest monadic soul which are reunited in the physical union and marriage of "soul-mates."

yeled; yeledim   Small child; children

Yeshua Ben-Sirach Author of *The Wisdom of Ben-Sirach* (OT Apocrypha).

yetzer The *Imago Dei* or Image of God that was breathed into Adam (Mankind) at the "creation" or emanation of God as humanity. The ancient Rabbis copied this word with a double *yod* in their manuscripts (*yyetzer*) to explain the origin of human evil through two yetzerim--the *Yetzer Ha-Tov* (Good or Divine Impulse) and the *Yetzer Ha-Ra* (Evil Impulse) implanted by God in the heart of humanity (Adam). The Good Impulse is comparable to the Pythagorean/Platonic microcosm, the "Son of God," in every human heart. Like Plato's doctrine of the two impulses (Way of the Right, Way of the Left), the spiritual path and goal of each person is to follow the Good Impulse in the heart, which in Plato's philosophy is the Path of the Philosopher, and in the Kabbalistic view the Path of the Jewish Saint.

Yetzirah "formation." The Kabbalistic view of so-called "Creation" codified in the ancient *Sepher Yetzirah* (Book of Formation) is not that of a demiurge or creator deity that stands apart from matter and shapes it, as in the theological view of Christianized Platonism dominating theistic religions like mainstream Christanity, Judaism, and Islam. Rather, the origin of all things derives from the Source of All Being Who emanates or manifests Itself by stages into what we know as form or reality. Thus everything that manifests in form on any level or plane is an expression of Godhead--not of a separate substance or nature. This is a thoroughgoing philosophical monism, as opposed to the dualism of Divine and Human that posits an original dualism between God and Nature. Plato's received tradition from Pythagoras described the Macrocosm or Universe as the "Son of God," but in his exposition based on a misunderstanding of the Hermetic Egyptian doctrine found in the *Timaeus* and the *Kore Kosmou*, Plato established the inherent dualism that characterizes "creation" theologies.

YHWH   The Tetragrammaton or four consonants of the Divine Name of God given to Moses, probably intoned as "Eeyahway." In the Palestinian Rabbinic Judaism that was coming into being at the time of Jesus, it was considered impious to pronounce "The Name" (*Ha Shem*), which would be done privately only once a year by the High Priest in the inner sanctum of the Temple on the Day of Atonement. This was not the convention in Galilean and Kabbalistic Judaism, where The Name was still pronounced. The Hebrew word *Adonai* (Lord, Master) came to be substituted for The Name YHWH in synagogue readings, and today pious Jews substitute the written English word G-d. The medieval Protestants substituted the vowel of *Adonai* into the four Hebrew consonants YHWH to create the name Jehovah. In the King James Version of the Bible, the YHWH is written as LORD (all capital letters) to distinguish it from the Hebrew word *Adonai* "Lord."

Yod The smallest Hebrew letter usually translitered as an English "y;" referred to in the early New Testament translations from Greek as the "jot.

Yod He Vav He   See YHWH

Zippori The Jewish city razed by Herod because of zealot rebellion and rebuilt as his capital called Sepphoris, where a great deal of construction in stone was being done during the youth of Jesus.

www.ingramcontent.com/pod-product-compliance
Lightning Source LLC
Chambersburg PA
CBHW081415230426
43668CB00016B/2239